Implementing AS/400 Security

Fourth Edition

Carol Woodbury & Wayne Madden

NEWS/400 Books™ is a division of
DUKE COMMUNICATIONS INTERNATIONAL

221 E. 29th Street • Loveland, CO 80538 USA
(800) 621-1544 • (970) 663-4700 • www.as400networkstore.com

Library of Congress Cataloging-in-Publication Data

Woodbury, Carol.
  Implementing AS/400 security / by Carol Woodbury and Wayne Madden.-- 4th ed.
    p. cm.
Includes bibliographical references and index.
 1. IBM AS/400 (Computer) 2. Computer security. I. Madden, Wayne, 1960- II. Title.
  QA76.8.I25919 W47 2000
  005.8--dc21
                                      00-011912

NEWS/400 Books™ is a division of
DUKE COMMUNICATIONS INTERNATIONAL
Loveland, Colorado USA

© 2000 by Carol Woodbury and Wayne Madden

All rights reserved. No part of this book may be reproduced in any form by any electronic or mechanical means (including photocopying, recording, or information storage and retrieval) without permission in writing from the publisher.

It is the reader's responsibility to ensure procedures and techniques used from this book are accurate and appropriate for the user's installation. No warranty is implied or expressed.

This book was printed and bound in Canada.

ISBN 1-58304-073-0

2002 2001 2000 WL 10 9 8 7 6 5 4 3 2 1

To my wife, Karen.

— *Wayne Madden*

To my sister and brother-in-law, Janet and Jack,
and my brother and late sister-in-law, Alan and Mary.
Thank you for so faithfully lifting me up to our Heavenly Father in prayer.

— *Carol Woodbury*

Acknowledgments

There are several people whom we need to thank for their part in completing the fourth edition of *Implementing AS/400 Security*. Thank you to Katie Tipton, editor of NEWS/400 Books, for being so flexible in working around several family emergencies and our work schedules. A big note of thanks goes to editors Barb Gibbens and Ann Hutchins for so craftily making sense out of our updates. Art director Mike Friehauf designed the new cover, and Martha Nichols worked with us on production.

Ernie Malaga contributed the output queue authority utility in Chapter 6. Dan Riehl of the PowerTech Group contributed the FTP exit program in Chapter 7. A special thanks goes to Carol's friend and former colleague, Patrick Botz of the IBM Enterprise Server Group, for his technical review of this edition. His insight, technical expertise, and humor were all very much appreciated. Mark Anderson and Scott Sylvester — also of the IBM Enterprise Server Group — gave of their time to explain new functions and review new material for technical accuracy. Thank you all for contributing to the success of this book.

Table of Contents at a Glance

Chapter 1 Security Is a Business Function	1
Chapter 2 Security at the System Level	11
Chapter 3 The Facts About User Profiles	45
Chapter 4 Object Authorization	63
Chapter 5 Database Security	89
Chapter 6 Output Queue and Spooled-File Security	129
Chapter 7 Network Security	165
Chapter 8 Communications Security	189
Chapter 9 Internet Security	215
Chapter 10 Thwarting Hackers	231
Chapter 11 Evaluating Your Current Strategy	249
Chapter 12 Establishing and Controlling System Access	267
Chapter 13 Building Object and Role Authorization	281
Chapter 14 Security for IT Professionals	301
Chapter 15 Security Implementation Example	313
Chapter 16 Is Your Strategy Working?	341
Chapter 17 Status Auditing	345
Chapter 18 Event Auditing	375
Chapter 19 Building a Business Contingency Plan — A Workbook	401
Appendix A Security APIs	423
Appendix B Security Journal Entry Types (Detail)	435
References	441
Index	443

Table of Contents
[*Italic type* indicates a sidebar.]

Part I: AS/400 Security Basics

Chapter 1 Security Is a Business Function 1
Evaluating Your Risks 1
   Confidentiality 2
   Integrity 2
   Availability 3
   Privacy 4
Evaluating the Threats 4
Managing the Strategic Issues 4
   Develop a Security Mentality 5
   Control Access to Applications, Data, and Systems 6
   Establish and Perform Security Auditing 7
   Build and Test a Business Contingency Plan 7
Getting Started 8

Chapter 2 Security at the System Level 11
The System Security Level 11
Security Level 10 12
Security Level 20 13
Security Level 30 14
Security Level 40 15
   State and Domain Restrictions 16
   Use of Restricted MI Instructions 16
   Job Initiation Validation 17
   Restoration of Modified Programs 17
   Why Use Security Level 40? 18
Security Level 50 19
   Parameter-Passing Validation 19
   Message Restrictions and Pointer Removal 19
   Prevention of Control Block Modification 20
   QTEMP Library Maintenance 20
   Why Use Security Level 50? 21
Security-Related System Values 21
   General System Values 21
   Password-Related System Values 33
   Audit-Related System Values 38
A Helpful Tool 42
Operations Navigator 42

Chapter 3 The Facts About User Profiles 45
Why User Profiles? 45
What Is a User Profile? 45
User Profile Attributes 46
    USRPRF (User Profile) 47
    PASSWORD (User Password) 49
    PWDEXP (Set Password to Expired) 50
    STATUS (Profile Status) 50
    USRCLS (User Class) and SPCAUT (Special Authority) 50
    Initial Sign-On Options 55
    System Value Overrides 57
    Group Profiles 57
    UID (User Identification Number) and GID (Group Identification Number) 59
    AUT (Authority) 59
Helpful Tools 59
Operations Navigator 61

Chapter 4 Object Authorization 63
Specific Authorities 63
    Object Authorities 64
    Data Authorities 65
    Authority Relationships 66
Authority Classes 66
Granting and Revoking Specific Authorities 68
Group Profiles 69
    Multiple Group Profiles 70
    Why Grant Authority to Group Profiles? 71
Public Authority 71
    Establishing Public Authority 71
    Using Default Public Authority 73
Authorization Lists 75
How OS/400 Checks Authority 77
Authority Cache 80
Adopted Authority 80
Authorities and Save/Restore Functions 83
Object Ownership 84
Limit User Function 86
Helpful Tools 88
Operations Navigator 88

Chapter 5 Database Security 89
Database File Authorities 89
Data Authorities and Logical Files 108

Field-Level Security 108
   Field-Level Security Before V4R2 109
   A Program Example 112
Row-Level Security 128
What About SQL Tables and Views? 128

Chapter 6 Output Queue and Spooled-File Security 129

The Security-Related Output Queue Attributes 129
   DSPDTA (Display Data) 130
   OPRCTL (Operator Control) 130
   AUTCHK (Authority Check) 131
   The AUT Parameter 131
Output Queue Ownership 132
Sample Output Queue Security Implementation 133
An Output Queue Security Management Utility 134
Helpful Tools 163
Operations Navigator 163

Chapter 7 Network Security 165

Physical Security 165
Network Configuration 166
Network Security Attributes 166
   JOBACN 167
   PCSACC 167
   DDMACC 168
DDM Security 168
   System-Related Security Attributes 170
   User--Profile–Related Security Attributes 171
   Object-Authorization–Related Security Attributes 172
   The Whole Picture 173
   Writing a DDM User Exit Program 176
Security Considerations for PCs 177
   Client Access 178
      Access Issues 178
      Password Issues 179
      Connection Issues 179
      Data Transfer and Remote Command Issues 180
      Running Client Access over TCP/IP 180
      Limiting Function from the Desktop 181
   ODBC Security Considerations 182
   Viruses 182
Using Exit Points 182
Installing USRFTPLOGC 187
Helpful Tools 187

Chapter 8 Communications Security ... 189
TCP/IP Security Considerations ... 189
   IP Packet Filtering ... 191
   Network Address Translation (NAT) ... 191
   PPP ... 191
   SLIP ... 192
   Telnet ... 194
   FTP ... 195
   LPR and LPD ... 196
   WSG ... 196
   SMTP ... 197
   POP ... 198
   BOOTP and TFTP ... 199
   DHCP ... 199
   DNS ... 200
   REXEC ... 200
   RouteD ... 200
   SNMP ... 201
   INETD ... 201
   IBM HTTP Server for AS/400 ... 201
   DRDA ... 202
   Dial-Up Line Security Considerations ... 203
      Control the Line Status ... 203
      Authorize Devices ... 203
      Dial-Back Security ... 203
Data Encryption ... 204
   Public Key Infrastructure (PKI) ... 204
   Digital Certificates ... 205
   Secure Sockets Layer (SSL) ... 206
   Digital Certificate Manager (DCM) ... 207
   Virtual Private Networks (VPNs) ... 207
   Other Encryption Options ... 208
   AS/400 Encryption Requirements ... 208
APPN/APPC Communications Configuration Security ... 209
   Line Description ... 209
   Controller Description ... 210
   Device Description ... 211
   APPN Filtering Support ... 213
Helpful Tools ... 213
Operations Navigator ... 213

Chapter 9 Internet Security 215
Corporate Security Policy 216
Internet Service Provider 217
Firewalls 217
AS/400 System Values 219
User Profiles 222
Use Resource Security 223
Control What Goes On 223
Write Secure Web Applications 224
Use Exit Points 226
Monitor 227
   Intrusion Detection 227
   Denial-of-Service Attacks 227
   Security Configuration 228
Test 228
Update Your Business Contingency Plan 229
The Good News 229

Part II: The Invisible Threat

Chapter 10 Thwarting Hackers 231
Hacker Terminology 231
Access — A Hacker's First Hurdle 232
   Minimizing Access Exposures 232
   Making the Hunt for User Profiles and Passwords More Difficult .. 236
Bypassing or Gaining Authority 238
   QSYSLIBL — The System Library List 238
   Adopted Authorities 238
   Profile Swapping 239
   Using OS/400 Objects Directly 239
   Subsystem Descriptions 239
   Job Descriptions with an Associated User Profile 240
   Program Evoke 240
   Remote Command Facilities 241
   Client Access Express Functions 241
   ODBC 241
   *SAVSYS Special Authority 241
   DB2 UDB for AS/400 Trigger Programs 242
   Too Much Public Authority 242
   Closing Off Authority Exposures 242
Preventing Trojan Horses 243
Preventing Viruses 245

Preventing Worms 246
Internet Attacks 247
Final Words of Advice 247

Part III: How to Build an AS/400 Security Strategy

Chapter 11 Evaluating Your Current Strategy 249
Common Authorization Models 249
   Menu Authorization Model 249
   Library and Directory Authorization Model 251
   Direct Authorization Model 252
   Group Authorization Model 253
   Program Adoption Authorization Model 255
   Changing the Process or Thread's Profile Authorization Model .. 256
Evaluating the Key Areas 257
   Physical Security 258
   Security Level 259
   System Configuration 259
   Communications and Device Configurations 261
   Initial Programs and Menus 261
   Resource Security 262
Determining Your Level of Threat 262
   Physical Threat 262
   Data and Public Access 263
   Competitive Information 264
   Source of Threat 264

Chapter 12 Establishing and Controlling System Access 267
Verify Security Level 267
Plan for User Profiles 267
Plan the Physical Connections 269
   The AS/400 System Unit 269
   Direct Workstation Access 270
   Dial-Up Workstation Sessions 271
   Passthrough Workstation Sessions 271
      Implementation 1 273
      Implementation 2 274
      Implementation 3 274
      Implementation 4 275
   PCs 276
   DDM 276
   Interactive Subsystems 277
   TCP/IP Applications 278

Printers and Output Queues 278
　　　Backup Media 279

Chapter 13 Building Object and Role Authorization 281

Fundamental Tenets 281
　　　Object Security Is a Continuum 281
　　　Object Security Is Flexible with System Organization 282
　　　Object Security Uses Multiple Methods 282
　　　Purchased Software Is Not Exempt from Object Security 282
Evaluating Object Security Requirements 283
Identifying Application Security Requirements 283
Identifying Data File Security Requirements 286
Identifying Program Security Requirements 288
Identifying Authorization Roles 291
Defining Enterprise Roles 291
Defining Authorizations 292
　　　Operations and Objects 293
Implementation Example 294
Documenting Role Authorizations 295

Chapter 14 Security for IT Professionals 301

Security and Your IT Staff 301
Identify the Business Functions 301
Define a Secure Environment for Each Business Function 302
　　　Operator 302
　　　Communications Administrator 304
　　　Programmer/Analyst 304
　　　Security Administrator 306
　　　Network Administrator 308
　　　Webmaster 309
Security for Vendors and Consultants 309
　　　The Super Program 309
　　　The Super Profile 310
　　　Vendor Dial-In Support 310
　　　Consultant Practices 311

Chapter 15 Security Implementation Example 313

Application Security Requirements 314
Organizational Chart 315
User Profile and Password Rules 316
Role-Authorization Samples 317
Network Security Considerations 332
　　　Firewall 332

VPN 332
Network Attributes 332
Port Restrictions 332
IP Packet Filtering 332
Antivirus Software 333
Exit Programs 333
Client Access User Exit Program 333
Application Administration 334
System Values 334
User Profile Listing 336
Special Authorities Listing 337
Library/Object Authorities Listing 337

Part IV: Auditing Your Security Strategy

Chapter 16 Is Your Strategy Working? 341
What Can Change? 341
Business Model Changes 341
Operating System Updates 341
New Products 342
Procedural Changes 342
New User Profiles 342
Changing Roles 342
Terminations and Resignations 343
New and Changed Objects 343
Deleted Objects 343
Temporary Authorities and Objects 343
Changes to System Values and Network Attributes 343
User Identification 343
Auditing Overview 344

Chapter 17 Status Auditing 345
Physical Security Auditing 347
System-Level Security Auditing 347
User Profile Monitoring 348
Expanded User Profile Auditing 355
Critical Objects and Object Authorities Monitoring 359
Miscellaneous Audit Activities 362

Chapter 18 Event Auditing 375
Monitoring the History Log 375
History Log Housekeeping 376
Inside Information 377

The Security Audit Journal 377
The Audit Journal 378
Auditing Controls 380
System-wide Auditing 381
User Auditing 382
Object Auditing 383
Event-Auditing Recommendations 386
Working with the Audit Journal 387
   Understanding Journal Entry Formats 387
Displaying and Printing the Audit Journal Entries 390
   Using the DSPJRN Command to Display Entries 391
   Using the DSPJRN Command to Print Entries 392
Helpful Tools 398
Operations Navigator 398

Chapter 19 Building a Business Contingency Plan — A Workbook 401

Have a Purpose 401
Find the Leaders 401
Recognize Reality 402
Risk Analysis 403
   Identifying Functional Exposures 403
   Identifying Functional Dependencies 403
   Identifying Functional Threats 404
   Evaluating Financial Risk — Expenses 405
   Evaluating Financial Risks — Losses 405
   Identifying Recovery Priorities 406
   Getting the Information You Need 406
Disaster Avoidance 410
   Avoiding Disaster Through Prevention 410
      Data Center Security 410
      System Security 411
      Network Security 411
      Fire Prevention and Natural Disaster Preparedness 411
      Employee Policies 411
      UPS 412
      Records/Data-Storage Options 412
      Preventive Maintenance 413
   Avoiding Disaster Through Effects Reduction 413
      Employee Training 413
      Alternative Facilities 414
Emergency Procedures 414
   Establishing Evacuation Procedures 414
   Establishing Notification Procedures 415

Establishing Shutdown Procedures 415
Establishing Departmental Procedures 415
A Complete Recovery Program 416
Building a Recovery-Program Document 416
Identifying Recovery-Program Tasks 416
Assigning Recovery-Program Teams 417
Evaluation Team Activities 417
Administration and Support Team Activities 417
Operations Team Activities 417
IT Operations/Recovery Team Activities 417
Salvage/Facilities-Recovery Team Activities 419
Communications Team Activities 419
Testing and Auditing 419
Performing a Level 1 Test 421
Performing a Level 2 Test 421
Auditing Your Contingency Plan 421

Appendices and References

Appendix A Security APIs 423
User and Group ID APIs 427
Digital Certificate APIs 429
Profile Token APIs 430
User Function Registration APIs 431
Validation-List APIs 432

Appendix B Security Journal Entry Types (Detail) 435
Action Auditing 435
Object Auditing 439

References 441
IBM Manuals 441
IBM Redbooks 441
IBM Web Sites 441
Articles from *NEWS/400* Magazine and *AS400 Network* 442
Other Publications 442

Index 443

Chapter 1

Security Is a Business Function

Security is a business function. You should keep this fundamental principle in mind as you build and implement your security plan. Security is a technology issue only in terms of its implementation.

The purpose of security is to enforce the guidelines that secure your organization's information assets. Suppose that tomorrow you take your entire IT staff to your company's human resources department. You tell the departmental manager that you and the staff are going to spend the day browsing personnel files, examining any documents that pique your interest, discussing those documents, and perhaps even copying some of them to take with you. What would the human resources manager say? Obviously, your staff doesn't have permission to access these documents, even if no written policy prohibits it.

But how many members of your IT organization have *ALLOBJ special authority or access to all production objects on your AS/400 system? Everyone who has *ALLOBJ authority can do electronically what they would never be permitted to do openly: access any production object on your system and do with it whatever they like. If anyone other than the security administrator has *ALLOBJ special authority to your system's human resources objects, you are allowing that person to violate a written or unwritten guideline limiting access to HR information.

Whether you're talking about locks on doors, restrictions on who can access documents in file cabinets, limitations on who can access files on your AS/400, or controls over the information your company makes available on the Internet, your organization's guidelines — formal or informal, written or unwritten — govern your business. You must take those guidelines into consideration as you develop your IT security plan. If you make enforcing guidelines a top concern, you'll plan security as you develop applications instead of trying to retrofit security to completed applications.

When you clearly understand that security is a business function, you're ready for a definition of information security:

> *Information security is the protection of information assets from accidental or intentional (but unauthorized) disclosure, modification, or destruction and from the inability to process that information.*

Your information security strategy and implementation must take into account all security violations, whether intentional or accidental, that result in modification, disclosure, or destruction of your information assets.

Evaluating Your Risks

What are the risks to your information assets? In other words, what are you protecting? You can answer this question with four words: confidentiality, integrity, availability, and privacy.

Confidentiality

Some information is absolutely confidential because it consists of private information about individuals (as in the case of HR information) or because it could give a competitor an advantage (e.g., early knowledge of an upcoming event, current financial status, proprietary product information, customer information). You must evaluate your information in terms of its confidentiality to determine what type of security that information needs.

We often hear about outsiders who approach someone in an IT department and request information from company files. A few years ago, an AS/400 programmer for a property development company reported that someone had offered him $1,000 for a printed list from his company's AS/400 system. The individual wanted a report listing the company's future property developments, which he could have used to make a tidy profit by buying and selling land near the development areas. What's surprising isn't that people make such attempts to obtain restricted information, but that, because of a lack of security, the programmer who related the story — and for that matter, probably most programmers reading this book — could have walked out the doors of his company's office building with virtually any printed report the AS/400 could produce or with a diskette containing proprietary or confidential information. Security often fails when it comes to restricting the access of IT personnel to information assets.

Integrity

Information security also addresses the integrity of your applications and data. Your applications and data must be authentic, accurate, and concurrent with your company's other applications and data. A problem such as an inventory control program that introduces errors in replenishing stock, an order entry program that loses order items, or customer invoice records that someone has tampered with could easily bring a business to a crawl or a standstill and endanger profits and even the company's long-term success. You can't afford to risk the integrity of your applications and data because of a nonexistent or weak information security implementation.

For instance, if you let users share user profiles and passwords, you immediately sacrifice your system's ability to authenticate changes to information. In other words, your AS/400 can't accurately identify who is doing what on the system because one profile might represent several people. Although limited profile sharing may be acceptable for a specific application, as a rule, system integrity requires that you prevent profile sharing.

What if users suddenly started doubting the accuracy of the data in your database? Perhaps someone mistakenly uploaded old data from a PC into a file. Or maybe a well-meaning programmer put into production a program that wasn't fully tested, which in turn introduced errors into the database. These two scenarios illustrate the importance of the integrity and accuracy of your programs and data. Your information security plan must minimize the opportunities for users and IT staff to accidentally introduce errors into your application repository or database.

Concurrence is another significant integrity issue. A banking application provides a classic example. Say a customer transfers $50 from savings to checking. Your application subtracts $50 from savings and then adds $50 to checking. But what happens if the system fails after it subtracts the $50 withdrawal from savings and before it adds the deposit to checking? Will the $50 be lost forever? Of course, you develop your applications to ensure concurrence, but your security implementation must also do its part. For example, by restricting *OBJREF (object reference) authority to tables in DB2 Universal Database (DB2 UDB) for AS/400, you can control which user profiles are able to define referential integrity constraints in the database. By restricting who can define referential integrity constraints, you can ensure that only a responsible person makes such changes or notifies the operations staff about the relationships of files for backup and restore purposes. Failing to synchronize your backup and recovery strategy could cause a major breakdown in your database's data concurrence.

Add to the concurrence issue the complexities of client/server computing, and you have even more security challenges related to applications control and data integrity. As your company implements Internet, intranet, and other network-based applications and makes more programs and database files available on a network, maintaining concurrence among these programs and files and acquiring the tools you need to do so become increasingly important.

Secure information assets are also vital to your company's integrity and reputation. Any security breach, if publicized, can damage a company's reputation. Say your business depends on the cash flow that its e-commerce Web site produces, and you have a highly publicized security breach in which consumers' credit card numbers are stolen. The company's integrity could be so severely damaged as a result that the company might not be able to continue doing business. A well-thought-out and -implemented security plan protects a company's integrity as well as its data.

Availability

At one company I (Wayne) worked for, a lead programmer once came in on Sunday to work on the order entry system. The programmer modified several programs in a programmer development library. When he finished working that day, he decided to delete all the order entry programs in the development library. He typed the command DLTPGM OE* because all those program names started with the letters OE. But he forgot that, for testing purposes, he had added the order entry production library to his library list during the session, and the production library now preceded the programmer development library in the list. As a result, he deleted all production order entry programs. Blissfully unaware of what he'd just done, he left for the evening.

The next morning, it took several hours to recompile order entry programs in the production library, and the company (which typically took about $1 million worth of orders each day) lost at least two hours of orders and probably alienated some good customers in the process.

This disaster could easily have been prevented by implementing security measures that controlled how programmers could access the system's production objects. Although the disruption was accidental, malicious attacks can also result in a similar "denial of service." A denial-of-service attack typically doesn't permanently damage data, but rather prevents the system or server application from performing its intended function, which in turn might significantly, and possibly permanently, harm the business.

Privacy

In recent years, concerns about privacy have increased dramatically. Consumers are becoming increasingly concerned about how companies use people's personal data, whether it's collected over the Web or on an employment or health insurance application. If you use very sensitive information, such as that collected from medical tests and credit reports, inappropriately or release it to the wrong organization, you could adversely affect an individual's life.

Although security alone doesn't guarantee privacy, you can't guarantee privacy *without* implementing good security policies and practices. Don't make the mistake of ignoring this rapidly growing area of concern. The United States and many European countries are either considering or already have legislation that mandates protection for personal information. In addition, many companies in the United States are attempting self-regulation. For example, IBM is one of several companies that won't advertise on Web sites that don't publish their privacy policy.

You need to analyze all data that you collect. If any of it is personal information, examine how you use and secure that data and be sure to tell the people who provide the data how you're going to use it. If you share personal data with individuals or organizations, obtain the source's permission to do so and be sure you're not breaking any laws by sharing the information.

Evaluating the Threats

What types of problems pose the greatest threat to your information security plan and implementation? A common thread you might have recognized in the scenarios we discussed in the preceding section is the role that accidents play in breaching confidentiality, accuracy, or availability. A little security can go a long way toward reducing these threats to your system. If you implement commonsense security measures, such as securing production data and programs from IT staff, auditing critical data and functions, and limiting access to PC downloads and uploads from and to the host database, you can eliminate many common sources of errors and omissions. Your security implementation will certainly need to address the threat from disgruntled employees, natural disasters, and hackers. But you should concentrate first on simple security basics, which can prevent accidents and employees from damaging the system, and on a good business contingency plan, which can reduce the effects of a natural disaster or other form of site loss or system outage.

Managing the Strategic Issues

Evaluating the risks and threats to your information assets is the key to getting management's attention. As you expose risks and threats, management begins to see the possible ramifications of inadequate or inappropriate security. However, once you have management's attention, it's important to follow through by fostering a security mentality within your organization and managing the strategic issues that surround any security plan and implementation. You must control access to your systems, applications, and data. You must establish and carry out security auditing procedures. And you must build and test a business contingency plan.

These tasks take time, but once complete, they provide the building blocks for the various security implementations you need to undertake on your enterprise's computer systems.

Develop a Security Mentality

The first step toward developing a security mentality within your enterprise is to publish a corporate-wide security policy. Perhaps your company has an employee handbook that is updated regularly and that all employees receive when they are hired. This book contains both guidelines and information. In many such handbooks, one guideline is something such as "Employees will not discuss their own or other employees' salaries with anyone else in the company. Violators are subject to discharge." In a similar vein, consider guidelines such as "Employees will not share their passwords. An employee's password is a key to our information assets and must be known to and used by only the employee assigned that password. Violators are subject to discharge." If you truly believe that security is a business function, you can readily deliver some simple, easily followed security guidelines in an employee handbook.

These guidelines should cover the following topics:

- Passwords
- PC and PC printer care
- PC access, including the use of physical keys
- Storage of information on PC clients vs. on servers
- Software licenses (pirated software)
- Use of Internet access, including
    - whether personal use is allowed
    - what code (if any) can be downloaded from the Internet and from what sources
    - what corporate information can be placed on the Internet

In addition to offering employees broad guidelines related to security, such policies send employees the right message: "Security is important to our business and is part of your job." Top-level management can take this opportunity to show support for information security efforts, which ultimately makes your job easier by motivating everyone in the company to become aware of and maintain information security.

Another step toward developing a security mentality is to clearly define the roles of information owner, information user, and information custodian. The IT department must recognize that it doesn't own all applications and data. Rather, each department owns its own applications and data. Because security is a business function, departments must relay their security requirements to IT, which must then design and build into the system the necessary security measures to deliver on those requirements. For instance, if a department allows only certain employees to modify data in a file the department owns, IT is responsible for implementing that restriction for that file, including restricting the IT department itself from modifying the data, if the originating department so wishes.

When you establish ownership in the minds of users, you prepare them for the subsequent application development process, during which you'll extract application requirements (including security requirements) from users in the department. At the same time, you can help users recognize themselves in a second role — that of information user. Although the department as a whole owns the application, each person in the department is a user who must live by the security guidelines the department establishes. Typically, a department supervisor or senior employee will work toward establishing the ownership security requirements, to which all users will then be subject.

In contrast to an owner or user, the IT department is the custodian of other departments' applications and data. IT must ensure that the applications and data are available, accurate, authentic, concurrent, and secure. However, these responsibilities don't authorize IT personnel to directly access the data or the applications beyond using some process or tool that enables IT's tasks or that provides auditing to monitor user access of data.

Control Access to Applications, Data, and Systems

Controlling access to your information resources involves physical security, managing user profiles and passwords, defining authorization roles, and implementing resource authorities and specific security programs to enforce and audit access to your system. This particular strategic issue constitutes most of the tasks usually associated with security implementation and consequently occupies the largest portion of this book.

In today's network-connected world, access is a critical part of a security implementation. Perhaps in the past you relied on more primitive security measures, such as menu systems, to secure your own application users on the system. Today, with numerous ways of accessing data that bypass traditional menus — such as Client Access data transfer, File Transfer Protocol (FTP), Open Database Connectivity (ODBC), and Distributed Data Management (DDM) — you must incorporate other approaches to ensure that you have a firm hold on access to your data and systems.

One specific subset of access control relates specifically to security within the IT department. IT professionals are sometimes blind to the need to secure the system from themselves. Some professionals perceive any form of security aimed at IT as, at best, making IT's job more difficult or, at worst, as a personal attack. However, because security is a business function and the IT professional's tasks, like all other users' tasks, require security, IT security is essential.

Some of the keys to a successful IT security implementation are apparent from a management perspective. You must commit yourself to supporting separate development, test, and production environments. The production environment on your systems must be completely stable except for planned and audited changes using a tool that can track changes to the system. You might elect to purchase a software configuration management tool (which should offer, as a minimum, change-control and version-control management), or you might decide to write your own tool.

IT professionals don't need authority to production data and applications as long as they have an emergency plan for dealing with critical problems that require immediate attention and have access to a tool that can manage the change process.

IT vendors (e.g., consultants, third-party software providers) should fall under the same guidelines as in-house developers: They should have access only to development and test environments — with no authority to the production environment without your assistance or without accessing a secure tool — and all access should be audited. Implementing these guidelines gives you more control over vendor tasks as well as a better grasp of the tasks outsiders perform on your system. Be cautious of third-party software providers that require users to have *ALLOBJ special authority to run their software. *ALLOBJ authority should be the exception, not the rule. Make such vendors explain why users need *ALLOBJ authority to use the software. There are some legitimate reasons for requiring *ALLOBJ authority, such as when the underlying operating system function requires it. However, vendors should not require *ALLOBJ authority simply to access the application database.

Overall, when you're dealing with IT, design security from the "least possible privilege" point of view. Start with the minimal authorities that you believe the IT professional requires, and add necessary additional authorities as you go, adding only the authorities necessary to enable the staff member to perform his or her job. For more information about implementing security for IT professionals, see Chapter 14.

Establish and Perform Security Auditing

In any security implementation, established security requirements and rules become less effective as time passes. Because your security requirements, as well as pieces of the system (e.g., operating system, application programs, procedures) aren't static, you must continually audit and adapt your security plan to stay current.

As Chapters 16, 17, and 18 show in detail, to maintain a well-tuned security implementation, you must audit your security "controls" as well as the security-related events that take place on your system each day. Many security implementations fall short of auditing, instead simply trusting that the security plan works and that "someone" will know when it needs to be changed.

Build and Test a Business Contingency Plan

The last strategic security issue you need to manage is business contingency planning. Several years ago in California, one company learned about this need the hard way. The company owned two buildings. One building was small and housed the IT staff and the company's primary host computer. The company had made a large investment in contingency planning for the IT department and for that site. In the event of a disaster, the company could quickly and efficiently make its host computer operational.

However, the company nearly went bankrupt when the larger building burned down — the building that housed all the users and their desks, PCs, printers, phones, documents, and forms. The company hadn't invested at all in true business contingency planning. Yes, it could make its host computer and a few terminals in the IT department operational, but where were 1,000 users supposed to do their jobs? What phone number were customers supposed to call to place an order? Who would answer that phone? How should orders be entered or fulfilled?

Your contingency plan must include the entire business. Don't make the mistake of worrying only about IT.

So where do you start? First, you must define contingency planning. Complete the following statement by selecting the correct choice from the list below:

Contingency planning is

A. never having to say you're sorry.
B. maintaining an up-to-date resume.
C. evaluating your enterprise's critical functions and establishing procedures that minimize the negative effect of some form of disaster and ensure that you can restore those critical functions to the level necessary for the enterprise to survive.
D. a waste of time for those who worry about events that can't be controlled.

C is obviously the correct response. When you break down this definition, you see that a contingency plan can do two things: It can minimize the effects of some form of disaster, and it can ensure that you can restore business-critical functions so your enterprise can survive. Those are the best results you can get from a contingency plan. To make sure you can realize these results, you need to go through a contingency planning process that includes the following steps:

- Evaluating the risks
- Establishing disaster avoidance procedures
- Establishing emergency procedures
- Documenting a complete recovery program
- Testing your contingency plan
- Auditing your contingency plan as an ongoing process

Chapter 19 focuses on business contingency planning and serves as a workbook for putting together a plan for your business.

Getting Started

The hardest part of security planning is getting started. As you read this chapter and look forward to the practical material in subsequent chapters, you can take a few simple steps to help you get started in your own company.

First, examine any potential risks to your company's information assets. Is there confidential information that your company wants to protect? Does your data need to be accurate? Does your contingency plan include departments other than IT? How much money would you lose each day in the event of a disaster that affects each department?

List these risks and present the list to management. Also list possible threats and specific examples of how your current applications and security implementation expose the company to those threats. This step is critical, especially if your enterprise has or is considering a Web presence.

Next, obtain management support to begin documenting corporate-wide security policies. After defining some broad policies, move to the department level to establish data ownership and build authorization roles that describe how users will access applications and data.

Only then are you ready to begin enforcing a security implementation. It is in the enforcing that you'll use the technical tools this book describes. System values, network attributes, exit programs, and object authorities all exist only so that you can enforce the information security that you have previously established as a set of guidelines or business rules for each department.

The final step in getting started, from a management point of view, is to commit to auditing your security implementation and plan. The only way to determine whether your implementation is working is to audit it on an ongoing basis. As you discover possible gaps in security, you can tighten your implementation. As you find areas where security is too limiting, you can make adjustments there as well. Auditing is a tool that lets you tune your security implementation as well as discover possible security breaches as they occur.

The remaining chapters in this book give you the technical skills and the right approach for implementing an AS/400 security plan. If you remember that security is a business function, you'll be able to see how using these tools will support your business.

Chapter 2

Security at the System Level

A successful AS/400 security plan considers all available security methods and tools, combining and tailoring them selectively to suit a particular installation. Chapters 3 through 8 describe OS/400's user profile, object, data, spooled file, network communications, and Internet security tools. But the security you build with these tools and policies is only as robust as the system-related security values you use to configure OS/400. This chapter discusses those system values and recommends the settings you need to provide a solid foundation upon which to structure security.

The System Security Level

The AS/400 is the product of a marriage between the best of the S/36 and S/38 technologies. This marriage affected system security as well as architecture. On the S/36, you can choose to activate resource security, or you can decide to use only password security without specifically securing objects. On the S/38, both password and resource security are required. OS/400 marries these two security implementations by letting the customer choose the level of security. Security levels range from level 20, which provides only password security, to level 50, which, in addition to password and resource security, provides system integrity security (i.e., the ability to prevent users and applications from executing restricted machine-level instructions) as well as specific security features that comply with the U.S. Department of Defense (DoD) Level C2 security specifications. Understanding these security levels and choosing the correct level for your circumstances is the first step in securing your system.

System value QSECURITY controls the system security level. The possible QSECURITY values of 20, 30, 40, and 50 correspond to the four available security levels. Before V4R3, security level 10, which provides no password or resource security, was also an option. However, IBM believed the availability of level 10 sent the wrong message and no longer supports that level.

Today, IBM ships all new AS/400 systems with a QSECURITY value of 40. Before OS/400 V3R7, the shipped default setting was level 10. You can view the current value on your system by executing the DSPSECA (Display Security Attributes) command. This command displays the current value and pending values for QSECURITY. (If you change QSECURITY, you must IPL your system for the new value to take effect. The pending value is the value of QSECURITY after your next system IPL.) You can use the DSPSYSVAL (Display System Value) command, but the value that command displays is equivalent to DSPSECA's pending value. DSPSYSVAL doesn't reveal whether QSECURITY will have a different value after an IPL.

You can change the security level by executing the CHGSYSVAL (Change System Value) command. For instance, to change the QSECURITY value to 40, you would enter

CHGSYSVAL SYSVAL(QSECURITY) VALUE('40')

Technical Note
When you modify QSECURITY, the new system security level takes effect at the next IPL. Until then, the current security level remains in effect. To display the current and pending values of QSECURITY, use the DSPSECA command.

Technical Note
If your system is set at security level 10 when you install V4R3 or a later release, the value is not changed, even though 10 is no longer a valid value for QSECURITY. However, if you subsequently change QSECURITY to something other than 10, you won't be able to reset it to 10.

Security Level 10

System security level 10 might more aptly have been called security level 0 or "physical security only": At level 10, the physical security measures you took, such as locking the door to the computer room, were the only security you had. If users had access to a workstation with a sign-on screen, they could simply type any user profile name and press Enter (no password was required). If that user profile didn't exist, the system simply created a new user profile for the session and let the user proceed. The profile the system created in such a case had *ALLOBJ special authority, which is sufficient for the user to delete any or all objects on the system.

Although user profiles were not required at level 10, you could still create and assign them and ask users to type in their assigned user profile at sign-on. You could then tailor the user profiles to have the appropriate special authorities — you could even grant or revoke authorities to objects. But because those accessing the AS/400 could create a new user profile at will, there was no way to enforce the use of those assigned profiles, and thus no way to enforce restricted special authorities or actual resource security. Level 10 provided no security whatsoever, so you can easily understand why IBM removed it.

Technical Note
At security level 10, the user profile's LMTCPB (Limit Capabilities) parameter isn't active, meaning that you can't limit users to an initial menu or program and can't restrict them from system commands, and that they can modify their current library. IBM doesn't support security level 10 after V4R2.

Security Level 20

Security level 20 provides password security. To access the system at level 20, a user must have a user profile and a valid password. By requiring users to have a user profile and password, level 20 institutes minimum security and deters unauthorized access. However, as with level 10, the default special authorities for each user class include *ALLOBJ special authority (see Table 2.1), so level 20 in effect bypasses resource security.

At security level 20, you can tailor the special authorities for individual user profiles by using the SPCAUT (Special Authorities) parameter on the CRTUSRPRF (Create User Profile) or CHGUSRPRF (Change User Profile) command. You can also specify LMTCPB(*YES) to restrict users to a specific initial program or menu (for a detailed discussion of the LMTCPB parameter, see "Initial Sign-On Options" in Chapter 3).

TABLE 2.1
Special Authorities for Level 20

User class	Special authorities				
*SECOFR	*ALLOBJ	*SECADM	*SAVSYS	*JOBCTL	*SERVICE
	*SPLCTL	*AUDIT	*IOSYSCFG		
*SECADM	*ALLOBJ	*SECADM	*SAVSYS		
*PGMR	*ALLOBJ		*SAVSYS		
*SYSOPR	*ALLOBJ		*SAVSYS	*JOBCTL	
*USER	*ALLOBJ		*SAVSYS		

Although these functions let you tailor the user profile, the inherent weakness of level 20 remains: By default, resource security is not implemented. The default *ALLOBJ special authority assigned to every user profile bypasses any form of resource security. To implement resource security at level 20, you must explicitly remove the *ALLOBJ special authority from all profiles that don't absolutely require it (only the security officer and security administrator need *ALLOBJ special authority), and you must remember to remove the special authority from every new user profile you create. But the drudgery of manually removing *ALLOBJ authority is pointless; by default, level 30 security does this for you. On a production system, you must be able to explicitly authorize or deny user authority to specific objects. Therefore, level 20 security is inadequate in the initial configuration, requiring you to make significant changes to mimic what level 30 provides automatically.

If you're running your AS/400 at security level 10 and you change QSECURITY to 20, the system assigns all existing user profiles a password that is the same as the user profile name and doesn't change any user profile special authorities. When you move from level 10 to level 20, you'll probably want to clean up your user profile list. (At level 10, when a user mistypes a profile, the system simply creates a new profile. Consequently, many incorrect user profiles probably exist on a level 10 system.)

First, list all user profiles on your system using the DSPAUTUSR (Display Authorized Users) command and eliminate all profiles you don't need. Then, create new user profiles or copy existing profiles and give the new profiles more meaningful names. Finally, ensure that users create new passwords immediately after they first sign on under the default password (which is the same as the user profile name) that the system assigns when you move to level 20. To require users to choose new passwords, set each user profile's password to "expired" (i.e., change each profile's PWDEXP keyword value to *YES) and then modify the password composition system values (for instructions, see "Password-Related System Values" later in this chapter) so that users can't select trivial passwords (e.g., their initials or phone extension, short passwords).

If you follow these tips, you can successfully move from system security level 10 to level 20 without any major impact on your applications or system interactions.

Technical Note

Resource security (i.e., the system requirement that users have authority to an object in order to access it) is active at all security levels. The difference between security levels lies in their ability to support resource security. Security level 10 offered no support at all. Level 20's support is minimal, ineffective, difficult to implement, and unmanageable. Levels 30, 40, and 50 effectively support resource security by assuming it as the default. In other words, at level 30 and above, users must obtain authority to objects; *ALLOBJ special authority isn't automatically granted.

Security Level 30

By default, security level 30 supports resource security (users don't receive *ALLOBJ authority by default). Resource security permits objects to be accessed only by users who have authority to the objects.

Table 2.2 shows the default special authorities for all user classes at level 30 (these special authorities are also the defaults at levels 40 and 50). Notice that *ALLOBJ special authority isn't a default for any user class except *SECOFR, the security officer class. Under level 30, user profiles don't automatically have the authority to create, modify, or delete objects on the system. The authority to work with, create, modify, or delete objects must be granted either specifically or because it's the default public authority.

TABLE 2.2
Special Authorities for Levels 30, 40, and 50

User class	Special authorities					
*SECOFR	*ALLOBJ	*SECADM	*SAVSYS	*JOBCTL	*SERVICE	
	*SPLCTL	*AUDIT	*IOSYSCFG			
*SECADM		*SECADM				
*PGMR	(no special authorities)					
*SYSOPR			*SAVSYS	*JOBCTL		
*USER	(no special authorities)					

Technical Note

In this book, we discuss how to properly secure a production machine using tools available when the system is at a minimum of security level 30. However, to effectively safeguard data, programs, and other production objects and prevent unintentional data loss or modification, production machines should be at least at level 40.

As we've explained, moving from security level 10 to level 20 isn't difficult. But moving from level 10 or 20 to the more secure level 30 requires careful thought and planning. When you move from a lower level to level 30, OS/400 removes all special authorities users have that level 30 doesn't allow by default. For planning purposes, compare Table 2.2 with Table 2.1. You can see that levels 30, 40, and 50 grant each user class different default special authorities than levels 10 and 20 do. OS/400 automatically revokes inappropriate special authorities when you move to level 30. If you don't anticipate and plan for these changes, some users may no longer have authorities to applications, database files, and some system functions.

Security Recommendation

Run all your production systems at least at security level 40.

Security Level 40

The need for level 40 security centers on a security gap that the AS/400 inherited from the S/38. This gap allowed languages that could manipulate Machine Interface (MI) objects (e.g., MI itself, C, C++) to access objects to which the user wasn't authorized by stealing an authorized pointer from an unsecured object. In other words, an MI program could access an unsecured object and use its authorized pointer as a passkey to an unauthorized object.

To level 30's resource security, level 40 adds operating system integrity (Table 2.2 lists the default special authorities for level 40). System integrity strengthens level 30 security in four ways:

- by providing program states and object domains
- by preventing use of restricted MI instructions
- by validating job initiation authority
- by preventing restoration of invalid or modified programs

State and Domain Restrictions

Regardless of security level, the AS/400 classifies all objects (e.g., programs, files, commands) into one of two domains: system or user. All programs and service programs also have a state assignment — again, either system or user. The concepts of object domain and program state work with level 40 to close the hole in level 30 security. Under level 40, system-state programs can reference (i.e., directly manipulate through pointers) all objects regardless of their domain, and user-state programs can reference only user domain objects.

At levels 10, 20, and 30, the system tests programs against these rules when the programs are executed. If the programs violate the rules, the system simply logs the violation in the audit journal (see Chapter 18 for a discussion of the audit journal). But at level 40, the system won't execute programs that violate these rules.

Object domain and program state also prevent users from abusing operating system objects by accessing them directly. Most OS/400 objects are in the system domain, and most programs and service programs, except Application Programming Interfaces (APIs), are in the system domain and have the system state. At security levels 40 and 50, operating system objects can't be accessed directly. Why is this important? Some interfaces that ship with the operating system can provide authorized pointers, change jobs to run under QSYS or QSECOFR, or let users who run jobs access objects to which they don't have authority. These are legitimate interfaces that OS/400 needs to run properly. At security levels 40 and 50, these interfaces can't be abused. Security levels 10, 20, and 30 allow these interfaces to be used to harm your system.

Use of Restricted MI Instructions

At security level 40, the system restricts access to certain MI instructions, including those that create system-domain objects, manage processes or events, and access the database. At all security levels, the system detects all attempts to create a program that uses restricted MI instructions and doesn't allow the program to be compiled. At levels 40 and 50, an attempt to execute an existing program that uses restricted instructions causes the program to fail; at all other security levels, the attempt simply logs an entry in the audit journal.

Job Initiation Validation

At security levels 40 and 50, an attempt to submit a job fails if the user submitting the job doesn't have authority to the user profile specified in the job description. At all other security levels, the system logs the attempt in the audit journal but lets the profile submit the job.

Technical Note

One attribute of a job description is the USER (User Profile) attribute. You can specify this attribute's value by changing the USER parameter on the CRTJOBD (Create Job Description) or CHGJOBD (Change Job Description) command. The possible values are

*RQD	The job using the job description must specify a user profile.
user_profile_name	You can specify a user profile to be associated with the job description. A job can then use this user profile for execution.

Security levels 10, 20, and 30 don't require that the user submitting the job have authority to the job description's default user profile. The resulting gap in security can be exploited by any user who has authority to a job description that contains a powerful default user profile.

Workstation entries whose job description specifies a user profile allow workstations that access the subsystem to sign on as that user without entering a user profile or password. Pressing Enter is all the user needs to do to sign on the workstation as the user specified in the job description. At all security levels, the system logs this action in the audit journal. But at security levels 40 and 50, an attempt to sign on using a workstation entry whose job description specifies a user profile on the USER parameter fails.

Security Recommendation

Specify JOBD(*USRPRF) for all workstation entries to ensure that users sign on to the system with a valid user profile and password.

Restoration of Modified Programs

Whenever a program is created, the system calculates a set of check bytes over the program object. The check bytes let the system determine whether a program being restored is identical to the original. If the program validation fails (e.g., because the program has been modified), the system attempts to retranslate the program.

If the retranslation succeeds, the system logs the validation failure and restores the program. If the retranslation is unsuccessful, the system restores the program and logs an entry to the audit journal regardless of which security level the system is at. However, when the system is at security level 40 or above and ALWOBJDIF(*NONE) is specified on the RSTOBJ (Restore Object) command, the system changes the program's owner to QDFTOWN (the IBM-supplied default owner) and sets public authority to *EXCLUDE. If ALWOBJDIF(*ALL) is specified, the system restores the program and logs an audit entry but lets the owner and public authorities stay the same.

Technical Note
Because the system must retranslate all programs when you move them from a CISC machine (V3R2 or earlier) to a RISC machine (V3R6 or later), you can't upgrade programs that contain blocked instructions.

Security level 40 is your primary defense against Trojan horses. A *Trojan horse* is a program disguised as a legitimate AS/400 program, such as QSYS/QSTRUP, the default system start-up program that your AS/400 executes each time you IPL. Someone with harmful intent could patch a program on another AS/400, name it QSYS/QSTRUP, and save it to tape or CD. If this person had access to a workstation at which another user was signed on with *SAVSYS authority and if your system were not at level 40 or 50, the hacker could restore the revised version of QSTRUP to your machine. The next time you IPLed, your AS/400 would execute the Trojan horse QSTRUP program.

Security Recommendation
Before moving to level 40, run at level 30 and monitor the audit journal for violations that level 40 guards against. If you find none, go to level 40 security. If the system logged violations, review them to determine their source. Some vendor software packages use restricted MI instructions and will fail. In these cases, you should consult your vendor. Some vendor programs will take a different code path depending on your system's security level. The vendor program might run at security level 40 or 50.

Why Use Security Level 40?

You might wonder what security level 40 buys you. As you purchase more third-party software and as systems become more widely networked, especially over the Internet, you need to give serious consideration to the security benefits that operating system integrity provides.

Level 40 lets you prevent anyone from creating or restoring programs on your system that might threaten system integrity at the MI level or that might abuse interfaces meant for use only by OS/400. We can't emphasize too strongly how important it is to run your system at least at security level 40 if you want to maintain system integrity.

Security Level 50

Security level 40 adds security for system integrity. Security level 50 adds additional system integrity features as well as the security functions required to meet the DoD Level C2 certification requirements as specified by the DoD Trusted Computer System Evaluation Criteria. (For the level 50 default special authorities, see Table 2.2.)

Before we explore the functions that security level 50 activates, you should be aware of one important fact: Security level 50 adds overhead to your system. How much overhead it adds depends on how your applications are written. If your system is CPU-bound, you'll need to consider the performance cost of level 50. Nevertheless, because of the additional system integrity features, we highly recommend that you run your system at security level 50.

When you use level 50, the system

- validates passed parameters
- imposes certain message restrictions and removes pointers from messages
- prevents control block modification
- maintains the QTEMP library

Parameter-Passing Validation

At level 50, each time a user application calls an OS/400 program that runs in system state (e.g., an OS/400 API, an application that performs any I/O), OS/400 checks every parameter passed between the programs. The system checks both the storage domain and the actual values passed to ensure that neither will cause OS/400 to perform an operation that compromises system integrity.

Message Restrictions and Pointer Removal

As we explained earlier, every AS/400 object belongs to either the system domain (*SYSTEM) or the user domain (*USER). Most IBM-supplied objects are in the system domain. All user-created objects and some IBM-supplied objects are in the user domain. In addition, every AS/400 program is either a system-state (*SYSTEM) program or a user-state (*USER) program. Most IBM-supplied programs are system state, and all user-created programs are user state. User-state programs can access only user-domain objects, but system-state programs can access both user- and system-domain objects.

The rules of object domains and program states mean that you can access system-domain objects only by using the appropriate command or API. Level 50 imposes the following message restrictions:

- Any system-state program can send a message of any type to any user- or system-state program.
- Any user-state program can send a message of any type to any other user-state program.
- A user-state program can send a nonexception message to any system-state program.

- A user-state program can send an exception-type message to a system-state program only if the system-state program is a request program (e.g., QCMD) or the system-state program called the user-state program.

In addition, OS/400 removes the pointers from replacement text in messages sent to a user application from another job. Removing pointers prevents the receiving job from using the pointers to compromise security and bypass system auditing.

Prevention of Control Block Modification

At level 50, no internal control blocks can be modified. A control block is an internal structure available to OS/400. OS/400 relies on control blocks to remain unmodified. However, some third-party vendors change internal control blocks so that their code runs instead of OS/400 code. Such changes often result in unpredictable results when the system runs and frequently require a lengthy debugging process to locate and fix the problem. Although level 40 prevents modification of some control blocks, level 50 covers all control blocks, including the open data path (ODP), the spaces for CL commands and programs, and the S/36E job control blocks. This feature may cause some third-party utilities to cease functioning, so you should check with your application and utility vendors before you move to level 50 security.

QTEMP Library Maintenance

On the surface, objects in library QTEMP appear to be temporary. The external view of QTEMP implementation is that for every job on the system, a unique QTEMP library exists; that you can access objects in QTEMP only from within its associated job; and that when a job ends normally, the job's QTEMP library as well as all the objects in it are deleted.

The facts of QTEMP implementation, however, are somewhat different. If your AS/400 doesn't run at security level 50, every QTEMP library is actually a permanent object on the system. When a job begins, OS/400 creates a QTEMP library for the job and assigns an address for the library and each object in it in OS/400's permanent root address system. If a job or the system ends abnormally, on the next IPL OS/400 uses these addresses to locate all stranded QTEMP libraries and objects and clears them from the system. So, internally, QTEMP and the objects in it are permanent.

Level 50 prevents hackers from using OS/400's internal permanent address system to access QTEMP library objects. At level 50, OS/400 no longer stores those addresses. Instead, the system actually does treat every QTEMP library and its objects as temporary.

That sounds fine, of course, but as a result, if a job or the system ends abnormally, OS/400 can't automatically locate and delete the "lost" QTEMP library and its objects when you IPL. Consequently, when you implement level 50, you need to execute the RCLSTG (Reclaim Storage) command more frequently to recover objects that get "lost," and then you need to specifically delete them.

Why Use Security Level 50?

Organizations that want the highest level of security should run at level 50. Level 50 provides the best defense against exploitation of internal interfaces and introduction of Trojan horses and viruses.

Security-Related System Values

After you've determined the security level at which you want to run, you can use the security-related system values to build the foundation for your system security structure. These system values fall into three categories: general security system values, system values related specifically to password creation and maintenance, and system values that control auditing.

General System Values

The general security-related system values provide a variety of system-level security functions. For instance, by changing a single system value, you can limit the number of successive incorrect sign-on attempts allowed at a workstation, thus minimizing password guessing and lowering your security risk. As another example, you can specify the length of time a workstation can remain inactive before the system takes action.

Table 2.3 summarizes the general security system values. Later, as we look at the details of each system value individually, we suggest values you should use.

TABLE 2.3
General Security System Values

System value	Description
QALWOBJRST	Determines whether security-sensitive objects (e.g., system-state objects, programs that adopt authority) can be restored to your system
QALWUSRDMN	Specifies in which libraries you can place *USRSPC, *USRIDX, or *USRQ objects
QAUTOVRT	Determines whether virtual device descriptions are created automatically
QCRTAUT	Specifies the default public authority
QDSPSGNINF	Specifies whether the sign-on information display appears when a user signs on
QINACTITV	Determines the interval (in minutes) that a workstation can remain inactive before the system sends a message to a message queue or terminates the job
QINACTMSGQ	Specifies the name of the message queue that receives messages about the workstation when the inactive time interval is reached, or specifies that the job at the workstation is to be terminated or disconnected when the interval is reached
QLMTDEVSSN	Determines whether users can have more than one device session concurrently
QLMTSECOFR	Determines whether users with *ALLOBJ or *SERVICE special authorities can sign on to devices without explicit authority
QMAXSIGN	Sets the maximum number of sign-on attempts allowed at a workstation

continued

TABLE 2.3 CONTINUED

System value	Description
QMAXSGNACN	Specifies the action taken when a user reaches the maximum number of invalid sign-on attempts
QRETSRVRSEC	Determines whether decryptable passwords are stored on your AS/400
QRMTSIGN	Specifies whether automatic sign-on from a remote system is allowed
QSECURITY	Determines the system security level
QUSEADPAUT	Defines which users can create programs that use adopted authority — USEADPAUT(*YES) program attribute

QALWOBJRST — Allow Restoration of Security-Sensitive Objects

System value	Description	Possible values	Default
QALWOBJRST	Determines whether security-sensitive objects (i.e., system-state objects, programs that adopt authority) can be restored to your system	*ALL *NONE *ALWSYSST *ALWPGMADP *ALWPTF *ALWSETUID *ALWSETGID	*ALL

QALWOBJRST lets you control whether anyone can restore system-state objects or programs that adopt authority to your system. The default value of *ALL lets a user with the appropriate authority restore any object. You can specify a value of *NONE to prevent anyone from restoring security-sensitive objects. The *ALWSYSST value lets anyone restore system-state objects, and *ALWPGMADP lets anyone restore programs that adopt authority.

The *ALWPTF value, which was added in V4R4, lets you restore system-state programs and programs that adopt authority when you load PTFs. IBM learned that many of you wanted to set QALWOBJRST to *NONE but found it impractical to do so because you needed to change the value whenever you applied PTFs or installed a Licensed Program Product. The *ALWPTF option makes this system value more usable.

New with V4R5 are the *ALWSETUID and *ALWSETGID values, neither of which pertain to many shops. *ALWSETUID lets Unix programs that have the S_ISUID attribute and run in the AS/400 Portable Application Solutions Environment (PASE) be restored. *ALWSETGID lets Unix programs that have the S_ISGID attribute and run in the AS/400 PASE be restored.

Security Recommendation

Set QALWOBJRST to *NONE so you have maximum control over the restoration of system-state objects and programs that adopt authority. If this setting is too restrictive, set the value to *ALWPTF so that you won't have to change the system value every time you load PTFs. If you frequently restore programs that adopt authority (for example, if you frequently distribute software to multiple AS/400s), set QALWOBJRST to *ALWPGMADP, but carefully examine all software that others restore to your systems.

QALWUSRDMN — *Allow User Domain Objects in These Libraries*

System value	Description	Possible values	Default
QALWUSRDMN	Specifies in which libraries you can place *USRSPC, *USRIDX, or *USRQ objects	*ALL *DIR library_names	*ALL

QALWUSRDMN specifies the names of the libraries that can contain *USRSPC (User Space), *USRIDX (User Index), or *USRQ (User Queue) objects. The default value of *ALL permits these objects to exist in all libraries and is generally acceptable for any system that doesn't have to comply with DoD Level C2 security specifications. The value *DIR allows user-domain objects in all directories on the system.

You can also name specific libraries that you want to be able to put *USRSPC, *USRIDX, and *USRQ objects into. System administrators who want to be able to track these objects easily might want to specify libraries.

If you need to comply with DoD Level C2, you must use security level 50 and specify the library name QTEMP (see the Technical Note below, which explains why you must also include library QRCL) for QALWUSRDMN. The system can't audit information that moves to and from *USRSPC, *USRIDX, and *USRQ objects. At level 50, library QTEMP is a temporary object, preventing the passing of confidential data between users.

Some people think that this system value takes effect at security level 50, but it's actually active at all security levels.

Technical Note

If you specify anything other than *ALL for QALWUSRDMN, you should include library QRCL in the list of libraries. When you execute the RCLSTG command, the system might need to move *USRSPC, *USRIDX, or *USRQ objects into library QRCL. For security purposes, you may also wish to change QRCL's public authority to *EXCLUDE.

> **Security Recommendation**
> Unless you must comply with DoD Level C2 security, specify *ALL for system value QALWUSRDMN.

QAUTOCFG — Automatic Device Configuration

System value	Description	Possible values	Default
QAUTOCFG	Specifies whether locally attached devices are configured automatically	0 (off) 1 (on)	0

QAUTOCFG determines whether you manually configure new local controllers and devices or let the system configure them. We recommend that you set this system value to 1 (on) when you install the system and when you add many new devices. Otherwise, set QAUTOCFG to 0 (off). This system value doesn't affect creation of virtual devices and thus is becoming less pertinent as virtual devices become more prevalent.

QAUTOVRT — Automatic Virtual Device Creation

System value	Description	Possible values	Default
QAUTOVRT	Determines whether virtual device descriptions are created automatically	0 (off) 1–32500 *NOMAX	0

QAUTOVRT determines whether incoming Display Station Passthrough (DSPT) and Telnet session requests create virtual devices automatically as needed. A value of 0 tells the system that you'll create the virtual devices to be used and the system isn't to create them automatically. A numerical value in the range 1–32500 indicates the maximum number of temporary devices the system can configure automatically for passthrough requests. *NOMAX specifies there is no limit imposed on the number of automatically created device descriptions.

> **Technical Note**
> QAUTOVRT doesn't affect whether IBM AS/400 Client Access for Windows Family automatically creates PC device descriptions when it runs over SNA. QAUTOVRT does affect automatic device creation when you run Client Access Express, which runs only over TCP/IP.

> **Security Recommendation**
> Set QAUTOVRT to 0 so that you can explicitly control the number and use of virtual devices on your system.

QCRTAUT — Create Authority

System value	Description	Possible values	Default
QCRTAUT	Specifies the default public authority	*ALL *CHANGE *USE *EXCLUDE	*CHANGE

In V2, IBM added the CRTAUT (Create Authority) parameter on the CRTLIB (Create Library) and CHGLIB (Change Library) commands. The CRTAUT parameter defines the default public authority for all objects created in the library and permits the following values:

*SYSVAL	Uses the value specified in the QCRTAUT system value
*ALL	Default public authority is *ALL
*CHANGE	Default public authority is *CHANGE
*USE	Default public authority is *USE
*EXCLUDE	Default public authority is *EXCLUDE
authorization_list_name	Default public authority is *AUTL, using the specified authorization list

The CRTAUT parameter's default is *SYSVAL, which references the QCRTAUT system value. Thus, when you create a library and specify no other value for the CRTAUT parameter, the public authority for new objects created in that library defaults to the authority specified in system value QCRTAUT. When you create objects in that library, the AUT (public authority) parameter on the CRTxxx command defaults to *LIBRCRTAUT, which instructs the system to refer to the library's CRTAUT attribute to determine the default public authority for the new object.

Security Recommendation

You have two choices for changing the default public authority for objects created in a library. One approach is to change QCRTAUT to either *USE or *EXCLUDE. If you take this approach, you must also set the CRTAUT parameter for library QSYS to *CHANGE so that device descriptions and their message queues will be usable after they are created (you need *CHANGE authority to the device descriptions and their message queues to sign on to a device). You'll also need to change the command default for the CRTLIB command to either *USE or *EXCLUDE.

The second approach is to leave QCRTAUT with its default value of *CHANGE and control the public authority at the library level. In other words, change the CRTAUT parameter for user libraries to either *USE or *EXCLUDE, depending on each library's contents. For more information, see "Public Authority" in Chapter 4.

QDSPSGNINF — Display User Sign-on Information

System value	Description	Possible values	Default
QDSPSGNINF	Specifies whether the sign-on information display appears when a user signs on	0 (off) 1 (on)	0 (off)

QDSPSGNINF controls the display of user sign-on information. A value of 1 causes the system to display certain information to users when they sign on to the system: the last date and time signed on and the number of failed sign-on attempts due to an invalid password. This type of information isn't valuable, and is often a nuisance, for most end users. However, IT personnel may find it useful for monitoring the security of their own profiles and passwords.

Technical Note

QDSPSGNINF controls the display of sign-on information systemwide. To override this system value at the user profile level, change the DSPSGNINF user profile parameter.

Security Recommendation

Set QDSPSGNINF to 0 and control sign-on information at the user profile level by modifying the DSPSGNINF parameter for individual user profiles.

System value	Description	Possible values	Default
QINACTITV — Inactivity Time-out Interval			
QINACTITV	Determines the interval in minutes that a workstation can be inactive before the system sends a message to a message queue or ends the job	*NONE 5 to 300	*NONE
QINACTMSGQ — Inactivity Message Queue			
QINACTMSGQ	Specifies either the action to be taken when the inactivity time-out interval is reached or the name of the message queue that will receive messages about the workstation	*ENDJOB *DSCJOB message_queue_name	*DSCJOB
QDSCJOBITV — Disconnect-Job Interval			
QDSCJOBITV	Specifies the interval (in minutes) that a job can be disconnected before the system ends the job	*NONE 5 to 1440	240

QINACTITV determines the length of time, in minutes, that a workstation is allowed to remain inactive before the system either ends the job, disconnects the job, or sends a message to the message queue specified in system value QINACTMSGQ. If you select *DSCJOB for the QINACTMSGQ system value, the system will disconnect a job that times out rather than ending it. The job will remain disconnected for the length of time specified in the QDSCJOBITV (Disconnect Job Interval) system value, and then it will end (the system will cancel the job, close all files and programs, and automatically roll back all uncommitted transactions running under commitment control). Users that sign back on to disconnected jobs are simply reconnected to the job and can continue processing.

It's important to realize that "inactive" refers not to the job itself, but to the workstation. Has the user pressed the Enter key? The System request key? Page up or Page down? In other words, a workstation is considered inactive when there is no user interaction for the specified time. If the workstation job is waiting for a user response, the workstation is inactive.

At first, you should set the value of QINACTITV to about 30 minutes and supply a message queue name in system value QINACTMSGQ. Monitor the message queue to determine how many workstations, if any, are timing out. If you don't have a problem with time-outs, you can go ahead and change QINACTMSGQ to *DSCJOB. If some terminals time out regularly, you should probably talk to the users before you change the system value. Because an available workstation is a veritable invitation for unauthorized access, you must prevent signed-on workstations from being left unattended.

As an alternative to ending or disconnecting the job, you can write a program to monitor the message queue specified in QINACTMSGQ and take action appropriate to the job in progress. This is often a good approach. Because the inactivity interval you specify is system-wide, a user-written message-queue-monitoring program is the only way to provide different inactivity intervals or consequences for specific workstations or user profiles.

If a system is the target system for DSPT sessions from another system, you'll probably want to write a program to monitor the inactive jobs to avoid disconnecting or canceling those particular sessions. After a DSPT session disconnects, it's difficult to reconnect using the same virtual device.

The QINACTITV system value also monitors the activity of Client Access emulation sessions. These sessions might appear inactive if the user isn't directly interacting with the AS/400 session (e.g., if the user is editing a document using a PC-based word processor or spreadsheet). Using the QINACTITV system value without a user-written program might inconvenience such users by unnecessarily ending their emulation sessions.

Security Recommendation

Set the value of **QINACTITV** to **30** and the value of **QINACTMSGQ** to ***DSCJOB**. Be sure to set the **QDSCJOBITV** system value to a reasonable number, such as **30**. With QDSCJOBITV at 30, if the user doesn't sign on again before the job has been disconnected for 30 minutes, the job will end.

QLMTDEVSSN — Limit Device Sessions

System value	Description	Possible values	Default
QLMTDEVSSN	Lets you specify whether a user can have concurrent device sessions	0 (off) 1 (on)	0 (off)

QLMTDEVSSN determines whether a user profile can be signed on to more than one workstation simultaneously. A value of 0 allows a user profile to work at more than one workstation simultaneously. A value of 1 restricts the user profile to a single workstation device. QLMTDEVSSN can't prevent users from sharing a single workstation and the user profile currently signed on.

Sharing user profiles decreases the effectiveness of auditing users' activities. However, sharing user profiles might be necessary in some situations, such as a retail operation in which clerks share sales-counter workstations. Signing on and off such terminals would be inconvenient, would cause the customer to wait, and would create a sales-counter bottleneck at busy times.

Technical Note
QLMTDEVSSN controls concurrent device sessions system-wide, but you can override this system value at the user profile level by changing the user profile parameter LMTDEVSSN (Limit Device Sessions).

Security Recommendation
Use a value of 1 for QLMTDEVSSN to discourage users from sharing user profiles.

QLMTSECOFR — Limit Security Officer Access to Workstations

System value	Description	Possible values	Default
QLMTSECOFR	Limits users with *ALLOBJ or *SERVICE special authority to authorized devices	0 (off) 1 (on)	1 (on)

QLMTSECOFR determines which workstations can be accessed by user profiles that have *ALLOBJ or *SERVICE special authority, such as QSECOFR and QSRV, the profile the system supplies for your Customer Engineer's use. If you set the value at 0 (off), users with *ALLOBJ or *SERVICE special authority can use any workstation attached to the system. When the value is 1 (on), these users are limited to accessing workstations to which they are specifically authorized (by virtue of granted authority or ownership). In most situations, there's no need for profiles with *ALLOBJ or *SERVICE special authorities to access workstations outside of the IT facilities, and we recommend setting QLMTSECOFR to 1.

We realize that this recommendation can occasionally cause a problem. For example, you might travel to a remote site and then discover that you need to access the system using a profile with *ALLOBJ special authority. With QLMTSECOFR set at 1, what choices do you have? You could have the operations staff specifically authorize the QSECOFR profile to one of the remote devices. Or you could prepare ahead of time by following these steps:

1. Create a user profile, specifying *USER as the user class and MAIN for the initial menu. This user profile should also have LMTCPB(*NO).

2. Create a CL program as follows:

   ```
   PGM
   CALL QCMD
   SIGNOFF
   ENDPGM
   ```

3. Compile the CL program as QSECOFR with USRPRF(*OWNER) to adopt the QSECOFR authority, and authorize only the user profile you created in step 1 to execute this program.

At the remote site, you can then use this special profile and call the CL program to access a command entry display with QSECOFR adopted authority. This solution doesn't create a security problem when only the security officer knows the password for the special user profile and only that profile is authorized to the CL program that adopts QSECOFR authority. Don't authorize any other user profile to this program. However, remember that any users who have *ALLOBJ (all object) special authority can call the program if they know its name, even if they don't have explicit authority to the program.

Security Recommendation

Set QLMTSECOFR to 1 to limit access to authorized workstations, and then grant authority to specific IT workstations. Regardless of the value you assign to QLMTSECOFR, the QSECOFR user profile can always sign on at the system console.

System value	Description	Possible values	Default
QMAXSIGN — Maximum Number of Sign-on Attempts			
QMAXSIGN	Determines the maximum number of sign-on attempts allowed for a workstation	*NOMAX any number	3 (as of V3R7)
QMAXSGNACN — Maximum Sign-on Action			
QMAXSGNACN	Specifies the action taken when a user reaches the maximum number of failed sign-on attempts	1 2 3	3

QMAXSIGN determines the number of invalid sign-on attempts the system allows before taking action to disable the device or user profile being used. Users cause invalid sign-on attempts by entering nonexistent user profiles or incorrect passwords or by trying to use a workstation without having authorization to it.

When you set a numeric value for QMAXSIGN, the system sends a message to the workstation when only one attempt remains. The message warns the user that the next incorrect sign-on will disable the device or user profile.

Setting QMAXSIGN to *NOMAX can cause a serious problem. One business discovered from its phone bill that a hacker had called repeatedly on the dial-up line and attempted to sign on by guessing user profiles and passwords. In this case, a value of *NOMAX resulted in a huge phone bill and could have resulted in the hacker guessing the QSECOFR password. A QMAXSIGN value of 3 would have varied off the device after the third unsuccessful attempt and alerted the operations staff that something was up.

QMAXSGNACN controls the action the system takes when a user reaches the maximum number of failed sign-on attempts specified in QMAXSIGN. The possible values are

- 1 — Disable the display device.
- 2 — Disable the user profile.
- 3 — Disable both the display device and the user profile.

As you can see, this system value lets you disable the user profile of a user who exceeds the maximum allowed number of sign-on attempts. After a user profile is disabled, you can restore it to active state only by using the STATUS(*ENABLE) parameter on the CHGUSRPRF command.

Security Recommendation

For maximum protection, retain the default value of 3 for QMAXSGNACN. The default value prevents multiple invalid sign-on attempts using the same profile or workstation and limits your exposure to profile and password guessing.

QRETSVRSEC — Retain Server Security

System value	Description	Possible values	Default
QRETSVRSEC	Determines whether you allow decryptable passwords to be stored on your system	0 (off) 1 (on)	0 (off)

QRETSVRSEC was created to let you control whether OS/400 will store decryptable passwords. This system value doesn't affect AS/400 user profile passwords, which are stored in a one-way–encrypted form. The passwords QRETSVRSEC controls are typically passwords used to sign on to another system. For example, Serial Line Internet Protocol (SLIP) requires a password that can be decrypted so it can be used to sign on to another system. In addition, in V4R2, you can store decryptable passwords in a validation list. (For a discussion of validation lists, see the section "Write Secure Web Applications" in Chapter 9.)

Technical Note

Changing the QRETSVRSEC value from 1 (on) to 0 (off) will remove all decryptable passwords that are stored on your system.

Security Recommendation

If you don't want to store decryptable passwords on your AS/400, leave the QRETSVRSEC system value at its default of 0 (off).

QRMTSIGN — Remote Sign-on Value

System value	Description	Possible values	Default
QRMTSIGN	Determines whether automatic sign-on from a remote system is allowed	*FRCSIGNON *SAMEPRF *REJECT *VERIFY program_name	*FRCSIGNON

The OS/400 command STRPASTHR (Start Pass-Through) lets a user enter a user profile name, password, initial program, initial menu, and current library to bypass the target system's typical sign-on procedures. This capability lets you automate passthrough services. The QRMTSIGN system value determines how your system handles automatic passthrough requests it receives. The allowed values are

- *FRCSIGNON — All passthrough sessions begin with the normal sign-on procedure (screen). If the user profile names on the source and target systems aren't the same, the attempt fails.
- *SAMEPRF — A passthrough session that bypasses the normal sign-on procedure is allowed only when the user profile names are identical on the source and target systems.
- *REJECT — All passthrough requests are rejected.
- *VERIFY — Automatic passthrough requests (those bypassing normal sign-on procedure) must contain a valid user profile and the profile's valid password.
- program_name — Designates a program to be executed at the beginning and end of every passthrough session. The specified program controls and logs access for every passthrough request. You can qualify this value by library name.

If you have programming expertise in your shop, writing a program to control passthrough is an excellent way to audit and flexibly control passthrough use.

Security Recommendation

If you don't use communications, give QRMTSIGN the value of *REJECT. If you participate in a network that allows passthrough, use *VERIFY to require both the user profile and password.

QSECURITY — System Security Level

See the detailed discussion in "The System Security Level" at the beginning of this chapter.

QUSEADPAUT — Use Adopted Authority

System value	Description	Possible values	Default
QUSEADPAUT	Specifies which users can create programs that adopt authority	authorization_list_name *NONE	*NONE

Many people misunderstand the USEADPAUT (Use Adopted Authority) program attribute. This attribute doesn't control whether the program adopts authority. USEADPAUT controls whether the program can *use* adopted authority propagated to it from another program higher in the call stack.

Many applications use programs that adopt a powerful profile (often QSECOFR) and call other programs but don't qualify the call by library. If a clever employee or hacker can create a program by the same name and put it into a library that precedes the real program's library in the library list, the hacker's program will be called instead of the real program and the hacker's program can use the adopted authority that the calling program provides.

The QUSEADPAUT system value lets you prevent users from being able to create programs that adopt authority. Create an authorization list and specify it for QUSEADPAUT. For the most security, you might want to create the authorization list as *PUBLIC(*EXCLUDE), then grant specific authority to only those users allowed to create programs that use adopted authority.

It's very appropriate to use this system value for a production system. However, if you implement it in an application development environment, it can seriously affect how programmers can do their jobs. Some application designs depend on programs that can use adopted authority.

Security Recommendation

For maximum protection in a production environment, use the QUSEADPAUT system value to determine which users (if any) are allowed to create programs that use adopted authority.

Password-Related System Values

Ten security-related system values are available for you to use with the CHGPWD (Change Password) command. When users use the CHGPWD command to change their current password, the system checks each of these system values to determine which rules to apply to the new password's format. If any of these system values restricts the format of the password and the user's new password violates that rule, the system sends an error message, and the user must select another password.

Remember that passwords should be secret, hard to guess, and changed regularly. However, sometimes "hard to guess" also translates into "hard to remember." When passwords are hard to remember, users tend to write them down near the workstation so they don't forget them. This practice is a major security problem. Carefully used, these system values can strengthen your security plan without creating a situation where users have difficulty selecting and remembering passwords. Table 2.4 lists the password-related system values.

TABLE 2.4
System Values Used with the CHGPWD Command

System value	Description
QPWDEXPITV	Specifies the maximum number of days a password is valid
QPWDRQDDIF	Determines whether the password must be different from previous passwords
QPWDMINLEN	Specifies the minimum number of characters in a password
QPWDMAXLEN	Specifies the maximum number of characters in a password
QPWDRQDDGT	Determines whether a digit is required in the password
QPWDLMTAJC	Determines whether passwords can contain adjacent digits
QPWDLMTCHR	Specifies characters that are not allowed in a password
QPWDLMTREP	Determines whether passwords can contain repeating characters
QPWDPOSDIF	Determines whether each position in a new password must contain a different character than the corresponding position in the old password
QPWDVLDPGM	Specifies the name of the user-written password approval program

We look at the function of each system value in turn. For an in-depth discussion of password creation and maintenance, see Chapter 3.

QPWDEXPITV — Password Expiration Interval

System value	Description	Possible values	Default
QPWDEXPITV	Determines the maximum number of days a password is valid	*NOMAX 1 to 366	*NOMAX

QPWDEXPITV determines the maximum number of days that a password is valid. When the limit is exceeded, the password expires, and the next attempt to sign on causes the system to prompt the CHGPWD command. The user must then select a new password to access the system.

Technical Note

The QPWDEXPITV system value controls the password expiration interval system-wide, but you can override it with the user profile parameter PWDEXPITV.

Security Recommendation

For most users, set QPWDEXPITV to a value of 60 or 90 days. For users who have special authorities or access to sensitive functions or data (e.g., human resources, IT), set a value of 30 or 45 days.

QPWDRQDDIF — Require Different Password

System value	Description	Possible values	Default
QPWDRQDDIF	Determines whether the password must be different from previous passwords	0 to 8	0

With QPWDRQDDIF, you can prevent users from selecting a new password that is the same as a selected number of previous passwords. You can tell the system to allow users to duplicate a previous password (specify the default value of 0) or prevent users from using the previous 4, 6, 8, 10, 12, 18, 24, or 32 passwords, depending on which non-zero value you enter. The meanings of the non-zero values are

- 1 — User can't duplicate previous 32 passwords
- 2 — User can't duplicate previous 24 passwords
- 3 — User can't duplicate previous 18 passwords
- 4 — User can't duplicate previous 12 passwords
- 5 — User can't duplicate previous 10 passwords
- 6 — User can't duplicate previous 8 passwords
- 7 — User can't duplicate previous 6 passwords
- 8 — User can't duplicate previous 4 passwords

This system value is a must for every organization. You should prevent users from duplicating at least the previous 4 passwords, and if you want tighter security, you probably should stretch that guideline to cover the previous 10 passwords.

Security Recommendation

Set QPWDRQDDIF to 5 to prevent users from reusing their past 10 passwords.

System value	Description	Possible values	Default
QPWDMINLEN — Minimum Number of Characters Required			
QPWDMINLEN	Determines the minimum number of characters in a password	1 to 10	6 (as of V3R7)
QPWDMAXLEN — Maximum Number of Characters Allowed			
QPWDMAXLEN	Determines the maximum number of characters in a password	1 to 10	8 (as of V3R7)

QPWDMINLEN determines the minimum number of characters a valid password must contain. QPWDMAXLEN determines the maximum number of characters a valid password can contain. Every AS/400 installation should use these password system values.

Security Recommendation

Set QPWDMINLEN to at least 7 to prevent the use of short names and initials. Change the value of QPWDMAXLEN to 10. (If you want to synchronize passwords with another system in your network that can't support 10-character passwords, you'll need to set QPWDMAXLEN to a value less than 10.)

QPWDRQDDGT — Require a Digit

System value	Description	Possible values	Default
QPWDRQDDGT	Determines whether a digit is required in a password	0 (off) 1 (on)	0 (off)

QPWDRQDDGT determines whether at least one digit (0 to 9) is required in a valid password. We recommend you set the value to 1 to require a digit in the password. This requirement doesn't ensure extraordinarily effective passwords, but it does at least make the guessing game a little more difficult.

Security Recommendation

Set QPWDRQDDGT to 1 to require users to put at least one digit in their passwords.

QPWDLMTAJC — Limit Use of Adjacent Digits

System value	Description	Possible values	Default
QPWDLMTAJC	Limits the use of digits next to each other in a password	0 (off) 1 (on)	0 (off)

QPWDLMTAJC restricts the use of adjacent digits, thus preventing passwords such as 11111111, phone numbers, and social security numbers.

> **Security Recommendation**
>
> Set QPWDLMTAJC to 1 to prevent the use of phone numbers or other numbers that someone could easily associate with the user.

QPWDLMTCHR — Limit Use of Specific Characters

System value	Description	Possible values	Default
QPWDLMTCHR	Limits the use of up to 10 specified characters in passwords	*NONE Specify up to 10 characters	*NONE

QPWDLMTCHR lets you specify up to 10 characters that aren't allowed in a valid password. The characters that can normally be used in a password are A through Z, 0 through 9, and the special characters #, $, and @.

Based on our knowledge and training, we're inclined to suggest specifying vowels here, thus eliminating words as a choice for passwords. However, our experience is that this restriction makes passwords hard to remember as well as hard to guess, resulting in the user writing the password down and keeping it close to the workstation for reference. So use your own judgment.

QPWDLMTREP — Limit Repeating Characters

System value	Description	Possible values	Default
QPWDLMTREP	Limits the use of a repeating character in a password	0, 1, 2	0

QPWDLMTREP lets you prevent more than one occurrence of an alphabetic character in a password. The default value of 0 allows the same character to be repeated in a password. Specifying the value 1 prevents the same character from being used anywhere in a password. For instance, the passwords "aaabbb" and "ababab" would be invalid because a character is repeated in some form. Specifying the value 2 prevents consecutively repeating characters only. In that case, the password "aaabbb" would not be allowed, whereas "ababab" would be, because the characters aren't repeated consecutively.

> **Security Recommendation**
>
> Set the value of QPWDLMTREP to 2 to prevent users from repeating any character consecutively in a password.

QPWDPOSDIF — Require Positions to Be Different

System value	Description	Possible values	Default
QPWDPOSDIF	Determines whether each position in a new password must contain a different character than the same position in the old password	0 (off) 1 (on)	0 (off)

QPWDPOSDIF lets you prevent the use of a character in a new password in the same position as that character occupied in the old password. This system value was designed to prevent a succession of passwords such as CRAZY1, CRAZY2, CRAZY3.

Again, the ideal doesn't match the pragmatic. This feature would be nice to enforce but makes it difficult for a user to diagnose the error when the system disallows a new password.

QPWDVLDPGM — Password Validation Program

System value	Description	Possible values	Default
QPWDVLDPGM	Specifies the name of the user-written password approval program	*NONE program_name	*NONE

QPWDVLDPGM provides a viable alternative to working with the many system values that control passwords. You can write your own password validation program, using any rules you want to enforce. The advantage is in the flexibility such a program provides. For example, you can check a file containing commonly used words and prevent their use, or you can make sure users don't use their own name or initials.

Figure 2.1 shows a simple shell for a password validity-checking CL program. This particular program prevents users from changing their password more than once a day. Some users try to bypass the QPWDRQDDIF system value limitation by changing their password again and again until they can reuse the same password they started with. A validation program like the one we show here at least forces users to work harder and wait longer to keep their old familiar password.

The disadvantage of using a password validation program is that the validation program provides users' passwords in clear text. If you create a password-validation program, you must monitor it to ensure that no one is storing the clear-text passwords.

FIGURE 2.1
Sample Password Validity-Checking Program

```
/*===================================================================*/
/* Password Validity Checking Program                                */
/* This program name defined as QPWDVLDPGM system value.             */
/* This program called as part of CHGPWD command process.            */
/*===================================================================*/
  PGM PARM( &i#oldpwd       /* IN   old password                    */ +
            &i#newpwd       /* IN   new password                    */ +
            &o#rtn_code     /* OUT  return code (0 = Good, 1 = Bad) */ +
            &i#user         /* IN   user changing password          */ +
          )
```

continued

FIGURE 2.1 *CONTINUED*

```
   DCL   &i#oldpwd        *char    10
   DCL   &i#newpwd        *char    10
   DCL   &o#rtn_code      *lgl      1
   DCL   &i#user          *char    10
   DCL   &jobdate         *char     6
   DCL   &pwdchgdat       *char     6
   DCL   &pwdexp          *char     4
   DCL   &@no             *char     4    VALUE('*NO ')
   DCL   &@yes            *char     4    VALUE('*YES')
   DCL   &@good           *lgl      1    VALUE('0')
   DCL   &@bad            *lgl      1    VALUE('1')
/* Preset return code                                              */
   CHGVAR   &o#rtn_code &@good

/*================================================================*/
/* Allow only one password change per day.                        */
/*================================================================*/

/* Get current job date                                           */
   RTVJOBA  DATE(&jobdate)
   CVTDAT   DATE(&jobdate) TOVAR(&jobdate) TOFMT(*YMD) TOSEP(*NONE)
/* Retrieve password change date                                  */
   RTVUSRPRF USRPRF(&i#user) PWDCHGDAT(&pwdchgdat) PWDEXP(&pwdexp)

/* If equal and password not expired, reject request              */
   IF (&pwdchgdat = &jobdate *AND &pwdexp = &@no) DO
      CHGVAR   &o#rtn_code &@bad
      SNDPGMMSG MSGID(CPF9898)                                    +
                MSGF(QCPFMSG)                                     +
                MSGDTA('Password can be changed only once per day') +
                MSGTYPE(*ESCAPE)
   ENDDO

   RETURN
   ENDPGM
```

Security Recommendation

If you implement a password validity-checking program, be certain to secure the source and program object to prevent anyone from modifying the program. If the program is unsecured, someone could use it to record passwords.

Audit-Related System Values

One area that continues to evolve significantly in AS/400 security is the auditing capabilities of the operating system. The system values listed in Table 2.5 are key to implementing AS/400 auditing functions.

TABLE 2.5
Auditing System Values

System value	Description
QAUDCTL	Turns OS/400 security auditing on or off
QAUDENDACN	Determines the action the system should take if it's unable to continue auditing (i.e., if the system can't write another audit record to the journal)
QAUDFRCLVL	Determines when new auditing journal entries are physically written to disk from memory
QAUDLVL	Determines which security-related events are recorded in the security audit journal for all system users
QCRTOBJAUD	Specifies the default auditing level for any new object

Here, we only introduce and give an overview of these system values. For the complete guide to AS/400 auditing, see Chapters 16, 17, and 18.

QAUDCTL — Auditing Control

System value	Description	Possible values	Default
QAUDCTL	Serves as the on/off switch for OS/400 security auditing	*NONE *AUDLVL *OBJAUD *NOQTEMP	*NONE

QAUDCTL is the on/off switch for OS/400 security auditing. The default value, *NONE, tells OS/400 not to perform security auditing. Entering the value *AUDLVL or *OBJAUD tells OS/400 to perform auditing. *AUDLVL activates event auditing by system or by user. *OBJAUD activates object auditing. *NOQTEMP prevents extraneous auditing entries for objects in library QTEMP.

QAUDENDACN — Auditing End Action

System value	Description	Possible values	Default
QAUDENDACN	Determines the action the system should take if it's unable to continue auditing (i.e., if the system can't write another audit record to the journal)	*NOTIFY *PWRDWNSYS	*NOTIFY

QAUDENDACN determines the action the system should take if it can't write another audit record to the journal and thus is unable to continue auditing. The default value *NOTIFY causes OS/400 to continue processing, but also to send a message to the system operator. The system also sends the message to QSYS/QSYSMSG if that message queue exists.

The other choice is *PWRDWNSYS, which instructs the system to immediately power down. Both *NOTIFY and *PWRDWNSYS trigger an automatic change to *NONE in the QAUDCTL system value. This means that auditing will be turned off. You must turn it back on manually after correcting the problem that prevented the system from writing to the journal. (See the "Auditing Controls" section of Chapter 18 for a detailed discussion of other implications of the *PWRDWNSYS value.)

Security Recommendation

Unless you must comply with DoD Level C2 security, use the QAUDENDACN default value, *NOTIFY.

QAUDFRCLVL — Auditing Force Level

System value	Description	Possible values	Default
QAUDFRCLVL	Determines when new auditing journal entries are physically written to disk from memory	*SYS number_of_records (1 to 100)	*SYS

QAUDFRCLVL determines the maximum number of audit records you let the system cache before forcing them to disk. You can specify any number in the range 1 to 100, or you can specify *SYS to let OS/400 control this number dynamically for performance purposes. If a system failure occurs, you might lose the audit records not yet written to disk. Systems that require DoD Level C2 compliance will specify 1 for this system value. For all other systems, however, we recommend the value *SYS, which maximizes performance when you use auditing.

Security Recommendation

Unless you must comply with DoD Level C2 security, use the QAUDFRCLVL default of *SYS.

QAUDLVL — Auditing Level

System value	Description	Possible values	Default
QAUDLVL	Determines the level of auditing on the system	*NONE *AUTFAIL, *CREATE, *DELETE, *JOBDTA, *NETCMN, *OBJMGT, *OFCSRV, *OPTICAL, *PGMADP, *PGMFAIL, *PRTDTA, *SAVRST, *SECURITY, *SERVICE, *SPLFDTA, *SYSMGT	*NONE

The AS/400 can help the security officer audit security by logging data concerning security-related events to a journal named QAUDJRN. QAUDLVL determines the level of auditing the system performs. You can specify one or more values (unless one of the values is *NONE, which causes other values to be ignored). The following list describes the types of journal entries made for each value.

- *NONE — No auditing occurs on the system.
- *AUTFAIL — Audit authority failures (e.g., user doesn't have authority to open file, user doesn't have authority to execute a program).
- *CREATE — Audit object creation operations.

- *DELETE — Audit object deletion operations.
- *JOBDTA — Audit job start and end.
- *NETCMN — Audit violations detected by APPN filter.
- *OBJMGT — Audit object management operations (e.g., move an object, rename an object).
- *OFCSRV — Audit office mail actions and changes to the system distribution directory.
- *OPTICAL — Audit use of optical storage volumes.
- *PGMADP — Audit use of programs that adopt authority.
- *PGMFAIL — Audit system integrity violations (e.g., use or attempted use of restricted machine instructions).
- *PRTDTA — Audit direct and spooled printing.
- *SAVRST — Audit restore operations.
- *SECURITY — Audit changes to security controls (e.g., system value changes, object authority changes, auditing control changes).
- *SERVICE — Audit use of the service tools (i.e., the STRSST, or Start System Service Tools, command and options).
- *SPLFDTA — Audit spooled file control (e.g., moving a spooled file, releasing a spooled file).
- *SYSMGT — Audit system management activities (e.g., changes to the power on/off schedule, system reply list, backup options, Distributed Relational Database Architecture — DRDA).

The most important thing to remember when you use QAUDLVL is to begin with only a few values. If you use many of these values concurrently, you're likely to spend most of your time managing the size of the journal receiver attached to the audit journal (it will grow quickly!). Some of the options, such as *SECURITY, *PGMFAIL, and *SERVICE, can help maintain tight security on an ongoing basis. Other values, such as *PGMADP, *AUTFAIL, *CREATE, and *DELETE, may prove more helpful for spot-checking or to solve specific security-related problems. The point is, use these wisely. For more information and guidance, see Chapter 18.

Security Recommendation
Start by setting QAUDLVL to *SECURITY, *SAVRST, *SERVICE, and *AUTFAIL, and then add the other values one at a time while monitoring the activity and size of the journal. Before attempting to move to level 40, use the *PGMFAIL audit log level to determine which, if any, system integrity violations are occurring.

QCRTOBJAUD — Auditing for New Objects			
System value	Description	Possible values	Default
QCRTOBJAUD	Specifies the default auditing level for new objects	*NONE *USRPRF, *CHANGE, *ALL	*NONE

QCRTOBJAUD and the library attribute CRTOBJAUD together determine the default object auditing level for new objects. QCRTOBJAUD works much like the QCRTAUT system value, which determines the default public authorities for new objects. When you create a new object, OS/400 checks the CRTOBJAUD attribute for the library in which the new object will reside. If the attribute's value is *SYSVAL, OS/400 refers to the QCRTOBJAUD system value to determine which of the object-auditing values (*NONE, *USRPRF, *CHANGE, or *ALL) to assign to the new object's OBJAUD attribute.

AS/400s ship with a CRTOBJAUD attribute value of *SYSVAL for every library on the system. Consequently, you could use the QCRTOBJAUD system value to control the object auditing level for every new object on your system. However, for existing objects, you must use the CHGOBJAUD (Change Object Auditing) command to change the OBJAUD value. For more detail about using the CHGOBJAUD command, see "Object Auditing," Chapter 18.

A Helpful Tool

OS/400 V3R2 provides integrated security tools. One tool that relates specifically to this chapter is the PRTSYSSECA (Print System Security Attributes) command, which is available on the SECTOOLS and SECBATCH menus and prints a list of the current security-related system values and network attributes. This tool also shows IBM's recommended values.

AS/400 security rests on a foundation of well-configured security-related system values. One of these (QSECURITY) sets the security level. Any production-environment AS/400 should be at least at security level 40 (resource security and system integrity). The other security-related system values enforce security measures relating to general workstation access, passwords, and communications. With a solid foundation underfoot, we can now move into a discussion of more specific OS/400 security methods and tools.

Operations Navigator

IBM provides a graphical user interface (GUI) to make your administrative tasks easier to carry out. This GUI is intended to replace green-screen commands. In fact, IBM has implemented most new functions in recent releases of OS/400 in a GUI but *not* in commands. So, like it or not, if you want to use new functions, you'll need to use Operations Navigator. Chapter 7 describes the security considerations that come into play with Operations Navigator. Here, we explain how Operations Navigator can make security administration easier.

First, to help you configure your AS/400, the security development team in Rochester implemented a security wizard. The security wizard can help you change your security plan, determine how your implementation compares to the IBM recommendations, and guide you if you just don't know where to start when it comes to securing your system. To access the wizard, click on the name of your AS/400 to expand your options, right-click on Security, and select Configure (Figure 2.2).

When you launch the wizard, it will ask you several questions about your security requirements and your system's configuration. After you answer the questions, the wizard will recommend settings for the security-related system values and network attributes. It will also provide recommendations for auditing and for running and scheduling the security tools. You can choose to apply the recommendations to your system or save them and apply them later (or never), if you wish. The wizard even provides an "oops" button — the Reset security controls button.

FIGURE 2.2
The Security Wizard Configuration Screen

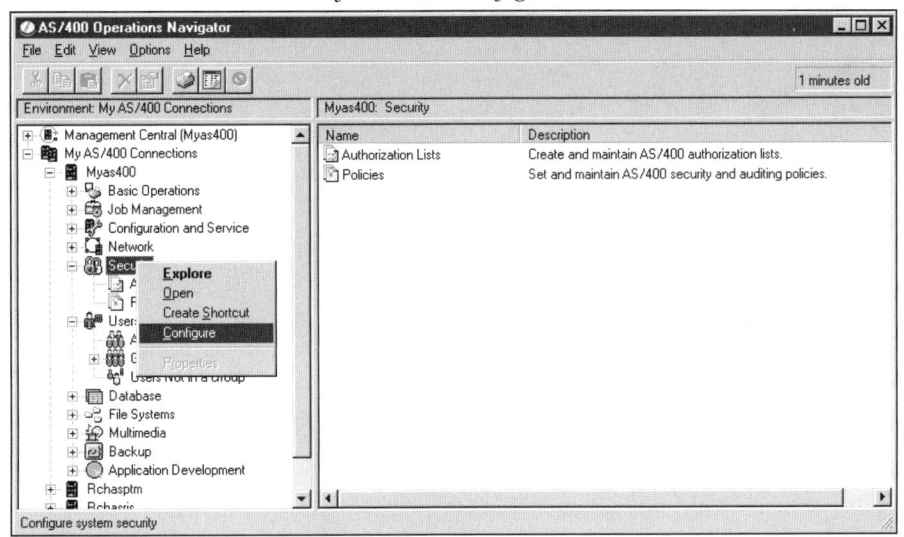

Technical Note

For those who don't have Client Access or choose not to use Operations Navigator, these security wizard recommendations are available from the AS/400e Security Advisor, on the Internet at http://www.as400.ibm.com/ebusiness/security.

If you apply the changes and then realize that you didn't investigate all of the ramifications of the new settings, you can reenter the security wizard and use the "Reset security controls" button to reset the values to their previous settings. The security wizard also provides two reports for your use. An administrator report describes the recommended settings by grouping similar system values and describing the interaction between them. The end user report describes the settings that affect end users, such as the password rules. You can store both reports on your PC and use your favorite word processing program to edit and print them. The administrator report helps you document your security implementation for management or auditors. You can use the end user report to communicate your company's security policy to employees.

Another Operations Navigator function lets you manage security-related system values. Operations Navigator calls system values *policies*. To manage policies, click the name of your AS/400 and choose Security, Policies. From the resulting screen (Figure 2.3), you can manage the auditing system values or the security-related system values.

FIGURE 2.3
Operations Navigator Policy Management Window

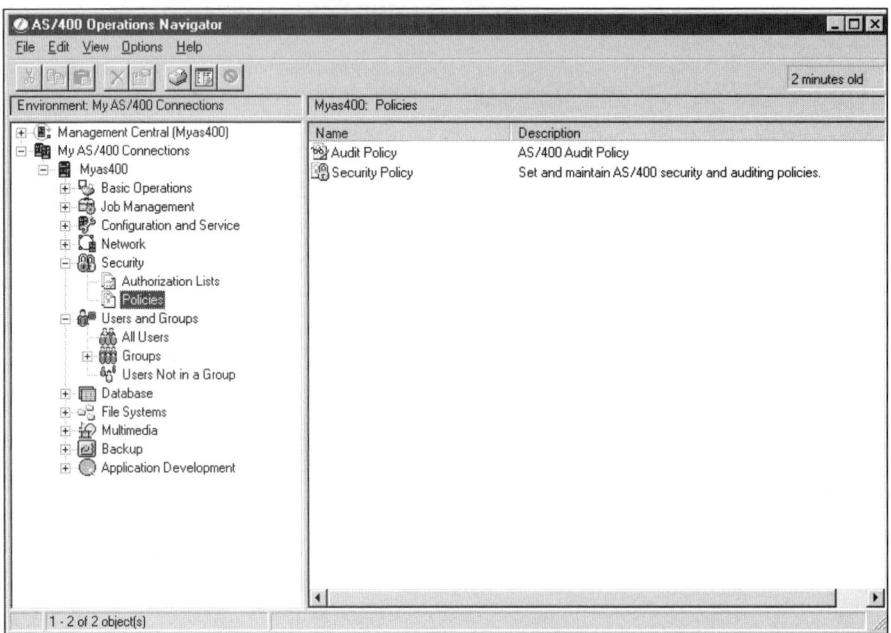

Chapter 3
The Facts About User Profiles

User profiles serve two purposes: They identify the user accessing the system, and they identify the objects the user is authorized to access or manipulate.

We suggest you read the preceding sentence again: It has as much to do with implementing security as any sentence that could be written or spoken. Permit us to explain.

Why User Profiles?

As we've said, user profiles serve to let the system identify authorized users. The ability to identify authorized users lets the system also recognize unauthorized attempts at access. These facts make evident the inadequacy of operating an AS/400 at security level 10, which didn't require that users identify themselves with a user profile known to the system.

Identifying authorized users is only the first step toward a secure system. The second step is authorizing those users to manipulate only the objects they need to manipulate to do their jobs. You can't achieve this goal at security level 20, which doesn't effectively support resource security. However, at levels 30, 40, and 50, after a user enters a valid user profile and password, the system checks every object that the user's job requests to determine whether the user has the authority to work with that object and what the user is authorized to do with it.

By requiring users to enter a user profile and password and by authorizing users to needed objects on the system, you can formalize a sound security strategy into an implementation that provides the proper levels of authorization. You can grant users authority based on their user profiles, you can group user profiles for authorization purposes, and you can establish audit trails that track which users made what changes.

What Is a User Profile?

To the AS/400, a user profile is an object. Although the object's name (e.g., WDAVIS, PGMR0234) is what you normally think of as the user profile, a user profile is much more than a name. The attributes of each user profile object define a particular user to the system, enabling it to establish a custom initial session (i.e., job) for that user at sign-on. To make the best use of user profiles, you need to understand those attributes and how they can help you implement your security strategy.

You must have *SECADM (security administrator) special authority to create and maintain user profiles on your system using the CRTUSRPRF (Create User Profile), CHGUSRPRF (Change User Profile), and DLTUSRPRF (Delete User Profile) commands. Thus, only the security officer profile (QSECOFR) or another profile that has *SECADM special authority can create, change, or delete user profiles.

User Profile Attributes

You use the CRTUSRPRF command to create a user profile. When you prompt the CRTUSRPRF command and press F10, the system displays the command's parameters (Figure 3.1). We've highlighted those that relate directly to security and discuss them below.

FIGURE 3.1
CRTUSRPRF Parameters

```
                  Create User Profile (CRTUSRPRF)

Type choices, press Enter.

    User profile . . . . . . . . . .   USRPRF
    User password  . . . . . . . . .   PASSWORD       *USRPRF
    Set password to expired  . . . .   PWDEXP         *NO
    Status . . . . . . . . . . . . .   STATUS         *ENABLED
    User class . . . . . . . . . . .   USRCLS         *USER
    Assistance Level . . . . . . . .   ASTLVL         *SYSVAL
    Current library  . . . . . . . .   CURLIB         *CRTDFT
    Initial program to call  . . . .   INLPGM         *NONE
      Library  . . . . . . . . . . .
    Initial menu . . . . . . . . . .   INLMNU         MAIN
      Library  . . . . . . . . . . .                    *LIBL
    Limit capabilities . . . . . . .   LMTCPB         *NO
    Text 'description' . . . . . . .   TEXT           *BLANK

    Special authority  . . . . . . .   SPCAUT         *USRCLS
                  + for more values
    Special environment  . . . . . .   SPCENV         *SYSVAL
    Display sign-on information  . .   DSPSGNINF      *SYSVAL
    Password expiration interval . .   PWDEXPITV      *SYSVAL
    Limit device sessions  . . . . .   LMTDEVSSN      *SYSVAL
    Keyboard Buffering . . . . . . .   KBDBUF         *SYSVAL
    Maximum allowed storage  . . . .   MAXSTG         *NOMAX
    Highest schedule priority  . . .   PTYLMT         3
    Job description  . . . . . . . .   JOBD           QDFTJOBD
      Library  . . . . . . . . . . .                    *LIBL
    Group profile  . . . . . . . . .   GRPPRF         *NONE
    Owner  . . . . . . . . . . . . .   OWNER          *USRPRF
    Group authority  . . . . . . . .   GRPAUT         *NONE
    Group authority type . . . . . .   GRPAUTTYP      *PRIVATE
    Supplemental groups  . . . . . .   SUPGRPPRF      *NONE
                  + for more values
    Accounting code  . . . . . . . .   ACGCDE         *BLANK
    Document password  . . . . . . .   DOCPWD         *NONE
    Message queue  . . . . . . . . .   MSGQ           *USRPRF
      Library  . . . . . . . . . . .
    Delivery . . . . . . . . . . . .   DLVRY          *NOTIFY
    Severity code filter . . . . . .   SEV            00
    Print device . . . . . . . . . .   PRTDEV         *WRKSTN
```

continued

Figure 3.1 *Continued*

```
Output queue  . . . . . . . . . . OUTQ        *WRKSTN
   Library   . . . . . . . . . . .
Attention program  . . . . . . . ATNPGM      *SYSVAL
   Library   . . . . . . . . . . .
Sort sequence  . . . . . . . . . SRTSEQ      *SYSVAL
   Library   . . . . . . . . . . .
Language ID . . . . . . . . . . . LANGID      *SYSVAL
Country ID . . . . . . . . . . .  CNTRYID     *SYSVAL
Coded character set ID . . . . .  CCSID       *SYSVAL
User options . . . . . . . . . .  USROPT      *NONE
                  + for more values _
User ID number . . . . . . . . .  UID         *GEN
Group ID number  . . . . . . . .  GID         *NONE
Home directory . . . . . . . . .  HOMEDIR     *USRPRF
Authority  . . . . . . . . . . .  AUT         *EXCLUDE
```

USRPRF (User Profile)

What's in a user profile name? Although selecting names for user profiles might seem simple enough, developing and following a naming strategy can help immensely in implementing and maintaining your security plan.

One approach to user profile names is that each one should be as similar as possible to the name of the person to whom they belong (e.g., WMADDEN, MJONES, MARYM, JOHNZ). This method can work well when you have only a few end users. Under such a strategy, each user needs only one profile, which simplifies design and administration of the security system and lets operations personnel identify employees by their user profiles. The drawback to this method is that the profiles can be easily guessed and thus provide a door for unauthorized sign-ons, leaving an intruder to guess only the password. One of my (Wayne's) friends bragged about his new LAN one evening and wanted to show me how it worked, but he didn't know his user profile or password. We were sitting at his secretary's desk, so I asked him what his secretary's name was. Within one minute we were signed on using her first name as the profile and her initials as the password. Good guess? No — a bad profile and password.

Another approach holds that user profile names should be completely meaningless (e.g., SYS23431, Q83S@06Y7B, LR50M3ZT4) and should be maintained in some type of user information file. Meaningless names make profiles difficult to guess and don't link the name to a department or location that might change as the employee moves within the company. The user information file documents security-related information, such as the individual to whom the profile belongs and the department in which the user works. This method is the most secure, but it often meets with resistance from the users, who have difficulty remembering their profiles.

A third approach is to use a naming strategy that aids system administration. Under such a strategy, each user profile name identifies the user's location and perhaps function, which makes it easier for you to effectively audit your system security plan. For instance, if you monitor the history log or use the security journal for auditing purposes, this approach lets you quickly identify users and the jobs they're doing.

To implement this strategy, your naming convention should incorporate the user's location or department and a unique identifier for the user's name. For example, if John Smith works at your Ohio distribution center in the inventory control department, you might assign one of the following profiles:

OHJSMITH	The first two letters of this 10-character profile represent the location (OH for Ohio), and the remainder consists of the first letter of the user's first name followed by as much of the last name as will fit in the remaining seven characters.
OHICJES	This name is similar, but the branch is followed by the department (IC for inventory control) and the user's initials. This method provides more departmental information while reducing the unique name identifier to initials.
B12ICJES	This example is identical to the second, but the Ohio branch is designated by a number (B12).

When profile names provide this type of information, programs in your system that supply user menus or functions can resolve the profiles at run time based on location, department, or group. As a result, both your security plan and your initial program drivers can be dynamic, flexible, and easy to maintain. Auditing is also more effective because you can easily spot departmental trends, and user profile organization and maintenance are enhanced by having a naming standard to follow. However, such profiles are less secure than meaningless profiles because someone who understands the naming scheme can easily deduce them, leaving only the password to guess.

Regardless of the naming strategy you follow, we recommend maintaining user profiles in a user information file. Using a file lets you easily maintain up-to-date user profile information such as initial menus, initial values for programs (e.g., branch number, department number), and the user's full name formatted for use in outgoing invoices or order confirmations. When a user transfers to another location or moves to a new department, you can deactivate the old profile and assign a new one to maintain a security history. A user information file helps you keep what amounts to a user profile audit trail and lets your applications retrieve information from the file and use it to establish each user's work environment, library list, and initial menu.

A final consideration in choosing a naming convention for user profiles is whether your users will have access to multiple systems. If they will, you can simplify DSPT functions by using the same name for each user's profile across all systems. To follow this strategy, however, you must take into consideration all limitations the other systems in the network place on user profile names and apply those limitations when you create the user profiles for your system. For instance, another platform in your network might limit the number of characters allowed for user profile names. For your user profiles to be valid across the network, they must respect that limitation.

It's up to you to decide which user profile naming convention will work best for your environment. For the most secure environment, random and meaningless profile names are best (unless users take to writing them down). User profiles that consist of the end user's name are the least secure and are often used in small shops where everyone knows (and is on good terms with) everyone else. A convention that incorporates the user's location and function is a compromise between security and system management and is an implementation that suits many shops.

> **Security Recommendation**
> If you can get away with it, enforce meaningless user profile names. If not, devise an informational profile naming standard. We strongly advise not using end-user names for profiles.

PASSWORD (User Password)

As we said in Chapter 2, passwords should be secret, hard to guess, and changed regularly. You can't ensure that users keep their passwords secret, but you can help make them hard to guess by controlling password format, and you can require users to change their passwords regularly.

This discussion assumes that you let users select and maintain their own passwords. No one in IT needs to — or should — know user passwords. The AS/400 maintains the first rule of passwords — that they be secret — by not allowing even the security officer to view passwords.

The PASSWORD parameter lets you specify a value of *NONE, a value of *USRPRF, or the password itself. *NONE means that the user profile can't sign on to the system. We recommend you use *NONE for group profiles, profiles of users who are on vacation and don't need access for a period of time, profiles of users who have been terminated but whose profiles you can't immediately delete, and other situations in which you want to ensure that a profile isn't used (in all these situations, you should also specify STATUS(*DISABLED) for those user profiles). The default value, *USRPRF, dictates that the password be the same as the user profile name. You should never use PASSWORD(*USRPRF). If you do, you forfeit the very important layer of security provided by having a password that differs from the user profile name.

> **Security Recommendation**
> Specify a password that's different from the user profile name.

You can control the format of passwords by using one or more of the password-related system values or by creating your own password validation program, all of which we discussed in Chapter 2. The format you impose should encourage users to create hard-to-guess passwords but shouldn't result in passwords that are so cryptic that users can't remember them without writing them down within arm's reach of the keyboard. In Chapter 2, we suggested the following guidelines:

- Enforce a minimum length of at least seven characters (use the QPWDMINLEN system value).

- Require at least one digit (use the QPWDRQDDGT system value).
- Don't allow adjacent numbers in a password (use the QPWDLMTAJC system value).
- Don't allow an alphabetic character to be repeated consecutively in a password (use the QPWDLMTREP system value).

To ensure that users change their passwords regularly, use system value QPWDEXPITV to specify the maximum number of days a password can remain valid. A good value for QPWDEXPITV is 60 or 90 days, which would require all users systemwide to change passwords every two or three months. You can use CRTUSRPRF's PWDEXPITV parameter, which we discuss later in this chapter, to specify a different password expiration interval for selected individual profiles.

PWDEXP (Set Password to Expired)

The PWDEXP parameter lets you set the user profile's password to the expired state. When you create new user profiles, you should specify PWDEXP(*YES) to prompt new users to choose a secret password the first time they sign on. You should also specify PWDEXP(*YES) when you reset passwords for users who have forgotten theirs.

STATUS (Profile Status)

The STATUS parameter specifies whether a user profile is enabled or disabled for sign-on. When the value is *ENABLED, the system lets the user sign on. If the value is *DISABLED, the system doesn't let the user sign on until an authorized user re-enables the profile (i.e., changes the value of STATUS to *ENABLED).

This parameter is used primarily with the QMAXSGNACN system value. When you set QMAXSGNACN to 2 or 3, the system disables a profile that attempts too many invalid sign-ons (the QMAXSIGN system value determines the maximum number of sign-on attempts allowed). When the system disables a profile, the system changes the value of STATUS to *DISABLED. An authorized user must reset the value to *ENABLED before the user can use the profile again.

> **Technical Note**
> If the QSECOFR profile is disabled, you can sign on as QSECOFR at the console and enable the profile.

USRCLS (User Class) and SPCAUT (Special Authority)

The USRCLS and SPCAUT parameters work together to determine the special authorities granted to the user. Special authorities let users perform certain system functions, such as save/restore operations, job manipulation, spooled-file manipulation, and user profile administration. We discuss the details of the special authorities themselves later in this chapter; here, we explain how USRCLS and SPCAUT work.

The USRCLS parameter lets you classify users by type according to their special authorities. Table 3.1 shows the five user classes recognized on the AS/400: *SECOFR (security officer), *SECADM, *PGMR (programmer), *SYSOPR (system operator), and *USER (user). These classes represent the types of users that are typical for an installation. By specifying a user class for each user profile, you can classify users based on their role on the system. You can display the USRCLS value by using the DSPUSRPRF (Display User Profile) command, which can be a valuable tool for printing lists of users and the user class to which they belong. Auditors love this type of information!

TABLE 3.1
User Classes for Levels 30, 40, and 50

User class	Special authorities				
*SECOFR	*ALLOBJ	*SECADM	*SAVSYS	*JOBCTL	*SERVICE
	*SPLCTL	*AUDIT	*IOSYSCFG		
*SECADM		*SECADM			
*PGMR	(no special authorities)				
*SYSOPR			*SAVSYS	*JOBCTL	
*USER	(no special authorities)				

When you assign a user profile to a class, the profile by default has the special authorities associated with that class. Table 3.1 also shows the default special authorities associated with each user class under security levels 30, 40, and 50. You can override these special authorities using the SPCAUT (Special Authority) parameter, but you'll find that the default authorities are often sufficient.

The default for the SPCAUT parameter is *USRCLS, which instructs the system to refer to the USRCLS parameter and assign the predetermined set of special authorities (Table 3.2 lists the values allowed for the SPCAUT parameter and the meaning of each). You can override the default by typing from one to eight individual special authorities that you want to assign to the user profile. After sending a message that the special authorities assigned don't match the user class, the system creates the user profile as requested.

TABLE 3.2
SPCAUT Parameter Values

Special authority	Description
*USRCLS	Determines the set of special authorities for the user profile.
*NONE	No special authorities are assigned.
*ALLOBJ	User is allowed to access any object on the system.
*AUDIT	User is allowed to change auditing characteristics on the system (e.g., turn auditing on/off, change auditing system values and auditing parameters on user profiles).
*IOSYSCFG	User is allowed to modify system configuration objects and attributes (e.g., creating or changing lines, controllers, and device descriptions and configuring and changing TCP/IP applications).
*JOBCTL	User can change, display, hold, release, cancel, and clear all jobs on the system. Spooled files must be in an output queue that specifies OPRCTL(*YES).
*SAVSYS	User can save, restore, and free storage for all objects.
*SECADM	User can create and change user profiles so long as the user is also authorized to the CRTUSRPRF and CHGUSRPRF commands.
*SERVICE	User can perform functions in the System Service Tools.
*SPLCTL	User can delete, display, hold, and release spooled files owned by other users, including spooled files existing in output queues that specify OPRCTL(*NO).

In the command

```
CRTUSRPRF USRPRF(B12ICJES) PASSWORD(password) +
          USRCLS(*SYSOPR)
```

the default value of *USRCLS is assumed for the SPCAUT parameter, so user profile B12ICJES will have *SAVSYS and *JOBCTL special authorities, which are the defaults for the *SYSOPR user class. The command

```
CRTUSRPRF USRPRF(B12ICJES) PASSWORD(password) +
          USRCLS(*SYSOPR)  SPCAUT(*NONE)
```

assigns user profile B12ICJES to the *SYSOPR class but gives the profile no special authorities.

You should give special authorities to very few user profiles. Many special authorities give the holder great power and can be dangerous if given to other than very trusted users. For example, *ALLOBJ special authority gives the user unlimited access to and control over *all* objects on the system: A user with *ALLOBJ special authority can perform any function on any object on your system. The danger in letting that power get into the wrong hands is clear.

Technical Note

Operations Navigator refers to special authorities as *privileges*. See the Operations Navigator section at the end of this chapter for an example.

Generally speaking, no profile other than QSECOFR should have *ALLOBJ authority. This is the primary reason all development and production machines should be at least at level 30, which lets you control resource security and *ALLOBJ special authority with confidence.

You should design your security implementation so as not to require *ALLOBJ authority to administer most functions. Reserve this special authority for QSECOFR, and use that profile or a special user profile that you create with QSECOFR as its group profile to make all changes that require *ALLOBJ authority.

Security Recommendation

Applications running on your system generally shouldn't require a profile with *ALLOBJ authority to manage the application or its objects. If you find that someone with this special authority is constantly required to maintain or modify an application, you may have a poorly designed or poorly implemented application. Reserve the use of the QSECOFR profile or another profile with *ALLOBJ special authority to those activities relating to security implementation or maintenance.

The *SECADM special authority can help you design a security system that gives users no more authority than they need to do their job. *SECADM special authority enables a user profile to create and maintain the system user profiles without requiring the profile to be in the *SECOFR user class or giving it *ALLOBJ authority.

The *SAVSYS special authority lets a user profile perform save/restore operations on any object on the system without having the authority to access or manipulate those objects. *SAVSYS shows clearly how the AS/400 lets you grant only the authority a user needs to do a job. What would the effect be on system security if your operations staff needed *ALLOBJ special authority or *OBJMGT authority (the object authority needed to save/restore an object; see "Object Authorities," Chapter 4) to every object on the system to perform save/restore operations? Without *SAVSYS, you would have to either give system operators *ALLOBJ authority (which would let them access such sensitive information as payroll and master files) or continually maintain the proper *OBJMGT authority for every object on your system, which would be a management nightmare. *SAVSYS avoids that authorization problem while providing operators the functional authority to perform save/restore operations.

However, *SAVSYS authority has an associated risk. If you use *PUBLIC authorities to secure an object that resides in a privately secured library, the operator could save and restore that file to a library that allows access and then use the *PUBLIC authorities to read and modify records.

*IOSYSCFG special authority lets the holder create, delete, and manage devices, lines, and controllers and configure and start any TCP/IP application, such as a Web server. Because IBM provides new capabilities that require *IOSYSCFG special authority with each new release of OS/400, *IOSYSCFG, too, has become a powerful authority that needs to be assigned with care.

*SERVICE is another special authority that you should guard. *SERVICE special authority lets a user profile use the System Service Tools. These tools let the user trace data on communications lines and view user profiles and passwords as they're transmitted when someone signs on to the system. These tools also let the user display or alter any object on the system. Be stingy with *SERVICE special authority.

Technical Note
In V4R2 and later releases of OS/400, you must have *SERVICE and *ALLOBJ special authorities to use the Display/Alter facility in the System Service Tools.

OS/400's QSRV and QSECOFR profiles have *SERVICE authority. You should check whether your systems still have the default passwords for the QSRV user profile. If they do, change those passwords to *NONE and assign a password only when a Customer Engineer needs to use the profile. Remember to change the password back to *NONE when the Customer Engineer no longer needs it.

Security Recommendation
Assign *SERVICE special authority only to the system-supplied profiles that require it, and possibly to the network manager (if large-scale communications debugging is needed).

Security Recommendation
IBM-supplied profiles QUSER, QSRV, QSRVBAS, QPGMR, and QSYSOPR can have passwords, but these profiles ship with PASSWORD(*NONE), so no one can use them to sign on. To ensure none of these profiles have passwords on your system, use the ANZDFTPWD (Analyze Default Password) command. In early releases of OS/400, these profiles shipped with default passwords that were the same as the profile name. Those passwords were common knowledge in the hacker community and, if left unchanged, were a very serious security exposure. QSECOFR still ships with a default password, but the first time you sign on as QSECOFR, you must change the password. Use the ANZDFTPWD command to determine whether QSECOFR still has a default password.

Initial Sign-On Options

Three user profile parameters work together to determine the user's initial sign-on options. The CURLIB, INLPGM, and INLMNU parameters determine the user profile's current library, initial program, and initial menu, respectively. These parameters establish how the user interacts with the system initially. The menu or program executed at sign-on determines the menus and programs available to the user. Let's look at two examples.

Example 1
Consider the user profile USER, which has the following values:

```
Current library . . . . . . . . CURLIB    ICLIB
Initial program to call . . . . INLPGM    *NONE
  Library . . . . . . . . . . .
Initial menu . . . . . . . . .  INLMNU    ICMENU
  Library . . . . . . . . . . .           ICLIB
```

When USER signs on, the user's current library is set to ICLIB and the display shows menu ICMENU from library ICLIB. All other menus or programs that the user can access through ICMENU and to which the user has authority are also available.

Now let's say USER has these values:

Example 2

```
Current library . . . . . . . . CURLIB    ICLIB
Initial program to call . . . . INLPGM    ICUSERON
  Library . . . . . . . . . . .           SYSLIB
Initial menu . . . . . . . . .  INLMNU    *SIGNOFF
  Library . . . . . . . . . . .
```

When USER signs on, ICLIB is the user's current library, and the system executes program ICUSERON from library SYSLIB. Again, any other menus or programs accessible through ICUSERON and to which the user is authorized are also available.

The value of *SIGNOFF for the INLMNU parameter is worth some discussion. When a user signs on, OS/400 executes the program, if any, specified in the INLPGM parameter. If the user or user program doesn't execute the SIGNOFF command when the initial program ends, the system displays the menu, if any, specified in parameter INLMNU. However, when you specify *SIGNOFF for the INLMNU parameter, OS/400 signs the user off the system.

The CURLIB, INLPGM, and INLMNU parameters are significant to security because users can modify their values at sign-on. Users can also execute OS/400 commands from the command line provided on AS/400 menus. Obviously, allowing all users these capabilities isn't a good idea from a security point of view, and that brings the LMTCPB (Limit Capabilities) parameter into the picture. LMTCPB controls users' ability to

- define (using the CHGPRF command) or change (at sign-on) their own initial program
- define (using the CHGPRF command) or change (at sign-on) their own initial menu
- define (using the CHGPRF command) or change (at sign-on) their own current library

- define (using the CHGPRF command) or change (at sign-on) their own attention key program
- execute OS/400 or user-defined commands from the command line on AS/400 native menus

Table 3.3 shows the effects of the possible values for LMTCPB.

TABLE 3.3
Effects of the LMTCPB Parameter

User can define, change, and execute:

LMTCPB	Initial program	Initial menu	Current library	Attention program	Commands
*NO	Yes	Yes	Yes	Yes	Yes
*PARTIAL	No	Yes	No	No	Yes
*YES	No	No	No	No	Limited*

*A user with LMTCPB(*YES) is limited to the SIGNOFF, SNDMSG (Send a Message), DSPMSG (Display Messages), DSPJOB (Display Job), DSPJOBLOG (Display Job Log), and STRPCO (Start PC Organizer) commands and to other commands that you create or change to specify ALWLMTUSR(*YES).

> **Technical Note**
> If you want to let users with LMTCPB(*YES) use a particular command, you can specify ALWLMTCPB(*YES) on the CRTCMD (Create Command) or CHGCMD (Change Command) command.

Production systems usually enforce LMTCPB(*YES) for most user profiles. The profiles that typically need LMTCPB(*NO) are IT personnel who frequently use the command line from OS/400 menus. You can still use resource security to secure sensitive data from these user profiles. Although you could specify LMTCPB(*PARTIAL) for IT personnel to ensure that they can't change their initial program, they could still change their initial menu, which would be executed at the conclusion of the initial program.

> **Technical Note**
> Although the LMTCPB parameter has value for green-screen menu environments, current technology has limited its effectiveness. Many interfaces, such as FTP, ODBC, remote command, and DDM, bypass menus altogether. The limited capability setting is ignored in most cases when the user doesn't actually sign on at a menu. Don't make the mistake of thinking that limited capabilities provide more protection than they do.

> **Security Recommendation**
> Change the LMTCPB parameter to *YES unless that user specifically needs the additional capabilities provided by LMTCPB(*NO).

System Value Overrides

As we mentioned in Chapter 2, you can override system values QDSPSGNINF, QPWDEXPITV, and QLMTDEVSSN by using the DSPSGNINF, PWDEXPITV, and LMTDEVSSN user profile parameters.

From Figure 3.1, you can see that these three parameters all have a default value of *SYSVAL, which lets the system value control these functions. To override the system values, specify the desired values in the user profile parameters. The available choices are the same as those for the system values themselves.

Group Profiles

All of the parameters we've discussed so far are used to define profiles for individual users. The GRPPRF (Group Profile), OWNER (Owner), GRPAUT (Group Authority), GRPAUTTYP (Group Authority Type), and SUPGRPPRF (Supplemental Groups) parameters let you associate an individual user profile with one or more group profiles. When you authorize a group profile to objects on the system, the authorization applies to all profiles in the group.

How is this accomplished? First you create a user profile for the group. You should specify PASSWORD(*NONE) for the group profile to prevent it from being used to sign on to the system — all members of the group should sign on using their own profiles. For instance, you might create a group profile called DEVPGMR for your programming staff. Then, for each user profile belonging to a member of the staff, use the CHGUSRPRF command and the GRPPRF, OWNER, and GRPAUT parameters to place the user profile in the DEVPGMR group.

The GRPPRF parameter specifies a group profile that will include the user profile. In other words, you would specify DEVPGMR as the GRPPRF value for the user profiles you put into the DEVPGMR group. You can use the SUPGRPPRF parameter to place a user profile in up to 15 additional groups. The authority that an individual user profile has on the system is additive within these multiple group profiles. For instance, if one group profile gives the user only *READ data authority to a file and another group profile provides *UPD data authority, a user profile that's in both groups will have both *READ and *UPD authority as long as that user profile has no private authorities to that file. (If a user profile has private authorities to an object, those authorities take precedence and any group authority is ignored.)

The ability to put a user into more than one group profile offers an advantage for building authorities across departments for end users such as supervisors. However, you need to be aware of the performance implications to implementing multiple group profiles. The system goes through the authority lookup process for each group profile that exists for an individual user profile, so the more groups a user belongs to, the slower the performance. Consequently, you should use multiple group profiles sparingly and only for user profiles that truly require multiple types of authorities. It's also smart to specify first the groups that are most likely to have the most authorities. You should aim to implement a group profile scheme that puts most individuals in only one group.

> **Security Recommendation**
> Use multiple group profiles sparingly. When you must use them, list the most-used groups (in terms of authority) first.

The OWNER parameter specifies whether the user profile or the group profile to which the user profile belongs owns objects that the user profile creates. There is an advantage to having the group profile own all objects created by its constituent user profiles. When the group profile owns the objects, every member of the group has *ALL authority to the objects. This is helpful, for instance, in a programming environment in which more than one programmer works on a project. However, you can provide authority to group members without giving them *ALL authority. If you specify OWNER(*USRPRF), the user profile owns the objects it creates. When a user profile owns an object, the group profile and other members in the group have only the authority specified in the GRPAUT parameter. The OWNER, GRPAUT, and GRPAUTTYP parameters apply only to the group specified in the GRPPRF parameter, not to any group profiles specified in the SUPGRPPRF parameter.

> **Technical Note**
> Objects created in the Integrated File System (IFS) are owned by the user profile regardless of the value of the OWNER parameter.

The GRPAUT parameter specifies the authority granted to the group profile (and thus to the other members of the group) when the value for OWNER is *USRPRF. Valid values for GRPAUT are *ALL, *CHANGE, *USE, *EXCLUDE, and *NONE. The first four are authorities, each of which represents a set of specific object and data authorities. We discuss *ALL, *CHANGE, *USE, and *EXCLUDE in detail in Chapter 4 as part of the discussion of specific authorities. If you specify one of these four values for the GRPAUT parameter, the individual user profile that creates an object owns it, and the group profile has the specified set of authorities to the object.

You must specify GRPAUT(*NONE) when you specify *GRPPRF as the owner of objects the user creates. Because the group profile automatically owns the object, all members of the group share that authority.

The GRPAUTTYP parameter determines the type of authority (i.e., private authority or primary group authority) the user's group profile has to objects the user creates. If you specify GRPAUTTYP(*PRIVATE), OS/400 grants the group profile the private authority specified in the GRPAUT parameter. If you specify GRPAUTTYP(*PGP), OS/400 assigns the group profile specified in the GRPPRF parameter as the primary group for the new object, and the primary group authorities will be those designated by the GRPAUT parameter's value.

Assigning private authorities or primary group authorities yields the same results in terms of authorization; however, the performance implications are different. Primary group authorities are stored with the object, while private authorities are stored with the user profile description. OS/400 can more quickly obtain information that's stored with the object. For more information about using primary group authority, see Chapter 4.

UID (User Identification Number) and GID (Group Identification Number)

The Integrated File System (IFS) requires every user profile to have a User Identification (UID) number. When you create a user profile, OS/400 by default assigns a UID to the user profile. The default UID is an arbitrary number from 100 to 4294967294. The UID parameter lets you assign the UID yourself if you wish, in which case you can choose any number from 1 to 4294967294. OS/400 uses the UID to verify the user's authority to access the objects in the IFS, so every user on the system must have a unique UID.

The Group Identification Number (GID) is identical in purpose to the UID, except that it is required only for group profiles.

AUT (Authority)

AUT indicates the *PUBLIC authority granted to the user profile object itself — in other words, the public authority other user profiles have to the user profile you're creating. The authority to a profile controls such activities as displaying and/or modifying a user profile, submitting a job under that user profile, or (for group profiles) adding members to the group. To prevent misuse of such activities, make sure the public authority to all user profiles is *EXCLUDE and grant specific authorities only when an application requires it.

Helpful Tools

Several security tools can help you manage user profiles on your system. Below is a listing and description of each of these tools. You can find these tools on the SECTOOLS and SECBATCH menus.

Security tool	Description
ANZDFTPWD	
(Analyze Default Passwords)	Prints a report listing all user profiles whose password is equal to the user profile name. Such profiles aren't secure and require attention.
ANZPRFACT	
(Analyze Profile Activity)	Checks user profiles' last sign-on date and last-used date every day and disables those profiles that haven't been used for a specified number of days (you supply the number). However, some applications that use profiles don't update the last sign-on or last-used date, making the profile look like it's been inactive. To exempt a profile from ANZPRFACT processing, use the CHGACTPRFL command to add the profile to the exemption list.
CHGACTPRFL	
(Change Active Profiles List)	Lets you add and remove user profiles from the ANZPRFACT command's exemption list. ANZPRFACT ignores all profiles that are on the active profile (i.e., exemption) list.
DSPACTPRFL	
(Display Active Profiles List)	Lists user profiles that are on the ANZPRFACT exemption list.
DSPACTSCD	
(Display Activation Schedule)	Lists the schedule information that controls enabling and disabling user profiles by date and time. This information includes the user profile and the valid inactive day and time you've specified for that user on the CHGACTSCDE command.
CHGACTSCDE	
(Change Activation Schedule Entry)	Creates and maintains user profile entries and their activation day and time periods. For each user profile, you can schedule days and times for which the user profile is inactive, thus controlling that user's system use.
DSPEXPSCDE	
(Display Expiration Schedule)	Lists user profiles that are scheduled to be removed or disabled.
CHGEXPSCDE	
(Change Expiration Schedule Entry)	Lets you create and maintain a list of user profiles that you want to remove or disable at some point in the future. This tool makes managing temporary profiles easier by scheduling their removal so you don't have to remember to remove them. Each day at one minute after midnight, the system runs a job that examines this list and takes the appropriate action.
PRTUSRPRF	
(Print User Profile)	Lets you print information about user profiles based on selection criteria that you supply (e.g., special authorities, user class, mismatch between user class and special authorities). You can print authority information, environment information, and password information.
PRTPRFINT	
(Print Profile Internals)	Lets you print information about how "full" a user profile is. User profiles contain an entry for each object owned, each private authority the user has, and each private authority another user has to objects the user owns. If there are too many of these entries, the user profile becomes full. (If a user profile is full, it can't own more objects, be authorized to additional objects, or allow any objects it owns to be authorized to another user.) This command produces a report indicating how full the profile is and the percentage of each type of entry.

Operations Navigator

You can use Operations Navigator instead of the CRTUSRPRF command to create user profiles. Expand the directory for the AS/400 on which you want to create the user and select Users and Groups. Right-click All Users and select New User (Figure 3.2). You'll notice that Operations Navigator's terminology for user profile attributes differs from the CRTUSRPRF command's terminology. You might find this difference a bit confusing if you're moving between Operations Navigator and green-screen commands, but IBM's intent was to better describe the attribute.

FIGURE 3.2
New User Configuration Window

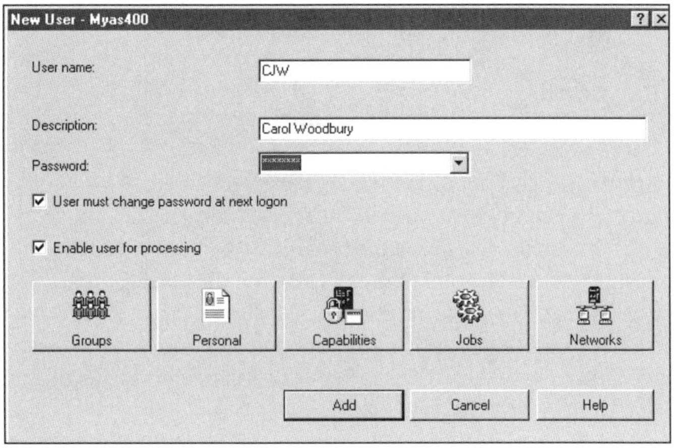

Operations Navigator provides a different path for creating user and group profiles. To create a new group profile, expand the directory for the AS/400 you want to create the new group profile on. Select Users and Groups, right-click Groups, and select New Group (Figure 3.3). You might notice that Operations Navigator doesn't include most of the user profile attributes for the group profile. That's because it often doesn't make sense to specify a particular attribute for a group profile. For example, Operations Navigator doesn't let you specify a password for a group profile, because group profiles shouldn't be used to sign on.

FIGURE 3.3
New Group Configuration Window

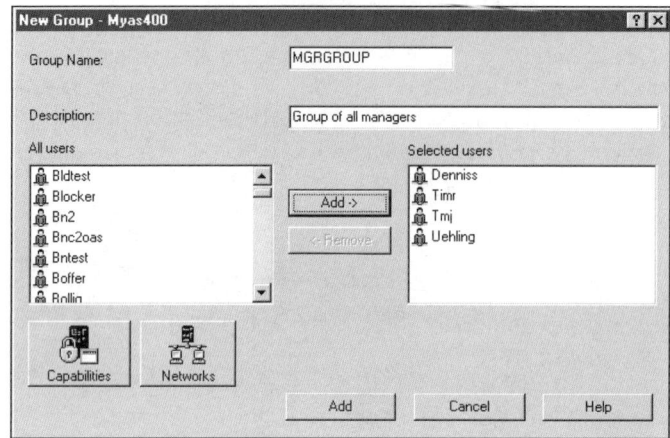

Another benefit of using Operations Navigator to create user profiles is the other things that Operations Navigator lets you do at the same time or automatically does for you. For example, it automatically creates a system distribution entry for user profiles. You can also choose to create a Lotus Notes client for the user profile.

Do you need to create the same user on multiple AS/400s? You can click the user profile you just created and drag it onto another AS/400. Operations Navigator will prompt you for the profile's password and then automatically create the profile on the target AS/400.

Chapter 4
Object Authorization

Chapter 3 noted that one purpose of a user profile is to identify the user's authority to specific objects on the system. Before a user profile can access an object, the profile must have authority to the object. In this chapter, we examine the kinds of specific authorities OS/400 gives you to work with, how you grant and revoke those authorities, and tools the system provides for organizing authorities.

The examples in this chapter generally use the QSYS file system (which uses the traditional AS/400 library/file/member structure), but we also discuss special considerations you need to be aware of for other file implementations supported by the Integrated File System (IFS). Before reading this chapter, you might want to take time to familiarize yourself with the IFS by reading the IBM manual *Integrated File System Introduction* (SC41-5711).

Specific Authorities

As we explained in Chapter 3, special authorities, sometimes called *privileges*, let users perform certain system functions. Specific authorities, sometimes called *private authorities*, let users access and use specific objects.

As Figure 4.1 illustrates, there are two categories of specific authorities: object authorities and data authorities. Object authorities authorize actions that affect the entire object, such as renaming, changing, saving, and deleting objects, as well as a few functions for specific types of objects, such as defining referential integrity rules for database files. Data authorities apply at the content level for objects (e.g., database files, data queues, libraries, output queues) and authorize very specific actions, such as adding, updating, reading, and deleting object contents (e.g., records, entries).

FIGURE 4.1
Specific-Authority Categories

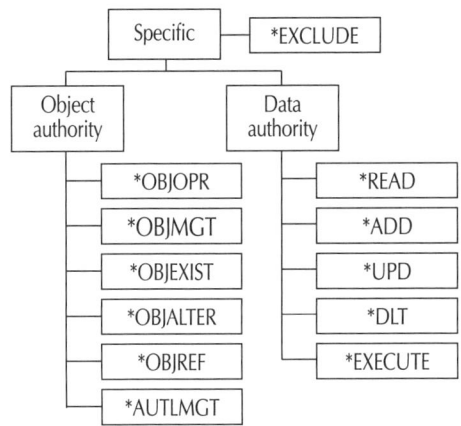

```
                    Specific ─── *EXCLUDE
                   /        \
            Object          Data
           authority        authority
              │                │
              ├─ *OBJOPR       ├─ *READ
              ├─ *OBJMGT       ├─ *ADD
              ├─ *OBJEXIST     ├─ *UPD
              ├─ *OBJALTER     ├─ *DLT
              ├─ *OBJREF       └─ *EXECUTE
              └─ *AUTLMGT
```

Object Authorities

OS/400 provides six object authorities, which we find helpful to classify into three categories. The first category consists of three object authorities that apply to all objects on your system: *OBJOPR, *OBJMGT, and *OBJEXIST.

*OBJOPR   Object Operation authority authorizes the use of an object.

*OBJMGT   Object Management authority authorizes the user to move and rename the object, to change its attributes, and to grant and revoke the authority of other user profiles to the object.

*OBJEXIST   Object Existence authority lets the user delete, save, and restore the object and transfer ownership of the object.

Users who have *OBJOPR authority to an object can use the object. What exactly does it mean to be able to "use" an object? *OBJOPR lets the user view the object's description, regardless of the object's type. If the object contains data or executable code, the user can access the object's description but can't access the data or run the program without having the appropriate data authority (we discuss data authorities a little later in this chapter).

*OBJMGT authority lets a user change the object's attributes, including the authorities other users have to the object. *OBJMGT is a superset of *OBJALTER and *OBJREF authorities (which we discuss below). If you don't want a user to have *OBJALTER or *OBJREF authority, you must revoke not only *OBJMGT authority but also the *OBJALTER and *OBJREF authorities specifically.

*OBJEXIST authority lets a user perform save/restore operations on the object, transfer object ownership, and delete the object.

To reduce the risk of an object being used improperly or inadvertently deleted, you should restrict *OBJMGT and *OBJEXIST authorities to the object's owner.

Security Recommendation
Give *OBJMGT and *OBJEXIST authorities only to the object's owner.

The second category consists of object authorities that apply primarily to database files and consists of *OBJALTER and *OBJREF authorities.

*OBJALTER   Object Alter authority authorizes the user to add, clear, reorganize, and initialize database file members and to alter the attributes of database files (SQL tables or physical and logical files). Authorized actions include adding and removing triggers and changing the attributes of tables, files, and SQL packages.

*OBJREF   Object Reference authority lets the user specify a database file or table as the parent file in a referential constraint.

A user with *OBJALTER authority to a database file can modify the file's attributes and can add and remove database file triggers. If you want to avoid granting a database administrator or programmer *OBJMGT authority, you can grant only *OBJALTER authority to limit the user to database-specific functions.

You should grant *OBJREF object authority to only the database administrator or programmer responsible for enforcing referential integrity constraints. This authority is necessary only for the parent file in a referential constraint. For example, say you want to ensure that every new order record in the ORD_MAST file references an existing customer in the CUST_MAST file. You can do so by adding a referential constraint linking the two files by the customer number that is common to both files. In this case, you must have *OBJREF authority to the CUST_MAST file to add the constraint.

The third category of object authorities consists of the *AUTLMGT (Authorization List Management) authority and applies only to authorization lists. *AUTLMGT authority lets you add and remove users' authorities to an authorization list.

Data Authorities

Data authorities apply to all object types, but they are most easily explained by using objects that have contents. For example, a physical file has an object description, and a physical file has contents — data records. Other objects that have contents include libraries (object type *LIB), data queues (object type *DTAQ), and output queues (object type *OUTQ).

The five data authorities are

*READ	Lets the user read and retrieve data and entries.
*ADD	Lets the user insert a new data record or entry.
*UPD	Lets the user modify existing data and entries.
*DLT	Lets the user delete and remove data and entries. (Remember that *OBJEXIST is required to delete the object itself.)
*EXECUTE	Lets the user execute a program, a service program, or an SQL package and locate an object in a library or directory.

The first four data authorities let you read and manipulate the contents of an object. You would typically grant users who need to manipulate data all four of these data authorities. However, if you wish, you can grant users only a subset of the four.

*EXECUTE authority lets you search the contents of a library or directory. To access an object, you need not only authority to the object itself, but also at least *EXECUTE authority to the library or directory in which the object resides. *EXECUTE authority is also one of the authorities you need to run a program, service program, or SQL package (you also need *OBJOPR authority).

As we mentioned earlier, data authorities also apply to objects that don't have contents. For example, to submit a job that uses a job description, you need *OBJOPR, *READ, and *EXECUTE authorities to that job description.

Authority Relationships

One point of confusion for many people when they first encounter the AS/400's object security implementation is the difference between having authority to a library and having authority to objects within the library. To access or use an object, you must have authority to the library the object is in as well as to the object itself. However, having authority to a library doesn't automatically give you authority to the objects in the library. Authority to a library and authority to the objects in the library are controlled separately.

Assume library MYLIB contains physical file MYFILE1. Users who need access to MYFILE1 must have at least *OBJOPR object authority and *READ or *EXECUTE data authority to MYLIB. You can think of library-level authority as a gate to what goes on with the objects that reside in the library. To access the objects, you must first open the gate: You must have appropriate authority to the library. For example, to look for objects in the library, you must have *OBJOPR authority to the library. To read the description of objects in the library, you must also have *READ authority to the library. To add more objects to the library, you must have *ADD authority. And so on.

*DELETE authority can also be confusing. You'd think that if you have *DELETE authority to the library, you could delete objects from the library. However, to delete an object from a library, you need only *OBJOPR, *READ, and *EXECUTE authorities to the library. Whether you can delete the object is determined by the authority you have to the object itself. To delete an object, you must have *OBJEXIST to the object. To delete a library, you'd need *OBJEXIST authority to the library.

If you work with directories on the AS/400 (i.e., if you work with a file system other than the QSYS file system), you need to know that the relationship between directory and object authorities is almost identical to the relationship we just described between library and object authorities. The only difference is that to access an object in the file system, you must have *EXECUTE authority to all directories in the directory path. For example, to access the product_directory/product_subdirectory/readme.txt file, you must have authority to every directory in the path that leads to the file (i.e., product_directory and product_subdirectory), as well as having proper authority to the readme.txt file itself.

Authority Classes

You can think of authority classes as shorthand: They let you specify commonly used combinations of object and data authorities with a single parameter value. Except when working with database files, most security administrators use authority classes rather than individual object and data authorities. You use one set of classes with the QSYS authority commands and another set of classes with the generic authority commands. Generic authority commands work on all objects in all file systems, including QSYS. Table 4.1 shows the authority classes you can use with QSYS and the object and data authorities they grant.

TABLE 4.1
Authority Classes for Use with QSYS Authority Commands

Object and data authorities	Authority classes			
	*ALL	*CHANGE	*USE	*EXCLUDE
*OBJOPR	X	X	X	(NONE)
*OBJMGT	X			
*OBJEXIST	X			
*OBJALTER	X			
*OBJREF	X			
*READ	X	X	X	
*ADD	X	X		
*UPD	X	X		
*DLT	X	X		
*EXECUTE	X	X	X	

Table 4.2 summarizes the authority classes you can use with the generic authority commands. As you can see, authority class *RWX assigns the same authorities as *CHANGE, and *RX assigns the same authorities as *USE. (No generic-authority equivalent to the *ALL class exists because POSIX has no equivalent to the AS/400's *OBJMGT, *OBJEXIST, *OBJALTER, and *OBJREF authorities.)

TABLE 4.2
Authority Classes for Use with Generic Authority Commands

Object and data authorities	Authority classes						
	*RWX	*RW	*RX	*R	*WX	*W	*X
*OBJOPR	X	X	X	X	X	X	X
*OBJMGT							
*OBJEXIST							
*OBJALTER							
*OBJREF							
*READ	X	X	X	X			
*ADD	X	X			X	X	
*UPD	X	X			X	X	
*DLT	X	X			X	X	
*EXECUTE	X		X		X		X

So, to use authority classes to grant user profile B01WER object operational and all data rights to physical file DEFPF in the QSYS file system, you could use the command

```
GRTOBJAUT OBJ(MYLIB/DEFPF) OBJTYPE(*FILE) USER(B01WER)   +
          AUT(*OBJOPR *READ *ADD *UPD *DLT *EXECUTE)
```

Or, you could use

```
GRTOBJAUT OBJ(MYLIB/DEFPF) OBJTYPE(*FILE) USER(B01WER)   +
          AUT(*CHANGE)
```

The effects of both commands are the same. To grant B01WER the same authorities using the CHGAUT command, you would enter

```
CHGAUT OBJ('/QSYS.LIB/MYLIB.LIB/DEFPF.FILE')   +
       USER(B01WER) DTAAUT(*RWX)
```

The *EXCLUDE authority class is a bit odd. Users who have *EXCLUDE private authority to a file are prevented from accessing the file. Many other operating systems prevent users from accessing a file by not granting any authority to the file. OS/400 uses a different model. On the AS/400, if you don't grant users authority to a file, they still have *PUBLIC authority to the file. (We explain *PUBLIC authorities in the section "Public Authority" later in this chapter.) To deny *all* access to an AS/400 object, you can use *EXCLUDE authority.

Granting and Revoking Specific Authorities

Any profile that has *ALLOBJ special authority and any profile that has *OBJMGT authority to an object can use one of the following commands to grant or revoke other users' authorities to the object:

- GRTOBJAUT (Grant Object Authority)
- RVKOBJAUT (Revoke Object Authority)
- EDTOBJAUT (Edit Object Authority)
- CHGAUT (Change Authority)
- DSPAUT (Display Authority)
- WRKAUT (Work with Authority)

The first three commands work only with the QSYS file system. The last three commands work for any object in any IFS file system, including the QSYS file system.

You can use these six commands to display, grant, and revoke specific authorities. If you use the CHGAUT or WRKAUT command to change authorities, you must manage two sets of authorities for each object, as Figure 4.2 shows. One set controls data authorities and lets you grant *R, *W, and *X authorities. The other set controls object authorities and uses the AS/400 object authority values of *OBJMGT, *OBJEXIST, *OBJALTER, and *OBJREF. (*OBJOPR is included with the data authorities in the file system commands.)

FIGURE 4.2
Sample Change Authority (CHGAUT) Screen

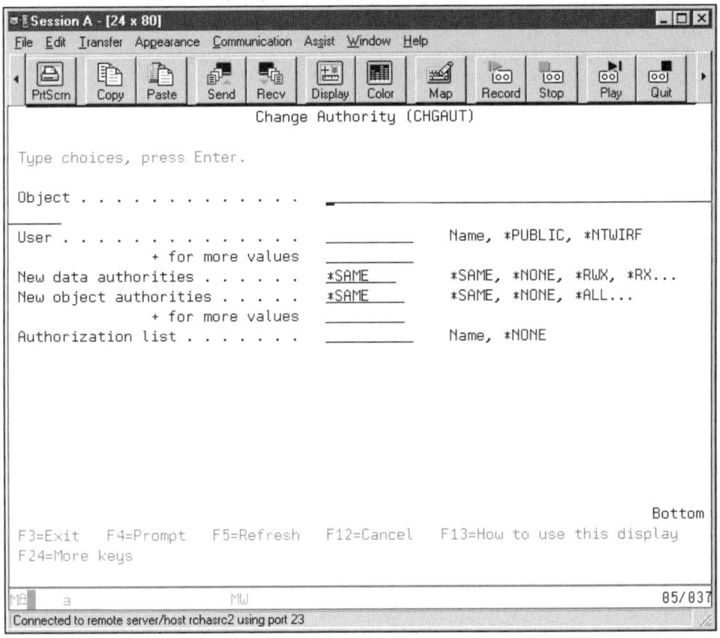

```
 Session A - [24 x 80]                                           _ □ ×
 File Edit Transfer Appearance Communication Assist Window Help
 ◄ [PrtScrn] [Copy] [Paste] [Send] [Recv] [Display] [Color] [Map] [Record] [Stop] [Play] [Quit] ►
                         Change Authority (CHGAUT)

 Type choices, press Enter.

 Object . . . . . . . . . . . . .  _____

 User . . . . . . . . . . . . .   _____    Name, *PUBLIC, *NTWIRF
               + for more values
 New data authorities . . . . . .   *SAME        *SAME, *NONE, *RWX, *RX...
 New object authorities . . . . .   *SAME        *SAME, *NONE, *ALL...
               + for more values
 Authorization list . . . . . . .   _____   Name, *NONE




                                                                 Bottom
 F3=Exit     F4=Prompt    F5=Refresh    F12=Cancel    F13=How to use this display
 F24=More keys

 MA       a               MW                                     05/037
 Connected to remote server/host rchasrc2 using port 23
```

Group Profiles

In addition to granting and revoking private authorities to individual users, you can manipulate private authorities for group profiles. Group profiles are a management tool that let you associate a group of users with a single set of authority requirements. You can use group profiles to, in effect, grant the same set of authorities to all members of a group. However, you can also fine-tune the authorities of selected group members.

Figure 4.3 illustrates an implementation of a sample group profile, PAYCLERK. PAYCLERK is the group profile for three payroll clerks who perform similar jobs and need similar authorities. As you can see, group profile PAYCLERK owns no objects and has *USE authority to library PAYLIB and *CHANGE authority to file PAYFILE.

FIGURE 4.3
Sample Group Profile Implementation

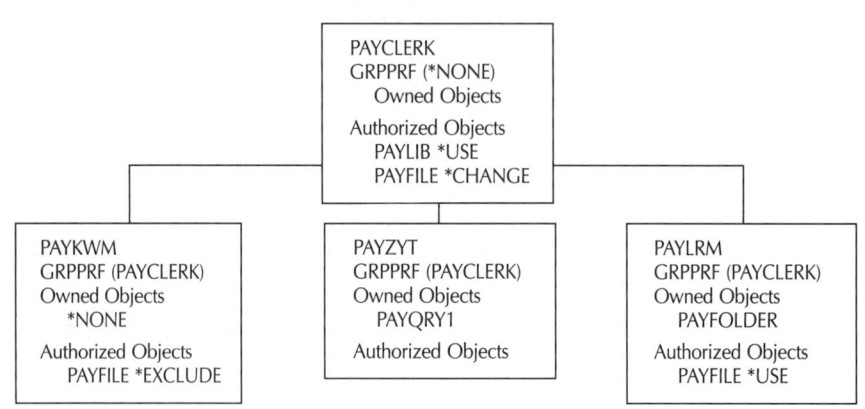

```
                    PAYCLERK
                    GRPPRF (*NONE)
                    Owned Objects
                    Authorized Objects
                    PAYLIB *USE
                    PAYFILE *CHANGE
      ┌────────────────┼────────────────┐
  PAYKWM            PAYZYT            PAYLRM
  GRPPRF (PAYCLERK) GRPPRF (PAYCLERK) GRPPRF (PAYCLERK)
  Owned Objects    Owned Objects     Owned Objects
  *NONE            PAYQRY1           PAYFOLDER
  Authorized Objects  Authorized Objects  Authorized Objects
  PAYFILE *EXCLUDE                    PAYFILE *USE
```

Individual user profile PAYKWM has *EXCLUDE authority to PAYFILE. This authority excludes PAYKWM from using PAYFILE, even though the group profile to which PAYKWM belongs has *CHANGE authority. As we explain in the section "How OS/400 Checks Authority" later in this chapter, the system checks a user's private authority before it checks group authority. And because private authorities take precedence over group authorities, you can grant a member of a group profile a private authority that is different from the group authority.

User profile PAYZYT owns the object PAYQRY1 and has no specific authority to PAYFILE. When the system searches for PAYZYT's authorities to PAYFILE, it finds the group profile's *CHANGE authority.

User PAYLRM also owns an object (PAYFOLDER) and has private *USE authority to PAYFILE.

Using group profiles is a very good way to define security because many users commonly function as a member of a group, doing similar work on the system as other users and needing similar authorities to objects. Chapter 13 discusses how to use group profiles to implement the security strategy you design for your system.

Multiple Group Profiles

You can specify a user profile as a member of up to 16 groups. First, specify a group in the user profile's GRPPRF parameter. Then use the SUPGRPPRF (Supplemental Group Profile) parameter to specify any other group profiles you want the user to be a member of. When a user is in more than one group, the user's authorities are additive. OS/400 first looks for enough authority in the user's individual private authorities. If the user doesn't have private authority to the object to perform the task, the system looks in each group, accumulating the authorities it finds (e.g., *READ, *ADD, *OBJEXIST), until either the user has enough authority to perform the task or the sum of all the authorities proves insufficient. (For more details about how the system searches for and sums authorities, see the section "How OS/400 Checks Authority" later in this chapter.)

When a member of multiple groups creates an object, OS/400 refers to the user profile's OWNER, GRPAUT, and GRPAUTTYP parameters to determine the authority, if any, the first group (i.e., the group profile named in the GRPPRF parameter) has to the new object. When you assign multiple groups to users, you should assign the most frequently used groups first. OS/400 searches each group profile listed in the user profile's GRPPRF and SUPGRPPRF parameters until it finds enough authority to perform the task (or determines that the user doesn't have sufficient authority). The fewer groups OS/400 has to search to accumulate sufficient authority, the better the performance.

Why Grant Authority to Group Profiles?

Group profiles simplify security management by letting you grant similar authorities to multiple user profiles that perform similar functions. Many user profiles in your organization probably have similar basic authorities. Combining like user profiles into a single group profile lets you administer authorities for the entire group instead of for each user individually. The ability to make a user profile a member of more than one group enhances this logical grouping of authority.

Performance is a consideration when you use group authority. When you authorize one or more groups to an object, you're using private authorities, so the system performs slightly slower than when you use only public authorities. However, if you need to grant private authority to a group, you might be able to use primary group authority. You can grant primary group authority for an object to only one group. Rather than give the primary group private authority to the object, you can grant the group primary group authority by using the CHGOBJPGP (Change Object Primary Group) or the WRKOBJPGP (Work with Objects by Primary Group) command. Primary group authority is a faster version of private authority for group profiles. Primary group authority isn't considered a private authority but is stored with the object itself, thus shortening the time the system needs to find the proper authorities during an authorization search.

Public Authority

When a user creates an object, OS/400 associates a default authority with the object. This authority, which is called *public authority,* is the authority given to users who haven't been granted authority to the object by any other means. You can use the EDTOBJAUT or DSPAUT command to view an object's authorities. The display for both commands includes an entry for *PUBLIC.

Establishing Public Authority

All objects on the system are created either by using one of the many CRTxxx (Create) commands or by restoring the object from a save file or from save media. Public authorities are established when the object is created. When you use a Create command to create an object, the command's AUT parameter establishes the object's public authorities. The AUT parameter has the following possible values:

*LIBCRTAUT	Uses the library's CRTAUT attribute to determine the object's *PUBLIC authorities
*ALL	Grants all object and data rights
*CHANGE	Grants *OBJOPR object authority and all data authorities
*USE	Grants *OBJOPR object authority and *READ and *EXECUTE data authorities
*EXCLUDE	Grants *PUBLIC *EXCLUDE authority
Authorization_list_name	Secures the object with an authorization list. *PUBLIC authority for the object comes from the authorization list's *PUBLIC authority. (You can't specify an authorization list for the AUT parameter of a user profile or of another authorization list.)

For most Create commands, the default value for the AUT parameter is *LIBCRTAUT, which causes the system to use the target library's CRTAUT attribute to determine the object's public authority. Thus, the CRTAUT library attribute specifies the default public authority that all new objects in that library will have unless you override the default authority on the Create command.

When you create or change a library description, you can use the library's CRTAUT parameter to define the default public authority for all objects subsequently created in that library (existing objects aren't affected). The CRTAUT parameter allows the following values:

*SYSVAL	Uses the value specified in the QCRTAUT system value
*ALL	Grants all object and data rights
*CHANGE	Grants *OBJOPR and all data rights
*USE	Grants *OBJOPR, *READ, and *EXECUTE rights
*EXCLUDE	Grants *PUBLIC *EXCLUDE authority
Authorization_list_name	Uses the specified authorization list to determine public authorities

The default value for the CRTAUT parameter is *SYSVAL, which instructs OS/400 to reference the QCRTAUT system value to determine the default public authorities for the objects in the library. When you create a library and don't specify a CRTAUT value, the *SYSVAL default value causes the library to use the value found in the QCRTAUT system value.

Technical Note

QCRTAUT has no effect on objects created in directories.

Figure 4.4 illustrates the trickle effect of the default values for the library's CRTAUT attribute and the object's AUT attribute. From right to left, the values shown for QCRTAUT, CRTAUT, and AUT are the defaults shipped with OS/400. As you can see, if you don't change these defaults, the system automatically gives the public *CHANGE authority to every object created on the system.

The only tricky part of how *PUBLIC authority is determined comes when you create a library. As OS/400 is implemented, it actually creates all libraries within library QSYS. You can think of QSYS as the "master" library. So, when you create a new library, say, PAYLIB, and specify *LIBCRTAUT for the library's AUT parameter, PAYLIB's public authority comes from the QSYS library's CRTAUT value.

FIGURE 4.4
*How *PUBLIC Authority Is Determined*

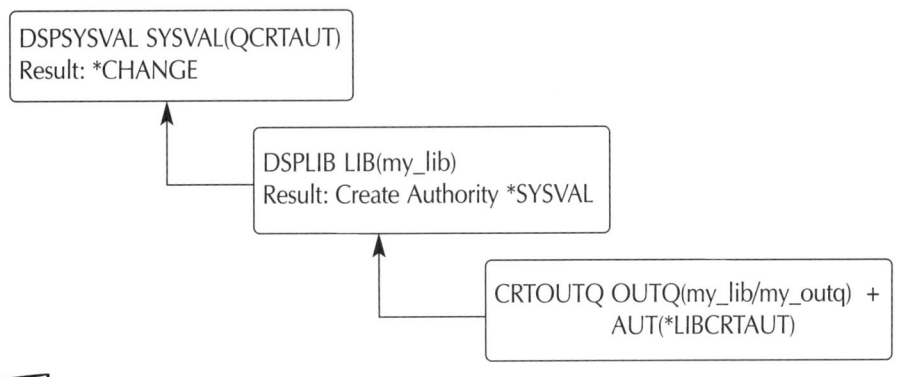

```
DSPSYSVAL SYSVAL(QCRTAUT)
Result: *CHANGE
         ▲
         │
    DSPLIB LIB(my_lib)
    Result: Create Authority *SYSVAL
              ▲
              │
         CRTOUTQ OUTQ(my_lib/my_outq) +
         AUT(*LIBCRTAUT)
```

Technical Note
A library's CRTAUT parameter has no effect when you move, duplicate, or restore an object to a library. Instead, the object's public authority is the public authority the object had before you moved, duplicated, or restored it.

Technical Note
When you create an object and specify REPLACE(*YES), the new object will have the public authority of the replaced object instead of the authority specified in the library's CRTAUT parameter.

Using Default Public Authority

The existence of default values for object attributes and system values seems to indicate that the default is the suggested or typical value. But that's not necessarily the case with security-related default values. Defaults that define the public authority for objects on your system are valid only if you plan to use those particular values as part of your overall security implementation.

The default public authority for most objects created in the QSYS file system is *CHANGE. In today's open interface environment, where users have access to tools such as File Transfer Protocol (FTP), Open Database Connectivity (OBDC), DDM, and DRDA, *CHANGE public authority isn't appropriate.

Your first inclination might be to change the QCRTAUT system value to *USE or even *EXCLUDE to limit public authority to new libraries and objects. However, you must take a couple additional steps if you use that approach. OS/400 automatically creates device descriptions and their associated message queues, and users must have *CHANGE authority to these objects in order to use them. If you don't take these additional steps, you'll have to individually authorize all users to the devices and message queues they need to use. To safely change QCRTAUT to *USE, take the following steps:

1. Change the CRTAUT value for library QSYS to *CHANGE.
2. Change the command default for the CRTLIB command to AUT(*USE).
3. Change QCRTAUT to *USE.

Now, with the exception of libraries, all commands that create objects in QSYS and normally have AUT(*LIBCRTAUT) will have *CHANGE public authority, and users will be able to use the devices and messages queues that OS/400 automatically creates.

*USE is the most appropriate public authority in today's environment. If you want to change QCRTAUT to *EXCLUDE, you'll have many more considerations. The exact procedure will depend on your applications and system configuration.

Another inclination might be to change QCRTAUT to *ALL to simplify object authorizations and make every object on the system easily accessible. This alternative would be like opening Pandora's box!

Another alternative is to leave QCRTAUT set to *CHANGE and then change each library's CRTAUT attribute to determine the public authority to new objects created in the library. But remember: The only good default public authority is planned default public authority!

To ensure that public authorities enhance rather than hinder security on your system, determine the appropriate public authority for each user-defined library. Check each one to see whether the currently defined public authority is right for the objects in the library as well as for the library itself. Then modify the CRTAUT attribute of each library to reflect the appropriate default public authority for objects created in that library.

Perhaps one library contains only utility program objects (e.g., date conversion routines, a binary-to-decimal conversion program, a check object/authority program) that various applications use. Because all the programs should be available for execution, it makes sense to set that library's CRTAUT attribute to *USE so that new objects created in that library will have *USE default public authority.

Suppose another library contains the payroll and employee data files. You probably want to restrict public access to this library and secure it by user profile, a group profile, or an authorization list. Any new objects created in this library should probably also have *EXCLUDE public authority unless the program or person creating the object specifically selects another public authority using the object's AUT attribute. This library should have a CRTAUT attribute value of *EXCLUDE.

If you follow these suggestions for the QCRTAUT system value and the CRTAUT library attribute, an AUT value of *LIBCRTAUT works well as a default. In many cases, public authority at the object level coincides with the public authorities the CRTAUT attribute establishes at the library level. However, be sure you make this a planned decision instead of a default decision.

If you're working with objects created in directories, how you set public authority depends on the method you use to create the object. In most cases, the object inherits its public authority from the directory in which the object resides. And, when objects in directories inherit public authority, more than just the public authority is inherited. The object also inherits authorization list, primary group, and private authorities. However, when you use UNIX-like APIs, such as mkdir(), open(), and creat(), to create objects, you specify the data authorities for the owner, the primary group, and public.

Understanding the AS/400's implementation of object security can help you plan your authorization scheme. You can secure many or most objects on your system simply through the object's *PUBLIC authority. You can then secure more sensitive objects by specifying *EXCLUDE authority for certain user or group profiles. Understanding OS/400's authority search order will also help you make these decisions. We explain the search order later, in the section "How OS/400 Checks Authority."

Authorization Lists

An authorization list is a management tool that helps you secure similar objects. Usually, the objects associated with an application all need the same type of security. Figure 4.5 shows an accounts receivable application that creates a new file each month. The same users need to have the same authority to each monthly file. The best way to secure these files is to use an authorization list.

To create an authorization list to secure an object, you run the CRTAUTL (Create Authorization List) command. Then you execute the EDTAUTL (Edit Authorization List) command to give selected user or group profiles authority to the authorization list. Next, you associate the authorization list with all the application's files by specifying the authorization list name in each file's AUT parameter.

By virtue of having authority to the authorization list, the users have authority to the objects. The type of authority each user has to the object is the same as the authority you grant the user to the authorization list. For example, in Figure 4.5, Kelsey has *CHANGE authority to the authorization list; therefore, she has *CHANGE authority to all objects associated with the authorization list. You can also grant *PUBLIC authority to an object from an authorization list.

Authorization lists have several advantages. They are a wonderful tool for securing files. When you use an authorization list, users can't alter the authority to a file when it's in use. For a 24×7 shop, managing authorities to files that are almost always in use can be a challenge. By associating an authorization list with those files, managing authorities simply requires changing authorities to the authorization list, which you can do even when the file is open. Once you've associated files with an authorization list, you simply manage authorities to the authorization list rather than to all the files.

FIGURE 4.5
Securing Similar Objects with an Authorization List

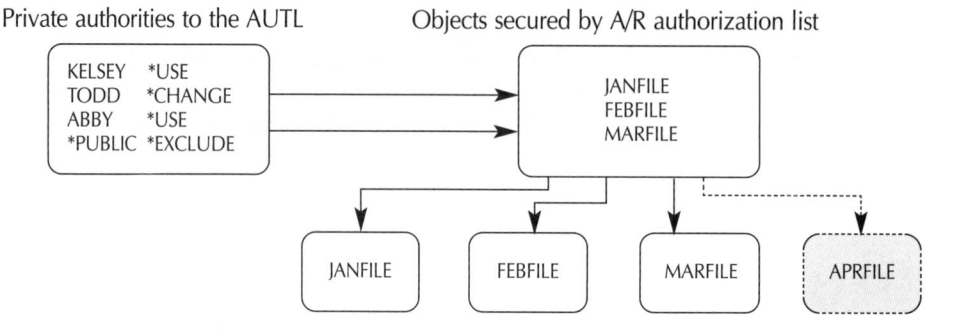

Private authorities to the AUTL

KELSEY	*USE
TODD	*CHANGE
ABBY	*USE
*PUBLIC	*EXCLUDE

Objects secured by A/R authorization list

JANFILE
FEBFILE
MARFILE

JANFILE FEBFILE MARFILE APRFILE

Technical Note

If you have trouble maintaining authorities for a file because the file is always open, secure the file with an authorization list. You can grant and revoke authority to the authorization list even when the file is open.

Another advantage to authorization lists is that they save room in the internal structure of user profiles. Rather than putting into a user profile an entry for each object the profile has private authority to, you put only an entry for the authorization list. Having fewer entries in a user's profile saves time when you run the SAVSECDTA (Save Security Data) and RSTAUT commands.

Authorization lists don't preclude using private authorities. You can still grant and revoke private authorities to an object using the GRTOBJAUT, RVKOBJAUT, and EDTOBJAUT commands. A user profile's private authorities supersede any authority the user has to an authorization list.

We're often asked whether it's better to use group profiles or authorization lists. Neither method is inherently better than the other. You should use the method that makes the most sense for what you're trying to do. Many people use a combination of both methods — giving a group profile authority to an authorization list, for example. Table 4.3 compares authorization list and group profile methods of implementing AS/400 security.

TABLE 4.3
Comparison of Authorization Lists and Group Profiles

Authorization list	Group profile
Groups similar objects	Groups similar user profiles
Can authorize multiple objects	Can authorize multiple objects
Each user profile can have different authorities	All users in the group have the same authorities
A user profile has the same authority to every object on the list	A user profile can have different authorities to objects
A user can be on multiple lists	A user can be in multiple groups
An object can be on only one authorization list	An object can be authorized to multiple groups
Many users authorized to the same objects with different authorities	Many users authorized to many objects with the same authorities
Must explicitly associate object with list	Can automatically authorize the group to an object that a member of the group creates

How OS/400 Checks Authority

We've discussed the different methods you can use to obtain authority — private authorities for users and groups, authorization lists, and *PUBLIC authorities. But how do they work together, and which one takes precedence?

OS/400 searches for authorities in a predetermined order. The authorization search order is a mystery to many people. But unless you understand how it works, securing your system will be a change-something-and-hope-it-works process that will be prone to error and impossible to explain or maintain.

The authorization search order is really quite simple once you see it. Figure 4.6 illustrates the progression of the authority search algorithm.

FIGURE 4.6
Authorization Search Progression

Access denied (because of *EXCLUDE authority or because authorities not sufficient)		Access granted (authority for task sufficient)
	Does user have *ALLOBJ authority? — Yes, *ALLOBJ →	
	No *ALLOBJ	
Insufficient authorities ←	Does user have private authority to the object?	→ Sufficient authorities
	No private authorities	
Insufficient authorities ←	Does user have authority via an authorization list?	→ Sufficient authorities
	No authorization list authorities	
	Is user part of a group profile that has *ALLOBJ authority? — Yes, *ALLOBJ →	
	No	
Insufficient authorities ←	Is user part of a group profile that has primary group authority?	→ Sufficient authorities
	No primary group authority	
Insufficient authorities ←	Is user part of a group profile that has authorities (check multiple groups if provided)?	→ Sufficient authorities
	No direct group profile authorities	
Insufficient authorities ←	Is user part of a group profile that has authority via an authorization list?	→ Sufficient authorities
	No group authority via authorization list	
Insufficient authorities ←	Is *PUBLIC authority sufficient?	→ Sufficient authorities

As you can see, the system first determines whether the profile has *ALLOBJ special authority. If it does, the system lets the user access the object because *ALLOBJ gives the user profile *ALL authority to every object on the system.

If the profile doesn't have *ALLOBJ authority, the system performs an authority lookup to determine whether the user profile has specific authority to the object. If the system finds the profile to have a specific authority, even if it's *EXCLUDE, the system uses that authority and doesn't go on to check group or *PUBLIC authorities.

If the user doesn't have specific authority, the system then determines whether the desired object is secured with an authorization list and whether the user has authority to the authorization list. If not, the system checks the user's first group profile, if there is one, for *ALLOBJ special authority, then for primary group authority to the object, then for a private authority to the object. If none of those authorities are available, the system checks whether the group has authority to the authorization list, if one is used to secure the object.

If the first group profile doesn't have sufficient authority, the system checks the user's next group and so on until sufficient authority is found or all groups have been checked. If a user has multiple group profiles, OS/400 sums the groups' authorities, if necessary, as it checks the groups. For example, if GROUP_TWO has *OBJOPR private authority and *READ authority to the file, GROUP_THREE has *ADD, *UPDATE, and *DELETE private authority, and GROUP_SIX has *EXECUTE authority to the file, the system accumulates the authorities and determines that the user has *CHANGE authority to the file.

Finally, if neither the user nor his or her group(s) has sufficient authority, OS/400 checks *PUBLIC authority. *PUBLIC authority can come from either the object itself or from an authorization list that secures the object.

During each step of the check at the user level and after all group profiles have been checked, when OS/400 finds some authority, sufficient or not, the system discontinues the search unless a program in the call stack adopts authority. (We explain adopted authority in detail later in this chapter.) In that case, the system checks the adopting program's owner for authority to the object. The system checks the program owner's authority for *ALLOBJ, private, and authorization list authority (the first three boxes in Figure 4.6).

This is how the authorization search works conceptually. However, IBM has made some enhancements to refine the search performance. First, OS/400 determines whether the user profile is authorized to the object by means of private authority (i.e., via specific authority granted to the user profile, to the group profile that includes the user profile, or to an authorization list that includes the user profile). If no private authorities are present (determined simply by checking a flag in the object's header), the system immediately examines the *PUBLIC authorities. (Every object has an internal part called a *header* that OS/400 maintains. The header contains basic object attributes, such as the owner and the owner's authorities, the name of the primary group profile and its authorities, and the *PUBLIC authority.) Another flag in the object header indicates whether existing private authorities are less restrictive than the public authorities. If existing private authorities are no less restrictive than the public authorities, the system bypasses the rest of the authority search algorithm and immediately checks whether public authority is sufficient. This modification to the search algorithm speeds search performance significantly.

Although OS/400's search algorithm supports flexibility by granting authorities broadly and then controlling certain authorities through exclusion, this model doesn't correlate well to the real world of security implementation. Normally, one thinks of user authority as additive, and most people find it more sensible to structure security that way. The problem with the model used for authorization searches is that after OS/400 identifies an authority for a user profile, the search ends. Consequently, you can't augment specific user authorities with group or authorization-list authorities. Or, if the user profile is in a group that has authority to an object, you can't augment the group authority with additional authorities from an authorization list. Small shops might benefit by allowing *PUBLIC access to most objects and then using exclusion methods for sensitive objects, but larger shops that use this approach might find themselves creating many detailed user profile authorities for exclusion purposes, thus building a complex environment that is difficult to manage.

Authority Cache

OS/400 uses an authority cache to look up private authorities to objects and to authorization lists. The first time the system performs an authority lookup to determine whether a user has specific authority to an object, OS/400 creates a cache for the user and adds the specific authority to the cache. The next time the system performs a lookup, it checks the user's cache before checking the profile. This procedure results in a much faster check than looking in the user profile. The cache contains up to 32 private authorities to objects and 32 authorities to authorization lists. Whenever a user's authority changes, the system automatically updates the user's cache. All users' authority caches are cleared at IPL.

The effect of the authority cache is that if users generally access the same objects and have private or authorization list authority to the objects, the impact on performance is very small. The authority cache gives you more flexibility in securing your objects, but it doesn't give you license to go wild with private authorities. Massive numbers of private authorities are still difficult to manage and maintain, still cause *USRPRF objects to grow very large, and still affect performance when you save and restore your system.

Adopted Authority

Another way a user can gain authority to an object is through adopted authority. You can use adopted authority to temporarily give a user sufficient authority to accomplish a sensitive task.

When you compile a program on the AS/400 (using the CRTxxxPGM commands), you can supply a value of either *USER or *OWNER for the USRPRF parameter. The default value, *USER, instructs the system to run the program under the authority of the user who is executing the program. A value of *OWNER instructs the system to run the program under the authority of the program's owner if the user's profile doesn't have enough authority to perform the program's tasks. Adopted authority remains in effect until the program ends — in other words, for as long as the program is in the program call stack. Any programs called by the program that adopts authority also use the adopted authority unless the called programs specifically use the USEADPAUT(*NO) parameter to block propagation of the adopted authority.

Figure 4.7 illustrates the concepts and implementation of authority adoption. Because PGM_A doesn't adopt authority (notice USRPRF(*USER)), OS/400 can use only USER_A's authority to execute the program. When PGM_A calls PGM_B, OS/400 uses USER_A's authority plus, if necessary, the program owner's (PRODOWN's) authority to complete the tasks. When PGM_B calls PGM_C, the authorities continue to add up. PGM_C specifies USRPRF(*OWNER), and the owner of PGM_C is SECUSER. The system first determines whether USER_A has sufficient authority to execute PGM_C and then adds the authority of PRODOWN and SECUSER if necessary to obtain the needed authorities. Finally, when PGM_C calls PGM_D, two things change. First, PGM_D ignores previously adopted authorities (USEADPAUT(*NO)). Second, because program PGM_D doesn't specify USRPRF(*OWNER), PGM_D doesn't adopt the program owner's authorities. As a result, PGM_D uses only USER_A's authorities.

FIGURE 4.7
Adopted Authority Concepts

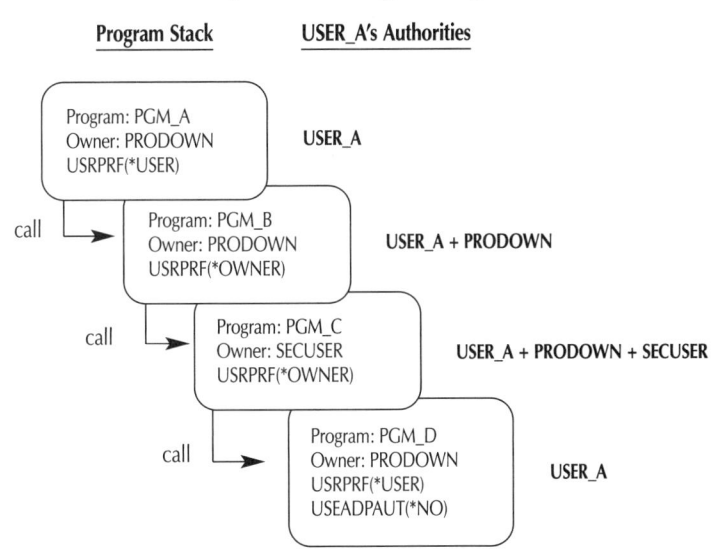

Program Stack   **USER_A's Authorities**

Program: PGM_A
Owner: PRODOWN   USER_A
USRPRF(*USER)

call → Program: PGM_B
Owner: PRODOWN   USER_A + PRODOWN
USRPRF(*OWNER)

call → Program: PGM_C
Owner: SECUSER   USER_A + PRODOWN + SECUSER
USRPRF(*OWNER)

call → Program: PGM_D
Owner: PRODOWN   USER_A
USRPRF(*USER)
USEADPAUT(*NO)

Let's consider an example. Physical file ICFPRC contains pricing data for every part a company sells. Only USER_ONE and USER_TWO are allowed to update the file, and all changes to the pricing file must be written to a log file for future reference and auditing. It's important that USER_ONE and USER_TWO have no way of updating prices that would circumvent writing changes to the log file. How would you implement security to fulfill these requirements? We would do it like this.

First, we would write a program — call it ICPRCUPD — that makes the price changes and writes the log records to the log file (ICFPLOG). We would revoke public authorities to files ICFPRC and ICFPLOG. USER_ONE and USER_TWO must be the only user profiles to have authority to those files, and they should have that authority only while they use program ICPRCUPD. If we were to give USER_ONE and USER_TWO private authority to the files, the users might be able to find a way to update the files without using program ICPRCUPD.

Instead, program ICPRCUPD itself must provide the authority to update the files. We would create another user profile (e.g., USER_PRICE), specify PASSWORD(*NONE) for the profile, and grant it *CHANGE authority to files ICFPRC and ICFPLOG (we would also need to grant USER_PRICE authority to the library in which the files reside). We would compile program ICPRCUPD with USRPRF(*OWNER) and then make USER_PRICE the owner of the program. Finally, we would grant only USER_ONE and USER_TWO the authority to use program ICPRCUPD.

The result is a single program for updating prices. This program has the authority to perform this task only, and only USER_ONE and USER_TWO have authority to use the program. No one can use any other method to change prices because no users have authority to change the price file directly.

Although using QSECOFR as the owner of programs that adopt authority is certainly the easiest way to ensure that the program has all the authority it needs, this strategy can cause serious security problems if the program incorrectly propagates QSECOFR authority to subsequent programs, command lines, or menus. The owner's special authorities (e.g., *ALLOBJ, *SERVICE, *JOBCTL) and private authorities are adopted.

Here is a summary of some things to keep in mind when you use programs that adopt authority.

- Adopted authority is additive.
- Adopted authority is checked only if existing authority is inadequate.
- The owner's special authorities (e.g., *ALLOBJ, *JOBCTL) are adopted.
- The owner's private authorities are adopted.
- The owner's group authorities are not adopted.
- Adopted authority is active as long as
  - the program that adopts authority is in the program stack (you can use the USEADPAUT program keyword to block propagation).
  - the program that adopts authority isn't interrupted by the System request or Attention key, transfer to a group job, break-message-handling program, or debug functions.
- Adopted authority can't be passed to submitted jobs.
- Adopted authority can't be used to execute the CHGJOB command.

Security Recommendation
If you use programs that adopt authority, make sure they perform only one task (e.g., update salary, update prices, retrieve personnel information) and that they don't call other programs (which might propagate authority unnecessarily) or that they call only programs that have USEADPAUT(*NO) specified. Be sure to document the programs thoroughly and make them easy to identify.

Create user profiles specifically to own the programs that adopt authority. Create these profiles with PASSWORD(*NONE) and with only enough authority for the program to perform its task. Don't let QSECOFR own programs that adopt authority.

Authorities and Save/Restore Functions

One subtlety of the issue of public and private authorities concerns how they are saved and restored. OS/400 saves and restores public authorities with the object, as part of the object header. In contrast, OS/400 maintains private authorities as part of the user profile; private authorities aren't saved with the object. When you restore an object and it already exists on the system (i.e., when the object you restore replaces an existing object), OS/400 maintains the existing object's public authorities, which may or may not be the same as the authorities of the object on the media. When you restore a new object, OS/400 restores the public authority from the media along with the object.

What happens when you restore a user profile? When you restore one or more user profiles, you must also execute the RSTAUT (Restore Authorities) command to restore the user profile's private authorities. This explains why, if you restore your complete system, including all user profiles and objects, but don't execute the RSTAUT command, only the public and primary group authorities work. No private authorities exist until you execute the RSTAUT command.

Another interesting point concerning the private and public authorities' save/restore functions relates to users who have *SAVSYS special authority. Let's assume you've given your system operator *SAVSYS authority. Let's also assume that you have a library called PAYROLL that holds all payroll files and that you've used library authority to secure those files. In other words, the library's public authority is *EXCLUDE, and you've authorized only a few users (not including your system operator) to the library. However, you've specified *CHANGE public authority to the files in library PAYROLL. In effect, you've secured the library from all users except those with private authorities. But if an unauthorized user can get inside the library, he or she can have public access to the files.

This security scenario is a "normal" and somewhat typical practice for securing some libraries. However, you need to be aware of a security exposure in this scenario related to saving and restoring the files that reside in the library. If the system operator (who has *SAVSYS authority) were to restore to a nonsecure library files saved from the PAYROLL library, he or she would then have complete public access to the files in the unsecured library. Because public authorities are saved with the object, the files' public *CHANGE authority is restored with the files to the unsecured library, and the system operator can retrieve, modify, and delete records in that library. The system operator could then simply save the modified version of the file and restore that version to the PAYROLL library.

Because you'll probably want to give *SAVSYS special authority to system operators so they can perform system backups, what's the solution to this exposure? First, you must have some level of trust with the system operator. Second, you should audit the restore operations on your system and monitor for any unusual restoration of files into libraries (e.g., unscheduled restores or restores into nonsecure libraries). For more information about this type of auditing, see Chapter 18.

Object Ownership

Every object on the system has an owner. When an object is created, the object's owner is the user profile that created it. You can use the CHGOBJOWN (Change Object Owner) command or the IFS CHGOWN (Change Owner) command to change the ownership of an object. But what exactly does it mean to own an object?

The user profile that owns an object is automatically granted *ALL authority to the object when the object is created or when ownership is transferred to a new owner. Having *ALL authority gives the owner all object and data rights. The owner or another user who has sufficient authority (e.g., *ALLOBJ special authority) can revoke one or more of the owner's authorities to the object. For example, the owner can revoke his or her own data rights to the object, thus protecting the data but retaining the ability to control the object. If for some reason the owner doesn't have sufficient authority to the library in which the object resides, the owner can't access or manage the object regardless of the object and data authorities the owner has to the object itself.

Object ownership isn't an authority per se, but because ownership is so powerful, you need to control and audit it as you would authority settings. Generally, the best way to do so is to create a few user profiles to own certain applications.

Let's say your system has the following libraries, applications, and files:

FINOLIB — all financial applications
FINFLIB — all financial database files
MFGOLIB — all manufacturing applications
MFGFLIB — all manufacturing database files
DEVLIB — all development files and applications

In this scenario, we recommend three owners: one for all financial objects, one for all manufacturing objects, and one for the development objects. We would implement this strategy in two steps:

1. Create three user profiles with PASSWORD(*NONE):
   - FINOWNER (financial owner)
   - MFGOWNER (manufacturing owner)
   - DEVOWNER (development owner)
2. Change the ownership of the libraries and corresponding objects as follows:
   - FINOWNER owns libraries FINOLIB and FINFLIB
   - MFGOWNER owns libraries MFGOLIB and MFGFLIB
   - DEVOWNER owns library DEVLIB

The names of the user profiles used as owners should indicate their use. The sole purpose of these profiles is to own the applications and associated objects. The profiles shouldn't be group profiles, and users shouldn't use them to sign on. To ensure that users can't use the profiles to sign on, create them with PASSWORD(*NONE). If you use purchased software, you'll notice that most third-party applications use one user profile to own all the application's objects.

In a development environment, depending on how your change control software works, you might need to assign ownership of development objects to a group profile. This approach lets programmers easily work with objects created by another member of the team without requiring you to implement an elaborate authority scheme. When each member of the development team is a member of the group profile, the group profile does all the work. Some organizations create their developers' profiles with OWNER(*GRPPRF) so that when a developer creates an object, the object is owned by the developer's primary group profile. This method works fairly well if all the users create objects in the QSYS file system. However, OS/400 ignores the OWNER parameter for objects in other file systems, and the user retains ownership. Given today's environment, in which programmers might be writing Java programs and creating stream files, this method doesn't work well. In this case, you can use the profile swapping APIs, which we discuss in Chapter 10.

Many shops use QSECOFR as the owner of production objects. This strategy is unwise for two reasons. First, it encourages the use of the QSECOFR profile to implement and modify production objects. QSECOFR should be used only to establish and maintain security or in emergencies. Second, when QSECOFR owns production objects, there's a temptation to use QSECOFR to create programs that adopt authority. Allowing programs to adopt the authority of QSECOFR, the most powerful profile on the system, is very dangerous. Programs that adopt authority should be owned by a profile with limited authority created specifically for that task.

Security Recommendation
Don't let QSECOFR or other IBM-supplied profiles own production objects.

This chapter has covered the two forms of specific authority — object and data — and the four authority classes OS/400 provides. We've explained how you can grant and revoke these authorities for individual user profiles, for group profiles, and through authorization lists. What we haven't explained yet is how to use these authorities to implement security on your system. That discussion begins in Chapter 11, after an explanation in Chapters 5 through 10 of the tools available for building database security, securing output queues and spooled files, establishing network and Internet security, and thwarting hackers.

Limit User Function

When you're designing the security aspects for a new application, you need to determine the ownership and *PUBLIC authority of the application's objects and how to control users' abilities to perform tasks within the application. A user's ability to perform a task within an application often depends on whether the user has authority to an object such as a command or file. However, sometimes you need to control whether a user can perform a task within an application when there is no associated object to check the user's authority to. The Limit User Function APIs let you define and register a function. You use the APIs in the application to determine whether the user has authority to perform the registered function.

Function definition isn't limited to user-written applications. For example, Client Access defines several functions that let you to control which Client Access features are displayed on a user's desktop, and OS/400 defines functions to control access to some service tools, such as some DASD management functions implemented in V4R5. You should consider functions defined to control what appears on the desktop (e.g., data transfer) to be the modern-day equivalent of menu security. In other words, you shouldn't count on those functions to secure your system. However, functions that control access on the AS/400 (e.g., the DASD management and Service trace functions) are relevant to security and should be monitored.

To administer these OS/400 functions, you must use Operations Navigator. Right-click the name of the AS/400 you're connected to and select Application Administration. The resulting dialog box (Figure 4.8) lists all registered functions and categorizes them under three tabs. The AS/400 Operations Navigator tab lists functions defined by Operations Navigator and Operations Navigator plug-ins. The Client Applications tab lists all other client functions (sometimes referred to as applications), including Client Access Express. The Host Applications tab lists applications that reside on the AS/400, not on the client. Business partners and other application providers can define and register their own functions. From Operations Navigator, you can see which functions a particular user is allowed to perform. Select the AS/400 you're connected to, expand Users and Groups, select All Users, right-click the user you're interested in, select Capabilities, and click the Applications tab. Figure 4.9 shows a sample window.

FIGURE 4.8
Operations Navigator Application Administration Window

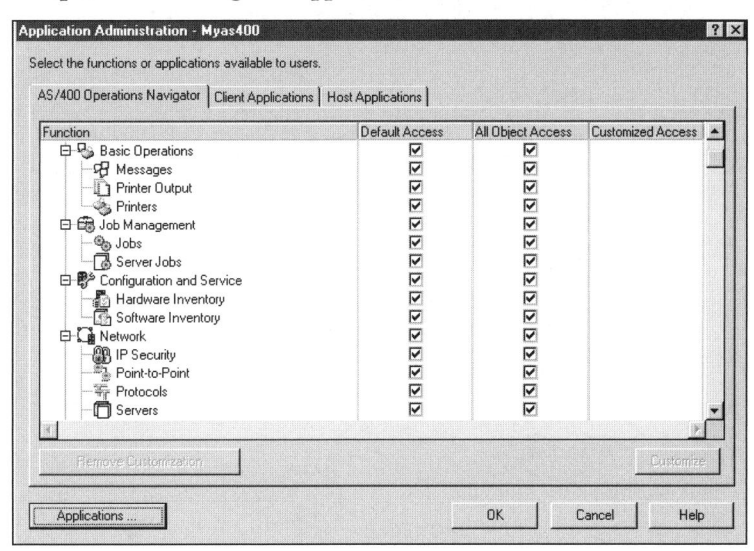

FIGURE 4.9
Viewing a User's Capabilities in Operations Navigator

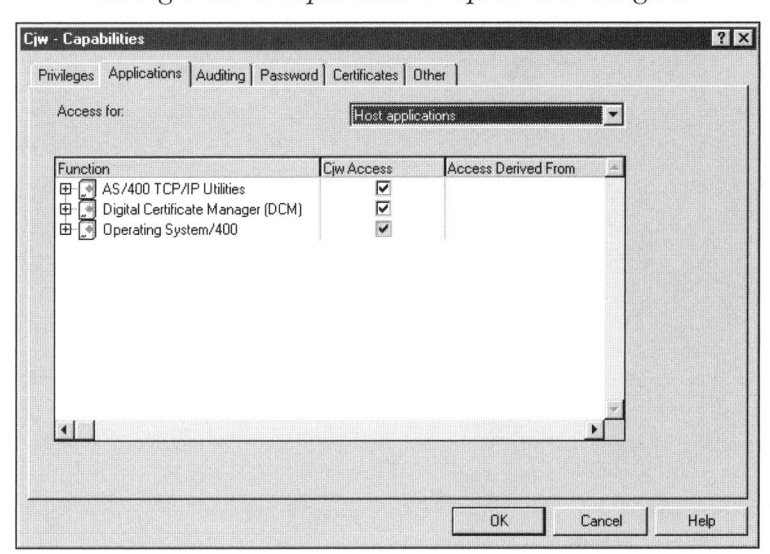

Helpful Tools

Several security tools are available on the SECTOOLS and SECBATCH menus to help you effectively manage object authorities on your system. Here is a list and description of those tools.

Security tool	Description
PRTADPOBJ (Print Adopting Objects)	Use this command to print a list of objects that adopt the authority of a specified user profile. You can specify one profile or specify a set of profiles generically (e.g., PGMR* for all user profiles that begin with PGMR).
PRTPVTAUT (Print Private Authorities)	This report lists the private authorities that exist for a specified type of object in a library or directory. PRTPVTAUT can list all objects of the specified type and those objects' private authorities, list only changes to the objects since the last time you ran the report, or even list the private authorities that have been deleted since the last time you ran the report.
RTPUBAUT (Print Public Authorities)	You can use this command to list all objects whose public authority is not *EXCLUDE. You can select objects by type and library or directory.

Operations Navigator

Operations Navigator provides an interface for managing object authorities. To manage object authorities (which Operations Navigator refers to as a user's "permissions" to an object), navigate to the object, right-click it, and choose the Permissions option. Operations Navigator will display a window like the one in Figure 4.10.

FIGURE 4.10
Operations Navigator Permissions Window

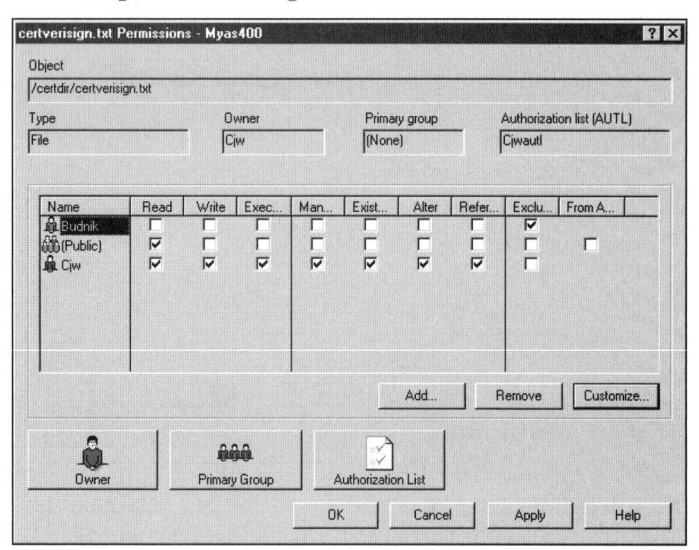

Chapter 5

Database Security

Most security measures you'll implement will pertain to securing data. The AS/400 provides ways to secure file objects and control the user's ability to read, add, update, and delete records in a file. OS/400 also provides field-level (or in SQL — column-level) security for the DB2 UDB for AS/400 database. For pre-V4R2 versions of OS/400, explicit field-level security wasn't a part of the AS/400's security implementation for database files; however, we discuss some OS/400 capabilities your applications can use to secure data at the field level.

Database File Authorities

At any release of DB2 UDB for AS/400, you can secure AS/400 database files (and SQL tables) at two levels. Because a database file is an object, the object authorities we covered in Chapter 4 apply (e.g., *OBJOPR, *OBJEXIST, *OBJREF). Object authorities are key to a few particular database operations. First, *OBJOPR determines whether a user can use the database file. Regardless of the data authorities a user has, the user needs *OBJOPR authority just to open the file. This fact becomes more significant when we talk about the relationship between physical and logical files or SQL tables and views.

Two other important object authorities for database files are *OBJALTER and *OBJREF (when you're working with an SQL collection, these two authorities are called ALTER and REFERENCES, respectively). If a user has *OBJALTER authority to a database file, the user can add and remove database triggers for that file. If a user has *OBJREF authority for a database file, that user can add and remove referential constraints to a physical file.

You can also grant data authorities to database files. You use data authorities to specify how users can manipulate a file's data records. You can grant data authorities to SQL tables and views and to both physical and logical files.

All applications that use database files should recognize and honor the data authorities of the user who executes the application. Unless you plan for data authorities in your application, if the application attempts to write a record to a file to which the user doesn't have *ADD authority, the application receives an error message and fails. A better solution is for the application either to determine in advance which data authorities are present and then act accordingly or to trap authority error messages and take appropriate action.

One popular way to control operations such as add, update, and delete is to create specific applications that perform the functions and then control user access to the menus that contain those applications. With this approach, your database applications don't have to check for OS/400 data authorities or grant and revoke such authorities at the OS/400 level. The downside to this technique is that it doesn't provide a secure environment for data files when a user has access to tools and applications such as DB2 UDB Query Manager, SQL Development Kit, third-party report writers, or ODBC, all of which would bypass such internal security methods.

A good solution is to write an application that filters users' authorities and sets appropriate authority for the files so users can do only what they're authorized to do. Were you to implement such a solution, you might decide to let the user attempt any operation (add, change, delete) and have the application catch authority errors after the fact. However, a much better approach is to eliminate options to which the user isn't authorized. Users will appreciate, too, not attempting an operation only to discover, too late, that they don't have the proper authority.

To create an application that gives users only the options they are authorized to perform, you need a tool to retrieve user authorities. The right tool for this job is the security API QSYRUSRA, which returns to the calling program a specific user profile's authority to a specified object. (This API won't retrieve a user's field-level authorities; to retrieve column authorities, you must use SQL.) The QSYRUSRA API requires the following parameters:

Parameter	Type	I/O
Receiver variable	CHAR(*)	O
Receiver variable length	BIN(4)	I
Format name	CHAR(8)	I
User name	CHAR(10)	I
Qualified object name	CHAR(20)	I
Object type	CHAR(10)	I
Error structure	CHAR(*)	I/O

The first three parameters pertain to the data the API returns to the calling program. The receiver variable's data structure contains the data identified by the format name variable. Format USRA0100 is the only format available for this API's return data. This format describes a structure 93 bytes long that contains the return data summarized in Table 5.1. (Note that Table 5.1 uses offsets to indicate the correct starting position. For example, offset 0 indicates the field starts in position 1; offset 25 means the field starts in position 26.) In the fields that deal with specific authorities, a return value of Y or N signifies whether the user has the authority. The "receiver variable length" parameter must contain the actual length of the return variable; because USRA0100 is the only format, the appropriate value is 93. (For a complete description of this format, see *AS/400 System APIs Information,* SC41-5801.)

TABLE 5.1

Format USRA0100

Offset	Type	Field
0	BINARY(4)	Bytes returned
4	BINARY(4)	Bytes available
8	CHAR(10)	Object authority

continued

TABLE 5.1 *CONTINUED*

Offset	Type	Field
18	CHAR(1)	Authorization list management
19	CHAR(1)	Object operational
20	CHAR(1)	Object management
21	CHAR(1)	Object existence
22	CHAR(1)	Data read
23	CHAR(1)	Data add
24	CHAR(1)	Data update
25	CHAR(1)	Data delete
26	CHAR(10)	Authorization list name
36	CHAR(2)	Authority source
38	CHAR(1)	Some adopted authority
39	CHAR(10)	Adopted object authority
49	CHAR(1)	Adopted authorization list management
50	CHAR(1)	Adopted object operational
51	CHAR(1)	Adopted object management
52	CHAR(1)	Adopted object existence
53	CHAR(1)	Adopted data read
54	CHAR(1)	Adopted data add
55	CHAR(1)	Adopted data update
56	CHAR(1)	Adopted data delete
57	CHAR(1)	Adopted data execute
58	CHAR(10)	Reserved
68	CHAR(1)	Adopted object alter
69	CHAR(1)	Adopted object reference
70	CHAR(10)	Reserved
80	CHAR(1)	Data execute
81	CHAR(10)	Reserved
91	CHAR(1)	Object alter
92	CHAR(1)	Object reference

The next three parameters identify the user and the object for which the API is to retrieve authorities. Normally, the user parameter has the value *CURRENT to refer to the calling program's current user. However, you can specify any valid user profile name for the user parameter. The qualified object name and object type parameters identify the object that the API is to check for user authorities. The special values *CURLIB and *LIBL are valid for the last 10 positions of the qualified object name, or you can use those positions to specify the library in which the object resides.

Finally, following IBM's standard API implementation, QSYRUSRA uses an error code structure that provides information to the calling program if the API fails.

To illustrate how to write an application that allows different authorities for different users, we provide a subfile program for working with customer records. Figures 5.1A and 5.1B show the DDS for sample physical file CUSTPF and sample logical file CUSTLFNM, respectively. Figure 5.2 shows RPG program CSTMAINT, which produces a work-with panel that lets a user read, add, change, and delete customer records depending on the user's object and data authorities.

FIGURE 5.1A
Physical File CUSTPF

```
*...1....+....2....+....3....+....4....+....5....+....6....+....7....+
      *==================================================================*
      * Sample Customer File (Partial)                                    *
      *==================================================================*
      *
     A                                              UNIQUE
     A          R CUSTPR                            TEXT('Customer Record')
      *
     A            CUSTNO         7P 0               COLHDG('Customer' 'Number')
     A                                              TEXT('Customer number')
     A            CNAME         30A                 COLHDG('Customer name')
     A                                              TEXT('Customer name')
     A            CSTRT         30A                 COLHDG('Street address')
     A                                              TEXT('Street address')
     A            CCITY         20A                 COLHDG('City')
     A                                              TEXT('City')
     A            CSTATE         2A                 COLHDG('State')
     A                                              TEXT('State')
     A            CZIP           9A                 COLHDG('Zip code')
     A                                              TEXT('Zip code')
     A            CCONT         30A                 COLHDG('Customer contact')
     A                                              TEXT('Customer contact')
     A            CCTITL        30A                 COLHDG('Contact title')
     A                                              TEXT('Contact title')
      *
     A                                              TEXT('Contact phone number')
     A            NOTES1        40A                 COLHDG('Notes 1')
     A                                              TEXT('Notes 1')
     A            NOTES2        40A                 COLHDG('Notes 2')
     A                                              TEXT('Notes 2')
     A            CLORDT         6S 0               COLHDG('Last order date')
     A                                              TEXT('Last order date')
     A            CBALNC        11P 2               COLHDG('Current' 'Balance')
     A                                              TEXT('Current balance')
     A                                              EDTCDE(J)
     A            CCRFLG         1A                 COLHDG('Good Credit Y/N?')
     A                                              TEXT('Credit Flag')
     A                                              VALUES('Y' 'N')
     A                                              DFT('N')
      *
     A          K CUSTNO
```

Figure 5.1B
Logical File CUSTLFNM

```
*...1....+....2....+....3....+....4....+....5....+....6....+....7....+

*==================================================================*
* Sample Customer File - Logical by name                           *
*==================================================================*
*
A          R CUSTPR                   PFILE(CUSTPF)
*
A          K CNAME
A          K CUSTNO
```

Figure 5.2
RPG Program CSTMAINT

```
*...1....+....2....+....3....+....4....+....5....+....6....+....7....+

*==================================================================*
* From "Work-With with Authority," NEWS 3X/400, February 1994      *
*                                                                  *
* COPYRIGHT (c) 1994 Duke Communications International,            *
* ALL RIGHTS RESERVED.  This program may not be reproduced         *
* or distributed in any form without permission in writing         *
* from the publisher, except for noncommercial, private use        *
* and adaptation granted by U.S. copyright law.                    *
* Redistribution of this program, or the distribution of           *
* derivative works, is expressly prohibited.  This copyright       *
* notice must remain in all private-use copies.                    *
*==================================================================*
* Program name: CSTMAINT                                           *
* Purpose.....: Customer Selection Window Program                  *
*                                                                  *
* Indicators:                                                      *
*     08   -   Controls SFLNXTCHG DDS keyword for CSFL subfile     *
*     09   -   Nondisplay for deleted subfile record fields        *
*     11   -   Toggles SFLDROP and SFLFOLD DDS keywords            *
*     40   -   Clear subfile                                       *
*     41   -   Display subfile control record SFLCTLDSP DDS kwd    *
*     42   -   Display subfile SFLDSP DDS keyword                  *
*     51   -   Record change authority (*ON if authority exists)   *
*     52   -   Record delete authority (*ON if authority exists)   *
*     53   -   Record add     authority (*ON if authority exists)  *
*     60   -   Cannot roll up or down in subfile                   *
*     98   -   EOF for read changed records in CSFL subfile        *
*     99   -   EOF for CUSTLFNM                                    *
*==================================================================*
FCUSTLFNMIF  E            K         DISK
FCUSTPF   UF E            K         DISK
FCUSTDF   CF E                      WORKSTN         KINFDS INFDS
F                                           CRRN KSFILE CSFL
F                                           CNFRRNKSFILE CNFSFL
*
```

continued

FIGURE 5.2 CONTINUED

```
*...1....+....2....+....3....+....4....+....5....+....6....+....7....+
 * File information data structure for workstation file
IINFDS        DS
I                                           369 369 KEY
I                                         B 378 3790PAGRRN
 *
 * Named constants
I                    '* Record deleted'    C           #DMSG
I                    '0'                   C           @TRUE
I                    '1'                   C           @FALSE
I                    'N'                   C           @NO
I                    'Y'                   C           @YES
 *
 * Named hexadecimal constants for function keys
I                    X'33'                 C           @F03
I                    X'36'                 C           @F06
I                    X'3C'                 C           @F12
I                    X'F4'                 C           @PAGUP
I                    X'F5'                 C           @PAGDN
 *
 * API parameter definitions
 *     ALNGTH = length of return data (see ARDS)
 *     AFMT   = return data format name (must be USRA0100)
 *     AUSER  = name of user
 *     AOBJ   = qualified object name
 *     AOBJT  = object type
 *     ERRCDE = API error code
I              DS
I I                  93                    B   1   40ALNGTH
I I                  'USRA0100'                5   12 AFMT
I I                  '*CURRENT   '            13   22 AUSER
I I                  'CUSTPF    *LIBL    '    23   42 AOBJ
I I                  '*FILE     '             43   52 AOBJT
I I                  X'00000000'              53   56 ERRCDE
 *
 * Authority receiver structure (format USRA0100) for QSYRUSRA API
IARDS          DS                                   93
I                                         B   1   40BRET
I                                         B   5    80BAVL
I                                              23  23 AREAD
I                                              24  24 AADD
I                                              25  25 AUPD
I                                              26  26 ADLT
 *
 *=================================================================*
 * Reset variables and clear subfile.                              *
 * In case program called again after *INLR = *OFF                 *
 * ensures that program starts again properly                      *
 *=================================================================*
 *
C                    RESET@EXIT
C                    EXSR @RESET
 *
```

continued

Figure 5.2 Continued

```
*...1....+....2....+....3....+....4....+....5....+....6....+....7....+

*================================================================*
* Program mainline                                               *
*================================================================*
*
C                   EXSR @LOAD
*
* Perform until exit requested
C         @EXIT     DOUEQ@TRUE
*
C                   WRITECSFLCMD
C                   EXFMTCSFLCTL
*
C                   Z-ADDPAGRRN    RCDNBR
*
* Process response
C         KEY       CASEQ@F03      @F03SR          F03 exit
C         KEY       CASEQ@F06      @F06SR          F06 add record
C         KEY       CASEQ@F12      @F12SR          F12 cancel
C         KEY       CASEQ@PAGDN    @PGDN           Page down
C                   CAS            @ENTKY          Enter
C                   ENDCS
*
C                   ENDDO
*
* End of program, you can modify to leave *INLR = *OFF
* and program will still work properly when called again
*
C                   MOVE *ON       *INLR
C                   RETRN
*
*================================================================*
* Subroutine Section of Program                                  *
*================================================================*
*
*================================================================*
* Initialization Subroutine                                      *
*================================================================*
*
C         *INZSR    BEGSR
*
C         *LIKE     DEFN CNAME     ENDNAM
C         *LIKE     DEFN CUSTNO    ENDCUS
*
* Create program exit flag and set value to @FALSE
C                   MOVE @FALSE    @EXIT    1
*
* Variable declarations
C                   Z-ADD0         CRRN     50
C                   Z-ADD0         ENDRN    50
C                   Z-ADD0         CNFRRN   50
C                   Z-ADD0         RRNSAV   50
C                   Z-ADD1         RCDNBR
C                   MOVE '0'       #FOLD    1
*
```

continued

FIGURE 5.2 CONTINUED

```
*...1....+....2....+....3....+....4....+....5....+....6....+....7....+
      * Set MODE to 0=Folded for first load of subfile
      * SFLMODE(&SFMODE) in DDS
     C                   MOVE '0'       SFMODE
      *
      * Complete file key
     C           FILKEY  KLIST
     C                   KFLD           CNAME
     C                   KFLD           CUSTNO
      *
      * End key for repositioning subfile
     C           ENDKEY  KLIST
     C                   KFLD           ENDNAM
     C                   KFLD           ENDCUS
      *
      * Determine physical file authorities and set proper indicators
     C                   CALL 'QSYRUSRA'
     C                   PARM           ARDS
     C                   PARM           ALNGTH
     C                   PARM           AFMT
     C                   PARM           AUSER
     C                   PARM           AOBJ
     C                   PARM           AOBJT
     C                   PARM           ERRCDE
      *
     C           AUPD    IFEQ @YES
     C                   MOVE *ON       *IN51
     C                   ENDIF
     C           ADLT    IFEQ @YES
     C                   MOVE *ON       *IN52
     C                   ENDIF
     C           AADD    IFEQ @YES
     C                   MOVE *ON       *IN53
     C                   ENDIF
      *
     C                   ENDSR
      *
      *================================================================*
      * Clear/Reset Subfile                                             *
      *================================================================*
      *
     C           @RESET  BEGSR
      *
      * Clear subfile and reset subfile display indicator.
     C                   MOVE *ON       *IN40
     C                   WRITECSFLCTL
     C                   MOVE *OFF      *IN40
     C                   MOVE *OFF      *IN42
      *
      * Reset subfile record number and subfile position fields.
     C                   RESETCRRN
     C                   RESETENDRN
     C                   RESETRCDNBR
      *
     C                   ENDSR
      *
```

continued

FIGURE 5.2 *CONTINUED*

```
*...1....+....2....+....3....+....4....+....5....+....6....+....7....+

*================================================================*
* Reposition file                                                 *
*================================================================*
*
C           @REPOS    BEGSR
 *
 * Clear subfile
C                     EXSR @RESET
 *
 * Reposition file by search value
C           CNAME     SETLLCUSTLFNM
C                     EXSR @LOAD
 *
C                     ENDSR
*
*================================================================*
* Load subfile                                                    *
*================================================================*
*
C           @LOAD     BEGSR
 *
 * Clear RCDNBR
C                     CLEARRCDNBR
 *
 * Read a page of records or until EOF.
C                     DO    15
C                     READ  CUSTLFNM                         99
 *
C           *IN99     IFEQ *ON
C                     LEAVE
C                     ELSE
 * Write subfile record.
C                     ADD   1            CRRN
 * First record on this page
C           RCDNBR    IFEQ 0
C                     Z-ADDCRRN          RCDNBR
C                     ENDIF
C                     WRITECSFL
C                     ENDIF
 *
C                     ENDDO
 *
 * Do not allow RCDNBR = 0
C           RCDNBR    IFEQ 0
C                     Z-ADD1             RCDNBR
C                     ENDIF
 *
 * Set endkey values
C                     EXSR @ENDKY
 *
```

continued

FIGURE 5.2 *CONTINUED*

```
*...1....+....2....+....3....+....4....+....5....+....6....+....7....+
 * If not EOF, read one more record to make sure.
C           *IN99     IFEQ *OFF
C                     READ CUSTLFNM                    99
C                     ENDIF
 *
 * If no records were added to subfile, set error indicators.
C           CRRN      IFEQ *ZEROS
C                     MOVE *OFF      *IN42
C                     ELSE
 * Else, set indicators to display subfile.
C                     MOVE *ON       *IN42
C                     ENDIF
 *
 * Determine which subfile mode (drop or fold)
 * is current, and display new records in that mode
C           SFMODE    IFEQ #FOLD
C                     MOVE *OFF      *IN11
C                     ELSE
C                     MOVE *ON       *IN11
C                     ENDIF
 *
C                     ENDSR
 *
 *===============================================================*
 * Update end keys and variables for file/subfile                *
 *===============================================================*
 *
C           @ENDKY    BEGSR
 *
C                     MOVE CNAME     ENDNAM
C                     MOVE CUSTNO    ENDCUS
C                     Z-ADDCRRN      ENDRN
 *
C                     ENDSR
 *
 *===============================================================*
 * Subfile page down                                             *
 *===============================================================*
 *
C           @PGDN     BEGSR
 *
C           *IN99     IFEQ *OFF
 * Continue with record after the last one read.
C           ENDKEY    SETGTCUSTLFNM
C                     Z-ADDENDRN     CRRN
C                     EXSR @LOAD
 * Page down beyond end of subfile
C                     ELSE
C                     MOVE *ON       *IN60
C                     ENDIF
 *
C                     ENDSR
 *
```

continued

Figure 5.2 Continued

```
*...1....+....2....+....3....+....4....+....5....+....6....+....7....+

 *================================================================*
 * Process enter key after subfile display                        *
 *================================================================*
 *
C           @ENTKY    BEGSR
 *
 * User request position to new name
C           NCNAME    IFNE *BLANKS
C                     MOVELNCNAME    CNAME
C                     EXSR @REPOS
C                     ELSE
C                     EXSR @SFLRD
C                     ENDIF
 *
C                     ENDSR
 *
 *================================================================*
 * Read changed records in subfile to check for selection         *
 *================================================================*
 *
C           @SFLRD    BEGSR
 *
 * Did user make a selection?
C                     READCCSFL                       98
 *
C           *IN98     DOWEQ*OFF
 *
 * Execute for appropriate selections
 *
 * Select group ....
C                     SELEC
 * Change selected
C           SELIO     WHEQ 2
C           *IN51     ANDEQ*ON                                        (D)
C                     EXSR @CCHG
C           KEY       IFEQ @F03
C                     LEAVE
C                     ENDIF
C                     Z-ADD0         SELIO
C                     UPDATCSFL
C                     Z-ADDCRRN      RCDNBR
 * Delete selected
C           SELIO     WHEQ 4
C           *IN52     ANDEQ*ON                                        (E)
C                     Z-ADDCRRN      RRNSAV
C                     EXSR @CDLT
C                     Z-ADDRRNSAV    RCDNBR
C           KEY       IFEQ @F12
C                     LEAVE
C                     ENDIF
```

continued

FIGURE 5.2 *CONTINUED*

```
*...1....+....2....+....3....+....4....+....5....+....6....+....7....+
 * View selected
C           SELIO     WHEQ 5
C                     EXSR @CVEW
C           KEY       IFEQ @F03
C                     LEAVE
C                     ENDIF
C                     Z-ADD0         SELIO
C                     UPDATCSFL
C                     Z-ADDCRRN      RCDNBR
 *
C                     ENDSL
 *
C                     READCCSFL                     98
C                     ENDDO
 *
C                     ENDSR
 *===============================================================*
 * Modify customer record                                         *
 *===============================================================*
 *
C           @CCHG     BEGSR
 *
 * Code to modify customer record
 * or code to call module to modify customer record
 *
C                     ENDSR
 *
 *===============================================================*
 * View customer record                                           *
 *===============================================================*
 *
C           @CVEW     BEGSR
 *
 * Code to view customer record
 * or code to call module to view customer record
 *
C                     ENDSR
 *
 *===============================================================*
 * Delete customer records                                        *
 *===============================================================*
 *
C           @CDLT     BEGSR
 *
C                     MOVE *ON       *IN40
C                     WRITECNFCTL
C                     MOVE *OFF      *IN40
C                     RESETCNFRRN
 *
 * Fill confirmation subfile with all deletion requests
C           *IN98     DOWEQ*OFF
C           SELIO     IFEQ 4
C                     ADD  1         CNFRRN
C                     WRITECNFSFL
C                     ENDIF
```

continued

FIGURE 5.2 *CONTINUED*

```
*...1....+....2....+....3....+....4....+....5....+....6....+....7....+
 * set SFLNXTCHG
C                       MOVE *ON        *IN08
C                       UPDATCSFL
C                       MOVE *OFF       *IN08
C                       READCCSFL                       98
C                       ENDDO
 *
 * Display confirmation subfile
C                       WRITECNFCMD
C                       EXFMTCNFCTL
 *
 * Other than F12=Cancel
C           KEY         IFNE @F12
 *
 * Process subfile records and delete the appropriate
 * database records, as well as update original subfile
C                       READCCNFSFL                     98
 *
C           *IN98       DOWEQ*OFF
 * Delete record
C           CUSTNO      DELETCUSTPR                     22
 * Update original subfile
C           CRRN        CHAINCSFL                       22
C                       CLEARSELIO
C                       MOVE *BLANKS    CCONT
C                       MOVEL#DMSG      CCONT
C                       MOVE *ON        *IN09
C                       UPDATCSFL
C                       MOVE *OFF       *IN09
 *
C                       READCCNFSFL                     98
C                       ENDDO
 *
C                       ENDIF
 *
C                       ENDSR
 *
 *===============================================================*
 * F03 key subroutine                                             *
 *===============================================================*
 *
C           @F03SR      BEGSR
 *
 * set exit program flag
C                       MOVE @TRUE      @EXIT
 *
C                       ENDSR
 *
```

continued

Figure 5.2 *Continued*

```
*...1....+....2....+....3....+....4....+....5....+....6....+....7....+

*================================================================*
* F06 key subroutine - add customer record                       *
*================================================================*
 *
C           @F06SR        BEGSR
 *
* code to add a customer record
* or call to module to add customer record
 *
C                         ENDSR
 *
*================================================================*
* F12 key subroutine                                             *
*================================================================*
 *
C           @F12SR        BEGSR
 *
* set exit program flag
C                         MOVE      @TRUE         @EXIT
 *
C                         ENDSR
 *
```

In program CSTMAINT, a data structure, including initial values (A in Figure 5.2), defines the API parameters. Notice that we supply the value *CURRENT for the user parameter and that object *LIBL/CUSTPF type *FILE is the object whose user authorities the API will check. To execute program CSTMAINT, the user must have *OBJOPR authority to logical file CUSTLFNM. The program also assumes that every user who has access to CUSTLFNM has at least *READ authority to both CUSTLFNM and CUSTPF. CSTMAINT uses the API to check for only *ADD, *UPD, and *DLT data authorities to the physical file because the program lets the user add, update, and delete records.

At B in Figure 5.2, the program defines data structure ARDS. The data structure length is 93, but we need only the four fields in positions 23 through 26 — the fields that return the user's data authorities (read, add, update, and delete). Fields AREAD, AADD, AUPD, and ADLT will contain either a Y or an N to indicate whether the current user has the corresponding authority to file CUSTPF.

At C, the program checks variables AUPD, ADLT, and AADD and sets on an indicator for each authority the user has (*IN51 for update authority, *IN52 for delete authority, and *IN53 for add authority). Display file CUSTDF (Figure 5.3) uses these indicators (at A, B, and C) to control the display of options 2=Change, 4=Delete, and F6=Create. Program CSTMAINT also uses these indicators (at D and E in Figure 5.2) to restrict access to the update and delete functions (because *IN53 conditions the CA06 key in the display file, subroutine @F06SR doesn't have to repeat the check for add authority).

FIGURE 5.3
Display File CUSTDF

```
*...1....+....2....+....3....+....4....+....5....+....6....+....7....+

*================================================================*
* From "Work-With with Authority," NEWS 3X/400, February 1994    *
*                                                                *
* COPYRIGHT (c) 1994 Duke Communications International,          *
* ALL RIGHTS RESERVED.  This program may not be reproduced       *
* or distributed in any form without permission in writing       *
* from the publisher, except for noncommercial, private use      *
* and adaptation granted by U.S. copyright law.                  *
* Redistribution of this program, or the distribution of         *
* derivative works, is expressly prohibited.  This copyright     *
* notice must remain in all private-use copies.                  *
*================================================================*
* Display file name: CUSTDF                                      *
*                                                                *
* Purpose: Work with Customer Records - add, update, delete      *
*          Include ability to toggle SFLDROP and SFLFOLD          *
*          Include ability to secure fields                      *
*================================================================*
 *
A                                          DSPSIZ(24 80 *DS3)
A                                          REF(*LIBL/CUSTPF)
A                                          PRINT
A                                          CA03
A                                          CA12
 *
A          R CSFL                          SFL
A 08                                       SFLNXTCHG
A            CUSTNO    R       H
A            SELIO           2Y 0B  7 2VALUES(0 2 4 5)
A                                          EDTCDE(4)
A 09                                       DSPATR(ND)
A 09                                       DSPATR(PR)
A            CNAME     R        0 7  6
A            CCONT     R        0 7 37
A            CPHONE    R        0 7 68EDTWRD('   -   -    0')
A 09                                       DSPATR(ND)
A            CCITY     R        0 8  6
A 09                                       DSPATR(ND)
A            CSTATE    R        0 8 27
A 09                                       DSPATR(ND)
A            CCTITL    R        0 8 37
A 09                                       DSPATR(ND)
A                                         9 3' '
 *
A          R CSFLCTL                       SFLCTL(CSFL)
A 53                                       CA06                    Ⓐ
A                                          PAGEDOWN
A                                          BLINK
A                                          OVERLAY
A 42                                       SFLDSP
```

continued

Figure 5.3 Continued

```
*...1....+....2....+....3....+....4....+....5....+....6....+....7....+
A N40                                   SFLDSPCTL
A  40                                   SFLCLR
A  99                                   SFLEND(*MORE)
A N11                                   SFLFOLD(CA11)
A  11                                   SFLDROP(CA11)
A                                       SFLMODE(&SFMODE)
A                                       SFLSIZ(0016)
A                                       SFLPAG(0005)
A  60                                   SFLMSG('Roll up or down beyond
A                                         first or last record in subfile
A                                         ' 60)
A               RCDNBR        4S  0H    SFLRCDNBR(CURSOR)
A               SFMODE        1A   H
A                                     1 31'Work with Customers'
A                                         DSPATR(HI)
A                                     3  2'Type options, press Enter.'
A                                         COLOR(BLU)
A  51                                 4  5'2=Change'
A                                         COLOR(BLU)
A  51
AA 52                                 4 16'4=Delete'
A                                         COLOR(BLU)
A  51
AAN52                                 4 16'5=View'
A                                         COLOR(BLU)
A  51
AA 52                                 4 27'5=View'
A                                         COLOR(BLU)
A N51
AA 52                                 4  5'4=Delete'
A                                         COLOR(BLU)
A N51
AA 52                                 4 16'5=View'
A                                         COLOR(BLU)
A N51
AAN52                                 4  5'5=View'
A                                         COLOR(BLU)
A                                     4 36'Position to customer . .'
A               NCNAME       20A  I  4 61CHECK(LC)
A                                     6  2'Opt'
A                                         DSPATR(HI)
A                                     6  6'Customer'
A                                         DSPATR(HI)
A                                     6 37'Contact/Title'
A                                         DSPATR(HI)
A                                     6 68'Phone number'
A                                         DSPATR(HI)
A                                     1  2'CSFL'
 *
```

continued

FIGURE 5.3 CONTINUED

```
*...1....+....2....+....3....+....4....+....5....+....6....+....7....+
A              R CSFLCMD
A                                      23  2'F3=Exit'
A                                          COLOR(BLU)
A N53                                  23 13'F11=Alt-View'
A                                          COLOR(BLU)
A N53                                  23 29'F12=Previous'
A                                          COLOR(BLU)
A   53                                 23 13'F6=Create'
A                                          COLOR(BLU)
A   53                                 23 26'F11=Alt-View'
A                                          COLOR(BLU)
A   53                                 23 42'F12=Previous'
A                                          COLOR(BLU)
A*
A              R CNFSFL                    SFL
A                                          SFLNXTCHG
A                SELIO       2Y 00  7  2EDTCDE(4)
A                CRRN        5Y 0H
A                CUSTNO   R         H
A                CNAME    R         0  7  6
A                CCONT    R         0  7 37
A                CPHONE   R         0  7 68EDTWRD('   -   -    0')
A                CCITY    R         0  8  6
A                CSTATE   R         0  8 27
A                CCTITL   R         0  8 37
A                                       9  3' '
A*
A              R CNFCTL                    SFLCTL(CNFSFL)
A                                          SFLSIZ(0006)
A                                          SFLPAG(0005)
A                                          BLINK
A                                          OVERLAY
A   42                                     SFLDSP
A N40                                      SFLDSPCTL
A   40                                     SFLCLR
A   98                                     SFLEND(*MORE)
A                                       1  2'CNFSFL'
A                                       1 27'Confirm Delete of Customers'
A                                          DSPATR(HI)
A                                       3  2'Press Enter to confirm your
A                                             choices for 4=Delete.'
A                                          COLOR(BLU)
A                                       4  2'Press F12 to return to change
A                                             your choices.'
A                                          COLOR(BLU)
A                                       6  2'Sel'
A                                          DSPATR(HI)
A                                       6  6'Customer'
A                                          DSPATR(HI)
A                                       6 37'Contact/Title'
A                                          DSPATR(HI)
A                                       6 68'Phone number'
A                                          DSPATR(HI)
A*
```

continued

FIGURE 5.3 CONTINUED

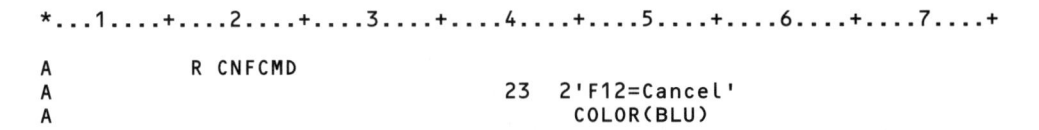

```
*...1....+....2....+....3....+....4....+....5....+....6....+....7....+
A          R CNFCMD
A                                      23  2'F12=Cancel'
A                                          COLOR(BLU)
```

Table 5.2 lists the authorities of user profiles KWM and USER_A and of *PUBLIC to file CUSTPF. Program CSTMAINT presents the panel shown in Figure 5.4A to user profile KWM and to *PUBLIC. But when USER_A calls program CSTMAINT, the program presents the panel shown in Figure 5.4B, which provides only option 5=View.

TABLE 5.2
User Authorities to File CUSTPF

Physical File: CUSTPF
Owner: KWM

User	Authority	Object Opr	Mgt	Exist	Alter	Ref	Data Read	Add	Update	Delete	Execute
KWM	*ALL	✓	✓	✓	✓	✓	✓	✓	✓	✓	✓
USER_A	USER DEF	✓					✓				
*PUBLIC	*CHANGE	✓					✓	✓	✓	✓	✓

Adding a little code to your application means you can maintain just one program instead of two or three. For many physical files, you may need to implement no security other than granting all five data authorities to all authorized users. However, adding a call to API QSYRUSRA to all your work-with panels lets you tighten or relax security without writing additional programs or having to find embedded user profile names in existing programs. Instead, you can use the authority structure OS/400 provides for database files, and your programs can act appropriately.

FIGURE 5.4A
Restricted Work-With Panel, Example 1

```
 CSFL                       Work with Customers

 Type options, press Enter.
   2=Change   4=Delete   5=View    Position to customer . . _____

 Opt Customer                      Contact/Title              Phone number
  _  A-1 Interiors                 Mary Lee Wilson            919-228-3495
     Raleigh              NC       Interior Decorator

  _  Acme Paint Distributors       Fred Short                 606-234-9323
     Franklin             KY       Owner

  _  Barnwall Fix-it-Yourself      Jim Henley                 205-865-2394
     Barnwall             AL       Owner

  _  Best Paints                   Betty White                919-439-2831
     Elizabethtown        NC       Store Manager

  _  Cain's Furniture and Hardware Martin Spencer             615-426-3492
     Waverly              TN       Store Manager

                                                                  More...

 F3=Exit     F6=Create    F11=Alt-View     F12=Previous
```

FIGURE 5.4B
Restricted Work-with Panel, Example 2

```
 CSFL                       Work with Customers

 Type options, press Enter.
   5=View                           Position to customer . . _____

 Opt Customer                      Contact/Title              Phone number
  _  A-1 Interiors                 Mary Lee Wilson            919-228-3495
     Raleigh              NC       Interior Decorator

  _  Acme Paint Distributors       Fred Short                 606-234-9323
     Franklin             KY       Owner

  _  Barnwall Fix-it-Yourself      Jim Henley                 205-865-2394
     Barnwall             AL       Owner

  _  Best Paints                   Betty White                919-439-2831
     Elizabethtown        NC       Store Manager

  _  Cain's Furniture and Hardware Martin Spencer             615-426-3492
     Waverly              TN       Store Manager

                                                                  More...

 F3=Exit     F11=Alt-View    F12=Previous
```

Data Authorities and Logical Files

Logical files contain no data. Rather, a logical file is a view of the data in a physical file. For example, a logical file might present the physical file's records in a particular sequence, display a subset of the physical file's fields, or use SELECT/OMIT logic to present a subset of the physical file's records. An SQL view is a logical file.

Physical and logical files have two significant relationships in terms of authority. First is what we'll call the "use" relationship. You can give users *OBJOPR (object use) authority to both the physical and logical file, or you can give users *OBJOPR authority to only the logical file, preventing them from directly using the physical file. Restricting the user to a logical file is an effective security technique when you use a logical file to subset fields or records and you want to give the user authority to only the data in the view instead of to all the physical file's fields and records. Because users don't have *OBJOPR authority to the physical file, they can't directly access it, regardless of the program or tool they use. But they can access the physical file's data through the logical file. The logical file definitions determine which fields and records users can access.

We'll call the second relationship between physical and logical files the "data authority" relationship. You need to remember two things about this relationship. First, a logical file can't provide more data authority than the physical file does. In other words, if you grant a user *READ, *ADD, and *UPD authorities to a logical file, you must also grant the user *READ, *ADD, and *UPD authorities to the associated physical file(s). Second, a logical file can support less authority. So, you can grant a user all data authorities to a physical file, or you can grant less data authority to a logical file that the user can access. If you plan to grant a user less authority to a logical file, you need to revoke the user's *OBJOPR authority to the physical file; otherwise, the user can bypass the logical file and use the physical file directly.

Field-Level Security

As we mentioned earlier, OS/400 lets you secure physical files or tables at the field level. (In this discussion, we use *field* and *column* synonymously.) Field-level security lets you implement security at a more granular level. Two types of field-level authority are available: reference and update.

Reference authority lets you use a physical file's fields as parent keys in a referential constraint associated with that physical file. For instance, if you create physical file CUSTPF and you grant reference authority to field CUST# in that file, the user can then add a referential constraint to that physical file and use the CUST# field in that referential constraint. Fields that you don't specifically grant reference authority to aren't eligible for use in a referential constraint. However, if you grant *OBJREF authority to a file, all the file's fields are eligible for referential constraints. In other words, *OBJREF authority to the file grants REFERENCE authority to all fields.

Granting update authority to specific fields in a file lets the user update those fields. If you grant a user update authority at the file level, the user can update all fields in the file. If you grant a user update authority only to certain fields, the user can update only those fields. Keep in mind that if a user has *READ data authority to the file, the user can see all fields even if you don't grant UPDATE authority to the fields.

You can't grant REFERENCE or UPDATE authority to fields in multiformat logical files, program-described files, source files, SQL indexes, or distributed database files that exist on systems in your network running a version of OS/400 earlier than V4R2. To grant and revoke reference and update authorities, you need to use either the SQL GRANT and REVOKE statements or the Permissions function in Operations Navigator; you can't use the EDTOBJAUT (Edit Object Authorities) command. You can see, but not manipulate, these authorities using the DSPOBJAUT (Display Object Authorities) and EDTOBJAUT commands. Also, you should use reference and update authorities only when absolutely necessary so as not to slow performance.

Field-Level Security Before V4R2

To implement field-level security on a version of OS/400 earlier than V4R2, you need to combine the use and data authority relationships between physical and logical files with a little programming and a database technique called *projection*.

Projection is the relational database term for a view (e.g., a logical file, an SQL view) of a table (e.g., a physical file, an SQL table) that shows only a subset of the table's fields. In AS/400 terms, a projection is a logical file (built over an existing physical file) that contains only the fields you want users to access. By implementing a projection as a logical file, you can use OS/400 object authorities to the logical file to restrict users to the fields in that particular projection.

Let's look at an example of implementing field-level security using projection. Consider CUSTPF, the sample database file of customer records that we used earlier in the chapter (Figure 5.1A). Figure 5.5A shows the DDS for logical file CUSTLFA, which is based on CUSTPF. Every logical file record format must reference the physical file on which it is based (CUSTPF in this case) in the PFILE keyword. The logical file definition also indicates which of the physical file's fields to include in the logical file. Because CUSTLFA uses the physical file's record format — CUSTPR — as the logical file record format, CUSTLFA includes all fields from the physical file. You can also put the fields in a different order and use other DDS functions, such as RENAME, CONCAT, and SST, in a logical file definition. (For more details about creating logical file record formats, see the manuals *DDS Reference*, SC41-5712, and *AS/400 Database Programming Information,* SC41-5612; see the *DB2 for AS/400 SQL Reference,* SC41-5612, for the additional derivations allowed.)

Figure 5.5A
DDS for Logical File CUSTLFA

```
*...1....+....2....+....3....+....4....+....5....+....6....+....7....+

*================================================================*
* Sample Customer File - Logical by name w/ all fields           *
*================================================================*
 *
A          R CUSTPR                    PFILE(CUSTPF)
 *
A            K CNAME
A            K CUSTNO
```

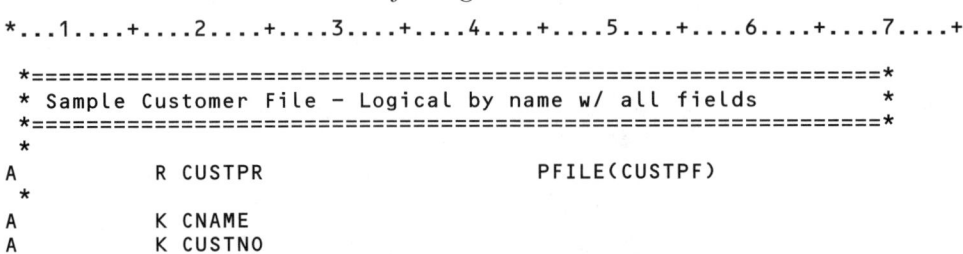

Figure 5.5B shows a definition for logical file CUSTLFB, which is a projection of CUSTPF. Instead of specifying physical file record format CUSTPR, this logical file defines a new record format, CUSTLRB, that includes a subset of the fields from the physical file. The omitted fields (CLORDT, CBALNC, CCRFLG) contain sensitive information that some users are not allowed to see. For documentation purposes, we left the omitted fields in the definition but commented them out.

Figure 5.5B
DDS for Logical File CUSTLFB

```
*...1....+....2....+....3....+....4....+....5....+....6....+....7....+

*================================================================*
* Sample Customer File - Logical by name - partial fields        *
*================================================================*
 *
A          R CUSTLRB                   PFILE(CUSTPF)
 *
A            CUSTNO
A            CNAME
A            CSTRT
A            CCITY
A            CSTATE
A            CZIP
A            CCONT
A            CCTITL
A            CPHONE
A            NOTES1
A            NOTES2
  * Fields not included in this logical file
A******      CLORDT
A******      CBALNC
A******      CCRFLG
 *
A            K CNAME
A            K CUSTNO
```

To see how we can use these two logical files to provide field-level security, let's look at the authorities in Table 5.3. As the table shows, only the owner has *OBJOPR authority to the physical file, so only the owner can actually use the physical file. Because no users have *OBJOPR authority, they can't access the physical file directly. They can access the data (because *PUBLIC has *READ, *ADD, *UPD, *DLT, and *EXECUTE data authorities to the physical file) but only via the logical files. Further, USER_A, who doesn't have individual authority to any of the files, has *CHANGE authority to both logical files (by way of the *PUBLIC authorities). Two other individual users — USER_B and USER_C — have *USE authority to logical file CUSTLFB but *EXCLUDE authority to logical file CUSTLFA. These two user profiles can't access CUSTLFA. They can access CUSTLFB, but this projection doesn't show the physical file's sensitive fields, and USER_B and USER_C can only *USE data (they have *OBJOPR, *READ, and *EXECUTE authorities). Thus, we limit USER_B's and USER_C's access to the projected subset of CUSTPF's fields and let them only read records, even though *PUBLIC has all data rights to the physical file.

TABLE 5.3
Physical and Logical File Authorities

Physical File: CUSTPF
Owner: SAMPOWNER

User	Authority	Opr	Mgt	Exist	Alter	Ref	Read	Add	Update	Delete	Execute
SAMPOWNER	*ALL	✓	✓	✓	✓	✓	✓	✓	✓	✓	✓
*PUBLIC	USER DEF						✓	✓	✓	✓	✓

Logical File: CUSTLFA
Owner: SAMPOWNER

User	Authority	Opr	Mgt	Exist	Alter	Ref	Read	Add	Update	Delete	Execute
SAMPOWNER	*ALL	✓	✓	✓	✓	✓	✓	✓	✓	✓	✓
USER_B	*EXCLUDE										
USER_C	*EXCLUDE										
*PUBLIC	*CHANGE	✓					✓	✓	✓	✓	✓

Logical File: CUSTLFB
Owner: SAMPOWNER

User	Authority	Opr	Mgt	Exist	Alter	Ref	Read	Add	Update	Delete	Execute
SAMPOWNER	*ALL	✓	✓	✓	✓	✓	✓	✓	✓	✓	✓
USER_B	*USE	✓					✓				✓
USER_C	*USE	✓					✓				✓
*PUBLIC	*CHANGE	✓					✓	✓	✓	✓	✓

A Program Example

Let's look at a sample application that implements the projection technique we just discussed for database access and update. The example builds on the work-with-customers function that we described earlier in the CSTMAINT program. Here, we add a Customer Master Record panel that lets authorized users view and update customer information. The application's RPG program uses API QSYRUSRA to determine the user's authority to the two logical files and then opens and processes the files accordingly. If the user has authority to logical file CUSTLFA, the program presents a panel that displays all fields (Figure 5.6A). If the user has authority only to logical file CUSTLFB, the application presents a panel that doesn't show the sensitive fields (Figure 5.6B).

FIGURE 5.6A
CMAST Panel Showing All Fields

```
                    Customer Master Record
        Type the following, then press Enter.

              Customer name  . . . . :  A-1 Interiors
              Street address . . . . :
              City, State, Zip . . . :  Raleigh                NC

              Customer contact . . . :  Mary Lee Wilson
              Contact title  . . . . :  Interior Decorator
              Contact Phone Number . :  919-228-3495

              Notes  . . . . . . . . :


              Last order date  . . . :  0/00/00
              Current Balance  . . . :                  .00
              Good Credit Y/N?   . . :




          F3=Exit    F12=Cancel
```

The only difference between CUSTDF2, the display file for this sample application, and CUSTDF, the display file in the earlier example, is the addition of record format CMAST (Figure 5.7), which displays the new Customer Master Record panel. In this record format, indicator *IN50 conditions the phrase "Type the following, then press Enter." and the underline and protect display attributes, DSPATR(UL) and DSPATR(PR).

FIGURE 5.6B
Restricted CMAST Panel

```
                     Customer Master Record
        Type the following, then press Enter.

            Customer name    . . . . :  A-1 Interiors
            Street address . . . . :
            City, State, Zip . . . :  Raleigh              NC

            Customer contact . . . :  Mary Lee Wilson
            Contact title  . . . . :  Interior Decorator
            Contact Phone Number . :  919-228-3495

            Notes  . . . . . . . . :




        F3=Exit    F12=Cancel
```

FIGURE 5.7
New Record Format CMAST for Display File CUSTDF2

```
 *...1....+....2....+....3....+....4....+....5....+....6....+....7....+
 *                                                                    *
A     R CMAST
A                                        CHGINPDFT
A                                     1 25'Customer Master Record'
A                                        DSPATR(HI)
A N50                                  3  2'Type the following, then press
A                                        Enter.'
A                                        COLOR(BLU)
A                                     5  4'Customer name  . . . . :'
A       CNAME         R        B      5 30CHECK(LC)
A N50                                    DSPATR(UL)
A  50                                    DSPATR(PR)
A                                     6  4'Street address . . . . :'
A       CSTRT         R        B      6 30CHECK(LC)
A N50                                    DSPATR(UL)
A  50                                    DSPATR(PR)
A                                     7  4'City, State, Zip . . . :'
A       CCITY         R        B      7 30CHECK(LC)
A N50                                    DSPATR(UL)
A  50                                    DSPATR(PR)
```

continued

Figure 5.7 Continued

```
*...1....+....2....+....3....+....4....+....5....+....6....+....7....+
A                   CSTATE      R       B   7 51
A N50                                          DSPATR(UL)
A  50                                          DSPATR(PR)
A                   CZIP        R       B   7 55
A N50                                          DSPATR(UL)
A  50                                          DSPATR(PR)
A                                           9  4'Customer contact . . . :'
A                   CCONT       R       B   9 30CHECK(LC)
A N50                                          DSPATR(UL)
A  50                                          DSPATR(PR)
A                                          10  4'Contact title  . . . . :'
A                   CCTITL      R       B  10 30CHECK(LC)
A N50                                          DSPATR(UL)
A  50                                          DSPATR(PR)
A                                          11  4'Contact Phone Number . :'
A                   CPHONE      R       B  11 30
A N50                                          DSPATR(UL)
A  50                                          DSPATR(PR)
A                                              EDTWRD('   -   -     ')
A                                          13  4'Notes . . . . . . . . :'
A                   NOTES1      R       B  13 30CHECK(LC)
A N50                                          DSPATR(UL)
A  50                                          DSPATR(PR)
A                   NOTES2      R       B  14 30CHECK(LC)
A N50                                          DSPATR(UL)
A  50                                          DSPATR(PR)
*
* *IN55 controls display of these optional fields for
*   security reasons.
A N55                                      16  4'Last order date  . . . :'
A N55               CLORDT      R       O  16 30
A                                              EDTCDE(Y)
A N55                                      17  4'Current Balance  . . . :'
A N55               CBALNC      R       O  17 30
A N55                                      18  4'Good Credit Y/N?  . . :'
A N55               CCRFLG      R       O  18 30
*
A                                          23  2'F3=Exit'
A                                              COLOR(BLU)
A                                          23 12'F12=Cancel'
A                                              COLOR(BLU)
```

When the RPG program CSTMAINT2 (Figure 5.8) sets *IN50 to *OFF and performs a send/receive (EXFMT) operation to CMAST, the user can enter data into the record's fields. If *IN50 is *ON, the user can't enter data in the fields and sees no underlines in the panel — in other words, when *IN50 is *ON, CSTMAINT2 presents a view-only screen. This implementation is one way of using just one record format to provide both a "view" and a "change" mode. Some programmers prefer to design two screen records — one for view and one for change — that implement the appropriate attributes without using indicators. One advantage of our approach is that you don't need to maintain two screens.

Note that indicator *IN55 in CMAST conditions the sensitive fields (CLORDT, CBALNC, and CCRFLG) and their associated constants. When *IN55 is *ON, these fields aren't displayed; when *IN55 is *OFF, the fields are displayed. Notice also that the three conditioned fields are always output-only, because they are updated by other programs rather than by users.

FIGURE 5.8

New "Work-with" Program CSTMAINT2

```
*...1....+....2....+....3....+....4....+....5....+....6....+....7....+

*===============================================================*
 * From "Implementing Field-Level Security,"                     *
 * NEWS 3X/400, March 1994                                       *
 *                                                               *
 * COPYRIGHT (c) 1994 Duke Communications International,         *
 * ALL RIGHTS RESERVED.                                          *
 *                                                               *
 * Program name: CSTMAINT2                                       *
 * Purpose.....: Customer Selection Window Program               *
 *                                                               *
 * Indicators:                                                   *
 *     08   -   Controls SFLNXTCHG DDS keyword for CSFL subfile  *
 *     09   -   Nondisplay for deleted subfile record fields     *
 *     11   -   Toggles SFLDROP and SFLFOLD DDS keywords         *
 *     40   -   Clear subfile                                    *
 *     41   -   Display subfile control record SFLCTLDSP DDS kwd *
 *     42   -   Display subfile SFLDSP DDS keyword               *
 *     50   -   Protect fields for view-only mode                *
 *     51   -   Record change authority (*ON if authority exists)*
 *     52   -   Record delete authority (*ON if authority exists)*
 *     53   -   Record add   authority (*ON if authority exists) *
 *     55   -   Display/nondisplay sensitive fields in DSPF      *
 *     60   -   Cannot roll up or down in subfile                *
 *     98   -   EOF for read changed records in CSFL subfile     *
 *     99   -   EOF for CUSTLFNM                                 *
*===============================================================*
FCUSTLFA  UF  E             K        DISK                          UC
FCUSTLFB  UF  E             K        DISK                          UC
FCUSTDF2  CF  E                      WORKSTN      KINFDS INFDS
F                                         CRRN  KSFILE CSFL
F                                         CNFRRNKSFILE CNFSFL
 *
 * File information data structure for workstation file
IINFDS         DS
I                                           369  369 KEY
I                                         B 378 3790PAGRRN
 *
```

continued

FIGURE 5.8 CONTINUED

```
*...1....+....2....+....3....+....4....+....5....+....6....+....7....+
    * Named constants
I                    '* Record deleted'    C                   #DMSG
I                    '0'                   C                   @TRUE
I                    '1'                   C                   @FALSE
I                    'N'                   C                   @NO
I                    'Y'                   C                   @YES
I                    'CUSTPF   '           C                   @PFILE
Ⓐ I                  'CUSTLFA  '           C                   @FILEA
I                    'CUSTLFB  '           C                   @FILEB
    *
    * Named hexadecimal constants for function keys
I                    X'33'                 C                   @F03
I                    X'36'                 C                   @F06
I                    X'3C'                 C                   @F12
I                    X'F4'                 C                   @PAGUP
I                    X'F5'                 C                   @PAGDN
    *
    * API parameter definitions
Ⓑ I              DS
I I                  93                    B    1   40ALNGTH   authority_length
I I                  'USRA0100'                 5   12 AFMT    authority_format
I I                  '*CURRENT   '             13   22 AUSER   authority_user
I I                  '          *LIBL    '     23   42 AOBJ    authority_object
I I                  '*FILE     '              43   52 AOBJT   authority_objtype
I I                  X'00000000'               53   56 ERRCDE  authority_error_code
I I                  ' '                       57   57 AFLAG   authority_flag
I I                  '*OBJOPR   '              58   67 AAUTH   authority_checked
I I                  1                     B   68   71 0ANBR   authority_nbr
I I                  0                     B   72   75 0ACLVL  authority_call_level
    *
    * Authority receiver structure for QSYRUSRA API
IARDS            DS                                 93
I                                          B    1   40BRET
I                                          B    5   80BAVL
I                                              23   23 AREAD
I                                              24   24 AADD
I                                              25   25 AUPD
I                                              26   26 ADLT
    *
    *===============================================================*
    * Reset variables and clear subfile                              *
    * in case program called again after *INLR = *OFF.               *
    * Ensures that program starts again properly                     *
    *===============================================================*
    *
C                    RESET@EXIT
C                    EXSR @RESET
    *
```

continued

FIGURE 5.8 CONTINUED

```
*...1....+....2....+....3....+....4....+....5....+....6....+....7....+

*================================================================*
* Program mainline                                                *
*================================================================*
*
C                     EXSR @LOAD
*
* Perform until exit requested
C           @EXIT     DOUEQ@TRUE
*
C                     WRITECSFLCMD
C                     EXFMTCSFLCTL
*
C                     Z-ADDPAGRRN     RCDNBR
*
* Process response
C           KEY       CASEQ@F03       @F03SR          F03 exit
C           KEY       CASEQ@F06       @F06SR          F06 add record
C           KEY       CASEQ@F12       @F12SR          F12 cancel
C           KEY       CASEQ@PAGDN     @PGDN           Page down
C                     CAS             @ENTKY          Enter
C                     ENDCS
*
C                     ENDDO
*
* End of program. You can modify to leave *INLR = *OFF
* and program will still work properly when called again
*
C                     MOVE *ON        *INLR
C                     RETRN
*
*================================================================*
* Subroutine Section of Program                                   *
*================================================================*
*
*================================================================*
* Initialization Subroutine                                       *
*================================================================*
*
C           *INZSR    BEGSR
*
C           *LIKE     DEFN CNAME      ENDNAM
C           *LIKE     DEFN CUSTNO     ENDCUS
*
* Create program exit flag and set value to @FALSE
C                     MOVE @FALSE     @EXIT    1
*
* Variable declarations
C                     Z-ADD0          CRRN     50
C                     Z-ADD0          ENDRN    50
C                     Z-ADD0          CNFRRN   50
C                     Z-ADD0          RRNSAV   50
C                     Z-ADD1          RCDNBR
C                     MOVE '0'        #FOLD    1
C                     MOVE *BLANKS    @FILE    8
*
```

continued

FIGURE 5.8 *Continued*

```
*...1....+....2....+....3....+....4....+....5....+....6....+....7....+
 * Set MODE to 0=Folded for first load of subfile
 * SFLMODE(&SFMODE) in DDS
C                        MOVE '0'       SFMODE
 *
 * Complete file key
C           FILKEY       KLIST
C                        KFLD           CNAME
C                        KFLD           CUSTNO
 *
 * End key for repositioning subfile
C           ENDKEY       KLIST
C                        KFLD           ENDNAM
C                        KFLD           ENDCUS
 *
 * Determine file authorizations
C                        MOVE @NO       AFLAG
C                        MOVEL@FILEA    AOBJ
C                        CALL 'QSYCUSRA'
C                        PARM           AFLAG
C                        PARM           AUSER
C                        PARM           AOBJ
C                        PARM           AOBJT
C                        PARM           AAUTH
C                        PARM           ANBR
C                        PARM           ACLVL
C                        PARM           ERRCDE
 *
C           AFLAG        IFEQ @YES
C                        MOVE @FILEA    @FILE
C                        ELSE
 *
C                        MOVE @NO       AFLAG
C                        MOVEL@FILEB    AOBJ
C                        CALL 'QSYCUSRA'
C                        PARM           AFLAG
C                        PARM           AUSER
C                        PARM           AOBJ
C                        PARM           AOBJT
C                        PARM           AAUTH
C                        PARM           ANBR
C                        PARM           ACLVL
C                        PARM           ERRCDE
 *
C           AFLAG        IFEQ @YES
C                        MOVE @FILEB    @FILE
C                        ENDIF
C                        ENDIF
 *
 * Open correct file
C           @FILE        IFEQ @FILEA
C                        OPEN CUSTLFA
C                        MOVE *OFF      *IN55
```

continued

Figure 5.8 Continued

```
*...1....+....2....+....3....+....4....+....5....+....6....+....7....+
C                    ELSE                                            (D)
C          @FILE     IFEQ @FILEB
C                    OPEN CUSTLFB
C                    MOVE *ON      *IN55
C                    ELSE
C                    MOVE *ON      *INLR
C                    RETRN
C                    ENDIF
C                    ENDIF
 *
 * Determine physical file authorities and set proper indicators
C                    MOVEL@PFILE   AOBJ
C                    CALL 'QSYRUSRA'
C                    PARM          ARDS
C                    PARM          ALNGTH
C                    PARM          AFMT
C                    PARM          AUSER
C                    PARM          AOBJ
C                    PARM          AOBJT
C                    PARM          ERRCDE
 *
C          AUPD      IFEQ @YES
C                    MOVE *ON      *IN51
C                    ENDIF
C          ADLT      IFEQ @YES
C                    MOVE *ON      *IN52
C                    ENDIF
C          AADD      IFEQ @YES
C                    MOVE *ON      *IN53
C                    ENDIF
 *
C                    ENDSR
 *
 *================================================================*
 * Clear/reset subfile                                             *
 *================================================================*
 *
C          @RESET    BEGSR
 *
 * Clear subfile and reset subfile display indicator.
C                    MOVE *ON      *IN40
C                    WRITECSFLCTL
C                    MOVE *OFF     *IN40
C                    MOVE *OFF     *IN42
 *
 * Reset subfile record number and subfile position fields.
C                    RESETCRRN
C                    RESETENDRN
C                    RESETRCDNBR
 *
C                    ENDSR
 *
```

continued

Figure 5.8 Continued

```
*...1....+....2....+....3....+....4....+....5....+....6....+....7....+

 *===============================================================*
 * Reposition file                                                *
 *===============================================================*
 *
C           @REPOS        BEGSR
 *
 * Clear subfile
C                         EXSR @RESET
 *
 * Reposition file by search value
(E) C         @FILE         IFEQ @FILEA
    C         CNAME         SETLLCUSTLFA
    C                       ELSE
    C         CNAME         SETLLCUSTLFB
    C                       ENDIF
    C                       EXSR @LOAD
 *
C                         ENDSR
 *
 *===============================================================*
 * Load subfile                                                   *
 *===============================================================*
 *
C           @LOAD         BEGSR
 *
 * Clear RCDNBR
C                         CLEARRCDNBR
 *
 * Read a page of records or until EOF.
C                         DO   15
C           @FILE         IFEQ @FILEA
C                         READ CUSTLFA               N       99
C                         ELSE
C                         READ CUSTLFB               N       99
C                         ENDIF
 *
C           *IN99         IFEQ *ON
C                         LEAVE
C                         ELSE
 * Write subfile record.
C                         ADD  1            CRRN
 * First record on this page
C           RCDNBR        IFEQ 0
C                         Z-ADDCRRN         RCDNBR
C                         ENDIF
C                         WRITECSFL
C                         ENDIF
 *
C                         ENDDO
 *
```

continued

FIGURE 5.8 *Continued*

```
*...1....+....2....+....3....+....4....+....5....+....6....+....7....+
 * Do not allow RCDNBR = 0
C           RCDNBR    IFEQ 0
C                     Z-ADD1         RCDNBR
C                     ENDIF
 *
 * Set end-key values
C                     EXSR @ENDKY
 *
 * If not EOF, read one more record to make sure.
C           *IN99     IFEQ *OFF
C           @FILE     IFEQ @FILEA
C                     READ CUSTLFA              N    99
C                     ELSE
C                     READ CUSTLFB              N    99
C                     ENDIF
C                     ENDIF
 *
 * If no records were added to subfile, set error indicators.
C           CRRN      IFEQ *ZEROS
C                     MOVE *OFF      *IN42
C                     ELSE
 * Else, set indicators to display subfile.
C                     MOVE *ON       *IN42
C                     ENDIF
 *
 * Determine which subfile mode (drop or fold)
 * is current, and display new records in that mode
C           SFMODE    IFEQ #FOLD
C                     MOVE *OFF      *IN11
C                     ELSE
C                     MOVE *ON       *IN11
C                     ENDIF
 *
C                     ENDSR
 *
 *================================================================*
 * Update end keys and variables for file/subfile                 *
 *================================================================*
 *
C           @ENDKY    BEGSR
 *
C                     MOVE CNAME     ENDNAM
C                     MOVE CUSTNO    ENDCUS
C                     Z-ADDCRRN      ENDRN
 *
C                     ENDSR
 *
 *================================================================*
 * Subfile page down                                              *
 *================================================================*
 *
C           @PGDN     BEGSR
 *
```

continued

FIGURE 5.8 Continued

```
*...1....+....2....+....3....+....4....+....5....+....6....+....7....+
C                    *IN99       IFEQ *OFF
 *
 * Continue with record after the last one read.
C                    @FILE       IFEQ @FILEA
C                    ENDKEY      SETGTCUSTLFA
C                                ELSE
C                    ENDKEY      SETGTCUSTLFB
C                                ENDIF
C                                Z-ADDENDRN        CRRN
C                                EXSR @LOAD
 * Page down beyond end of subfile
C                                ELSE
C                                MOVE *ON          *IN60
C                                ENDIF
 *
C                                ENDSR
 *
 *===============================================================*
 * Process enter key after subfile display                       *
 *===============================================================*
 *
C                    @ENTKY      BEGSR
 *
 * User request position to new name
C                    NCNAME      IFNE *BLANKS
C                                MOVELNCNAME       CNAME
C                                EXSR @REPOS
C                                ELSE
C                                EXSR @SFLRD
C                                ENDIF
 *
C                                ENDSR
 *
 *===============================================================*
 * Read changed records in subfile to check for selection        *
 *===============================================================*
 *
C                    @SFLRD      BEGSR
 *
 * Did user make a selection?
C                                READCCSFL                      98
 *
C                    *IN98       DOWEQ*OFF
 *
 * Execute for appropriate selections
 *
 * Change selected
C                    SEL IO      IFEQ 2
C                    *IN51       ANDEQ*ON
C                                EXSR @CCHG
C                    KEY         IFEQ @F03
C                                EXSR @F03SR
```

continued

FIGURE 5.8 CONTINUED

```
*...1....+....2....+....3....+....4....+....5....+....6....+....7....+
C                       LEAVE
C                       ENDIF
C                       Z-ADD0         SELIO
C                       UPDATCSFL
C                       Z-ADDCRRN      RCDNBR
C                       ELSE
 * Delete selected
C           SELIO       IFEQ 4
C           *IN52       ANDEQ*ON
C                       Z-ADDCRRN      RRNSAV
C                       EXSR @CDLT
C                       Z-ADDRRNSAV    RCDNBR
C           KEY         IFEQ @F12
C                       LEAVE
C                       ENDIF
C                       ELSE
 * View selected
C           SELIO       IFEQ 5
C                       EXSR @CVEW
C           KEY         IFEQ @F03
C                       EXSR @F03SR
C                       LEAVE
C                       ENDIF
C                       Z-ADD0         SELIO
C                       UPDATCSFL
C                       Z-ADDCRRN      RCDNBR
 *
C                       ENDIF
C                       ENDIF
C                       ENDIF
 *
C                       READCCSFL                    98
C                       ENDDO
 *
C                       ENDSR
*================================================================*
 * Modify customer record                                        *
*================================================================*
 *
C           @CCHG       BEGSR
 *
 * Chain to correct file
C           @FILE       IFEQ @FILEA
C           FILKEY      CHAINCUSTLFA                 21
C                       ELSE
C           FILKEY      CHAINCUSTLFB                 21
C                       ENDIF
 *
 * Present customer master record
C                       EXFMTCMAST
 *
```

continued

FIGURE 5.8 CONTINUED

```
*...1....+....2....+....3....+....4....+....5....+....6....+....7....+
 * Code to edit the customer record changes ......
 *
 * Update appropriate file
C           @FILE     IFEQ @FILEA
C                     UPDATCUSTPR
C                     ELSE
C                     UPDATCUSTLRB
C                     ENDIF
 *
C                     ENDSR
 *
 *================================================================*
 * View customer record                                           *
 *================================================================*
 *
C           @CVEW     BEGSR
 *
 * Set *IN50 = *ON for view-only mode
C                     MOVE *ON      *IN50
 *
 * Chain to correct file
C           @FILE     IFEQ @FILEA
C           FILKEY    CHAINCUSTLFA              N21
C                     ELSE
C           FILKEY    CHAINCUSTLFB              N21
C                     ENDIF
 *
 * Present customer master record
C                     EXFMTCMAST
 *
C                     MOVE *OFF     *IN50
 *
C                     ENDSR
 *
 *================================================================*
 * Delete customer records                                        *
 *================================================================*
 *
C           @CDLT     BEGSR
 *
C                     MOVE *ON      *IN40
C                     WRITECNFCTL
C                     MOVE *OFF     *IN40
C                     RESETCNFRRN
 *
 * Fill confirmation subfile with all deletion requests
C           *IN98     DOWEQ*OFF
C           SELIO     IFEQ 4
C                     ADD  1        CNFRRN
C                     WRITECNFSFL
C                     ENDIF
```

continued

FIGURE 5.8 CONTINUED

```
*...1....+....2....+....3....+....4....+....5....+....6....+....7....+
 * set SFLNXTCHG
C                   MOVE *ON       *IN08
C                   UPDATCSFL
C                   MOVE *OFF      *IN08
C                   READCCSFL                     98
C                   ENDDO
 *
 * Display confirmation subfile
C                   WRITECNFCMD
C                   EXFMTCNFCTL
 *
 * Other than F12=Cancel
C         KEY       IFNE @F12
 *
 * Process subfile records and delete the appropriate
 * database records, as well as update original subfile
C                   READCCNFSFL                   98
 *
C         *IN98     DOWEQ*OFF
 * Delete record from appropriate file
C         @FILE     IFEQ @FILEA
C         FILKEY    DELETCUSTPR                   22
C                   ELSE
C         FILKEY    DELETCUSTLRB                  22
C                   ENDIF
 * Update original subfile
C         CRRN      CHAINCSFL                     22
C                   CLEARSELIO
C                   MOVE *BLANKS   CCONT
C                   MOVEL#DMSG     CCONT
C                   MOVE *ON       *IN09
C                   UPDATCSFL
C                   MOVE *OFF      *IN09
 *
C                   READCCNFSFL                   98
C                   ENDDO
 *
C                   ENDIF
 *
C                   ENDSR
 *
*================================================================*
 * F03 key subroutine                                             *
*================================================================*
 *
C         @F03SR    BEGSR
 *
 * Set exit program flag
C                   MOVE @TRUE     @EXIT
 *
C                   ENDSR
 *
```

continued

FIGURE 5.8 CONTINUED

```
*...1....+....2....+....3....+....4....+....5....+....6....+....7....+

 *================================================================*
 * F06 key subroutine - add customer record                       *
 *================================================================*
 *
C                   @F06SR        BEGSR
 *
 * code to add a customer record
 * or call to module to add customer record
 *
C                                 ENDSR
 *
 *================================================================*
 * F12 key subroutine                                             *
 *================================================================*
 *
C                   @F12SR        BEGSR
 *
 * set exit program flag
C                                 MOVE  @TRUE     @EXIT
 *
C                                 ENDSR
 *
```

RPG program CSTMAINT2 is based on program CSTMAINT but performs the additional tasks of determining which file the user is authorized to, setting conditioning indicator *IN55 to control presentation of the sensitive fields, opening the correct file, and reading or updating it. In the I-specs, CSTMAINT2 defines named constants and data structure definitions. The program initializes named constants @FILEA and @FILEB (A) to CUSTLFA and CUSTLFB, respectively. The program initializes fields for security API QSYCUSRA at B.

QSYCUSRA lets you determine whether a user has one or more specific authorities to an object. You supply the user profile, the object name, and the authorities you want to check. The API returns a one-character variable containing either a Y, to indicate that the user has all the specified authorities, or an N, to indicate that the user does not. This API doesn't let you check authority to an individual field, only to the file itself. To check authority to a field, you must use SQL.

QSYCUSRA has the following parameters:

Parameter	Type	I/O
Authority flag	CHAR(1)	O
User name	CHAR(10)	I
Qualified object name	CHAR(20)	I
Object type	CHAR(10)	I
Authorities	CHAR(*)	I
Number of authorities	BIN(4)	I
Call level	BIN(4)	I
Error code	CHAR(*)	I/O

The authority flag is the parameter you interrogate to determine whether the user has the authorities you're trying to verify. The user name parameter is the name of the user profile whose authorities you want to check (you can use *CURRENT to specify the current user). The next two parameters identify the object to which you're checking the user's authority. The next two parameters specify which authorities to check and the number of authorities to check, respectively.

The call-level parameter identifies the program stack call level for the API to check. If the user adopts authority in the current program stack, you can specify a different call level (the one that immediately precedes the program that adopts authority) to interrogate the user's own authority to the object.

Finally, following IBM's standard API implementation, QSYCUSRA uses an error code structure to provide information to the calling program if the API fails.

At C, in the initialization subroutine, CSTMAINT2 calls API QSYCUSRA to check whether the user has *OBJOPR authority to file CUSTLFA. When the user has the authority, the subroutine moves file name CUSTLFA to field @FILE. Otherwise, the program calls the API again to check the user's authority to file CUSTLFB. If the user is authorized to CUSTLFB (AFLAG = @YES), the subroutine moves file name CUSTLFB into variable @FILE.

At D, the initialization subroutine checks variable @FILE to open the appropriate file and set conditioning indicator *IN55. Before performing database I/O in subsequent subroutines, the program checks the value of @FILE to determine which logical file to access and which version of the panel to display (the code at E shows an example of this processing).

You might wonder what happens when you write to a logical file that contains only a subset of the physical file's fields. For instance, let's say you modified CSTMAINT2 to include an add function. Users can't write the new record directly to the physical file because they don't have authority to the physical file. Users who have authority to CUSTLFA can write to logical file CUSTLFA, which contains all the fields from the physical file. But for users who have authority only to CUSTLFB, what happens to the three sensitive fields during a write operation?

When you write to a logical file record format implemented as a projection of a physical file, the system initializes the missing fields before writing the record to disk. If you've specified the ALLNULL keyword, the system initializes missing fields to NULL; otherwise, the system sets character fields to blanks and numeric fields to zeros. Alternatively, you can specify a default (DFT) value for a missing field in the physical file's record format, and the system initializes the field to the default value (instead of null, blanks, or zeros).

This approach to field-level security requires thoughtful programming, but it is still easier than maintaining hard-coded user profiles along with conditioned fields. And as time passes, your investment in this implementation method pays off in lower maintenance costs and easier maintenance of security. You never have to recompile the RPG program to change authorities — to change which users can view the sensitive fields, you can simply change the authorities to the logical files. Another benefit is that your application can take advantage of OS/400's integrated security.

Row-Level Security

You can use the SELECT statement in SQL to implement row-level security. The SELECT statement lets you create a subsetted list of the rows in a table. You can select which rows to present based on several things, one of them being the value in a particular column or columns.

For example, if you have a database of patient information and you want to restrict doctors from seeing data for patients other than their own, you could dynamically determine which rows to present by passing the doctor's name to a SELECT statement. SQL would look at the values in the Physician column and present only the rows that contain the specified doctor's name in that column.

You can accomplish the same thing using logical files or views. However, logical files aren't dynamic, so you would have to build one for each doctor. As you can imagine, this method would quickly become unmanageable if you have many doctors or you often have to add or remove doctors from your application.

Another method for dynamically determining which rows to select is to use User Defined Functions (UDFs). Because a UDF is a program you write, you can check literally anything you want to before presenting the row. If it made sense for your data's security, you could write a program to determine whether the moon is full before selecting a row! For a useful example of a UDF that does authority checking for an application, go to http://www.as400.ibm.com/db2.

What About SQL Tables and Views?

You may have picked up this fact early in the chapter, but for readers who didn't, we'll spell it out: The same authority model that we've described for physical and logical files applies to SQL tables (physical files) and views (logical files). With SQL, you use the GRANT and REVOKE SQL statements to grant and revoke object and data authorities. SQL also provides some powerful functions, such as the SELECT statement and UDFs, that your applications can use to provide access control at the row level.

Chapter 6
Output Queue and Spooled-File Security

Many shops neglect their printers when they formulate a security plan. But access to printed data can be just as damaging as access to data files. You should review both user access to printers and the way that users request printed output.

In many organizations, printers are everywhere — in public areas as well as on employees' desks — and they produce countless documents and reports containing significant customer and corporate information. For some companies, the proliferation of printers and printouts could constitute a vulnerability. It's not at all unusual for competitors to try to bribe programmers and operators for printed reports containing strategic information. Most programmers and operators, and even many end users, can print a plethora of reports and walk right out of the building with the information. To reduce the chances of printed output getting into the wrong hands, you might need to secure output queues, reorganize menus, and even move printers to more secure locations.

Output queues are a functional necessity on the AS/400, but that doesn't mean that all users need to have access to data in all output queues. In one company I (Wayne) worked for, the payroll supervisor made a big deal about guarding the printer while the payroll checks were being printed. She wanted to make sure that no one, especially the system operators, could see the checks. I didn't have the heart to tell her that on their system, anyone who had access to the DSPOUTQ (Display Output Queue) command on the S/38 could easily view the payroll spooled file.

To appreciate the importance of controlling access to output queues, remember that you can use them not only to print spooled files but also to display them. Output queue security is one of the trickiest forms of security on the AS/400. To achieve the desired results, you need to carefully plan and design your output queue security.

The Security-Related Output Queue Attributes

You create output queues using the CRTOUTQ (Create Output Queue) command. The values you specify for a few security-related CRTOUTQ command parameters determine how you control user access to output queues and spooled data. (You can also modify these output queue attributes using the CHGOUTQ (Change Output Queue) and WRKOUTQD (Work with Output Queue Description) commands.) Three attributes — DSPDTA (Display Data), OPRCTL (Operator Control), and AUTCHK (Authority Check)

— work with the output queue's existing public and private authorities to determine who can and can't view and manipulate the output queue's spooled files. Before you start to design your output queue security, you need to fully comprehend the role of each of these attributes.

DSPDTA (Display Data)

DSPDTA specifies the kind of output queue access allowed for users who have at least *READ authority to the output queue. A value of *YES means that a user who has *READ access to the output queue can display, copy, and send (e.g., using the SNDNETSPLF or SNDTCPSPLF command) the data from any spooled file on the queue. A value of *NO specifies that users who have *READ authority to the output queue can display, copy, and send the output data only from their own spooled files, unless

- they have *JOBCTL special authority and the output queue's OPRCTL attribute value is *YES,
- they have *CHANGE authority to the output queue and the output queue's AUTCHK attribute value is *DTAAUT, or
- they own the output queue and AUTCHK is *OWNER.

If the value of DSPDTA is *OWNER, only the owner of a spooled file can display, copy, send, or move the spooled file. *OWNER is the appropriate DSPDTA value for operators who manage output queue entries but who shouldn't be able to view the contents of spooled files. When you specify OPRCTL(*YES) and DSPDTA(*OWNER) for the output queue, a user profile with *JOBCTL special authority can hold, change, delete, and release spooled files on that output queue but can't display, copy, send, or move the spooled files.

OPRCTL (Operator Control)

OPRCTL specifies whether a user who has *JOBCTL special authority can manage or control the files on an output queue. When you specify OPRCTL(*YES), a user profile with *JOBCTL special authority can control the output queue (e.g., hold, release, start a writer to the queue) and manage the spooled file entries (e.g., hold, release, change, delete). As we saw above, when the output queue's DSPDTA attribute value is *NO, user profiles with *JOBCTL special authority can still display, copy, send, and move all users' spooled files.

Before giving *JOBCTL authority to users only so they can start their own print writer, you should consider using a program that adopts authorities. Programs that adopt authority also adopt the owner's special authorities (e.g., *JOBCTL). For users who don't need *JOBCTL special authority to start, change, and end writers to the queue, you can provide a program that performs such writer functions by adopting the program owner's *JOBCTL authority. When the program ends, the user no longer has *JOBCTL authority.

AUTCHK (Authority Check)

The AUTCHK parameter specifies whether the commands that check the requesting user's authority to the output queue should check whether the user owns the output queue (*OWNER) or just has data authority (*DTAAUT) to the output queue. When the AUTCHK value is *OWNER, only the user who owns the output queue can change or delete spooled files owned by other user profiles. When the value is *DTAAUT, any user with *READ, *ADD, and *DLT authority to the output queue can change or delete other users' spooled files on that output queue.

The AUT Parameter

Finally, the AUT parameter specifies the initial level of authority allowed for the public. You can use the EDTOBJAUT (Edit Object Authority), GRTOBJAUT (Grant Object Authority), or RVKOBJAUT (Revoke Object Authority) command to modify this level of authority.

The last and perhaps most important point to remember is that a user who has *SPLCTL special authority has complete access to all output queues and spooled files regardless of which output queue attributes and authorities are specified. This means that if any user has *SPLCTL special authority on your system, you truly can't secure any output queue.

Table 6.1 shows a chart from IBM's *OS/400 Security — Reference* manual (SC41-5302, used with permission) that describes the printing function you want to secure and the parameter values required to do so.

TABLE 6.1
Authority Required to Perform Printing Functions

Printing function	Output queue parameters DSPDTA	AUTCHK	OPRCTL	Output queue authority	Special authority
Add spooled files to queue[1]	Any Any	Any Any	Any *YES	*READ Any	None *JOBCTL
View list of spooled files (WRKOUTQ command[2])	Any Any	Any Any	Any *YES	*READ Any	None *JOBCTL
Display, copy, or send spooled files (DSPSPLF, CPYSPLF, SNDNETSPLF, SNDTCPSPLF[2])	*YES *NO *NO *YES *NO *OWNER[4]	Any *DTAAUT *OWNER Any Any Any	Any Any Any *YES *YES Any	*READ *CHANGE Owner[3] Any Any Any	None None None *JOBCTL *JOBCTL AnyChange,
delete, hold, and release spooled file (CHGSPLFA, DLTSPLF, HLDSPLF, RLSSPLF[2])	Any Any Any	*DTAAUT *OWNER Any	Any Any *YES	*CHANGE Owner[3] Any	None None *JOBCTL
Change, clear, hold, and release output queue (CHGOUTQ, CLROUTQ, HLDOUTQ, RLSOUTQ)	Any Any Any	*DTAAUT *OWNER Any	Any Any *YES	*CHANGE Owner[3] Any	None None *JOBCTL
Start a writer for the queue (STRPRTWTR, STRRMTWTR[2])	Any Any	*DTAAUT Any	Any *YES	*CHANGE[4] Any[4]	None *JOBCTL

[1] This authority is required to direct output to an output queue.
[2] Using these commands or equivalent options from a display.
[3] You must own the output queue.
[4] You must own the spooled file or have *SPLCTL special authority.
[5] Also requires *USE authority to the printer device description.

Reprinted from *OS/400 Security — Reference V4R5*, ©2000, by permission from International Business Machines Corporation.

Output Queue Ownership

The issue of output queue security also raises the question of who should create output queues. Although this may seem like a simple question, it's important for two reasons: First, the owner can modify the output queue attributes as well as grant and revoke authorities to the output queue, which means the owner controls who can view and work with spooled files on that queue. Second, the AUTCHK parameter checks the ownership of the output queue as part of the authorization test when the output queue is accessed.

The system operator should be responsible for creating and controlling output queues that hold data considered public or unsecured. You can use this ownership with the authority parameters on the CRTOUTQ command to create an environment that lets users control their own print files and print on various printers in their work areas.

For secured data (e.g., payroll, human resources, financial statements), the department supervisor profile (or a similar profile) should own the output queue. The person who owns the output queue is responsible for maintaining its security and can even explicitly deny access to IT personnel.

Sample Output Queue Security Implementation

For example purposes, consider an organization that has output queues in the IT department, human resources, the financial area (e.g, GL, AR, AP), the order/sales departments, and the warehouse. Let's assume that you want to secure the human resources output queue — an output queue named HROUTQ — and spooled files. You want no one except HR personnel to manage this output queue and its spooled files. Let's also say that you want to secure the financial spooled files — in output queue FINOUTQ — but you want the operator to manage the queues. The remaining output queues should have minimum security and allow complete access to any spooled file and to the output queue itself. How would you accomplish this?

First, you would create all the output queues except FINOUTQ and HROUTQ and make the system operator profile the owner of the queues. You would enter the following CRTOUTQ command for each of the output queues you created:

```
CRTOUTQ    OUTQ(outq_lib/outq_name)    +
           DSPDTA(*YES)                +
           OPRCTL(*YES)                +
           AUTCHK(*OWNER)              +
           AUT(*USE)
```

The combination of DSPDTA(*YES), AUTCHK(*OWNER), and AUT(*USE) for the public authority means that any user can display, copy, or send any spooled files on the output queue, and that only spooled-file owners can change, hold, release, or delete their own spooled files. (The owner of the output queue can change, hold, release, or delete any spooled file in the output queue, regardless of who owns it.) The one exception to the limitation of AUTCHK(*OWNER) is that a user profile that has *JOBCTL special authority and OPRCTL(*YES) can change, hold, release, or delete any spooled file. This implementation lets you give system operators *JOBCTL authority to manage these output queues while limiting other users to managing their own spooled files. However, all users with at least *READ data authority can display, copy, and send any spooled file on the queue.

Next, create FINOUTQ, which will hold confidential financial reports. You want all profiles to have access only to their own reports, and you want the operator to manage the queue without being able to view the spooled files. You would create FINOUTQ as follows, with FINUSER as the owner:

```
CRTOUTQ    OUTQ(outq_lib/FINOUTQ)     +
           DSPDTA(*OWNER)             +
           OPRCTL(*YES)               +
           AUTCHK(*OWNER)             +
           AUT(*USE)
```

Although everyone, including the system operator, can access this output queue, each user profile can display, copy, or send only the user's own spooled files. The system operator, by virtue of *JOBCTL special authority and the OPRCTL(*YES) attribute on the output queue, can manage the queue but can't look at any reports other than the ones the system operator places on the queue. The DSPDTA(*OWNER) attribute ensures that only the owner of a spooled file can display, copy, or send that spooled file.

Note that if you specify DSPDTA(*OWNER) in this scenario, even user profiles that have *ALLOBJ authority can't access spooled files other than their own.

> **Technical Note**
> Users who have *ALLOBJ authority but not *SPLCTL authority can view only their own spooled files on output queues whose DSPDTA attribute has the value *OWNER.

The last output queue is HROUTQ, which is extremely confidential. Only those in the HRUSER group should be able to access this output queue or these spooled files. To create the output queue, use the following CRTOUTQ command:

```
CRTOUTQ      OUTQ(outq_lib/HROUTQ)     +
             DSPDTA(*YES)              +
             OPRCTL(*NO)               +
             AUTCHK(*DTAAUT)           +
             AUT(*EXCLUDE)
```

Make the HRUSER group profile the owner, and revoke all other authorities from the queue.

Profiles with *JOBCTL authority can't access this queue because of the queue's OPRCTL(*NO) attribute. Only the owner has any object or data authority to the queue. Only the owner can start or stop a writer to the queue. All users in the HRUSER group can display, copy, or send any spooled file on the output queue. As a result of the AUTCHK(*DTAAUT) attribute and the fact that the HRUSER group profile owns the output queue, all users in the group can also change, hold, move, or delete any spooled file.

An Output Queue Security Management Utility

The following utility — command DSPOUTQAUT and its supporting programs — lets you display and manage output queue authorities. To use DSPOUTQAUT, you execute the command and enter an output queue name (which can be qualified). Then you simply press Enter, and the system displays the names of all user profiles on the system, along with their output queue authorities, in a subfile display (Figure 6.1A). You can use this screen to check and change authorities for many user activities on the specified output queue.

FIGURE 6.1A
Sample DSPOUTQAUT Utility Subfile Display

```
                      Display Output Queue Authorities
                      Output Queue:   *LIBL/QPRINT
    Position to user: _____
    Type options, press Enter.
      2=CHGUSRPRF    5=DSPUSRPRF    15=GRTOBJAUT    16=RVKOBJAUT
                     STR     *--------OUTQ--------*   *-------SPLF-------*
                     PRT              CHG, CLR    DSP,           CHG, DLT
    Opt  User        WTR  Add  WRK    HLD, RLS    CPY, SND       HLD, RLS
    __   EDISON       Y    Y    Y       Y          Y              Y
    __   EINSTEIN     N    N    N       N          Y              Y
    __   JEFFERSON    Y    Y    Y       Y          Y              Y
    __   LINCOLN      N    N    N       N          N              N
    __   MARCONI      Y    N    Y       N          Y              N
    __   QPGMR        Y    Y    Y       Y          Y              Y
    __   QSECOFR      Y    Y    Y       Y          Y              Y
    __   QSYSOPR      Y    Y    Y       Y          Y              Y
    __   WASHINGTON   N    Y    Y       N          N              N

                                                                  Bottom
    F3=Exit    F7=CHGOUTQ    F8=CHGOBJOWN    F9=DSPOBJAUT    F12=Cancel
```

This subfile display lets you see whether each user on the system can

- start a printer writer and specify this output queue as the source
- add spooled files to the output queue
- work with the output queue
- change the output queue attributes, clear the output queue of all reports, hold the output queue so no reports print from it, and release the output queue
- display a spooled file contained in the output queue, copy a spooled file, and send the spooled file to another system
- change a spooled file's attributes, delete a spooled file, hold a spooled file so it doesn't print, and release a spooled file

Using the options on the screen, you can

- position the cursor next to a user profile name, type option 2, and press Enter to change the user profile. The utility displays the CHGUSRPRF (Change User Profile) prompt, from which you can change special authorities and other user profile attributes
- enter option 5 to display a user profile
- enter option 15 to grant a user profile additional private authorities to QPRINT, or enter option 16 to revoke private authorities. The utility displays the GRTOBJAUT or RVKOBJAUT command prompt, respectively
- press F7 to change QPRINT's attributes, such as its DSPDTA or AUTCHK setting

- press F8 to change QPRINT's owner
- press F9 to display all users' private authorities to QPRINT

When you press a function key, make changes, and press Enter, the system recalculates the authorities (Y or N) for all user profiles and displays the refreshed information.

You can also move the cursor to the "Position to user" input field, type a partial or complete user profile name, and press Enter. The program repositions the subfile to display the user profile you specified (or the closest one, if you typed the name of a nonexistent profile). The workstation controller moves the subfile to the page where the requested profile is located. Although the workstation controller doesn't position that profile at the top of the screen, it does move the cursor to the appropriate record.

Figures 6.1B through 6.1G provide the code for the DSPOUTQAUT command, the command processing program, the DSPOQAD display file, RPG program DSPOQAR, a Cobol version of the program (DSPOQAK), and CL program DSPOQAC1, which the utility calls to carry out some of the options.

FIGURE 6.1B
Command Definition for DSPOUTQAUT

```
/* From "Are Your Output Queues Secure?,"            */
/* NEWS 3X/400, August 1994                          */
/*                                                   */
/* COPYRIGHT (c) 1994 Duke Communications            */
/* International                                     */

CMD     'Display OutQ Authorities'

        PARM    outq   q1                              +
                MIN( 1 )                               +
                PROMPT( 'Output queue' )

Q1:                                                    +
        QUAL    *NAME   10                             +
                MIN( 1 )                               +
                EXPR( *YES )
        QUAL    *NAME   10                             +
                DFT( *LIBL )                           +
                SPCVAL( ( *LIBL ) )                    +
                EXPR( *YES )
                PROMPT( 'Library' )
```

FIGURE 6.1C
Command Processing Program DSPOQAC

```
/* From "Are Your Output Queues Secure?,"             */
/* NEWS 3X/400, August 1994                           */
/*                                                    */
/* COPYRIGHT (c) 1994 Duke Communications             */
/* International                                      */

PGM    (                                              +
          &qual_outq    /* Qualified output queue name */  +
       )

   DCL   &outq          *CHAR   10
   DCL   &outqlib       *CHAR   10
   DCL   &qual_outq     *CHAR   20

   MONMSG  cpf0000   EXEC( GOTO error )

   /*                                                 +
    | Break qualified output queue name, then validate it.  +
    */
   CHGVAR   &outq      %SST( &qual_outq  1 10 )
   CHGVAR   &outqlib   %SST( &qual_outq 11 10 )

   CHKOBJ   &outqlib/&outq   *OUTQ

   SNDPGMMSG  MSGID( cpf9898 )                        +
              MSGF( qcpfmsg )                         +
              MSGDTA( 'Gathering data.  Please wait' ) +
              MSGTYPE( *STATUS )                      +
              TOPGMQ( *EXT )
   DSPOBJD   *ALL    *USRPRF                          +
             OUTPUT( *OUTFILE )                       +
             OUTFILE( qtemp/qadspobj )                +
             OUTMBR( *FIRST *REPLACE )
   OVRDBF   qadspobj   TOFILE( qtemp/qadspobj )
   CALL   dspoqar  (                                  +
                     &outq                            +
                     &outqlib                         +
                   )
   RETURN

ERROR:
   MOVPGMMSG
   MONMSG   cpf0000
   RSNESCMSG
   MONMSG   cpf0000

ENDPGM
```

FIGURE 6.1D
DDS for Display File DSPOQAD

```
*...1....+....2....+....3....+....4....+....5....+....6....+....7....+....8
A* From "Are Your Output Queues Secure?" NEWS 3X/400,            *
A* August 1994                                                   *
A*                                                               *
A* COPYRIGHT (c) 1994 Duke Communications International          *
A                                        DSPSIZ(24 80 *DS3)
A                                        PRINT
A                                        INDARA
A                                        CA03
A                                        CA07
A                                        CA08
A                                        CA09
A                                        CA12
A *_____
A          R FKEYS
A                                        LOCK
A                                    23  2'F3=Exit    F7=CHGOUTQ    F8=CHGOBJOW-
A                                        N   F9=DSPOBJAUT    F12=Cancel'
A                                        COLOR(BLU)
A *_____
A          R USRRCD                      SFL
A            OPTNBR        2   B  9  3VALUES(' ' '2 ' ' 2' '5 ' ' 5' '15-
A                                        ' '16')
A                                        ALIAS(OPTION_NUMBER)
A            USRPRF       10   O  9  7ALIAS(USER_PROFILE)
A            STRWTR        1   O  9 20ALIAS(START_PRTWTR)
A            ADDOQ         1   O  9 26ALIAS(ADD_TO_OUTQ)
A            WRKOQ         1   O  9 32ALIAS(WORK_WITH_OUTQ)
A            CHGOQ         1   O  9 40ALIAS(CHANGE_OUTQ)
A            DSPSF         1   O  9 51ALIAS(DISPLAY_SPLF)
A            CHGSFA        1   O  9 62ALIAS(CHANGE_SPLF_ATTRIB)
A            SAVRRN        4   0H       ALIAS(SAVED_RECORD_NUMBER)
A *_____
A          R USRCTL                      SFLCTL(USRRCD)
A                                        SFLSIZ(0014)
A                                        SFLPAG(0013)
A                                        BLINK
A                                        OVERLAY
A                                        SFLCSRRRN(&RRN)
A                                        SFLDSPCTL
A N80                                    SFLDSP
A  80                                    SFLCLR
A N81                                    SFLEND(*MORE)
A            RRN          5S   0H       ALIAS(SUBFILE_RRN)
A            POSSFL       4S   0H       ALIAS(POSITION_SUBFILE_AT_RECORD)
A                                        SFLRCDNBR(CURSOR)
A                                     1 25'Display Output Queue Authorities'
A                                        DSPATR(HI)
A                                     2 23'Output Queue:'
A            QOUTQ       21A   O     2 38ALIAS(QUAL_OUTPUT_QUEUE)
A                                     4  2'Type options, press Enter.'
A                                        COLOR(BLU)
```

continued

Figure 6.1D *Continued*

```
*...1....+....2....+....3....+....4....+....5....+....6....+....7....+....8
A                                      5 3'2=CHGUSRPRF   5=DSPUSRPRF   15=GRT-
A                                          OBJAUT   16=RVKOBJAUT'
A                                          COLOR(BLU)
A                                      6 19'STR'
A                                          DSPATR(HI)
A                                      6 25'*___-OUTQ___-*'
A                                          DSPATR(HI)
A                                      6 48'*___SPLF___-*'
A                                          DSPATR(HI)
A                                      7 19'PRT'
A                                          DSPATR(HI)
A                                      7 37'CHG, CLR'
A                                          DSPATR(HI)
A                                      7 48'DSP,'
A                                          DSPATR(HI)
A                                      7 59'CHG, DLT'
A                                          DSPATR(HI)
A                                      8  2'Opt'
A                                          DSPATR(HI)
A                                      8  7'User'
A                                          DSPATR(HI)
A                                      8 19'WTR'
A                                          DSPATR(HI)
A                                      8 25'Add'
A                                          DSPATR(HI)
A                                      8 31'WRK'
A                                          DSPATR(HI)
A                                      8 37'HLD, RLS'
A                                          DSPATR(HI)
A                                      8 48'CPY, SND'
A                                          DSPATR(HI)
A                                      8 59'HLD, RLS'
A                                          DSPATR(HI)
A                                      3 51'Position to user:'
A            POSUSR         10A   I    3 70ALIAS(POSITION_TO_USER)
 *
A            R MSGRCD                      SFL
A                                          SFLMSGRCD(24)
A              MSGKEY                      SFLMSGKEY
A              PGMQ                        SFLPGMQ
 *
A            R MSGCTL                      SFLCTL(MSGRCD)
A                                          SFLDSP
A                                          SFLDSPCTL
A                                          SFLINZ
A N82                                      SFLEND
A                                          SFLSIZ(0002)
A                                          SFLPAG(0001)
A                                          OVERLAY
A              PGMQ                        SFLPGMQ
```

continued

FIGURE 6.1E
RPG Program DSPOQAR

```
*...1....+....2....+....3....+....4....+....5....+....6....+....7....+....8
F* From "Are Your Output Queues Secure?" NEWS 3X/400,        *
F* August 1994                                                *
F*                                                            *
F* COPYRIGHT (c) 1994 Duke Communications International       *
FDSPOQAD CF  E                    WORKSTN
F                                            SFLRRNKSFILE USRRCD
F                                                  KINFDS INFDS
FQADSPOBJIF  E                    DISK
*******************************************************************
 * API error structure parameter.
IAPIERR      DS
I I               96              B   1   40BYTPRV
I I                0              B   5   80BYTAVL
I                                     9  15 EXCPID
I                                    17  96 EXCPDT
 *
 * Object authority structure.  Used as receiving variable by
 * QSYRUSRA system API.  Each subfield contains '0' or '1',
 * depending on whether the specified user enjoys each authority.
IAUTDS       DS                       96
I                                    20  20 OBJOPR
I                                    21  21 OBJMGT
I                                    22  22 OBJEXS
I                                    23  23 DTARD
I                                    24  24 DTAADD
I                                    25  25 DTAUPD
I                                    26  26 DTADLT
I                                    27  80 FILL1
I                                    81  81 DTAEXC
I                                    82  93 FILL2
 *
 * Command string to be executed.
ICMDSTR      DS                     3000
 *
 * Information data structure for display file.
IINFDS       DS
I                                   369 369 FKEY
I                                 B 376 379 SFLPAG
 *
 * Object description data structure.  Used as receiving variable
 * by the QUSROBJD system API to retrieve the object's owner.
IOBJDS       DS                       90
I                                    53  62 OBJOWN
 *
 * Output queue description data structure.  Used as receiving
 * variable by the QSPROUTQ system API to retrieve information
 * about the output queue being worked on.
IOUTQDS      DS                      202
I                                    39  48 DSPDTA
I                                    53  62 OPRCTL
I                                    83  92 AUTCHK
 *
```

continued

FIGURE 6.1E CONTINUED

```
*...1....+....2....+....3....+....4....+....5....+....6....+....7....+....8
 * User profile description data structure.  Used as receiving
 * variable by the QSYRUSRI system API.
IUSRDS          DS                            83
I                                       29  29 ALLOBJ
I                                       30  30 FILL3
I                                       31  31 JOBCTL
I                                       32  32 SPLCTL
 *_____
 * A few binary variables needed in the program.
IBINARY         DS
I I            96                   B    1  40AUTLEN
I I            90                   B    5  80OBJLEN
I I           206                   B    9 120OUTQLN
I I            83                   B   13 160USRLEN
I I             0                   B   17 200PGMSTK
 *_____
 * Program constants.
I              '?CHGOBJOWN ?*OBJ('    C          CHGO01
I              ') ?*OBJTYPE(*OUTQ) ?-C          CHGO02
I              '?NEWOWN() ??CUROWNAU-
I              'T()'
I              '?CHGOUTQ ?*OUTQ('     C          CHGOQ1
I              ') ??DSPDTA('          C          CHGOQ2
I              ') ??AUTCHK('          C          CHGOQ3
I              ') ??OPRCTL('          C          CHGOQ4
I              '?CHGUSRPRF ?*USRPRF('C           CHGUP1
I              '?DSPOBJAUT ?*OBJ('    C          DSPOA1
I              ') ?*OBJTYPE(*OUTQ)'   C          DSPOA2
I              '?DSPUSRPRF ?*USRPRF('C           DSPUP1
I              X'33'                  C          F3
I              X'37'                  C          F7
I              X'38'                  C          F8
I              X'39'                  C          F9
I              X'3C'                  C          F12
I              '?GRTOBJAUT ?*OBJ('    C          GRTAU1
I              ') ?*OBJTYPE(*OUTQ) ?-C           GRTAU2
I              '*USER('
I              X'F1'                  C          ENTER
I              'N'                    C          NO
I              '?RVKOBJAUT ?*OBJ('    C          RVKAU1
I              ') ?*OBJTYPE(*OUTQ) ?-C           RVKAU2
I              '*USER('
I              'Y'                    C          YES
 ****************************************************************
 * Mainline.                                                     *
 ****************************************************************
C              *ENTRY     PLIST
C                         PARM           OUTQ   10
C                         PARM           OUTQLB 10
 *
C                         EXSR INZPGM
C                         EXSR PRCPGM
 *
```

continued

Figure 6.1E Continued

```
*...1....+....2....+....3....+....4....+....5....+....6....+....7....+....8
C                       MOVE *ON        *INLR
 *
 * Subroutine to declare work variables and initialize them.
C           #DCL        BEGSR
C           OUTQ        CAT  OUTQLB     APIQOQ 20 P
C                       MOVEL'USRA0100'AUTFMT  8 P
C                       Z-ADD3000       CMDLEN 155
C                       MOVE *BLANK     CMDSTR
C                       MOVE *BLANK     ERRFND  1
C                       MOVE *BLANK     ENDPGM  1
C                       MOVE *BLANK     MORRCD  1
C                       MOVEL'*ALL'     MSGRMV 10 P
C                       MOVEL'OBJD0100'OBJFMT  8 P
C                       MOVEL'OUTQ0100'OUTQFM  8 P
C                       MOVEL'*OUTQ'    OUTQTP 10 P
C                       MOVE *BLANK     RLDSFL  1
C                       Z-ADD*ZERO      RRNDIF 50
C                       Z-ADD*ZERO      RRNHI  50
C                       Z-ADD*ZERO      RRNLO  50
C                       Z-ADD*ZERO      RRNTTL 50
C                       Z-ADD*ZERO      SFLRRN 40
C                       MOVEL'USRI0200'USRFMT  8 P
C                       Z-ADD1          USRRRN 110
C                       ENDSR
 *
 * BINSCH: Perform binary search in the records loaded to the
 * subfile in order to quickly scan them and reposition subfile.
C           BINSCH      BEGSR
C           RRNHI       ADD  RRNLO      SFLRRN
C                       DIV  2          SFLRRN
C           SFLRRN      CHAINUSRRCD                    99
C           USRPRF      IFLT POSUSR
C                       Z-ADDSFLRRN     RRNLO
C                       ELSE
C                       Z-ADDSFLRRN     RRNHI
C                       ENDIF
C                       ENDSR
 *
 * CLCYES: Calculate all "Y" (yes) values for authority to the
 * output queue so they can be written to the subfile.
C           CLCYES      BEGSR
 * Determine whether the user can start the printer writer.
C           JOBCTL      IFEQ YES
C           OPRCTL      ANDEQ'*YES'
C           OBJOPR      OREQ YES
C           DTARD       ANDEQYES
C           DTAADD      ANDEQYES
C           DTAUPD      ANDEQYES
C           DTADLT      ANDEQYES
C           DTAEXC      ANDEQYES
C                       MOVE YES        STRWTR
```

continued

FIGURE 6.1E CONTINUED

```
*...1....+....2....+....3....+....4....+....5....+....6....+....7....+....8
* Determine whether the user can add reports to the output queue
* and work with the output queue.
C           DTARD     IFEQ YES
C           OPRCTL    OREQ '*YES'
C           JOBCTL    ANDEQYES
C                     MOVE YES       ADDOQ
C                     MOVE YES       WRKOQ
C                     ENDIF
* Determine whether the user can change the output queue.
C           AUTCHK    IFEQ '*DTAAUT'
C           OBJOPR    ANDEQYES
C           DTARD     ANDEQYES
C           DTAADD    ANDEQYES
C           DTAUPD    ANDEQYES
C           DTADLT    ANDEQYES
C           DTAEXC    ANDEQYES
C           AUTCHK    OREQ '*OWNER'
C           OBJOWN    ANDEQODOBNM
C           OPRCTL    OREQ '*YES'
C           JOBCTL    ANDEQ'*YES'
C                     MOVE YES       CHGOQ
C                     ENDIF
* Determine whether the user can display spooled files.
C           DSPDTA    IFEQ '*YES'
C           DTARD     ANDEQYES
C           DSPDTA    OREQ '*NO'
C           AUTCHK    ANDEQ'*DTAAUT'
C           OBJOPR    ANDEQYES
C           DTARD     ANDEQYES
C           DTAADD    ANDEQYES
C           DTAUPD    ANDEQYES
C           DTADLT    ANDEQYES
C           DTAEXC    ANDEQYES
C           DSPDTA    OREQ '*NO'
C           AUTCHK    ANDEQ'*OWNER'
C           OBJOWN    ANDEQODOBNM
C           DSPDTA    OREQ '*YES'
C           OPRCTL    ANDEQ'*YES'
C           JOBCTL    ANDEQYES
C           DSPDTA    OREQ '*NO'
C           OPRCTL    ANDEQ'*YES'
C           JOBCTL    ANDEQYES
C           DSPDTA    OREQ '*OWNER'
C                     MOVE YES       DSPSF
C                     ENDIF
* Determine whether the user can change spooled files.
C           AUTCHK    IFEQ '*DTAAUT'
C           OBJOPR    ANDEQYES
C           DTARD     ANDEQYES
C           DTAADD    ANDEQYES
C           DTAUPD    ANDEQYES
C           DTADLT    ANDEQYES
```

continued

FIGURE 6.1E Continued

```
*...1....+....2....+....3....+....4....+....5....+....6....+....7....+....8
C           DTAEXC    ANDEQYES
C           AUTCHK    OREQ '*OWNER'
C           OBJOWN    ANDEQODOBNM
C           OPRCTL    OREQ '*YES'
C           JOBCTL    ANDEQYES
C                     MOVE YES       CHGSFA
C                     ENDIF
C                     ENDSR
*_____
* CLCSFL: Calculate each subfile record.
C           CLCSFL    BEGSR
C                     MOVE ODOBNM    USRPRF
C                     EXSR GETSPC
* If the user has *ALLOBJ or *SPLCTL special authority, the user
* can do everything with the output queue.
C           ALLOBJ    IFEQ YES
C           SPLCTL    OREQ YES
C                     MOVE YES       STRWTR
C                     MOVE YES       ADDOQ
C                     MOVE YES       WRKOQ
C                     MOVE YES       CHGOQ
C                     MOVE YES       DSPSF
C                     MOVE YES       CHGSFA
* Otherwise, initialize all subfile fields to "N" (no), get the
* user's private authority to the output queue, and calculate
* all "Y" values.
C                     ELSE
C                     MOVE NO        STRWTR
C                     MOVE NO        ADDOQ
C                     MOVE NO        WRKOQ
C                     MOVE NO        CHGOQ
C                     MOVE NO        DSPSF
C                     MOVE NO        CHGSFA
C                     EXSR GETPRV
C                     EXSR CLCYES
C                     ENDIF
C                     ENDSR
*_____
* CHGOWN: Change the output queue's owner if user pressed F8.
C           CHGOWN    BEGSR
C           CHG001    CAT  OUTQLB:0  CMDSTR    P
C                     CAT  '/':0     CMDSTR
C                     CAT  OUTQ:0    CMDSTR
C                     CAT  CHG002:0  CMDSTR
C                     CALL 'DSPOQAC1'
C                     PARM           CMDSTR
C                     PARM           CMDLEN
C                     PARM           ERRFND
C           ERRFND    IFEQ NO
C                     EXSR LODSFL
C                     ENDIF
C                     ENDSR
*_____
```

continued

Figure 6.1E Continued

```
*...1....+....2....+....3....+....4....+....5....+....6....+....7....+....8
 * CHGOUT:  Change the output queue attributes if user pressed F7.
C           CHGOUT    BEGSR
C                     CHGOQ1    CAT  OUTQLB:0   CMDSTR     P
C                               CAT  '/':0      CMDSTR
C                               CAT  OUTQ:0     CMDSTR
C                               CAT  CHGOQ2:0   CMDSTR
C                               CAT  DSPDTA:0   CMDSTR
C                               CAT  CHGOQ3:0   CMDSTR
C                               CAT  AUTCHK:0   CMDSTR
C                               CAT  CHGOQ4:0   CMDSTR
C                               CAT  OPRCTL:0   CMDSTR
C                               CAT  ')':0      CMDSTR
C                               CALL 'DSPOQAC1'
C                               PARM            CMDSTR
C                               PARM            CMDLEN
C                               PARM            ERRFND
C           ERRFND    IFEQ NO
C                     EXSR LODSFL
C                     ENDIF
C                     ENDSR
*
 * CHGUSR:  Change the user profile if option 2 selected.
C           CHGUSR    BEGSR
C                     CHGUP1    CAT  USRPRF:0   CMDSTR     P
C                               CAT  ')':0      CMDSTR
C                               CALL 'DSPOQAC1'
C                               PARM            CMDSTR
C                               PARM            CMDLEN
C                               PARM            ERRFND
C           ERRFND    IFEQ NO
C                     MOVE *ON            RLDSFL
C                     ENDIF
C                     EXSR ERSOPT
C                     ENDSR
*
 * CLRPQ:   Clear the interactive program message queue.
C           CLRPQ     BEGSR
C                     CALL 'QMHRMVPM'
C                     PARM '*'            PGMQ
C                     PARM 0              PGMSTK
C                     PARM *BLANK         MSGKEY
C                     PARM '*ALL'         MSGRMV
C                     PARM                APIERR
C                     ENDSR
*
 * DSPINF:  Display information via the subfile panel.
C           DSPINF    BEGSR
C                     WRITEFKEYS
C                     WRITEMSGCTL
C                     EXFMTUSRCTL
C                     EXSR CLRPQ
C                     SELEC
C           FKEY      WHEQ F3
C           FKEY      OREQ F12
C                     MOVE *ON            ENDPGM
```

continued

FIGURE 6.1E CONTINUED

```
*...1....+....2....+....3....+....4....+....5....+....6....+....7....+....8
C                   FKEY      WHEQ F7
C                             EXSR CHGOUT
C                   FKEY      WHEQ F8
C                             EXSR CHGOWN
C                   FKEY      WHEQ F9
C                             EXSR DSPAUT
C                   FKEY      WHEQ ENTER
C                             EXSR PRCENT
C                             ENDSL
C                             ENDSR
 *
 * DSPAUT:  Display the output queue authority if user pressed F9.
C                   DSPAUT    BEGSR
C                   DSPOA1    CAT  OUTQLB:0  CMDSTR     P
C                             CAT  '/':0     CMDSTR
C                             CAT  OUTQ:0    CMDSTR
C                             CAT  DSPOA2:0  CMDSTR
C                             CALL 'DSPOQAC1'
C                             PARM           CMDSTR
C                             PARM           CMDLEN
C                             PARM           ERRFND
C                             ENDSR
 *
 * DSPUSR:  Display the user profile if option 5 selected.
C                   DSPUSR    BEGSR
C                   DSPUP1    CAT  USRPRF:0  CMDSTR     P
C                             CAT  ')':0     CMDSTR
C                             CALL 'DSPOQAC1'
C                             PARM           CMDSTR
C                             PARM           CMDLEN
C                             PARM           ERRFND
C                             EXSR ERSOPT
C                             ENDSR
 *
 * ERSOPT:  Erase option number from subfile record.
C                   ERSOPT    BEGSR
C                   SAVRRN    CHAINUSRRCD                99
C                             CLEAROPTNBR
C                             UPDATUSRRCD
C                             ENDSR
 *
 * EXCOPT:  Execute option number from subfile record.
C                   EXCOPT    BEGSR
C                             SELEC
C                   OPTNBR    WHEQ '2 '
C                   OPTNBR    OREQ ' 2'
C                             EXSR CHGUSR
C                   OPTNBR    WHEQ '5 '
C                   OPTNBR    OREQ ' 5'
C                             EXSR DSPUSR
C                   OPTNBR    WHEQ '15'
C                             EXSR GRTAUT
```

continued

FIGURE 6.1E CONTINUED

```
*...1....+....2....+....3....+....4....+....5....+....6....+....7....+....8
C                   OPTNBR    WHEQ '16'
C                             EXSR RVKAUT
C                             ENDSL
C                             ENDSR
 *
 * FNDOPT:  Find all options entered into subfile records, such
 * as 5=Display, etc.
C                   FNDOPT    BEGSR
C                             MOVE *OFF     RLDSFL
C                             MOVE *ON      MORRCD
C                   MORRCD    DOUEQ*OFF
C                             READCUSRRCD                         99
C                   *IN99     IFEQ *ON
C                             MOVE *OFF     MORRCD
C                             ELSE
C                             EXSR EXCOPT
C                             ENDIF
C                             ENDDO
C                   RLDSFL    IFEQ *ON
C                             EXSR LODSFL
C                             ENDIF
C                             ENDSR
 *
 * GETOQI:  Get output queue information.
C                   GETOQI    BEGSR
C                             CALL 'QSPROUTQ'
C                             PARM          OUTQDS
C                             PARM          OUTQLN
C                             PARM          OUTQFM
C                             PARM          APIQOQ
C                             PARM          APIERR
C                             ENDSR
 *
 * GETOQO:  Get output queue's owner.
C                   GETOQO    BEGSR
C                             CALL 'QUSROBJD'
C                             PARM          OBJDS
C                             PARM          OBJLEN
C                             PARM          OBJFMT
C                             PARM          APIQOQ
C                             PARM          OUTQTP
C                             PARM          APIERR
C                             ENDSR
 *
 * GETPRV:  Get user profile's private authority to output queue.
C                   GETPRV    BEGSR
C                             CALL 'QSYRUSRA'
C                             PARM          AUTDS
C                             PARM          AUTLEN
C                             PARM          AUTFMT
C                             PARM          ODOBNM
C                             PARM          APIQOQ
C                             PARM          OUTQTP
C                             PARM          APIERR
C                             ENDSR
 *
```

continued

FIGURE 6.1E CONTINUED

```
*...1....+....2....+....3....+....4....+....5....+....6....+....7....+....8
 * GETSPC:  Get user profile's special authorities.
C           GETSPC    BEGSR
C                     CALL 'QSYRUSRI'
C                     PARM            USRDS
C                     PARM            USRLEN
C                     PARM            USRFMT
C                     PARM            ODOBNM
C                     PARM            APIERR
C                     ENDSR
 *
 * GRTAUT:  Grant authority to output queue if user selected
 * option 15.
C           GRTAUT    BEGSR
C           GRTAU1    CAT  OUTQLB:0  CMDSTR      P
C                     CAT  '/':0     CMDSTR
C                     CAT  OUTQ:0    CMDSTR
C                     CAT  GRTAU2:0  CMDSTR
C                     CAT  USRPRF:0  CMDSTR
C                     CAT  ')':0     CMDSTR
C                     CALL 'DSPOQAC1'
C                     PARM           CMDSTR
C                     PARM           CMDLEN
C                     PARM           ERRFND
C           ERRFND    IFEQ NO
C                     MOVE *ON       RLDSFL
C                     ENDIF
C                     ENDSR
 *
 * INZPGM:  Initialize program.  Prepare displayable output queue
 * name, prepare message subfile, get output queue's owner,
 * initialize work variables, and load subfile.
C           INZPGM    BEGSR
C           OUTQLB    CAT  '/':0     QOUTQ       P
C                     CAT  OUTQ:0    QOUTQ
C           OUTQ      CAT  OUTQLB    APIQOQ
C                     MOVEL'*'       PGMQ
C                     MOVE *OFF      *IN82
C                     EXSR GETOQO
C                     Z-ADD1         POSSFL
C                     EXSR #DCL
C                     EXSR LODSFL
C                     ENDSR
 *
 * LODSFL:  Load subfile with information.
C           LODSFL    BEGSR
C                     MOVE *ON       *IN80
C                     MOVE *OFF      *IN81
C                     WRITEUSRCTL
C                     EXSR GETOQO
C                     EXSR GETOQI
C                     MOVE *ON       MORRCD
C                     Z-ADD1         USRRRN
C                     Z-ADD0         SFLRRN
```

continued

FIGURE 6.1E CONTINUED

```
*...1....+....2....+....3....+....4....+....5....+....6....+....7....+....8
C                   OPTNBR      WHEQ '16'
C                               EXSR RVKAUT
C                               Z-ADD0                RRNTTL
C                   MORRCD      DOUEQ*OFF
C                               EXSR READ
C                               ENDDO
C                   SFLRRN      IFGT 0
C                               MOVE *OFF             *IN80
C                               ELSE
C                               MOVE *ON              *IN80
C                               ENDIF
C                               ENDSR
 *
 * PRCENT:  Process the Enter key.
C                   PRCENT      BEGSR
C                               EXSR FNDOPT
C                   POSUSR      IFNE *BLANK
C                               EXSR REPOS
C                               ENDIF
C                               ENDSR
 *
 * PRCPGM:  Process this program until exit program is signaled.
C                   PRCPGM      BEGSR
C                               MOVE *OFF             ENDPGM
C                   ENDPGM      DOUEQ*ON
C                               EXSR DSPINF
C                               ENDDO
C                               ENDSR
 *
 * READ:  Read a record from the input file.
C                   READ        BEGSR
C                   USRRRN      CHAINQADSPOBJ                  99
C                   *IN99       IFEQ *ON
C                               MOVE *OFF             MORRCD
C                               ELSE
C                               EXSR CLCSFL
C                               EXSR WRTSFL
C                               ADD  1                USRRRN
C                               ENDIF
C                               ENDSR
 *
 * REPOS:  Reposition subfile to user profile name entered.
C                   REPOS       BEGSR
C                               Z-ADD1                RRNLO
C                               Z-ADDRRNTTL           RRNHI
C                   RRNHI       SUB  RRNLO            RRNDIF
C                   RRNDIF      DOULE1
C                               EXSR BINSCH
C                   RRNHI       SUB  RRNLO            RRNDIF
C                               ENDDO
C                   SFLRRN      IFLT 1
C                               Z-ADD1                SFLRRN
C                               ELSE
C                   POSSFL      IFGT RRNTTL
C                               Z-ADDRRNTTL           SFLRRN
C                               ENDIF
```

continued

FIGURE 6.1E *Continued*

```
*...1....+....2....+....3....+....4....+....5....+....6....+....7....+....8
C                    ENDIF
C                    Z-ADDSFLRRN    POSSFL
C                    ENDSR
 *
 * RVKAUT:  Revoke authority to output queue if option 16 selected.
C           RVKAUT   BEGSR
C           RVKAU1   CAT   OUTQLB:0  CMDSTR     P
C                    CAT   '/':0     CMDSTR
C                    CAT   OUTQ:0    CMDSTR
C                    CAT   RVKAU2:0  CMDSTR
C                    CAT   USRPRF:0  CMDSTR
C                    CAT   ')':0     CMDSTR
C                    CALL  'DSPOQAC1'
C                    PARM            CMDSTR
C                    PARM            CMDLEN
C                    PARM            ERRFND
C           ERRFND   IFEQ  NO
C                    MOVE  *ON       RLDSFL
C                    ENDIF
C                    ENDSR
 *
 * WRTSFL:  Write a record to the subfile.
C           WRTSFL   BEGSR
C                    ADD   1         SFLRRN
C                    ADD   1         RRNTTL
C                    Z-ADDSFLRRN     SAVRRN
C                    WRITEUSRRCD
C                    ENDSR
```

FIGURE 6.1F
Cobol Program DSPOQAK

Note: If you choose to implement the Cobol version, you must change DSPOQAC to call Cobol program DSPOQAK instead of RPG program DSPOQAR.

```
      PROCESS FS9MTO0M.

      IDENTIFICATION DIVISION.
      PROGRAM-ID.  dspoqak.

     *******************************************************************
      ENVIRONMENT DIVISION.
     *_____
      CONFIGURATION SECTION.
      SPECIAL-NAMES.   I-O-FEEDBACK IS file-i-o-feedback.
     *_____
      INPUT-OUTPUT SECTION.
      FILE-CONTROL.
          SELECT display-file ASSIGN TO WORKSTATION-dspoqad-SI
                              ORGANIZATION IS TRANSACTION
                              ACCESS MODE IS DYNAMIC
                              RELATIVE KEY IS subfile-record-number.
          SELECT user-file    ASSIGN TO DATABASE-qadspobj
                              ORGANIZATION IS RELATIVE
                              ACCESS MODE IS RANDOM
                              RELATIVE KEY IS user-file-rrn.

     *******************************************************************
      DATA DIVISION.
     *_____
      FILE SECTION.
      FD  display-file.
      01  display-record            PIC X(2000).

      FD  user-file.
      01  user-record.
          COPY DD-ALL-FORMATS OF qadspobj
              REPLACING odobnm BY user-profile-name.
     *_____
      WORKING-STORAGE SECTION.
      01  all-display-records.
          02  usrrcd-data.
              COPY DD-USRRCD-O OF dspoqad.
          02  usrctl-i-data.
              COPY DD-USRCTL-I OF dspoqad.
          02  usrctl-o-data.
              COPY DD-USRCTL-O OF dspoqad.
          02  msgrcd-o-data.
              COPY DD-MSGRCD-O OF dspoqad.
          02  msgctl-o-data.
              COPY DD-MSGCTL-O OF dspoqad.

      01  display-indicators.
          COPY DD-ALL-FORMATS-INDIC OF dspoqad.
```

continued

Figure 6.1F *Continued*

```
01  work-variables.
    02  api-error-structure.
        03  bytes-provided          PIC 9(9) BINARY
            VALUE 96.
        03  bytes-available         PIC 9(9) BINARY
            VALUE 0.
        03  exception-id            PIC X(7).
        03  FILLER                  PIC X(1).
        03  exception-data          PIC X(80).
    02  api-qualified-output-queue  PIC X(20).
    02  authority-data-structure.
        03  FILLER                  PIC X(19).
        03  object-operational      PIC X(1).
        03  FILLER                  PIC X(2).
        03  data-read               PIC X(1).
        03  data-add                PIC X(1).
        03  data-update             PIC X(1).
        03  data-delete             PIC X(1).
        03  FILLER                  PIC X(54).
        03  data-execute            PIC X(1).
        03  FILLER                  PIC X(12).
    02  command-string              PIC X(3000).
    02  display-i-o-feedback.
        03  FILLER                  PIC X(146).
        03  key-pressed             PIC X(1).
        03  FILLER                  PIC X(6).
        03  subfile-page-rrn        PIC 9(4) BINARY.
    02  error-found-switch          PIC X(1).
        88  error-found             VALUE "Y".
        88  no-error-found          VALUE "N".
    02  exit-program-switch         PIC X(1).
        88  exit-program            VALUE "Y".
        88  stay-in-program         VALUE "N".
    02  more-records-switch         PIC X(1).
        88  more-records            VALUE "Y".
        88  no-more-records         VALUE "N".
    02  object-data-structure.
        03  FILLER                  PIC X(52).
        03  object-owner            PIC X(10).
        03  FILLER                  PIC X(28).
    02  outq-data-structure.
        03  FILLER                  PIC X(38).
        03  dspdta-setting          PIC X(10).
        03  FILLER                  PIC X(4).
        03  oprctl-setting          PIC X(10).
        03  FILLER                  PIC X(20).
        03  autchk-setting          PIC X(10).
        03  FILLER                  PIC X(110).
    02  reload-subfile-switch       PIC X(1).
        88  reload-subfile          VALUE "Y".
        88  do-not-reload-subfile   VALUE "N".
    02  rrn-high                    PIC S9(5) PACKED-DECIMAL.
    02  rrn-low                     LIKE rrn-high.
    02  rrn-total                   LIKE rrn-high.
    02  subfile-record-number       PIC 9(4) PACKED-DECIMAL.
```

continued

Figure 6.1F Continued

```
    02  user-data-structure.
        03  FILLER              PIC X(28).
        03  all-object          PIC X(1).
        03  FILLER              PIC X(1).
        03  job-control         PIC X(1).
        03  spool-control       PIC X(1).
        03  FILLER              PIC X(51).
    02  user-file-rrn           PIC 9(11) PACKED-DECIMAL.

01  constants.
    02  authority-api-format    PIC X(8)
        VALUE "USRA0100".
    02  authority-structure-length PIC 9(9) BINARY
        VALUE 93.
    02  command-string-length   PIC 9(10)V9(5) PACKED-DECIMAL
        VALUE 3000.
    02  F3-pressed              PIC X(1)
        VALUE X"33".
    02  F7-pressed              PIC X(1)
        VALUE X"37".
    02  F8-pressed              PIC X(1)
        VALUE X"38".
    02  F9-pressed              PIC X(1)
        VALUE X"39".
    02  F12-pressed             PIC X(1)
        VALUE X"3C".
    02  Enter-pressed           PIC X(1)
        VALUE X"F1".
    02  ind-off                 PIC 1
        VALUE B"0".
    02  ind-on                  PIC 1
        VALUE B"1".
    02  message-key             PIC X(4)
        VALUE SPACES.
    02  messages-to-remove      PIC X(10)
        VALUE "*ALL".
    02  program-queue-name      PIC X(10)
        VALUE "*".
    02  program-stack-counter   PIC 9(9) BINARY
        VALUE 0.
    02  no-value                PIC X(1)
        VALUE "N".
    02  object-api-format       PIC X(8)
        VALUE "OBJD0100".
    02  object-structure-length PIC 9(9) BINARY
        VALUE 90.
    02  output-queue-object-type PIC X(10)
        VALUE "*OUTQ".
    02  outq-api-format         PIC X(8)
        VALUE "OUTQ0100".
    02  outq-structure-length   PIC 9(9) BINARY
        VALUE 206.
    02  user-api-format         PIC X(8)
        VALUE "USRI0200".
```

continued

FIGURE 6.1F CONTINUED

```cobol
    02  user-structure-length       PIC 9(9) BINARY
        VALUE 83.
    02  yes-value                   PIC X(1)
        VALUE "Y".
*
 LINKAGE SECTION.
 01  output-queue-parm              PIC X(10).
 01  output-queue-library-parm      PIC X(10).

 ********************************************************************
 PROCEDURE DIVISION USING output-queue-parm
                          output-queue-library-parm.
*
 mainline.
     PERFORM initialize-program.
     PERFORM process-program.
     PERFORM terminate-program.
     GOBACK.
*
 binary-search.
     COMPUTE subfile-record-number
        = ( rrn-high + rrn-low ) / 2.
     READ SUBFILE display-file
        INTO usrrcd
        FORMAT IS "USRRCD"
     END-READ.
     IF user-profile OF usrrcd < position-to-user OF usrctl-i
        MOVE subfile-record-number TO rrn-low
     ELSE
        MOVE subfile-record-number TO rrn-high
     END-IF.
*
 calculate-column-yes-values.
     IF job-control        = yes-value AND
        oprctl-setting     = "*YES"    OR
        object-operational = yes-value AND
        data-read          = yes-value AND
        data-add           = yes-value AND
        data-update        = yes-value AND
        data-delete        = yes-value AND
        data-execute       = yes-value THEN
        MOVE yes-value TO start-prtwtr OF usrrcd
     END-IF.

     IF data-read       = yes-value OR
        oprctl-setting = "*YES"     AND
        job-control     = yes-value THEN
        MOVE yes-value TO add-to-outq      OF usrrcd
                          work-with-outq   OF usrrcd
     END-IF.
```

continued

FIGURE 6.1F *Continued*

```
IF autchk-setting     = "*DTAAUT"          AND
   object-operational = yes-value          AND
   data-read          = yes-value          AND
   data-add           = yes-value          AND
   data-update        = yes-value          AND
   data-delete        = yes-value          AND
   data-execute       = yes-value          OR
   autchk-setting     = "*OWNER"           AND
   object-owner       = user-profile-name  OR
   oprctl-setting     = "*YES"             AND
   job-control        = yes-value          THEN
     MOVE yes-value TO change-outq OF usrrcd
END-IF.

IF dspdta-setting     = "*YES"             AND
   data-read          = yes-value          OR
   dspdta-setting     = "*NO"              AND
   autchk-setting     = "*DTAAUT"          AND
   object-operational = yes-value          AND
   data-read          = yes-value          AND
   data-add           = yes-value          AND
   data-update        = yes-value          AND
   data-delete        = yes-value          AND
   data-execute       = yes-value          OR
   dspdta-setting     = "*NO"              AND
   autchk-setting     = "*OWNER"           AND
   object-owner       = user-profile-name  OR
   dspdta-setting     = "*YES"             AND
   oprctl-setting     = "*YES"             AND
   job-control        = yes-value          OR
   dspdta-setting     = "*NO"              AND
   oprctl-setting     = "*YES"             AND
   job-control        = yes-value          OR
   dspdta-setting     = "*OWNER"           THEN
     MOVE yes-value TO display-splf OF usrrcd
END-IF.

IF autchk-setting     = "*DTAAUT"          AND
   object-operational = yes-value          AND
   data-read          = yes-value          AND
   data-add           = yes-value          AND
   data-update        = yes-value          AND
   data-delete        = yes-value          AND
   data-execute       = yes-value          OR
   autchk-setting     = "*OWNER"           AND
   object-owner       = user-profile-name  OR
   oprctl-setting     = "*YES"             AND
   job-control        = yes-value          THEN
     MOVE yes-value TO change-splf-attrib OF usrrcd
END-IF.
```

*―――――――――――――――――

continued

FIGURE 6.1F CONTINUED

```
calculate-subfile-record.
    MOVE user-profile-name TO user-profile OF usrrcd.
    PERFORM get-special-authorization.
    IF all-object    = yes-value OR
       spool-control = yes-value THEN
        MOVE yes-value TO start-prtwtr        OF usrrcd
                         add-to-outq          OF usrrcd
                         work-with-outq       OF usrrcd
                         change-outq          OF usrrcd
                         display-splf         OF usrrcd
                         change-splf-attrib   OF usrrcd
    ELSE
        MOVE no-value  TO start-prtwtr        OF usrrcd
                         add-to-outq          OF usrrcd
                         work-with-outq       OF usrrcd
                         change-outq          OF usrrcd
                         display-splf         OF usrrcd
                         change-splf-attrib   OF usrrcd
    PERFORM get-private-authorization
    PERFORM calculate-column-yes-values
    END-IF.
*_____
change-object-owner.
    INITIALIZE command-string.
    STRING "?CHGOBJOWN ?*OBJ("          DELIMITED BY SIZE
           output-queue-library-parm    DELIMITED BY SPACE
           "/"                          DELIMITED BY SIZE
           output-queue-parm            DELIMITED BY SPACE
           ") ?*OBJTYPE(*OUTQ) ??NEWOWN() ??CUROWNAUT()"
                                        DELIMITED BY SIZE
        INTO command-string
    END-STRING.
    CALL "DSPOQAC1" USING command-string
                          command-string-length
                          error-found-switch.
    IF no-error-found THEN
       PERFORM load-subfile
    END-IF.
*_____
change-output-queue.
    INITIALIZE command-string.
    STRING "?CHGOUTQ ?*OUTQ("           DELIMITED BY SIZE
           output-queue-library-parm    DELIMITED BY SPACE
           "/"                          DELIMITED BY SIZE
           output-queue-parm            DELIMITED BY SPACE
           ") ??DSPDTA("                DELIMITED BY SIZE
           dspdta-setting               DELIMITED BY SPACE
           ") ??AUTCHK("                DELIMITED BY SIZE
           autchk-setting               DELIMITED BY SPACE
           ") ??OPRCTL("                DELIMITED BY SIZE
           oprctl-setting               DELIMITED BY SPACE
           ")"                          DELIMITED BY SIZE
        INTO command-string
    END-STRING.
```

continued

FIGURE 6.1F CONTINUED

```
    CALL "DSPOQAC1" USING command-string
                          command-string-length
                          error-found-switch.
    IF no-error-found THEN
       PERFORM load-subfile
    END-IF.
*_____
 change-user-profile.
    INITIALIZE command-string.
    STRING "?CHGUSRPRF ?*USRPRF("   DELIMITED BY SIZE
           user-profile OF usrrcd   DELIMITED BY SPACE
           ")"                      DELIMITED BY SIZE
      INTO command-string
    END-STRING.
    CALL "DSPOQAC1" USING command-string
                          command-string-length
                          error-found-switch.
    IF no-error-found THEN
       SET reload-subfile TO TRUE
    END-IF.
    PERFORM erase-option.
*_____
 clear-program-queue.
    CALL "QMHRMVPM" USING program-queue-name
                          program-stack-counter
                          message-key
                          messages-to-remove
                          api-error-structure.
*_____
 display-information.
    WRITE display-record
       FORMAT IS "FKEYS"
    END-WRITE.
    WRITE display-record
       FROM msgctl-o
       FORMAT IS "MSGCTL"
    END-WRITE.
    WRITE display-record
       FROM usrctl-o
       FORMAT IS "USRCTL"
       INDICATORS ARE usrctl-o-indic
    END-WRITE.
    READ display-file
       INTO usrctl-i
       FORMAT IS "USRCTL"
    END-READ.

    ACCEPT display-i-o-feedback
       FROM file-i-o-feedback
       FOR  display-file.
    PERFORM clear-program-queue.
    EVALUATE TRUE
       WHEN key-pressed = F3-pressed OR
            key-pressed = F12-pressed
            SET exit-program TO TRUE
```

continued

FIGURE 6.1F CONTINUED

```
        WHEN key-pressed = F7-pressed
            PERFORM change-output-queue
        WHEN key-pressed = F8-pressed
            PERFORM change-object-owner
        WHEN key-pressed = F9-pressed
            PERFORM display-object-authority
        WHEN key-pressed = Enter-pressed
            PERFORM process-Enter-key
        WHEN OTHER
            CONTINUE
    END-EVALUATE.
*_____
 display-object-authority.
    INITIALIZE command-string.
    STRING "?DSPOBJAUT ?*OBJ("        DELIMITED BY SIZE
           output-queue-library-parm  DELIMITED BY SPACE
           "/"                        DELIMITED BY SIZE
           output-queue-parm          DELIMITED BY SPACE
           ") ?*OBJTYPE(*OUTQ)"       DELIMITED BY SIZE
        INTO command-string
    END-STRING.
    CALL "DSPOQAC1" USING command-string
                          command-string-length
                          error-found-switch.
*_____
 display-user-profile.
    INITIALIZE command-string.
    STRING "?DSPUSRPRF ?*USRPRF(" DELIMITED BY SIZE
           user-profile OF usrrcd DELIMITED BY SPACE
           ")"                    DELIMITED BY SIZE
        INTO command-string
    END-STRING.
    CALL "DSPOQAC1" USING command-string
                          command-string-length
                          error-found-switch.
    PERFORM erase-option.
*_____
 erase-option.
    MOVE saved-record-number OF usrrcd TO subfile-record-number.
    READ SUBFILE display-file
        INTO usrrcd
        FORMAT IS "USRRCD"
    END-READ.
    MOVE SPACES TO option-number OF usrrcd.
    REWRITE SUBFILE display-record
        FROM usrrcd
        FORMAT IS "USRRCD"
    END-REWRITE.
*_____
```

continued

FIGURE 6.1F CONTINUED

```
 execute-option.
     EVALUATE TRUE
         WHEN option-number OF usrrcd = "2 " OR
              option-number OF usrrcd = " 2"
              PERFORM change-user-profile
         WHEN option-number OF usrrcd = "5 " OR
              option-number OF usrrcd = " 5"
              PERFORM display-user-profile
         WHEN option-number OF usrrcd = "15"
              PERFORM grant-object-authority
         WHEN option-number OF usrrcd = "16"
              PERFORM revoke-object-authority
         WHEN OTHER
              CONTINUE
     END-EVALUATE.
*_____
 find-options-selected.
     SET do-not-reload-subfile TO TRUE.
     SET more-records TO TRUE.
     PERFORM UNTIL no-more-records
         READ SUBFILE display-file NEXT MODIFIED
             INTO usrrcd
             FORMAT IS "USRRCD"
             AT END
                 SET no-more-records TO TRUE
             NOT AT END
                 PERFORM execute-option
         END-READ
     END-PERFORM.
     IF reload-subfile THEN
         PERFORM load-subfile
     END-IF.
*_____
 get-output-queue-info.
     CALL "QSPROUTQ" USING outq-data-structure
                           outq-structure-length
                           outq-api-format
                           api-qualified-output-queue
                           api-error-structure.
*_____
 get-output-queue-owner.
     CALL "QUSROBJD" USING object-data-structure
                           object-structure-length
                           object-api-format
                           api-qualified-output-queue
                           output-queue-object-type
                           api-error-structure.
*_____
 get-private-authorization.
     CALL "QSYRUSRA" USING authority-data-structure
                           authority-structure-length
                           authority-api-format
                           user-profile-name
                           api-qualified-output-queue
                           output-queue-object-type
                           api-error-structure.
*_____
```

continued

FIGURE 6.1F CONTINUED

```
get-special-authorization.
    CALL "QSYRUSRI" USING user-data-structure
                          user-structure-length
                          user-api-format
                          user-profile-name
                          api-error-structure.
*_____
grant-object-authority.
    INITIALIZE command-string.
    STRING "?GRTOBJAUT ?*OBJ("          DELIMITED BY SIZE
           output-queue-library-parm    DELIMITED BY SPACE
           "/"                          DELIMITED BY SIZE
           output-queue-parm            DELIMITED BY SPACE
           ") ?*OBJTYPE(*OUTQ) ?*USER(" DELIMITED BY SIZE
           user-profile OF usrrcd       DELIMITED BY SPACE
           ")"                          DELIMITED BY SIZE
       INTO command-string
    END-STRING.
    CALL "DSPOQAC1" USING command-string
                          command-string-length
                          error-found-switch.
    IF no-error-found THEN
       SET reload-subfile TO TRUE
    END-IF.
*_____
initialize-program.
    OPEN INPUT user-file
         I-O   display-file.
    INITIALIZE work-variables
               all-display-records
               display-indicators.
    STRING output-queue-library-parm DELIMITED BY SPACE
           "/"                       DELIMITED BY SIZE
           output-queue-parm         DELIMITED BY SIZE
       INTO qual-output-queue OF usrctl-o
    END-STRING.
    STRING output-queue-parm         DELIMITED BY SIZE
           output-queue-library-parm DELIMITED BY SIZE
       INTO api-qualified-output-queue
    END-STRING.
    MOVE program-queue-name TO pgmq OF msgrcd
                               pgmq OF msgctl-o.
    MOVE ind-off TO in82 OF msgctl-o-indic.

    PERFORM get-output-queue-owner.

    MOVE 1 TO position-subfile-at-record OF usrctl-o.
    PERFORM load-subfile.
*_____
load-subfile.
    MOVE ind-on  TO in80 OF usrctl-o-indic.
    MOVE ind-off TO in81 OF usrctl-o-indic.
    WRITE display-record
       FORMAT IS "USRCTL"
       INDICATORS ARE usrctl-o-indic
    END-WRITE.
```

continued

FIGURE 6.1F CONTINUED

```
    PERFORM get-output-queue-owner.
    PERFORM get-output-queue-info.

    SET more-records TO TRUE.
    MOVE 1 TO user-file-rrn.
    MOVE 0 TO subfile-record-number
             rrn-total.
    PERFORM read-one-record UNTIL no-more-records.
    IF subfile-record-number > 0 THEN
       MOVE ind-off TO in80 OF usrctl-o-indic
    ELSE
       MOVE ind-on  TO in80 OF usrctl-o-indic
    END-IF.
*_____
 process-Enter-key.
    PERFORM find-options-selected.
    IF position-to-user OF usrctl-i NOT = SPACES THEN
       PERFORM reposition-subfile
    END-IF.
*_____
 process-program.
    SET stay-in-program TO TRUE.
    PERFORM display-information UNTIL exit-program.
*_____
 read-one-record.
    READ user-file
       INVALID KEY
          SET no-more-records TO TRUE
       NOT INVALID KEY
          PERFORM calculate-subfile-record
          PERFORM write-subfile-record
          ADD 1 TO user-file-rrn
    END-READ.
*_____
 reposition-subfile.
    MOVE 1         TO rrn-low.
    MOVE rrn-total TO rrn-high.
    PERFORM binary-search
       UNTIL rrn-high - rrn-low <= 1.
    IF subfile-record-number < 1 THEN
       MOVE 1 TO subfile-record-number
    ELSE
       IF subfile-record-number > rrn-total THEN
          MOVE rrn-total TO subfile-record-number
       END-IF
    END-IF.
    MOVE subfile-record-number TO
         position-subfile-at-record OF usrctl-o.
*_____
 revoke-object-authority.
    INITIALIZE command-string.
    STRING "?RVKOBJAUT ?*OBJ("          DELIMITED BY SIZE
           output-queue-library-parm    DELIMITED BY SPACE
           "/"                          DELIMITED BY SIZE
```

continued

FIGURE 6.1F CONTINUED

```
            output-queue-parm              DELIMITED BY SPACE
            ") ?*OBJTYPE(*OUTQ) ?*USER("   DELIMITED BY SIZE
            user-profile OF usrrcd         DELIMITED BY SPACE
            ")"                            DELIMITED BY SIZE
      INTO command-string
   END-STRING.
   CALL "DSPOQAC1" USING command-string
                         command-string-length
                         error-found-switch.
   IF no-error-found THEN
      SET reload-subfile TO TRUE
   END-IF.
*_____
terminate-program.
   CLOSE user-file
         display-file.
*_____
write-subfile-record.
   ADD 1 TO subfile-record-number
           rrn-total.
   MOVE subfile-record-number TO saved-record-number OF usrrcd.
   WRITE SUBFILE display-record
      FROM usrrcd
      FORMAT IS "USRRCD"
   END-WRITE.
```

FIGURE 6.1G
CL Program DSPOQAC1

```
/* From "Are Your Output Queues Secure?,"                        */
/* NEWS 3X/400, August 1994                                      */
/*                                                               */
/* COPYRIGHT (c) 1994 Duke Communications                        */
/* International                                                 */

PGM   (                                                          +
         &cmd         /* Command string requested */             +
         &cmdlen      /* Command string length    */             +
         &errcde      /* Error code               */             +
      )

   DCL  &cmd     *CHAR   3000
   DCL  &cmdlen  *DEC    ( 15 5 )
   DCL  &errcde  *CHAR   1

   /*                                                            +
     | Execute the command requested from the interactive program. +
     | If the command ends in error or is canceled by the user (by +
     | pressing F3 or F12), send an error code of 'Y'; otherwise,  +
     | send an error code of 'N'.                                  +
   */
   CHGVAR  &errcde  'N'
   CALL   qcmdexc  ( &cmd &cmdlen )   MONMSG  cpf0000  EXEC( DO )
      CHGVAR  &errcde  'Y'
   ENDDO

   MOVPGMMSG  MSGTYPE( *ALL )
   MONMSG  cpf0000

ENDPGM
```

Helpful Tools

You can find the PRTQAUT (Print Queue Authority Report) security tool on the SECTOOLS and SECBATCH menus. This utility prints the security settings for both output queues and job queues on your system. The full report lists all the queues that meet the selection criteria. This utility also provides a report that lists the changes since the last time you ran the report and any new output or job queues that have been added in the interim.

Operations Navigator

To manage spooled files through Operations Navigator, click on the name of your AS/400 and choose Basic Operations, Printer output.

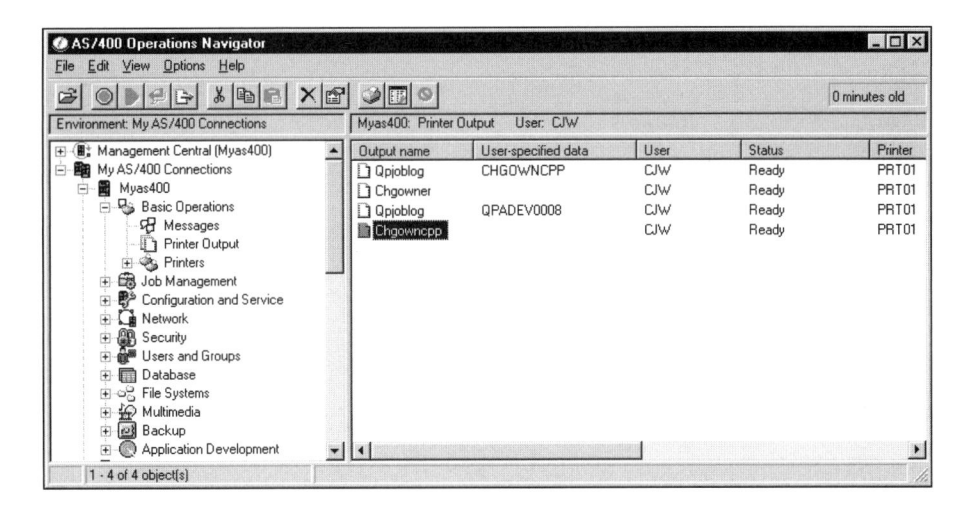

Chapter 7
Network Security

What AS/400 today doesn't exist in some form of network (even if the network consists only of attached PCs)? Network security must be part of your security plan and implementation. By definition, a network lets users access your AS/400 who don't have a direct connection to it. Many times, attachment is not by way of terminal emulation. You might have program-to-program communications, Distributed Data Management (DDM) communications, Open Database Connectivity (ODBC), and file transfer and download requests through Client Access, for example. In most of these cases, users are accessing your AS/400 data and programs via another program or a job running on another system that doesn't have the menu-based security safeguards that are part of workstation (5250) emulation.

To understand the security problems and solutions in a networked environment, you must understand a variety of AS/400 concepts, including physical network security, network configuration security and network security attributes, and DDM, Client Access, and ODBC security. (We cover communications-configuration security, including SNA and TCP/IP, dial-up security, and data encryption, in Chapter 8.) Although not all types of security are appropriate in every network environment, you need to understand those that fit your situation so you can apply the level of security your organization needs.

Physical Security

Physical network security helps prevent inadvertent damage as well as intentional abuse and misuse. If you don't physically secure your network, inevitably a janitor or an employee's child will trip over a wire and possibly sustain personal injury as well as damage your equipment. Some parts of a network can't be physically secured (e.g., phone lines, vendor-controlled switch boxes); however, by taking some practical, commonsense steps, you can achieve an acceptable level of physical security.

To begin, you should put all communications equipment together in a single location at each network site. If you operate a host computer that supports remote access from many locations, place all host communications equipment (e.g., modems, protocol converters, cables, vendor line blocks) in one locked cabinet or closet in an area with no traffic except that necessary to maintain the equipment.

Similar precautions are also necessary — and often even more important — at remote sites. Many remote sites that dial in to the host have a small remote controller or system but don't have IT personnel on site. In such cases, you have to rely on the people at the site to maintain the communications equipment securely. You can prevent many accidents with a little planning and by moving equipment to a safe, secure location.

If your installation uses communications lines between buildings on the same property, these lines should be secured underground where possible to prevent mishaps caused by natural forces or carelessness on the part of employees or service providers.

Network Configuration

When your AS/400 is installed, it autoconfigures the console and internal system features. After installation, however, you should turn off the autoconfiguration option except while you're physically adding devices to the system. It's important that you control how physical devices are attached to your system.

To turn off autoconfiguration, change system value QAUTOCFG to 0:

```
CHGSYSVAL QAUTOCFG VALUE('0')
```

(If you're not sure what the current value is, you can use the DSPSYSVAL (Display System Value) command to display it.)

> **Security Recommendation**
> Restrict authority to the AS/400 configuration commands to the IT person responsible for creating and maintaining the network configuration.

Perhaps even more important in today's networked environment, where most devices are virtual devices, is the QAUTOVRT system value. QAUTOVRT controls the automatic creation of virtual devices. After you have enough virtual devices to meet your needs, you should set the value to 0 so that the system won't automatically create any more virtual devices. Alternatively, set QAUTOVRT to the number of virtual devices you think you need to do business. Don't give an intruder the chance to overload your system by creating thousands of virtual devices.

```
CHGSYSVAL QAUTOVRT VALUE('0')
```

*IOSYSCFG special authority is required to configure all lines, controllers, and devices. After disabling the QAUTOCFG system value, you should also restrict who has *IOSYSCFG special authority. The objective is to ensure that IT has control over all additions and changes to your system configuration.

Network Security Attributes

The system stores network-related values in network attributes, a collection of data that drives the AS/400's original, high-level networking functions. Together, the network attributes determine whether — and how — your system responds to requests of any kind (e.g., PC Support, DDM, network job requests) from another system.

Three network attributes relate specifically to security:

JOBACN	Job Action
PCSACC	PC Support Access
DDMACC	DDM Access

You can use the DSPNETA (Display Network Attributes) command to view the values for these attributes. Any user profile that has *ALLOBJ and *SECADM special authority can use the CHGNETA (Change Network Attributes) command to modify the network attribute values. Let's look at each attribute and its function.

JOBACN

JOBACN determines how your AS/400 responds to incoming job streams from other systems in your network. This network attribute can have one of three values: *REJECT, *FILE, or *SEARCH.

*REJECT causes the target system to reject the input job stream. When a job is rejected, the system sends a message to both the originating user profile and the intended recipient stating that the input stream was rejected.

*FILE causes the system to file the input job stream in the recipient's network file queue. The intended recipient (a user profile) can display the job stream, cancel it, receive it into a database file, or submit it to a job queue for processing. Again, the system sends a message to the sender and receiver notifying them that the incoming stream was filed.

*SEARCH instructs the system to search the network job action table for information about how to control the incoming job stream. The network job action table holds information about how the system is to handle specific requests. Each record in the table consists of the sender's ID, the action the local system is to take for that sender's requests, the user profile to use when submitting the job if the action desired is *SUBMIT, and the job queue to use for submitting the job. (For detailed information about how to use the network job action table, see the IBM manual *OS/400 SNA Distribution Services V4R4*, SC41-5410.)

Security Recommendation

Give the JOBACN attribute a value of *REJECT unless the remote system uses System Network Architecture Distribution Services (SNADS) to submit jobs to your system. If SNADS is used, specify a value of *SEARCH to explicitly control the job actions.

PCSACC

PCSACC determines how the local system processes requests from PCs that use PC Support or from Original Client Access clients. PCSACC can have one of four values: *REJECT, *REGFAC, *OBJAUT, or the name of an exit program.

This network attribute has lost its importance because it has no effect whatsoever on any current client. In other words, if you're using Client Access Express or Client Access's optimized clients (Client Access for Windows 95/NT, Client Access Enhanced for Windows 3.1, Client Access for Windows 3.1, or Client Access Optimized for OS/2), the system ignores this network attribute.

If you need to define exit programs for Client Access Express or Client Access Optimized clients, you must do so through the registration facility. These clients don't call programs you specify in the PCSACC parameter. You don't need to specify *REGFAC for the

PCSACC parameter to have Client Access Express or Optimized clients call programs defined in the registration facility.

For a discussion of how to use exit programs to enhance network security, see "Using Exit Points" later in this chapter. For more information about the use of exit programs for Client Access servers, see the IBM manual *Client Access Express Host Servers V4R4M0* (SC41-5740).

> **Security Recommendation**
> Set the PSACC network attribute to *REJECT to cause the target system to reject all PC Support requests.

DDMACC

DDMACC determines how your system processes DDM requests from remote systems. The local system receives a DDM request when a remote system attempts to access data using a file, data area, or data queue whose type is *DDM.

The three possible values for the DDMACC attribute are *REJECT, *OBJAUT, or the name of an exit program. We discuss these values in detail in the section "System-Related Security Attributes" a little later in this chapter.

> **Security Recommendation**
> For local systems that explicitly control object authority, use a value of *OBJAUT for the DDMACC attribute. For systems on which object authority is minimal, you might need a user-written exit program to maintain explicit control of DDM requests.

DDM Security

DDM security is often perceived as a puzzle of intertwining system values, numerous object parameters, and confusing interrelationships. As IBM presents it, it can be perplexing, and people who don't consider jigsaw puzzles fun might conclude that implementing DDM security is too much trouble. But you can master the topic with an organized approach and a grasp of a handful of basic concepts.

Visualizing the final picture always helps when you begin putting a puzzle together. (That's why the picture is usually on the outside of the box, right?) A security solution is no different. Figure 7.1 illustrates the final picture for a simple DDM environment. DDM identifies one system as the requester — the source system upon which DDM requests originate. The target system is the one on which the database file exists (when DDM is used for data retrieval or update) or on which the requested remote CL command is executed (when the source system executes a SBMRMTCMD (Submit Remote Command) command).

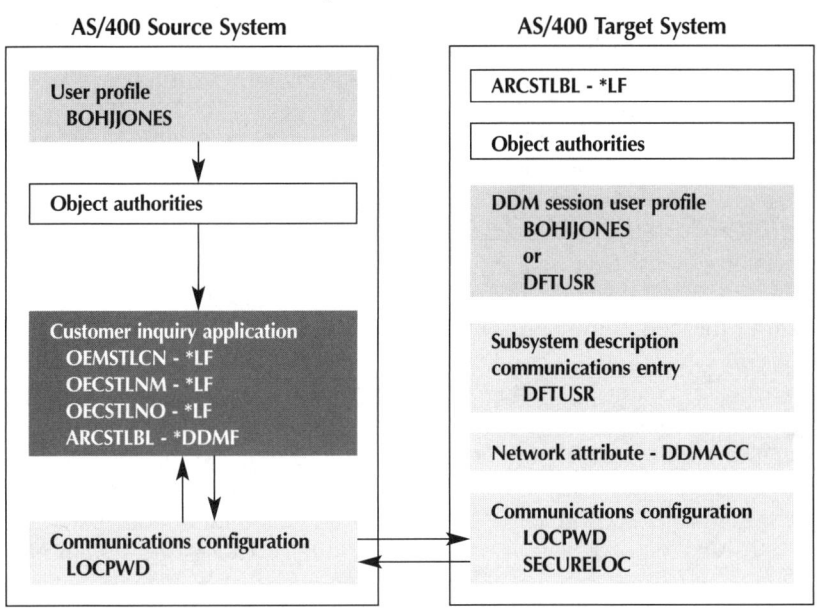

FIGURE 7.1
A Simple DDM Environment

AS/400 Source System

- User profile: BOHJJONES
- Object authorities
- Customer inquiry application
  - OEMSTLCN - *LF
  - OECSTLNM - *LF
  - OECSTLNO - *LF
  - ARCSTLBL - *DDMF
- Communications configuration: LOCPWD

AS/400 Target System

- ARCSTLBL - *LF
- Object authorities
- DDM session user profile: BOHJJONES or DFTUSR
- Subsystem description communications entry: DFTUSR
- Network attribute - DDMACC
- Communications configuration: LOCPWD, SECURELOC

In Figure 7.1, user BOHJJONES initiates a DDM request from the source system via a customer inquiry application. The application uses a local DDM file called ARCSTLBL to query an accounts-receivable customer file of the same name that resides on the target system. As the figure shows, many system resources come into play in a DDM transaction.

First, the user must be authorized to the local application and files, including the local DDM file, and to the APPC device descriptions — both source and target. When the application opens the DDM file, the operating system establishes a DDM conversation with the target system via communications. The source and target systems might require a location password (LOCPWD) to establish the communications session.

Once the session is established (which can occur either at the time of the DDM request or in advance, via a previous connection for another DDM request, passthrough, or an APPC request), the target system checks its SECURELOC communications configuration parameter to determine whether to verify the user profile. The target system also checks the DDMACC network attribute to verify that DDM requests are accepted. Depending upon the SECURELOC value, the target system then associates the DDM job either with a default user profile defined as part of a communications entry on the subsystem description or with a target-system user profile having the same name as the source-system user profile. The profile must also have authority to the system resources needed to satisfy the DDM request.

When proper object authorities exist for the DDM user, the database file on the target system is opened, and the source system application is notified. Finally, the target system verifies that the user profile has the data authorities (e.g., read, add, update, delete) needed to accomplish the task.

When you implement DDM security, it helps to separate the attributes into categories — kind of like separating all the corner and border puzzle pieces from the rest and then sorting both groups by color or background. The DDM attributes fall into three major groups: system-, user profile-, and object authorization-related attributes.

System-Related Security Attributes

System-level security attributes (the light gray boxes in Figure 7.1) constitute one group of DDM puzzle pieces. Before we discuss these attributes, we should mention one piece purposely left off the figure: the QSECURITY system value, which determines the security level under which your AS/400 runs.

You can achieve secure DDM communications at level 20, but object authorities could be compromised if the target user profile has level 20's default *ALLOBJ special authority. The level of DDM security we discuss henceforth can be established with confidence only under security level 30, 40, or 50.

The first system-level security piece is the LOCPWD communications parameter. On the AS/400, LOCPWD has a default value of *NONE, which causes the system to use a null password (in effect ignoring the password requirement). You can also specify a password (in hexadecimal) of up to eight characters. By designating a password, you require the source system to use the correct location password to connect to the target system.

You specify the LOCPWD parameter value on both the source and target systems as part of the remote configuration list entry (in an APPN environment) or as part of the APPC device description (in a non-APPN environment). If you use APPC, you can use the CRTDEVAPPC (Create Device Description (APPC)) or CHGDEVAPPC (Change Device Description (APPC)) command to set both the LOCPWD and the SECURELOC attributes. In an APPN environment, you first execute the CRTCFGL (Create Configuration List) command to create the QAPPNRMT configuration list, then you use elements 6 and 7 of the APPNRMTE parameter on the ADDCFGLE (Add Configuration List Entries) or CHGCFGLE (Change Configuration List Entries) command to specify the LOCPWD and SECURELOC attribute values.

The LOCPWD parameter is particularly important to security in X.25 networks and switched-line communications, which open your system to dial-up access from a variety of sources. However, if your network is large and any-to-any connectivity is the goal, you might need to have numerous location passwords. In this situation, using the null password default eliminates the headaches, although it also eliminates this line of security.

The CHGNETA command controls the second system-level security piece, the DDMACC network attribute. The value of DDMACC on the target system determines how the target system processes DDM requests. You have three choices for this attribute: *REJECT, *OBJAUT, and the name of a user-written exit program.

*REJECT causes the system to reject all DDM requests from all source systems. This value doesn't affect the system's ability to act as a source system. (Because Distributed Relational Database Architecture, or DRDA, runs over DDM, specifying *REJECT deactivates DRDA as well.)

The *OBJAUT default lets DDM requests be processed in accordance with the system's object authorities; that is, the target system governs whether the user profile associated with the DDM request has authority to the objects being accessed.

Alternatively, you can specify the name of a user-written exit program, which must exist on the target system. In this case, the exit program processes DDM requests and determines the functions and objects to which to allow access. Such a program lets you identify specific user profiles and the DDM functions authorized for each profile, as long as the target system's object authorities — which still apply, as they do with the *OBJAUT value — provide access.

An exit program is a good choice when few or no object authorities are implemented on the target system — a common situation when menu- or application-based security is the primary form of authorization (i.e., users are restricted only by the menu options they can access or by something internal to the application, such as an authority table). On such systems, a lack of object security might grant too much authority to the DDM target user profile. An exit program lets you provide an extra measure of detailed, lower-level security tailored specifically to the environment. "Writing a DDM User Exit Program" later in this chapter provides a sample exit program and more information about how to write one.

User-Profile–Related Security Attributes

The second category of DDM security attributes relates to the target-system user profile used for the DDM session. When a user initiates a DDM conversation with a target system, which user profile is associated with the DDM job on the target system? On the AS/400, the answer is determined by the SECURELOC parameter, which is on the device description (for APPC devices) or on the remote configuration list entry (in an APPN environment). Figure 7.1 shows the user-profile-related security pieces in dark gray.

The SECURELOC parameter specifies whether the target system "trusts" the source system. If it does, the target system lets the source system verify the user profile and password and send an "already verified" indicator with the DDM request. If the source system is secure (i.e., it rigorously verifies the user profile and password), you might consider using a value of SECURELOC(*YES). In this case, the target AS/400 uses the name of the source-system profile to accomplish the work. A user profile of the same name must exist on the target system; however, the password can be different, because passwords aren't revalidated.

Alternatively, you can use the value of SECURELOC(*VFYENCPWD). If you use this value, a user profile with the same name and the same password must exist on the target system. Beginning in V4R2, if this profile's password is expired, the request fails.

If you allow source-system user verification, be sure that the only source-system user profiles duplicated on the target system are those that require target-system access through

DDM, passthrough, or other communications functions you use. Also, limit the authority of each target-system profile to the required task.

Yet another option is to use SECURELOC(*NO) to indicate that source-system verification is not allowed (i.e., the target system must verify the user profile independently of the source system). In this case, the target system runs the DDM job under the default user profile specified in the communications entry of the subsystem that handles communications requests. When using SECURELOC(*NO), you can specify the default user profile to be used in the DFTUSR parameter of the ADDCMNE (Add Communications Entry) or CHGCMNE (Change Communications Entry) command. Authorize that user profile to only the data files required by DDM requests. Unless another user profile is specified in the communications entry, DDM requests run under QUSER.

The weakness of SECURELOC(*NO) is that you can't discriminate between remote users. You can specify a default user in the communications entry based only on the RMTLOCNAME parameter or on the mode. Any application (e.g., DDM, APPC) using that remote location name runs under the same default user.

QSECOFR isn't a valid choice for the default user profile, and you shouldn't try to circumvent that system restriction. You should also avoid the other system-supplied profiles (because release-to-release authorization changes might cause problems with established procedures) and profiles that have *ALLOBJ special authority. If you choose the default-user approach, the most secure implementation is to create a unique, properly authorized profile for the purpose of DDM request processing. Authorize this user profile to only the device descriptions used for DDM.

A default user profile might be practical in certain instances, but remember that any shared user profile violates a basic objective of security — the ability to uniquely identify each user on the system. When users share profiles, you can identify only the user profile and the source system responsible for a particular action; the actual user can be difficult or impossible to track down. Remember, too, that all audit entries on the target system are logged under the default user, not the user that makes the request.

Object-Authorization–Related Security Attributes

The third category of DDM security is object authorities (shown in white in Figure 7.1). Object authorization plays an important role on both the source and target system. First, the user must be authorized to the APPC device descriptions on both the source and target systems. Then, on the source system, you can secure the DDM files themselves to allow access to only authorized user profiles. If a source-system user can't open the DDM file, that user can't even access the target system, much less open the remote database file.

On the target system, as long as the DDMACC network attribute is either *OBJAUT or an exit program, the user profile associated with the DDM session must have specific authority to use or manipulate files. If the DDM request is to update a record, for example, the target-system user profile must have *UPD data rights to the physical file in which the data resides. This authority can be granted either specifically to the user profile or via public authority.

The Whole Picture

Now that we've identified the pieces, we can assemble the picture.

On the source system, you must first identify the applications that require DDM and create the DDM files to reference the target database. Use the AUT parameter on the CRTDDMF (Create DDM File) command to set the public authority. We recommend that you put all DDM files into one library. Having all the files together simplifies documentation and management. Then, authorize user profiles to the appropriate DDM files. Grant authority to each DDM file as you would to the actual database file if it were on the local machine.

If you create a DDM file for the purpose of using the SBMRMTCMD command, you should specifically authorize that file to only users who are allowed to issue the remote commands. Because all users who can access the DDM file can execute commands directly on the remote system, an unsecured DDM file is a serious security risk. Another lock you can put on DDM is to secure the device descriptions used. The device descriptions on both the target and source systems are checked before the connection is even made. You can also restrict who has *CHANGE authority to these device descriptions.

Finally, determine whether a location password is required. If it is, enter the password and relay it to the target-system network administrator.

On the target system, the process of implementing security basically works in reverse. If a location password is required, enter the password in the LOCPWD parameter of the device description or the remote configuration list entry, whichever is appropriate for your network environment.

Next, determine the value you want to use for the SECURELOC parameter. Modify this parameter on the device description or the remote configuration list entry, whichever is appropriate. If you use SECURELOC(*YES) or SECURELOC(*VFYENCPWD), you should also modify the DFTUSR parameter of the communications entry that controls DDM. Give this parameter a value of *NONE to prevent DDM requests from being processed by the default user profile. If you use SECURELOC(*NO), make sure the DFTUSR parameter reflects the user profile you want all DDM requests to use.

Then set the DDMACC value. *REJECT is valid only when no DDM requests are to be allowed. The *OBJAUT value is normally sufficient to allow DDM requests to be processed while maintaining normal resource security. Finally, grant the user profile — either the default user profile or the user profiles that access data from the source system — authority to the appropriate database files on the target system.

Figure 7.2 is a flow chart of the DDM authorization process. At each decision point, you implement one of the security measures discussed above. You can use this figure as your guide to a fill-in-the-blanks approach to implementing DDM security.

FIGURE 7.2
The DDM Authorization Process

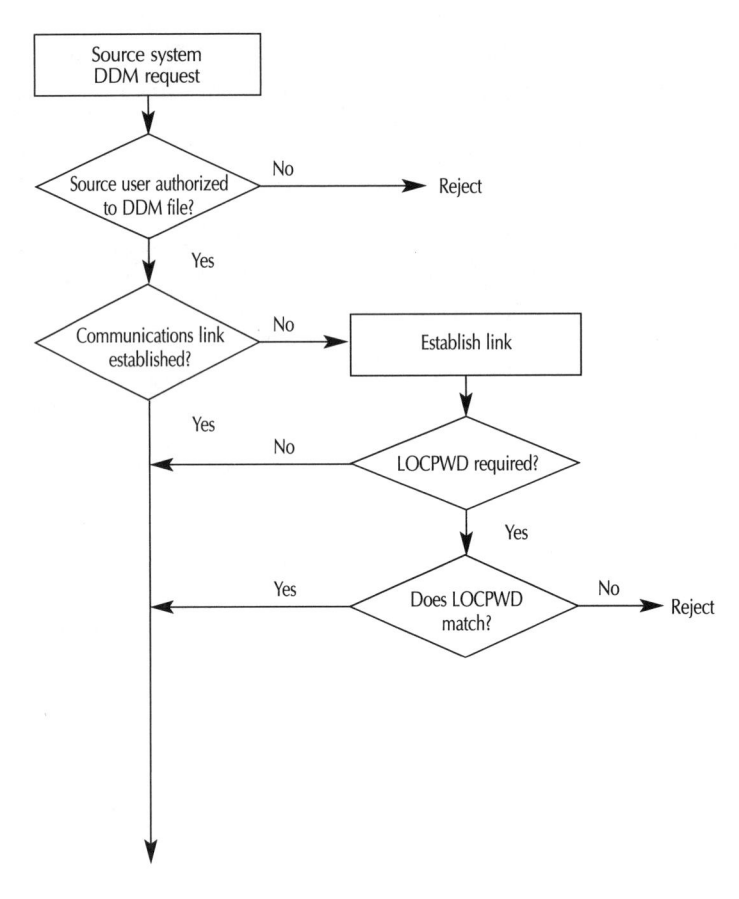

continued

Chapter 7 Network Security 175

FIGURE 7.2 *CONTINUED*

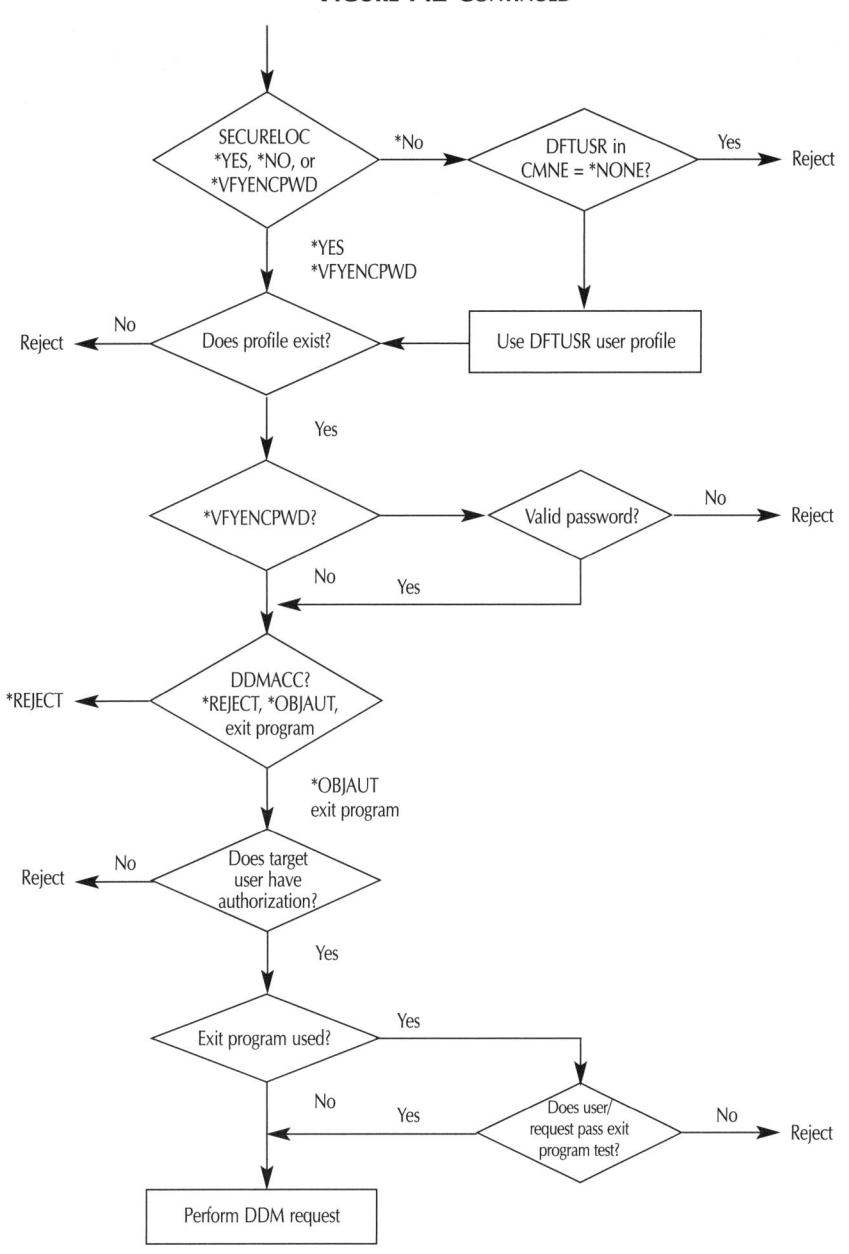

Writing a DDM User Exit Program

One way to have a user-defined exit program control processing is to identify the target-system user profile executing the request and then search a database file to determine whether that user profile is allowed to perform the requested DDM function. Figures 7.3A and 7.3B show a sample user-written DDM exit program and user-created DDM exit database file, respectively.

FIGURE 7.3A
Sample DDM User Exit Program

```
*...1....+....2....+....3....+....4....+....5....+....6....+....7
FDDMEXITFIF  E           K         DISK
 * Array required to bypass field length restriction
E                          IOTH      1921 1
 *
IDDMDTA      DS
I                                          1  10 INUSR
I                                         11  20 INAPP
I                                         21  30 INSUB
I                                         31  40 INOBJ
I                                         41  50 INLIB
I                                         51  60 INMBR
I                                         61  70 INFMT
I                                         71  75 INLGTH
I                                         76  85 INLUN
I                                         86  95 INSRS
I                                         96  96 INIRQ
I                                         97  97 INORQ
I                                         98  98 INURQ
I                                         99  99 INDRQ
I                                        100 111 INAOB
I                                        112 174 INADR
I                                        1752095 IOTH
 *
C           *ENTRY    PLIST
C                     PARM O#RTN      I#RTN   1
C           DDMDTA    PARM            I#DTA2095
 *
C           *LIKE     DEFN I#RTN      O#RTN
 *
C           DDMKEY    KLIST
C                     KFLD            INOBJ
C                     KFLD            INLIB
C                     KFLD            INUSR
C                     KFLD            INAPP
C                     KFLD            INSUB
 *
 * Does request match a valid record in exit file?
C           DDMKEY    CHAINDDMEXITF                21
 *
 * If found, then approve DDM request O#RTN='1'
 *   if not, then disapprove request  O#RTN='0'
C           *IN21     IFEQ *OFF
C                     MOVE '1'        O#RTN
C                     ELSE
C                     MOVE '0'        O#RTN
C                     ENDIF
 * End of Program
C                     MOVE *ON        *INLR
C                     RETRN
```

FIGURE 7.3B
Sample DDM User Exit Database File

```
 *...1....+....2....+....3....+....4....+....5....+....6....+....7

 *=================================================================*
 *   DDM User Exit Program Data File                               *
 *=================================================================*
 *
 A             R DDMEXITR                TEXT('DDM User Exit Record')
 *
 A               DDMUSR        10A       COLHDG('User' 'Name')
 A               DDMAPP        10A       COLHDG('Application' 'Name')
  **                                     VALUE = *DDM
 A               DDMSUB        10A       COLHDG('Function' 'Requested')
  **                                     ADDMBR   DELETE      RENAME
  **                                     CHANGE   EXTRACT     RGZMBR
  **                                     CHGMBR   INITIALIZE  RMVMBR
  **                                     CLEAR    LOAD        RNMMBR
  **                                     COMMAND  LOCK        UNLOAD
  **                                     COPY     MOVE
  **                                     CREATE   OPEN
 A               DDMOBJ        10A       COLHDG('File' 'Name')
  **                                       *N when DDMSUB=COMMAND
  **                                       *SPC when file is
  **                                          document or folder
 A               DDMLIB        10A       COLHDG('Library' 'Name')
  **                                       *N when DDMSUB=COMMAND
  **                                       *SPC when file is folder
 A               DDMMBR        10A       COLHDG('Member' 'Name')
  **                                       *N when N/A
 A               DDMFMT        10A       COLHDG('N/A')
 A               LENGTH         5S 0     COLHDG('Length of' 'next field')
 A               DDMLUN        10A       COLHDG('Remote' 'Logical' 'Unit')
 A               DDMSRS        10A       COLHDG('Remote' 'System' 'Name')
 A               DDMIRQ         1A       COLHDG('Input' 'Request')
 A               DDMORQ         1A       COLHDG('Output' 'Request')
 A               DDMURQ         1A       COLHDG('Update' 'Request')
 A               DDMDRQ         1A       COLHDG('Delete' 'Request')
 A               DDMAOB        12A       COLHDG('Alternate' 'Object' 'Name')
 A               DDMADR        63A       COLHDG('Alternate' 'Directory')
  **
 A             K DDMLIB
 A             K DDMOBJ
 A             K DDMUSR
 A             K DDMAPP
 A             K DDMSUB
```

After you create the exit file, enter the user profiles and the requests you allow each user profile to make. Create the RPG program, and then use the CHGNETA command to modify the DDMACC network attribute to reflect the name of the program and the library in which it resides. For more information about creating and using a DDM user-exit program, see the IBM manual *Distributed Data Management* (SC41-5307).

Security Considerations for PCs

PCs and the technology they enable are one of the biggest challenges to face AS/400 security administrators. Security administrators who don't have to deal with the security risks of attaching PCs to their AS/400 are the exception rather than the rule. Given the power and ease-of-use of desktop software today, the security risks are significant and definitely a challenge. Nothing has underscored the inadequacies of menu-based security more than attaching PCs to the AS/400. If you have PCs attached to your AS/400 and you still rely solely on menu security to control your sensitive and confidential information (in other words, you don't use object-level security), your security has holes. Let's look at Client Access Express and some of the security issues you'll have to deal with.

Client Access

Client Access for Windows 95/NT and Client Access Express clients provide several PC-based applications, including ODBC, data transfer, Operations Navigator, and 5250 emulation, for accessing an AS/400. These applications make it convenient to manipulate AS/400 data using desktop applications such as Microsoft Excel. In fact, when you install Client Access Express on a client PC on which Excel is also installed, Client Access adds an Excel icon that lets the user download AS/400 data into a spreadsheet with the click of a mouse.

You must couple Client Access with good resource security on the AS/400 to ensure that users can access only data you want them to access. We discuss Client Access security in this section, but we also encourage you to monitor the Client Access Web site at http://www.as400.ibm.com/clientaccess for information about the latest features and issues.

Access Issues

Carol has received numerous complaints from security administrators who say that the Windows clients have security exposures because users can now access data they once couldn't. But of course, it's not the Windows clients that cause the security exposures — it's the security implementation on the AS/400. In other words, depending on how you or your vendor software has implemented object-level authorities, your data might now be accessible through client applications. Windows clients don't let Client Access users access objects they're not authorized to access, but the object authorities on most systems don't protect against access with desktop tools.

One exposure that administrators encounter occurs when users start to use tools, such as Windows Explorer, that access files through the root file system to manipulate AS/400 objects (i.e., objects in the QSYS file system). When a PC drive is mapped to an AS/400, Windows Explorer presents the QSYS file system as a structure that the user can manipulate like all other directories and files on the PC. For example, if a user has sufficient authority to a production file (that is, *OBJEXIST authority) he or she could drop the file onto the desktop shredder! Good object-level authority can prevent inadvertent and malicious destruction of production objects, but to entirely prevent users from accessing QSYS file system objects through such tools, you can explicitly revoke the authority of user profiles, group profiles, or *PUBLIC to the QPWFSERVER authorization list. Users who have authority to this authorization list can manipulate AS/400 objects through Windows Explorer. QPWFSERVER is shipped with public authority *USE, so by default, everyone can access QSYS objects.

However, the QPWFSERVER authorization list doesn't alter QSYS objects' public authority. If a sensitive file has *CHANGE public authority, you can prevent users from updating the file through the Explorer interfaces by removing their authority to the QPWFSERVER authorization list, but doing so doesn't prevent access through other interfaces, such as FTP, ODBC, or DDM.

Finally, you need to understand that QPWFSERVER doesn't control all Client Access access to QSYS objects. For example, QPWFSERVER doesn't control access to objects through Operations Navigator.

Password Issues

Whenever you use Client Access, the system stores, in some form, the user ID and password you use to sign on to Client Access (some long-time users of Client Access refer to this sign-on as "signing on to the router"). The system uses this password to establish the initial connection with the AS/400 and passes the user ID and password to the AS/400 whenever an application doesn't prompt you separately for identification. How this password is stored and used varies depending on which Client Access client you use.

You should never hard-code this user ID and password in a configuration file that automatically signs the user on to Client Access when someone powers up the PC. Instead of relying on just a software implementation, you should protect the PC with a hardware lock or a password that is implemented as part of the hardware.

The Client Access Express client (and the Win95/NT client, when installed on Windows 95 or Windows 98) provides the capability to store the user's password in more than just memory. In fact, by default, these clients store the user ID and password on disk. (When you install the Win95/NT client on Windows NT, the client doesn't store passwords on disk.) You can choose not to cache the password, but this option appears only when you change your password, and again, it's not the default. So how might a user exploit this? Let's say that you sign on to a user's PC as security officer but don't power down the workstation. The client stores your user ID and password. If someone else subsequently uses a Client Access interface that doesn't require a user ID and password, your user ID will be used. We leave the possibilities to your imagination.

In V4R2, IBM made the option not to store the password more obvious and added an option to flush the cache. Whenever you sign on to a PC other than your own, you must discipline yourself to either flush the cache or power down the workstation. Teach your users to do the same.

Connection Issues

Another consideration with the Windows clients (both Win95/NT and Client Access Express) is that they don't disconnect you from the AS/400 when you sign off Client Access. When you select the option to disconnect Client Access, the status on your connections list changes and your Client Access license is released, but the connection isn't physically disconnected because of the way Client Access works with the communications stack in Windows.

Let's say that you use your PC to administer your system through Operations Navigator on Thursday. You disconnect (but don't power down) and go home for the evening. You're out of the office on Friday, but you give your screen-saver password to a colleague so he can use your PC because his isn't working. Because you only disconnected and didn't power down, he will be you for any connection you made on Thursday that wasn't disconnected. He could potentially exploit the power of your user ID through the file server, file manager, ODBC (depending on how the application is written), and — worse — Operations Navigator. Powering down is the only way you can be certain that someone can't exploit the power of the user profile used to initially sign on to Client Access.

You need to take special care when users share PCs. If a system administrator shares a PC, the administrator must either power down the PC or close all the applications before letting someone else sign on. Remember, the first user to sign on to Client Access is the one whose profile all Client Access applications that don't specifically request a user ID and password will use.

> *Security Recommendation*
> **When you are finished for the day, don't just disconnect from Client Access; power down your workstation.**

Data Transfer and Remote Command Issues

Client Access provides the ability to transfer data and run remote commands. If you let users take advantage of these capabilities (i.e., if you don't use an exit program, policy, or Application Administration to disallow them), you need to be aware of the consequences with regard to the confidentiality of your data. Remember, all files with *PUBLIC(*USE) authority can be downloaded. Files with *PUBLIC(*CHANGE) authority can be downloaded, changed, and uploaded.

Letting users run remote commands is like letting users submit batch commands: The AS/400 doesn't check the user profile's LMTCPB parameter. However, IBM uses the remote command server to implement Operations Navigator, so if you write an exit program to totally disallow use of the remote command server, you effectively disable most of Operations Navigator as well.

> *Technical Note*
> **See Informational APAR II12227 for a list of Client Access functions and which servers are required to perform the function. This APAR gives you an idea of what functions will no longer work if you choose not to start a server.**

Running Client Access over TCP/IP

If you use Client Access Express, you must use the TCP/IP communications protocol; Client Access Express doesn't support the SNA protocol. However, with the Client Access for Windows 95/NT client, you had a choice. To run Client Access over TCP/IP, you must start the TCP/IP servers that enable the Client Access applications you want to run. For example, to use 5250 emulation, you must start the Telnet server and then use the

STRHOSTSVR (Start Host Servers) command to start the corresponding host servers. If you want to prevent users from using a particular Client Access application, you can either not start the TCP/IP server or not start the corresponding host server.

In V4R2, running the STRTCP (Start TCP/IP) command also runs the STRHOSTSVR command. The STRTCP command starts only the TCP/IP servers with the AUTOSTART value of *YES, but by default, STRHOSTSVR starts all of the host servers. You can use Operations Navigator to customize which servers are started, or you can edit the QATOCSTART file in QUSRSYS to customize which servers you want to start. Unfortunately, if TCP/IP fails or the ENDTCP (End TCP/IP) command is run, you must use the ENDHOSTSVR (End Host Servers) command manually to end the host servers.

Limiting Function from the Desktop

Client Access for Windows 95/NT and Client Access Express clients provide several ways, including Microsoft policies, Application Administration, and selective install, to limit what users can do from their desktops. Consider these alternatives as a modern-day form of menu access control. In other words, none of these methods can substitute for object level security. Nevertheless, limiting what is on a user's desktop is good practice because it reduces complexity and confusion for the end user.

Microsoft Policies

Microsoft policies support is inherent to the Windows operating system. The administrator uses templates to determine what function is allowed for a particular user or group or for a particular PC. Client Access provides two templates that let you use policies to govern some Client Access function. This support assumes that the client PC is connected to a server from which the policy is downloaded whenever the user signs on to the Windows workstation.

This method isn't foolproof, however. Knowledgeable users who can manipulate the Windows Registry could subvert the Registry updates that policies make. Additionally, the tools available to the system administrator for setting policies aren't easy to use, and the administrator must hand-configure each PC to download the policies at sign-on.

Application Administration

The Application Administration interface, which is included in Operations Navigator, lets you administer parts of Client Access. The effect is the same as enforcing Microsoft policies, except that controlling whether users can perform a particular function is much easier through the Operations Navigator GUI. For instructions on accessing Application Administration, see the "Limit User Function" section of Chapter 4.

Selective Install

System administrators can configure which components of Client Access they want users to have installed on their PCs. This is a good place to begin to control what function is available from users' desktops. This configuration isn't foolproof, however. If Joan has more capabilities than Dan, Dan might simply go to Joan's PC and copy the additional Client Access components onto his own PC.

ODBC Security Considerations

ODBC is set of standard interfaces developed to provide easy access to databases. Vendors who provide ODBC have four choices when accessing DB2 UDB for AS/400. They can

- use the ODBC server provided with Client Access,
- use DDM,
- use DRDA, or
- write their own ODBC server.

Most vendors seem to use DRDA to access DB2 data. Because most vendors use DRDA, exit programs written for the Client Access ODBC server exit points are not called. Exit programs for ODBC running over either DRDA or DDM are registered under the DDMACC network attribute using the CHGNETA command. Programs registered for the ODBC exit points in the registration facility are called only when the IBM ODBC server is used.

If your users use ODBC, you need to carefully monitor that use. ODBC is designed to make it easy to write an application to access information stored in a database. Any database file that has public authority of at least *USE can be read through ODBC.

With stored procedures, you can secure your data and still use ODBC. Because stored procedures are programs, you can use adopted authority to access data while the stored procedure runs and protect the file containing the data from access through other interfaces by setting its public authority to *EXCLUDE. (For more information about programs that adopt authority, see "Adopted Authority" in Chapter 4.) Alternatively, after you authenticate a user in a stored procedure, you can use the Security APIs to swap to a user profile that has authority to the database while retaining *EXCLUDE public authority. (For more information about profile swapping, see the "Profile Swapping" section in Chapter 10.)

Viruses

Network-attached PCs are susceptible to viruses. A new virus seems to be in the news at least once a month. Although a virus that can infect a PC or an executable attached to an e-mail message won't affect OS/400, OS/400 can be a "carrier" for these types of viruses.

Because data stored in shared folders or the IFS is PC data (not AS/400 data), you should scan it regularly for viruses. You could encounter a virus on a PC and remove it, only to promptly reinfect the PC when the user next downloads data from the AS/400. To scan for a virus in the IFS, you can map a PC drive to your AS/400 and run a PC virus scanner against the appropriate IFS directory.

Using Exit Points

Exit points are places throughout OS/400 where a user-written program can be called to customize the behavior of the function or server being used at the time. Exit points are defined for OS/400 servers, such as FTP and Telnet, as well as for functions, such as creating a user profile or changing a password. Registering an exit program requires you to use various system values and parameters (e.g., the QPWDVLDPGM system value, network attributes such as the DDMACC parameter on the CHGNETA command) depending on the exit point you're using. However, registration for most new exit programs is consolidated in a registration facility that you can access by using the WRKREGINF (Work with Registration Information) command.

Although you shouldn't use exit programs as the sole means of securing your AS/400, there are good reasons to include them in your security implementation. Exit programs can provide more granularity than object-level security can provide. For example, although Pat has authority to update the payroll file, you can use an exit program to prevent him from using that authority to download the file using FTP or data transfer. Exit programs let you turn off functions for specific users (e.g., prevent QSECOFR from using Telnet) or prevent functions or parts of functions from being used altogether (e.g., you might allow FTP downloads but not FTP uploads). Exit programs also let you implement specialized functions, such as named Telnet devices and anonymous FTP.

You can also use exit programs to provide more authority than your security configuration allows. For example, if a third-party application uses adopted authority and sets *PUBLIC authority for all application objects to *EXCLUDE, you might have a problem obtaining the necessary authority to download data from OS/400 into a spreadsheet. You might write an exit program for Client Access data transfer, for instance, that adopts enough authority to let a particular user download a file containing inventory data to an Excel spreadsheet.

Finally, you can use exit programs as a stopgap measure to help stem the flood of security exposures caused by software vendors who irresponsibly give their application objects a public authority of *CHANGE or, worse, *ALL. When you can't turn off functions such as data transfer, ODBC, FTP, or DDM, exit programs can help curtail which data can flow into and out of your system until you can implement a good object authority scheme or convince your software vendor to change the application's security implementation.

As we've said, exit programs aren't a substitute for object authority, but they do have their place in some security configurations. Figure 7.4 provides the code for a CL exit program you can use to control which FTP functions are allowed. For installation instructions, see "Installing USRFTPLOGC" (page 187).

FIGURE 7.4
FTP Server Logon Exit-Point Program USRFTPLOGC

```
/* Program name: USRFTPLOGC                                          */
/* From: "Who's Accessing My FTP Server?" by Dan Riehl, NEWS/400,    */
/*       June 1997.                                                  */
/* Copyright:  (c) 1997 Dan Riehl. Used with permission.             */
/* Purpose: This is the FTP server Logon Exit Point Program to       */
/*          record all FTP logon attempts to a message queue.        */
/*          Exit point is QIBM_QTMF_SVR_LOGON.                       */
/*          Parameter format is TCPL0100.                            */
/* ----------------------------------------------------------------- */
/* Instructions: Place source code in a secure library.              */
/*               Create program into a secure library                */
/*                  (i.e., PUBLIC(*EXCLUDE)).                        */
/*               Do not allow retrieval of CL source.                */
/*               Create the CL program:                              */
/*                  CRTCLPGM PGM(ASecureLibrary/USRFTPLOGC)   +      */
/*                           SRCFILE(ASecureLibrary/QCLSRC)  +      */
/*                           LOG(*NO)                         +      */
/*                           ALWRTVSRC(*NO)                   +      */
/*                           AUT(*EXCLUDE)                           */
/*               Create a secure message queue:                      */
/*                  CRTMSGQ MSGQ(ASecureLibrary/FTPSVRLOG)    +      */
/*                          AUT(*EXCLUDE)                            */
/*               Grant the QTCP user profile *CHANGE to the          */
/*                  message queue and *USE to both the secure        */
/*                  library and the USRFTPLOGC CL program            */
/*                                                                   */
/* ----------------------------------------------------------------- */

     PGM     ( &P_AppID    +
               &P_User     +
               &P_UserLen  +
               &P_Pwd      +
               &P_PwdLen   +
               &P_IP       +
               &P_IPLen    +
               &P_RtnOut   +
               &P_UserOut  +
               &P_PwdOut   +
               &P_LibOut   )

 /* Parameters for exit point interface FORMAT TCPL0100              */

 /* Input parms */
     DCL     &P_AppID      *CHAR   4    /* Application ID (%bin)     */
                                        /* 1 = FTP                   */
     DCL     &P_User       *CHAR 999    /* User ID                   */
     DCL     &P_UserLen    *CHAR   4    /* User ID length (%bin)     */
     DCL     &P_Pwd        *CHAR 999    /* Password                  */
     DCL     &P_PwdLen     *CHAR   4    /* Password length (%bin)    */
     DCL     &P_IP         *CHAR  15    /* Requester IP address      */
     DCL     &P_IPLen      *CHAR   4    /* IP address length (%bin)  */
     DCL     &P_IPLen      *CHAR   4    /* IP address length (%bin)  */
```

continued

FIGURE 7.4 CONTINUED

```
/* Output parms */
  DCL        &P_RtnOut      *CHAR    4     /* Return code out                 */
                                           /* Values are:                     */
                                           /* 0=Reject                        */
                                           /* 1=Accept, w/Usrprf Curlib       */
                                           /* 2=Accept, w/ &P_LibOut          */
                                           /* 3=Accept, w/UsrPrf Curlib       */
                                           /*          and &P_UserOut         */
                                           /*          and &P_PwdOut          */
                                           /* 4=Accept, w/ &P_LibOut          */
                                           /*          and &P_UserOut         */
                                           /*          and &P_PwdOut          */
                                           /* 5=Accept, w/UsrPrf Curlib       */
                                           /*          and &P_UserOut         */
                                           /*          Password bypass        */
                                           /* 6=Accept, w/ P_LibOut           */
                                           /*          and &P_UserOut         */
                                           /*          Password bypass        */
  DCL        &P_UserOut     *CHAR   10     /* User profile out                */
  DCL        &P_PwdOut      *CHAR   10     /* Password out                    */
  DCL        &P_LibOut      *CHAR   10     /* CURLIB out                      */
/* End of FORMAT TCPL0100                                                     */

/* Variables for binary conversions */
  DCL        &AppID         *DEC    (1 0)
  DCL        &UserLen       *DEC    (3 0)
  DCL        &PwdLen        *DEC    (3 0)
  DCL        &IPLen         *DEC    (3 0)

/* Misc. work variables              */
  DCL        &Time          *CHAR    6
  DCL        &Date          *CHAR    6
  DCL        &Message       *CHAR  256
  DCL        &Accept1       *DEC     1    Value(1)
  DCL        &MsgQ          *CHAR   10    Value('FTPSVRLOG')
  DCL        &MsgQLib       *CHAR   10    Value('USRTCPIP')

/* Message-handling variables */
  DCL        &MsgID         *CHAR    7
  DCL        &MsgF          *CHAR   10
  DCL        &MsgFLib       *CHAR   10
  DCL        &MsgDta        *CHAR  100

  MonMsg    (CPF0000 MCH0000) Exec(GoTo Error)

  ChgVar    &AppID     %Bin(&P_AppID)
  ChgVar    &UserLen   %Bin(&P_UserLen)
  ChgVar    &PwdLen    %Bin(&P_PwdLen)
  ChgVar    &IPLen     %Bin(&P_IPLen)

  RtvSysVal QTIME      &Time
  RtvSysVal QDATE      &Date
```

continued

FIGURE 7.4 CONTINUED

```
    ChgVar      &Message    +
                ('FTP Logon'                           +
                *BCAT %SST(&P_User 1 &UserLen)         +
                *BCAT 'From IP Addr'                   +
                *BCAT %SST(&P_IP 1 &IPLen)             +
                *BCAT 'at'                             +
                *BCAT %SST(&Time 1 2)                  +
                *CAT  ':'                              +
                *CAT  %SST(&Time 3 2)                  +
                *CAT  ':'                              +
                *CAT  %SST(&Time 5 2)                  +
                *BCAT 'on'                             +
                *BCAT %SST(&Date 1 2)                  +
                *CAT  '/'                              +
                *CAT  %SST(&Date 3 2)                  +
                *CAT  '/'                              +
                *CAT  %SST(&Date 5 2))

    SndPgmMsg   MsgID(CPF9897)                         +
                Msgf(QCPFMSG)                          +
                MsgDta(&Message)                       +
                ToMsgQ(&MsgQLib/&MsgQ)

    ChgVar      %Bin(&P_RtnOut)   Value(&Accept1)  /* Return "Accept" */

    Return      /* Normal end of program */

ERROR:
    RcvMsg      Msgtype(*LAST)                         +
                MsgDta(&MsgDta)                        +
                MsgID(&MsgID)                          +
                MsgF(&MsgF)                            +
                SndMsgFLib(&MsgFLib)

    /* Prevent loop, just in case        */
    MonMsg      CPF0000

    SndPgmMsg   MsgID(&MsgID)                          +
                MsgF(&MsgFLib/&MsgF)                   +
                MsgDta(&MsgDta)                        +
                MsgType(*ESCAPE)

    /* Prevent loop, just in case        */
    MonMsg      CPF0000
    EndPgm
```

Exit point documentation and examples are scattered among several IBM manuals, including *Client Access Express for Windows Host Servers* (SC41-5740), *System API Reference* (SC41-5801), and *OS/400 TCP/IP Configuration and Reference V4R4* (SC41-5420). The Client Access manual also maps out which of the Original Servers invoke an exit program in the registration facility when you specify *REGFAC for the CHGNETA command's PCSACC parameter.

Installing USRFTPLOGC

To enable program USRFTPLOGC as the exit program for the FTP server log-on exit point, QIBM_QTMF_SVR_LOGON, follow these steps:

1. Sign on as QSECOFR.
2. Create library USRTCPIP with AUT(*EXCLUDE).
3. Grant user QTCP *USE authority to the library.
4. Create source file QCLSRC with AUT(*EXCLUDE).
5. Enter the source for CL exit program USRFTPLOGC.
6. Create the program in USRTCPIP with AUT(*EXCLUDE).
7. Create message queue FTPSVRLOG in USRTCPIP with AUT(*EXCLUDE).
8. Grant user QTCP *CHANGE authority to the message queue.
9. Register the exit point with the WRKREGINF (Work with Registration Information) or ADDEXITPGM (Add Exit Program) command.

Helpful Tools

Here's a tool that can help you monitor aspects of network security.

Security tool	Description
WRKREGINF (Work with Registration Information)	Prints a list of all registered exit points and the programs associated with them. Use this command to track exit programs in the registration facility.

Chapter 8

Communications Security

In Chapter 7, we discussed security considerations that arise when you network your AS/400 and let clients connect to it. In this chapter, we explore security considerations associated specifically with using the two primary communications protocols — TCP/IP and APPC/APPN. We also provide an overview of encryption and how it enables much of today's network security technology and explain how OS/400 uses encryption options in your own applications.

TCP/IP Security Considerations

If you don't yet use Transmission Control Protocol/Internet Protocol (TCP/IP), you probably will in the not-too-distant future. TCP/IP, the communications protocol used on the Internet, enables such applications as Telnet and FTP. TCP/IP is also the required networking protocol for Web serving and for many newer intranet products such as Domino, Java, and IBM Network Stations. TCP/IP has fewer integrated security features than SNA, not because of the way TCP/IP is implemented on the AS/400, but as a consequence of its design. However, the AS/400 provides a few security knobs you can turn to help you manage security when using TCP/IP applications.

*IOSYSCFG special authority lets you configure and manage all aspects of TCP/IP on the AS/400. *IOSYSCFG special authority is included in only the *SECOFR user class for a reason: *IOSYSCFG is very powerful and should be given only to trusted individuals.

The basic security rule for TCP/IP servers is: Until you need the function, don't start the server. To follow this rule, you need to understand and control which application servers start when you start TCP/IP.

When you execute the STRTCP (Start TCP/IP) command, the system examines each server's AUTOSTART parameter and starts only those with AUTOSTART(*YES). Table 8.1 lists the servers that autostart by default. However, executing the STRTCPSVR (Start TCP/IP Server) command overrides the AUTOSTART parameter of all servers and starts all servers by default.

TABLE 8.1
TCP/IP Application Servers That Autostart by Default

FTP — File Transfer (Data)
FTP — File Transfer (Control)
Telnet — Remote Terminal Protocol
SMTP — Simple Mail Transfer Protocol
SNMP — Simple Network Management Protocol
LPD — Line Printer Daemon
Client Access Express using IP

To ensure you don't start servers you don't need, you can use the CHGCMDDFT (Change Command Defaults) command to change the SERVER parameter of the STRTCPSVR command to specify the server you want to start. For example,

`CHGCMDDFT CMD(STRTCPSVR) NEWDFT('SERVER(*FTP)')`

starts only the FTP server. (You can specify only one server to start on the CHGCMDDFT command.)

The STRTCP and STRTCPSVR commands have *EXCLUDE public authority. IBM-supplied profiles QPGMR, QSYSOPR, QSRV, and QSRVBAS have *USE private authority to these commands and can execute them; *IOSYSCFG special authority isn't necessary. You should carefully monitor who can run these commands, and you might want to explicitly exclude some users from being able to do so.

The Internet Assigned Numbers Authority (IANA) assigns specific ports to well-known TCP/IP applications. To find the ports defined on the AS/400, run the CFGTCP (Configure TCP/IP) command and take Option 21 (Configure related tables) and then Option 1 (Work with service table entries).

All users can use programs that listen on ports. To limit the damage that someone could do by eavesdropping, you should restrict ports you don't use. You can restrict a port by configuring it to run under a profile that has been deleted. First, be sure that you don't want to use the port's application, because restricting the port causes the application not to start. Then, create a profile:

`CRTUSRPRF TCP_USER PASSWORD(*NONE)`

After you create the profile, follow these steps to restrict the port:

1. Go to the TCP/IP Configuration menu (GO CFGTCP).
2. Take Option 4 (Work with TCP/IP port restrictions).
3. Specify Option 1 (Add).
4. Specify the port associated with the application you're restricting and enter that number for the lower port range.
5. Specify *ONLY for the upper port range.
6. Specify *TCP for the protocol.
7. Specify the user profile you just created to use this port.
8. Repeat these steps specifying *UDP for the protocol.

Then, after following these steps for all the ports you want to secure, delete the user profile:

`DLTUSRPRF TCP_USER`

The port restriction will take effect the next time TCP/IP is started. If an application running as QSECOFR issues a bind() to that port, the bind will fail.

When you configure the TCP/IP addresses of your devices, consider using "reusable" addresses. Reusable addresses are those outside the range of addresses that are valid for use on the Internet (i.e., they are in reserved ranges, such as 10.*.*.* or 192.168.*.*). Several security mechanisms let you control processing based on IP addresses. Using reusable addresses within your organization can help you separate "inside" requests from "outside" requests.

Now let's look at some of the features of TCP/IP as well TCP/IP applications and their associated security issues.

IP Packet Filtering

IP packet filtering, which is integrated into OS/400 beginning in release V4R3, lets you prevent unwanted packets from coming onto or leaving your system. To filter packets, you set up filter rules that specify the types of packets you want to allow. The information you filter is contained in the packet's header and can include source IP address, protocol (e.g., TCP or UDP), destination IP address, source port, destination port, IP datagram direction (i.e., inbound, outbound, or both), forwarded or local, packet fragments, and TCP SYN bit. For example, you might want to allow inbound FTP requests only when they come from a particular TCP/IP address in your network. After you define filters, any request that doesn't match a filter is expressly denied. Therefore, if someone requests a Telnet connection to your system and your filter rules don't allow Telnet, the request is denied.

IP packet filtering is part of OS/400's integrated firewall technology. Although packet filtering is not recommended as the sole replacement for a standalone firewall product in all configurations, it might provide necessary support in some cases, such as in your intranet. In all configurations, native IP packet filtering provides another layer of defense in your network security configuration.

Network Address Translation (NAT)

NAT, also added in V4R3, lets you hide or map TCP/IP addresses. NAT lets you join networks that implement different addressing schemes and hide internal TCP/IP addresses from the outside world by mapping them to external addresses. It's very important that you keep your internal addresses private. If you publish your internal addresses externally, you give intruders a roadmap to your network and make it easier for them to launch an attack. We recommend you use reusable TCP/IP addresses internally and map them to an external or "real" address when going outside your internal network.

PPP

You use Point-to-Point Protocol (PPP) to establish TCP/IP communications between your AS/400 and another system via modems. PPP is referred to as a point-to-point link because it connects only two systems. PPP is the Internet standard for point-to-point connections and is available on the AS/400 in V4R2. You can use PPP to establish a high-speed connection between your AS/400 and an Internet Service Provider (ISP), and remote users can use PPP to dial in to your AS/400 while traveling or working from home. After a PPP connection is made, another application, such as Telnet or FTP, is used over the connection. PPP provides additional function beyond what is available by using

Serial Line Internet Protocol (SLIP, described below) and is the preferred method for point-to-point connections. To configure PPP, you must use Operations Navigator.

PPP provides several security mechanisms not available with SLIP. Unlike SLIP, which requires a connection script to authenticate the user, the PPP protocol includes authentication. By default, PPP requires a user ID and password to make a connection. With PPP, you can configure your system to require Challenge Handshake Authentication Protocol (CHAP), which, when used on both ends of the connection, ensures that the user ID and password are encrypted and eliminates the possibility that the profile and password will be sniffed. You can also configure your system to use Password Authentication Protocol (PAP) to connect to systems that don't support CHAP. PAP is less secure because the user IDs and passwords are sent in clear text.

With PPP, you don't have to create "real" AS/400 user profiles for authentication. Instead, you can define a user with a validation list that is valid for use only on the PPP connection. (For more information about validation lists, see Chapter 9.)

To protect your system from users piggybacking on an active session, you can configure PPP to periodically rechallenge to ensure the session is still coming in on the same IP address and under the same authentication. The rechallenge takes place without the user's knowledge. If piggybacking is detected, the session is dropped.

Another feature of PPP lets you accept (or reject) connections based on the incoming user ID and the corresponding IP address of the request after the user ID is authenticated via PAP/CHAP. This mechanism is subject to IP address spoofing, however, and might be more appropriate for an intranet application than for an Internet connection.

> **Technical Note**
> **Because passwords must be decryptable, you must set the QRETSVRSEC system value to 1 to enable authentication in PPP and SLIP.**

SLIP

SLIP is a very simple point-to-point protocol. Unlike PPP, SLIP isn't an Internet standard. With both SLIP and PPP, you can configure your AS/400 to accept calls (*ANS) or dial out (*DIAL). The system will not do either by default. To configure SLIP, you create point-to-point connection profiles that define how the AS/400 will communicate with other systems.

By default, users dialing in to an AS/400 don't need an AS/400 user ID and password to make a SLIP connection (*ANS). They need only the phone number (which should be unlisted). However, you can configure SLIP to require a valid AS/400 user ID and password. The purpose of requiring a user ID and password isn't to define the profile SLIP runs under (SLIP is just the connection) but to let you control who can dial in to your system.

To require SLIP to validate incoming callers, specify an authorization list in the System Access Authorization List parameter in your SLIP *ANS profile. Then use the ADDAUTLE (Add Authorization List Entry) command to assign user profiles to the authorization list.

Finally, create a connection dialog script for the configuration profile that handles the user validation function. (File QATOCPPSCR in library QUSRSYS provides an example of such a dialog script.) Then, when someone attempts to connect to your AS/400, the caller must provide an AS/400 user ID and password. The system searches the authorization list, and if the user isn't authorized to the authorization list named in the System Access Authorization List parameter, or if the password isn't valid, the connection fails.

After making a SLIP connection to your AS/400, a user can start a TCP/IP application on your AS/400 or can start an application (such as FTP) to another system in your network. Intruders use this approach to establish connections to systems that don't allow dial-in. To prevent dial-in users from avoiding application security by establishing connections to other systems without starting an application on your AS/400, specify N (No) for the Allow IP Datagram Forwarding parameter in your *ANS configuration profile.

If you provide dial-out capability, you might need to configure your AS/400 to provide a user ID and password when it connects to another system. Once again, you must write a connection dialog script to send the user ID and password on the connection. You specify the user profile on the Remote service access name parameter of your SLIP *DIAL profile, and you specify the user's password on the Remote Service Access Password parameter. OS/400 must store the password in a decryptable form so that the system can send the password in clear text on the connection. The QRETSVRSEC system value controls whether you allow decryptable passwords to be stored on your AS/400. If you need to perform user authentication on the *DIAL SLIP connection, you must change the QRETSVRSEC system value to 1 so passwords can be decrypted for use with SLIP.

User profiles that you use to authenticate SLIP connections should be used for that purpose only. Because you must either store the password on your system (for *DIAL) or give out the password (for *ANS), you must take precautions so the user profile can't be used maliciously. The profile(s) should have the following attributes:

No initial program	INLPGM(*NONE)
No initial menu	INLMNU(*SIGNOFF)
Limited capabilities	LMTCPB(*YES)
No special authorities	SPCAUT(*NONE)
No group profiles	GRPPRF(*NONE)
Own no objects	
Excluded from sensitive or confidential information	

To prevent intruders from misusing your SLIP configurations, define different profiles for your *ANS and *DIAL profile configurations and turn off IP datagram forwarding.

Telnet

Telnet is a TCP/IP-based terminal emulation application protocol that lets users sign on to your AS/400 and run applications. Users are required to sign on to the AS/400 before running an application. Telnet specifications don't provide a way of encrypting passwords, so user IDs and passwords are sent in clear text when users connect to your AS/400 via Telnet.

Telnet honors the setting of the QMAXSIGN system value and takes the action specified by the QMAXSGNACN system value. However, you need to make sure you set the QAUTOVRT system value to either the number of virtual devices your enterprise needs or 0. (Recall that if QAUTOVRT is *NOMAX, a hacker has more opportunities to guess a user ID and password to gain access to your system.) Explicit device ID support is available via a Telnet exit point, so you can assign a device description to a particular IP address.

When users access your AS/400 via Telnet, you must also think about the setting for the QLMTSECOFR system value. Recall from Chapter 2 that if QLMTSECOFR is set to 0, users with *ALLOBJ or *SERVICE special authority can sign on to any workstation attached to the system. If QLMTSECOFR is set to 1, such users must be specifically authorized to sign on to a workstation. Using device ID support with Client Access Express, IBM Network Stations, or one of the Telnet exit points, you can assign a device description to a particular IP address. Assuming that a user with *ALLOBJ or *SERVICE special authority always comes in on the same IP address, you can authorize that user to that device description so the user can use Telnet.

In V4R2, Telnet honors the QINACTITV system value. In earlier releases, Telnet has its own configuration option to set a time-out value and to specify the time a Telnet session can be inactive before the Telnet server closes the connection. In those earlier releases, you use the CHGTELNA (Change Telnet Attributes) command to set the inactivity time-out (INACCTTIMO) parameter. If you're on V4R4 or later, however, you need to instead use the QINACTITV system value. As of V4R4, the INACTTIMO parameter on the CHGTELNA command is no longer supported and any value you specified is ignored.

Another exit point defined for Telnet lets you control the functions of Telnet based on an IP address. For example, if you used reusable addresses (as we discuss earlier in this chapter), you could reject any attempt to use a "real" address to access your system. Or, you could use the exit program to implement a guest user ID for your system. If you do so, you should create the guest profile with very limited access to your system's resources. Remember, restricting access to your system based on IP address shouldn't be your only security mechanism, because IP addresses can be spoofed. You must also use object-level security to truly secure your system.

A Telnet feature added in V4R2 is the ability to bypass the sign-on display by sending the user ID and password with the Telnet session request. This is a configurable option when you use PCOMM (the 5250 emulator that comes with Client Access) or the Host OnDemand product. The QRMTSIGN system value determines whether your system permits users to bypass sign-on. QRMTSIGN was originally designed to determine how the system responded to automatic sign-on requests for passthrough. Table 8.2 summarizes how QRMTSIGN works with Telnet.

TABLE 8.2
Effect of QRMTSIGN Value on Telnet

QRMTSIGN value	Effect on Telnet
*REJECT	Sessions requesting automatic sign-on are not allowed
*VERIFY or *SAMEPRF	Telnet session starts if the user ID and password are valid
*FRCSIGNON	User is forced to sign on via the Sign On display

Bypassing the Sign On screen doesn't give the user making the request an opportunity to enter a different (and potentially more powerful) user ID and password. For that reason, this capability is useful in certain instances, such as if you implement the guest user ID support.

In V4R4, Telnet was Secure Sockets Layer (SSL)-enabled. In other words, you can configure Telnet so that all data, including user IDs and passwords, are sent encrypted. For more details about SSL, see "Data Encryption" later in this chapter. In V4R5 (and via PTF in V4R4), IBM added support for authenticating users via digital certificates. Configuration options for user authentication let you very tightly control who can access your system using Telnet.

FTP

File Transfer Protocol (FTP) lets users download files from and upload files to your system. FTP also provides facilities to rename, add, and delete files. Before manipulating a file, the user must provide a valid AS/400 user ID and password (this information is sent in clear text). Remember, however, that because the user doesn't sign on via a Sign On display, the user's initial program and initial menu are never run. This is another case in which menu-based security is insufficient.

FTP ignores the setting of the QMAXSIGN system value. It allows five attempts to provide a valid user ID and password before dropping the connection (this number is hard-coded, and you can't change it). However, FTP does honor the QMAXSGNACN system value when you set it to 2 or 3 (the values that disable a user profile). In other words, if a user hits the limit of five unsuccessful attempts to provide a user ID and password, the system disables the user ID.

FTP uses the INACTTIMO parameter in its configuration to set the length of time an FTP session can be inactive before the system closes the connection. It ignores the QINACTITV system value.

FTP lets users submit remote commands through its RCMD (Remote Command Facility) subcommand. However, unlike with the Client Access Express remote command server, limited-capability FTP users can't run remote commands.

You can use exit points to implement anonymous FTP, which lets a system define a well-known user ID and password for guests to use to sign on and download data. You can use these exit points to enable a tightly controlled FTP environment that lets users download only a predefined set of files. For example, a company might enable anonymous FTP to let customers download beta code for its newest product. You can also use exit programs to disable downloading of specific files and prevent execution of RCMD while still permitting file transfer. See the IBM manual *OS/400 TCP/IP Configuration and Reference V4R4* (SC41-5420) or visit http://www.as400.ibm.com/tcpip for a sample exit program that implements anonymous FTP. Figure 7.4 in Chapter 7 provides a sample exit program that limits FTP functions.

Before enabling FTP, you should closely examine the public authority of your sensitive objects. Any user who has *USE authority to an object can download the object. Any user who has *CHANGE authority to an object can download and upload the object. So, a file that contains inventory data and has *PUBLIC(*CHANGE) authority can be downloaded, changed with a PC spreadsheet, and then uploaded.

One method intruders like to use is to store stolen data (e.g., credit card numbers, pornographic photographs) on someone else's system. To protect your system, you might want to write your exit program to make sure that a user can't execute both PUT and GET subcommands to the same library or directory (i.e., if you allow PUTs to a directory, disallow GETs, and vice versa). This precaution removes some of the allure of using your system because intruders can't retrieve information they store on your system.

LPR and LPD

Line Printer Requester (LPR) sends spooled files to another system in a network. Line Printer Daemon (LPD) receives files sent by LPR. Using LPR and LPD, users can print remotely on your AS/400.

For a user to receive a spooled file, LPD requires that the user who sends the file exist on the receiving AS/400 or that the sending user have authority to the QTMPLPD user profile, which is the default owner of spooled files. You can restrict who can print on your system by controlling public authority to the QTMPLPD user profile. You can further limit remote printing to your system by controlling the authority on your output queues. Use the PRTQAUT (Print Queue Authority) command to list all your output queues and their security-relevant fields.

A popular denial-of-service attack is to swamp a system by filling it up with unwanted files — in this case, spooled files. To prevent such an attack, make sure you've set adequate threshold limits for your auxiliary storage pools (ASPs), which you can manage through either Dedicated Service Tools (DST) or System Service Tools (SST).

WSG

Workstation Gateway (WSG) converts AS/400 5250 green-screen applications on the fly to Hypertext Markup Language (HTML) so they can be viewed with a Web browser. You must remember that when you use WSG, the communication between the browser and the AS/400 isn't encrypted, so all data, including AS/400 user IDs and passwords, is sent in clear text. In other words, all information is passed through the Internet for all to see (and sniff and steal, if so inclined). The sign-on screen also gives hackers an opportunity to guess user IDs and passwords and gain access to your system.

Rather than present a sign-on screen, you can create an exit program that bypasses the sign-on screen and runs a specific application. This approach is safer than using a sign-on screen because no user information is transmitted; however, sensitive or confidential data is still sent in clear text. Use the Display Sign-on Panel parameter in the WSG configuration to control whether a sign-on screen will be displayed. WSG honors the QLMTSECOFR system value, so you can use it to control whether users with *ALLOBJ or *SERVICE special authority can sign on with WSG.

Until V4R2, WSG ignored the QINACTITV system value. In pre-V4R2 releases, you must use the INACTTIMO parameter in the WSG configuration to control how long WSG waits before it ends a session.

WSG does honor the QMAXSGNACN system value. But because WSG creates virtual devices, you need to use the QAUTOVRT system value to control how many virtual devices can be created on your system.

Logging is available to track user accesses. Use the Access Logging parameter and specify *YES in the configuration to enable logging. You can find the log records in the QUSRSYS/QATMTLOG physical file.

SMTP

Simple Mail Transfer Protocol (SMTP) lets you send and receive e-mail. Flooding a system with misdirected e-mail (i.e., e-mail that has an invalid recipient) is another popular denial-of-service attack. To protect your system from being a router for misdirected e-mail, don't use *ANY *ANY in the system distribution directory. Removing the *ANY *ANY entry causes OS/400 to reject misdirected e-mail when it isn't addressed to a user in your network. If you don't reject misdirected e-mail, it could be routed around your network, taking up valuable system resources.

You can also have a problem if your system redirects misdirected e-mail to another system on the Internet. If your system has been found to do this, other systems can "blackball" your system on the Internet and refuse to accept e-mail from your system. If the blackballed system is your Web server, which is sending out order confirmations via e-mail, then you have a problem. On the other hand, you want to protect your own AS/400 from systems that are known to route misdirected e-mail. Three PTFs let you configure your system to control SMTP's RELAY and CONNECTIONS functions:

- V4R2 5769TC1 SF52864
- V4R3 5769TC1 SF53421
- V4R4 5769TC1 SF54014

Another hacker trick is to mail-bomb a system, flooding it with e-mail from many locations. If you configure SMTP to automatically register users in the System Distribution Directory, such an attach will also flood the System Distribution Directory. To avoid this exposure, specify *NO for the AUTOADD attribute in the SMTP configuration.

Viruses attached to e-mail are an increasing problem. IBM added support to the SMTP server (by way of PTFs in V4R4 and V4R5) for scanning e-mail attachments and the subject line of all e-mail that comes in or goes out through the SMTP server, the POP server, or the mail framework for the SNADs gateway. This support looks for known virus titles and file types. Had you had this support when the "I Love You" virus made the rounds of the world's e-mail systems early in 2000, you could have configured a filter to scan the subject line of all e-mail for the known titles of the virus attachment. When the virus was found, you could have either deleted the attachment or sent it to a specified location for possible repair. For the PTF numbers of this new support, go to the AS/400 TCP/IP Web site at http://www.as400.ibm.com/tcpip.

You can also use an alias table to hide the profile name of AS/400 users who send and receive e-mail. If hackers can find user profile names, they are halfway to signing on to your system. Use the WRKNAMSMTP (Work with Names for SMTP) command to define aliases.

POP

The name of this TCP/IP application, Post Office Protocol, pretty well describes its function. POP is an electronic mailbox that receives e-mail and stores it until the user retrieves it. To retrieve e-mail, a user must have an entry in the System Distribution Directory and an AS/400 user profile and password. The password is passed to the AS/400 as clear text. You can't control whether clients (e.g., Web browsers) store the AS/400 user profile and password. If a user has a reason to access your AS/400 other than to access e-mail, you might want to create two profiles: one for accessing the user's personal mailbox and another for the user to use to sign on and access AS/400 applications. If you use this approach, create the mailbox profile with the following attributes so that the user can't use the mailbox profile to sign on to and exploit your system.

Initial program	INLPGM(*NONE)
Initial menu	INLMNU(*SIGNOFF)
Limited capabilities	LMTCPB(*YES)
Special authorities	SPCAUT(*NONE)
Group profiles	GRPPRF(*NONE)

Unfortunately, a user who can't sign on also can't change passwords. Therefore, you need to set the password expiration interval to *NOMAX (so it never expires) or write a program that changes the password and runs at a regular interval.

To prevent your system from being mail-bombed, make sure you set the size of your ASPs to an appropriate value. This value should be large enough to store and serve your users' e-mail but small enough to reach the limit without wasting too much room for unwanted e-mail in the event of a mail bomb.

POP stores e-mail in the Integrated File System (IFS) on the AS/400. To prevent users from snooping through other users' e-mail, you must monitor the authority of

/QTCPTMM/SMTPBOX in the IFS. E-mail sent to the AS/400 through SMTP is stored in this subdirectory before being delivered to a user's mailbox. The files that store the e-mail use the naming convention QTCPTMM/MAIL/user_profile_name. Anyone with *RX authority can see the contents of these files, and anyone who has *RW authority can update or change the files. You can use the PRTPUBAUT (Print Publicly Authorized Objects) and PRTPVTAUT (Print Private Authority) commands to monitor who has authority to these files.

BOOTP and TFTP

Bootstrap Protocol (BOOTP), in combination with Trivial File Transfer Protocol (TFTP), is used to support IBM Network Station for AS/400. BOOTP provides the dynamic IP address and initial program load (IPL) source for medialess network clients (i.e., PCs without hard drives). The client makes a request of the BOOTP server, and BOOTP returns the client's IP address and the name of the IPL file. The client then makes a request of TFTP, which downloads the IPL file and ends the TFTP session. If you aren't using network stations, you don't need to run either BOOTP or TFTP servers.

BOOTP doesn't provide a way for a user to gain access to your AS/400. The only aspect of BOOTP that may be cause for concern is the integrity of the BOOTP table that manages the IP addresses for the network stations. If a user inappropriately updates this table, your network stations might not work.

On the other hand, you do need to monitor TFTP. TFTP is a simple file transfer mechanism. Unlike FTP, TFTP doesn't require or allow a user ID and password before transferring a file. All requests run under the QTFTP user profile. As initially configured, TFTP downloads only the files the network station needs. However, the directory from which the files are downloaded is configurable in the TFTP configuration, so you should monitor the following:

- who has authority to the CHGTFTPA (Change TFTP Attributes) command
- the directory specified for the Alternate Target Directory parameter on CHGTFTPA
- the public and private authorities of this directory
- what resources the QTFTP user profile has authority to

You can change TFTP to perform other file transfers, but you must control it very carefully. Use an exit program to validate each request.

DHCP

Dynamic Host Configuration Protocol (DHCP) autoconfigures devices (using a DHCP-enabled client) attaching to your system via TCP/IP. (If you use DHCP, you don't need to run BOOTP.) If you want to use this TCP/IP server, you should analyze how accessible your LAN is. How easy is it for someone to walk into your enterprise and attach a laptop to your LAN? If DHCP were active, the laptop would be autoconfigured to access your network. You can protect your system from this type of attack by creating the list of hardware addresses DHCP will automatically configure. Unknown hardware (such as the intruder's laptop) would not be configured.

You should monitor who has *RW authority to two IFS files that contain configuration information for DHCP:

- /QIBM/UserData/OS400/DHCP/dhcpsd.cfg
- /QIBM/UserData/OS400/DHCP/dhcprd.cfg

Anyone who has *RW authority can update these files.

DNS

Domain Name Server (DNS) provides name lookups: Given a host name, DNS finds the corresponding IP address, and vice versa. The DNS that the AS/400 provides should be used within your intranet. You shouldn't use the same DNS for both intranet and Internet (or public) systems. Think of the DNS as a phone directory. You typically don't publish your employees' internal phone extensions in a public directory, but you publish your company's toll-free number widely. The DNS on the AS/400 is your "private" directory; your "public" directory is on your firewall or provided by an Internet Service Provider (ISP). To an intruder, a DNS provides a topology of your network, complete with IP addresses. Some networks are partitioned into subnets. You might not want users in one subnet to know the topology of the other subnets. To define which IP addresses or network interfaces can view your topology, you can define protection directives for your DNS.

To protect your DNS configuration, monitor who has authority to the \QIBM\UserData\OS400\DNS and \QIBM\UserData\OS400\DNS\TMP directories and the files they contain. Only the user who created the DNS file or the users who have to maintain those files should have authority to them. Public authority should be *EXCLUDE.

REXEC

The Remote Execution (REXEC) server allows an REXEC client to run commands on your AS/400. REXEC provides the same type of function as FTP's RCMD subcommand (see "FTP" earlier in this chapter). Just like FTP, REXEC requires a user ID and password and checks the value of the user profile's limited capability (LMTCPB) parameter before running the accompanying command. If the user has LMTCPB (*YES), REXEC rejects the request. You can also use exit points to validate incoming requests.

If you don't normally let users access an AS/400 command line, don't start the REXEC server. When you start this server, you in effect provide a command line.

RouteD

Route Daemon (RouteD) provides support for Routing Information Protocol (RIP). You use RouteD to increase the efficiency of network traffic. Using RouteD, systems update other systems within a network on how best to route IP packets. An intruder with access to your RouteD server could reroute packets through a system so they could be sniffed or modified.

AS/400 RIP support in V4R2 and later (RIPv2) provides some authentication mechanisms. The earlier version doesn't, and you should use it only within a network in which you "trust" every system.

SNMP

Simple Network Management Protocol (SNMP) lets the AS/400 act as an agent to manage gateways, routers, and hosts in the network. An SNMP agent gathers information about the system and performs functions that remote SNMP network managers request. Some of the information gathered could be information that you've hidden by using aliases or by using the DNS server. An intruder could use SNMP to gain information about the topology of your network and possibly to alter the network.

Access to SNMP requires a *community name*. A community name is somewhat analogous to a password, but it isn't encrypted. To limit the possibility of someone masquerading as a legitimate SNMP network manager, change the value of the Internet Address parameter (INTNETADR) on the ADDCOMSNMP (Add Community for SNMP) command from *ANY to the IP address of your SNMP network manager.

INETD

Unlike most TCP/IP servers, the INETD server performs multiple services, including time, daytime, echo, and discard. On most systems, the INETD server is the "master" server that receives all requests and starts the appropriate server, such as Telnet or FTP, based on the incoming request. The AS/400 implements separate servers for each of these services, and those servers' incoming requests aren't routed through INETD. However, some services do remain routed through the INETD server on the AS/400 and can be used throughout the network to obtain the system time, determine whether a system is active, and so on. Because of the nature of those services, they are also powerful tools for denial-of-service attacks. For example, intruders can configure system ABC to send an echo request to system XYZ, which returns the echo request to ABC. The intruder could then configure system ABC to route the echo request back to system XYZ, producing a continuous loop that consumes processor time and network bandwidth.

Should you decide you need one of the services provided by the INETD server, you should configure the server to permit only the required services. You should also monitor who has access to the /QIBM/UserData/OS400/inetd/inetd.conf and /QIBM/ProdData/OS400/inetd/inetd.conf configuration files. These files determine which services are started when you start the INETD server and under which user profile the services run. You should let only the system administrator have access to these files. Set public authority to the files to *EXCLUDE.

IBM HTTP Server for AS/400

The IBM HTTP Server for AS/400 is the Web server that ships with OS/400. The HTTP Server provides protection directives to let you control the information your system serves to the Internet. The HTTP Server also lets you perform basic authentication and enables the concept of Internet users. (For details about Internet access, see Chapter 9.)

Whenever you start the IBM HTTP Server for AS/400, you have what is called an *instance* of the server. You can have multiple instances of the server. One instance can be an *ADMIN instance that lets you perform administrative tasks. The Uniform Resource Locator (URL) for the administration home page is published in IBM manuals, so it's probably also published on hacker Web sites. To protect the *ADMIN instance of your Web server, you can do any or all of the following:

- Use a firewall to protect your AS/400 from direct access from the Internet and to hide your internal system and domain names, which make up part of your URL.
- Configure the *ADMIN instance to use SSL to ensure that the AS/400 user ID and password required to perform administrative tasks are encrypted.
- Run the *ADMIN instance only when performing administrative tasks.

If you need to ensure that the information being served or the data being sent from a Web browser is kept confidential or that an *ADMIN instance of the IBM HTTP Server for AS/400 is secure, you can use protection directives to configure the use of SSL for all pages being served or for specific pages. For information about SSL, see the section "SSL" later in this chapter.

DRDA

Distributed Relational Database Architecture (DRDA) defines the protocols for communication between an application program and a remote relational database. DRDA on the AS/400 uses Distributed Data Management (DDM) to communicate to the remote system that contains the relational database. DRDA can run over Advanced Program to Program Communications (APPC) or TCP/IP.

When run over APPC, DRDA uses the conversation-level security inherent in APPC. However, TCP/IP provides no comparable security feature. When you run DRDA over TCP/IP, by default the connection requires a user name and password to be sent to the system on which the relational database resides. The request runs under this user profile on the remote system. The user can provide the user ID and password on the SQL CONNECT statement when connecting to the relational database. Alternatively, you can use the ADDSVRAUTE (Add Server Authentication Entry) command to define a server authorization entry:

```
ADDSVRAUTE USRPRF(application_requester_job_profile) +
           SERVER(remote_RDB_name)                    +
           USERID(server_job_profile)                 +
           PASSWORD(password)
```

When trying to connect to the distributed database, the system uses the user ID and password from this entry. When the ADDSVRAUTE command runs, OS/400 encrypts the password and populates the authentication entry with the user ID and encrypted password. However, the system needs to retrieve the password in clear text. To allow authentication entry passwords to be decrypted, you must change the QRETSVRSEC system value to 1.

DRDA gives you the option of sending only a user ID and not a password. However, this option isn't very secure, and the remote system must be configured to allow such a connection. In V4R4, you can send an encrypted password on the connection if the client supports the password substitution feature. AS/400 Java Toolbox and Client Access OLE DB Provider are clients known to support password substitution.

Dial-Up Line Security Considerations

Using a dial-up line is scary for many IT shops. Security-conscious network managers imagine a hacker getting into their system and hacking away at proprietary or sensitive information. Although the risks are real, a few simple precautions can significantly reduce them.

Control the Line Status

Callers who can't establish a communications session can't sign on. If you use dial-up lines for outgoing calls only, be sure lines are varied off when they aren't being used. When the line is varied off, no one can dial in to the system.

If you accept incoming calls, use AUTOANS(*NO) when possible (e.g., when you have someone to answer the message). The modem will connect, but the system won't allow the connection to be completed until the system operator answers an inquiry message.

Authorize Devices

Where possible, authorize configured devices to only the user profiles that will be dialing in for access. This precaution is usually feasible because typically only a few users have dial-up access to a system. You reduce your risk by authorizing the device to only those profiles. Along with device authorization, you should use the QLMTSECOFR system value discussed in Chapter 2 to limit users' ability to sign on to a dial-up device using a user profile that has *ALLOBJ or *SERVICE special authority. When you eliminate the danger of an outside source signing on with profiles that have these authorities, you are limiting your security exposure.

Dial-Back Security

If you use dial-up communications, dial-back security is a feature that might be worth purchasing. When you use dial-back security, the system identifies each user that calls in, and then the modem or software hangs up and calls the user back at a known, previously verified telephone number. Dial-back security eliminates random hacking by those who find your dial-up number listed on some bulletin board.

Dial-back security comes in two forms: fixed and variable. In fixed dial-back security, the local system disconnects after identifying the caller and then calls the number associated with the user ID that placed the incoming call. Variable security requires the caller to enter a password to establish the connection (the password isn't an AS/400 password). After the connection is made, the user can enter a phone number for the local system to use when calling back. The system disconnects and returns the call at the specified phone number. Although the advantage of fixed dial-back is lost, at least the user is required to enter a password. This method of dial-back security is necessary when dial-in users are traveling.

Dial-back modems function like other modems except that dial-back modems physically disconnect and then redial the caller after user verification. Communications software on the user's receiving system must be configured to accept the incoming call immediately to establish the connection.

Data Encryption

The use of encryption is becoming increasingly common, especially for enterprises doing business over the Internet. If you want to protect your data from being sent over the Internet in clear text, you must use encryption. Modern data encryption is accomplished primarily through two popular standards: the Data Encryption Standard (DES), defined by the United States government, and the RSA encryption algorithm, offered by RSA Data Security of Redwood City, California. Besides protecting data so that it can't be read without being decrypted, encryption enables much of today's Internet security technology.

Let's take a quick look at how some of this technology works before we describe OS/400's encryption features. Don't worry, we won't discuss the derivation of the various encryption algorithms. We'll keep this explanation at the conceptual level.

Public Key Infrastructure (PKI)

Public key infrastructure (PKI) uses encryption to let you send data securely and privately over an essentially unsecure public network, such as the Internet. When using an encryption algorithm, you feed the encryption algorithm an element called the *encryption key*, which the system uses to encrypt the data. There are two types of keys: symmetric and asymmetric.

If you use an algorithm that takes a symmetric key, you use the same key to both encrypt and decrypt the data. Although symmetric keys are simple and fast, they have drawbacks. Say you encrypt an e-mail message with a symmetric key. How do you securely give that key to the e-mail recipient? Send it in another e-mail? Not very secure. Send it via certified letter? Not very practical. Give it to the recipient over the phone? It's easy to introduce an error either providing the key or copying it.

You might instead choose to use an algorithm that requires an asymmetric key. Asymmetric keys are actually two keys: one key to either encrypt or decrypt and a second key to do the reverse operation. (Figure 8.1 illustrates the differences between symmetric and asymmetric keys.)

FIGURE 8.1
Symmetric and Asymmetric Keys

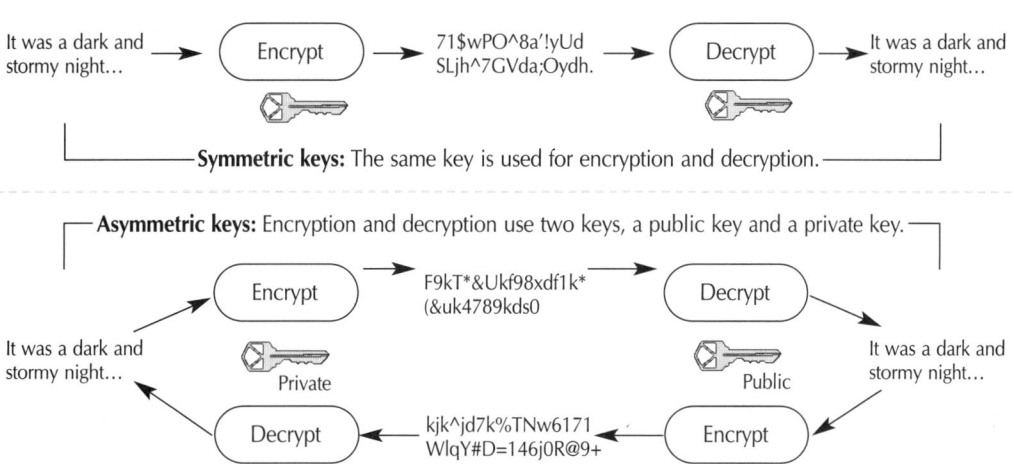

These two keys, one a *private key* and the other a *public key,* are known as a public/private key-pair. When you send an e-mail message, the sender encrypts her message with the recipient's public key and the recipient decrypts the e-mail message with his own private key. When he responds, he encrypts the reply with her public key and she decrypts his response using her private key.

Let's see how public/private key-pairs are used with digital certificates.

Digital Certificates

A digital certificate has many similarities to a passport, but in electronic form. Like a passport, a digital certificate must be issued by a particular agency (in this case a Certificate Authority — CA) and is valid for a particular time period. You must present some form of identification to have a CA issue you a digital certificate. Once issued, the certificate can be used to identify a user, server, company, or other entity. And just as some countries don't allow entry by people holding passports from certain other countries, servers can choose to disallow digital certificates issued by particular CAs.

Part of the process of creating a digital certificate includes the generation of a public/private key-pair. Users typically store private keys in their browser on their PC. A public key is included as part of the digital certificate. Let's look at how a popular Internet technology makes use of digital certificates and the public/private key-pairs associated with them.

Secure Sockets Layer (SSL)

Secure Sockets Layer, better known as SSL, is a protocol that lets applications using a sockets connection ensure that all data is encrypted. Telnet and HTTP are two examples of applications that use SSL to encrypt data that flows between the client and server.

When an application requests SSL services from a server, the client will always verify the server. To do this, the client will send some random data to the server, along with a challenge that in effect says, "Tell me who you are." When the server receives the challenge from the client, the server uses its private key to encrypt the random data and returns the encrypted data and the server's digital certificate to the client. The client then takes the public key from the server's digital certificate, decrypts the random data, and compares it to the data originally sent.

Also, as part of verification, the client will determine what CA signed or issued the server's digital certificate and check that the CA is included in the client's list of trusted signers. In other words, the client makes sure that it trusts the CA that issued the server's digital certificate. If the random data didn't decrypt properly or if the server's digital certificate isn't in the client's list of trusted CAs, the connection isn't established.

When the decrypted random data is the same as the original data and the server trusts the CA that issued the digital certificate, the client and server negotiate a session key. The client and server then encrypt the rest of the transmission using a symmetric key.

These steps are always followed when a client requests an SSL session. Optionally, after server authentication, you can request SSL to authenticate the client. For client authentication, the steps discussed above are reversed — in other words, the server sends the client random data and a "Tell me who you are" request, and authentication proceeds as it did in the other direction.

Let's look at a practical example. John is doing some Christmas shopping and goes to the Web site http://www.savemefromgoingtothemall.com. When he finds the perfect gift for his wife, he clicks the Purchase It button, which takes him to the payment page, where he is asked to enter his credit card number.

The link to the payment page is coded as HTTPS, or HTTP secure. The HTTPS code lets the browser know that it must verify the Web server. Before John even sees the payment page, the browser sends a challenge request and validates the Web server. After validation, the rest of the transmission, including John's credit card number, is encrypted. John can verify that the transmission is encrypted by looking at his browser. If John is using Netscape Communicator, the padlock in the lower left-hand corner is closed when an SSL session has been established. If John is running Microsoft Internet Explorer, the skeleton key in the lower left-hand corner is closed.

The IBM HTTP Server for AS/400 has been SSL-enabled since V4R1. In V4R4, IBM SSL-enabled the Telnet, DDM, DRDA, Lightweight Directory Access Protocol (LDAP), Management Central, Java Toolbox, Open Database Connectivity (ODBC), and Client Access Express servers (i.e., data transfer, 5250 emulation, data queues, remote queues, and print servers). To configure these servers to use SSL, you must use the AS/400's digital certificate facility, Digital Certificate Manager (DCM), which we discuss in the next section.

You must also go into the *ADMIN instance of the Web server and enable the server instance to use SSL. Then, in your HTML, you must code the link to the page that requires an SSL connection to be HTTPS rather than HTTP. You can also use a protection directive to ensure that certain pages aren't served if the connection isn't SSL. For the Client Access Express servers, you must also configure the client to request verification of the server for the services you want to run using SSL.

As of V4R5 (V4R4 by PTF), both the HTTP Server and Telnet server provide optional client-side SSL authentication. Client-side SSL authentication requires that users who make a request of either the HTTP server or the Telnet server have a digital certificate so that the server can validate the users. Client-side SSL authentication is a very powerful feature that lets the system administrator very tightly control who can access the system. As a system administrator, you can configure the server to accept only digital certificates issued by a particular CA. You could choose to set up your AS/400 as a CA and then issue the certificates to only the individuals you want to connect to your system.

This approach is especially valuable for Telnet when you want to very tightly control who can sign on to the system over the Internet. For example, say you have four system operators who rotate on-call duty. By issuing each operator a digital certificate for his or her home PC, you can let those operators sign on from home to manage the system and perhaps save them trips to the office in the middle of the night. Because those operators are the only ones you've issued certificates for, they will be the only users able to establish a session to the Telnet server.

Digital Certificate Manager (DCM)

DCM lets you set up your AS/400 as a CA, create digital certificates, and receive digital certificates from well-known CAs, such as VeriSign, Equifax, and Thawte. You use DCM to associate a digital certificate with SSL-enabled servers such as Telnet, IBM HTTP Server for AS/400, Java Toolbox, and various Client Access Express servers, so that your system knows what digital certificate to use when a client makes an SSL request.

Although you can use DCM to create user certificates, it lacks the management tools to manage large numbers of digital certificates. If you need to create fewer than 50 digital certificates, DCM probably supplies adequate management capabilities for you to use it as a CA. If you want to issue more than that, however — and certainly if you want to issue hundreds or thousands of digital certificates — you will probably want to establish a relationship with a well-known CA to obtain your digital certificates.

Virtual Private Networks (VPNs)

VPNs are another method of ensuring that data is encrypted during transmission. VPNs let you establish a secure, private connection over a public network. VPNs use three standards: IP Security (IPSec), which provides authentication, integrity, and encryption; Internet Key Exchange (IKE), which manages the encryption keys; and Layer 2 Tunneling Protocol (L2TP), which extends PPP connections to a destination network.

The difference between VPN and SSL is that VPN uses IPSec, which is implemented lower in the TCP/IP communications stack than SSL is. After an IPSec session is established, all subsequent traffic is encrypted. Unlike with SSL, you don't have to change an application to ensure encryption of the application's data.

A VPN might be a good choice to replace a leased line. Rather than having a dedicated physical connection, you could use a VPN to establish a private connection using the Internet's bandwidth, yet be assured that the data from any application that uses the connection is transmitted securely.

OS/400 takes its integrated VPN support very seriously. At least twice a year, IBM's VPN development team participates in a VPN "bake-off," which gathers VPN vendors to test the latest enhancements to their VPN solutions. IBM's participation ensures that the OS/400 VPN solution interoperates with other vendors' solutions.

Other Encryption Options

If you need to implement data encryption within your own applications, you have several options. You can use the APIs provided with the AS/400's hardware or software products to encrypt data before it's transmitted or stored. IBM offers both hardware — the 4758 Cryptographic Coprocessor for AS/400 (new with V4R5) and the 2620 Cryptographic Processor (being discontinued after V4R5) — and software — IBM Cryptographic Support for AS/400. You can use these products to perform encryption before transmitting data or writing it to media. These products use DES encryption. If you choose to implement the cryptography algorithms from RSA, you can use RSA's BSAFE ToolKit for AS/400. All methods require that the application and all other applications using or receiving the data implement the respective encryption APIs.

Another option, if you're writing a sockets application (i.e., an application that runs over the TCP/IP protocol), is to use the Internet standard Transport Layer Security (TLS), which is available in V4R5 or, in earlier releases, in SSL. (TLS is basically the industry-standard version of SSL.) AS/400 SSL APIs that use encryption algorithms from RSA are shipped with the operating system.

If you're using APPC, you can configure OS/400's APPC mode to use session-level encryption (SLE). You configure SLE through the CRTMODD (Create Mode Description) or CHGMODD (Change Mode Description) command. Data decryption at the other end of the transmission requires modes on both ends to be configured to use SLE. SLE requires the 2620 Cryptographic Processor hardware feature as well as the Common Cryptographic Architecture Services (CCAS/400) PRPQ software. Because the new 4758 hardware coprocessor doesn't support SLE, SLE won't be supported after V4R5.

AS/400 Encryption Requirements

To enable the encryption key and algorithms that OS/400 can use for encryption (including the 4758 hardware coprocessor, the IBM Cryptographic Support for AS/400 software product, and the encryption used for SSL and VPN), you must install one of IBM's encryption-enabling products (i.e., product 5769-AC1, 5769-AC2, or 5769-AC3). Export laws in the United States have relaxed considerably in recent years, so you can use the strongest encryption enabler (5769-AC3) in most countries. However, at one time, the United States disallowed export of the most powerful encryption, resulting in three enabler products. Nevertheless, the two strongest encryption enablers will probably both remain because some countries don't allow strong encryption to be imported and because the United States still prevents the export of strong encryption to some countries.

Although data encryption can be CPU-intensive, it provides considerable protection for those who need that level of security in data transmissions or storage.

APPN/APPC Communications Configuration Security

To set up your AS/400 to participate in a network using Advanced Peer-to-Peer Networking (APPN) or APPC, you must create configuration objects (i.e., line descriptions, control unit descriptions, and device descriptions) and specify the communications parameters necessary to let the AS/400 function in that network. When you set up these configuration objects, you need to be aware of the security ramifications of several of the object parameters.

Line Description

Four line-description parameters affect security:

SECURITY	Security for Line
AUTOCRTCTL	Autocreate Controller
AUTOANS	Autoanswer
AUTODIAL	Autodial

The SECURITY parameter identifies to the network the physical line's security attributes. You need to specify a value for this parameter when the configuration is part of an APPN environment that facilitates route calculation. The system uses the specified value to determine the best route for communications to take between systems. The interesting thing about this parameter is that the system has no way of determining whether the value you supply is valid; an "honor system" is in effect. In other words, the value describes rather than determines the security characteristics of the line. It's important to understand that, apart from network route calculation, this value doesn't affect any of the configuration's communications elements.

The possible values for the SECURITY parameter are

*NONSECURE	No security on the line
*PKTSWTNET	Packet-switched network (the traffic doesn't take a fixed route, and so is more secure than if it did)
*UNDGRDCBL	Underground cable (considered secure)
*SECURECND	Secure, but not guarded, conduit (e.g., pressurized pipe)
*GUARDCND	Guarded conduit, protected against physical tapping
*ENCRYPTED	Data encrypted before transmission
*MAX	Guarded conduit, protected against physical and radiation tapping

A more useful security parameter is AUTOCRTCTL, which specifies whether the local system automatically creates a controller description when no existing controller matches an incoming request. The possible values for AUTOCRTCTL are *YES and *NO. If you specify AUTOCRTCTL(*YES), anyone with access to the line can connect to your system.

AUTOANS determines whether the local system automatically responds to a dial-up call. The possible values for AUTOANS are *YES and *NO. *YES specifies that when the line receives a dial-up call — after the modem establishes the connection — the AS/400 is to automatically start communicating. A value of *NO causes the local system to first prompt the system operator, who can then determine whether the call should be connected. This value ensures that the system operator knows when someone is dialing in to the system and can verify that the user profile is a valid dial-up participant.

AUTODIAL determines whether a switched line can make outgoing calls without operator intervention. The valid values for AUTODIAL are *YES and *NO. Specifying AUTODIAL(*YES) allows anyone with access to your system to dial out to other systems.

Controller Description

When you create a controller description, two security parameters are used in an APPN or APPC environment to describe the remote system to which the AS/400 attaches:

RMTCPNAME	Remote Control Point Name
EXCHID	Exchange ID

RMTCPNAME specifies the location name of the remote system to which the control unit refers. This parameter ensures that only the named system can use the control unit for communications.

The EXCHID parameter further identifies the remote system to be connected. The EXCHID defined on the local control unit must match that provided by the remote system. If the two don't match, communications are not allowed. EXCHID is required for synchronous data link control (SDLC) switched connections but is optional for other line types.

In addition to RMTCPNAME and EXCHID, you should understand the ramifications of the three other parameters:

AUTOCRTDEV	Automatically Create Device Description
CPSSN	Control Point Sessions
DSCTMR	Disconnect-Timer

AUTOCRTDEV determines whether the system automatically creates a device description when an incoming request doesn't find the matching device description. For APPN-capable controllers, this parameter is ignored and devices are automatically created.

APPN-capable controllers use the CPSSN parameter to determine whether they should automatically establish an APPC connection with the remote system. This connection is used to exchange information about the network to ensure that it stays up-to-date. Specifying *YES for the CPSSN parameter means that the switched line used for the connection isn't automatically dropped, leaving your system open to another session "riding in" or "piggybacking" on your established connection.

DSCTMR specifies the timers used for dropping the connection when there are no active sessions on the controller. Specifying a large value for this parameter leaves your system vulnerable to piggybacking.

Device Description

Most of the configuration security options for an APPC environment are in the device description. In an APPN network, most device description parameters are defined on the remote configuration list entry, which you create by executing the CRTCFGL (Create Configuration List) and ADDCFGLE (Add Configuration List Entry) commands. APPN networks require an entry on the QAPPNRMT configuration list for each remote system whose attributes you want to be different from the defaults (to see what the APPN defaults are, use the CRTDEVAPPC (Create Device APPC) command). Let's start with the following three parameters.

RMTLOCNAME	Remote Location Name
LOCPWD	Location Password
SECURELOC	Secure Location

When defining an APPC, asynchronous (ASC), bisynchronous (BSC), Intra, System Network Architecture Upline Facility (SNUF), or SNA host (HOST) device, you must use the RMTLOCNAME parameter to specify the name of the remote location associated with the device. The communications link is established only when the remote location name specified by the device matches the attached system's local location name.

The LOCPWD parameter lets you require a password for access to APPC devices (i.e., those created with the CRTDEVAPPC command). The location password isn't associated with a user profile. During an attempt to connect to an APPC device, the remote system sends the password to the local system to prove that the remote system is who it claims to be. A value of *NONE means that no system password is required to validate the connection with the device. Alternatively, you can specify, in hexadecimal, a password of up to eight characters. Any incoming request for connection must include this password.

Security Recommendation
In an APPN environment, use the LOCPWD parameter with all systems that support it. LOCPWD provides additional security, especially if you're using the SECURELOC(*YES) parameter to verify security from the remote system.

SECURELOC specifies whether the local system is to let the remote system verify the user profile and password and send an "already verified" indicator with the DDM request or with the program start request (when using program-to-program communications). A value of *NO specifies that security validation by the remote system isn't allowed. A value of *YES indicates that the local system should accept the remote system's verification of the user profile and password. A value of *VFYENCPWD tells the local system that remote verification is allowed provided the user ID and password on the local system match the user ID and password on the remote system. To determine whether the user ID and password match, APPC compares the local user's and remote user's encrypted passwords. Although *VFYENCPWD requires that you maintain the same passwords on all systems that connect, this value provides a much higher degree of security than does the *YES value.

In an APPN network, the device description's SECURELOC parameter is ignored. Instead, the parameter is specified for the remote configuration list entry associated with the remote system. To check or change the remote configuration list entries in an APPN network, use the WRKCFGL (Work with Configuration Lists) command.

> **Technical Note**
> You can use the PRTCMNSEC (Print Communications Security) command to monitor the values of the security-relevant parameters for lines, controllers, devices, and configuration lists.

Four other device-description parameters also affect security:

APPN	APPN-Capable
SNGSSN	Single Session
PREESTSSN	Pre-Establish Session
PGMSTRQS	SNUF Program Start Fields

The APPN parameter determines whether the device can be used to roam elsewhere in your network or is limited to the target system. You need to determine how much you want to control where your users roam in your network.

Settings for the SNGSSN and PREESTSSN parameters can make your system more or less vulnerable to piggybacking. SNGSSN(*NO) says that you can use the same device description for multiple sessions. For example, if a user establishes a session between System A and System B, SNGSSN(*YES) prevents a user from piggybacking on that connection to connect from System B to System A.

When a remote system contacts the local system, the PREESTSSN parameter determines whether a session is established immediately or only after an application requests a session with the local system. Although specifying PREESTSSN(*YES) minimizes the time it takes for an application to complete a connection, PREESTSSN(*NO) is safer because the connection is made only when a request is made and the connection is dropped when the line is no longer in use.

The PGMSTRQS parameter (valid only for SNUF devices) determines whether users on the remote system can start and run programs on the local system. SNUF allows APPC-like program invokes so, conceivably, any program could be invoked.

APPN Filtering Support

Some people refer to OS/400's APPN filtering support as "APPN firewall support" because filtering is a widely used firewall technique. APPN filtering lets you control which systems can connect to your system and which systems can pass through your system to access another system. The control is based on APPN location names and control point names. Filtering is a very powerful function that gives you great control over who can roam your network. See the IBM manual *AS/400 Tips and Tools for Securing Your AS/400 V4R5* (SC41-5300) for details about how to set up filtering support.

Helpful Tools

The PRTCMNSEC tool helps you monitor aspects of network security, including the security-related parameters for lines, controllers, devices, and configuration lists.

Security tool	Description
PRTCMNSEC (Print Communications Security)	Use this command to monitor the values of the security-relevant parameters for lines, controllers, devices, and configuration lists.

Operations Navigator

Operations Navigator can simplify management of TCP/IP servers. In fact, you can administer some functions, such as IP packet filtering, only through Operations Navigator.

To manage TCP/IP through Operations Navigator, expand the icon for the AS/400 you're connected to and then expand Network. Click IP Security to configure IP packet filtering. Click Protocols, and then click TCP/IP to configure port restrictions and which servers autostart. Expand Servers and then click TCP/IP, as Figure 8.2 shows, to see which TCP/IP servers are started. Right-click a server that is started and choose Properties to see the server's configuration properties. Right-click a server that is stopped, and you can change the configuration properties.

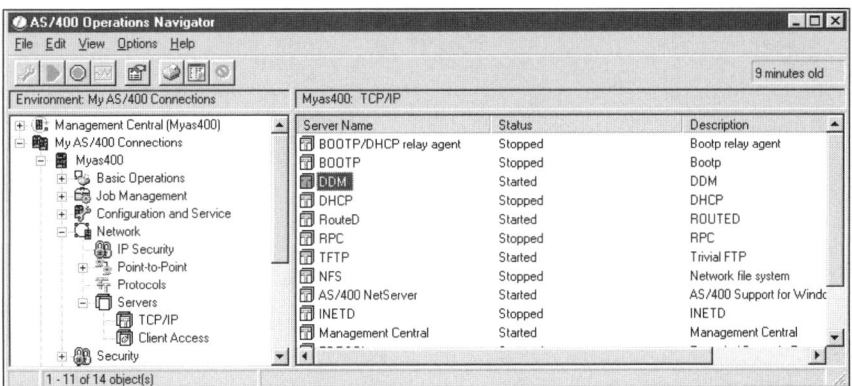

FIGURE 8.2
Viewing TCP/IP Servers

Chapter 9

Internet Security

The Internet isn't just for serving static Web pages any more. In the business world, the Internet provides technology so that customers can obtain product information, order products, track their orders, and get help if the product fails. Beyond the typical business to consumer (B2C) business model, business to business (B2B) models are in place. Now, instead of using a leased phone line, you can connect directly with your vendors or suppliers through virtual private networks (VPNs). You can purchase supplies through electronic markets rather than ordering from paper catalogs, or maybe you supply goods to those markets and provide an electronic catalog for your customers to order from. You also might be using the Internet to let traveling employees dial into your system.

However you're using the Internet, securing your information assets in this networked world requires much more than simply securing your AS/400 as part of your internal network. When you use the Internet, you open up your system to the outside, uncontrollable, and sometimes dangerous world. It's a frightening thought, we know; but we think market forces are going to require most companies to do at least some portion of their business on the Internet, or else go out of business altogether.

So, where do you start? First, you need to determine your level of risk tolerance. That is, how determined are you and to what lengths are you willing to go to prevent your system from being broken into? Then, assume that someone has broken into your system. What damage could be done? Let's look at some of the issues you need to consider.

What data is stored on the system that is accessible to the Internet? If the data is highly confidential (e.g., business data that your competitors would like to get their hands on), sensitive (e.g., credit card numbers), or private (e.g., patient medical records), your risk tolerance will be lower than it would be if your system is only serving static Web pages about your products. You can easily restore such pages should someone break in and delete them.

How dependent are you on the system that is accessible to the Internet? Does that system need to be available 24×7? Some businesses, such as Amazon.com, do business only on the Web. If Amazon.com's Web site is down, the business is, in effect, closed.

How much damage would your reputation suffer if a hacker were to break into your system and steal data or "graffiti" your Web site? What if a hacker broke into an online stockbroker's system and entered invalid trades and transferred money into and out of accounts? You can imagine that the brokerage's reputation — and its future success — would be greatly damaged.

Your level of risk tolerance will determine how many layers of defense you need to use to protect your system. If you were dressing for a cold January day in Minnesota, you'd need many layers of clothing — long underwear, thermal socks, turtleneck, wool sweater, flannel-lined pants, down coat, scarf, hat, mittens, and boots — to stay warm. The lower your risk tolerance, the more layers of defense you need to dress your network in to be as safe as possible from outside attack. Your level of risk tolerance will also feed into the requirements you implement in your corporate security policy.

Corporate Security Policy

You need to update your corporate security policy to take into account your use of Internet technology. *Don't skip this step!* If you don't update your policy to consider Internet technology before you deploy the technology, soon, when you want to expand your use of the Internet, you won't know how it fits into your corporate policy. Consequently, you won't know what security measures to take or whether Internet technology should even be allowed in your configuration. The lower your risk tolerance, the more restrictive your security policy will be and the more layers of protection your systems will require.

To formulate your policy, you need to decide how you're going to deploy Internet technology throughout your network and what your network configuration must include. You also need to form a policy about appropriate use of the Internet by employees. Put the policy, along with the consequences of noncompliance, in writing and communicate it throughout your enterprise. Here are some of the topics you need to address.

- Where are you going to deploy firewall technology?
- What TCP/IP applications are required?
- Are you going to allow downloads from or uploads to your Web site?
- Does your Web site require real-time data from systems in your internal network? How are you going to implement the connection to your internal network?
- Will you let users connect to your system over the Internet? How are you going to protect that connection — VPN? Secure Sockets Layer (SSL)?
- Are you going to monitor the Web sites your users visit? For example, IBM monitors users' activity, but it doesn't filter Web sites. Unless employees access certain types of Web sites (e.g., pornographic sites) excessively, IBM takes no action, because it's easy for someone to land on an indecent Web site by following a link from a legitimate page. But maybe your organization would prefer to purchase software to prevent access to certain Web sites.
- What does the company want to do if pornographic material is found on users' workstations or if users repeatedly visit pornographic Web sites?
- Will you let users use corporate e-mail systems for personal messages?
- Will you let employees download code from the Internet?
- Are users allowed to run Java applets in browsers?
- How should employees handle suspected "social engineering" probes? Typically, someone calls an employee and pretends to be a fellow employee. The caller asks probing questions in search of inside secrets. Are your users aware of this practice? Encourage employees to verify the authenticity of the calls they receive before giving out information. Users also need to understand what constitutes sensitive information.

What may seem like an innocent piece of information might be the piece of the puzzle a hacker needs to gain access to your network.

After you've determined your level of risk tolerance and updated your security policy, it's time to decide how you're going to implement your policy. The rest of this chapter describes some of the layers of defense that you can use to protect your network. You'll need to examine each potential layer and determine whether you want to deploy it. Understand that there isn't one right answer. Each business must determine for itself what approach will serve its business needs. Not every company will find it practical or necessary to implement every layer. You might also find and want to deploy some layers of defense that we don't discuss. The important thing is that, given your business needs, you and your management feel comfortable with the layers of defense you put in place.

Internet Service Provider

Your first layer of defense lies with your ISP. When choosing an ISP, you need to determine whether the service provider cares about security. Does the ISP have an emergency contact person you can call if you're under a denial-of-service or hacker attack? A cooperative ISP is priceless when you're trying to track down an intruder or discover who launched the denial-of-service attack. Another question to ask the ISP you're considering is whether it has a contingency plan and what that plan is. Also look into the services the ISP provides. Most ISPs will provide packet filtering or other firewall services. Some enterprises might want to control their own firewall configurations, but small organizations without firewall skills will need to rely on the ISP's expertise.

Firewalls

Most Internet-connected networks require firewall technology for security. Firewalls can perform a number of functions. The functions of basic firewalls include using network address translation (NAT) to hide your system's TCP/IP address from the rest of the Internet world (therefore protecting your system's identity) and filtering unwanted incoming and outgoing requests or IP packets. Firewalls can also monitor for attacks and take action if one is detected. Some firewalls now include VPN capabilities and virus scanners to scan incoming e-mail.

Not long ago, such firewall technology was available only with a separate, standalone system loaded with firewall software. Recently, however, firewall technology has evolved. Today, it's often integrated into routers, appliances or *bricks*, and operating systems, such as OS/400. Where you implement the technology in your network depends on the functions you want, how much network traffic you anticipate, and how many layers of defense you want to employ.

To determine where to implement firewall technology, you must take your network configuration into consideration. Figure 9.1 illustrates a dedicated AS/400 connected to an internal network. This is an example of a network configuration that uses a dedicated AS/400 as either a Web server or a commerce server for a company that hosts an online catalog and takes orders. To protect this production AS/400, you would put the firewall between the Web server or commerce server and your internal network. Depending on the number of users that need to access the Internet, a firewall appliance might be sufficient. Beyond that, you might need to buy a more traditional hardware firewall. You might also want to use IP packet filtering in either your router or your dedicated AS/400 to block unwanted IP traffic.

FIGURE 9.1
A Dedicated Web Server Connected to an Internal Network

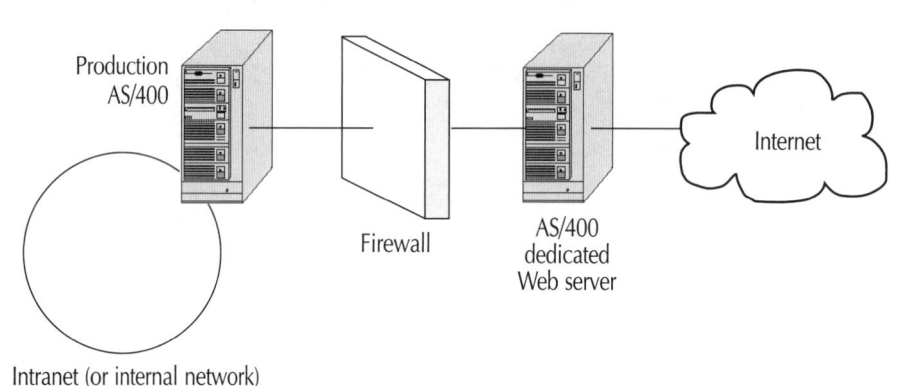

The configuration in Figure 9.2 provides Internet access as well as production operations. An enterprise that uses this type of network configuration might have a VPN connection from the production AS/400 to suppliers over the Internet. Another configuration might have the production AS/400 doing double duty as an Internet Web server. Although doing Web serving and production work on the same server isn't as secure a configuration as having a separate Web server, some operations might have business reasons for choosing this configuration. In the case of a VPN connection, a router with IP packet filtering might meet your needs. However, if your production system also acts as a Web server, you probably want the services, such as proxy or SOCKS servers, found in traditional firewalls.

Before you purchase a firewall, you should determine which features you really need and decide where to implement the technology. If you need a traditional firewall — a standalone system with firewall software — compare several vendors' firewalls that provide the features you need. Keep one thing in mind: The more functions and capabilities built into the firewall, the more complex it can be to configure. Most firewall breaches are due to configuration errors.

FIGURE 9.2
A System That Performs Web Serving and Production Operations

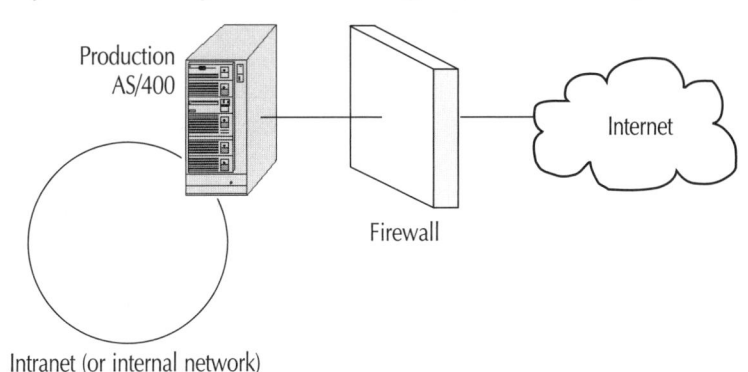

AS/400 System Values

Although a firewall is your first line of defense when connecting your AS/400 to the Internet, a firewall alone won't protect you. Errors in firewall configuration can leave your system vulnerable. Also, hackers and crackers are always looking for new ways to penetrate firewalls or fool them into thinking that an intruder's requests are valid ones. You need to assume that, at some point, your firewall won't keep out intruders. What then? What's your next line of defense?

Setting the AS/400 system values listed in Table 9.1 to the recommended settings is critical if you connect your AS/400 to the Internet. If you also need SNA connections to the AS/400, you'll want to also set the last three system values that appear in the table. To view recommendations for auditing your system and running the integrated security tools for this environment, use the Security Configuration Wizard available through Operations Navigator or the Security Advisor available via the Web (http://www.as400.ibm.com/ebusiness/security). If you implement the wizard's recommendations only to find them too restrictive, you can use the wizard to easily back out the changes you made.

TABLE 9.1
Recommended Settings for Selected AS/400 System Values When Connecting to the Internet

System value	Recommended setting	Rationale
QSECURITY (Security Level)	50	This system value is the most important. It sets the tone of your system security. Because you don't want hackers to be able to subvert your operating system, you need the system integrity OS/400 provides at level 50.

continued

TABLE 9.1 CONTINUED

System value	Recommended setting	Rationale
QAUTOCFG (Automatic Device Configuration)	0 (No)	You don't want someone adding to your system devices that you didn't specifically authorize.
QAUTOVRT (Automatic Virtual Device Creation)	0 (None)	Turn this value on once to create the virtual devices you need. Then set QAUTOVRT to 0. If you allow unlimited virtual devices, a hacker can continuously attack your system by creating virtual devices until your system becomes overloaded with devices and crashes.
QALWOBJRST (Allow Restoring of Security-Sensitive Objects)	*NONE	Unless you're upgrading or applying PTFs, there is no reason to ever restore system-state programs to your system. Programs that adopt authority must be carefully monitored. Disallowing both types of programs from being restored helps you maintain your system's integrity. If business partner software requires you use a different value for QALWOBRST, be wary of that software.
QDEVRCYACN (Device Recovery Action)	*DSCMSG or *ENDJOB	*DSCMSG ensures that during device recovery on a communications line, users must sign on to the system to reconnect to their original job (instead of reconnecting automatically, perhaps to someone else's job).
QDSPSGNINF (Display User Sign-on Information)	1 (On)	This setting causes the system to display a screen after a user signs on. The screen displays the last date and time the user signed on, so the user can detect whether someone else (presumably an intruder) has used or tried to use the user's profile. It is especially important to use this system value for powerful profiles. Educate your users about what the information on the screen means and what to do if they suspect their profile has been "hacked."
QLMTDEVSSN (Limit Device Sessions)	1 (On)	This system value prevents a user profile, including an intruder who guesses or otherwise obtains a user profile, from signing on to more than one workstation simultaneously.
QLMTSECOFR (Limit Security Officer Access to Workstations)	1 (On)	This system value requires users who have *ALLOBJ or *SERVICE special authority to have an additional private authority to the device in order to sign on. QLMTSECOFR limits the power of intruders who manage to gain access to your system.

continued

Table 9.1 Continued

System value	Recommended setting	Rationale
QMAXSIGN (Maximum Number of Sign-on Attempts)	3	This system value limits the number of sign-on attempts at a workstation. Assigning QMAXSIGN a small value gives a would-be hacker only a few tries to guess a password. The more tries you give intruders, the more likely they are to succeed.
QMAXSGNACN (Maximum Sign-on Action)	3 (Disable the display device and user profile)	After the maximum number of failed sign-on attempts, the system should disable both the display device and user profile. This system value, combined with QAUTOVRT, limits the number of times a hacker can attempt to guess your users' passwords.
QRETSRVSEC (Retain Server Security)	0 (Don't allow decryptable passwords)	Some AS/400 applications let you save decryptable passwords on your AS/400. Although decryptable passwords aren't AS/400 user profile passwords, decryptable passwords are inherently less secure than one-way encrypted passwords. If you have no need to store decryptable passwords, set this value to 0.
QUSEADPAUT (Use Adopted Authority)	Name of an authorization list whose public authority is *EXCLUDE	If an intruder accesses your system and compiles a program, you don't want the program to be able to inherit the authority of a powerful user.

If you need SNA connections:

System value	Recommended setting	Rationale
QINACTITV (Inactivity Time-out Interval)	30 (minutes)	Set this system value to a reasonably small number; don't give an intruder time to use your system while you go out for lunch.
QINACTMSGQ (Inactivity Message Queue)	*ENDJOB	If the job has been inactive for the length of time specified in QINACTITV, make hackers sign on again if they want to reuse the same user ID.
QRMTSIGN (Remote Sign-on Value)	*REJECT (preferably) or, if necessary, *FRCSIGNON or *VERIFY	The best choice is to not allow passthrough at all. But if you must, then make the intruder provide a valid user ID and password, or at least require that the passwords be the same on both the target and source machines.

In addition to setting the system values listed in Table 9.1, you should set the Inactivity Time-Out parameter, INACTTIMO, for each TCP/IP application. (The system ignores the INACTTIMO value for Telnet connections. As of V4R4, Telnet uses only the QINACTITV system value; for an explanation, see the "Telnet" section of Chapter 8.) To set the INACTTIMO value, you use the appropriate Change command to change the application's attributes; for example, you would use the CHGFTPA (Change FTP Attributes) command to set INACTTIMO for an FTP application.

On an AS/400 connected to the Internet, you'll want to use all of the password composition (QPWDxxx) system values. The more strict your password composition requirements are, the less likely a hacker will be able to guess a valid password. Unfortunately, this is a double-edged sword. When you make it difficult for a hacker to guess a password, you also make it difficult for legitimate users to compose passwords and to remember them after they do. If you don't use all of the password system values (see Chapter 2), you should use at least those shown in Table 9.2. Note that because this chapter assumes your AS/400 is connected to the Internet, this table recommends some stricter values than we recommended in Chapters 2 and 3.

TABLE 9.2
Minimum Recommended Password Composition System Values

System value	Recommended setting	Rationale
QPWDMINLEN (Minimum Length)	At least 7	Difficulty guessing passwords increases exponentially with password length. Given the computing power available today, you should make this value as large as possible.
QPWDRQDDGT (Require a Digit)	1 (On)	Requiring a digit prevents a hacker from using a dictionary attack to guess a password.
QPWDEXPITV (Password Expiration Interval)	30 (days)	Assuming a hacker does guess a password, you want to limit the amount of time the password is valid.
QPWDRQDDIF (Require Different Password)	4 or less	Don't let passwords be repeated very often. If an intruder guesses a password, you don't want it to be valid again in the near future.

After you've set your system values, you need to examine your next line of defense — the users you've defined for your system.

User Profiles

As we discussed in Chapter 3, to sign on to the AS/400, you must have a user profile. To reduce the possibility of someone maliciously getting to your AS/400 from the Internet, you want to severely restrict the number of user profiles on your system. You also want to ensure that the IBM-supplied profiles aren't usable. IBM profiles are well documented in both IBM and hacker publications. In fact, at least one posting on a hacker Web page has listed the IBM profiles and suggested that you try to sign on with them using a password that is the same as the profile name.

Don't give hackers such an obvious door into your system. Execute the ANZDFTPWD (Analyze Default Password) command and make sure the passwords for QPGMR, QSYSOPR, QUSER, QSRV, and QSRVBAS are set to *NONE. QSECOFR is the other well-published profile. To make it unusable to hackers, create a profile and make QSECOFR its group profile. Then set QSECOFR to a status of *DISABLED. In the event of an emergency, you can always sign on as QSECOFR at the console even when QSECOFR's status is *DISABLED. To protect all active profiles on your system, you can use the CHGACTSCDE (Change Activation Schedule Entry) command to set these profiles' status to *DISABLED during hours you don't expect them to be used.

For the few remaining user profiles on your system, use a cryptic naming convention. Profile names such as Alan, Mary, SECOFR, MASTER, and OPERATOR are too easily guessed. Profile names can always be guessed, but the more cryptic they are, the longer guessing will take. Increase the odds that an intruder will run out of time before making a successful guess.

Use Resource Security

Another layer of defense available to you is object-level (resource) security. We've found that most AS/400s give users broad authority to most functions on the system and exclude them from only sensitive functions, such as the payroll application.

If your AS/400 is in a networked environment, you need to take a 180 degree turn from that approach. Your philosophy should be to close off all access to all functions on the system and give each user access to only the functions he or she actually needs to perform his or her job. Consider setting most libraries and directories to *PUBLIC(*EXCLUDE) and then giving explicit access to only those users that need it. At the very least, you must secure your critical assets and confidential information. By closing down your system, you also prevent hackers from using it to store inappropriate data. Hackers don't keep stolen data, pornography, illegal copies of software, or hacking tools on their own systems; they find systems — including yours, if they can get to it — and store such data there.

Control What Goes On

Don't be lax about what happens on your system. If you don't want an intruder to be able to perform some function and you don't need the function for business purposes, don't allow it on your system. The more services and applications available on your AS/400, the more likely it is that an unintentional avenue exists into your system. If a tool or application doesn't exist on your system, a hacker can't use it to break in or cause damage.

In addition to the system-value recommendations we described earlier, we recommend the following steps:

- Start the TCP/IP servers for only the applications you're running. For example, if you don't use LPD (line printer daemon), don't start it.
- Follow the directions in Chapter 8 to ensure that you start only the TCP/IP servers that you need and to secure the ports these applications use.
- Remove or secure compilers on your system and secure the CRTxxxPGM commands.

- If you aren't using SNA, create your Token-Ring line to allow only TCP/IP by specifying only the value AA for the SSAP (Source Service Access Point) parameter on the CRTLINTRN (Create Line Description — Token-Ring) command.
- Turn off IP packet forwarding by specifying N (No) for the Allow IP Datagram Forwarding parameter when you add or change a configuration profile from the WRKTCPPTP (Work with Point-to-Point TCP/IP) command.
- Be careful how much validity you place in the data you receive over the Internet. Some AS/400 shops use FTP exit programs to allow or deny the use of FTP based on the user's IP address. Validating a user based on an IP address can be dangerous because IP addresses can be spoofed. (*Spoofing* occurs when someone alters an IP address to look like another — legitimate — one.)
- If you need a connection from your internal network to your Web server, you might want to make that connection using Advanced Peer-to-Peer Networking (APPN). Then, you can use the APPN Filtering support described in Chapter 8 to further protect your internal network.

Write Secure Web Applications

The IBM HTTP Server for AS/400 gives you another layer of defense by providing the following mechanisms:

- directives within the configuration file that provide access control to Web server resources
- separation of who can access HTML source and CGI-BIN programs
- Secure Sockets Layer (SSL)

The AS/400 HTTP server doesn't serve information unless you specifically tell it to. You use directives within a configuration file to tell the HTTP server what information to serve and who to serve it to. The HTTP server by itself can't grab confidential information out of your database files and serve it to the world.

Just as you have a separate library for each of your native AS/400 applications, you need to separate your HTML source and CGI-BIN programs from other applications that might be on your Web server. By default, the AS/400 serves all CGI-BIN programs out of the QTCP library. Don't propagate that design. Create a library for each Web application and put that application's CGI-BIN programs there. Set public access for these libraries to *USE or *EXCLUDE to control who can add programs to the library. You should also create a separate directory for all your HTML source. Set public access for this directory to *R (the equivalent of *READ).

Separating HTML source and CGI-BIN programs from other applications is necessary because the directives in the configuration file allow wild cards or generic rules. For example, you can add a directive to let users execute any program in a particular library. When you do that, any program in that library is accessible over the Internet. Another reason not to mix applications is that if you have programs and files with the same name or that both fit a generic directive, you might not be able to predict what program or file the system will serve.

Other directives enable basic authentication. An application that enables basic authentication challenges the requester for a user ID and password when a request comes to the server. For example, when checking the balance of a TDSP (Tax Deferred Savings Plan), customers must enter their name and password in order to obtain the information. The AS/400's HTTP server lets you enable basic authentication in two ways — one way with AS/400 users and another way with Internet users.

You can configure your Web application to require requesters to provide a valid AS/400 user profile and password before serving any information to them. Although browsers don't transmit passwords in clear text over the connection, they aren't encrypted. We don't recommend requiring AS/400 user profiles and passwords for authentication unless you're operating in an intranet environment or using SSL.

Internet users aren't true AS/400 users because they don't have a corresponding *USRPRF object, so no job ever runs under their profile. You implement Internet users using an object type called a validation list (*VLDL). Validation lists associate an entity (typically a user) with authentication information (e.g., a password, account number, digital certificate). You can specify a validation list for your Web application to use to authenticate users. When your application requires basic authentication, the system checks the user name and password against the information in the specified validation list. The Web application doesn't have to store or know of the actual authentication information because the browser and server handle authentication between themselves.

Another feature of the AS/400's Web server is the ability to configure Web pages to be served using SSL. When a Secure Hypertext Transfer Protocol (HTTPS) request initiates an SSL session, the browser ensures that it is talking to the server you pointed to. After the browser validates the server, the connection is established and all subsequent flows are encrypted. Encryption is critical for ensuring privacy and integrity of confidential data over the Internet. All data sent via a nonsecure (non-SSL) connection is passed in clear text and is subject to being altered or sniffed (i.e., read from the communications flow). Because the Internet is a public network, you can't determine how many or which systems your data is routed through. (To be realistic, although sniffing certainly occurs, it's not something the average user can do. If your data is sniffed, it's most likely to be sniffed by someone inside your own organization who is able to attach a line-tracing device in your network.) Using SSL protects your data from both external and internal hackers. However, you should use SSL on only your confidential data, because making an SSL connection and subsequently encrypting data incurs overhead.

Another feature of SSL — and an HTTP server configuration option — is client-side authentication. When you configure client-side authentication and the browser identifies the server, the server (e.g., your AS/400 HTTP server) authenticates the user that made the request. Client-side authentication uses digital certificates. A digital certificate can be associated with either a real AS/400 user profile or an Internet user.

When you use digital certificates for either basic authentication or client-side authentication and the users you're authenticating are real AS/400 users, you can configure your Web server to run as that user. This is a powerful feature for intranet applications because it lets you use traditional AS/400 object security to secure your data.

Let's look at an example of how you might use several features of the AS/400 Web server to write a secure Web application.

An insurance company has decided to write a rate calculating program and make it available to its agents over the Internet. Because the application is available only to the company's agents and not to the general public, agents will have to enter a user ID and password to access the application from the company's Web site. The agents will be Internet users — that is, they will have meaning to only the application that uses the validation list in which they are registered.

Because the agents won't have an AS/400 user profile, the Web application will run under a user profile, WEB_PROF, created especially for this purpose (Figure 9.3 illustrates the authorities to the application). The WEB_OWNER user profile owns the rate calculating program. All the application objects are PUBLIC(*EXCLUDE). WEB_PROF is excluded from all other application libraries and directories and has authority only to the first program of the rate calculating application. The first program adopts its owner's (WEB_OWNER's) profile. Setting up the rate calculation application in this way ensures that the only way a user can access the application's programs or files is to go through the application itself. Having the Web server run as WEB_PROF instead of WEB_OWNER ensures that if an intruder broke into the Web server, the intruder would have access to only the first program in the rate calculating application on the Web server.

FIGURE 9.3
An Example of a Secure Web Application

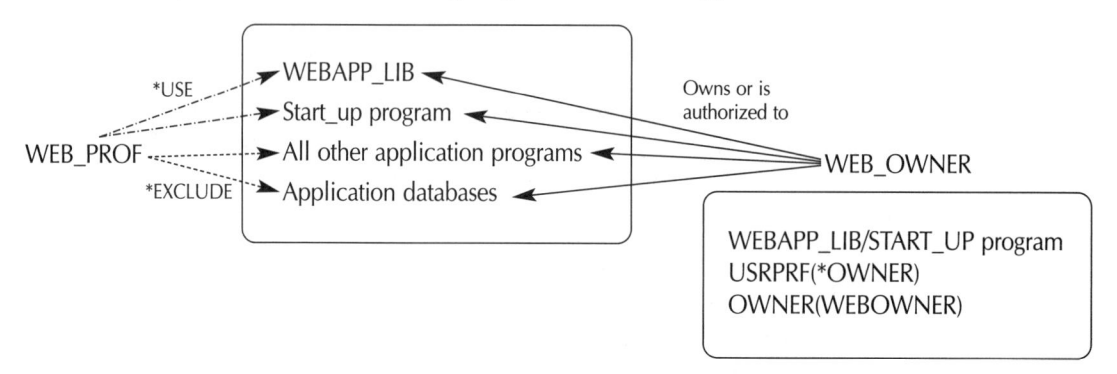

Use Exit Points

Exit programs can provide another layer of defense. You can write exit programs that enable a function (e.g., anonymous FTP), disallow a feature altogether (e.g., Client Access Express data transfer uploads to your system), or allow a function for some users or objects but not others.

For example, you can allow FTP on your system but make sure no one can use it to download the file of customer credit card numbers from your database. You set the credit card file to *PUBLIC(*EXCLUDE), of course. But because you're really risk-averse, you also write an exit program that lets visitors to your Web site download all files on your Web site except the credit card file. The exit program provides a secondary line of defense should someone with *ALLOBJ special authority try to download the credit card file.

Monitor

It's one thing to set up your system for an Internet connection, but it's another thing entirely to maintain the security of that system. To ensure that your security mechanisms remain effective and adequate, you need to do several types of monitoring.

Intrusion Detection

Intrusion detection isn't just one type of monitoring, but three. First, you should analyze your system proactively for known vulnerabilities. For the AS/400, vulnerability analysis includes making sure you've applied all the integrity PTFs. Starting only the TCP/IP servers you need and securing the ports of the ones you don't also fall into this category.

The second type of intrusion-detection monitoring is active monitoring. When your network is up and running, you need to do continuous real-time monitoring to detect whether anyone is trying to do something on your system that you didn't intend. For example, on the AS/400, you can monitor the QSYSMSG message queue for messages that indicate invalid sign-on attempts. If you receive a certain number of messages within a specified timeframe (e.g., 50 messages within two minutes), you could send an alert to an operator or system administrator.

For active monitoring to be successful, it must include a plan of action that you'll follow if you do detect an intrusion. It won't do you much good to detect that your system is being attacked if you don't know what to do about it.

The third type of intrusion-detection monitoring is after-the-fact detection that someone accessed your system without your permission. Part of this analysis includes determining what was accessed, changed, or stolen. There are several ways to log system accesses on the AS/400. The auditing capabilities integrated into OS/400 provide good information for this type of intrusion detection. The AS/400 HTTP server also includes access and error logs that are useful in determining who accessed your system.

Typically, the problem isn't an inability to monitor. Rather, many companies that don't audit extensively or log Web accesses think they don't need that type of information and consider such monitoring a waste of system resources. Unfortunately, you can't go back and recreate the audit entries after a break-in has occurred. Which objects and actions you're going to audit are choices you must make based on the needs of your business and your security policy before a break-in occurs.

Denial-of-Service Attacks

A denial-of-service attack is one that attempts to make your system unavailable for its intended purpose. One type of denial-of-service attack is mail spamming, in which an attacker floods your system with so much invalid e-mail that the AS/400 has no time left to serve Web pages. Another type of denial-of-service attack could occur if you enable Telnet and leave system value QAUTOVRT set at a value other than 0. In this case, a hacker could repeatedly sign on to your system and create hundreds of thousands of virtual devices, filling up your storage.

Denial-of-service attacks can be difficult to defend against. Because they come in many forms, they require defenses at different points in your network. OS/400 has changed its IP stack and some of its TCP/IP applications to better defend against some denial-of-service attacks. Other attacks are better defended against farther out in your network, such as at your firewall or router. When you choose a firewall or router vendor, ask the vendor about the product's denial-of-service features.

Your system can never be 100 percent safe from denial-of-service attacks, because intruders continually create new types. The important thing is to have enough monitoring in place to be able to detect when a denial-of-service attack is occurring and to have a plan for thwarting such an attack.

Security Configuration

Organizations aren't static; they change. And their systems and security needs change with them. You should regularly monitor the status of your security configuration — your user profiles, system values, and object authorities. Use the integrated security tools or tools from AS/400 Business Partners to detect changes to your security configuration and to keep it current. For example, you can use the ANZPRFACT (Analyze Profile Activity) command to set profiles to a status of *DISABLED after a short period of inactivity (e.g., 30 days) to ensure that intruders can't exploit old profiles (profiles belonging to users who no longer work for the company or who have changed jobs within your company and no longer sign on to the system).

Test

Test, test, and retest. Obviously you should test your network configuration for holes before you go live with your Internet connection. You don't want to face a situation like the Internal Revenue Service faced. The IRS provided a Web site before properly securing the site. The Web site, which provided personal information for U.S. citizens, gave out this information too freely because the IRS didn't properly test the access control mechanisms for the information.

Whoever does your testing must think deviously and be very creative. It's not enough for testers to ensure that your Web application works. They must attempt to access your system from every conceivable angle and in unconventional ways. They need to find the vulnerabilities in each layer.

Consider hiring an outside organization to test your configuration. IBM has an ethical hacking service, as do other companies. At least find someone who hasn't worked on your network-configuration project to test your setup. Or hire some computer "nerds" from a local college or university!

Update Your Business Contingency Plan

Last, but certainly not least, are the changes you need to make to your business contingency plan. Some of the areas you need to consider are

- Does your backup or hot site have Internet access?
- Do you have an alternative route to your ISP or an alternative ISP if your current ISP's connection is severed? I (Carol) saw exactly that happen when a backhoe severed the optical line between Rochester and Minneapolis, where one of IBM Rochester's ISPs is located.
- If you're monitoring for network intrusions and detect one, do you have plans in place for handling it?
- Is your virus scanner up to date? As we were revising this book, a virus infested e-mail attachments. How would you detect and recover from one of these viruses — or any other?

For an in-depth discussion of business contingency planning, see Chapter 19.

The Good News

Are there risks associated with connecting your system to the Internet? Yes. But most companies feel the risks are worth taking.

Today, the Internet is an attractive place to do business, and avoiding the Internet might cost you your business. However, risk is part of life and part of doing business. Connecting your AS/400 to the networked world shouldn't paralyze you. The secret to doing business safely on the Internet is to analyze your risks and then mitigate them by implementing as many layers of defense as your business needs dictate.

Chapter 10

Thwarting Hackers

The AS/400 has a history as a secure system. But that doesn't mean an operating system as powerful as OS/400 doesn't have security-sensitive interfaces that need to be guarded. The trick is to keep valuable OS/400 functions out of the wrong hands. As we've discussed, IBM provides ample tools to secure the AS/400. If you take the time to use these tools, you can effectively defend your system against accidental errors and omissions that occur when security is lax and against direct attacks by intruders. In this chapter, we look at such exposures and offer advice to minimize the risks of a breach in your system security.

Hacker Terminology

Computer culture has spawned a few terms we use within this chapter that we want to define here. First is the term hacker. A *hacker* is an outsider (someone who doesn't have system access) or an insider (someone who does) who might access your system to explore unauthorized areas. A hacker wants to gain access with as much authority as possible. The intent of most hackers is simply to access your system or network for the challenge or "fun of it." Nevertheless, a hacker might cause damage to your system, applications, or data. A *cracker* is a hacker with malicious intent. After gaining access to your system, a cracker will purposefully try to harm the system (e.g., make it crash, compromise the integrity of your data, steal corporate information). All references we make to hackers also pertain to crackers.

Unfortunately, the threat from inside your network is greater than the threat from those you would think of as traditional hackers. We refer to users who might threaten your system from inside as disgruntled employees because they typically are unhappy with their employer. Disgruntled employees are often planning to leave the company or know they are about to be fired or laid off and exact some retribution in advance. Disgruntled employees have a leg up on the traditional hacker because they already have a valid user ID and password along with some knowledge of your system. The term *hacker* in the rest of this chapter also pertains to disgruntled employees.

In addition to the harm a hacker might cause by exploring your system during an interactive session, three specific types of attack have been made popular by PC and Unix hackers: Trojan horses, viruses, and worms.

A Trojan horse is an executable program that masquerades as an "official" program on your system — that is, a program that is supposed to be there. The program might seem to provide some useful function, but it can also harm the system or give a hacker additional authorities.

A virus is some form of executable code that normally attaches itself to a particular object type (e.g., files with .exe or .com extensions) and propagates itself to other systems. The code might be benign, or it might be harmful. If you think your AS/400 can't host a virus, you're wrong. The Integrated File System (IFS) gives hackers the opportunity to extend their habits to the AS/400.

A worm is a form of executable code that replicates itself over and over, normally causing damage only in terms of monopolizing disk space or CPU usage and taking your time as you try to eliminate the worm from the system.

A hacker may or may not try to attack your system with one of these types of tools. First, however, the hacker must have access to your system.

Access — A Hacker's First Hurdle

The first hurdle hackers face is gaining access to your system or gaining access with a higher authority than they might already have. In the hacker-heaven Unix world, hackers learned to go straight after the root-level security access to gain complete control over the system. The hacker ideal is no different on the AS/400. Whether hackers are insiders or outsiders, they will attempt to gain access at the QSECOFR level.

Before we talk about combating such an attempt, understand that "the QSECOFR level" can mean any user profile on your system that has *ALLOBJ authority. The *ALLOBJ special authority (not necessarily the QSECOFR profile itself) is actually the golden egg. Also, keep in mind that hackers don't always use a direct approach. As you'll see, some types of Trojan horses gradually climb up the authority ladder or simply lay in wait for the right opportunity until they finally gain *ALLOBJ authority. To combat any form of attack or unauthorized access to your system, it's important that you assess the various ways you currently allow access or that someone might gain access. You certainly can't deny users system access, so you always have some exposure. But by knowing the possible access options, you can minimize your risk with the right preventive measures.

Minimizing Access Exposures

A normal workstation that is an everyday tool for your end users can be an exposure in the hands of a hacker. To explore your system, the first thing hackers need to have is access through a physical workstation or remote connection. An active (signed-on) workstation is an invitation to hackers. A physical workstation whose end user has made sign-on convenient by using the keyboard's record/playback feature to record his or her user profile and password sequence is a road map for a hacker. If hackers can find an active workstation session or a way to start a session, they might find a way to do harm or to plant a Trojan horse that can enable further access.

To prevent hackers from finding an active workstation they can use, you must guard against:

- public access to the physical key to your system
- unattended signed-on workstations
- unattended workstations that are turned off but not locked
- an autoconfig option that lets a hacker create new devices

- dial-up devices that let any user profile access a session
- an existing session on another system in the network

Rather than discuss solutions for each exposure, we present general suggestions concerning access, then mention how each of these exposures is included in that discussion.

SUGGESTION #1 — REMOVE THE PHYSICAL KEY TO YOUR AS/400 AND STORE THE KEY IN A SAFE PLACE THAT YOU CAN ACCESS WHEN YOU NEED TO.

If a hacker has access to your key (known technically as a *keystick*), the hacker has access to functions that can compromise your security. A hacker can perform a manual IPL to access the Dedicated Service Tools (DST). If you haven't changed the master DST security password (which ships as QSECOFR, just like the QSECOFR profile) or if the hacker can guess the password, he or she can reset the QSECOFR password to any other value, even QSECOFR, patch programs to plant a virus or Trojan horse on your system, or dump main storage to prowl about in the AS/400 internals in search of a way into the system.

Using the key, a hacker can also perform an alternate IPL using a personal copy of OS/400 to boot the system. Although the hacker might be able to do this only once (because you would then discover that your operating system had been tampered with), that opportunity might be all the hacker needs to steal or harm data on your system. The result could be very costly.

Unfortunately, many low-end models of the AS/400 don't come with a key. Furthermore, most of these systems are in smaller companies that might not have a separate computer room. Systems that don't have a key are very vulnerable to these exposures. If you have such a system, your only course of action is to locate it in a room that you can physically secure.

SUGGESTION #2 — USE AN AUTOMATED FACILITY TO SIGN OFF IDLE USERS FROM WORKSTATIONS.

In Chapter 2 we looked at using the QINACTITV and QINACTMSGQ system values to prevent users from walking away from their workstations and leaving them signed on (idle) for long periods of time. You should take advantage of these system values or purchase a third-party package that offers similar protection. Even if hackers have only an end-user's profile, they might steal or harm data. If the end user happens to have additional authorities (e.g., security administrator for Domino, system operator), hackers might even be able to gain additional access.

For example, let's say a hacker finds a PC workstation signed on to the system and idle. The user signed on happens to be the database application administrator and can assign trigger programs to database files. The hacker writes a short CL program on the PC (using the PC editor), uploads the program to the AS/400, and uses the RMTCMD (Remote Command) facility in Client Access Express to compile the CL program and make it the trigger program for a database file. This program attempts to create a user profile that has *ALLOBJ authority and monitors for failure (because the program will work only if someone with the authority to create profiles runs the database application that invokes the trigger program). This sounds like a longshot for the hacker, but it does give the hacker a fighting chance to eventually get a profile that works as a backdoor to your system. The hacker simply waits and occasionally checks for the profile.

Although this scenario relies on a few open security holes, perhaps these holes exist on your system: unsecured remote command, unsecured file transfer, unsecured CRTxxxPGM commands, and no auditing for failed sign-on attempts.

> *Technical Note*
> **Until V4R2, all TCP/IP applications ignore the QINACTITV system value. In V4R2 and later releases, Telnet and Workstation Gateway (WSG) honor this system value. In releases earlier than V4R2 and for all other TCP/IP applications, you must set the INACCTTIMO attribute for each application.**

SUGGESTION #3 — USE THE WORKSTATION KEY TO LOCK WORKSTATIONS THAT AREN'T LOCATED IN A SECURE AREA.

Hackers still need to have a profile and password, but securing the physical devices certainly helps prevent access.

SUGGESTION #4 — USE THE QLMTSECOFR SYSTEM VALUE AND SPECIFIC AUTHORITY TO DEVICES TO REDUCE YOUR EXPOSURE TO HACKING ON CERTAIN PROFILES.

In Chapter 2 we discussed the QLMTSECOFR system value, which lets you explicitly control devices that any profile with *ALLOBJ or *SERVICE authority has access to. Because most hackers want *ALLOBJ authority, it makes sense to limit your exposure to specific devices.

Whether or not you use QLMTSECOFR, it's a good idea to authorize certain devices to only certain user profiles at a time. For instance, if you support dial-in access, authorize only specific user profiles to the dial-up device descriptions so that fewer user profiles and passwords exist that can provide hackers dial-up access.

> *Technical Note*
> **If you find that you must regularly sign on with *ALLOBJ special authority from a variety of workstations to support applications, consider it a strong indication that your application security model is inadequate. Application maintenance shouldn't require *ALLOBJ authority.**

SUGGESTION #5 — TURN OFF AUTOCONFIGURATION (QAUTOCFG SYSTEM VALUE).

Authorization to devices does little good if someone can simply turn the device off, change the address, and turn it on again and let OS/400 configure a new device. Autoconfiguration is useful only for initial installations and can be inactivated during production use of your AS/400.

SUGGESTION #6 — TURN OFF AUTOMATIC CONFIGURATION OF VIRTUAL DEVICES (QAUTOVRT SYSTEM VALUE).

Unless you control the number of virtual devices on your system, you give hackers an unlimited number of attempts to hack your system via the Telnet TCP/IP application and other emulators that use virtual devices to present a sign-on screen.

SUGGESTION #7 — DON'T PUBLISH ANY OF YOUR DIAL-UP NUMBERS.

SUGGESTION #8 — USE THE DIAL-UP CALL-BACK FEATURE WHEN POSSIBLE.

Using a dial-back mechanism greatly reduces your risk of dial-up hacking. For more information, see the section "Dial-Up Line Security Considerations" in Chapter 8.

SUGGESTION #9 — IF YOU'RE NOT ABSOLUTELY CERTAIN THAT A NETWORKED SYSTEM (E.G., ANOTHER AS/400) IS SECURE, REQUIRE ALL INCOMING DISPLAY STATION PASSTHROUGH (DSPT) SESSIONS TO SIGN ON SPECIFICALLY TO YOUR LOCAL SYSTEM, REQUIRE SECURITY INFORMATION IN ALL PROGRAM INVOCATION REQUESTS (E.G., APPC PROGRAM CONNECTIONS), AND SECURE DISTRIBUTED DATA MANAGEMENT (DDM) ACCESS (E.G., REMOTE COMMANDS, DDM FILES).

This precaution is especially necessary when the system accessing your AS/400 is a PC client. Force PC clients to sign on to your AS/400 again for a workstation session. Users that automate start-up of a workstation session by bypassing the sign-on screen cause security exposures. If a user leaves a Client Access Express connection active and you don't require sign-on for new workstation sessions, anyone can use that connection without entering the user profile and password.

SUGGESTION #10 — SET THE QDEVRCYACN SYSTEM VALUE TO *DSCJOB, NOT TO *MSG.

If you set QDEVRCYACN to *MSG, another user might dial in during device recovery and get a passthrough session, thus bypassing any additional sign-on request. If the QDEVRCYACN value is *DSCJOB, the user must again sign on to the system to reconnect to the original job.

SUGGESTION #11 — GIVE *IOSYSCFG SPECIAL AUTHORITY TO TRUSTED INDIVIDUALS ONLY.

If a user can change a device description, that user can change the description's SECURELOC attribute to create a security exposure on the target machine. For example, a user passing through to the target machine might change SECURELOC to *YES and then try again to pass through using a different profile with no password. If your QRMTSIGN system value allows automatic sign-on from a remote system, the user could bypass the target machine's security. *IOSYSCFG authority also lets a user configure and start all

TCP/IP applications. A hacker who has *IOSYSCFG authority might be able to start an application that violates your security policy.

Making the Hunt for User Profiles and Passwords More Difficult

If a hacker has access to a sign-on screen and wants to submit a program invocation request in a communications job or attempt to download or upload a file via FTP, two pieces of information are required: a valid user profile and password. Both are necessary and important, so you should craft both defensively.

Every AS/400 has a QSECOFR profile and a few other IBM-supplied profiles. Profiles common to all AS/400s and their default passwords have been spelled out in the hacker magazine *2600: The Hacker Quarterly* as well as on hacker Web sites on the Internet. Hackers generally feel that AS/400s are easy prey because so many shops don't implement anything more than minimum security measures. Certainly, you should change the default password for QSECOFR and make sure the other IBM-supplied profiles have PASSWORD(*NONE). (Since V3R7, AS/400s have shipped with QSECOFR's password expired, forcing a change the first time you sign on to the system.)

Many organizations have a John, a Mary, a Sue, a J. Smith, an M. Smith, an S. Johnson, or the like. It just doesn't make sense to believe that a hacker isn't going to try user profiles such as JOE, JOHN, SUE, MARY, MSMITH, and JSMITH. Yes, it is convenient to base user profile names on the user's name, but it's *not* secure. If you want to tighten security, you should make user profiles more difficult to guess.

This logic applies equally to passwords. Simple names, phone extensions, birthdays, and telephone numbers all make for bad passwords. To make passwords more difficult for hackers to guess, review the discussion of passwords in Chapter 3 and the discussion of the system values that determine how valid passwords must be constructed in Chapter 2 and follow the security recommendations in those chapters. Here are a few suggestions to help minimize your exposure to easy-to-guess passwords.

SUGGESTION #1 — USE THE QMAXSIGN AND QMASIGNACN SYSTEM VALUES (SEE CHAPTER 2) TO LIMIT THE NUMBER OF TIMES SOMEONE CAN UNSUCCESSFULLY ATTEMPT TO SIGN ON TO A WORKSTATION.

SUGGESTION #2 — FORCE USERS TO CREATE SECRET, HARD-TO-GUESS PASSWORDS AND TO CHANGE THEM FREQUENTLY.

Chapter 3 contains an in-depth discussion of the password requirements you should implement. The essence is that you should use the system values that control password content and, if necessary, write a password validation program to aid in that process. For example, use the QPWDRQDDGT system value to ensure that all passwords contain at least one number. Including digits in passwords prevents dictionary attacks (attempts to access your system by using an online dictionary to guess passwords).

SUGGESTION #3 – CHANGE THE SIGN-ON ERROR MESSAGES TO USE THE SAME TEXT.

Change CPF1107, *Password not correct for user profile*, and CPF1120, *User xxx does not exist*, to read *Password or user profile incorrect*. Following this tip prevents hackers from knowing which part of the user name/password combination they tried is incorrect.

SUGGESTION #4 — AS WE SUGGESTED IN THE PRECEDING SECTION, USE THE QLMTSECOFR SYSTEM VALUE TO RESTRICT PROFILES THAT HAVE *ALLOBJ OR *SERVICE SPECIAL AUTHORITY TO SPECIFIC DEVICES.

SUGGESTION #5 — LIMIT AUTHORITIES TO ANY PASSWORD VALIDITY-CHECKING EXIT PROGRAM YOU IMPLEMENT. DO NOT STORE THE PASSWORD THAT IS PASSED TO THE VALIDITY-CHECKING PROGRAM.

SUGGESTION #6 — RESTRICT THE USE OF AND AUDIT THE OVRDSPF COMMAND.

SUGGESTION #7 — GIVE *SERVICE SPECIAL AUTHORITY TO ONLY THOSE PROFILES THAT ABSOLUTELY NEED IT.

SUGGESTION #8 — USE YOUR SECURITY POLICY TO PROHIBIT USERS FROM AUTOMATING THEIR PC-TO-AS/400 LOG-ON PROCESSES, AND ENFORCE THIS POLICY AS STRICTLY AS YOU CAN.

Protection against stolen passwords is another issue. Hackers who are accustomed to Unix systems call programs that steal passwords *sniffers*. The AS/400 isn't immune to sniffers if the hacker has sufficient access to certain functions.

For instance, if you write a password validity-checking program (for details, see the discussion of the QPWDVLDPGM system value in Chapter 2), you must secure it with public *USE authority and have the owner be the only user with any additional authorities. If you give hackers the opportunity to replace your password validation program or to write their own password validation program and change the QPWDVLDPGM system value to use the hacker program, they can then record each user profile and password as it's changed. You should definitely audit any changes to security-related system values (for details about AS/400 auditing, see Chapters 16 through 18). You should also ensure that any password validity-checking program and its source are secure.

A second way hackers might intercept passwords is by presenting a mock sign-on screen before the actual system sign-on screen. You must secure and audit the use of the OVRDSPF (Override with Display File) command to make sure that no one overrides a display file to a specific device and bypasses the initial sign-on screen with a hacker-created display file record format. A hacker who mimics the sign-on screen might then use a Trojan horse to record the profile and password the user enters and then end. The AS/400 at that point would present the real sign-on screen. Unsuspecting users might think that something happened when they entered the password the first time and that it "didn't take."

Hackers could also steal passwords by gaining access to the System Service Tools (SST). A user must have *SERVICE authority to use these tools. The SST (the command is STRSST) lets you monitor a communications line and output the network traffic for examination. Unless you specifically implement an encryption solution, none of the data transmitted across a communications line is encrypted, including the user profile and password data when someone signs on to the system. It would be easy with SST access to watch for this information and record it for future use.

PCs that use automatic sign-on are easy prey for hacker attacks. Some users like to store their user ID and password in a file on the PC, use that stored information to automatically sign on to the AS/400 when the PC boots, and then bypass the sign-on screen in an emulation session. This is dangerous because PCs are more vulnerable to hacking than the AS/400 is. Someone could easily turn on the PC and have fun on the AS/400 (the janitor might do this at night looking for Solitaire) or read the file that stores the user profile and password data.

Bypassing or Gaining Authority

After hackers gain access to your system, their next step (unless they've been able to log on with QSECOFR or another profile that has *ALLOBJ authority) is to seek as much authority as possible. Several features and functions on your AS/400 lend themselves to hacker attacks or provide possible loopholes that hackers might exploit to gain additional authorities. In the sections that follow, we discuss these possibilities. The last section provides a list of suggestions to close off these possible exposures.

QSYSLIBL — The System Library List

If a hacker can add a library that precedes QSYS in your system library list (QSYSLIBL), the hacker can write a Trojan horse to replace an IBM-supplied command or program.

Adopted Authorities

Using adopted authorities isn't bad in and of itself. But if you're not careful, it's easy to be a little sloppy and create possible doorways to additional authorities. One possible problem is that unless you specifically block authority propagation on the called program, any program the adopting program subsequently calls will automatically adopt the same authorities as the adopting program itself. Propagating adopted authority is unnecessary in most cases and can lead to unintended, unnecessary, and dangerous authorities in applications that have many levels of program calls.

A second problem can occur if programs that adopt authority fail and then neglect to clean up temporary objects and the library list. For instance, say a user calls a program that adopts authority. What if this program adds library PAYROLL to the user's library list and then fails with an error message? Unless the program specifically removes library PAYROLL from the user's library list, the user will continue to have authority to that library even after the program fails. Depending on the user's object authorities, he or she might then have access to objects in the PAYROLL library.

Applications that adopt authority and that don't use library-qualified calls to other programs can present a risk. Hackers can take advantage of the adopted authority if they can place a program in a library higher in the library list than the program the application should call. The best approach is to rewrite all applications to use library-qualified calls. If that isn't immediately feasible, you should control who can create programs that use adopted authority — in effect, stopping the propagation of adopted authority — by using the QUSEADPTAUT system value. Although this system value is very useful on a production system, it might not be appropriate for a development system.

Profile Swapping

Another way to gain enough authority to perform some function is to actually swap the profile under which the job is running. Two problems can occur with profile swapping: A user can keep the swapped profile's authority even after the application is completed, or an application writer might unintentionally provide an interface someone can use to swap to a powerful profile.

If a program swaps to a powerful profile, such as QSECOFR, to perform an operation, and then the program fails, the program must have error handling to swap back to the original profile, or else the job will remain under the more powerful profile. The other problem occurs with the program that does the actual profile swap. Say an application performs a function that requires the user to have *ALLOBJ special authority, so the application developer decides to swap to QSECOFR. To swap to a user profile, the application developer must either know the profile's password or the user running the profile swap APIs must have *USE authority to the user profile. Rather than give all users *USE authority to QSECOFR, the application developer uses program adoption to ensure the swap works. If the program doing the swap has a public authority of *USE or greater, anyone can call the program and swap to QSECOFR.

Using OS/400 Objects Directly

At security level 30 or lower, objects (e.g., programs, files, data areas) that ship with OS/400 can be called or accessed directly. For example, as long as you have the parameter structure correct, you can call most OS/400 programs directly. Using some of these OS/400 objects gives a hacker the authority of the user profile of his choice or the ability to run as QSECOFR or QSYS. The only way to prevent inappropriate use of operating system objects is to run at security level 40 or higher. We strongly urge you to run at security level 50 to achieve the best protection.

Subsystem Descriptions

If we were hackers and found out that we could change or create subsystem descriptions on your system, we would be in hacker heaven. The subsystem description presents several opportunities to write and implement a Trojan horse on your system. Consider routing entries for a minute. Let's say we know that all of your users' profiles specify QDFTJOBD as the default job description. So we change the routing data of that job description (if one of us has the authority to change the job description). We then add a routing entry to the subsystem that matches the new routing data. This routing entry causes the following CL routing program to be executed:

```
PGM
CRTUSRPRF  USRPRF(QSRVSEC)  USRCLS(*SECOFR)
MONMSG     CPF0000
RRTJOB     RTGDTA('QCMDI')
ENDPGM
```

Any time a profile with the QDFTJOBD job description signs on to the system using that subsystem, or any time a batch job is run using QDFTJOBD in that subsystem, this routing program attempts to create a security-officer–like profile. When the right user signs on, this program works, giving us a powerful profile for exploring your system.

Of course, this attack assumes the user can change this job description, add a subsystem routing entry, and write and compile the routing program. These assumptions aren't all that unlikely when you consider the authorities your programmers probably have to these items. Even a system operator with the right authorities could mount this Trojan horse attack.

A hacker might also get curious about communications entries. When you define a communications entry in a subsystem, you can define a default user. For some situations, using a default user is desirable. In many situations, however, defining a default user profile isn't good practice. Instead, you should keep the DFTUSER parameter value set at *NONE to ensure that APPC jobs or DDM requests that don't include security information won't use a default user, but instead will require a user profile and password.

Job Descriptions with an Associated User Profile

One possible exposure that we mentioned in Chapter 2 is a job description that includes a user profile. At level 30 security or lower, a user who has *USE authority to the job description can submit the job and let the job description's user profile be the user of the job. The user who submits the job doesn't need authority to that user profile.

This loophole would let a hacker execute a job as another user, possibly one with more authority, and would certainly confuse the audit trail. At security level 30, this occurrence is audited. At level 40, a user profile that doesn't have authority to the user profile associated with the job description can't use the job description to submit a job, and any attempt to do so is audited.

Another loophole associated with this type of job description is the possibility that someone will use the job description in a workstation entry. If that happens, any job that uses the workstation entry can start without the user entering a user profile and password. At level 30, users who attempt to sign on without a user ID and password are audited but are not prevented from signing on. At level 40, the system doesn't allow the job description to supply the user profile at sign-on; the user must actually sign on to the AS/400 by entering the user profile and password as usual.

Program Evoke

Invoking a program after an APPC session has been acquired is a situation that a hacker could exploit. The QCMN and QBASE subsystem descriptions have a PGMEVOKE routing entry. This routing entry lets the requesters call any program they have the authority to invoke. You might want to remove the default entry and add entries for the specific programs you want users to be able to run. This is not a topic for the faint of heart, however. You need to understand how AS/400 Work Management processes routing entries as well as which system programs you need to add routing entries for. For more information about which routing entries you might need to add, see *AS/400 Tips and Tools for Securing Your AS/400 V4R5* (SC41-5300).

Remote Command Facilities

The AS/400 has several remote command facilities, including DDM (SBMRMTCMD), RMTCMD through Client Access Express, the Remote Execution (REXEC) server, and FTP's RCMD function. Users who use remote command facilities bypass the security built into your menus or applications, so you must depend on resource-level security to protect your system. (Although FTP and REXEC check the LMTCPB attribute of the user profile, Client Access and DDM do not.) A hacker can do great damage if you don't implement resource security. Say that a user running Client Access Express leaves her workstation unattended and signed on. The hacker could use the RMTCMD function and submit the command PWRDWNSYS *IMMED. If the user who was signed on had authority to the Power Down System command, your system would be powered down! You must ensure that you know who is using remote-command capabilities and secure those capabilities where possible.

Client Access Express Functions

Client Access Express uses the user's authority to access AS/400 objects and run Client Access Express functions. Chapter 7 describes in detail what can happen when a user only disconnects from Client Access or when a user leaves the workstation unattended and someone else uses the workstation. A hacker can easily exploit the authority of the signed-on user in this case.

ODBC

ODBC is another facility that bypasses all menu and application security when accessing database files. Data on systems that haven't implemented resource security could be severely compromised. Anyone can read data residing in files that have *PUBLIC(*USE) authority and can update data in files that have *PUBLIC(*CHANGE) authority. Although exit points exist for the IBM ODBC driver, other ODBC drivers don't necessarily use these exit points. Other drivers either have their own ODBC server or use Distributed Relational Database Architecture (DRDA). For V4R1 and V4R2, PTFs are available that provide exit-program support for DRDA. However, we don't recommend that you depend solely on exit programs. Before you implement ODBC applications, it's essential that you have in place a sound security methodology that implements resource security.

*SAVSYS Special Authority

A user who has *SAVSYS special authority can save objects from libraries to which he or she isn't authorized. If the user could restore that object to a library that has more authority available, he or she could certainly explore the system and, depending on whether the object itself is secure, might be able to modify data.

DB2 UDB for AS/400 Trigger Programs

The arrival of referential integrity and triggers in DB2 UDB was certainly welcome. Powerful capabilities are often associated with security risks, however, and that's certainly true of triggers. Let's say you have a development environment. A programmer decides to write a trigger program that contains a virus. The programmer has *OBJALTER authority to development database files, so the trigger is added and the program is executed every time the trigger condition occurs. When the code is promoted, the promotion tool automatically moves the trigger program as well, or maybe an unsuspecting manager promotes the trigger. Either way, no one takes the time to identify what the trigger does, and the hacker successfully gets the virus into the production library.

Too Much Public Authority

Unmanaged public authority is dangerous. The QCRTAUT system value, the CRTAUT library attribute, and the AUT parameter on CRTxxx commands control the level of public authority granted when an object is created. If the default public authority is excessive (e.g., *ALL), the result could be a security loophole that gives users too much authority. If a hacker can use file transfer through Client Access or FTP, the hacker can download any file that has *PUBLIC(*CHANGE) authority, use a PC editor to alter the file, and upload the file to your system. *USE authority might even be too much for files that contain sensitive data because *USE lets the hacker download the file. Public authority with too much access is probably the biggest threat to AS/400s today.

Closing Off Authority Exposures

Here are our suggestions for closing off authority exposures.

SUGGESTION #1 — GUARD THE SYSTEM LIBRARY LIST (*SYSLIBL) AND AUDIT ALL OBJECTS IN ALL LIBRARIES THAT PRECEDE QSYS IN THE SYSTEM LIBRARY LIST.

SUGGESTION #2 — RUN MACHINES AT SECURITY LEVEL 40 OR 50.

SUGGESTION #3 — SPECIFICALLY PLAN PUBLIC AUTHORITIES.

SUGGESTION #4 — USE THE PRTPUBAUT (PRINT PUBLICLY AUTHORIZED OBJECTS) REPORT TO MONITOR THE PUBLIC AUTHORITY OF SENSITIVE OBJECTS.

SUGGESTION #5 — DON'T HAVE PROGRAMS THAT ADOPT AUTHORITY CALL OTHER PROGRAMS.

SUGGESTION #6 — MAKE SURE THAT PROGRAMS THAT ADOPT AUTHORITY OR SWAP PROFILES "CLEAN UP" WHETHER THEY END NORMALLY OR ABNORMALLY.

SUGGESTION #7 — USE THE QUSEADPAUT SYSTEM VALUE TO PREVENT CREATION OF PROGRAMS THAT MALICIOUSLY USE ADOPTED AUTHORITY.

SUGGESTION #8 — AUDIT USERS WHO HAVE SPECIAL AUTHORITIES.

SUGGESTION #9 — DON'T USE PROFILES WITH *ALLOBJ AUTHORITY FOR NORMAL WORK.

SUGGESTION #10 — LIMIT OWNERSHIP OF OBJECTS TO PROFILES THAT HAVE NO PURPOSE OTHER THAN TO OWN THE OBJECTS.

SUGGESTION #11 — DON'T USE IBM-SUPPLIED PROFILES TO OWN OBJECTS.

SUGGESTION #12 — LIMIT AUTHORITIES TO SUBSYSTEMS, AND AUDIT CHANGES TO THEM.

SUGGESTION #13 — AUDIT RESTORE OPERATIONS TO THE SYSTEM.

SUGGESTION #14 — AUDIT ALL OUTSIDE CONSULTANTS AND VENDORS USING AUDLVL(*CMD).

SUGGESTION #15 — DON'T ALLOW LIBRARIES IN THE SYSTEM PORTION OF THE LIBRARY LIST TO HAVE *PUBLIC(*CHANGE) OR GREATER AUTHORITY.

SUGGESTION #16 — QUALIFY PROGRAM CALLS TO PROTECT AGAINST TROJAN HORSES THAT MIGHT EXIST IN A LIBRARY THAT PRECEDES THE PROGRAM'S LIBRARY IN THE LIBRARY LIST.

SUGGESTION #17 — WRITE EXIT PROGRAMS TO EXPLICITLY CONTROL AND AUDIT DSPT, DDM, AND CLIENT ACCESS FUNCTIONS.

SUGGESTION #18 — USE THE PRTTRGPGM (PRINT TRIGGER PROGRAM) COMMAND TO MONITOR TRIGGER PROGRAMS.

Preventing Trojan Horses

Trojan horses are one of the most popular tools for hackers trying to gain authorities to your system. A hacker who wants to plant a successful Trojan horse looks for the opportunity to substitute the Trojan horse for a normal program, add a Trojan horse to an otherwise normal flow of program calls, or simply place on the system a Trojan horse that someone might execute directly in the belief that it is a normal application program.

For instance, if the applications on your system typically call programs without qualifying the call with a library name, a hacker could place a program with the same name as one of the called programs in a library that precedes the program library in a job's library list. Then, when the application makes its unqualified call to the program, the Trojan horse program is invoked instead of the application's program. With this approach, the hacker needs authority only to a library in the library list. QGPL, which normally has public authority of *CHANGE, is a good candidate library. You might decide to change the authority to library QGPL or audit the library.

Another ideal opportunity for a Trojan horse is the DB2 UDB database trigger function. As we've discussed, if you don't secure the process for adding triggers to database files or audit triggers, you leave the door open for a hacker to put a Trojan horse on your system as a trigger.

Numerous third-party software packages implement exit programs. You also might have written your own. Regardless, the exit programs registered on your system provide an excellent opportunity for a hacker to introduce a Trojan horse. For that reason, you need to vigilantly monitor exit programs. Hacker bulletin boards list potentially damaging sample programs. For example, one such listing provides code that captures the clear-text passwords passed to an FTP exit program.

Here are some specific steps you can take to protect your system against Trojan horses:

SUGGESTION #1 — AUDIT ALL LIBRARIES THAT PRECEDE QSYS IN THE SYSTEM LIBRARY LIST (OR ELSE DON'T ALLOW LIBRARIES TO PRECEDE QSYS).

SUGGESTION #2 — CAREFULLY PLAN EACH JOB'S LIBRARY LIST — THE SYSTEM PORTION, THE PRODUCT PORTION, AND THE USER PORTION — AND APPLICATION CALL STATEMENTS TO REDUCE EXPOSURE FROM UNQUALIFIED PROGRAM CALLS.

SUGGESTION #3 — SECURE SUBSYSTEM DESCRIPTIONS TO PREVENT SOMEONE FROM INTRODUCING A ROUTING ENTRY THAT CONTAINS A TROJAN HORSE.

SUGGESTION #4 — RUN AT SECURITY LEVEL 40 OR 50 TO ENSURE THAT THE SYSTEM DETECTS PROGRAMS THAT HAVE BEEN MODIFIED.

SUGGESTION #5 — LIMIT AUTHORITY TO ADD TRIGGERS TO DB2 UDB, AND AUDIT TRIGGERS.

SUGGESTION #6 — RESTRICT AND AUDIT USE OF THE OVRMSGF (OVERRIDE WITH MESSAGE FILE) COMMAND. THE SYSTEM USES MESSAGES (SPECIFICALLY CPX2313) TO DETERMINE AND MAINTAIN COMMANDS THAT THE SYSTEM REQUEST MENU WILL EXECUTE.

SUGGESTION #7 — RESTRICT CHANGE AND DEBUG ACCESS TO, AND AUDIT, ALL EXIT PROGRAMS (THOSE DEFINED IN THE REGISTRATION FACILITY AS WELL AS DDM, PC SUPPORT/400 — OR PCS, DSPT, PASSWORD VALIDATION).

SUGGESTION #8 — RESTRICT AUTHORITIES TO THE PRODUCTION ENVIRONMENT.

Preventing Viruses

Many AS/400 IT personnel probably haven't worried much about the threat of a virus on their AS/400 because, until recently, we've all primarily associated viruses with PCs. But as we said at the beginning of this chapter, the AS/400 isn't immune to viruses. Remember that the IFS provides a PC-like root file system, and — beginning with V4R2 — the Network Neighborhood lets the AS/400 act as a network file server. The IFS file systems can store Unix and PC executables (e.g., COM and EXE files) and so can store and propagate any virus that attacks those types of executables. The same antivirus measures that work in Unix and on PCs will work in the IFS.

However, even the traditional AS/400 environment has a few places that can let someone attach a virus to an executable (e.g., CL command, subsystem routing step). A command, for example, can have a command processing program, a validity-checking program (VCP), and a prompt override program. Many of you probably don't use VCPs. However, if a hacker has *OBJMGT authority to a command, the hacker can introduce a generic VCP that works like a virus. The hacker could define dummy VCP parameters, and the command and its processing program would function normally. But the VCP could attach itself to other commands that the current user has *OBJMGT authority to change and could launch batch jobs, execute commands, or do whatever else it wants and has the authority to do, depending on the authority of the user who is executing the command at the time.

Attaching a program to a database file in the form of a trigger might be considered a virus, depending on the program's purpose — we've already established that a hacker could substitute a Trojan horse for a trigger program.

A hacker could add an auto-start job entry to a subsystem, and that job could start other jobs or perform mischief on the system. A hacker could write an exit program for an exit point on the system (e.g., a DDM user exit program, password validation user exit program, or an exit program for one of the exit points in the Registration Facility).

Here are specific steps you can take to protect your system from someone who wants to plant a virus:

SUGGESTION #1 — RUN YOUR SYSTEM AT SECURITY LEVEL 50. SECURITY LEVEL 50 BEST PROTECTS YOUR SYSTEM AGAINST HACKERS TRYING TO INTRODUCE DESTRUCTIVE PROGRAMS.

SUGGESTION #2 — LIMIT OWNERSHIP AUTHORITIES (E.G., *OBJMGT, *OBJEXIST) TO ALL COMMANDS AND PROGRAMS.

SUGGESTION #3 — LIMIT AUTHORITY TO ADD TRIGGERS TO DB2 UDB, AND AUDIT TRIGGERS.

SUGGESTION #4 — RESTRICT ACCESS TO, AND AUDIT, ALL EXIT PROGRAMS (WRKREGINF — WORK WITH REGISTRATION INFORMATION, DDM, PCS, DSPT, PASSWORD VALIDATION).

SUGGESTION #5 — LIMIT AUTHORITIES TO CHANGE SUBSYSTEMS.

SUGGESTION #6 — LIMIT WHO YOU ALLOW TO RESTORE OBJECTS TO YOUR SYSTEM.

SUGGESTION #7 — LIMIT ACCESS TO SST AND DST (A HACKER CAN PATCH PROGRAMS USING THESE FUNCTIONS).

SUGGESTION #8 — LIMIT ACCESS TO API QPRCRTPG, WHICH LETS THE USER ASSEMBLE AN MI PROGRAM OBJECT.

Preventing Worms

Although some well-known PC viruses have been worms, worms get little attention. OS/400 has some places that can be susceptible to worm attacks. Remember, a worm usually attacks by filling disk space or filling memory until the system can't function. Limit your AS/400's exposure to worms by taking the steps that follow.

SUGGESTION #1 — RESTRICT ACCESS TO THE CHGCLS (CHANGE CLASS) COMMAND AND RELATED COMMANDS. A HACKER COULD CHANGE A *CLS OBJECT TO HAVE AN UNREALISTIC TIME-SLICE AND HOG MEMORY FOR MANY JOBS THAT USE THAT *CLS.

SUGGESTION #2 — RESTRICT ACCESS TO THE CHGSBSD COMMAND AND RELATED COMMANDS.

SUGGESTION #3 — CHECK YOUR SYSTEM FOR SUBSYSTEMS THAT HAVE THE MAXJOBS PARAMETER SET TO *NOMAX. SET THE PARAMETER TO A FINITE NUMBER FOR ALL SUBSYSTEMS.

SUGGESTION #4 — CHECK FOR JOB DESCRIPTIONS THAT SUBMIT TO THE QCTL JOB QUEUE AND RESTRICT USE OF THOSE JOB DESCRIPTIONS. QCTL HAS THE HIGHEST PRIORITY OF ALL SUBSYSTEMS, SO ONE JOB COULD TAKE ADVANTAGE AND HOG THE CPU.

SUGGESTION #5 — RESTRICT ACCESS TO THE TFRJOB (TRANSFER JOB) AND RRTJOB (REROUTE JOB) COMMANDS WHERE POSSIBLE.

SUGGESTION #6 — USE THE CRTUSRPRF (CREATE USER PROFILE) COMMAND'S MAXSTG PARAMETER TO MAINTAIN REALISTIC MAXIMUM STORAGE VALUES FOR EACH USER PROFILE ON THE SYSTEM. BY LIMITING THE AMOUNT OF STORAGE EACH USER CAN USE, THE MAXIMUM STORAGE VALUE PREVENTS ANY USER FROM USING A JOB THAT REPEATEDLY DUPLICATES OR CREATES AN OBJECT TO FILL DISK STORAGE.

SUGGESTION #7 — SET REASONABLE AUXILIARY STORAGE POOL (ASP) THRESHOLDS.

Internet Attacks

Every week seems to bring a new, sensational attack by a hacker who has gained access to a system via the Internet. Although no major news story has implicated the AS/400, it isn't immune to Internet-based hacking. Common attacks include getting "graffitied" (in which the hacker alters the Web site, typically with unflattering and undesirable images), spoofing (in which a hacker pretends to be someone he or she isn't, often by changing the IP address of your device or system), sniffing (monitoring or eavesdropping on transmissions), flooding (overflowing your e-mail system with misdirected e-mail, which is also known as a mail-bomb), and denial-of-service (making your system unavailable for its intended purpose). Your susceptibility to such attacks depends on your network configuration and which TCP/IP applications you enable. For specific recommendations for preventing Internet attacks and protecting your AS/400, see Chapters 8 and 9.

Final Words of Advice

We close this chapter by recommending several general-security steps for improving your overall defense against hackers.

SUGGESTION #1 — TO HELP ENSURE MANAGEMENT SUPPORT AND FOSTER EMPLOYEE AWARENESS, DEVELOP AND ENFORCE GOOD SECURITY POLICIES FOR YOUR BUSINESS.

SUGGESTION #2 — TO HELP MOTIVATE ADMINISTRATORS NOT TO ABUSE THEIR POWER OVER THE SYSTEM OR NETWORK, SEPARATE THE NETWORK ADMINISTRATION, SECURITY ADMINISTRATION, AND AUDITING FUNCTIONS AMONG DIFFERENT USERS.

SUGGESTION #3 — ENFORCE GOOD SECURITY FOR IT PERSONNEL, INCLUDING SOFTWARE VENDORS AND CONSULTING IT PROFESSIONALS.

SUGGESTION #4 — TO MANAGE YOUR SOFTWARE DEVELOPMENT AND MAINTENANCE, PURCHASE A SOFTWARE-DEVELOPMENT AND SOURCE-CODE-CONTROL PACKAGE THAT INCLUDES GOOD SECURITY TRACKING.

SUGGESTION #5 — IMPLEMENT AS MANY LAYERS OF DEFENSE AS MAKES BUSINESS SENSE.

SUGGESTION #6 — AUDIT, AUDIT, AUDIT!

Chapter 11

Evaluating Your Current Strategy

Having studied the security tools we have to work with on the AS/400, we can now turn our attention to using those tools to develop and implement an effective security strategy. As the first step in this process, you need to study your current strategy and its implementation. This step is important, whether or not you were involved in designing and implementing that strategy.

This chapter introduces some common authorization models that customers and vendors alike employ on the AS/400. These models describe the strategies you can use to implement security on your AS/400. We then present a series of questions and exercises to help you evaluate your current implementation. When you finish this chapter, you'll understand your current implementation well enough to make the decisions necessary to ensure that you have a secure environment that protects your company's data and physical IT assets.

Common Authorization Models

IBM customers and software vendors typically implement one of several authorization models on the AS/400. These models shouldn't be regarded as security solutions in and of themselves, but rather as methods often used to build a security solution. The menu authorization model, for example, is used to some extent at almost every AS/400 installation. However, many shops have gone beyond menu authorization and are using concepts from one or more of the other models. If your shop is one of those that has been content to stay with menu authorization and your users have access to tools such as File Transfer Protocol (FTP), Open Database Connectivity (ODBC), file transfer, and Distributed Data Management (DDM), you need to rethink this decision.

This chapter discusses the strengths and weaknesses of each model so that, as you begin to build your own security strategy, you'll understand how best to use each type of authorization.

Menu Authorization Model

The pure menu authorization model assumes that no specific authority is granted to system users. Security is achieved simply by presenting to each user only menus that provide the functions that user needs to perform his or her job. Users can access anything on their set of menus and can access the objects and data associated with those menu options. Figure 11.1 shows a diagram of the menu authorization model.

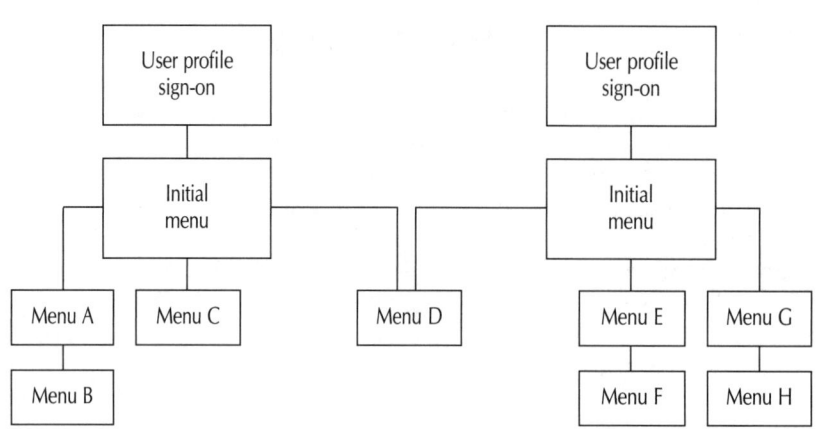

FIGURE 11.1
The Menu Authorization Model

```
    User profile                    User profile
      sign-on                          sign-on
         |                                |
      Initial ─────────────────────────Initial
       menu                             menu
     /   |   \                         /   |   \
Menu A Menu C Menu D              Menu E     Menu G
   |                                 |          |
Menu B                            Menu F     Menu H
```

Properly used, the menu authorization model requires that each user's initial menu reflect only the options the user needs to do his or her job. You design the initial menu for each user individually using the Initial Program (INLPGM) or Initial Menu (INLMNU) parameter of the user profile or, in the case of some packaged software applications, by means of initial user data entered and maintained by your organization's employees. The menu authorization model is many software vendors' method of choice simply because it's the least complex for customers to implement and because it can be used under a security level of 20 or higher.

Menus are a logical way to provide access to software applications. Because you don't want end users entering commands from a command line, you provide menus that logically group end-user functions. Whether the menu is a pull-down, pop-up, or plain, full-screen menu, end users are much more productive when they can select tasks from a list than when they must memorize cryptic commands or program names.

By logically grouping the tasks users can perform, menus also secure the system by restricting users to the tasks on the menus. You might wonder whether the resulting security is sufficient. The proper question, however, is "Can someone get around menu security accidentally or intentionally?" The answer, of course, is "Yes."

The most basic problem associated with menu-based security is managing the proliferation of menus. Users commonly begin performing tasks that weren't originally part of their set of menus. After a while, the users need additional options that exist on other menus, but those other menus also contain options and authorizations the users don't need. Therefore, you must create a new menu or set of menus for those special users, and you must make sure the new menus maintain a secure environment. It starts to get complicated, doesn't it?

Another problem occurs as a result of end-user requirements for tools such as ODBC, DDM, FTP, and file transfer. The system provides no specific object authority to prevent someone who uses such tools from accessing any file on the system. Consequently, you must create the objects the user needs (e.g., queries, reports, and upload and download procedures) and then place a special option on a separate menu for those users to access. Again, the result is a management headache, and you're tempted to become a little lax in enforcing your security strategy.

Without object authorizations that secure libraries, directories, data files, and program objects, there are many ways that someone can, accidentally or intentionally, corrupt or steal data. Consider the loopholes that can develop in any menu system. As menu requirements grow and the number of menus increases, so do the chances that users can access menus containing options that have nothing to do with their jobs and required tasks. Your security strategy is built squarely on a very shaky foundation — the assumption that users simply won't use menu options that don't relate to their jobs.

As a method of security in the IT department, the menu model is a complete failure. IT personnel normally aren't restricted to certain menus. Instead, they have access to programming languages, system utilities, OS/400 commands, and other means of reading, manipulating, and deleting objects and data. Does this mean that IT personnel are exempt from a security strategy? Certainly not! It does mean that you must use something more than menus to secure the system and ensure that IT personnel have authority to only the objects they need to perform their jobs.

Library and Directory Authorization Model

The library and directory authorization model uses object authority to grant user profiles specific authority to the libraries or directories they need. Users have specific authority to only the libraries or directories they need and can't access objects in libraries or directories to which they aren't authorized.

Figure 11.2 shows how one user might have access to one set of libraries while another user has access to a different set of libraries. The key to implementing the library authorization model is to authorize each user to the correct libraries and to make sure the user's initial program or job description provides the user with the right library list.

On the AS/400, all objects are kept in libraries or directories. Because all applications and data must exist in some library, the logical course of action is to divide applications and data among libraries or directories by function. For some shops, this organization means having all data in one directory and all programs in an application library. For others, it means having multiple data and application libraries and directories and defining each library and directory by the type of application (e.g., order entry, general ledger, purchasing).

With the library authorization model, end users and IT personnel both receive specific authority to certain libraries. If users attempt to access objects in libraries to which they don't have authority, the system generates an error. Even an IT user can't use an OS/400 command or a programming tool to get to an object unless the user has authority to the library or directory in which the object resides.

FIGURE 11.2
The Library Authorization Model

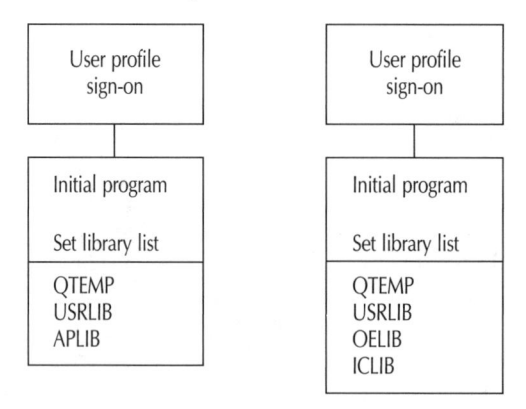

```
┌──────────────────┐      ┌──────────────────┐
│   User profile   │      │   User profile   │
│     sign-on      │      │     sign-on      │
└────────┬─────────┘      └────────┬─────────┘
         │                         │
┌────────┴─────────┐      ┌────────┴─────────┐
│ Initial program  │      │ Initial program  │
│                  │      │                  │
│ Set library list │      │ Set library list │
│                  │      │                  │
│     QTEMP        │      │     QTEMP        │
│     USRLIB       │      │     USRLIB       │
│     APLIB        │      │     OELIB        │
│                  │      │     ICLIB        │
└──────────────────┘      └──────────────────┘
```

Although this model secures the library, the problem of securing objects in the library remains. Because authority exists only at the library level, DDM, Client Access, and other tools that work independently of menu systems still cause problems — only now the problems are limited to specific libraries of data or application programs. The consequences depend on the nature of the objects in the library.

Exceptions are still difficult. This model grants authority to the entire library, even if a user needs access to only one or two objects in the library. The solution again requires creating many special menu or application programs.

Direct Authorization Model

With the direct authorization model, specific authority is granted to each object on the system. As Figure 11.3 shows, users are granted authority individually to the libraries, directories, applications, and data files the users require. If necessary, more than one user can be authorized to certain objects. By granting specific authorities to each user, the direct authorization model provides the most comprehensive security possible at the object level.

This model requires that the security implementer fully understand how the system functions and which users need which authorities. With the menu and library authorization models, public authority of at least *CHANGE is necessary for all objects (other than libraries) on the system, which means that only menus or library authorities control access to objects. With the direct authorization model, control over who can access an object is determined by the authority given to each user for each object.

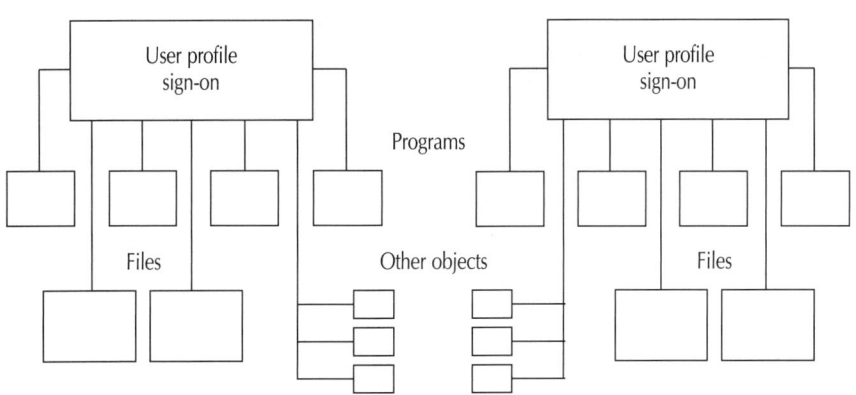

FIGURE 11.3
The Direct Authorization Model

However, a strict implementation of the direct model can be disastrous. Performance is one problem. Private authorities increase the number of authority look-ups the system performs and can thus degrade performance. Nevertheless, with improvements in the efficiency of the authority checking algorithm and the addition of the authority cache, a manageable, understandable authority scheme doesn't need to cause performance problems. In other words, you should be able to secure your system using the direct authorization model in a way that makes sense to you, is easily maintained, and performs satisfactorily. If that means using private authorities in some cases, then go ahead and use private authorities.

Another problem with the direct authorization model is administration, as we just mentioned. Who gets to document all those user authorities? Who has to maintain them? And how do you keep them all straight? The time required to save the system also increases dramatically because the system must track all private authorities associated with each user profile. It's easy to see why following this method exclusively could cost you some sleep.

Group Authorization Model

The group authorization model is similar to the direct authorization model, except that in the group model, you grant specific object authorities to group profiles, which in turn authorize members of the group to those objects (Figure 11.4 is a diagram of the group model). Specific authority is still granted to all objects. Users are assigned to groups whose members share common authority needs, and exceptions are handled by granting or revoking specific authorities.

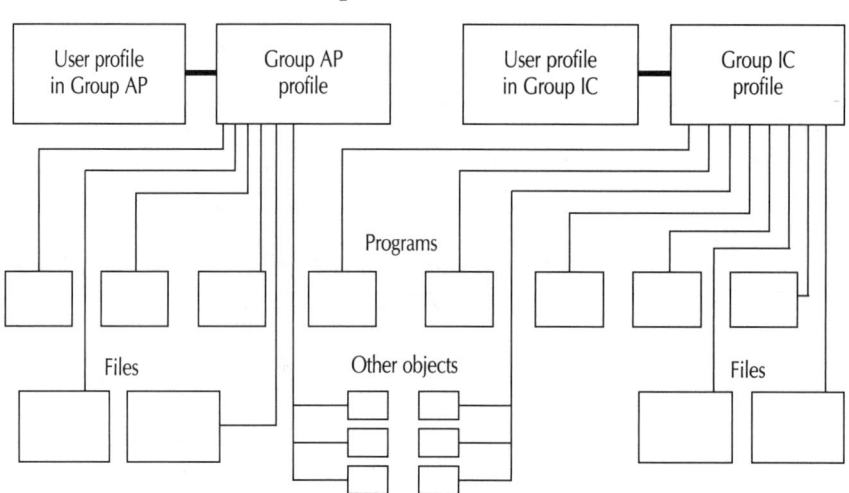

FIGURE 11.4
The Group Authorization Model

One advantage of the group model is that it more accurately reflects the function-based organization of most companies. An organization generally has several people who perform similar jobs. The order-entry department, for instance, often consists of several people who have similar roles and thus require similar authorities. All accounts receivable clerks generally require similar authorities, as do all billing clerks and all human resources staff. (Chapter 13 discusses the concept of role authorization in detail.)

Like the direct authority model, the group model requires specific authorities. The security implementer must be familiar with the business, the various jobs in the organization, and the authorities needed to perform the jobs.

Group profiles can be authorized to many objects, with each object authorization including the necessary operational and data rights. The group model is much easier to manage than the direct model because it reduces the number of private authorities granted to objects and is more easily documented. Adding user profiles to and removing them from groups is easy, and the authorities provided through the group profile are automatically granted or revoked, respectively.

Again, one potential drawback of the group authorization model is performance. Using group profiles where public authority would suffice causes the system to perform additional authority look-ups to determine a user's authority to those objects. However, the ease of management of the group model, the multiple-group capability, and the flexibility that groups offer for adding and removing users from the system offset performance implications as long as you don't overuse groups when public authority would suffice. You can improve performance by using the primary group function when possible.

Software vendors frequently use the group authorization model as an easy way to secure their software packages. A vendor might deliver a package with a group profile that owns all objects. Anyone enrolled in the product is simply added to the group and is thus authorized to all objects that the group owns. The vendor then uses menus to control who has access to objects via calls to programs on the menus. Those not enrolled in the product have no authority to any of its objects.

This particular example brings up one last drawback of a group implementation. When a user exits an application secured in this manner, the user retains *ALL authority to the application objects by virtue of belonging to the group that owns the objects, but upon exiting, the user is no longer governed by the application's security provisions. Consequently, any use of DDM, FTP, or ODBC can use the user's *ALL authority to the application objects. When used to implement authorities in this way, the group authorization model can seduce you into granting too much authority. It's important to resist this temptation.

Program Adoption Authorization Model

The ability of a program to adopt its owner's authority eliminates the need to authorize users to the program's objects, instead requiring only that the program's owner be authorized to perform the program's tasks. (The section "Adopted Authority" in Chapter 4 explains how programs adopt authority.) Adopted authority is preferable in situations that require a high level of control and in which you want only one program to be able to perform certain tasks. Figure 11.5 shows how program authority adoption can let a user access data without having object authority to the data files. In this scenario, neither user profile is authorized to FILE_A, FILE_B, FILE_C, or FILE_D, which are all owned by FIL_OWNER. Instead, PROGRAM_F adopts FIL_OWNER's authority, which then lets PROGRAM_F perform the required I/O to the files. This implementation lets you exclude all other users from the files and ensure that the only means of changing the files is through PROGRAM_F.

FIGURE 11.5
The Program Adoption Authorization Model

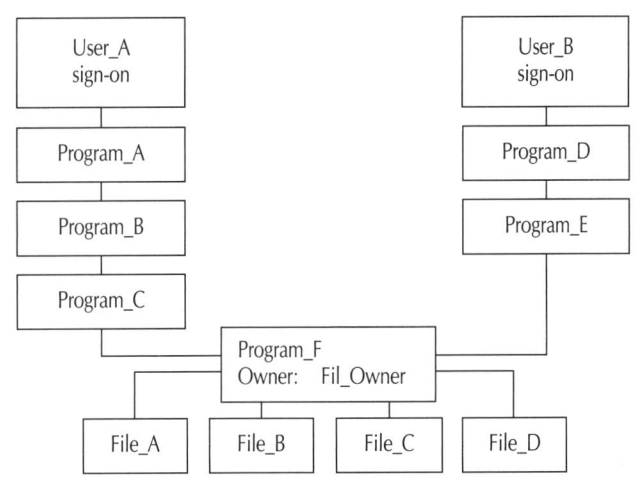

Program adoption isn't normally practiced on a system-wide basis but is instead used for specific security implementations. As a method of implementing security, adopted authority does have some drawbacks. First, it's often difficult to manage because of a lack of documentation. If you use programs that adopt authority, you must carefully and thoroughly document them. Second, applications containing programs that adopt authority must be carefully designed to prevent unwanted propagation of that authority to subsequent programs in the program invocation stack. Finally, program adoption doesn't work for objects accessed through the Integrated File System (IFS).

Changing the Process or Thread's Profile Authorization Model

Changing the user profile under which a process or thread is running is another way of giving temporary authority to the process or thread to perform a piece of work. (Hereafter, we use "process" to also imply "thread" unless otherwise noted.) For example, although you can't use adopted authority to access files in the IFS, you can change the user profile under which the process runs to let users access files. There are three ways to do this: using profile swapping APIs, profile token APIs, or the QSYSETUID/QSYSETGID APIs.

You can use the QSYGETPH (Get a User Profile Handle) and QWTSETP (Set Profile) APIs to "swap" to a profile that has the authority to perform the process. When you swap a profile, the process runs with the new profile's authority. For example, say Jonathan signs on to the system and runs an application. Initially, the application runs with Jonathan's authority. However, at some point the application needs to access files in the IFS that Jonathan is excluded from. The application swaps to a user profile, UPD_FILE, that has explicit authority to update the file. After the swap, the application runs as UPD_FILE, not as Jonathan. Note that swapping the profile also changes the user profile's group(s), limited capability attribute, and group authority attributes for the job.

As you can tell, profile swapping is a powerful function that must be used very carefully. In particular, application writers must ensure that they swap back to the original profile in the event of abnormal job termination as well as normal job termination.

A variation of profile swapping available in V4R5 is the use of profile tokens. Tokens are much like profile handles, but tokens can be passed to and utilized by other jobs on the system. When you create tokens, you can request one that can be used only one time, one that can be used multiple times, or one that can be used multiple times and regenerated. Tokens time out if they aren't used within the time period for which they are valid. Tokens provide more flexibility than profile handles. But if you need to change a profile only within a job, we recommend that you use profile handles instead of tokens. Profile handles are more secure, and profile tokens should be protected by the application: An application shouldn't generate a profile token for QSECOFR and then place it into a data area that the public can access! However, tokens are more secure than passing user names and passwords between applications.

Another set of APIs available in V4R5 consists of several variations of the QSYSETUID (Set User ID) and QSYSETGID (Set Group ID) APIs. Unix programmers will recognize these variations. To explain how these APIs work, we need to take a side trip and explain how the IFS performs authority checking.

Rather than using the name of the user profile associated with the job to check authority, the IFS uses the user ID (UID). (Remember that the IFS is a file system based on POSIX standards, which dictate that the system identifies users by their UID.) The UID is a number that represents the user and is one of the AS/400 user profile attributes. You can use the DSPUSRPRF (Display User Profile) command to see the UID.

The QSYSETUID and QSYSETGID APIs operate on the same principles as profile handles and tokens, but these APIs change only the currently running thread's UID *or* GID (group identifier), whereas profile handles and tokens change both the user and the user's groups. In other words, depending on whether you use QSYSETUID or QSYSETGID, you can change either the thread's user or its group. For example, if the current user Michelle is a member of five group profiles and you use the QSYSETUID API to run the process as Christopher, the process runs under Christopher's user ID but still has Michelle's five group profiles. The reverse is true for the QSYSETGID API. When you use QSYSETGID, only the process's first group profile is changed. The process's user ID and the original user's other group profiles remain unchanged. We describe these APIs in a bit more detail in Appendix A.

Unlike with program adoption, no commands or tools are available to list programs that perform swapping via handles or tokens or that set the UID or GID. To determine which programs change the UID or GID, you must turn on auditing, run your applications, and look for PS audit entries. You should ask your application providers whether their applications use either of these APIs and the purpose for doing so. Don't misunderstand: There are legitimate reasons for using QSYSETUID and QSYSETGID, but those reasons should be well understood, and as with program adoption, their use should be very carefully documented.

As we stated at the beginning of this chapter, our purpose in presenting these authorization models isn't to propose a complete security solution with any particular one, but to point out the models' strengths and weaknesses. The next step in the process is to walk through the evaluation of your current security implementation.

Evaluating the Key Areas

The questionnaire on the next page lists the key questions you need to answer to evaluate your current security strategy. As you identify the security measures currently implemented on your system, list your findings for later use in updating your plan.

> **Security Evaluation Questionnaire**
>
> Is your AS/400 physically secure?
> _____
> _____
>
> Is your system at security level 40 or 50? If not, what is preventing you from going to security level 40 or 50?
> _____
> _____
>
> What security principles have you applied to your system configuration?
> _____
> _____
>
> What security principles have you applied to your device configuration?
> _____
> _____
>
> What security principles have you applied to the manner in which your system is accessed (e.g., initial programs, menus)?
> _____
> _____
>
> Are you relying solely on menu security, or have you secured your system resources (e.g., libraries, files, programs)?
> _____
> _____
>
> Is your system connected to the Internet or in a network that is?
> _____
> _____

Physical Security

Is your AS/400 physically secure? At a minimum, your system should be in a room with limited traffic, and possibly one that is locked. Physical security is important for several reasons. By limiting physical access to the system, you reduce the risk of both accidental and intentional harm.

A news story once reported on the first convicted felon to be accepted into Harvard Law School. She had served five years in jail for chopping up a mainframe computer with an axe. The woman had worked at a government installation that housed a large mainframe that she believed controlled "the button" that the President of the United States could use to launch nuclear weapons. Being radically antinuclear, she walked into the computer center and destroyed the computer with an axe.

This admittedly extreme tale illustrates the need for physical security. You certainly don't want to invite vandalism. Nor do you want a visiting child to wander into the computer room and begin playing with disk-drive buttons. Even a simple form of physical security can prevent such incidents.

Another form of physical security involves simple common sense. You wouldn't want to learn that the closet next to your computer room contained dynamite. Neither would you want to walk into the computer room to find that pipes had burst in the ceiling and that you now needed a rowboat to traverse the room. Yet pipes have burst in computer-room ceilings. Corrosive chemicals have been stored too close to wiring. These and similar situations illustrate the importance of using common sense when you install computer equipment.

Using your inventory of computer-related equipment, determine where each piece is located and what, if any, security measures protect the equipment and discourage attempts to violate the system. Where is the key to your AS/400? We hope it isn't in the keyhole on the computer's front panel; but for now, just find it. (We discuss the use of the key in Chapter 12.) Also note the key-switch position setting on the front panel. The key-switch will be in the position of SECURE, AUTO, MANUAL, or NORMAL.

Remember, you are only evaluating the physical security in place today. List each physical security measure you can find.

Security Level

Under what security level is your system running? A production machine should have system value QSECURITY set at a minimum of 40. Security levels 10 and 20 don't provide the capability to establish the proper levels of application security. Level 30 provides object-level security but contains interfaces that hackers can exploit to bypass security. If your system is at level 30, you can't secure it. Security level 40 is a far better choice because those interfaces that can be exploited at level 30 aren't usable at level 40. So strongly does IBM believe that you should use at least level 40 that it ships the AS/400 with the QSECURITY system value set at 40 by default. We believe that security level 50 is the only choice if you want the best protection for your system. We recommend level 50, and it is a must if your system is running as a Web server or you have high security requirements.

System Configuration

In Chapter 2, we discussed the security-related system values. In Chapter 7, we covered security-related network attributes. Take the time now to determine how you are using these system values and network attributes. Figures 11.6 and 11.7 will help you record the values you find and compare them with the recommended values. If you find one that conflicts with the recommended value, you should review the discussion of that system value or network attribute.

FIGURE 11.6
Recommended System Value Settings

System value	Default value	Recommended value	Current value
QALWOBJRST	*ALL	*NONE or *ALWPTF	
QALWUSRDMN	*ALL	*ALL	
QAUDCTL	*NONE	*AUDLVL	
QAUDENDACN	*NOTIFY	*NOTIFY	
QAUDFRCLVL	*SYS	*SYS	
QAUDLVL	*NONE	*AUTFAIL, *SECURITY	
QAUTOVRT	0	0	
QCRTAUT	*CHANGE	*USE or *CHANGE	
QCRTOBJAUD	*NONE	*NONE	
QDSPSGNINF	'0' = No	'0' = No	
QINACTITV	*NONE	30	
QINACTMSGQ	*ENDJOB	*DSCJOB	
QLMTDEVSSN	'0' = No	'1' = Yes	
QLMTSECOFR	'1' = Yes	'1' = Yes	
QMAXSGNACN	3	3	
QMAXSIGN	3	3 to 5	
QPWDEXPITV	*NOMAX	120 to 180 (60 to 90 for powerful profiles)	
QRETSRVRSEC	0	0	
QRMTSIGN	*FRCSIGNON	*SAMEPRF	
QSECURITY	40	50	
QUSEADPAUT	*NONE	authorization_list_name	
QPWDMINLEN	6	7	
QPWDMAXLEN	8	10	
QPWDRQDDGT	'0' = No	'1' = Yes	
QPWDLMTAJC	'0' = No	'1' = Yes	
QPWDLMTCHR	*NONE	*NONE	
QPWDLMTREP	0	2	
QPWDPOSDIF	'0' = No	'0' = No	
QPWDRQDDIF	0	6	
QPWDVLDPGM	*NONE	*NONE	

FIGURE 11.7
Recommended Network Attribute Settings

Network attribute	Default value	Recommended value	Current value
JOBACN	*FILE	*REJECT — if not using remote job entries	_____
		*SEARCH — to maintain a network job action table for security	
DDMACC	*OBJAUT	*REJECT — if not participating in DDM activities or participating only as a source system	_____
		*OBJAUT — if in a DDM network, to ensure that proper object authority is enforced	
PCSACC	*OBJAUT	*REJECT — if no PC Support is used	_____
		*REGFAC — for optimum control of users and types of requests	

Communications and Device Configurations

Next, determine who can create communications devices, controllers, lines, and so on by examining the authority for the respective CRTxxx (Create) commands and determining who has *IOSYSCFG special authority. Public authority to the CRTxxx commands should be *EXCLUDE. Keep in mind our recommendation that you not autoconfigure communications devices. You should control the creation of all devices that will use your system, or at least activate autoconfiguration only for specific purposes. Although autoconfiguration is easier than manual configuration, it also means that devices can be created without your knowledge.

When you know who is authorized to the CRTxxx commands and who has *IOSYSCFG authority, find out who actually has the responsibility for creating devices. Also, determine who owns the devices created and whether specific authority has been granted to any devices. There should be one user profile on the system that owns all the communications and device configuration objects. Don't use QSECOFR as the device owner, or you'll invalidate the QLMTSECOFR system value.

Note: Users who have *IOSYSCFG special authority have a lot of power. Not only can they create devices, but also they can start, stop, and configure all TCP/IP applications on your system.

Initial Programs and Menus

List every initial program and initial menu available in your user profiles. It is especially important to note the user profiles that have LMTCPB(*NO) because those profiles can alter their initial programs and menus at will.

Resource Security

Evaluating your resource security will take some investigation. We suggest the following five steps:

1. List the libraries and directories on your system and determine the authorities necessary to access each: *PUBLIC, group authority, authorization list, or individual user profile.
2. Find out who owns each library and the objects in each library and directory.
3. Determine which files are secured by private authorities (i.e., authorized specifically by user profile, group profile, or authorization list). This step will identify files to which access is restricted.
4. Determine which programs, if any, are secured by private authorities.
5. Determine which production programs, if any, adopt authorities.

When you finish these five steps, you should have a good idea of exactly how resource security is implemented on your system. There's a good chance you'll discover that most objects have public access of some type and that few private authorities have been granted.

Determining Your Level of Threat

After you've quantified the security on your system, it's time to identify the threats to your system. In other words, what are you securing your system from? Until you know, you can't plan your security strategy. The questionnaire on page 263 lists the questions you need to answer.

Physical Threat

What damage could someone who has physical access to your computer equipment do? You might not be concerned about vandalism, but look at the security your organization uses in normal day-to-day operations. Your organization takes common-sense security measures to protect its investment in its building, office equipment, and personnel. The investment in your computer and computer-related equipment is large, and you put it at risk with every person who can touch it. Remember the woman with the axe!

Physical threat is easy to quantify. The more people who have access to your equipment, the greater the chance for someone to misuse or abuse the equipment. Access to a workstation is the first requirement for someone attempting to achieve unauthorized access to your system. Access to a printer is the first requirement for someone attempting to steal or copy corporate data.

Don't forget laptop computers. As these computers become more popular, you must consider the physical security aspects of the computer itself as well as the data it holds. Laptops are a prime target for thieves — both when the user is traveling and at the office.

> **Level-of-Threat Questionnaire**
>
> What damage could be done by someone having physical access to your IT equipment?
>
> _____
> _____
> _____
>
> Does your company allow any employee access to company files? Are some file cabinets locked? Are there storage areas with limited key access?
>
> _____
> _____
> _____
>
> Does your system store information that competitors could use to harm your company's market position?
>
> _____
> _____
> _____
>
> Who would benefit from harming or stealing programs or data?
>
> _____
> _____
> _____

Data and Public Access

Does your company consider public access a threat? In other words, does your company maintain data that isn't available to the general public or to all employees? Of course it does. Payroll is the classic example. Printed payroll documentation is kept under lock and key, and few employees are permitted to see the payroll records. The customer list is another example. Your company probably wouldn't want its customer list copied and distributed publicly.

When you stop to consider the data your company works with every day, you'll discover what data is of a public nature and what isn't. You can find the answer simply by observing normal business practices. Remember our fundamental approach to information security — information security is a business function and enforces the written or unwritten rules that secure your information assets. Do departments keep certain data in locked filing cabinets? Are certain documents stored off site or in a vault for protection in the event of a disaster? Take your cues from your business's external practices. If special security measures are taken with printed or handwritten source documents, it makes sense to take similar precautions with that data as it is stored on your computer system.

Competitive Information

Does your organization have information that competitors could use to compromise the organization's market position? Who, if anyone, would be able to print a report containing that kind of data and then leave the building with it? Who, if anyone, would be able to use FTP to transfer a file that contains confidential information to someone outside your organization? After you identify the threat in this arena, management must decide how to ensure the correct handling of the information.

Numerous IT employees have been approached by someone outside their company and offered money in exchange for documents that reveal sensitive corporate information such as strategic company decisions, plans, and customers. Unfortunately, many businesses don't take this problem seriously and don't institute measures directed at the security of such data.

Source of Threat

The final exercise in determining your level of threat is to consider just who could benefit from harming or stealing programs or data. Think about groups as well as individuals. Although this exercise might seem like chasing after windmills, it often generates candidates who have both the knowledge and the access to pose a threat.

Don't overlook the IT staff itself. You must consider the staff members simply because of the large-scale access usually granted to them. We don't believe that IT employees should have automatic access to all files and programs on the system. IT staff have no inherent right to corporate data solely because of the technical nature of their job. Like everyone else in the organization, they should have authority only to the objects and functions they need to perform their job.

The accounting people comprise another group you should think about specifically and in detail. Accounting personnel have access to the very heart of the financial transactions that sustain your business. An inadvertent upload of the wrong spreadsheet using Client Access could accidentally clear a vital file. A third-party software package might provide access to files that your own applications secure and let users print reports. The possibilities are numerous, but the point is that corporate spies aren't the only threats to your operations.

Then, of course, you can't overlook the outside hacker who might not intend to do damage but might still attempt to access your system or network just for the fun of it or the thrill of the challenge. Although the hacker's intent might not be to do damage, intent and reality are often two different things. Also, the damage might not be to the system itself, but to your company's reputation if its Web site is vandalized or if confidential information, such as credit card numbers, is stolen and news of the theft reaches the press.

However, your biggest threat is from disgruntled employees, and security surveys of IT managers have shown that this threat has been increasing in recent years.

As you apply the ideas and exercises in this chapter, try to think with your "business brain" rather than with your "technical brain." Evaluating your current security implementation and level of threat should give you a clear picture of the work you need to do.

Chapter 12

Establishing and Controlling System Access

After you evaluate your existing security using the ideas and techniques from Chapter 11, you can develop and implement a strategy that reflects your current security requirements. Although the task is enormous in terms of its effect on the everyday operations of your system, the steps needed to accomplish this objective are few. The first task is to establish who can use your system and how those users will access the system. To ensure success in this area, you must understand all the ways people can access your system.

Individuals can gain access to your system in a variety of ways. A user can sign on to a workstation. Someone can pick up a report that was thrown in the wastebasket or left on a printer in a public area. A programmer or an operator with access to your backup media might modify a saved program and then restore it to your system or simply use the backup media to restore data files to another system. If you're on a network, outside users might pass through to your system or use the SBMRMTCMD (Submit Remote Command) command to execute a command on your system from a remote AS/400. Client Access users can access your AS/400 easily. And if your AS/400 is connected to the Internet, literally the world has access to your system.

It's up to you to prevent unauthorized access by planning and controlling all access rather than simply assuming that unauthorized access won't occur. This chapter helps you define principles and guidelines for planning and controlling access to your AS/400. In this chapter, you'll begin to apply many of the tools and recommendations we discussed in Part I of this book.

Verify Security Level

First, verify that your system is at a minimum security level of 30. You can't effectively secure your system at level 20, and level 10 provides no security whatsoever. Our recommendation is that you move to security level 50 after you verify that all of your purchased software will operate in that security environment. If you can't run at level 50, you should run at least at level 40. Level 50's additional protection from possible security exposures to pointer-based languages is essential now that more and more AS/400s house or run applications written using one of these languages. Also, the protection OS/400 offers in preventing unauthorized restoration of modified programs to the system is extremely valuable in guarding against those who might try to place a Trojan horse or virus on your system. This protection is available only at security levels 40 and 50.

Plan for User Profiles

A few basic guidelines concerning user profiles will help you control system access. Although user profiles are covered in detail in Chapter 3, it's worth reiterating some of those recommendations here.

First, don't let users share user profiles. Unless it's functionally impossible to do so, prevent users from sharing profiles by specifying a value of 1 for system value QLMTDEVSSN. This value prevents any user profile from being signed on to more than one workstation simultaneously, effectively eliminating profile sharing. Allowing shared profiles nullifies any auditing you use because the user identifiers are not unique. Profile sharing also tends to propagate because new users find it easier to share a profile than to request one for themselves.

Security Recommendation
Give system value QLMTDEVSSN a value of 1 to prevent user profile sharing.

Technical Note
In some situations (e.g., when only one workstation is available to several people who all perform the same job), profile sharing is practical. By using the user profile parameter LMTDEVSSN, you can override the QLMTDEVSSN value for selected profiles for which two or more sessions should be allowed.

Second, require hard-to-guess, secret, and frequently changed passwords. Develop a password methodology you can enforce. As discussed in Chapter 3, your password rules should be ones the end-user community can follow without resorting to writing the password down to remember it. You should require users to change their passwords frequently and enforce a few simple rules to prevent easily guessed passwords.

Third, be stingy with special authorities. Special authorities let user profiles perform functions that are independent of object authorities (e.g., changing security-related system values, accessing a spooled file on the system, accessing the System Service Tools) and therefore should be guarded closely. You should give special authority only when you do so for a specific purpose.

Fourth, make certain that none of the system-supplied user profiles (QSECOFR, QSYSOPR, QPGMR, QUSER, QSRV, or QSRVBAS) have default passwords — in other words, passwords the same as their profile name. Recheck these passwords every time you load a new release or restore your system from a SAVSYS tape or original software media.

Security Recommendation
For all except QSECOFR, set the system-supplied profiles to have a password of *NONE.

And last, use the QMAXSIGN and QMAXSGNACN system values to control the number of invalid sign-on attempts allowed for a profile and workstation. This makes it much more difficult for someone to guess the password for a profile. The message queue, QSYSMSG, records attempts to sign on using a profile with an invalid password and is a good way to monitor for these attempts.

Plan the Physical Connections

All access begins with a physical link to the system. As we mentioned earlier, you can and must control these physical links. Let's start with the most basic link and work our way to the more complex network scenario.

The AS/400 System Unit

The place to start, as they say, is at the beginning — with the AS/400 system and expansion racks, including any attached tape, optical, or CD units. The more people you have walking around, chatting by, leaning on, or standing next to your system, the more likely it is that Murphy's Law will catch up with you. Limit the number of people with direct access to your AS/400 system and expansion racks. Although many AS/400s can be installed in an open office environment, you should place yours in a locked room, or at least in a controlled-access area. For most installations, a computer room is the best way to secure the system.

Secure your system with its key, and then remove the key. We notice one thing consistently in AS/400 shops: The key is kept in the keyhole on the system unit. When IBM's designers decided to include a key on the AS/400, they did so with a specific purpose in mind: security. With that key, someone can place your system in dedicated service mode, reload your (or their own) microcode or operating system, and retrieve secured information from the system by accessing offsets in the microcode data. Need we say that this security exposure is not desirable except for legitimate service reasons?

Following is a list of the key positions and the services each position enables:

Key position	Enabled services
MANUAL	Remote Power Off
	Local Power On
	Alternate IPL (new source)
	Dedicated Service Tools
NORMAL	Remote Power Off
	Remote IPL
	Local Power On
AUTO	Remote Power Off
	Remote IPL
SECURE	Remote Power Off

As you can see, SECURE, which is the most secure setting, allows only the Remote Power Off function. Turn the key to the secure position, remove it, and keep it in a safe place. You'll need it to perform various maintenance functions.

Protect all external switches with covers. In the days of the IBM 3370 disk drive for the S/38, there was a simple and elegant product for this purpose: a plastic cover that protected the buttons on top of the disk drives. This product probably saved many a database rebuild on S/38s and does so now on AS/400s. You can buy covers for each panel on the AS/400 system, disk drives, racks, and tape units. Although this sounds like a trivial matter, please believe that securing these switches can prevent a major blunder when someone decides to relax by leaning against your system or rolling a chair across the room!

Direct Workstation Access

The second area to focus on is access to workstations directly attached to the AS/400 (i.e., excluding dial-up and network-attached workstations). Workstations provide authorized users the physical device at which to perform their work; they also provide unauthorized users a physical connection with which to attempt to gain access.

Physically secure all workstations. Make sure offices are locked when not in use, install workstations in a place safe from harmful elements and away from idle traffic, and lock workstations that have keys when they're not being used. If you don't use workstation keys because they seem impractical, we suggest you re-evaluate this decision for sensitive work areas — those where access to an active workstation could be costly. Workstation keys afford a high degree of physical security by preventing unauthorized people from using the keyboard. While the workstation remains active, the key can prevent use of the keyboard.

Use the QLMTSECOFR system value to limit the workstations authorized to profiles that have *ALLOBJ or *SERVICE special authorities. In terms of threat, someone who gains unauthorized access using the QSECOFR user profile or a user profile that has *ALLOBJ or *SERVICE special authority can do the most damage. Limiting the number of profiles that have these special authorities is one security measure, as is frequently changing the password for such profiles. But another highly effective tool for preventing unauthorized access using these powerful profiles is to specify a value of 1 for system value QLMTSECOFR.

As we explained in the discussion of QLMTSECOFR in Chapter 2, a value of 1 requires profiles having the *ALLOBJ or *SERVICE special authority to be authorized specifically to the workstation where the profile signs on. By activating this limitation, you can drastically reduce the number of workstations available to anyone who attempts to use these profiles without authorization. We suggest authorizing these profiles only to workstations in the IT department and possibly only in the computer room itself.

Security Recommendation
Set QLMTSECOFR to 1 and then authorize user profiles with *ALLOBJ or *SERVICE special authority to the specific workstations those profiles will use.

This suggestion might raise alarms for you. You may be wondering, "If we change the system value before we authorize the profiles to any workstations, what happens?" The answer is that QSECOFR and QSRV can always access the workstation designated as the system console, even if they aren't authorized to the device. However, it's certainly best to authorize the profiles to the proper workstations before changing the system value.

> **Technical Note**
> *PUBLIC authority for the physical device does not provide the authorization needed by the QSECOFR and QSRV profiles or other profiles with *ALLOBJ and/or *SERVICE special authority when QLMTSECOFR is set to 1. These user profiles must have private authority to the physical device. However, once you grant QSECOFR private authority to a device, all users with *ALLOBJ or *SERVICE special authority can access it. You can use this knowledge as a shortcut method for giving all powerful users access to a particular device without having to authorize them individually.

Dial-Up Workstation Sessions

For dial-up lines, specifically authorize devices to allow access only to designated profiles. If you have a dial-up line that vendors use for support or that internal staff members use to work from offsite locations, that physical connection is available to anyone with the phone number and the correct hardware configuration. If someone familiar with AS/400 technology dials your system and gains access to the AS/400 sign-on screen, he or she can attempt to use standard AS/400 system-supplied profiles or other commonly used profiles. For that reason, it's important to limit the authority of user profiles authorized to dial-up device descriptions. For instance, you should not authorize QSECOFR, QSYSOPR, QPGMR, QSRV, or any other system-supplied profile to these devices (the previous discussion of system value QLMTSECOFR applies to these devices as well). If those dialing in need more authority, a utility program written specifically for the purpose can handle the exception. Authorizing only designated profiles to dial-up devices limits your exposure.

A second precaution in the area of dial-up lines is to use call-back procedures where possible. In Chapter 8 we discussed two forms of dial-back facilities: fixed and variable. For most situations, combining device authorization with a fixed dial-back (returning the call to a predetermined number associated with the user profile) provides effective dial-in security.

A third possibility you should consider is using the AS/400's auto-answer capabilities. If vendors will dial in to provide programming services or download PTFs, you should consider disabling the auto-answer feature, thus requiring the system operator to answer a message before connecting the line to the dial-up caller. This precaution ensures your explicit knowledge of dial-up attempts and gives you the opportunity to validate the need for the dial-up session.

Passthrough Workstation Sessions

For workstation access via the AS/400 Display Station Passthrough (DSPT) function, ensure that sessions are established only by authorized user profiles. The key to passthrough security lies in understanding a few important parameters on the STRPASTHR (Start Passthrough) command and how you can use them to initiate a passthrough session.

The key STRPASTHR command parameters that relate to security are

RMTLOCNAME	Remote location name. Name of the remote location that's the target of the passthrough session.	
RMTUSER	Remote user profile. User profile for automatic sign-on to the target system. The possible values are	
	*NONE — No user profile is specified; thus, automatic sign-on does not occur.	
	*CURRENT — The current user profile (i.e., the user profile of the job issuing the command) is sent to the target system. This value requires that the current user profile exist on the target system.	
	User_profile_name — The name of any user profile that exists on the target system can be used.	
RMTPWD	Remote password. Possible values are	
	*NONE — No password is provided.	
	Password — valid password for the remote user. This password is sent in clear text (i.e., unencrypted) across the communications line.	
RMTINLPGM	Remote initial program. Specifies the initial program to be run after automatic sign-on. Possible values are	
	*NONE — no program specified.	
	*RMTUSRPRF — Use the initial program defined for the user profile on the remote system.	
	Program_name — name of a program on the target system that becomes the remote user's initial program.	
RMTINLMNU	Remote initial menu. Specifies the initial menu to be executed after automatic sign-on and after the initial program is run. Possible values are	
	*SIGNOFF — After the initial program is run and completed, no initial menu is presented. The user is signed off the system.	
	*RMTUSRPRF — Use the initial menu defined for the user profile on the remote system.	
	Menu_name — Specify a menu to be shown after the execution of the initial program.	
RMTCURLIB	Remote current library. Specifies the name of the library on the target system that will be the remote user's current library. Possible values are	
	*RMTUSRPRF — Use the current library defined for the user profile on the remote system.	
	Library_name — Specify a library on the target system to be the remote user's current library.	

One of the difficulties associated with the STRPASTHR command is that you can use many parameter combinations, and their effect depends on other security-related values we will examine. The following examples of the STRPASTHR command can give you an idea of these many different effects:

```
STRPASTHR  RMTLOCNAME(ATLANTA)      +
           VRTCTL(VWCTL)
STRPASTHR  RMTLOCNAME(LOVELAND)     +
           VRTCTL(VWSC)             +
           RMTUSER(*CURRENT)
STRPASTHR  RMTLOCNAME(NASHVILLE)    +
           VRTCTL(VCTL)             +
           RMTUSER(CORPJDOE)        +
           RMTPWD(WRF3F3)
```

You can use the security-related STRPASTHR parameters, along with the QRMTSIGN system value and the SECURELOC (Secure Location) device description parameter — discussed in Chapters 9 and 8, respectively — to allow several different passthrough security implementations. In the following discussion, we present four workstation passthrough scenarios and then recommend how security should be implemented in each situation. (This discussion assumes that your system is the target system.)

Implementation 1	Require all passthrough sessions to begin with a sign-on screen at which the source user must enter a valid user profile and password.
Implementation 2	Allow a passthrough session to bypass the normal sign-on screen when the target user profile (specified in the STRPASTHR command's RMTUSER parameter) is the same as the name of the source user executing the command. This implementation requires a valid remote password on the target system that matches the user's password.
Implementation 3	Allow a passthrough session to bypass the normal sign-on screen when a valid remote user and remote password are provided on the STRPASTHR command, regardless of whether the source user profile matches that of the remote user.
Implementation 4	Require all passthrough requests to be processed by a passthrough filter program on the target system and evaluated by criteria known to that program.

These are the four possible types of implementation for securing a system that's a target for passthrough sessions. Now let's discuss each in more detail.

Implementation 1

To require everyone who passes through to your system to enter a valid user profile and password at the sign-on screen, just change system value QRMTSIGN to *FRCSIGNON. Each passthrough session will begin with a sign-on screen regardless of the values specified for STRPASTHR's RMTUSER and RMTPWD parameters. In this situation, the remote device description's SECURELOC parameter can be *YES or *NO.

Security Recommendation

If automatic sign-on is not a requirement, specify QRMTSIGN(*FRCSIGNON) to require the use of the normal sign-on screen.

Implementation 2

This implementation uses automatic sign-on (letting the user on the source system bypass the target system's normal sign-on screen) but requires that the user profile specified in the RMTUSER parameter be the same as the user profile sending the passthrough request. You can configure this implementation in one of three ways, depending on the source system's security.

> ***Security Recommendation***
> **Where automatic sign-on is required, specify QRMTSIGN(*SAMEPRF) to require that the remote user be the same as the user making the passthrough request. This requires additional configuration of user profiles but limits the use of passthrough to users specifically configured for that purpose.**

If the source system is secure (i.e., you feel confident that the user making the passthrough request has been identified using solid user profile/password security — not level 10 security on the source AS/400), you can specify SECURELOC(*YES) on the remote device description. This value instructs your system to accept the remote system's security verification. If you then change the value of QRMTSIGN to *SAMEPRF or *VERIFY, automatic sign-on will be allowed as long as the STRPASTHR command uses RMTUSER(*CURRENT) and the user profile exists on your system. In other words, no password is required, and the RMTPWD parameter may be *NONE.

If you're somewhat sure of the source system's security but want extra verification, you can specify SECURELOC(*VFYENCPWD) on the device configuration for the remote system to instruct OS/400 to make the remote sign-on connection when the user has the same password on both the target and source systems. This provides an extra level of verification without requiring the user to enter a password that then flows in clear text.

If the source system's security is unknown or untrustworthy, however, you can specify SECURELOC(*NO) on the device configuration for that remote system. You can also change the QRMTSIGN system value to *SAMEPRF. This combination of values allows automatic sign-on for passthrough sessions only when the remote user has the same name as the current source user and a valid password is supplied in the RMTPWD parameter. If the source user ID is CORPJDOE and the STRPASTHR command uses RMTUSER(QPGMR), your system will issue error message CPF8936 ("Password failed for security reasons - invalid password"). Even when a valid password is supplied, the system will generate this message because the profiles don't match.

Implementation 3

This implementation enables automatic sign-on to the target system whenever a valid remote user and password are supplied, regardless of the name of the source user profile making the passthrough request. Change the QRMTSIGN system value to *VERIFY to allow passthrough without the sign-on screen as long as a valid user profile and password are specified in the STRPASTHR command. In this scenario, the source user CORPJDOE could specify RMTUSER(QPGMR) as long as he or she also specifies a valid password in the RMTPWD parameter.

Implementation 4

This implementation processes all passthrough requests using a special program filter that determines which requests will be rejected, which will be forced to use the sign-on screen, and which will be allowed to sign on to the target system automatically. To use this implementation, specify the qualified name of your CL or high-level language (HLL) filter program in system value QRMTSIGN. Figure 12.1 shows a CL shell for a sample DSPT filter program. For more information about Display Station Passthrough programs, see the IBM manual *Remote Work Station Support* (SC41-5402).

FIGURE 12.1
Display Station Passthrough Exit Program

```
/*==================================================================*/
/* Display Station Pass-through Exit Program - Filter               */
/*                                                                  */
/* Incoming parameters:    &dptdata = pass-through data             */
/*                         &rtncode = return code                   */
/*                                                                  */
/* Parameters output..:    &rtncode = '0' Reject request            */
/*                                   '1' Force sign-on screen       */
/*                                   '2' Allow automatic sign-on    */
/*==================================================================*/

    PGM PARM(&dptdata &rtncode)

    DCL &dptdata    *char   128 /* display pass-through data */
    DCL &rtncode    *char   1   /* return code */

    DCL &zero       *char   1   /* '0' literal    */
    DCL &one        *char   1   /* '1' literal    */
    DCL &two        *char   1   /* '2' literal    */
    DCL &reason     *char   1   /* reason exit program called    */
                                /*   '1' STRPASTHR command request */
                                /*   '0' ENDPASTHR command request */
    DCL &srcuser    *char   1   /* source user profile *
    MONMSG CPF9999 EXEC(GOTO ERR_FOUND)

    CHGVAR &rtncode &zero
    CHGVAR &srcuser %SST(&dptdata 17 10)
    CHGVAR &reason  %SST(&dptdata 37 1)

    IF (&reason = '0') RETURN /* No action required for ENDPASTHR */

/* Do not allow pass-through when RMTUSER begins with "Q" */
    IF (%SST(&srcuser 1 1) = 'Q') GOTO END_PGM
```

continued

FIGURE 12.1 *CONTINUED*

```
/* Any other tests against the input data */
.
.
.
more testing as desired
.
.
.
 CHGVAR &rtncode &two
 GOTO END_PGM

 ERR_FOUND:
   CHGVAR &rtncode &zero

 END_PGM:
   RETURN
   ENDPGM
```

PCs

The use of PCs as AS/400 workstations has become commonplace. However, not all security administrators have recognized the inherent security threat these PCs pose. The use of Client Access and third-party emulation and file-transfer programs raises several serious security issues.

In such situations, we highly recommend using object authority. On AS/400s that don't employ object authority (i.e., the public has wide authority to objects, and security is implemented primarily through menus and applications), there is no easy way to control an end user's ability to transfer files. Very easy-to-use utilities display lists of libraries, files, directories, and folders, letting users circumvent application menus and download or upload any data to which they are authorized. Consequently, when you don't use object authority, your security exposure increases.

> **Security Recommendation**
> Write a user exit program to control who can perform what types of Client Access requests. A user exit program can provide an authority audit trail and a consistent means of determining who can perform specific requests.

In addition to the protection object authority provides, you can obtain protection by using exit programs written for Client Access servers, File Transfer Protocol (FTP), and Open Database Connectivity (ODBC). (Chapter 7 discusses the use of exit programs in detail.)

DDM

If you don't want to allow any Distributed Data Management (DDM) requests, change the DDMACC network attribute to *REJECT. A value of *OBJAUT instructs the system to apply its own object authorizations to the DDM requests. You can also specify a user-written exit program for the DDMACC network attribute and have that program control DDM requests; system object authorities will continue to apply.

DDM access is a powerful feature. As DDM evolves in future releases of OS/400 and becomes more widespread, you will continually have to re-evaluate your security strategy and how it accommodates DDM. Take the time to review Chapter 7 in this book and the AS/400 documentation about DDM to understand your security options.

Security Recommendation

If passthrough is not a requirement, use a value of *REJECT for QRMTSIGN. Set QAUTOVRT to 0 to prevent automatic configuration of virtual devices that specify VRTCTL(*NONE) for the STRPASTHR command. All user profiles created on the target system for the purpose of passthrough should specify LMTCPB(*YES) to prevent the use of the RMTINLPGM, RMTINLMNU, and RMTCURLIB parameters on the STRPASTHR command. For maximum flexibility of passthrough security, implement a passthrough exit program tailored for your system.

Interactive Subsystems

The subsystem is the key to letting batch and interactive jobs be executed. Subsystem descriptions have some security-related elements you must understand and control so you can establish a secure method for jobs to enter the subsystem and be processed.

One of these elements is the workstation entry, which provides the means for the subsystem to allocate workstations. As we mentioned in Chapter 2, you can use the user profile JOBD parameter to bypass the normal sign-on procedure of entering a user profile and password. If the job description named in a workstation entry's JOBD parameter has an associated default user (an actual user profile name specified in the USER parameter of the job description), a user at any workstation allocated by that workstation entry can sign on to the system without entering a user profile or a password simply by pressing Enter. The default user specified in that job description becomes the user for that interactive job. Although some people recommend this approach for particular applications, this type of environment has too many security risks to manage. All workstation entries should have the value *USRPRF specified for the JOBD parameter to ensure that a user profile and password are required for sign-on.

A second element that's similar to the first is the communications entry. The communications entry has a DFTUSER (Default User) parameter that lets you specify a default user for any communications jobs started using that communications entry. Any communications job can be started using the default user profile; the communications request isn't required to send a valid user profile and password. This presents the same type of security problem associated with the workstation entry JOBD parameter.

The final element to be considered when planning subsystem security is the routing entry. Routing entries provide the means for intercepting a job as it enters the subsystem and establishing the routing step for the job. The standard subsystem routing step program is QCMD (the command processor); however, new routing entries could be added to use programs that would compromise security.

For instance, a programmer could temporarily obtain the security officer's password for a task. Using the security officer profile, the programmer could create a program to call QCMD, compile the program, and have it adopt the QSECOFR authority. The programmer could use the program on a routing entry to start a routing step for his or her job each time he or she signs on to the system. Thereafter, that programmer would operate under QSECOFR's authorities. This is just an example, but the point is that routing entries provide a means to bypass normal programs and menus, and thus security.

Security Recommendation
For every workstation entry, specify JOBD(*USRPRF) to make sure a valid user profile and password are entered to initiate an interactive job.

The solution is to restrict authority to the ADDRTGE (Add Routing Entry) and CHGRTGE (Change Routing Entry) commands and to use the audit journal (discussed in Chapter 18) to monitor for routing entry changes.

Security Recommendation
Do not specify a default user profile on communications entries unless absolutely necessary.

TCP/IP Applications

A user with *IOSYSCFG special authority can easily start any TCP/IP server or application. The more TCP/IP services available on your system, the more opportunities you give users to try to exploit the services' vulnerabilities. Regularly monitor which TCP/IP applications you allow to be started, and take the steps to ensure this policy is enforced. Chapter 8 describes TCP/IP applications and methods for securing them.

Printers and Output Queues

You must also consider access to printed output. As more printers are installed in your network, it's important to manage access to printed output to prevent unauthorized disclosure of information. Chapter 6 offers a detailed look at output queue and spooled file security. Make it a priority to think of security when you create new output queues. Involve your users in determining how security for this medium should be handled.

Backup Media

Your backup media are important for two reasons. The most obvious is that you may need the media to restore your system. But backup media also represent all the data and programs on your system, which makes the media valuable to someone attempting to harm your system or organization. You must secure backups from all except people whose business function it is to perform save/restore operations. This security protects backup media two ways. First, it limits the possibility of someone stealing your data. Second, it limits the possibility of someone compromising your data or programs and then restoring the backup to your system.

The most common method of attempting to introduce a virus to a system is by restoring a modified copy of a program — something that the AS/400 can detect at all security levels. Modified programs can be restored; however, the restoration will generate a log entry in the audit journal, which can be monitored and thus prompt you to appropriate action.

Security Recommendation
Use QAUDJRN, the audit journal, to monitor for restoration of modified programs (set system value QAUDLVL to *SAVRST).

All the steps discussed in this chapter for establishing and maintaining access to your system and data are worth little unless you audit your system. Auditing is especially important today because of the increasingly open nature of networks and systems. Chapters 17 and 18 discuss auditing.

As the methods of accessing your system become even more varied, you must rise to meet greater challenges to maintain control of that access. You should take pains to learn all you can about securing your system in a network — especially when that network includes the Internet. You'll find that knowledge will soon pay off.

Chapter 13

Building Object and Role Authorization

Once an authorized user is on your system, your security strategy must enforce guidelines you establish for determining the objects and operations the user can access. You develop these guidelines by evaluating the security requirements for the objects on your system and then building role-authorization models for how individual users can access those objects. This chapter focuses on organizing your applications, identifying the data and programs that must be secured, and building the role-authorization models.

Fundamental Tenets

For today's AS/400, with its many available utilities, such as Client Access Express, File Transfer Protocol (FTP), Open Database Connectivity (ODBC), and data transfer tools, object security is an absolutely necessary component of authorization models. Four fundamental tenets underlie our approach to object security:

- Object security is a continuum.
- Object security is flexible with system organization.
- Object security uses multiple methods.
- Purchased software is not exempt from object security.

Object Security Is a Continuum

Object security is not an all-or-none proposition. Between the extremes of object "public authority" (available to all) and "private authority" (available to specific users) exists a broad continuum of security options. Good AS/400 object security implementations include objects secured by private authorities and objects secured only with public authorities. You might question how any objects can be secured only with public authorities, because public authority seems to indicate "no security." In fact, the use of public authority, when planned, is a form of good security.

Let's say your application relates to paint manufacturing, and two data files on your system contain information critical to the application. One file contains the formulas required to produce your line of paint colors. The other file contains the formulas for your paint's special texture, a quality that makes the paint unique and highly competitive. Do both files require the same security? No. Why not? You can secure the color data file by letting the public have "read-only" access — in other words, through *PUBLIC(*USE). A subset of user profiles has the private authority needed to modify records, but the general public authority suffices for the remainder of the user population because color formulas are widely published and so represent no real threat to the company if they are stolen.

In contrast, the file containing textural formulas should have no public authority — or *PUBLIC(*EXCLUDE). Instead, only private authorities, via individual or group profiles, should secure this data because it's vital to the company's market position.

For another example, suppose you have a library that contains only simple utility programs used by applications on your system (e.g., date-conversion routines, binary-to-decimal conversion, string-manipulation programs). Does this library require private authorities? We argue that it does not. You can secure the library and programs with *PUBLIC(*USE), letting the public use but not modify or delete the programs. Here again, public authority is a planned form of security that does everything required in this case.

Proper security doesn't necessarily require every object to be accessed only by means of private authorities. On the contrary, you serve your company best by avoiding extremism in either direction (i.e., no security or too much security). The use of public authority where possible not only makes sense but enhances your system's performance. The excessive use of private authorities where required may degrade performance somewhat. However, judicious use of private authorities won't cause a performance problem. In any case, the requirement for security always takes precedence over performance, because the loss, damage, or unauthorized knowledge of certain data could drastically affect your organization's financial well-being.

Object Security Is Flexible with System Organization

We've heard many variations of the statement "Because our data and programs are all in one big library, security is not feasible." To be brutally frank, that's baloney! Security is always feasible, whether your objects reside in one library or a hundred. The work required to create and maintain security may vary greatly depending on the way your system is organized, but the need for security is constant. You may even decide to reorganize your system to enhance or simplify security implementation.

Object Security Uses Multiple Methods

You must learn and use multiple methods for securing objects. In Chapter 11, we introduced some common AS/400 authorization models. These models represent methods that can — and, in most cases, should — be combined to achieve a secure system. For instance, menu security is effective, but only to a point. Someone who can avoid the menus must be presented with other barriers to block his or her access to sensitive data and programs. Thus, object security must back up all menu security or your system is only partially protected.

Purchased Software Is Not Exempt from Object Security

As you evaluate the data and program security your system needs, you must not exempt any software applications, even those your organization has bought from reliable, respectable vendors. You may discover that a third-party package lacks the security needed to satisfy your requirements. The exercise of building your authorization models will give you insight into your security requirements and the documentation necessary to help you resolve concerns that might arise with the vendor. In Chapter 14 we take a closer look at the issue of securing third-party applications to be consistent with the degree and type of security your installation requires.

Evaluating Object Security Requirements

The consequences of inadequate system security are too dire for you to go about establishing that security haphazardly. If you know your system inside out, you may be tempted to begin securing objects, relying on your knowledge of your application systems and their interrelationships. Don't do this! Such an approach inevitably results in either an implementation filled with security loopholes waiting to be discovered or the security version of spaghetti code, in which you go back and throw a little more security at things that didn't work right the first time. A structured approach will pay off in security you can count on and grow with.

Identifying Application Security Requirements

The first step in understanding application security requirements is to refer to your security policy. Your security policy will dictate your applications' security requirements. The next step in identifying the objects that must be secured is to list all the applications on your system. Include applications you've written and those you've bought. We realize that the term "application" means different things to different people, so let's explain in a bit more detail what exactly you need to identify.

By "application," we mean a group of related programs and data files. Common applications are order entry, inventory control, purchase orders, and accounts receivable. An application consists of many objects that work together. For instance, an order entry application might include the customer and order files; the order inquiry, order entry, and order-print programs; all the source members for the various files and programs and the HTML, Extensible Markup Language (XML), and CGI-BIN programs if the application is Web enabled. Although some common files and programs are shared among applications, there exists an identifiable body of files, programs, and other objects that can be called an application.

Although multiple applications may use some of the same files, that doesn't create a problem at this point. Simply list the library or directory in which the data file resides under each application that uses the file.

For each application listed, determine the general level of security required. Base your definition on the following categories:

PUBLIC	These applications contain no sensitive data files or programs and can be made available to everyone. The utility library we mentioned earlier that contains date conversion, binary-to-decimal conversion, and string-manipulation routines is a good candidate for this security category.
APPLICATION	An application in this category should be restricted to people whose jobs require use of the application. However, anyone authorized to the application should also have authority to all related objects. An example might be the purchase order application. Although purchase order data and programs should be protected from general access, those who have authority to the application might need access to these objects.
RESTRICTED	This category contains applications that should be restricted to people whose jobs require use of the applications. However, these applications include objects that will require additional security — sensitive data objects or programs. Human resources is an example of an application in this category. Although all employees in the human resources department probably require access, only a few might require access to sensitive salary and performance-evaluation data.

Security Recommendation

The PUBLIC category should not include source code of any type. Keep all source code in a different library from the object code and secure the source-code library by specific authority.

Using these categories as a guide, list all your applications on a form similar to the one on the following page.

For applications you've grouped in the PUBLIC category, you can now evaluate and implement the security needed for each library or directory and the objects in it. For instance, if the utility programs mentioned above were all in library TOOLLIB, you could grant *USE authority for *PUBLIC to library TOOLLIB and then grant the public authority of *USE to each object that exists in that library; or you could use the CRTAUT library attribute to establish the new default public authority for objects created in that library. (If objects already have *PUBLIC(*USE), no authority changes are required.) You should revoke any existing private authorities, except for the owner's. Granting *PUBLIC the authority needed to execute the programs in TOOLLIB is based on good security planning, and the system will save valuable time when accessing these objects because it won't have to check private authorities.

In other situations, one or more of the libraries or directories associated with a PUBLIC application might contain objects also used in other, non-PUBLIC applications. In these cases, you should continue the process described in the following sections to identify the additional security needed in those libraries and directories.

Application Security Requirement List

Application	Library(ies) or directory(ies)	Security category

For an application identified as requiring APPLICATION authority, you should specifically authorize the user profiles that need the application to the appropriate libraries and directories. The most effective way to do this is by using a group profile or an authorization list. *PUBLIC should have *EXCLUDE authority to the libraries and directories that support these applications. Thus, the difference between the PUBLIC and APPLICATION levels of security is simply who has authority to the library or directory. In APPLICATION-level security, you control who has access to the library or directory, the gateway to the other objects in the application.

The objects contained in those libraries and directories, however, should not be specifically authorized. As with the PUBLIC category, you grant the public *USE or *CHANGE authority to all objects in the library. For a directory, you grant the public *RX or *RWX authority to all objects in the directory. Because the public is excluded from the library or directory, these data authorities propagate only to the users who have specific authority to the library or directory. You should revoke existing private authorities, except for the owner's. We recommend this strategy because, if the library or directory itself is secure and if no additional authority is required for individual objects, you achieve the best performance by using *PUBLIC authority for the objects.

Identifying Data File Security Requirements

For applications you've identified as belonging to the RESTRICTED category, or for libraries or directories in applications defined as PUBLIC- or APPLICATION-level security, you'll have to list the data files and determine the security they require. Any library or directory that's part of a RESTRICTED application should not allow *PUBLIC to have authority at the library or directory level. Instead, you should grant *EXCLUDE authority to the public to explicitly deny authority to the library or directory. Then you can grant the appropriate private authorities to the library or directory using individual profiles, group profiles, or an authorization list.

When you list the data files in an application library or a directory, you again assign a specific security level based on the following categories:

APPLICATION	This data file can be fully accessed (read, add, update, and delete authorities) by anyone authorized to the application. This is equivalent to the public having *CHANGE authority to the file.
USE	This data file can be fully accessed only by authorized individuals. The public has *EXCLUDE authority, and the authorized user profiles have *USE or *CHANGE authority.
OPERATIONS	This data file can be accessed only by authorized individuals. Again, the public is granted *EXCLUDE authority to the file. However, user profiles are granted operation authority individually based on each profile's requirements to read only, add, update, or delete records. (Many third-party packages achieve this type of authority by using programs that restrict the operations users can perform on the data. Although this approach is valid for secure applications, without data authorities, utilities such as ODBC and FTP might let a user perform unauthorized operations on the data.)

Data File Security Requirement List

File	Library or directory	Security category

To build your list, you can use a form similar to the one on page 287. Because files identified as requiring APPLICATION security are safeguarded by specific library or directory authority, you can grant the public *CHANGE (or *RWX) authority at the object level. For files that fall into the USE category (operation authority, read authority, and execute authority only), you must first revoke public authority by specifying AUT(*EXCLUDE) for those files. Then you can grant *USE authority for each user profile that should have read access to the data files.

To properly authorize the OPERATIONS files, which require specific data operations authorities, you identify the users and the data operations each requires. For instance, you might determine that only certain key employees should be able to modify or add records in a file, while the remaining application users need only be able to read data. The process of further defining the specific data authorities users need is explained in more detail in the discussion of role authorizations in this chapter. After identifying these data operation requirements, you can grant the appropriate data authorities for each file.

Identifying Program Security Requirements

An often-overlooked item in a security strategy is securing the program objects. Programs are typically controlled by application interfaces such as menus or Web pages, but there is still a significant risk in not securing certain types of programs by specific authorization. What type of programs need securing? Those that perform large-scale updates on data files (e.g., payroll check runs, inventory adjustments, end-of-month accounts receivable summaries). Because only authorized employees can access the menu option for the program or submit the job, there is much less chance for a mistake or an irresponsible decision. You should also secure report programs for month-end or year-end reports by menu and object authority. Other examples of programs that require something more stringent than menu security are programs that perform batch updates (e.g., purges, end-of-month cleanups, batch posting programs); programs that access or update sensitive data (e.g., employee records, payroll, pricing information); and programs that adopt authority or use profile swapping to perform tasks.

To identify the security requirements for program objects on your system, you must first identify each program and its function. Which programs produce listings? Which are interactive maintenance programs, and which perform batch updates or purges? Which adopt authority? Which swap profiles?

As with data files, you should start by identifying all programs in each application area. If you don't have the proper documentation, you can use the DSPPGMREF (Display Program References) command to create a program-file cross-reference listing that shows which files and programs each program uses. For instance, if you're examining library ICLIB, you can enter the command

```
DSPPGMREF PGM(ICLIB/*ALL) OUTPUT(*PRINT)
```

to generate a listing of all the programs in ICLIB and the programs and files they reference. This command also shows you how each program uses the referenced files (i.e., whether they are opened for read only, write only, or update). You can optionally choose to send this output to an output file for processing by a high-level language (HLL) program or SQL.

The point is to understand the purpose of all programs in an application. This task is extremely difficult in shops that have little or no documentation. It's also complicated in shops where the program names and text descriptions provide no clue about the application or purpose of the programs being examined. We highly recommend you buy a good documentation package that includes reports that cross-reference programs, files, and fields. This type of software can help you immensely in understanding how you should secure the programs on your system.

Next, use the PRTADPOBJ (Print Adopting Objects Report) command to determine which programs adopt authority. When you execute the command, you specify a user profile and the system lists all programs that adopt the special and private authorities of that profile. The first profiles to check when looking for programs that adopt authority are the QSECOFR profile and any other profiles that have *ALLOBJ special authority. For instance, the command

```
PRTADPOBJ USRPRF(QSECOFR)
```

generates a list of all programs that adopt the QSECOFR profile's authority during execution.

You should next execute the PRTADPOBJ command for all group profiles and for any other profiles that own objects. The objective is to identify all programs that adopt their owner's authority, what that authority is, and who has authority to those programs. The PRTADPOBJ command produces a report that provides all this information in one step. We recommend that any program that adopts authority not be authorized to the public (i.e., *PUBLIC should have *EXCLUDE authority). These programs exist for a specific reason, and you should restrict access to them.

To determine which programs swap profiles, you'll have to first turn on auditing using the *SECURITY attribute, run your applications, and then query the audit journal to see whether you have any PS entries that indicate that a profile handle or token has been generated.

From there, you can build a list of programs that require specific authorization, such as batch purges or updates, programs that adopt authority, and programs that access extremely sensitive data. For this task, use the form on page 290.

At this point, you've identified applications and their security level, files in restricted applications that need further security, and programs to which access must be restricted. This process acts as a funnel to show how much of your system can use *PUBLIC authorization and to identify the relatively few objects that require more restrictive security.

Program Object Authorization Requirement List

Program	Library	Adopt? (Y/N)	Swap? (Y/N)	Owner

Identifying Authorization Roles

Now that you know what you have to secure, you need to identify the user profiles that must be authorized to those objects. You're probably familiar with object authorization, but you might not be familiar with the concept of role authorization, at least not as we discuss it here. Role authorization is an essential part of a successful security implementation.

When you have to add a user to your system, how do you determine the authorities the user requires? You probably look at a similar user in the same department, examine the authorities that user has and to what objects, and then grant those same authorities and the same initial menu to the new user. Or you may simply determine the menu options the new user needs and then decide which, if any, authorities are required to work with those menu options. Both of these methods are variants of the concept of role authorization.

Role authorization is the process of identifying the classes of users on your system, how they'll access the system, and which object and data authorities they need to accomplish their tasks. When you use another user as a model for adding a new user profile, you do so because the new profile performs a similar task and requires similar authorities. When you investigate which menus a new user requires, you're thinking in terms of the tasks that user must perform.

The following discussion of role authorizations explains how to identify the roles of individual user profiles and authorize those users based on their roles. In this process, you can see how users on your system naturally fall into groups with similar tasks. From there, it becomes clear how to use tools such as group profiles, menus, and authorization lists to implement the object authority you need.

Defining Enterprise Roles

Four simple questions help you determine the proper authority for an individual system user:

- What is the individual's role?
- What privilege is needed to perform that role?
- What operations must users in that role perform?
- What objects must those users have authority to?

You can apply these questions to any profile you create on the system. Based on your answers, you will either specifically authorize that user profile to certain objects, place the user in a group profile or on authorization lists, or place the individual in a group profile or on authorization lists and provide additional authorities to specific objects the user requires. You might also give that user or its group specific privileges or special authorities to let the user or group perform certain functions.

Roles are the business functions performed by the people who use your system. Think about the departments in your business environment. (Don't forget IT.) What do people in those departments do? Sum up each job type (e.g., receptionist, order entry clerk, invoice clerk, programmer/analyst, inventory control specialist, shop floor supervisor, Webmaster) in one sentence or phrase. Then list each department in the company, and list each individual in the department and the role that person performs. Some roles will probably be occupied by more than one user. Your list will appear something like this:

Person	Department	Role
John Doe	Inventory Control	Verifies and maintains inventory numbers.
Jim Smith	Inventory Control	Verifies and maintains inventory numbers.
Jane Smith	Order Entry	Order entry supervisor; manages order entry employees and resolves any problems related to order entry.
Bill Jones	Order Entry	Order entry clerk; takes orders on the phone and enters them into the computer.
Susan Hayes	Order Entry	Order entry clerk; takes orders on the phone and enters them into the computer.

You should then organize the list by role. If your organization is large, you might want to use a database to make the organization easier. The reason for organizing by role is to identify which individuals perform related jobs and can be grouped together for authorization purposes.

This is a good point to begin involving the people who determine the level of authority granted to each person in each department — probably the department supervisor or another responsible manager. Remember, security is a business function, and it should involve your business people. Although they may reject your initial request to become involved, you should encourage their involvement. Point out that your job is simply to enforce their authorizations.

Another hazard is the manager who says, "Oh, we don't need security." It's up to you to point out the dangers of a relaxed security policy. The need for auditing can be an effective motivator, too. Accountability for the data can be maintained only through some form of security enforcement of your company's security policy.

Once you've defined enterprise roles, you can define the specific authorizations each role needs.

Defining Authorizations

An authorization describes the business functions performed by an individual and comprises two elements: the operations a person performs and the objects (i.e., business entities) to which the person requires access. If you recall the point we made in Chapter 1, think of what would happen if you took your programming staff to the payroll department and informed the payroll supervisor that your programmers would spend the day browsing through the employee files because they require this knowledge for their jobs. We'd bet money that it wouldn't take the payroll supervisor more than a few seconds to kick you out of his or her office.

Each person has a defined business function, and security should be based on the business rules that define the authorization the person needs to perform that function.

Programmers need no access to payroll records, and payroll employees need no access to source members. The idea is to minimize the number of authorizations while maintaining enough security to prevent accidental or intentional damage and unauthorized access to data.

Let's define an authorization based on a previously defined role. Bill Jones is an order entry clerk. What is the authorization model for an order entry clerk? A sample answer might be:

1. Bill Jones takes incoming customer calls and enters the orders those customers place.
2. Bill verifies stock levels and prices.
3. Bill modifies orders that have not been shipped.
4. Bill prints the necessary paperwork, mails the appropriate copies to the customer, and files copies in the filing cabinet.

Operations and Objects

Now let's identify the two elements of this authorization model. What operations does Bill perform?

Bill *enters* orders.

Bill *verifies* stock levels and prices.

Bill *modifies* orders.

Bill *prints* paperwork.

What objects does Bill access?

Bill enters *orders*.

Bill verifies *stock levels* and *prices*.

Bill modifies *orders*.

Bill prints *paperwork*.

You may notice that the terminology we've used is not related to the design of the application, system, or database. In other words, authorization roles are not initially described in terms of files or using actual data-manipulation language (e.g., read, add, update, delete). The business is not run on those constructs, but instead on functions and objects described in business language. Operations should be described in business terms: adjust, increase, modify, validate. So should objects: inventory item, customer account, sales transaction, W-2 form. Any one of these nouns could describe multiple records in multiple files in terms of your system's design.

You'll have to translate the operations and objects defined in the authorization model into actual data and program authorities and sometimes into actual programming routines that enforce the model. Using the sample authorization model we've just defined, let's look at a basic security implementation that supports this model in varying degrees.

Implementation Example

Each branch office in your company has an order entry department. Although the number of clerks varies, all the clerks perform the same job: They all enter orders into the order entry system, maintain orders, and print orders. In addition, one clerk at each office is responsible for entering the time clock information each week into a payroll file. How would one establish security for this role?

Let's make a few assumptions:

- Order files are in library OEFLIB.
- The customer file for order entry is also in OEFLIB.
- All order entry programs are in library OEPLIB.
- The inventory master file is in library ICFLIB.
- The payroll time file is in library PRFLIB.
- The payroll time card entry program is PRP100 in library PRPLIB.

The implementation steps are

1. Create a group profile OECLERK and specify GRPPRF(OECLERK) when you create each order entry clerk's user profile.
2. Authorize group profile OECLERK with

    OEFLIB — *USE authority

    OEPLIB — *USE authority

    ICFLIB — *USE authority

3. Authorize only those user profiles that enter payroll time card information with

    PRFLIB — *USE authority

    PRPLIB — *USE authority

    You must be careful here. You've probably defined the payroll application as a RESTRICTED application, so you must specifically revoke public authority from all the payroll data files and grant private authorities to the appropriate group/user profiles. If you do this correctly, you'll be able to grant only the specific authority needed for the OECLERK profile to enter the time card data without compromising security for the rest of the files in the payroll application library.

4. Authorize only specific users to program PRP100. *PUBLIC authority is *EXCLUDE for this program. Group profile OECLERK is not authorized to this program.
5. Create a single menu containing all order entry options. This menu is in library OEPLIB, and the public is granted *USE authority. One option on that menu is "Enter payroll time-card information," and that option is displayed on the menu only when the user has *USE authority to program PRP100. The menu program uses the CHKOBJ (Check Object) command or the QSYCUSRA security API to determine whether that authorization is valid before displaying the menu. (See Appendix A for a complete list of the security APIs and a description of each.)

This implementation accomplishes several things. First, it uses as much group authority as possible. By virtue of the group's *USE authority to OEFLIB and OEPLIB, the order entry clerks all have authority to perform their order entry tasks. When a new clerk is hired, the only security-related task is to add the new user profile to the group and make sure the initial program provides the right menu.

Second, the order entry clerks responsible for time-card entry are the only ones who see that option or have authority to program PRP100. Because those clerks have *USE authority to libraries PRFLIB and PRPLIB, additional security must be in place for sensitive files in those libraries. The rest of the group does not receive authority to the payroll file or payroll entry program because that authority is specifically granted to individual profiles.

Documenting Role Authorizations

Whether you're starting from scratch with a newly installed AS/400 or you already have hundreds of users, documenting the role authorizations you've set up provides an excellent auditing tool. Although you must document the role of every user on the system, in many cases you can simply acknowledge that a particular user belongs to a group and identify the group itself only once as an authorization role. What form would this documentation take? Figures 13.1 through 13.4 show an example for our order entry clerk case.

Figure 13.1 (page 296) describes the order entry clerk role authorization. The user name is defined as *ROLE to indicate that this is the definition of a role authorization rather than an individual user. Figure 13.2 (page 297) defines a user who fills the order entry clerk role. Notice that the documentation simply references the general role definition of an order entry clerk.

Figure 13.3 (page 298) describes the role of the clerks who enter time card information as well as orders. Again, this is only a role definition. Figure 13.4 (page 299) defines an individual user who fills this role and references the role for authorization.

These are only examples of how you might document the user role authorizations on your system. You can provide the same information in any form of documentation you want, but do not disregard the need for it. Documentation of this type is critical to your understanding how your system is secured. Having such documentation doesn't mean you must have an elaborate, complicated security implementation. Even if you use *PUBLIC to authorize everything (although we don't recommend it!), documenting the user role authorizations for that method is essential to maintaining security in the future.

The process of role authorization produces a range of results, varying among departments and depending on security requirements. It's the only effective means of identifying security concerns in business terms. You must determine how to best complete this task, document the results, and then apply the results to your system, taking into account the objects on the system and their specific security requirements, to implement the most secure environment for those role authorizations. This is where the "business" security implementation and the "computer system" security implementation become one.

FIGURE 13.1
Order Entry Clerk Role Authorization Form

User Role Authorization Form

General Information

User name: *ROLE
Department: Order Entry
Role: Order Entry Clerk

Role Authorization

(1) Takes incoming customer calls and enters the orders those customers place. (2) Verifies stock levels and prices. (3) Modifies orders that have not been shipped. (4) Prints the necessary paperwork, mails the appropriate copies to the customer, and files the appropriate copies in the filing cabinet.

System Authorization Description

User profile name: OECLERK - Group Profile

  Group profile name: *NONE
           OWNER: *USRPRF
           GRPAUT: *NONE

Initial program: *NONE
Initial menu: *SIGNOFF
Current library: SYSLIB
Limit Capabilities: *YES

Authorized to the following:

Library	Object	Object type	Authorities
QSYS	OEFLIB	*LIB	Private authority - *USE
QSYS	OEPLIB	*LIB	Private authority - *USE
QSYS	ICFLIB	*LIB	Private authority - *USE
OEFLIB	*ALL	*FILE	Public authority - *CHANGE
OEPLIB	*ALL	*ALL	Public authority - *USE
ICFLIB	*ALL	*FILE	Public authority - *CHANGE

FIGURE 13.2
Order Entry Clerk User Authorization Form

User Role Authorization Form

General Information

User name: Bill Johnson
Department: Order Entry
Role: Order Entry Clerk

Role Authorization
(See previously defined role - Order Entry Clerk)

System Authorization Description

User profile name: OEBJOHNSON
Group profile name: OECLERK
       OWNER: *USRPRF
       GRPAUT: *NONE

Initial program: SYSLIB/USERON
Initial menu: *SIGNOFF
Current library: SYSLIB
Limit Capabilities: *YES

Authorized to the following:

Library	Object	Object type	Authorities

* see "Order Entry Clerk" role & group profile - OECLERK

FIGURE 13.3
Time Card/Order Entry Clerk Role Authorization Form

User Role Authorization Form

General Information

User name: *ROLE
Department: Order Entry
Role: Order Entry Clerk / Entry Payroll Time Card Information

Role Authorization
same as "Order Entry Clerk" role.

Plus these additional authorizations: (1) Enters payroll time card information. (2) Verifies and corrects time card entries.

System Authorization Description

User profile name: Individual user profile name
Group profile name: OECLERK
            OWNER: *USRPRF
            GRPAUT: *NONE

Initial program: SYSLIB/USERON
Initial menu: *SIGNOFF
Current library: SYSLIB
Limit Capabilities: *YES

Authorized to the following:

Library	Object	Object type	Authorities
* see "Order Entry Clerk" role & group profile - OECLERK			
QSYS	PRFLIB	*LIB	Private authority - *USE
QSYS	PRPLIB	*LIB	Private authority - *USE
PRFLIB	*ALL	*FILE	Public authority - *EXCLUDE
PRPLIB	*ALL	*ALL	Public authority - *EXCLUDE
PRFLIB	PRFTIMC	*FILE	Private authority - *CHANGE
PRPLIB	PRP100	*PGM	Private authority - *USE

FIGURE 13.4
Time Card/Order Entry Clerk User Authorization Form

User Role Authorization Form

General Information

User name: Judy Simms

Department: Order Entry

Role: Order Entry Clerk / Entry Payroll Time Card Information

Role Authorization

* see "Order Entry Clerk / Entry Payroll Time Card Information" role authorization form.

System Authorization Description

User profile name: OEJSIMMS
Group profile name: OECLERK
         OWNER: *USRPRF
         GRPAUT: *NONE

Initial program: SYSLIB/USERON
Initial menu: *SIGNOFF
Current library: SYSLIB
Limit Capabilities: *YES

Authorized to the following:

Library	Object	Object type	Authorities

* see "Order Entry Clerk / Entry Payroll Time Card Information" role

Chapter 14

Security for IT Professionals

Until now, this book has focused primarily on end-user security. We've discussed how to identify user authorization roles and how to use system and application security to implement those roles. But one particular group of users requires further attention: the IT department, in which we include the IT professionals on staff, software vendors who supply applications used on your system, and IT consultants.

Security and Your IT Staff

IT is one of the most difficult departments to establish a security strategy for, yet IT personnel pose more of a threat than those in any other department in your organization. Not that many years ago, a company that participated in a user group Wayne was associated with had to prosecute an IT employee who deliberately corrupted data and programs on the company's system. The downtime and person-hours that the company expended to resolve the problems were enormous compared to what the company would have spent to implement an effective security plan.

As with all other employees, IT personnel should be authorized to only the objects and functions they need to perform their jobs. The IT staff should no more be permitted to view or manipulate production data at will than any other employee. Yet a security policy that limits the authority of IT personnel is foreign to the midrange arena. Many shops with AS/400s enforce no particular security restrictions for IT personnel. Why not? Generally, because the IT staff are considered to be trusted individuals who would be offended at the thought of anyone doubting their integrity.

But the principle of security for IT isn't based on a lack of trust or a desire for control. As for all other departments in the organization, security in IT is, purely and simply, a business function. Your responsibility as security administrator is to ensure that *all* users are properly authorized to perform their jobs and are otherwise restricted so as to ensure system and data integrity.

Identify the Business Functions

The first step toward achieving security in the IT department is the same one you take in all other departments: Identify the authorization roles in the department. Chapter 13 presented a series of exercises designed to help you develop authorization roles for every user profile on your system. At the time, you might have listed and developed roles only for end users. If you haven't already done so, use the same procedure now to develop authorization roles for your IT personnel. You should find roles similar to those listed in Table 14.1. Some shops will have more roles in IT and some will have fewer, but these represent a general starting point.

TABLE 14.1
Typical IT Authorization Roles

Role	Responsibilities
Operator	Coordinate with end users to resolve workstation status, job status, and printing problems. Perform save/restore operations. Schedule batch jobs daily, weekly, and monthly.
Communications Administrator	Create and maintain all device descriptions, communications objects, and network configurations. Is sometimes the same person(s) as the system operator.
Programmer/Analyst	Design applications. Edit, compile, test, and debug programs (problem resolution). (For our purposes, this group includes all levels of programmer/analysts.)
Security Administrator	Create and maintain all user profiles. Implement security strategy, including putting in place the authorizations and system programs required to achieve the implementation.
Network Administrator	Design and possibly maintain all technology associated with the organization's network, including hardware, such as firewalls; connections, such as LANs, WANs, and VPNs; and service, such as intrusion detection. In smaller shops, is probably the same person as the Communications Administrator.
Webmaster	Design and possibly maintain your organization's Web site. In smaller shops, may be a Programmer/Analyst.

Define a Secure Environment for Each Business Function

After identifying the business authorization roles within IT, you need to define a functional, but secure, environment for each role.

Operator

The first decision to make about the operator role is whether you should use the QSYSOPR user profile (the IBM-supplied system operator user profile) or a unique user profile created for each system operator in your shop. Because a key function of security is to identify authorized users and their authorized objects and functions, using the QSYSOPR profile is acceptable if you have only one system operator. In this case, QSYSOPR uniquely identifies that user. However, the QSYSOPR profile and password must not be used by any other user.

For shops that have more than one system operator, we recommend that each operator have a unique user profile. This approach enables the history log, message queues, and audit journal entries to provide an audit trail of actions taken. To facilitate implementation and authorizations, the operator user profiles should be part of a group profile, which can be either QSYSOPR or a user-defined group profile such as OPERATOR or SYSOP. Alternatively, these profiles should be placed on an authorization list used to secure specific objects.

You shouldn't authorize operators to production data or production program libraries. Neither should you authorize an operator to the development libraries unless the operator's duties include programming. The operator role definition in Table 14.1 lists several business functions. Let's look at each function and how you might constructively implement security.

Because the operator is generally involved in problem resolution related to the status of workstations, jobs, and printing, he or she needs some control over these areas. Granting *JOBCTL (Job Control) special authority lets operators manipulate interactive workstation jobs and batch jobs, start and stop printers, and manipulate spooled output files that reside in output queues defined with the attribute of OPRCTL(*YES). You should use the OPRCTL(*NO) attribute to define output queues that contain sensitive spooled files to secure them from user profiles that have *JOBCTL authority (review Chapter 6 for more specific information about securing output queues from system operators).

Giving operators *SPLCTL (Spool Control) special authority lets them view spooled output even in output queues defined with OPRCTL(*NO). *SPLCTL authority is unnecessary and might tempt operators to view the data in those files. Operators need no specific authority to perform their functions.

Another system operator function is to perform save/restore operations. Again, this function requires no specific authority to production or development libraries. It used to be that having *SAVSYS (Save System) special authority was all operators needed to perform save/restore functions on any objects on the system. However, in V3R2 and V3R7, IBM set the public authority for all RSTxxx commands to *EXCLUDE to help you better control who can restore objects to your system. If you want everyone who has *SAVSYS special authority to be able to restore anything to your system, you can change the public authority for these commands back to *USE. However, we recommend that you secure all restore commands with an authorization list and give only a few trusted individuals authority to the authorization list.

Technical Note

A profile that has *SAVSYS special authority could access a secured object via the save/restore function. If the object is secured by public authorities but resides in a library secured by private authorities, a user who has *SAVSYS authority could save the object and restore it to a library to which the user has authority. Because the object isn't secured by private authorities at the object level, the user could then access the restored object.

Finally, system operators typically must be able to submit your shop's regularly scheduled batch jobs. This is the arena in which many security strategies fail to perform. Many administrators believe that because an operator submits the jobs that update accounts receivable and general ledger and that print invoices and checks, the operator must be authorized to those data files. This belief causes unnecessary authorizations that could prove costly if they are abused.

You can avoid such unnecessary authorization by creating CL-driven menus that contain the options the operator needs to submit batch jobs. These menu programs should adopt the security administrator's authority and should be authorized only to operators. When an operator selects an option, the program should submit the job using a job description that specifies a user profile to be used for the batch job. For instance, the job description for the batch job might be PRODJOBD, and the user profile defined for that job description might be PRODUSER. The SBMJOB (Submit Job) command would use the parameters JOBD(PRODJOBD) and USRPRF(*JOBD) to submit the job. The job would then be executed using the authority of the PRODUSER user profile.

There are two key elements to this implementation. First, only the security administrator should have the authority to use job description PRODJOBD. This restriction prevents the operator from using the job description to submit jobs from a command line. Second, these menus must contain only options that submit jobs. Accessing any other option from these menus should end the menu, and thus end the adopted authority.

As you can see, system operators can do all three business functions defined for them without having authority to access production data or programs. Implementing security for system operators requires a little work on your part as the security administrator, but the security achieved is well worth the effort.

Communications Administrator

All the business functions normally identified for the role of communications administrator can be performed with very little specific authority as long as the communications administrator owns all communications objects and has *IOSYSCFG special authority. As the owner of these objects, the communications administrator can create and maintain the objects in the network. If more than one user is responsible for these tasks, you should either have a group profile own the objects or set up an appropriate authorization list.

The only authority the communications administrator may lack under this implementation is that needed to change communications-related system values or network attributes. Rather than granting such authority, the security administrator should make such changes at the communications administrator's request. Typically, you should allow no one other than the security administrator to change system values or system network attributes. Because these values control security, performance, and other system-wide attributes, authority to them should be tightly controlled and well documented. This control is best achieved by restricting authority to modify these values (you can restrict authority to the WRKSYSVAL (Work with System Values) and the CHGSYSVAL (Change System Value) commands and not give the communications administrator *SECADM special authority).

Programmer/Analyst

Security for programmer/analysts is the most difficult both from a technical and an employee-relations point of view. Programmers typically resist security because they see it only as a limitation. Their jobs call for designing applications and writing, testing, and debugging the code to implement those applications. However, although programmers provide the physical framework for the data, the data itself belongs to those who administer it.

Normally a group profile works well for the programming staff. We suggest creating a user profile specifically for the purpose, remembering to specify PASSWORD(*NONE). We recommend not using QPGMR because, as an IBM-supplied profile, QPGMR's default authorities could change in future releases. Also, if you make QPGMR your programmers' group profile, you give them *JOBCTL and *SAVSYS special authorities. Few programmers we know really need these capabilities. When you create the individual profiles for the programmer/analysts, place them in the group using the GRPPRF parameter on the CRTUSRPRF (Create User Profile) or CHGUSRPRF (Change User Profile) command.

Don't authorize the programmer/analyst group profile (let's call it PROGRAMMER) to the production data or production program libraries, and don't give this group profile *ALLOBJ special authority. Instead, create either a single development library or one for each programmer, and create one or more test libraries to hold copies of production files for testing. The data files will contain either a subset of actual production data (if the data isn't sensitive) or a sample data set (if the actual data is sensitive) that accurately represents the actual data. Authorize the PROGRAMMER group profile to these development and test libraries, and specify *EXCLUDE public authority. The PROGRAMMER group should also be authorized to the necessary edit, compile, and debug commands, and these commands should be excluded from all other users.

Security Recommendation
Don't authorize programmer/analysts to modify production data or production programs.

To link the development environment to the production environment, as security administrator, you should write a few basic tools. These tools don't have to be elaborate. For instance, you can create a command that lets programmers copy source members from the production environment to the development environment. Programmers can then edit and compile source code in the development environment without fear of modifying the actual production code. You can compile the command processing program (CPP) for the command to adopt the security administrator's authority to perform the task. The CPP can also send a message to a special message queue that can be monitored to audit programming activity.

Programmers should also use a tool to promote completed and tested development objects into the production environment. The tool should let programmers put compiled and tested code into production either as a new program or as a replacement for an existing object, and the tool should move the object's source from the development to the production environment.

You can write such a tool or purchase a software configuration management tool that at least addresses both application version control and change-management functions. Although such tools are an added cost to your department, they can justify their cost by saving the security administrator's time and by providing complete audit trails of documentation as changes occur on your system.

Although the security measures we've mentioned are necessary to safeguard the development and production environments, occasionally programmers will need to view, and possibly modify, production data. Rather than design your security strategy around these situations, you should handle such situations as exceptions by having the security officer either temporarily authorize the programmer to the file or copy the records into the development environment for testing.

Security Administrator

The security administrator might be the most poorly implemented of all IT roles in the average shop. In most shops, the security administrator is whoever possesses the QSECOFR profile and password, and that person often does all his or her work, whether the work is security-related or not, under that profile. This is not an effective way to handle the role of security administrator.

The security administrator should be a separate profile used only for security-related functions. To manage object authorities for group profiles, the security administrator can have either *ALLOBJ special authority or simply enough authority to administer these authorizations. If you choose *ALLOBJ authority, the security administrator should be the only user other than QSECOFR with that special authority.

Security Recommendation
Don't use the QSECOFR profile as the security administrator profile; instead, create a unique and distinct profile for this person.

It's best for the security administrator profile to have no significant authority, but instead to rely on a few tools that adopt QSECOFR authority for such administrative functions as changing ownership and granting authority. Under this approach, when the security administrator is signed on, there is less risk of making a serious mistake, because the profile doesn't have *ALLOBJ authority. The tools should provide only enough authority to administer security. The QSECOFR profile would then be used only to create the necessary tools, not as a profile for security maintenance.

An example of a useful tool is the CHGOWNER command for changing object ownership. Figure 14.1 shows the command definition, and Figure 14.2 shows the CPP, CHGOWNCPP. The CHGOWNER command utilizes the OS/400 CHGOWN command, which you must use to change the ownership of objects in the Integrated File System (IFS). Using a path name, you can change the ownership of any OS/400 object, including objects that you specify in the traditional manner using a library, object name, and object type.

FIGURE 14.1
Command Definition CHGOWNER

```
CHGOWNER:   CMD         PROMPT('Change Ownership of Objects')
            PARM        KWD(OBJ) TYPE(*PNAME) LEN(5000) RSTD(*NO)      +
                        MIN(1) MAX(1) FILE(*NO) EXPR(*NO)              +
                        VARY(*YES *INT4) PASSATR(*NO)                  +
                        CASE(*MIXED) PROMPT('Path name of object')
            PARM        KWD(NEWOWN) TYPE(*NAME) LEN(10) RSTD(*NO)      +
                        MIN(1) MAX(1) FILE(*NO) FULL(*NO)              +
                        EXPR(*YES) VARY(*NO) PASSATR(*NO)              +
                        PROMPT('Name of new owner')
            PARM        KWD(RVKOLDAUT) TYPE(*CHAR) LEN(4) RSTD(*YES)   +
                        DFT(*YES) SPCVAL((*NO) (*YES)) MIN(0)          +
                        MAX(1) FILE(*NO) FULL(*NO) EXPR(*YES)          +
                        VARY(*NO) PASSATR(*NO) PROMPT('Revoke old     +
                        owner''s authority?')
```

FIGURE 14.2
Command Processing Program CHGOWNCPP

```
PGM   PARM(&OBJ &NEWOWN &RVKCUROWN)

/* Program input */
            DCL         VAR(&OBJ) TYPE(*CHAR) LEN(5004)
            DCL         VAR(&OBJPATH) TYPE(*CHAR) LEN(5000)
            DCL         VAR(&NEWOWN) TYPE(*CHAR) LEN(10)
            DCL         VAR(&RVKCUROWN) TYPE(*CHAR) LEN(4)
/* Variables needed to swap profiles */
            DCL         VAR(&PH1) TYPE(*CHAR) LEN(12)
            DCL         VAR(&CURPH) TYPE(*CHAR) LEN(12)

/* Monitor for any unexpected errors to make sure swap back occurs */
            MONMSG      CPF0000 EXEC(GOTO CMDLBL(DONE))

/* Swap to QSECOFR to have authority to change owner */
            CALL        PGM(QSYGETPH) PARM('CJW       ' '*NOPWD    ' +
                                        &PH1)
            MONMSG      MSGID(CPF22E4) EXEC(GOTO CMDLBL(PHERROR))
            CALL        PGM(QSYGETPH) PARM('*CURRENT  ' '          ' +
                                        &CURPH)
            MONMSG      MSGID(CPF22E4) EXEC(GOTO CMDLBL(PHERROR))
            CALL        PGM(QWTSETP) PARM(&PH1)
            MONMSG      MSGID(CPF22E4) EXEC(GOTO CMDLBL(PHERROR))

/* Parse out the path length */
            CHGVAR      VAR(&OBJPATH) VALUE(%SST(&OBJ 5 2004))

/* Change the ownership of the object(s) */
            CHGOWN      OBJ(&OBJPATH) NEWOWN(&NEWOWN) +
                        RVKOLDAUT(&RVKCUROWN)

/* Program cleanup */
DONE:       CALL        PGM(QWTSETP) PARM(&CURPH)
PHERROR:    RETURN
            ENDPGM
```

Another advantage of the CHGOWNER command over the OS/400 CHGOWN command is that CHGOWNER lets you use generics. For example, the following command changes the ownership of all objects in library CJWLIB:

```
CHGOWNER OBJ(QSYS.LIB/CJWLIB.LIB/*.*) NEWOWN(ABBY)
```

Because adopted authority doesn't work on objects in the IFS, simply creating the CPP for the CHGOWNER command in an attempt to adopt authority won't produce the desired effect. In other words, creating the CPP won't let the security administrator change the ownership of objects he or she doesn't have authority to. That's why CHGOWNCPP uses the profile swapping APIs to run the job under a user profile (CJW, as the CPP is written) that has enough authority to change the object's owner. (For this example, we created the CJW profile with *ALLOBJ and *SECADM special authorities. The CPP will still have to adopt authority to obtain enough authority to allow the profile swap.)

After the QSECOFR user profile creates the CHGOWNER command, the security administrator can use it (with no additional authorities) to modify object ownership.

Network Administrator

Your network administrator is the second-most powerful position in the IT organization after your security administrator. Some argue that the network administrator is the most powerful position. This argument typifies the power struggle that often occurs between the security administrator and the network administrator. The people in these positions often wage wars over function and security. The network administrator frequently wants to provide more services than the security administrator is comfortable with. To avoid these power struggles, you need to develop a clear, enforceable security policy so both individuals understand the position of the organization regarding security. It's also important that the network administrator, who typically controls the firewall and other security mechanisms, understands the business need for security.

The security administrator and network administrator shouldn't be the same person. The old saying about not putting all your eggs in one basket applies to these two positions. Because the security and network administrators are so powerful, you should have checks and balances between these two jobs. Giving one person all the power of both responsibilities makes it too easy for a disgruntled employee to do too much damage. Not too long ago, an individual who was both network administrator and security administrator for a large firm knew he was about to be fired. Before he was dismissed, he planted a logic bomb in one of the firm's applications. After he was terminated, the logic bomb triggered, and vital company information was deleted. He was later caught and prosecuted, but that was of little comfort to the firm, which lost millions of dollars during the resulting computer downtime and disaster recovery process.

Webmaster

Your Webmaster will need access to the libraries holding the programs and the directories that contain the HTML for your Web applications. He or she will have to work with the security administrator to set up authorities on your data files so that the Web application can access this data. The Webmaster also must work with the network administrator to get the application served on the Internet or intranet. The Webmaster role requires many of the same considerations as the programmer/analyst role. Because Internet applications are being served literally to the world, this person must take every precaution to make sure the application is written securely and serves only the information intended. Just like the programmer/analyst role, the Webmaster shouldn't have access to production data when testing the Web application.

Security for Vendors and Consultants

Third-party software vendors and consultants are an integral part of most IT environments. All third-party packages bring a new element to your IT shop: menus, applications, and usually some form of security as part of the package. With these packages come some security risks. You not only need to be aware of these risks, but — as the security administrator — you must manage them, obtaining help from the vendor when necessary. Remember that, although you've purchased software from the vendor, the data belongs to the enterprise, and that is where your responsibility lies. You can't afford to surrender the enterprise's security to the vendor.

A few basic weaknesses commonly occur in vendor applications and with consultant practices. We want to point these out and make a few recommendations for how to deal with these potential security threats.

The Super Program

Some vendor-supplied packages use the *super program* concept to negate system security and ensure that users aren't restricted except by the vendor's software. A super program is one that every user executes (e.g., the initial program that accesses the application menus and programs) and that adopts some powerful authority (e.g., QSECOFR, the program owner's authority). When a user profile executes the super program and it in turn calls other programs, the user profile can have authority to every object in the application (and sometimes in the whole system) as a result of the super program's adopted authority.

This approach to application security is dangerous. If the application provides a command line at some point, the user will be vastly overauthorized. And if the application calls products such as Open Database Connectivity (ODBC), Query/400, or third-party report writers, propagation of the adopted authority could let those users access files directly.

The justification for super programs is weak. Typically, vendors claim that their own applications handle security. If you own a product with such a program, you should revoke public authorities to data files in the application to ensure that no one outside of the application can access the files. You should also make sure that no authority adopted by an initial program is propagated outside of the application by means of a called program or menu program. You should insist that the vendor work with you to bring the security of the application up to your standards.

The Super Profile

Another tendency in many vendor applications is to use a *super profile* — a single group profile that the vendor uses to own all the application's objects. That practice is certainly acceptable. The problem arises when the vendor requires that every user enrolled in the application belong to the group whose profile owns the objects. This means that all application users have *ALL authority to every object in the application.

Having all users belong to the super profile group is another poor practice. The vendor claims that security is controlled by the application menu driver or through some other means embedded in the software. But today, as more and more end users participate in Client Access, ODBC, FTP, and other utility products outside of the vendor application, the application-specific group profile concept becomes both inadequate and dangerous. A user could replace an entire data file accidentally using Client Access file transfer. Any user could query any data from within the vendor's application using Query/400. You can't rely on the vendor-written application security to provide security outside the application.

Vendors claim this is a problem that IBM should work out. However, we believe this is clearly a vendor issue rather than an IBM-caused problem. When customers want more control, vendors must be willing to work with them to allow a more effective object-oriented authorization scheme. You must make a decision about the threat this type of security poses to your organization and then take any necessary steps to tighten that security.

Vendor Dial-In Support

Some vendors who support their software packages by dialing in to your system often claim more authority than they need. For instance, if a vendor says he or she must sign on as QSECOFR when dialing in to your system, you should let the vendor know that using QSECOFR is unacceptable. Ask the vendor to work with you to create a support profile whose authority is limited to the tools needed to update the software. Don't let the vendor use more authority than is required.

You certainly want to audit all vendor profiles any time they are signed on to the system. Chapter 18 introduces event auditing and explains how to audit at the user profile level for actual commands that a user enters. Activate this command-level auditing for all vendor support profiles. You can also use this method to audit the commands the security administrator and even QSECOFR enter.

Consultant Practices

There has been a substantial growth in the number of midrange consulting firms in recent years. These firms offer specialists in particular areas who can help develop and maintain application software on your system. Generally, consultants try to get as much authority as they can on your system — it makes their job easier. However, consultants should justify this requirement. You should evaluate the business function of each consultant as you would any IT staff position and then create specific user profiles and, where necessary, a group profile to authorize consultants. Give consultants a development environment; don't authorize them to production data and production programs. As the system's security administrator, you should offer tools and assistance to promote finished applications to the production environment. You should also audit consultant activities using the security audit journal that you will read about in Chapter 18.

Here we also add that you should require consultants to furnish ample documentation for every program they create on your system. Track these objects and understand their function. If a consultant asks to load a tool kit on your system, get documentation that explains exactly which tools are being loaded and be sure you know whether any of them adopt the authority of any of the system profiles.

In this chapter we've suggested and offered support for a few principles that can ensure security in the IT department:

- Evaluate and enforce security for IT personnel, vendors, and consultants just as you do for all other users on the system.

- Maintain separate development and production environments, and make sure objects being promoted into production are explicitly controlled.

- When using vendor-supplied software applications, maintain control of how those applications implement security. Work with the vendor if necessary to create a secure environment that doesn't undercut your security standards.

These few rules will help you make sure your security doesn't end outside the door to the IT department.

Chapter 15
Security Implementation Example

We've covered a lot of ground in the first 14 chapters. You've become acquainted with the AS/400 tools you use to facilitate your security implementation, and you've learned how to plan, organize, and implement your security strategy. This chapter provides an overview of what a security implementation might look like.

Our sample security implementation is a fictitious company, Initial-It, a small firm specializing in personalized stationery that sells primarily to corporate customers. Only a small group of employees actually interact with the company's main computer system, an AS/400. All employees who need computer access have PCs and run AS/400 applications via 5250 emulation in Client Access Express. The system administrator uses Operations Navigator. All computer users have Internet access. Initial-It's primary applications are order entry, inventory control, purchasing, accounting, payroll, and IT.

As a midsized company, typical of many AS/400 sites, Initial-It's strategy is to provide basic security, including basic communications network security. This chapter explains the development of a security strategy and implementation from the ground up simply by showing Initial-It's security-planning documentation and implementation strategy. This chapter consists almost entirely of figures and lists that comprise Initial-It's

- planning documentation
  - application security requirements
  - organizational chart by department
  - user profile and password rules
  - role-authorization forms
- implementation characteristics
  - network security considerations
  - system values
  - user profile listing
  - special authorities listing
  - library/object authorities listing
    - exit programs
    - application administration settings

As mentioned, these samples are intended to provide an example for a typical company. The Initial-It example represents only a basic security and network security configuration. More complex environments (e.g., where the AS/400 is in a large network or is acting as a Web server) require additional network security planning.

Application Security Requirements

Figure 15.1 provides an overview of Initial-It's application security requirements.

FIGURE 15.1
Application Security Requirements Checklist

Application Security Requirements List

Application	Library(ies)	Owner
Order Entry	OEFLIB - OE Files	OE_ICOWNER
	OEPLIB - OE Programs	OE_ICOWNER
Inventory Control	ICFLIB - IC Files	OE_ICOWNER
	ICPLIB - IC Programs	OE_ICOWNER
Purchasing	PUFLIB - Purch Files	PU_OWNER
	PUPLIB - Purch Programs	PU_OWNER
Accounting	APFLIB - Payables Files	AU_OWNER
	APPLIB - Payables Programs	AU_OWNER
	ARFLIB - Receivable Files	AU_OWNER
	ARPLIB - Receivable Programs	AU_OWNER
	GLFLIB - GL Files	AU_OWNER
	GLPLIB - GL Programs	AU_OWNER
Payroll	PRFLIB - Payroll Files	PR_OWNER
	PRPLIB - Payroll Program	PR_OWNER
IT	DEVLIB - Development Library	IT_OWNER
	OPLIB - Operations Library	IT_OWNER
	TOOLLIB - IT Tools	IT_OWNER
	SECLIB - Security/Audit Library	IT_OWNER

Marie Young, Initial-It's IT manager and security administrator, has taken a restrictive approach to security. She realized several years ago when her users switched from direct-connect 5250 terminals to PCs that menu security was no longer sufficient to protect the information on the AS/400. Therefore, only users who must run an application have access to that application's library. Everyone else is excluded from the library; *PUBLIC authority is *EXCLUDE. In addition, most of the applications were rewritten to let application users view files but not update them unless they made the updates through the application interface; thus, most application objects are *PUBLIC(*USE). The program that updates the files adopts the application owner's authority to perform the updates. As is the case with many applications, logic is coded into the application (using the Limit User Access APIs) to ensure that the user running the application is allowed to perform the update.

Organizational Chart

To determine who needed authority to which applications and objects, Marie first created the organizational chart in Figure 15.2.

FIGURE 15.2
Organizational Chart by Department

Department	User name	Title
Order Entry	Barry Swizer	Order Entry Clerk
	Felicia Rose	Order Entry Clerk
	Martha Blue	Order Entry Clerk
	Rick Donally	Order Entry Clerk
Inventory Control	John Carney	Inventory Control
	Jane Emory	Inventory Control
Order Entry/Inventory Control	Mary Spencer	Order Entry/Inventory Control Supervisor
Shipping/Receiving	Derek Smith	Shipping/Receiving Supervisor
	Tim Pack	Shipping/Receiving Clerk
	Wendy Upton	Shipping/Receiving Clerk
Purchasing	Patsy Clynd	Purchasing Supervisor
	Jose Rios	Purchasing Clerk
	Tyne Meek	Purchasing Clerk
General Accounting	Mark Willis	Accounting Manager
	Rita Taylor	Accounts Receivable Clerk
	Eve Simmons	Accounts Receivable Clerk
	Jolanda Damon	Accounts Payable Clerk
Payroll	Arlene Breden	Payroll Supervisor
	Wendell Olson	Payroll Clerk
IT	Marie Young	IT Manager
	Sylvia Johnson	Programmer/Analyst
	Juan Garcia	Operator

User Profile and Password Rules

Marie wanted to create user profile names that would help associate each user with a department and would also let her quickly identify the user by name. She settled on a standard that attached a departmental prefix to an abbreviation of the user's name.

> *Security Recommendation*
>
> **When you use a well-known or an easily guessed naming convention for user profile names, you make it easy for someone attempting to gain access to your system to guess a user's password. In other words, you've already given the intruder half of the information needed to break into your system. This is an example of a tradeoff between easier system operations and tighter security.**

All user-created user profiles begin with one of the following prefixes:

Prefix	Department
OE	Order Entry
IC	Inventory Control
PU	Purchasing
S_R	Shipping/Receiving
PR	Payroll
AC	Accounting
	AR Accounts receivable
	AP Accounts payable
	GL General ledger
IT	IT

The prefix is followed by the first letter of the first name and as many letters of the last name as possible. Figure 15.3 shows the user profile names created for each user identified in the organizational chart.

Here are the rules that govern password creation:

- All passwords must be a minimum length of seven positions.
- All passwords must contain at least one numeric digit.
- Passwords must not repeat characters consecutively.
- Passwords must not have adjacent numeric digits.
- All passwords expire every 180 days.
- Security officer passwords expire every 60 days.

FIGURE 15.3
Initial-It User Profiles

Department	Name	User profile
Order Entry	Barry Swizer	OEBSWIZER
	Felicia Rose	OEFROSE
	Martha Blue	OEMBLUE
	Rick Donally	OERDONALLY
Inventory Control	John Carney	ICJCARNEY
	Jane Emory	ICJEMORY
Order Entry/Inventory Control	Mary Spencer	ICMSPENCER
Shipping/Receiving	Derek Smith	S_RDSMITH
	Tim Pack	S_RTPACK
	Wendy Upton	S_RWUPTON
Purchasing	Patsy Clynd	PUPCLYND
	Jose Rios	PUJRIOS
	Tyne Meek	PUTMEEK
Accounting	Mark Willis	ACMWILLIS
	Rita Taylor	ACRTAYLOR
	Eve Simmons	ACESIMMONS
	Jolanda Damon	ACJDAMON
Payroll	Arlene Breden	PRABREDEN
	Wendell Olson	PRWOLSON
IT	Marie Young	ITMYOUNG
	Sylvia Johnson	ITSJOHNSON
	Juan Garcia	ITJGARCIA

Marie enforced these rules through the password-related system values on the AS/400. She forced the security officer password to be changed more often by setting the PWDEXPITV (Password Expiration Interval) parameter in the user profile. If a user changes his or her password, the user must supply a new password that follows these rules.

Role-Authorization Samples

The next step in the process of defining security for the system was to identify the role authorizations that existed in the organization. Marie interviewed all department supervisors to determine the exact functions department employees performed and then mapped those functions to the specific libraries, menus, programs, and objects required on the system. Figures 15.4 through 15.17 represent the role authorizations for each role identified in the departments listed in the organizational chart.

FIGURE 15.4
Order Entry Role Authorization Form

User Role Authorization Form

General Information

User name: *ROLE
Department: Order Entry
Role: Order Entry Clerk

Role Authorization

(1) Takes incoming customer calls and enters the orders those customers place. (2) Receives orders that have come in via e-mail and enters those orders as well. (3) Verifies stock levels and prices. (4) Modifies orders that have not been shipped. (5) Prints the necessary paperwork, mails the appropriate copies to the customer, and files the appropriate copies in the filing cabinet.

System Authorization Description

User profile name: OECLERK - Group Profile
Group profile name: *NONE
Initial program: QGPL/OESIGNON
Initial menu: *SIGNOFF
Current library: *CRTDFT
Limit Capabilities: *YES

Authorized to the following:

Library	Object	Object type	Authorities
QSYS	OEFLIB	*LIB	Private Authority - *USE
QSYS	OEPLIB	*LIB	Private Authority - *USE
QSYS	ICFLIB	*LIB	Private Authority - *USE
OEFLIB	*ALL	*FILE	Public Authority - *USE
OEPLIB	*ALL	*ALL	Public Authority - *USE
ICFLIB	*ALL	*ALL	Public Authority - *USE

FIGURE 15.5
Inventory Control Role Authorization Form

User Role Authorization Form

General Information

User name: *ROLE
Department: Inventory Control
Role: Inventory Control Clerk

Role Authorization

(1) Performs periodic stock level counts to determine accuracy of stock inventory. (2) Makes adjustments to stock levels when required. (3) Verifies computer-generated stock reorder. (4) Forwards reorder to Purchasing.

System Authorization Description

User profile name: ICCLERK - Group Profile
Group profile name: *NONE

Initial program: QGPL/ICSIGNON
Initial menu: *SIGNOFF
Current library: *CRTDFT
Limit Capabilities: *YES

Authorized to the following:

Library	Object	Object type	Authorities
QSYS	ICFLIB	*LIB	Private Authority - *USE
QSYS	ICPLIB	*LIB	Private Authority - *USE
ICFLIB	*ALL	*ALL	Public Authority - *USE
ICPLIB	*ALL	*ALL	Public Authority - *CHANGE

FIGURE 15.6
Order Entry/Inventory Control Supervisor Role Authorization Form

User Role Authorization Form

General Information

User name:	*ROLE
Department:	Order Entry/Inventory Control
Role:	OE/IC Supervisor

Role Authorization

(1) Has the ability to perform all tasks of the Order Entry Clerk or the Inventory Control Clerk.
(2) Makes price changes and has those changes recorded as an audit trail.

System Authorization Description

User profile name:	ICMSPENCER - Mary Spencer
Group profile name:	ICCLERK
OWNER:	*USRPRF
GRPAUT:	*NONE
SUPGRPPRF:	OECLERK
Initial program:	QGPL/ICSIGNON
Initial menu:	*SIGNOFF
Current library:	*CRTDFT
Limit Capabilities:	*YES

Authorized to the following:

Library	Object	Object type	Authorities
QSYS	OEFLIB	*LIB	Private Authority - *USE
QSYS	OEPLIB	*LIB	Private Authority - *USE
QSYS	ICFLIB	*LIB	Private Authority - *USE
QSYS	ICPLIB	*LIB	Private Authority - *USE
OEFLIB	*ALL	*FILE	Public Authority - *USE
OEPLIB	*ALL	*ALL	Public Authority - *USE
ICFLIB	ICFPRCA	*FILE	Public Authority - *USE
			all others in ICFLIB - Public Authority - *EXCLUDE
ICPLIB	ICPPRCU	*PGM	Private Authority - *USE
			Adopts authority to *CHANGE prices from program ICPPRCU
ICPLIB	*ALL	*ALL	Public Authority - *USE

FIGURE 15.7
Shipping/Receiving Role Authorization Form

User Role Authorization Form

General Information

User name: *ROLE
Department: Shipping/Receiving
Role: Shipping/Receiving Clerk

Role Authorization

(1) Uses shipping papers printed in Order Entry to determine what to ship to customers. (2) Ships orders to customers. (3) Receives goods from vendors and sends papers to Inventory Control for stock level update.

System Authorization Description

User profile name: S_RCLERK - Group Profile
Group profile name: *NONE

Initial program: QGPL/S_RSIGNON
Initial menu: *SIGNOFF
Current library: *CRTDFT
Limit Capabilities: *YES

Authorized to the following:

Library	Object	Object type	Authorities
QSYS	S_RFLIB	*LIB	Private Authority - *USE
QSYS	S_RPLIB	*LIB	Private Authority - *USE
S_RFLIB	*ALL	*FILE	Public Authority - *USE
S_RPLIB	*ALL	*ALL	Public Authority - *USE

FIGURE 15.8
Purchasing Role Authorization Form

User Role Authorization Form

General Information

User name: *ROLE
Department: Purchasing
Role: Purchasing Personnel

Role Authorization

(1) Uses a virtual private network connection to order supplies from company's paper and ink vendors. (2) Updates purchase orders as necessary. (3) Marks complete purchase orders after order is fulfilled.

System Authorization Description

User profile name: PUCLERK - Group Profile
Group profile name: *NONE

Initial program: QGPL/PUSIGNON
Initial menu: *SIGNOFF
Current library: *CRTDFT
Limit Capabilities: *YES

Authorized to the following:

Library	Object	Object type	Authorities
QSYS	PUFLIB	*LIB	Private Authority - *USE
QSYS	PUPLIB	*LIB	Private Authority - *USE
PUFLIB	*ALL	*FILE	Public Authority - *USE
PUPLIB	*ALL	*ALL	Public Authority - *USE

FIGURE 15.9
Accounts Receivable Role Authorization Form

User Role Authorization Form

General Information

User name: *ROLE
Department: General Accounting
Role: Accounts Receivable

Role Authorization

(1) Processes invoice payments. (2) Ensures that batch balance matches actual check payments. (3) Ensures that the appropriate orders are marked as paid.

System Authorization Description

User profile name: ARCLERK - Group Profile
Group profile name: *NONE

Initial program: QGPL/ARSIGNON
Initial menu: *SIGNOFF
Current library: *CRTDFT
Limit Capabilities: *YES

Authorized to the following:

Library	Object	Object type	Authorities
QSYS	ARFLIB	*LIB	Private Authority - *USE
QSYS	ARPLIB	*LIB	Private Authority - *USE
ARFLIB	*ALL	*FILE	Public Authority - *USE
ARPLIB	*ALL	*ALL	Public Authority - *USE

FIGURE 15.10
Accounts Payable Role Authorization Form

User Role Authorization Form

General Information

User name: *ROLE
Department: General Accounting
Role: Accounts Payable

Role Authorization

(1) Processes payable invoices and produces check payments. (2) Assists vendors with questions concerning payments.

System Authorization Description

User profile name: APCLERK - Group Profile
Group profile name: *NONE

Initial program: QGPL/APSIGNON
Initial menu: *SIGNOFF
Current library: *CRTDFT
Limit Capabilities: *YES

Authorized to the following:

Library	Object	Object type	Authorities
QSYS	APFLIB	*LIB	Private Authority - *USE
QSYS	APPLIB	*LIB	Private Authority - *USE
APFLIB	*ALL	*FILE	Public Authority - *USE
APPLIB	*ALL	*ALL	Public Authority - *USE

FIGURE 15.11
General Ledger Role Authorization Form

User Role Authorization Form

General Information

User name: *ROLE
Department: General Accounting
Role: General Ledger

Role Authorization

(1) Processes general ledger transactions.

System Authorization Description

User profile name: GLCLERK - Group Profile
Group profile name: *NONE

Initial program: QGPL/GLSIGNON
Initial menu: *SIGNOFF
Current library: *CRTDFT
Limit Capabilities: *YES

Authorized to the following:

Library	Object	Object type	Authorities
QSYS	GLFLIB	*LIB	Private Authority - *USE
QSYS	GLPLIB	*LIB	Private Authority - *USE
GLFLIB	*ALL	*FILE	Public Authority - *USE
GLPLIB	*ALL	*ALL	Public Authority - *USE

FIGURE 15.12
Accounting Manager Role Authorization Form

User Role Authorization Form

General Information

User name: *ROLE
Department: General Accounting
Role: Accounting Manager

Role Authorization

(1) Oversees work performed by Accounts Payable, Accounts Receivable Clerks, and Payroll department. (2) Maintains the general ledger.

System Authorization Description

User profile name: ACMWILLIS - Mark Willis
Group profile name: GLCLERK
    SUPGRPPRF: ARCLERK
                  APCLERK
                    PRCLERK
Initial program: QGPL/GLSIGNON
Initial menu: *SIGNOFF
Current library: *CRTDFT
Limit Capabilities: *YES

Authorized to the following:

Library	Object	Object type	Authorities
PRFLIB	*ALL	*FILE	Private Authority - *CHANGE
			Public Authority - *EXCLUDE

FIGURE 15.13
Payroll Clerk Role Authorization Form

User Role Authorization Form

General Information

User name: *ROLE
Department: Payroll
Role: Payroll Clerk

Role Authorization

(1) Enters new employee master information and deduction records. (2) Maintains deduction file. (3) Processes bimonthly payroll checks.

System Authorization Description

User profile name: PRCLERK - Group Profile
Group profile name: *NONE

Initial program: QGPL/PRSIGNON
Initial menu: *SIGNOFF
Current library: *CRTDFT
Limit Capabilities: *YES

Authorized to the following:

Library	Object	Object type	Authorities
QSYS	PRFLIB	*LIB	Private Authority - *USE
QSYS	PRPLIB	*LIB	Private Authority - *USE
PRFLIB	PRFMSTA	*FILE	Private Authority - *OBJOPR *READ *ADD
	PRFDEDA	*FILE	Private Authority - *USE
	PRFCHKA	*FILE	Private Authority - *USE
	*ALL	*FILE	Public Authority - *USE
			Public Authority - *USE
PRPLIB	*ALL	*ALL	Public Authority - *USE

FIGURE 15.14
Payroll Supervisor Role Authorization Form

User Role Authorization Form

General Information

User name: *ROLE
Department: Payroll
Role: Payroll Supervisor

Role Authorization

(1) Oversees and backs up the Payroll Clerk. (2) Maintains proper payroll master information.

System Authorization Description

User profile name: PRABREDEN - Arlene Breden
Group profile name: *NONE
Initial program: QGPL/PRSIGNON
Initial menu: *SIGNOFF
Current library: *CRTDFT
Limit Capabilities: *YES

Authorized to the following:

Library	Object	Object type	Authorities
QSYS	PRFLIB	*LIB	Private Authority - *USE
QSYS	PRFLIB	*LIB	Private Authority - *USE
PRFLIB	*ALL	*FILE	Private Authority - *CHANGE
PRPLIB	*ALL	*FILE	Private Authority - *CHANGE

FIGURE 15.15
IT Programmer/Analyst Role Authorization Form

User Role Authorization Form

General Information

User name: *ROLE
Department: IT
Role: Programmer/Analyst

Role Authorization

(1) Edits, compiles, and debugs development source code. (2) Tests development code.
(3) Moves development code into the production libraries. (4) Acts as backup to System Operator.

System Authorization Description

User profile name: ITPGMR - Group Profile
Group profile name: *NONE
Initial program: *NONE
Initial menu: MAIN
Current library: *CRTDFT
Limit Capabilities: *NO

Authorized to the following:

Library	Object	Object type	Authorities
QSYS	DEVLIB	*LIB	Private Authority - *CHANGE
QSYS	TOOLLIB	*LIB	Private Authority - *CHANGE
DEVLIB	*ALL	*ALL	Private Authority - *CHANGE
TOOLLIB	*ALL	*ALL	Private Authority - *CHANGE

FIGURE 15.16
IT Operator Role Authorization Form

User Role Authorization Form

General Information

User name: *ROLE
Department: IT
Role: Operator

Role Authorization

(1) Peforms save/restore functions. (2) Submits jobs for night processing. (3) Monitors system performance. (4) Assists end users with submitted jobs and spooled output.

System Authorization Description

User profile name: ITSYSOP - Group Profile
Group profile name: *NONE
Initial program: *NONE
Initial menu: MAIN
Current library: *CRTDFT
Limit Capabilities: *NO

Authorized to the following:

Library	Object	Object type	Authorities
QSYS	OPLIB	*LIB	Private Authority - *CHANGE
OPLIB	*ALL	*ALL	Private Authority - *CHANGE

In addition, this group profile owns all line, controller, and device configurations. This profile owns all output queues except those used in Accounting, which are owned by the Accounting Manager.

FIGURE 15.17
IT Manager Role Authorization Form

User Role Authorization Form

General Information

User name: Marie Young
Department: IT
Role: IT Manager

Role Authorization

(1) Assists in design of applications. (2) Edits, compiles, and debugs development source code. (3) Tests development code. (4) Moves development code into the production libraries. (5) Serves as the System Security Administrator.

System Authorization Description

User profile name: ITMYOUNG - Marie Young
Group profile name: *NONE
       GRPPRF: ITPGMR
   SUPGRPPRF: ITSYSOP
Initial program: *NONE
Initial menu: MAIN
Current library: *CRTDFT
Limit Capabilities: *NO

Authorized to the following:

No additional authorities are required. All the authorities Marie requires are acquired through her group profiles and her special authority, *SECADM.

Network Security Considerations

Firewall
Initial-It uses a digital subscriber line (DSL) connection to its Internet Service Provider (ISP). DSL connections are typically much faster than dial-up ones, but unlike dial-up connections, they have an "always-on" characteristic. Therefore, it was imperative that Initial-It protect its network with a firewall. Marie chose an inexpensive firewall "appliance," which lacks many of the features and the capacity of a more expensive firewall but provides adequate protection for Initial-It's network. The firewall was relatively easy to install and also was preconfigured to prevent access to the company's network from the Internet.

VPN
Initial-It uses a Virtual Private Network (VPN) connection with the AS/400 as the VPN client to link to its paper and ink vendors and place stock orders. Initial-It would have to program or configure the firewall to allow a VPN connection, but Marie, after analyzing Initial-It's security policy and business needs for connecting to its vendors, deemed that an acceptable risk.

Network Attributes
Following are the current settings for security-related network attributes at Initial-It:

Attribute	Setting
JOBACN	*REJECT
DDMACC	*REJECT
PCSACC	*REJECT

It was easy to decide that the attribute values should be *REJECT. The AS/400 wouldn't receive remote job streams from another system, and no applications use Distributed Data Management (DDM).

Port Restrictions
Marie restricted all ports except those that let Client Access communicate with the AS/400 and the port required for the VPN connection to Initial-It's suppliers. Marie used the ADDTCPPORT (Add TCP/IP Port) command to add the port restrictions, first creating a user profile, then adding the port restriction, and then deleting the profile.

IP Packet Filtering
Although the firewall protects the company's network from unwanted Internet traffic, Marie used the AS/400's IP packet-filtering capabilities to provide an additional layer of network security, defining rules (through Operations Navigator) that block incoming and outgoing HTTP and FTP requests. Also, because Marie set up the company's network to use an "invalid" TCP/IP address, the firewall rejects all requests from valid (i.e., Internet) TCP/IP addresses.

Antivirus Software

Because Initial-It's users have Internet access, Marie bought an antivirus software package and installed it on each PC. She chose a product with a subscription service that sends users periodic automatic updates of new virus signatures. This ensures that the PCs have the most up-to-date software and that users don't forget to update their antivirus software.

Exit Programs

Marie implemented an additional layer of security to supplement her AS/400 object security setup by installing a third-party software package that helps implement exit programs. This measure further ensures that only users who are supposed to perform a function may do so.

Client Access User Exit Program

Most exit programs simply reject the function a user is attempting to perform; however, Initial-It uses a Client Access exit program that selectively allows user access to AS/400 files. Initial-It accounting manager Mark Willis must download database files from the AS/400 to spreadsheet software on his PC to produce financial reports. Marie used the Client Access user exit program in Figure 15.18 to turn off database access for all users except Mark Willis.

FIGURE 15.18
Sample Client Access Exit Program

```
/**********************************************************************/
/*                                                                    */
/* Program Name          : CASTOPFT - Stop Database Access            */
/*                                                                    */
/* Exit Point Name       : QIBM_QZDA_INIT                             */
/*                                                                    */
/* Program Description   : This program rejects all requests to       */
/*                         use the Client Access Database server.     */
/*                         This will prevent use of file transfer     */
/*                         and ODBC requests (from an IBM ODBC        */
/*                         driver.)  Only Mark Wills is allowed to    */
/*                         use this interface.                        */
/*                                                                    */
/**********************************************************************/
PGM (&STATUS &REQUEST)
/**********************************************************************/
/* Parameter declarations                                             */
/**********************************************************************/
DCL VAR(&STATUS)   TYPE(*CHAR) LEN(1)    /* Accept or Reject indicator */
DCL VAR(&REQUEST)  TYPE(*CHAR) LEN(34)   /* Parameter structure        */

/**********************************************************************/
/* Other declarations                                                 */
/**********************************************************************/
DCL VAR(&USRPRF)   TYPE(*CHAR) LEN(10)   /* User making request        */
DCL VAR(&SERVERID) TYPE(*CHAR) LEN(10)   /* Database server            */
DCL VAR(&FORMAT)   TYPE(*CHAR) LEN(8)    /* Format (ZDAI0100)          */
DCL VAR(&FUNCTION) TYPE(*CHAR) LEN(4)    /* Function being requested   */
/**********************************************************************/
```

continued

FIGURE 15.18 *Continued*

```
/* Get values passed in from &REQUEST                                 */
/**********************************************************************/
CHGVAR VAR(&USRPRF)   VALUE(%SST(&REQUEST  1 10))
CHGVAR VAR(&SERVERID) VALUE(%SST(&REQUEST 11 10))
CHGVAR VAR(&FORMAT)   VALUE(%SST(&REQUEST 21  8))
CHGVAR VAR(&FUNCTION) VALUE(%SST(&REQUEST 28  4))
/**********************************************************************/
/* Program - Main                                                     */
/**********************************************************************/
CHGVAR VAR(&STATUS) VALUE('0')       /* Initialize to not allow   */
                                     /* database access           */

IF (&USRPRF *EQ 'ACMWILLIS') THEN(DO) /* If the user is Mark Willis */
    CHGVAR VAR(&STATUS) VALUE('1')    /* Allow him access           */
ENDDO

ENDPGM
```

This program prevents access to database files on the AS/400 through both Client Access's Data Transfer function and IBM's Open Database Connectivity (ODBC) driver. The exit program is registered using the WRKREGINF (Work with Registration Facility) command at the QIBM_QZDA_INIT exit point. Note that you must end all prestarted jobs associated with the TCP/IP server, QZDASOINIT, before running this program.

Application Administration

To keep users' PC desktops as simple as possible, Marie used Operations Navigator's Application Administration function and Client Access Express's selective install feature. For most users, Marie configured the desktop so that only the 5250 emulator is displayed when the user starts Client Access. For system operators and herself, Marie configured the PCs so Operations Navigator is displayed on the desktop.

System Values

Next, Marie ran the Operations Navigator Security Wizard to help her determine which security-related system values would provide functions that enhanced her security implementation. Table 15.1 shows the settings she used.

Notice that she used the security audit journal to record security information (e.g., *AUTFAIL, *DELETE, *SAVRST, *SECURITY). This information, along with other information gathered at periodic intervals, serves as an audit of the security implementation. Also notice the system values (QPWDEXPITV, QPWDMINLEN, QPWDMAXLEN, QPWDRQDDGT, and QPWDLMTAJC) used to support the password rules defined earlier in this chapter.

Because Initial-It's AS/400 is a production system, Marie created an authorization list named USEADOPTED and assigned it to the QUSEADPAUT system value. (See Chapter 2 for an explanation of the appropriate use of the QUSEADPAUT system value.) The authorization list has public authority *EXCLUDE.

TABLE 15.1
Security-Related System Values

System value	Value
QALWOBJRST	*NONE
QALWUSRDMN	*ALL
QAUDCTL	*AUDLVL
QAUDENDACN	*NOTIFY
QAUDFRCLVL	*SYS
QAUDLVL	*AUTFAIL, *DELETE, *SAVRST, *SECURITY
QAUTOCFG	0
QAUTOVRT	0
QCRTAUT	*CHANGE
QCRTOBJAUD	*NONE
QDEVRCYACN	*DSCMSG
QDSCJOBITV	120
QDSPSGNINF	'0' = No
QINACTITV	30
QINACTMSGQ	*DSCJOB
QLMTDEVSSN	'1' = Yes
QLMTSECOFR	'1' = Yes
QMAXSGNACN	3
QMAXSIGN	3
QPWDEXPITV	60
QPWDLMTAJC	'1' = Yes
QPWDLMTCHR	*NONE
QPWDLMTREP	2
QPWDMAXLEN	10
QPWDMINLEN	7
QPWDPOSDIF	'0' = No
QPWDRQDDGT	'1' = Yes
QPWDRQDDIF	6
QPWDVLDPGM	*NONE
QRETSVRSEC	'0' = No
QRMTSIGN	*SAMEPRF
QRMTSRVATR	'0' = No
QSECURITY	40 or 50
QUSEADPAUT	USEADOPTED

User Profile Listing

Table 15.2 lists the group and user profiles created at Initial-It, along with the user class, initial program, and initial menu assigned to each.

TABLE 15.2
Initial-It User Profiles

Group profile	User profile	No password	Class	INLPGM	INLMNU
APCLERK		X	*USER	*NONE	*SIGNOFF
	ACJDAMON		*USER	QGPL/APSIGNON	*SIGNOFF
ARCLERK		X	*USER	*NONE	*SIGNOFF
	ACRTAYLOR		*USER	QGPL/ARSIGNON	*SIGNOFF
	ACESIMMONS		*USER	QGPL/ARSIGNON	*SIGNOFF
GLCLERK		X	*USER	*NONE	*SIGNOFF
	ACMWILLIS		*USER	QGPL/GLSIGNON	*SIGNOFF
ICCLERK		X	*USER	*NONE	*SIGNOFF
	ICJCARNEY		*USER	QGPL/ICSIGNON	*SIGNOFF
	ICJEMORY		*USER	QGPL/ICSIGNON	*SIGNOFF
	ICMSPENCER		*USER	QGPL/ICSIGNON	*SIGNOFF
ITPGMR		X	*PGMR	*NONE	*SIGNOFF
	ITSJOHNSON		*PGMR	*NONE	MAIN
ITSYSOP		X	*SYSOPR	*NONE	*SIGNOFF
	ITJGARCIA		*SYSOPR	*NONE	MAIN
OECLERK		X	*USER	*NONE	*SIGNOFF
	OEBSWIZER		*USER	QGPL/OESIGNON	*SIGNOFF
	OEFROSE		*USER	QGPL/OESIGNON	*SIGNOFF
	OEMBLUE		*USER	QGPL/OESIGNON	*SIGNOFF
	OERDONALLY		*USER	QGPL/OESIGNON	*SIGNOFF
PRCLERK		X	*USER	*NONE	*SIGNOFF
	PRWOLSON		*USER	QGPL/PRSIGNON	*SIGNOFF
PUCLERK		X	*USER	*NONE	*SIGNOFF
	PUPCLYND		*USER	QGPL/PUSIGNON	*SIGNOFF
	PUJRIOS		*USER	QGPL/PUSIGNON	*SIGNOFF
	PUTMEEK		*USER	QGPL/PUSIGNON	*SIGNOFF
S_RCLERK		X	*USER	*NONE	*SIGNOFF
	S_RDSMITH		*USER	QGPL/S_RSIGNON	*SIGNOFF
	S_RTPACK		*USER	QGPL/S_RSIGNON	*SIGNOFF
	S_RWUPTON		*USER	QGPL/S_RSIGNON	*SIGNOFF
*NONE					
	ITMYOUNG		*SECADM	*NONE	MAIN
	PRABREDEN		*USER	QGPL/PRSIGNON	*SIGNOFF

This type of listing is essential to auditing the user profiles that can access the system. Marie printed a copy of the list using the PRTUSRPRF (Print User Profile) command with the "full report" option to list all the AS/400 user profiles and their attributes. She filed the printed copy of the original list and periodically runs PRTUSRPRF with the "changed only" option to print changes to user profiles since the last time the report was run. This saves her from having to manually compare the new report with the previous one.

Special Authorities Listing

Table 15.3 lists all profiles that have special authorities. Again, such a list is essential to security auditing. It's important to be aware of which special authorities your users have.

TABLE 15.3
Special Authorities

User profile	Special authorities
ITSYSOP	*JOBCTL *SAVSYS
ITJGARCIA	*JOBCTL *SAVSYS
ITMYOUNG	*SECADM
QSECOFR	*ALLOBJ *SECADM *JOBCTL *SAVSYS *SERVICE *SPLCTL *AUDIT *IOSYSCFG

Library/Object Authorities Listing

Table 15.4 gives an overview of Marie's implementation of library and object authorities for the applications at Initial-It. Starting with the application security requirements and then using the role authorizations, she determined exactly what public, group, and private authorities were needed to secure libraries and objects.

TABLE 15.4
Library and Object Authorities

Library	Object	Object type	Authorities
APFLIB		*LIB	ACAPCLERK — *USE
			ACMWILLIS — *USE
			*PUBLIC — *EXCLUDE
	*ALL	*FILE	*PUBLIC — *USE
APPLIB		*LIB	ACAPCLERK — *USE
			ACMWILLIS — *USE
			*PUBLIC — *EXCLUDE
	*ALL	*ALL	*PUBLIC — *USE
ARFLIB		*LIB	ACARCLERK — *USE
			ACMWILLIS — *USE
			*PUBLIC — *EXCLUDE
	*ALL	*FILE	*PUBLIC — *USE

continued

TABLE 15.4 *CONTINUED*

Library	Object	Object type	Authorities
ARPLIB		*LIB	ACARCLERK — *USE
			ACMWILLIS — *USE
			*PUBLIC — *EXCLUDE
	*ALL	*ALL	*PUBLIC — *USE
GLFLIB		*LIB	ACMWILLIS — *USE
			*PUBLIC — *EXCLUDE
	*ALL	*FILE	*PUBLIC — *USE
GLPLIB		*LIB	ACMWILLIS — *USE
			*PUBLIC — *EXCLUDE
	*ALL	*ALL	*PUBLIC — *USE
ICFLIB		*LIB	ICCLERK — *USE
			*PUBLIC — *EXCLUDE
	ICFPRCA	*FILE	ICMSPENCER — *USE
			*PUBLIC — *USE
	*ALL (other than ICFPRCA defined above)	*FILE	*PUBLIC — *USE
ICPLIB		*LIB	ICCLERK — *USE
			*PUBLIC — *EXCLUDE
	*ALL	*ALL	*PUBLIC — *USE
OEFLIB		*LIB	OECLERK — *USE
			*PUBLIC — *EXCLUDE
	*ALL	*FILE	*PUBLIC — *USE
OEPLIB		*LIB	OECLERK — *USE
			*PUBLIC — *EXCLUDE
	*ALL	*ALL	*PUBLIC — *USE
PUFLIB		*LIB	PUCLERK — *USE
			*PUBLIC — *EXCLUDE
	*ALL	*FILE	*PUBLIC — *USE
PUPLIB		*LIB	PUCLERK — *USE
			*PUBLIC — *EXCLUDE
	*ALL	*ALL	*PUBLIC — *USE
PRFLIB		*LIB	PRCLERK — *USE
			PRABREDEN — *USE
			*PUBLIC — *EXCLUDE
	PRFMSTA	*FILE	PRCLERK — *OBJOPR, *READ, *ADD
			PRABREDEN — *CHANGE
			*PUBLIC — *EXCLUDE
	*ALL (other than PRFMSTA defined above)	*FILE	PRCLERK — *CHANGE
			PRABREDEN — *CHANGE
			*PUBLIC — *EXCLUDE

continued

TABLE 15.4 *Continued*

Library	Object	Object type	Authorities
PRPLIB		*LIB	PRCLERK — *USE
			PRABREDEN — *USE
			*PUBLIC — *EXCLUDE
	*ALL	*ALL	*PUBLIC — *USE

Once the planning was complete, all that remained for Marie to do was to set the system values, put her user profile and password rules into effect, implement the role authorizations, grant the object and special authorities, and create the Client Access exit program. The time invested in planning and documenting security strategy, coupled with a dedicated auditing program, paid off in an effective and efficient security implementation for Initial-It.

Chapter 16

Is Your Strategy Working?

You create user profiles, grant and revoke authorities to objects, set system values and network attributes, configure communications objects, and design or modify applications — all with the goal of securing your system. These objects, authorities, and values are the barriers you erect to limit access to your system. But the system and its users aren't static. In any security strategy, the established security requirements and rules tend to become less effective as time passes. Employees, programs, and operating systems change, as do business requirements to safeguard data. Thus, you must audit these objects, authorities, and values to ensure that the barriers remain effective as time goes by.

Security auditing monitors security-related events and serves to verify the implementation of your security strategy. In this chapter and the following two, we address the need for auditing and the specific types of auditing and auditing activities. To get off to the right start, you should be aware of the types of changes that can affect your security plan.

What Can Change?

Many types of changes can require adjustments in your security plan. Let's look at some of the changes you'll most likely face — things such as business model changes, operating system updates, new products, procedural changes, new user profiles, changing roles, terminations and resignations, and object tracking.

Business Model Changes

Many businesses are adopting an e-business business model, which involves moving from a private network to doing business on the Internet. Of all the changes described in this chapter, this one will cause you the most work in terms of ensuring that your security policies are updated and enforced in the new environment. It will also require the biggest learning curve to evaluate the potential security risks and decide how (or whether) you'll defend against them. It's vital to your business that someone knowledgeable in security be involved in planning for the transformation of your company into an e-business.

Operating System Updates

One of the AS/400's strongest features is that security is integrated into the system in the form of object authorities, security-related system values, user profiles, and other operating system functions. However, this strength can also cause security problems. Operating system changes — such as new versions, releases, and PTFs — could change AS/400 security and can disrupt your implementation of that security.

Consider the upgrade from V2R3 to V3R1. Operating system changes included the addition of the AS/400 Integrated File System (IFS), two additional object authorities (*OBJREF and *OBJALTER) and one new data authority (*EXECUTE), and a new user profile special authority (*IOSYSCFG), among other enhancements. If you overlooked these additions, they might have affected your system's security without your knowledge.

The AS/400's operating system has continued to change. For example, V4R3 included additions such as Application Administration and the ability to limit access to functions within your programs. Given the importance of security on the AS/400, we anticipate that IBM will continue to enhance the system's security with each release. Before you upgrade to a new release, be sure to read all PTF documentation, the *System Handbook*, and the "Memo to Users" that IBM publishes for each new release so you know about such changes and how they'll affect your security implementation.

New Products

Over time, you'll probably buy and install new products on your system. Security planning is an important part of installation planning. You must participate in determining how a new product will change your security strategy and how the new product implements security. For example, before enabling IBM's HTTP Server for AS/400 or installing Client Access Express, you should understand the security implications of these products for the AS/400 itself and for the rest of your enterprise.

Procedural Changes

Any department that uses packaged or custom-written software has procedures that guide employees in the use of that software. Some of those procedures are security-related — for example, those dealing with who can access records, who can make changes, and which operations are valid. These procedures are the backbone of what we've defined in earlier chapters as the authorization role, and they change as a process matures or is altered. You must adjust your security strategy and implementation to reflect those changes.

New User Profiles

You must have a procedure for adding new user profiles to the system. Usually, the difficulty isn't in assigning the new user profile and providing the necessary authorities but in learning that a new employee needs system access. You can obtain this information more easily by discouraging profile sharing (via the QLMTDEVSSN system value and by encouraging department supervisors not to allow or condone sharing). If you let users share profiles, new employees are likely to begin using someone else's profile, and it could be months before you find out a new user exists. This is a security problem because one goal of security is to properly identify authorized users.

Changing Roles

Users can change departments or positions or transfer to another location within your company. When such a change occurs, you must document it and make the necessary authorization adjustments to provide the proper menus, applications, and objects to that user. You should revoke previous authorities that no longer apply to a user.

Terminations and Resignations

Auditing for terminations often poses some problems. You rely on someone to notify you when an employee is terminated so you can revoke the user profile. If an employee has announced a departure but has not yet left, you must monitor the employee's system activity to ensure that he or she does nothing improper. You should also update your user profile list periodically to ensure that no terminated employees have active user profiles on the system. Be sure that the HR department and department supervisors and managers know the importance of notifying you promptly in the event of a termination or resignation.

New and Changed Objects

As the security administrator, you must have the means to audit any new or changed objects on your system. You must ensure that such objects have the correct owner and are properly authorized. This is especially true in the case of an entirely new application or a major modification to an application. You must also be involved with development to the extent that you can be sure the new software integrates security in keeping with your standards. Security should be a major analysis and design consideration.

Deleted Objects

When an object is deleted from the production system, you must know about it. You must know the answers to these questions: Was the object replaced by another object? Is the deleted object no longer required? Must you change your security implementation to reflect the object's deletion?

Temporary Authorities and Objects

Sometimes temporary authorities must be granted, or even entirely new programs written, to provide temporary authority to objects. You must monitor temporary authorities and objects to ensure that they're deleted once they're no longer required. Such temporary authorities and objects are common problems in that they can remain active on the system long after they're no longer needed. They are a documentation nightmare as well as a security problem.

Changes to System Values and Network Attributes

We've discussed a variety of system values and network attributes that directly affect your security implementation. Changes to these values could invalidate your security implementation.

User Identification

Another major purpose of security auditing is to monitor the system for any attempts to violate or bypass a security point (e.g., repeated attempts to sign on using profiles such as QSECOFR or QPGMR, attempts to use objects without authorization). Such infractions provide vital security information by telling you either that someone is attempting to access objects that should remain secure or that your security plan has incorrectly prohibited a user from accessing an object.

Auditing Overview

Auditing on the AS/400 is facilitated by various OS/400 commands and is supported by OS/400's security audit journal. As you'll see in the next two chapters, security auditing is primarily a manual procedure, assisted to some extent by the use of a few automated functions. You can use the auditing commands to create tools that can provide the information you need to satisfy the two auditing purposes: monitoring security-related events and verifying the implementation of your security strategy.

Security auditing is optional. You may choose to audit only sporadically. However, to maintain a healthy security implementation, you should schedule certain auditing tasks at specific intervals — some daily; others weekly, monthly, or annually. The next chapter takes a practical look at security auditing by identifying specific auditing tasks and recommending frequencies for completing those tasks. You might want to have a workstation handy for the next two chapters so you can follow along as we examine each OS/400 auditing command and the objects that assist security auditing.

Chapter 17
Status Auditing

As Chapter 16 points out, the fact that your system and its users aren't static makes it critical that you have a method of auditing objects, authorities, and values to ensure that security remains effective. To do this, you should understand the auditing methods and tools available on the AS/400.

Security auditing on the AS/400 takes two forms: status auditing and event auditing. Status auditing is the process of checking security implementation objects, authorities, and values to verify that they exist as planned and configured. You can perform status-auditing tasks as often as you want. Event auditing, covered in Chapter 18, involves daily monitoring for security-related events that occur on your system.

Status-auditing tasks give you "snapshots" of particular physical conditions, system values, user attributes and authorities, and object ownership and authorities. These snapshots help you determine whether conditions or values are set according to your security plan. This chapter follows the checklist on the next page to present and discuss the tasks that status auditing comprises.

Security Recommendation

Keep all printed reports generated by status-audit tasks in a file folder or notebook. The next time you perform an audit task, compare the results to the previous audit, and then replace the previous records with current documentation.

Status Auditing Checklist

Physical Security Auditing
- [ ] Secure the system key and console
- [ ] Ensure that Dedicated Service Tools (DST) passwords have been changed
- [ ] Secure the computer room

System-Level Security Auditing
- [ ] Verify that system value QSECURITY is set to 40 or greater
- [ ] Verify that the remaining security-related system values and network attributes are properly set

User Profile Monitoring
- [ ] Audit profiles with special authorities
- [ ] Audit group profiles
- [ ] Audit users who own programs that adopt authority
- [ ] Monitor IBM-supplied user profiles
- [ ] Audit user profiles with password the same as the user profile
- [ ] Audit ownership of objects
- [ ] Audit the size of user profiles

Critical Objects and Object Authorities Monitoring
- [ ] Monitor authority for critical objects
- [ ] Audit authorization lists
- [ ] Audit the functions users may perform

Miscellaneous Audit Activities
- [ ] Verify security policy
- [ ] Verify organizational chart
- [ ] Monitor changes to the list of users
- [ ] Audit job descriptions
- [ ] Audit job and output queues
- [ ] Audit communications entries
- [ ] Audit lines, controllers, and devices
- [ ] Monitor TCP/IP applications
- [ ] Audit trigger programs
- [ ] Audit exit programs
- [ ] Audit Management Central tasks
- [ ] Audit new and changed objects

Physical Security Auditing

Auditing your system's physical security should be a regular part of your audit process. Checking the following three items requires very little time, yet all three are significant elements in maintaining a secure environment.

☑ Secure the system key and console.

Verify that the keylock switch is in the SECURE or AUTO position and that the key is removed and in a safe place. Access to the system key and console gives a knowledgeable person potentially unlimited access to your system. For example, the person could use the Dedicated Service Tools (DST) interface to reset the QSECOFR profile password, access a dump of main storage to locate particular address structures, or perform an alternate IPL from distribution media to replace all or part of OS/400.

☑ Ensure that the DST passwords have been changed.

The defaults for the DST user IDs and passwords are well known. Changing these passwords is another way to ensure you control who can use the DST and reload your system.

☑ Secure the computer room.

If your computer room doors require an entry code, make sure the code is changed regularly. If keys are used to gain entry to the computer room, make sure all keys are accounted for. Limiting physical access to the AS/400 reduces the chance of accidents and malicious damage that could disable your system for days.

Security Recommendation

To execute the audit tasks described here and in Chapter 18, you must be signed on as a user profile with *ALLOBJ, *AUDIT, and *SECADM authority. Create a library to hold audit tools and generated output, and secure the library and objects by eliminating public authority. Create a user profile (e.g., SECAUDIT) specifically for the purpose of status audits, and use that profile only to perform audit functions.

System-Level Security Auditing

The AS/400 offers several security-related system values and system network attributes that are important to the security of your system and network. As a part of your regular audit, take a few minutes to check that these values are properly set.

☑ **Verify that system value QSECURITY is set to 40 or greater.**

☑ **Verify that the remaining security-related system values and network attributes are properly set.**

Use the PRTSYSSECA (Print System Security) command to generate a list of the security-related system values and network attributes and their current and recommended values. PRTSYSSECA lists IBM's recommendations, which may be more restrictive than your security policy requires, especially in regard to system value settings for passwords. You should compare these recommendations with your security requirements to determine whether you should follow the recommended settings. You'll find the network attributes at the end of the PRTSYSSECA report.

Another monitoring tool is the security wizard available through Operations Navigator. You may have overlooked this tool because, typically, a wizard is used for setup or configuration. However, using the security wizard is a great way to learn the recommended system value, network attribute, auditing, and security tool settings for your system's configuration. You can also use the wizard to ensure the security settings you've chosen don't change.

User Profile Monitoring

User profiles are the focal point of any security implementation because they identify users' authorizations to all functions and objects on the AS/400. A security plan should establish guidelines for creating profiles (e.g., naming conventions, user classes, special authorities, group profile, object ownership). But again, time has a way of changing things. By auditing user profiles, you can determine whether your security guidelines are being followed for existing profiles and ensure that they're applied to new profiles.

The next several items on the checklist cover the user profile audit reports you should regularly produce and review.

☑ **Audit profiles with special authorities.**

Special authorities provide authorization to system functions that only certain user profiles require. Your security implementation limits the use of special authorities, so you should periodically audit user profiles that have such authorities to ensure that only the desired profiles have those authorities and that each profile has only the special authorities it requires.

To generate this audit report, use the PRTUSRPRF (Print User Profile) command and select one or more special authorities.

☑ **Audit group profiles.**

If you implement group profiles, it's essential that you periodically audit the groups to verify that the correct members are in each group. You can generate this audit report two ways, depending on the level of detail you want. The first method is to use the DSPAUTUSR (Display Authorized User) command:

```
DSPAUTUSR SEQ(*GRPPRF) OUTPUT(*PRINT)
```

This sample command instructs the system to generate a report (to the printer) of all users on the system in group sequence. The results will be similar to the listing in Figure 17.1.

FIGURE 17.1
Sample Group Profile Audit Listing

```
                                       Authorized Users
                    Password
Group       User    Last        No
Profile     Profile Changed     Password  Text
ADMNGRP
            ADAHARG  07/09/91             Administration - Ann Hargis
            ADCCHIN  06/17/91             Administration - Cynthia Chin
            ADRTAYL  06/25/91             Administration - Robert Taylor
OEGRP
            OEPZYT   06/25/91             Order Entry - Patty Zytler
            OEJJEN   07/23/91             Order Entry - Jim Jenson
            OEHJEN   05/05/91             Order Entry - Helen Jenson
            OEBWIN   06/15/91             Order Entry - Bob Winchell
QSYSOPR
            OPMNEL   03/25/91             Operations - Michelle Nelson
*NO GROUP
            PASSTHRU   05/06/91           Pass-through to S/36
            PCTRAN     04/25/91           User profile for PC file transfers
            PRODOWNER                     Production Object Owner
            QDBSHR     09/17/88    X      Internal Data Base User Profile
            QDFTOWN    09/17/88    X      Default Owner for System Objects
            QDOC       09/17/88    X      Internal Document User Profile
            QDSNX      09/17/88    X      QDSNX User Profile
            QFNC       09/17/88    X      Internal QFNC User Profile
            QGATE      09/17/88    X      Internal QGATE user profile
            QLPAUTO    05/18/91    X      QLPAUTO User Profile
            QLPINSTALL 05/18/91    X      QLPINSTALL User Profile
            QPGMR      01/22/91    X      Programmer and Batch User
            QRJE       01/22/91           Internal RJE User Profile
            QSECOFR    07/03/91           Security Officer
            QSNADS     09/17/88    X      Internal SNADS User Profile
            QSPL       09/17/88    X      Internal Spool User Profile
            QSPLJOB    09/17/88    X      Internal Spool User Profile
            QSRV       01/22/91    X      Service User Profile
            QSRVBAS    01/22/91    X      Basic Service User Profile
            QSYS       09/17/88    X      Internal System User Profile
            QSYSOPR    01/22/91    X      System Operator
            QTSTRQS    09/17/88    X      Test Request User Profile
            QUSER      01/22/91    X      Work Station User
```

As you can see, this type of report shows each group profile, the individual profiles in the group, and profiles that are not part of any group. Only the last password change date and text are shown. An X in the No Password column means that no password is provided for the user profile.

Another method that lets you generate a more descriptive report uses the DSPUSRPRF (Display User Profile) command to produce a work file. First type the following command:

```
DSPUSRPRF USRPRF(*ALL)           +
          TYPE(*BASIC)           +
          OUTPUT(*OUTFILE)       +
          OUTFILE(QGPL/DSPGRP)
```

This command creates file DSPGRP in library QGPL. The generated file is the basic user profile information file that uses the record format for file QADSPUPB. (See the section "Expanded User-Profile Auditing" later in this chapter.) Although the file is already sequenced (in arrival sequence only) by user profile name, this method requires that you create a logical file using field UPGRPF (group profile) as the key field. Create the DDS source member defined in Figure 17.2 and compile logical file DSPGRPLF in the library in which DSPGRP resides. RPG/400 program PRTGRPRPT in Figure 17.3 is an example of how the DSPGRP physical file and the DSPGRPLF logical file might be used to generate a detailed group profile report.

FIGURE 17.2
DDS for Logical File DSPGRPLF

```
*...1....+....2....+....3....+....4....+....5....+....6....+....7

 *=============================================================*
 * DSPGRPLF - Member used to create logical view over          *
 *            file DSPGRP created by the DSPUSRPRF command     *
 *=============================================================*
 *
A          R QSYDSUPB                      PFILE(DSPGRP)
 *
A            K UPGRPF
```

FIGURE 17.3
RPG Program PRTGRPRPT

```
*...1....+....2....+....3....+....4....+....5....+....6....+....7

 *=============================================================*
 * Program:   PRTGRPRPT                                        *
 * Purpose:   Print a detailed group profile report            *
 *=============================================================*
 * Outfile for DSPUSRPRF TYPE(*BASIC) command.
FDSPGRP    IF  E                    DISK
 * Logical file over DSPGRP keyed by UPGRPF Group Profile
FDSPGRPLFIF E           K           DISK
F                QSYDSUPB                         KRENAMEGRPRCD
 * Print file
FQPRINT   O   F     132        OF   PRINTER
 *
 * Read physical file.
C                     READ DSPGRP                      99
C                     EXCPTHDG
 *
```

continued

FIGURE 17.3 CONTINUED

```
*...1....+....2....+....3....+....4....+....5....+....6....+....7
 * Loop to read all records.
C           *IN99     DOWEQ*OFF
 *
 * If record is a group profile, print record and
 *   execute subroutine to print all members of this
 *   group.
C           UPGRPI    IFEQ '*YES'
 * Concatenate subroutine.
C                     EXSR @CAT
 * Overflow?, and print group detail.
C    OF               EXCPTHDG
C                     EXCPTGRPDTL
 * Execute subroutine to print all members of group.
C                     MOVELUPUPRF    UPGRPF
C                     EXSR @GDTL
C                     ENDIF
 *
 * Read physical file.
C                     READ DSPGRP                    99
C                     ENDDO
 * End of Program
C                     MOVE *ON       *INLR
C                     RETRN
 *
 *==============================*
 * Print all members of a group *
 *==============================*
C           @GDTL     BEGSR
 *
 * Set lower limits and read equal for group profile.
C           UPGRPF    SETLLDSPGRPLF
C           UPGRPF    READEDSPGRPLF                  98
 *
 * Loop for READE.
C           *IN98     DOWEQ*OFF
 * Concatenate.
C                     EXSR @CAT
 * Print member detail.
C    OF               EXCPTHDG
C                     EXCPTMBRDTL
 * Read logical file.
C           UPGRPF    READEDSPGRPLF                  98
C                     ENDDO
 *
C                     ENDSR
 *==============================*
 * Concatenate work             *
 *==============================*
C           @CAT      BEGSR
 *
```

continued

FIGURE 17.3 CONTINUED

```
*...1....+....2....+....3....+....4....+....5....+....6....+....7
 * Concatenate initial program and initial program library
C                     MOVE *BLANKS    INLPGM 21
C           UPINPG    IFEQ '*NONE'
C                     MOVEL'*NONE'    INLPGM
C                     ELSE
C           UPINPL    CAT  '/':0      INLPGM
C           INLPGM    CAT  UPINPG:0   INLPGM
C                     ENDIF
 *
 * Concatenate initial menu and initial menu library
C                     MOVE *BLANKS    INLMNU 21
C           UPINMN    IFEQ '*SIGNOFF'
C                     MOVELUPINMN     INLMNU
C                     ELSE
C           UPINML    CAT  '/':0      INLMNU
C           INLMNU    CAT  UPINMN:0   INLMNU
C                     ENDIF
 *
C                     ENDSR
 *
OQPRINT E   204          HDG
O                        UDATE Y
O                              +  5 'Group Profile Report'
O                                127 'Page'
O                        PAGE Z  132
 *
O       E   1            HDG
O                                  5 'Group'
O                                 16 'User'
 *      E   1            HDG
O                                  7 'Profile'
O                                 19 'Profile'
O                                 29 'Class'
O                                 51 'Initial Program'
O                                 71 'Initial Menu'
O                                 94 'User Profile'
O                                    ' Description'
 *
O       E   11           GRPDTL
O                        UPUPRF  10
O                        UPUSCL  34
O                        INLPGM  57
O                        INLMNU  80
O                        UPTEXT 132
 *
O       E   1            MBRDTL
O                        UPUPRF  22
O                        UPUSCL  34
O                        INLPGM  57
O                        INLMNU  80
O                        UPTEXT 132
```

✓ Audit users who own programs that adopt authority.

In Chapter 4, we covered the benefits and dangers associated with using programs that adopt authority. It's important to maintain a record of which user profiles own such programs and to make sure you're aware of each program's purpose. You can do this by running the PRTADPOBJ (Print Adopting Objects) command and specifying USRPRF(*ALL). For each user profile, this command produces a report containing all the objects that adopt that user profile's authority. Included in each report are the *PUBLIC authority of both the object and its library and any private authorities users have to the object. After you identify all the programs that adopt authority and verify that each of those objects is valid, you can periodically run this command, requesting a "Changed report only" so you can focus on programs new since the last time you ran the report.

✓ Monitor IBM-supplied user profiles.

Verify that passwords for the IBM-supplied user profiles are either *NONE (where appropriate) or changed regularly. Table 17.1 shows the IBM-supplied profiles, the default passwords when the system was shipped, and the recommended passwords. You can use the OS/400 Setup menu to make necessary changes to these passwords.

TABLE 17.1
IBM-Supplied User Profiles

User profile	Version 2 default password	Versions 3 and 4 default password	Recommended password
QSECOFR	QSECOFR	QSECOFR	user_defined
QPGMR	QPGMR	*NONE	*NONE
QSRV	QSRV	*NONE	*NONE
QSRVBAS	QSRVBAS	*NONE	*NONE
QSYSOPR	QSYSOPR	*NONE	*NONE
QUSER	QUSER	*NONE	*NONE

✓ Audit user profiles with password the same as the user profile.

Use the ANZDFTPWD (Analyze Default Passwords) command to find and potentially take action on user profiles with a default password (i.e., the password is the same as the user profile name). If the password matches the user profile, you can choose to set the profile to a status of *DISABLED, set the password to a status of *EXPIRED, or simply generate a report of the offending profiles.

✓ Audit ownership of objects.

An object-ownership audit report lets you see which user profiles actually own objects. As mentioned in Chapter 4, it's best to have only a few profiles that own objects, although you should be judicious in the number of objects each profile owns.

Again, you can use the DSPUSRPRF command, but this time with TYPE(*OBJOWN) to generate a work file for the report. Remember, when using TYPE(*OBJOWN), a value of USRPRF(*ALL) is invalid. Each user profile must be displayed and the results added to the work file. Figure 17.4 is a CL program (BLDOWNCL) that creates the needed work file complete with records of all user profiles on the system and any objects those users own.

FIGURE 17.4
CL Program BLDOWNCL

```
/*===================================================================*/
/* BLDOWNCL  - Build User Ownership Information File CL              */
/*                                                                   */
/* The purpose of this program is to build a work file that          */
/* contains records of user profiles and any objects they own.       */
/*                                                                   */
/*===================================================================*/
       PGM
/* Declare object description work file                              */
       DCLF FILE(QADSPOBJ)
/* Display all user profile objects, output to work file.            */
       DSPOBJD OBJ(*ALL)                       +
               OBJTYPE(*USRPRF)                +
               DETAIL(*BASIC)                  +
               OUTPUT(*OUTFILE)                +
               OUTFILE(QTEMP/ALLUSERS)
/* Override file declared to file created by DSPOBJD command.        */
       OVRDBF QADSPOBJ QTEMP/ALLUSERS
/* Delete the required work file if it already exists.               */
       DLTF QTEMP/DSPOBJOWN
       MONMSG CPF2105 /* Monitor for CPF2105 - File not found        */

/* Loop to load owned objects file                                   */
       RCD_LOOP:
       RCVF   /* Read record from ALLUSERS file                      */
       MONMSG CPF0864 EXEC(GOTO FINISH)
/* Display this user profile (from ALLUSERS) to add records          */
       DSPUSRPRF USRPRF(&ODOBNM)               +
                 TYPE(*OBJOWN)                 +
                 OUTPUT(*OUTFILE)              +
                 OUTFILE(QTEMP/DSPOBJOWN)      +
                 OUTMBR(*FIRST *ADD)
       MONMSG CPF0000 /* In case no records exist */

       GOTO RCD_LOOP

FINISH:
       DLTF QTEMP/ALLUSERS
       MONMSG CPF2105
       RETURN
       ENDPGM
```

After generating work file DSPOBJOWN using CL program BLDOWNCL, you can use a high-level language (HLL) program or a query to list those user profiles and the objects they own. This report will help you decide where to make ownership changes.

> **Technical Note**
> To reduce the size of the object-ownership report, you may want to tailor it to either bypass user profile QSYS or bypass objects that exist in library QSYS and are owned by QSYS.

☑ **Audit the size of user profiles.**

If you discover, in your object-ownership report, that only a handful of user profiles own all the objects on your system, you may have to be concerned about those profiles' size. If a user profile becomes full, the user profile cannot own or be given authority to more objects, and applications might fail.

Don't confuse a profile's size (i.e., the size of the user profile objects) with the profile's maximum storage setting. A user profile's size depends on how many entries the profile contains. Profiles can contain four types of entries (one entry per type): object-owned, private authority, private authority that another profile has to an object this profile owns (called authorized object entries), and primary group authority.

To complicate matters, some OS/400 object types comprise several internal objects. Profile entries are made for each internal object. For example, source files have several internal objects for each source file member. Thus, when a profile owns a source file with 100 members and five users have private authorities to the file, the owning profile ends up with approximately 2 internal objects × 100 members, or 200 objects owning entries, plus 2 × 100 × 5 users with private authorities, or 1,000 authorized objects owning entries, for a total of 1,200 entries for just one file.

Before V4R4, user profiles could contain up to 1 million entries. In V4R4, a user profile can contain up to 5 million entries. You can see how profiles could quickly get "full" in pre-V4R4 releases, especially when they owned many files and excessive amounts of private authorities were used. To reduce the number of entries in a user profile, use authorization lists, which would reduce the previous example to a total of five authorized objects entries (one for each of the five users who have a private authority to the authorization list securing the file). You can use the PRTPRFINT (Print Profile Internals) command to determine how "full" a user profile is.

Expanded User Profile Auditing

When you can't find an OS/400 command to audit user profile information, you can use one common technique to retrieve the user profile information stored on your AS/400. This technique involves using the DSPUSRPRF command, directing the output to an output file, and then writing an HLL report program or using SQL or a third-party report writer to print a report of the audit.

You can use the DSPUSRPRF command to perform common auditing tasks. For example, to display all — TYPE(*ALL) — information for the QSYSOPR user profile on your workstation display, enter the command

```
DSPUSRPRF  USRPRF(QSYSOPR)              +
           TYPE(*ALL)                   +
           OUTPUT(*)
```

To place basic information for all user profiles on the system in database file QTEMP/DSPUSRS, enter the command

```
DSPUSRPRF  USRPRF(*ALL)                 +
           TYPE(*BASIC)                 +
           OUTPUT(*OUTFILE)             +
           OUTFILE(QTEMP/DSPUSRS)       +
           OUTMBR(*FIRST *REPLACE)
```

If the output file doesn't exist, the system generates it. If the file exists, the system clears the file and then adds the new records.

The DSPUSRPRF command builds work files (using the OUTFILE parameter) according to one of four model files provided in library QSYS:

- QADSPUPA receives output for the CL commands, system devices, and objects to which the user profile is authorized (when TYPE is *OBJAUT, *DEVAUT, or *CMDAUT). Figure 17.5 shows QADSPUPA's record format.

FIGURE 17.5
Record Format for File QADSPUPA

```
File . . . . . . . . . :    QADSPUPA
Record format:    QSYDSUPA
OACEN           1A   Display century: 0-19xx, 1-20xx
OADDAT          6A   Display date: YYMMDD
OAUSR          10A   User profile name
OAOBJ          10A   Object name
OALIB          10A   Library
OATYPE          8A   Type of object
OAOWN          10A   Object owner
OAOPR           1A   Object operational auth: X-auth, blank-not auth
OAOMGT          1A   Object management auth: X-auth, blank-not auth
OAEXS           1A   Object existence auth: X-auth, blank-not auth
OAREAD          1A   Read authority: X-auth, blank-not auth
OAADD           1A   Add authority: X-auth, blank-not auth
OAUPD           1A   Update authority: X-auth, blank-not auth
OADLT           1A   Delete authority: X-auth, blank-not auth
OAAMGT          1A   Auth. list mgt auth: X-auth, blank-not auth
OASYST          8A   System name
OADTIM          6A   Display time: HHMMSS
OAEXCL          1A   Exclude authority: X-exclude, blank-not exclude
OAEXEC          1A   Execute Authority: X-auth, blank-not auth
OAALT           1A   Object alter authority: X-auth, blank-not auth
OAREF           1A   Object reference authority: X-auth, blank-not auth
OARES1         10A   Reserved
OAPGRP         10A   Primary group name
```

- QADSPUPB receives user description information (when TYPE is *BASIC). Figure 17.6 shows the record format.

FIGURE 17.6
Record Format for File QADSPUPB

```
File . . . . :   QADSPUPB
Record format:   QSYDSUPB
UPDCEN           1A      Display century: 0-19xx, 1-20xx
UPDDAT           6A      Display date: YYMMDD
UPDTIM           6A      Display time
UPSYST           8A      System
UPUPRF          10A      User Profile Name
UPUSCL          10A      User class
UPDSIN           7A      Display sign-on information
UPPWCC           1A      Password change century: 0-19xx, 1-20xx
UPPWCD           6A      Password change date: YYMMDD
UPPWCT           6A      Password change time
UPPWEI          5P 0     Password expiration interval
UPPWEX           4A      Password expired
UPPWON           4A      Password of *NONE: *YES or *NO
UPPSOC           1A      Previous sign-on century: 0-19xx, 1-20xx
UPPSOD           6A      Previous sign-on date: YYMMDD
UPPSOT           6A      Previous sign-on time
UPNVSA         11P 0     Sign-on attempts not valid
UPLDVS           7A      Limit device sessions
UPSPAU         150A      Special Authorities
UPMXST         15P 0     Max Storage
UPMXSU         15P 0     Storage used
UPPRLT           1A      Priority limit
UPINPG          10A      Initial Program
UPINPL          10A      Initial program library
UPJBDS          10A      Job description
UPJBDL          10A      Job description library
UPOWNR          10A      Owner
UPGRPF          10A      Group profile
UPGRAU          10A      Group authority
UPGRPI           4A      Group profile indicator: *YES
UPACCD          15A      Accounting code
UPMGQU          10A      Message queue
UPMGQL          10A      Message queue library
UPOTQU          10A      Output queue
UPOTQL          10A      Output Queue library
UPTEXT          50A      Text description
UPSPEN          10A      Special environment
UPCRLB          10A      Current Library
UPINMN          10A      Initial menu
UPINML          10A      Initial menu library
UPLTCP          10A      Limited capability
UPDLVY          10A      Message queue delivery
UPSVRT          2P 0     Message queue severity
UPPRDV          10A      Printer device
UPATPG          10A      Attention Program
UPATPL          10A      Attention program library
UPUSOP         240A      User options
UPUPLK           1A      User profile locked
UPUPDM           1A      User profile damaged
```

continued

Figure 17.6 Continued

```
UPSTAT       10A    Status
UPKBDB       10A    Keyboard buffering
UPASTL       10A    Assistance level
UPLANG       10A    Language identifier
UPCNTR       10A    Country identifier
UPCCSI       5P 0   Coded character set identifier
UPSRT        10A    Soft sequence
UPSRTL       10A    Sort sequence library
UPOBJA       10A    Object auditing value
UPAUDL       640A   Action auditing value
UPGATY       10A    Group authority type
UPSUPG       150    Supplemental group profiles
UPUID        10P 0  User ID number
UPGID        10P 0  Group ID number
UPSET        160A   Locale job attributes
UPCHID       10A    Character Identifier Control
```

- QADSPUPO receives the name, library, and type for each object the profile owns (when TYPE is *OBJOWN). Figure 17.7 shows the record format.

Figure 17.7
Record Format for File QADSPUPO

```
File . . . . :  QADSPUPO
Record format:  QSYDSUPO
OOCEN        1A    Display century: 0-19xx, 1-20xx
OODDAT       6A    Display date: YYMMDD
OOUSR        10A   User profile name
OOOBJ        10A   Object name
OOLIB        10A   Library
OOTYPE       8A    Type of object
OOAHLR       1A    Authority holder: X-authlr, blank-not authlr
OOSYST       8A    System name
OODTIM       6A    Display time: HHMMSS
```

- QADSPUPG receives primary group authorization information (when TYPE is *OBJPGP). Figure 17.8 shows the record format.

Figure 17.8
Record Format for File QADSPUPG

```
File . . . . . . . :  QADSPUPG
Record format: QSYDSUPG
OGSYST       8A    System name
OGCEN        1A    Display century: 0-19xx, 1-20xx
OGDDAT       6A    Display date:  YYMMDD
OGDTIM       6A    Display time:  HHMMSS
OGUSR        10A   User profile name
OGOBJ        10A   Object name
OGLIB        10A   Library name
OGTYPE       8A    Type of object
```

continued

FIGURE 17.8 CONTINUED

```
OGAHLR      1A   Authority holder
OGALT       1A   Object alter authority: X-auth, blank-not auth
OGOPR       1A   Object operation authority: X-auth, blank-not auth
OGOMGT      1A   Object management authority: X-auth, blank-not auth
OGEXS       1A   Object existence authority: X-auth, blank-not auth
OGREF       1A   Object reference authority: X-auth, blank-not auth
OGRES1     10A   Reserved
OGREAD      1A   Read authority: X-auth, blank-not auth
OGADD       1A   Add authority: X-auth, blank-not auth
OGUPD       1A   Update authority: X-auth, blank-not auth
OGDLT       1A   Delete authority: X-auth, blank-not auth
OGEXEC      1A   Execute authority: X-auth, blank-not auth
OGRES2     10A   Reserved
OGAMGT      1A   Authorization list management authority: x-auth,blank-none
OGEXCL      1A   Exclude authority; x-exclude, blank-not exclude
```

Note that you can obtain TYPE(*BASIC) information only for all user profiles (when USRPRF is *ALL) or for generic names (when USRPRF is a generic name). The remaining types of information (e.g., *OBJAUT, *CMDAUT) can be captured for only one user profile at a time.

> **Technical Note**
> You can obtain only TYPE(*BASIC) information for all user profiles at once. The other types of information can be captured for only one user profile at a time.

> **Technical Note**
> Field UPSPAU in file QADSPUPB is 150 characters. Because only eight special authorities exist (*ALLOBJ, *IOSYSCFG, *SECADM, *SAVSYS, *JOBCTL, *SPLCTL, *SERVICE, and *AUDIT), only the first 80 characters are used. When special authorities exist for the user profile, those values are placed in 10-character subfields in the first 80 characters.

After you execute the DSPUSRPRF command, you can write an HLL program or use a report writer, such as Query/400 or your favorite third-party package, to generate an audit report from the work file. With the four model files as a guide, you can generate a variety of audit reports.

Critical Objects and Object Authorities Monitoring

✓ **Monitor authority for critical objects.**

We suggested in Chapter 13 that you identify certain objects on your system as critical objects that require restricted security. You should regularly review the authorities granted these objects to ensure that no changes have been made without your knowledge. We offer three methods for accomplishing this task.

The first is to use the PRTPVTAUT (Print Private Authorities) command to print the private authorities of one or more objects of a specific type. This is helpful in monitoring objects that have critical private authorities. For example, the following command lists the private authorities of all stream files found under the root (/) directory:

```
PRTPVTAUT OBJTYPE(*STMF) DIR(/)
```

The second method is a manual process. To generate a listing of authorities for each critical object identified, type the command

```
DSPOBJAUT OBJ(library/object) OBJTYPE(object_type)  +
          OUTPUT(*PRINT)
```

Note: The DSPOBJAUT (Display Object Authority) command does not support objects in the AS/400 Integrated File System (IFS).

The third method is to create a file to store the names of the critical objects you've identified. The source for such a file would be similar to that for file SECPF in Figure 17.9. You can then key the object names and types into this file (using the AS/400's Data File Utility) and use program PRTOBJAUT (Figure 17.10) to process the file and produce an object-authorization listing for each object name. You should compare the results to previous reports, note any changes, and verify that the changes are legitimate.

Don't forget your critical objects that reside in the AS/400 IFS. In V4R3, IBM enhanced the PRTPVTAUT command to let you monitor the private authorities for directories and stream files. Before this, OS/400 provided no automated tools to keep track of these authorities and programming such a function was difficult because of the variable length of the path name to the object. Therefore, if you run an OS/400 version earlier than V4R3, you'll probably have to keep track of these objects manually by running the DSPAUT (Display Authority) command and specifying OUPUT(*PRINT).

FIGURE 17.9
DDS for File SECPF

```
*...1....+....2....+....3....+....4....+....5....+....6....+....7

     *================================================================*
     * SECPF1 - Critical Objects Physical File                        *
     *================================================================*
     *
     A          R SECPR1                    TEXT('Critical Objects')
     *
     A            OBJLIB        10A         COLHDG('Object' 'Library')
     A            OBJNAM        10A         COLHDG('Object' 'Name')
     A            OBJTYP         8A         COLHDG('Object' 'Type')
     *
     A          K OBJLIB
     A          K OBJNAM
     A          K OBJTYP
```

FIGURE 17.10
CL Program PRTOBJAUT

```
/*==================================================================*/
/* PRTOBJAUT - Print object authorizations.                         */
/*                                                                  */
/*             Produce object authorization listings for each       */
/*             critical object identified in file SECPF1            */
/*                                                                  */
/*==================================================================*/

             PGM

/* Message handling variables */
             DCL  &MSGDTA     *CHAR 256
             DCL  &MSGF       *CHAR  10
             DCL  &MSGFLIB    *CHAR  10
             DCL  &MSGID      *CHAR   7

/* Declare user profile work file TYPE(*BASIC) */
             DCLF FILE(SECPF)
/* Program-level monitor message */
             MONMSG CPF9999 EXEC(GOTO RSND_LOOP)

/* Loop to load object ownership file */
RCD_LOOP:    RCVF   /* Read record from SECPF1 file */
             MONMSG CPF0864 EXEC(GOTO FINISH)

/* Display object authorities for the object */
             DSPOBJAUT OBJ(&OBJLIB/&OBJNAM)      +
                       OBJTYPE(&OBJTYP)          +
                       OUTPUT(*PRINT)
             MONMSG CPF0000  /* In case no records are found */

             GOTO RCD_LOOP
/* Resend error messages to calling program */
 RSND_LOOP:  RCVMSG RMV(*YES)                    +
                    MSGDTA(&MSGDTA)              +
                    MSGID(&MSGID)                +
                    MSGF(&MSGF)                  +
                    MSGFLIB(&MSGFLIB)
             MONMSG CPF9999 EXEC(GOTO RSND_END)
             IF (&MSGID = ' ') GOTO RSND_END /* no more messages */
             SNDPGMMSG MSGID(&MSGID)             +
                       MSGF(&MSGFLIB/&MSGF)      +
                       MSGDTA(&MSGDTA)           +
                       MSGTYPE(*DIAG)
             GOTO RSND_LOOP

 RSND_END:   SNDPGMMSG MSGID(CPF9898)            +
                       MSGF(QSYS/QCPFMSG)        +
                       MSGDTA('Operation ended in error. See +
                         previously listed messages')        +
                       MSGTYPE(*COMP)

 FINISH:
             RETURN
             ENDPGM
```

☑ **Audit authorization lists.**

One problem with using authorization lists is that they're difficult to manage. A useful tool for managing — and auditing — those lists is one that prints one or more authorization lists and the objects each list secures. The PRTPVTAUT command lets you do just that. When you specify OBJTYPE(*AUTL) and AUTLOBJ(*YES), the command prints a report that lists the private authorities for each authorization list on your system and a report for each authorization list that shows all the objects secured by the list.

☑ **Audit the functions users may perform.**

Another way to control users' access to perform certain functions is through the limit access to program function support introduced in V4R3. Operations Navigator makes extensive use of this function to control what appears on a user's desktop. You need to monitor the functions users are allowed to perform. The AS/400 provides APIs to do this (not automated tools, however). (For more information about the APIs, see Appendix A.)

Miscellaneous Audit Activities

☑ **Verify security policy.**

Verify that a security policy exists. It's shocking how many organizations attempt to run their businesses without a security policy. How do you know whether you're in compliance unless security policies are in place? How do you know how to measure your security risks when you don't know whether the enterprise requires a strict policy (everyone is excluded, only a few objects have public access) or allows an open policy (most objects are available to the public, only the most sensitive objects are restricted). How can a security officer know whether a particular software product should be allowed on the system unless he or she knows the security policies the software must follow?

☑ **Verify organizational chart.**

Verify that an organizational chart exists for all system users and that it includes the group roles. An organization chart facilitates the formal audit process and initiates interaction with end-user departments to identify recent employee or authorization-role changes.

☑ **Monitor changes to the list of users.**

The purpose of auditing the user list is to make sure no profiles exist for terminated or absent employees. This process also ensures that all new employees have their own user profiles. Use the command

```
DSPAUTUSR OUTPUT(*PRINT)
```

and compare the results to a list of valid users submitted by each department. It's difficult to ensure that departments notify IT of employee status changes. Two tools are available to help you clean up "old" profiles — that is, profiles left after users have retired, taken an extended leave, or for whatever reason no longer work for your organization.

Use the CHGEXPSCDE (Change Expiration Schedule Entry) command to delete or set a profile's status to *DISABLED on a specific date. When you're notified that an employee is leaving, you can run this command to automatically act on the profile the day after the employee leaves. To make sure you don't miss any profiles, you can use the CHGACTSCDE (Change Activation Schedule Entry) command to automatically set a profile's status to *DISABLED after a certain period (e.g., 60 days) of inactivity.

✓ Audit job descriptions.

Audit the job descriptions on the system to verify which of them have specific user profiles for the USER parameter. Check the authorities of those user profiles and the authority granted to the job description itself. The PRTJOBDAUT (Print Job Description Authority) command lets you print a list of job descriptions whose public authority is not *EXCLUDE.

✓ Audit job and output queues.

Audit the output queues on your AS/400 to verify that sensitive output is secure. Audit the job queues to ensure that confidential jobs cannot be rerouted to an unsecure queue or cancelled altogether. Use the PRTQAUT (Print Queue Authority) command to produce a report that lists all the security-relevant attributes of job and output queues.

✓ Audit communications entries.

Audit communications entries in subsystems to make sure a default user profile doesn't exist in an entry unless absolutely necessary. If a default user profile does exist, it should have little authority. You can use the PRTSBSDAUT (Print Subsystem Description Authority) command to print a list of the communications entries with default user profiles.

✓ Audit lines, controllers, and devices.

Audit the security-relevant attributes of lines, controllers, and devices. Use the PRTCMNSEC (Print Communications Security) command to monitor and manage these attributes.

✓ Monitor TCP/IP applications.

Today, most platforms use the TCP/IP communications protocol, so it's more important than ever that you monitor all TCP/IP applications running on your AS/400. Several monitoring methods are available. One is to use a manual process and run the CHGxxxA command (xxx is the TCP/IP application; for example, CHGTELNA for Telnet) to determine the current settings for each application. You'll want to ensure that the AUTOSTART and INACTTIMO parameters have appropriate values for your security requirements. You can also view the AUTOSTART attribute for all servers by going to Operations Navigator and then clicking Network, Protocols, TCP/IP, and the Servers to Start tab. Alternatively, you can view the autostart values, which are stored in file QUSRSYS/QATOCSTART, by using the DSPPFM (Display Physical File Member) command or running an SQL query.

✓ Audit trigger programs.

You can monitor trigger programs using the PRTTRGPGM (Print Trigger Program) command. As with programs that adopt authority, you must ensure that the trigger programs are valid.

✓ Audit exit programs.

You must validate and monitor exit programs defined through OS/400's registration facility. You can obtain a list of all programs associated with each exit point by running the WRKREGINF (Work with Registration Information) command and specifying OUTPUT(*PRINT).

✓ Audit Management Central tasks.

Management Central, a facility included in Operations Navigator, helps you manage multiple AS/400s in your network. One Management Central function lets you define a command that's run after a task is run. Management Central uses the concept of a central or controlling system and "endpoint" or other systems in your network. You define a task on the central system and run it on the endpoint systems. The task and command run with the authority of whoever owns the task. To monitor commands that run after a task is completed, go into Management Central, right-click the task, and click Properties and then Definition. This is where you define the command string.

✓ Audit new and changed objects.

You should have a tool that lets you audit new and changed objects on the system. New objects must be authorized, and changed objects may require different authorizations than the current implementation. Figure 17.11 shows the command definition for PRTCHGOBJ, which generates a report for new or changed objects (or both) by using a date as the trigger. The entered date serves as the baseline, and the report lists any objects that are new or have changed since that date. In addition to its usefulness in security auditing, this type of report lets you ensure that your backup/recovery methods are effective.

FIGURE 17.11
PRTCHGOBJ Command Definition

```
/*======================================================================*/
/* PRTCHGOBJ - Print New or Changed Objects by Date                     */
/* CPP: PRTCOCPP                                                        */
/*                                                                      */
/* Parameter Descriptions                                               */
/*                                                                      */
/*                  Prompt                                              */
/*     Parameter    Sequence    Description and values                  */
/*     ---------    --------    --------------------                    */
/*                                                                      */
/*     LIB             1        Library to search for new or changed    */
/*                              objects.  Valid values are: single      */
/*                              library name, *LIBL (library list),     */
/*                              *USRLIBL (User library list), *ALLUSR   */
/*                              (all user libraries), or *ALL (all      */
/*                              libraries).  If anything other than     */
/*                              a single library is entered, I recommend*/
/*                              executing the program as a batch job.   */
/*                                                                      */
/*     DATE            4        The date to reference for determining   */
/*                              if an object is new or changed.  Any    */
/*                              object created or changed since the     */
/*                              date entered in this parameter will     */
/*                              appear on the report.                   */
/*                                                                      */
/*     OBJTYPE         2        The object types to include in search.  */
/*                                                                      */
/*     OPTION          3        Search option.  Search for new objects  */
/*                              (*NEW), changed objects (*CHG), or both */
/*                              (*BOTH).                                */
/*                                                                      */
/*     USER            5        User profile to search.  If a user      */
/*                              profile is specified, only objects      */
/*                              owned by that user will be searched     */
/*                              for the report.                         */
/*                                                                      */
/*======================================================================*/
             CMD         PROMPT('Print new or changed objects')

             PARM        KWD(LIB) TYPE(*NAME) LEN(10) SPCVAL((*ALL)     +
                           (*LIBL) (*USRLIBL) (*ALLUSR)) MIN(1)         +
                           PROMPT('Library name' 1)
             PARM        KWD(DATE) TYPE(*DEC) LEN(6 0) MIN(1)           +
                           PROMPT('From date (YYMMDD)' 4)

             PARM        KWD(OBJTYPE) TYPE(*CHAR) LEN(8) RSTD(*YES)     +
                           DFT(*ALL) VALUES(*ALRTBL *AUTL *BNDDIR *CFGL +
                           *CHTFMT *CLD *CLS *CMD *CNNL *COSD *CRQD *CSI +
                           *CSPMAP *CSPTBL *CTLD *DEVD *DTAARA *DTADCT  +
                           *DTAQ *EDTD *FCT *FILE *FNTRSC *FNTTBL *FORMDF +
                           *FTR *GSS *IPXD *JOBD *JOBQ *JRN *JRNRCV *LIB +
                           *LIND *LOCALE *M36 *M36CFG *MENU *MODD *MODULE +
```

continued

Figure 17.11 Continued

```
                  *MSGF *MSGQ *NODGRP *NODL *NTBD *NWID *NWSD      +
                  *OUTQ *OVL *PAGDFN * PAGSEG *PDG *PGM *PNLGRP    +
                  *PRDAVL *PRDDFN *PRDLOD *PSFCFG *QMFORM *QMQRY   +
                  *QRYDFN *RCT *S36 *SBSD *SCHIDX *SPADCT *SQLPKG  +
                  *SRVPGM *SSND *SVRSTG *TBL *USRIDX *USRPRF       +
                  *USRQ *USRSPC *VLDL *WSCST) EXPR(*YES)           +
                  ROMPT('Object type:' 2)

         PARM     KWD(OPT) TYPE(*CHAR) LEN(5) RSTD(*YES)           +
                  DFT(*BOTH) VALUES(*BOTH *NEW *CHG)               +
                  PROMPT('Select *NEW,*CHG,*BOTH' 3)

         PARM     KWD(USER) TYPE(*CHAR) LEN(10) DFT(*ALL)          +
                  PROMPT('User name or *ALL' 5)

         PARM     KWD(OPT) TYPE(*CHAR) LEN(5) RSTD(*YES)           +
                  DFT(*BOTH) VALUES(*BOTH *NEW *CHG)               +
                  PROMPT('Select *NEW,*CHG,*BOTH' 3)

         PARM     KWD(USER) TYPE(*CHAR) LEN(10) DFT(*ALL)          +
                  PROMPT('User name or *ALL' 5)
```

Figure 17.12 shows the command processing program (CPP) for the PRTCHGOBJ command. Figure 17.13 shows RPG program PRTCORPG, which the CPP calls to print new and changed objects by date. Figure 17.14 shows the DDS for logical file DSPOBJLF, and Figure 17.15 shows the DDS for logical file DSPMBRLF. Program PRTCORPG uses DSPOBJLF to sequence the report, and it uses DSPMBRLF to search for the most recently changed or created file member.

Figure 17.12

CPP for the PRTCHGOBJ Command

```
/*==================================================================*/
/* PRTCOCPP - Print new or changed objects by date - CPP            */
/* PRTCHGOBJ is command this program processes.                     */
/*==================================================================*/
             PGM PARM(&LIB &DATE &OBJTYPE &OPT &USER)

/* Command parameters */
             DCL &LIB       *CHAR    10
             DCL &DATE      *DEC    (6 0)
             DCL &OBJTYPE   *CHAR    5
             DCL &OPT       *CHAR    5
             DCL &USER      *CHAR    10

/* Delete object work files if they already exist */
             DLTF QTEMP/DSPOBJLF
             MONMSG CPF2105
             DLTF QTEMP/DSPOBJS
             MONMSG CPF2105
```

continued

FIGURE 17.12 CONTINUED

```
/* Delete member work files if they already exist */
          DLTF QTEMP/DSPMBRLF
          MONMSG CPF2105
          DLTF QTEMP/DSPMBRS
          MONMSG CPF2105

/* Display selected objects to work file                    */
          DSPOBJD OBJ(&LIB/*ALL)                          +
                  OBJTYPE(&OBJTYPE)                       +
                  DETAIL(*SERVICE)                        +
                  OUTPUT(*OUTFILE)                        +
                  OUTFILE(QTEMP/DSPOBJS)
/* If &OBJTYPE *EQ "FILE" OR "*ALL" then display member list */
          IF (&OBJTYPE *EQ '*ALL' *OR &OBJTYPE *EQ '*FILE') DO
             DSPFD FILE(&LIB/*ALL)                        +
                   TYPE(*MBR)                             +
                   OUTPUT(*OUTFILE)                       +
                   OUTFILE(QTEMP/DSPMBRS)
          ENDDO

/* Create logical files for report processing */
          CRTLF FILE(QTEMP/DSPOBJLF) SRCFILE(SOURCE)   +
                OPTION(*NOSRC *NOLIST)
          CRTLF FILE(QTEMP/DSPMBRLF) SRCFILE(SOURCE)   +
                OPTION(*NOSRC *NOLIST)

/* Print list of changed/new objects using HLL */
          CALL PRTCORPG PARM(&LIB &DATE &OBJTYPE &OPT &USER)

          ENDPGM
```

FIGURE 17.13
RPG Program PRTCORPG

```
   *...1....+....2....+....3....+....4....+....5....+....6....+....7

    *================================================================*
    * PRTCORPG - Print new or changed objects by date               *
    * Called from PRTCOCPP which is CPP for PRTCHGOBJ               *
    *================================================================*
    *
    FDSPOBJLFIF  E            K         DISK
    FDSPMBRLFIF  E            K         DISK
    FQPRINT  O   F   132         OF     PRINTER
    *
    E                 LINE        132  1              PRINT LINE --
    *
    I            DS
    I                                   1   50 ODOBTX
    I                                   1   35 TEXT35
    I            DS
    I                                   1   10 ODLBNM
    I                                   1    1 ODLB1
```

continued

FIGURE 17.13 CONTINUED

```
*...1....+....2....+....3....+....4....+....5....+....6....+....7
I                                          1   2 ODLB2
I                                          1   4 ODLB4
I            DS
I                                          1  10 ODOBAT
I                                          1   8 ATTR08
 * Object creation date
I            DS
I                                          1   6 ODCDAT
I                                          1  20CRMO
I                                          3  40CRDA
I                                          5  60CRYR
 * Object change date/time
I            DS
I                                          1   6 ODLDAT
I                                          1  20CHMO
I                                          3  40CHDA
I                                          5  60CHYR
I                                          7  12 ODLTIM
I                                          7 120CHTIM
 * Character save object date/time to numeric
I            DS
I                                          1   6 ODSDAT
I                                          1  20SVMO
I                                          3  40SVDA
I                                          5  60SVYR
I                                          7  12 ODSTIM
I                                          7 120SVTIM
 * Character member creation date to numeric
I            DS
I                                          1   6 MBCDAT
I                                          1  60MBCRDT
 * Character member change date to numeric
I            DS
I                                          1   6 MBCHGD
I                                          1  20MBMO
I                                          3  40MBDA
I                                          5  60MBYR
I                                          1  60MBRCDT
 * Character member change time to numeric
I            DS
I                                          1   6 MBCHGT
I                                          1  60MBRCTM
 * Compare data (input)
I            DS
I                                          1  60CMPDTE
I                                          1  20YY
I                                          3  40MM
I                                          5  60DD
 *
C           *ENTRY    PLIST
C                     PARM           LIB   10
```

continued

FIGURE 17.13 CONTINUED

```
*...1....+....2....+....3....+....4....+....5....+....6....+....7
C                      PARM           DATE   60
C                      PARM           OBJTYP  5
C                      PARM           OPT     5
C                      PARM           USER   10
 *
C           FKEY       KLIST
C                      KFLD           ODLBNM
C                      KFLD           ODOBNM
 *
C                      MOVEA*ALL'-'   LINE
C                      TIME           CURTIM 60
C                      Z-ADD0         COUNT  50
 *
 * Read record from object work file
C                      READ DSPOBJLF                  99          In
C                      MOVE *BLANK    LIBSAV 10
 *
 * Loop to process all records from DSPOBJLF
C           *IN99      DOWEQ*OFF
 *
 * Only "QGPL" is valid "Q" Library, bypass all other system libraries
C           ODLB1      IFEQ 'Q'
C           ODLB4      ANDNE'QGPL'
C                      GOTO NXTRCD
C                      ENDIF
 *
C           USER       IFNE '*ALL'
C           USER       CABNEODOBOW    NXTRCD
C                      ENDIF
 *
 * If object type if *FILE, execute member subroutine
C           ODOBTP     CASEQ'*FILE'   @GETMB
C                      ENDCS
 *
 * Check dates for create selection
C           OPT        IFEQ '*BOTH'
C           OPT        OREQ '*NEW '
C                      Z-ADDCRMO      MM
C                      Z-ADDCRDA      DD
C                      Z-ADDCRYR      YY
C           CMPDTE     CABGEDATE      GOOD
C           *IN21      IFEQ *OFF
C           MBCHGD     ANDNE*BLANK
C           MBRCDT     CABGEDATE      GOOD
C                      ENDIF
C                      ENDIF
 *
 * Check dates for change selection
C           OPT        IFEQ '*BOTH'
C           OPT        OREQ '*CHG '
C           ODLDAT     IFNE *BLANK
C                      Z-ADDCHMO      MM
```

continued

FIGURE 17.13 CONTINUED

```
*...1....+....2....+....3....+....4....+....5....+....6....+....7
C                       Z-ADDCHDA      DD
C                       Z-ADDCHYR      YY
C           CMPDTE      CABGEDATE      GOOD
C                       ENDIF
C           *IN21       IFEQ *OFF
C           MBCHGD      ANDNE*BLANK
C           MBRCDT      CABGEDATE      GOOD
C                       ENDIF
C                       ENDIF
 *
 * Bypass this record
C                       GOTO NXTRCD
 *
 * "GOOD" - print record
C           GOOD        TAG                           GOOD        Tag
C                       ADD  1         COUNT
 *
 * Condition output
C           ODLDAT      COMP *BLANK                   51
C           ODLTIM      COMP *BLANK                   52
C           ODSDAT      COMP *BLANK                   53
C           ODSTIM      COMP *BLANK                   54
C           MBCHGD      COMP *BLANK                   55
C           MBCHGT      COMP *BLANK                   56
C           MBCDAT      COMP *BLANK                   57
C           ODCDAT      COMP *BLANK                   58
 *
 * Save library name for level breaks
C           ODLBNM      IFNE LIBSAV
C                       EXCPTHDG
C                       MOVE ODLBNM    LIBSAV
C                       ENDIF
 *
C    OF                 EXCPTHDG                      HDG         Out
C                       EXCPTDTL                      DTL         Out
 *
C           NXTRCD      TAG                           NXTRCD      Tag
C                       READ DSPOBJLF             99              In
C                       ENDDO
 *
C                       EXCPTTOTL                     TOTL        Out
C                       SETON                         LR
C                       RETRN
 *
*=====================================================*
* Subroutine to check member change and create dates  *
*=====================================================*
C           @GETMB      BEGSR
 *
 * Initialize work fields and indicator
C                       Z-ADD0         LLDAT     60
```

continued

FIGURE 17.13 CONTINUED

```
*...1....+....2....+....3....+....4....+....5....+....6....+....7
C                       Z-ADD0         LLTIM     60
C                       SETON                              21
 *
 * Read member records
C           FKEY        SETLLDSPMBRLF
C           FKEY        READEDSPMBRLF                      98
 * Loop for all records
C           *IN98       DOWEQ*OFF
 * For determining correct output
C                       SETOF                              21
 * Determine most recent member date/time
C           MBCHGD      IFNE *BLANK
C                       Z-ADDMBMO      MM
C                       Z-ADDMBDA      DD
C                       Z-ADDMBYR      YY
C           CMPDTE      IFGT LLDAT
C                       Z-ADDMBRCDT    LLDAT
C                       Z-ADDMBRCTM    LLTIM
C                       ENDIF
C                       ENDIF
 * Read next record
C           FKEY        READEDSPMBRLF                      98
C                       ENDDO
 *
 * Use most recent data/time as member data/time
C                       Z-ADDLLDAT     MBRCDT
C                       Z-ADDLLTIM     MBRCTM
 *
C                       ENDSR
 *
 *
OQPRINT  E   203        HDG
O                       CURTIM              '  :  :  '
O                                        55 'DOCUMENTATION - OBJECT'
O                                      +  1 'CREATION/CHANGE LIST'
O                       UDATE Y      90
O                                       127 'PAGE'
O                       PAGE  Z     132
O        E   2          HDG
O                                           'SELECTIONS ====>'
O                                      +  2 'OBJECT TYPE:'
O                       OBJTYP         +  1
O                                      +  2 'LIBRARY:'
O                       LIB            +  1
O                                      +  2 'CREATE/CHANGE?:'
O                       OPT            +  1
O                                      +  2 '*GE TO DATE:'
O                       DATE  Y        +  1
O                                      +  2 'SELECT USER:'
O                       USER           +  1
O        E   0          HDG
O                                           'LIBRARY NAME ====>'
```

continued

FIGURE 17.13 CONTINUED

```
*...1....+....2....+....3....+....4....+....5....+....6....+....7
 O                              ODLBNM   +  1
 O          E  1                HDG
 O                                                'LIBRARY NAME ====>'
 O                              ODLBNM   +  1
 O          E  1                HDG
 O                              LINE       132
 O          E  1                HDG
 O                                           6 'OBJECT'
 O                                          15 'TYPE'
 O                                          24 'ATTR'
 O                                          40 'DESCRIPTION'
 O                                          70 'OWNER'
 O                                          84 'CREATED'
 O                                         103 'CHANGE DATE/TIME'
 O                                         112 'SAVE CMD'
 O                                         132 'SAVE DATE / TIME'
 O          E  1                HDG
 O                              LINE       132
 O          E  1                DTL
 O                              ODOBNM      10
 O                              ODOBTP      19
 O                              ATTR08      28
 O                              TEXT35      64
 O                              ODOBOW      75
 *
 O              N21N57          MBCRDTY     84
 O              N21N55          MBRCDTY     94
 O              N21N56          MBRCTM     103 ' : : '
 *
 O               21N58          CRYR        78
 O               21N58                      79 '/'
 O               21N58          CRMO        81
 O               21N58                      82 '/'
 O               21N58          CRDA        84
 O               21N51          CHYR        88
 O               21N51                      89 '/'
 O               21N51          CHMO        91
 O               21N51                      92 '/'
 O               21N51          CHDA        94
 O               21N52          CHTIM      103 ' : : '
 *
 O                              ODSCMD     114
 *
 O               N53            SVYR       117
 O               N53                       118 '/'
 O               N53            SVMO       120
 O               N53                       121 '/'
 O               N53            SVDA       123
 O               N54            SVTIM      132 ' : : '
 *
 O          E  2                TOTL
 O                                                'ITEMS REPORTED -'
 O                              COUNT Z +  1
```

FIGURE 17.14
DDS for Logical File DSPOBJLF

```
*...1....+....2....+....3....+....4....+....5....+....6....+....7

     *===============================================================*
     * DSPOBJLF - Logical File                                       *
     *                                                               *
     * Logical file for object work file - PRTCOCPP program          *
     *                                                               *
     *    In order to compile the program and execute the job,       *
     *    first you must use the DSPOBJD command to create           *
     *    outfile DSPOBJS.  Then create this logical file and        *
     *    compile the program.                                       *
     *===============================================================*
     *
     A          R QLIDOBJD                  PFILE(DSPOBJS)
     *
     A            K ODLBNM
     A            K ODOBTP
     A            K ODOBNM
     A            K ODOBAT
```

FIGURE 17.15
DDS for Logical File DSPMBRLF

```
*...1....+....2....+....3....+....4....+....5....+....6....+....7

     *===============================================================*
     * DSPMBRLF - Logical File                                       *
     *                                                               *
     * Logical file for member work file - PRTCOCPP program          *
     *                                                               *
     *    In order to compile the program and execute the job,       *
     *    first you must use the DSPFD command to create outfile     *
     *    DSPMBRS.  Then create this logical file and compile        *
     *    the program.                                               *
     *===============================================================*
     *
     A          R QWHFDMBR                  PFILE(DSPMBRS)
     *
     A            K MBLIB
     A            K MBFILE
```

Status auditing works only as well as the effort you're willing to invest in it. To properly audit the status of the various security values and authorities, you must schedule a regular time to perform the tasks and then follow that schedule. If you consistently follow the guidelines in this chapter for auditing your security system, you can maintain a security plan that meets your organization's ever-changing security requirements. You'll find this time-consuming but rewarding. And, when the time arrives for a formal audit, you'll also save many hours by having up-to-date information ready for the auditors.

Chapter 18

Event Auditing

When IBM first announced the AS/400, the only way to audit events on the system was to monitor the OS/400 history log (QHST). Because this log still exists (as a remnant of the S/38), we briefly discuss using the history log, but keep in mind that it's a primitive means of auditing and offers only a minimal benefit. As IBM improved OS/400, it added the OS/400 security audit journal and extensive event-auditing features. The primary focus of this chapter is the OS/400 security audit journal and these event-auditing features that you can — and should — take advantage of to help you better manage your security implementation.

Monitoring the History Log

The history log records high-level activities, such as the start and completion of each job, device status changes, system operator messages, and failed sign-on attempts. The history log records these events in the form of messages and stores them in system-created files. Although IBM is slowly reducing the number of security-related messages available in the history log and instead opting to audit those using the audit journal, you can still learn from your system's history. An accurate history log helps you monitor system activities and reconstruct events to aid problem-determination and debugging efforts. The text description that the system maintains contains the beginning and ending date and time for the messages in that file, information useful for tracking activities that occurred in a particular time period.

You can display the contents of the history log by executing the DSPLOG (Display Log) command:

```
DSPLOG LOG(QHST)
```

The resulting display resembles the screen in Figure 18.1. Because system events such as job completions, invalid sign-on attempts, and line failures are stored as messages in file QHST, you can place the cursor on a particular message and press the Help key to display second-level help text for the message.

FIGURE 18.1
Sample History Log

```
                    Display History Log Contents
Job 160839/QPGMR/DCP100 released by user QPGMR.
Job 160839/QPGMR/DCP100 started on 10/08/90 at 06:00:04 in subsystem QBATCH
Receiver ACG0239 in JRNLIB never fully saved. (I C)
C
Job 160839/QPGMR/DCP100 completed on 10/08/90 at 06:02:05. 32 seconds process
Vary Configuration (VRYCFG) command completed for line EAST.
Line EAST varied on successfully.
Vary Configuration (VRYCFG) command completed for controller CHICAGO.
Vary Configuration (VRYCFG) command completed for device CHICAGO.
Job 160921/DALLMKW/DSP10 started on 10/08/90 at 06:50:23 in subsystem QINTER.
Controller CHICAGO contacted on line CHICAGO.
Communications device CHICAGO was allocated to subsystem QCMN.
Password from device DSP23 not correct for user QSECOFR.
Writer 160934/QSPLJOB/PGMRWTR started.
Load form type '*STD' device PGMRWTR writer PGMRWTR. . (H C G I R)
A parity error or stop bit error detected while communicating with device
CHICAGO.
Password from device BPC01023S1 not correct for user DALLDDW.
                                                              More...
Press Enter to continue.
F3=Exit    F10=Display all    F12=Cancel
```

The DSPLOG command has several parameters that provide flexibility for history log inquiries. These are fairly self-explanatory:

LOG	The history log is QHST.
PERIOD	You can enter a specific time period or take the defaults for the beginning and ending periods. The default for the beginning time is the earliest available time, and the default for the beginning date is the current date. Enter values as six-digit numbers (i.e., time as *hhmmss* and date as *mmddyy*).
OUTPUT	This parameter is familiar from many other AS/400 commands. The asterisk value (*) sends output to the screen, and *PRINT sends it to a spool file.
JOB	You can use the JOB parameter to search for a specific job name. You can enter just the job name, in which case the system might find several jobs with the same name that ran during a given time period. Or you can enter the specific job name, user name, and job number to retrieve history information for a specific job.
MSGID	Like the JOB parameter, MSGID helps narrow the search. You can specify one or more messages.

History Log Housekeeping

The history log consists of a message queue and system files that store history messages. The files are in library QSYS and have names that follow the convention QHST*yydddn*. The *yyddd* stands for the Julian date on which the log was created, and *n* is a sequence number (0 through 9 or A through Z) appended to the date. The system creates a new file whenever the existing file reaches its size limit, which is controlled by system value

QHSTLOGSIZ (History Log Size). Because the system does not automatically delete files, it's important to develop a strategy for deleting the log files and for using the data before you delete the files.

It's wise to save previous versions of the log to media so you can retrieve them if necessary. We recommend making a save copy of the QHST files once a month. You should maintain enough recent history on disk so you can easily inquire into the log to resolve problems. We recommend that you use Operational Assistant's automatic cleanup capabilities.

Inside Information

A careful daily review of history logs lets you monitor security-related events and alerts you to unusual system activity. If, for example, the message "Password from device DSP23 not correct for user QSECOFR" appears in the log frequently, you might want to find out who uses DSP23 and why he or she is trying to sign on with the system security officer profile. Or, you might notice the message "Receiver ACG0239 in JRNLIB never fully saved (I C)." The second-level help text would tell you which program was attempting to delete the journal receiver. Bringing these types of events to your attention could help you prevent the loss of important information.

One especially useful DSPLOG command option is the ability to select all security-related messages with one parameter. All security-related messages (excluding some network and communications messages that might relate indirectly to security) are within the message identifier range of CPF2200 to CPF2299. If you enter the command

```
DSPLOG LOG(QHST) MSGID(CPF2200) PERIOD(time_period)
```

you can view security-related messages for the specified period. However, as mentioned earlier, IBM is slowly removing security-related messages from QHST as more customers use the OS/400 audit journal's superior capabilities. Even so, maintaining a history log lets you easily reconstruct events that occurred on the system. For example, when reviewing its history log, one company discovered that a programmer had planted a system virus. A history log can also alert you to less serious offenses (e.g., a specific sequence of jobs wasn't performed exactly as planned). Using and maintaining a history log is straightforward and is time well spent.

The Security Audit Journal

The primary tool for event auditing is the OS/400 security audit journal. This is a system-supplied journaling function that records specific security-related events based on your configuration of auditing controls (e.g., system values, user profile parameters, object-auditing attributes). In its initial implementation in V1R3, the auditing journal offered only one option: You could use the system audit-journaling capabilities to audit for specific activities on a system-wide basis. To accomplish this, you first created an initial journal receiver in a user library and the QAUDJRN audit journal in library QSYS. You then started auditing by modifying the QAUDLVL (Audit Level) system value to include one or more of the values that control the activities the audit journal captures. The obvious limit to this approach is the fact that you must control this auditing at a system level.

This function has evolved greatly since its inception. You now have many choices when you use the security audit journal approach to AS/400 auditing — choices that give you the flexibility you need to create and manage an effective auditing implementation. The following discussion introduces you to the six essential areas of knowledge you need to effectively implement and use the security audit journal:

- the audit journal
- auditing controls
- system-wide auditing
- user auditing
- object auditing
- displaying and printing the audit journal entries

The Audit Journal

When you install OS/400, no audit journal exists on the system. You must create the security audit journal before implementing any of the auditing features we discuss. OS/400 expects you to create a journal named QAUDJRN in library QSYS. Indeed, OS/400 can use a journal with only that name to log entries. Creating this journal is actually a two-step process: first creating a journal receiver, then creating the journal itself.

Use the CRTJRNRCV (Create Journal Receiver) command to create a journal receiver (of any name) in a library of your choice. Figure 18.2 shows the CRTJRNRCV prompt screen with appropriate values. Devise a descriptive naming convention for the audit journal receivers (e.g., AUDRCV0001).

FIGURE 18.2
CRTJRNRCV Prompt Screen

```
                    Create Journal Receiver (CRTJRNRCV)

 Type choices, press Enter.

 Journal Receiver  . . . . . . . .   AUDRCV0001     Name
   Library  . . . . . . . . . . .     AUDLIB       Name, *CURLIB
 Auxilliary storage pool ID  . . .   *LIBASP        1-16, *LIBASP
 Journal receiver threshold  . . .   *NONE          1-1919999, *NONE
 Text 'description'  . . . . . . .   Security Audit Journal Receiver




                                                                        Bottom
 F3=Exit     F4=Prompt     F5=Refresh     F10=Additional parameters    F12=Cancel
 F13=How to use this display           F24=More keys
```

Next, you use the CRTJRN (Create Journal) command to create the QSYS/QAUDJRN journal. Figure 18.3 is an example of the CRTJRN prompt screen with appropriate sample values.

FIGURE 18.3
Sample CRTJRN Prompt Screen

```
                         Create Journal (CRTJRN)

 Type choices, press Enter.

 Journal  . . . . . . . . . . . . . JRN
   Library  . . . . . . . . . . .                   *CURLIB
 Journal receiver . . . . . . . . . JRNRCV         _____
   Library  . . . . . . . . . . .                   *LIBL
                                                    *LIBL
 Auxiliary storage pool ID  . . . . ASP             *LIBASP
 Journal threshold msgq . . . . . . MSGQ            QSYSOPR
   Library  . . . . . . . . . . .                   *LIBL
 Manage receivers . . . . . . . . . MNGRCV          *USER
 Delete receivers . . . . . . . . . DLTRCV          *NO
 Receiver size options  . . . . . . RCVSIZOPT       *NONE
 Text 'description' . . . . . . . . TEXT            *BLANK

                                                                  More...

                         Additional Parameters

 Authority  . . . . . . . . . . . . AUT             *LIBCRTAUT




                                                                  Bottom
 F3=Exit    F4=Prompt   F5=Refresh   F12=Cancel   F13=How to use this display
 F24=More keys
```

You associate the journal with the journal receiver you created in the previous step. You can't create a journal without associating a journal receiver with it. This journal and the associated receiver function exactly like a normal database journal and receiver except that OS/400 automatically uses this journal for specific entries instead of your assigning the journal to one or more physical database files. For more information about journals and managing journals and receivers, see *OS/400 Backup and Recovery* (SC41-5304).

> **Technical Note**
> When you get ready to turn on event auditing, object auditing, or both, don't forget to activate auditing using system value QAUDCTL. You must create the security audit journal (QSYS/QAUDJRN) before starting the audit process.

Auditing Controls

When you create a user profile (see Chapter 3), you notice the *AUDIT special authority. *AUDIT special authority is required for any user who will manage AS/400 auditing (e.g., change auditing-related system values, modify auditing-related attributes on user profiles and/or objects, create and use the security audit journal).

Recall from Chapter 2 that the system value QAUDCTL (Auditing Control) turns OS/400 security auditing on or off. The default value *NONE indicates that you don't want to perform any security auditing. Entering the value *AUDLVL and/or *OBJAUD tells OS/400 to perform auditing. *AUDLVL activates event auditing by system or by user. (More about this in the "System-wide Auditing" and "User Auditing" sections later in this chapter.) *OBJAUD activates object auditing (more about this in "Object Auditing" later in this chapter). Specifying *NOQTEMP along with *OBJAUD or *AUDLVL tells OS/400 not to log most audit entries for actions against objects in QTEMP. Using the *NOQTEMP value removes many extraneous entries, leaving entries that you really care about.

Also recall from Chapter 2 that the system value QAUDFRCLVL (Auditing Force Level) determines the maximum number of audit records the system will cache before forcing them to disk. You can specify any number from 1 to 100, or you can specify *SYS to let OS/400 dynamically control this number for performance purposes. Be aware that if you've specified *SYS and a system failure occurs, you may lose audit records not yet written to disk. Thus, systems that require DoD Level C2 compliance should specify 1 for this system value. However, for all other systems, we recommend the value *SYS to maximize performance when auditing.

As we discussed briefly in Chapter 2, the system value QAUDENDACN (Auditing End Action) determines the action the system should take when it's unable to continue auditing (i.e., the system can't write another audit record to the journal). The default value *NOTIFY causes OS/400 to send a message to the system operator while the AS/400 continues processing; the system also sends the message to QSYS/QSYSMSG if this message queue exists.

Specifying *PWRDWNSYS as the value for QAUDENDACN instructs the system to power down immediately. The power down is similar to a "force power off," so the rebuild process after the next IPL will be lengthy. In addition, the next IPL returns the system in a restricted state, and a user profile with *ALLOBJ and *AUDIT authority must sign on to the system to restore auditing before the system can be restarted. As you can plainly see, the *PWRDWNSYS value is not recommended for the normal AS/400 shop; however, for those requiring strict auditing compliance, it's the only way to ensure that no auditing entries are lost.

Both *NOTIFY and *PWRDWNSYS trigger an automatic change to *NONE in the QAUDCTL system value as soon as the system executes the *NOTIFY or *PWRDWNSYS option. This means that auditing is turned off. You must turn it back on manually after correcting the problem that prevented the system from writing to the journal.

System-wide Auditing

As we mentioned earlier, the QAUDLVL system value determines the level of system-wide event auditing. Table 18.1 lists the possible values for QAUDLVL; you can specify one or more of these values.

TABLE 18.1
Possible Values for QAUDLVL System Value

Value	Description
*NONE	No auditing occurs on the system.
*AUTFAIL	Audit authority failures (e.g., user doesn't have authority to open file, user doesn't have authority to execute a program).
*CREATE	Audit object-creation operations.
*DELETE	Audit object-deletion operations.
*JOBDTA	Audit job start and end.
*NETCMN	Audit violations detected by the APPN filter. This is important if you're using APPN filtering support because it acts as a log for users who are attempting to access your system.
*OBJMGT	Audit object-management operations (e.g., move or rename an object).
*PGMADP	Log a journal entry each time someone uses authorities adopted from a program.

Let's look more closely at some of the most important QAUDLVL values.

First, we recommend that you include *AUTFAIL. *AUTFAIL instructs the system to audit events relating to insufficient authorities — events such as a user entering an incorrect user ID or password or a user trying to access an object with authorities he or she doesn't have. This type of auditing is useful in determining whether you have frequent attempts to gain access to specific user profiles without the correct password (i.e., is someone trying to guess a password?). This value is also useful in determining whether you've properly assessed which authorities are required for users on your system. A high number of entries probably means that you're getting frequent phone calls from unhappy users complaining they don't have enough authority. You can track which objects they're trying to access and correct either their procedures or your implementation.

The *CREATE and *DELETE values fall into a similar category. Is it important for you to know who places new objects on your system? Is it important to know which objects are deleted?

*CREATE instructs the system to create a journal entry each time someone creates (e.g., compiles, duplicates) a new object on your system, including new objects that simply replace objects already on the system. (Note that it excludes any new objects created in library QTEMP because those objects are temporary.) Knowing about new objects on your system can be helpful for managing programming activities as well as for preventing someone from placing programs on your system that might pose a security threat. You may want to add *CREATE to QAUDLVL only periodically (e.g., once a month or bimonthly) for spot-checking, during specific timeframes when you use outside consultants, or in other situations that increase your security exposure.

We recommend that you use *DELETE periodically as well. You may find it helpful because you rarely delete objects from your system except as part of a development project. You may catch mistakes or find unusual activities when you audit these *DELETE entries.

If you want to audit who submits and works with batch jobs, specify *JOBDTA as a QAUDLVL value. OS/400 will then audit job submissions, changes, and cancellations. However, using this audit value may cause numerous journal entries, so you should use it only occasionally for spot-checking.

*OBJMGT lets you keep track of users who perform operations such as moving or renaming an object. Specifying this value lets you spot users who might try to create a duplicate program or copy a master file and hide it by moving it into a private library or directory.

*PGMADP is another key audit value you may want to specify. You can use this value to log a journal entry each time someone uses authorities adopted from a program. Note, however, that OS/400 generates a journal entry only when you use adopted authority.

User Auditing

User auditing is relatively new to OS/400. Before V2R3, you could piece together a minimal audit trail of a user's activity from the history log, the system-wide security-audit–journal entries discussed above, and job logs (if you have them), but this method left far too much room for unaudited actions, especially for knowledgeable people with sufficient authorities to cover their own trail. With V2R3, IBM added two attributes to the user profile, AUDLVL (Audit Level) and OBJAUD (Object Auditing), that provide the ability to effectively audit at a user profile level. When you view the prompt for the CRTUSRPRF (Create User Profile) command or the CHGUSRPRF (Change User Profile) command, you see neither of these attribute parameters because IBM deliberately offers a separate command, the CHGUSRAUD (Change User Auditing) command, to maintain these user profile options. This approach allows the separation of security duties from auditing duties.

The AUDLVL attribute associated with a user profile is similar to the QAUDLVL system value in that it controls the type of security-related events the system audit journal will monitor. However, there are two primary differences. First, the actions you specify in the AUDLVL user profile attribute apply to that particular user only, letting you control how much auditing to perform for each user. Second, there are a few QAUDLVL values for AUDLVL that you cannot specify, and there is one significant value that you can specify only for an individual user's AUDLVL. Table 18.2 lists all the possible values for both QAUDLVL and the AUDLVL user profile attribute. Note that many of the values available for QAUDLVL are also available for the AUDLVL user profile attribute. This lets you specify those values at a user level instead of a system-wide level when appropriate.

TABLE 18.2
QAUDLVL and AUDLVL Values

Value	Description	System value QAUDLVL	User profile AUDLVL
*NONE	No actions audited at system level	Yes	Yes
*AUTFAIL	Authority failure events	Yes	No
*CMD	Commands	No	Yes
*CREATE	Object create operations	Yes	Yes
*DELETE	Object delete operations	Yes	Yes
*JOBDTA	Actions that affect a job	Yes	Yes
*NETCMN	APPN filtering violations	Yes	No
*OBJMGT	Object move and rename operations	Yes	Yes
*OFCSRV	Changes to the system distribution directory and office mail actions	Yes	Yes
*OPTICAL	Optical functions	Yes	Yes

The primary eye-catcher in Table 18.2 is the *CMD value, which is available only for the user profile AUDLVL attribute. *CMD lets you audit every command (including OS/400 and CL commands and S36E procedures, CL statements, and operator control commands) that a user executes. This is an excellent tool for spot-auditing users with *ALLOBJ special authority, consultants, and vendors who dial in and perform some unknown tasks. But keep in mind that this level of auditing is for spot-checking and not intended for use with every user profile every minute of the day. Can you imagine the size of the audit journal each day if you audited every command that users executed? You'd soon need that near-line storage system!

Object Auditing

OS/400's object auditing lets you track which objects a particular user accesses or which users access a particular object. You use the OBJAUD attribute associated with a user profile to track the former and the OBJAUD attribute associated with the object description to track the latter. The OBJAUD user profile attribute has direct control over the auditing of a user's successful access to objects. The OBJAUD value for an object and the OBJAUD value for a user profile work together to provide OS/400 object auditing.

Two types of events trigger an audit entry for object auditing: using an object and changing an object. Table 18.3 lists the read and change operations that can be audited for all objects and operations that can't be audited.

Table 18.3
OBJAUD Values

Object OBJAUD	User profile OBJAUD		
	*NONE	*CHANGE	*ALL
*NONE	None	None	None
*CHANGE	Change	Change	Change
*ALL	Change/Use	Change/Use	Change/Use
*USRPRF	None	Change	Change/Use

To trigger object auditing at the user profile level, you use the CHGUSRAUD command (Figure 18.4) and specify either *NONE, *CHANGE, or *ALL for the OBJAUD parameter. Entering *NONE activates no object auditing for that user. Entering *CHANGE tells OS/400 to audit only changes to an object. Entering *ALL tells OS/400 to audit any access (read or change) to an object for that user. Keep in mind that this applies to any object for a particular user.

Figure 18.4
CHGUSRAUD Prompt Screen

```
                    Change User Auditing (CHGUSRAUD)

 Type choices, press Enter.

 User profile . . . . . . . . . .   USRPRF
                            + for more values
 Object auditing value  . . . . .   OBJAUD         *SAME
 User action auditing . . . . . .   AUDLVL         *SAME
                            + for more values
```

You use the CHGOBJAUD (Change Object Auditing) command to change the object-access auditing control for one or more objects on the system. Figure 18.5 shows the prompt screen. You can enter the same values discussed above for the user profile OBJAUD attribute as well as the value *USRPRF, which tells OS/400 to refer to the OBJAUD attribute of the user profile to determine the auditing to perform.

FIGURE 18.5
CHGOBJAUD Prompt Screen

```
                    Change Object Auditing (CHGOBJAUD)

 Type choices, press Enter.

 Object . . . . . . . . . . . . . OBJ
   Library  . . . . . . . . . . .                 *LIBL
 Object type  . . . . . . . . . . OBJTYPE
 Object auditing value  . . . . . OBJAUD
```

The relationship between the object OBJAUD attribute and the user profile OBJAUD attribute is the key to understanding the control of object auditing on your system. You must remember one fundamental rule: The OBJAUD value for an object takes precedence over the OBJAUD value of a user profile. This means that when you specify *NONE for the object OBJAUD attribute, OS/400 does not audit that object, regardless of the OBJAUD attribute on a user profile. If you specify *CHANGE or *ALL for the object OBJAUD attribute, OS/400 performs that auditing, regardless of the value of OBJAUD on the user profile. OS/400 uses the user profile OBJAUD value only when you specify *USRPRF as the value for the object OBJAUD attribute.

The implications of this rule are simple. To implement any form of user-oriented auditing for access to objects (i.e., auditing for a specific user's access to objects), you must first specify OBJAUD(*USRPRF) for the objects you want to audit and then specify either OBJAUD(*CHANGE) or OBJAUD(*ALL) for that user profile. If you want to audit specific access to one or more objects regardless of which user profile is accessing the objects, you simply modify the OBJAUD attribute of the objects with no regard to the OBJAUD attribute of any user profiles. Figure 18.6 summarizes your options as you use system value QAUDCTL to control your auditing implementation.

For new objects, the system value QCRTOBJAUD (Create Object Auditing) and the library attribute CRTOBJAUD (Create Object Auditing) together determine the default object-auditing level. QCRTOBJAUD works much like the QCRTAUT system value, which determines the default public authorities for new objects. When you create a new object, OS/400 checks the CRTOBJAUD attribute for the library in which the new object will reside. If this value is *SYSVAL, OS/400 refers to QCRTOBJAUD to determine which object-auditing value (*NONE, *CHANGE, *ALL, or *USRPRF) to assign to the OBJAUD attribute of the new object. When you load OS/400, *SYSVAL is assigned as the default value for the CRTOBJAUD attribute for every library on your system. This means that you could control the object-auditing level for every new object on your system using the QCRTOBJAUD system value. However, for any existing objects, you must use the CHGOBJAUD command to change the OBJAUD value.

FIGURE 18.6
System Value QAUDCTL Options

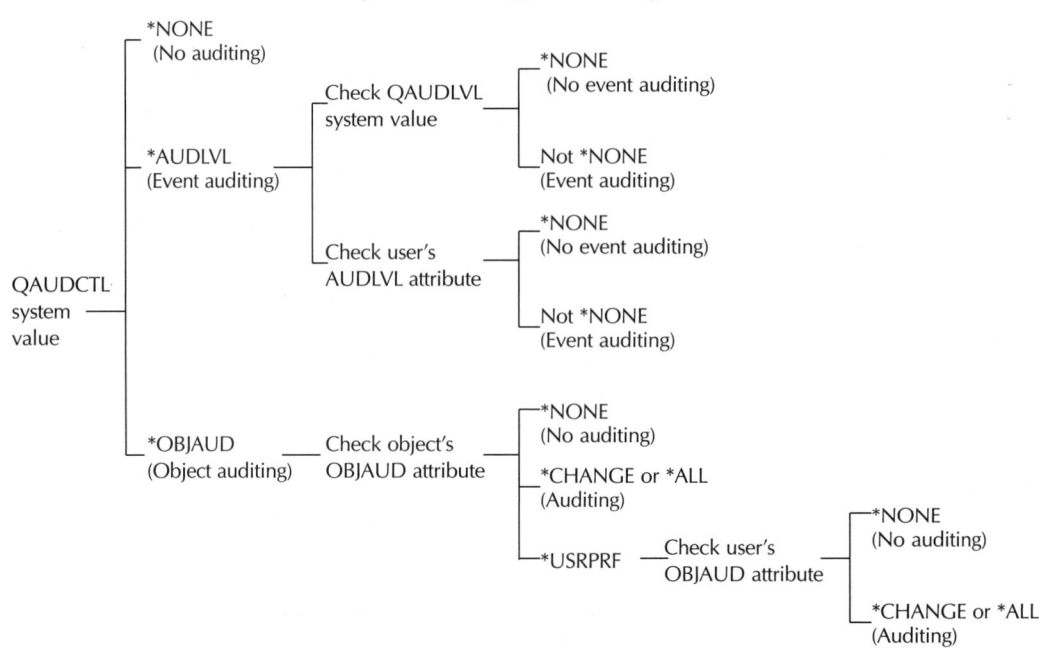

```
QAUDCTL          ┌── *NONE
system              (No auditing)
value
                 ├── *AUDLVL ──┬── Check QAUDLVL ──┬── *NONE
                    (Event         system value        (No event auditing)
                    auditing)                      └── Not *NONE
                                                       (Event auditing)
                                 └── Check user's ──┬── *NONE
                                     AUDLVL attribute   (No event auditing)
                                                   └── Not *NONE
                                                       (Event auditing)

                 └── *OBJAUD ── Check object's ──┬── *NONE
                    (Object       OBJAUD attribute   (No auditing)
                    auditing)                    ├── *CHANGE or *ALL
                                                 │    (Auditing)
                                                 └── *USRPRF ── Check user's ──┬── *NONE
                                                                OBJAUD attribute   (No auditing)
                                                                              └── *CHANGE or *ALL
                                                                                   (Auditing)
```

Note that you can specify *ALL for the OBJ keyword on the CHGOBJAUD command; however, you should execute the command using OBJ(*ALL) only when your system is in a dedicated mode to prevent interruptions to this process and to ensure that the system encounters no object-lock problems when attempting to change the attribute for all objects.

Event-Auditing Recommendations

Technology is generally worthless if you don't use it properly, and this maxim holds true for the auditing technologies now available on the AS/400. It's important that you apply the audit features correctly to audit your system effectively. The following is our list of recommendations concerning the use of the OS/400 auditing functions.

Auditing Controls Security Recommendations

- Set QAUDCTL to the value (*OBJAUD *AUDLVL) so you can perform both types of auditing.
- Leave both QAUDFRCLVL and QAUDENDACN at their default values of *SYS and *NOTIFY, respectively, unless you must comply with DoD Level C2.

System and User Event-Auditing Security Recommendations

- Start with only one or a small set of system-wide event-auditing values in the QAUDLVL system value. The most significant of these at the system level are *AUTFAIL, *PGMFAIL, and *SAVRST. However, there's one caution concerning the use of *PGMFAIL. Unless you're running at level 40 or level 50 security, when you first specify *PGMFAIL, watch the journal closely to see whether any of your programs are generating many of these entries. If you own a third-party utility package for file editing, documentation, or similar tasks, you may find that the vendor didn't rewrite the package to run at level 40 security, thereby leaving you with a high number of *PGMFAIL entries. You may want to turn off *PGMFAIL until those issues are resolved to avoid performance- and storage-related concerns.

- Use the AUDLVL attribute at a user profile level only to spot-check users you have concerns about and also to monitor the actions of QSECOFR, vendor user profiles, or other profiles that might have a large number of authorities on the system.

General Recommendations

- Set the QCRTOBJAUD system value to *USRPRF to assign this value for all new objects on the system.

- Use the CHGOBJAUD command to set the OBJAUD value to *USRPRF for all objects already on the system (remember to do this in a dedicated mode). This gives you maximum flexibility to easily switch between object-focused or user-profile–focused auditing for sets of objects or a particular user. When you want to audit a particular object or set of objects for every user access, use the CHGOBJAUD command to change only those objects to *CHANGE or *ALL. Audit only a small group of objects at a time to control overhead.

- With all objects using OBJAUD(*USRPRF), you can spot-check specific user profiles at will by modifying the OBJAUD attribute on the user profile to *CHANGE or *ALL. Audit only a small group of users at a time.

Working with the Audit Journal

Once you begin using the audit journal, the next step is to examine the audit-journal entries regularly for specific events, trends, or possible security exposures. The remainder of this chapter provides the information you need to accomplish this task. First we look at what a journal entry is and how security information is presented as a journal entry. Then we discuss how to display or print the journal entries.

Understanding Journal Entry Formats

All journal entries have common fields (e.g., date, time, journal sequence number, entry type, job name) followed by data specific to the type of entry. Table 18.4 lists the standard fields you'll find in every security-audit–journal entry. This new layout enables the audit journal entries for the year 2000.

Table 18.4
Standard Journal Entry Fields

Field	Definition	Description
Entry length	5S 0	Total length of journal entry
Sequence number	10S 0	Sequence number of entry
Journal code	1A	Always T or J
Entry type	2A	Security entry type
Date of entry	6A	System date of entry
Time of entry	6S 0	System time of entry
Timestamp	26A	Date and time of entry (replaces Date of entry and Time of entry fields)
Job name	10A	Name of job that caused the entry
User name	10A	Name of job user profile
Job number	6S 0	Job number
Program name	10A	Name of the program that made the entry
Object name	10A	Name of the object
Library name	10A	Name of the library the object is in
Member name	10A	Name of the member (if a file)
Count/RRN	10S 0	Change of count or relative record number
Flag	1A	Flag byte: 1 or 0
Commit cycle ID	10S 0	Commit cycle identifier
User profile	10A	Name of current user profile
System name	8A	AS/400 system name
Reserved	10A[1]	Not used
Referential constraint	1A	Not used for audit journal entries
Trigger	1A	Not used for audit journal entries
Reserved	8A	Not used for audit journal entries
Null value indicators	50A	Not used for audit journal entries
Entry-specific data length	Bin(4)	Length of entry-specific data

[1] Before V3R2 and V3R7, defined as 20A

Notice the field named "Entry type." Each journal entry type is identified with a two-character "entry type," and 68 types of journal entries are possible in QAUDJRN. Table 18.5 lists all 68 journal entry types. Each event action that you might audit (e.g., *AUTFAIL, *CMD, *SECURITY) using the QAUDLVL system value, user-action auditing, or object-access auditing has one or more entry types that OS/400 creates when adding a journal entry for those events. Appendix B provides a complete listing of each auditing action (e.g., *AUTFAIL, *CMD, *SECURITY) and the corresponding entry types that you can expect in the audit journal.

TABLE 18.5
Auditing Journal Entry Types

Entry type	Description
AD	Auditing changes
AF	Authority failure
AP	Obtaining adopted authority
CA	Authority changes
CD	Command string audit
CO	Create object
CP	User profile changed, created, or restored
CQ	Change of *CRQD object
CU	Cluster operations
CV	Connection verification
DO	Delete object
DS	DST security password reset
EV	System environment variables
GR	Generic records
GS	Give descriptor
IP	Interprocess communication
IR	Actions on IP rules
IS	Internet security management
JD	Change to user parameter of a job description
JS	Actions that affect jobs
KF	Key ring file
LD	Link, unlink, or look up directory entry
ML	Office services mail actions
NA	Network attribute changed
ND	APPN directory search filter violation
NE	APPN endpoint filter violation
OM	Object move or rename
OR	Object restore
OW	Object ownership changed
O1	(Optical Access) Single file or directory
O2	(Optical Access) Dual file or directory
O3	(Optical Access) Volume
PA	Program changed to adopt authority
PG	Change of an object's primary group
PO	Printed output
PS	Profile swap
PW	Invalid password

continued

Table 18.5 Continued

Entry type	Description
RA	Authority change during restore
RJ	Restoring job description with user profile specified
RO	Change of object owner during restore
RP	Restoring adopted authority program
RQ	Restoring a *CRQD object
RU	Restoring user profile authority
RZ	Changing a primary group during restore
SD	Changes to system distribution directory
SE	Subsystem routing entry changed
SF	Actions to spooled files
SG	Asynchronous signals processed
SK	Secure sockets connections
SM	System management changes
SO	Server security user information actions
ST	Use of System Service Tools
SV	System value changed
VA	Changing an access control list
VC	Starting or ending a connection
VF	Closing server files
VL	Account limit exceeded
VN	Logging on and off the network
VO	Validation list actions
VP	Network password error
VR	Network resource access
VS	Starting or ending a server session
VU	Changing a network profile
VV	Changing service status
YC	DLO object accessed (change)
YR	DLO object accessed (read)
ZC	Object accessed (change)
ZR	Object accessed (read)

Displaying and Printing the Audit Journal Entries

You can display or print QAUDJRN's contents by using the DSPJRN (Display Journal) or DSPAUDJRNE (Display Audit Journal Entries) command.

Using the DSPJRN Command to Display Entries

To view journal entries using DSPJRN, enter the command

`DSPJRN QAUDJRN`

This generates a screen like that in Figure 18.7.

FIGURE 18.7
Sample DSPJRN Screen

```
                       Display Journal Entries
    Journal . . . . . :  QAUDJRN        Library . . . . . :  QSYS

    Type options, press Enter.
      5=Display entire entry

    Opt     Sequence   Code  Type   Object    Library   Job        Time
            12003      T     PW                         QINTER     09:10:05
     5      12004      T     PW                         QINTER     09:15:36
            12005      T     AF                         DSP12      10:34:48
            12006      T     AF                         DSP24      11:56:21
            12007      T     AF                         DSP12      12:21:12
            12008      J     PR                         DSP32      12:02:52
            12009      T     SV                         DSP21      12:03:44
            12010      T     DO                         DSP01      12:04:25
            12011      T     NA                         DSP23      12:05:52
            12012      T     NA                         DSP01      12:05:59




    F3=Exit    F12=Cancel
```

Typing 5 in front of an entry gives you a detail screen similar to the one in Figure 18.8.

You can use parameters on the DSPJRN command to select only specific entry types or narrow your search based on a specific time period, job, or — in some cases — user profile. If you become familiar with the 17 entry codes and don't mind looking at several screens to research the entries, this method may appeal to you. However, this option does not give you any practical method of making the information available to another person and is time consuming.

FIGURE 18.8
Sample Journal Entry Detail Screen

```
                        Display Journal Entry
     Journal  . . . . . . :   QAUDJRN       Library . . . . . . :   QSYS
     Sequence . . . . . . :   12004

     Code . . . . . . . . :   T - Audit trail entry
     Type . . . . . . . . :   PW - Invalid password or user ID

     Object . . . . . . . :                 Library . . . . . . :
     Member . . . . . . . :

     Position to  . . . . .                 (Column)

              Entry specific data
     Column        *...+...1...+...2...+...3...+...4...+...5
     0001          'OESDER     DSP08                                 '
     0002          ' '

                                                                  Bottom
     Press Enter to continue.

     F3=Exit   F6=Display only entry specific data
     F10=Display only entry details   F12=Cancel   F24=More keys
```

Using the DSPJRN Command to Print Entries

Another option is to first use the DSPJRN command to output entries to a database file and then print those entries using a high-level language (HLL) program (e.g., RPG IV, Cobol) or a query tool. Although the DSPJRN command does have parameters that enable certain selection criteria, using this two-step process lets you use additional selection logic as well as create any form of custom output.

You can use the DSPJRN command to generate two different types of database files. The first type of database file is the standard audit–journal-entry output file. If you enter the command

```
DSPJRN  JRN(QSYS/QAUDJRN)         +
        ENTTYP(*ALL)              +
        OUTPUT(*OUTFILE)          +
        OUTFILFMT(*TYPE4)         +
        OUTFILE(QTEMP/AUDFILE)
```

OS/400 creates the file AUDFILE using record format QJORDJE4. You can obtain the external field names and descriptions using the DSPFFD (Display File Field Descriptions) command. The first 223 bytes of this record format conform to the field listing presented earlier in Table 18.4. The information in the rest of the record format is specific data relating to each record's entry type. The actual length will vary based on the "entry type" field.

In the above example, the OUTFILFMT(*TYPE4) parameter instructs OS/400 to use the QJORDJE4 record format. This particular format, as opposed to *TYPE1 or *TYPE2, includes a field that identifies the specific user profile associated with the journal entry as well as a 26-byte timestamp, providing support for the year 2000. Thus, it's important to use the *TYPE4 format for auditing purposes to make the profile information available and to accommodate the year 2000 and beyond.

> **Technical Note**
> Take special notice of parameter OUTFILFMT (Output File Format), which allows a value of *TYPE1, *TYPE2, or *TYPE4. Using *TYPE4 guarantees that when the journal entries are converted (journal entries are actually messages and must be converted to a physical record format), they will contain the user profile field and support for the year 2000. *TYPE1 allows the entries to be converted without the user profile field. *TYPE2 has the user profile field but does not accommodate the year 2000.

After you create this file, you can then write programs to display and/or print specific entry information. Program PRTAUDJRN in Figure 18.9 prints a sample audit report.

FIGURE 18.9
RPG Program PRTAUDJRN to Print Audit Journal

```
*...1....+....2....+....3....+....4....+....5....+....6....+....7

 *==========================================================*
 *  Program:  PRTAUDJRN                                      *
 *  Purpose:  Print audit journal general information        *
 *            from outfile generated by DSPJRN command.      *
 *            The format is QJORDJE4 - FILFMT(*TYPE4)        *
 *==========================================================*
 * Outfile generated for DSPJRN command (general format).
FAUDFILE IF  E                    DISK
 *
FQPRINT  O   F    132    OF       PRINTER
 *
C                   EXCPTHDG
 *
C                   READ AUDJRNF                          99
C                   MOVE JODATE      DATESV  6
 *
C           *IN99   DOWEQ'0'
 *
C           JODATE  IFNE DATESV
C                   EXCPTSPACE
C                   MOVE JODATE      DATESV
C                   ENDIF
 *
C           JONBR   IFNE 0
C                   MOVE *BLANKS     JOBNAM 28
C                   MOVE JONBR       JONBRC  6
C           JONBRC  CAT  '/':0       JOBNAM
```

continued

FIGURE 18.9 CONTINUED

```
*...1....+....2....+....3....+....4....+....5....+....6....+....7
C           JOBNAM    CAT  JOUSER:0   JOBNAM
C           JOBNAM    CAT  '/':0      JOBNAM
C           JOBNAM    CAT  JOJOB:0    JOBNAM
C                     ENDIF
 *
C                     MOVE JODATE     JOD       60
 *
C    OF              EXCPTHDG
C                    EXCPTDTL
 *
C                    READ AUDJRNF                         99
C                    ENDDO
 *
C                    MOVE *ON         *INLR
C                    RETRN
 *
OQPRINT  E  204          HDG
O                        UDATE Y
O                                  +10 'Audit Journal Report -'
O                                      'General Information'
O        E   1           HDG
O                                   4 'Jrnl'
O                                  11 'Entry'
O        E   2           HDG
O                                   4 'Code'
O                                  10 'Type'
O                                  18 'Date'
O                                  28 'Time'
O                                  40 'Job name'
O                                  69 'Program'
O                                  80 'Object'
O                                  93 'Library'
O                                 104 'Member'
O                                 122 'User Profile'
 *
O        E   1           DTL
O                        JOCODE     2
O                        JOENTT     9
O                        JOD    Y  20
O                        JOTIME    30 '  :  :  '
O                        JOBNAM    60
O                        JOPGM     72
O                        JOOBJ     84
O                        JOLIB     96
O                        JOMBR    108
O                        JOUSPF   120
 *
O        E   1           SPACE
```

You can customize this type of program to provide selection criteria for your own reports. However, you must remember that the QJORDJE4 format (which program PRTAUDJRN uses in the AUDFILE file) maps only the basic entry information into fields.

To extract the detailed audit data that exists after offset 224 of record format QJORDJE4, you need another technique that generates the second type of database file available for the DSPJRN command — the entry-specific database file. For each audit journal entry type, there is a model database file in library QSYS whose record format maps the entire journal entry into a physical record format. Table 18.6 lists these model files. Using your knowledge of these formats, you can generate an output file for a particular type of entry and then use an HLL program or a query tool to perform reporting.

TABLE 18.6
Model Files for Audit Journal Entry Types

Entry type	*TYPE2 (Model file name)	*TYPE4	Description
AD	QASYADJE	QASYADJ4	Auditing changes
AF	QASYAFJE	QASYAFJ4	Authority violation
AP	QASYAPJE	QASYAPJ4	Obtaining adopted authority
CA	QASYCAJE	QASYCAJ4	Authority changes
CD	QASYCDJE	QASYCDJ4	Command string audit
CO	QASYCOJE	QASYCOJ4	Create object
CP	QASYCPJE	QASYCPJ4	User profile changed, created, or restored
CQ	QASYCQJE	QASYCQJ4	Change of a *CRQD object
CU		QASYCUJ4	Cluster operations
CV		QASYCFJ4	Connection verification
DO	QASYDOJE	QASYDOJ4	Delete object
DS	QASYDSJE	QASYDSJ4	Reset DST security password
EV		QASYEVJ4	Environment variable entries
GR		QASYGRJ4	Generic records
GS	QASYGSJE	QASYGSJ4	Give descriptor
IP	QASYIPJE	QASYIPJ4	Authority failure for an IPC request
IR		QASYIRJ4	Actions on IP rules
IS		QASYISJ4	Internet security management
JD	QASYJDJE	QASYJDJ4	Job description change to user name
JS	QASYJSJE	QASYJSJ4	Actions that affect jobs
KF		QASYKFJ4	Key ring file actions
LD	QASYLDJE	QASYLDJ4	Link, unlink, or look up a directory entry
ML	QASYMLJE	QASYMLJ4	Office services mail actions
NA	QASYNAJE	QASYNAJ4	Network attribute changes
ND	QASYNDJE	QASYNDJ4	APPN filter violation when the Directory search filter is audited

continued

TABLE 18.6 *CONTINUED*

Entry type	Model file name *TYPE2	*TYPE4	Description
NE	QASYNEJE	QASYNEJ4	APPN filter violation when the End point filter is audited
OM	QASYOMJE	QASYOMJ4	Object move or rename
OR	QASYORJE	QASYORJ4	Object restore
OW	QASYOWJE	QASYOWJ4	Ownership change
O1	QASYO1JE	QASYO1J4	Optical data changes
O2	QASYO2JE	QASYO2J4	Optical actions
O3	QASYO3JE	QASYO3J4	Optical volume actions
PA	QASYPAJE	QASYPAJ4	Change program to adopt
PG	QASYPGJE	QASYPGJ4	Change object's primary group
PO	QASYPOJE	QASYPOJ4	Output of print file
PS	QASYPSJE	QASYPSJ4	Swap user profile
PW	QASYPWJE	QASYPWJ4	Invalid password on sign-on attempt
RA	QASYRAJE	QASYRAJ4	Authority change during a restore
RJ	QASYRJJE	QASYRJJ4	Restore of JOBD with user name defined
RO	QASYROJE	QASYROJ4	Restore of object with ownership change
RP	QASYRPJE	QASYRPJ4	Restore of programs that adopt authority
RQ	QASYRQJE	QASYRQJ4	Restore a *CRQD object
RU	QASYRUJE	QASYRUJ4	Restore of authority for user
RZ	QASYRZJE	QASYRZJ4	Restore of object with change in primary group
SD	QASYSDJE	QASYSDJ4	Change to system distribution directory
SE	QASYSEJE	QASYSEJ4	Routing entry changed
SF	QASYSFJE	QASYSFJ4	Actions (e.g., hold, release) to a spooled file
SG		QASYSGJ4	Asynchronous signals processed
SK		QASYSKJ4	Secure sockets connections
SM	QASYSMJE	QASYSMJ4	System management changes
SO		QASYSOJ4	Changing security object entries
ST	QASYSTJE	QASYSTJ4	Use of System Services Tools
SV	QASYSVJE	QASYSVJ4	System value changes
VA	QASYVAJE	QASYVAJ4	Changing an access control list
VC	QASYVCJE	QASYVCJ4	Starting or ending a connection
VF	QASYVFJE	QASYVFJ4	Closing server files
VL	QASYVLJE	QASYVLJ4	Account limit exceeded
VN	QASYVNJE	QASYVNJ4	Logging on and off the network
VO		QASYVOJ4	Validation list actions
VP	QASYVPJE	QASYVPJ4	Network password error

continued

TABLE 18.6 *Continued*

Entry type	Model file name *TYPE2	*TYPE4	Description
VR	QASYVRJE	QASYVRJ4	Network resource access
VS	QASYVSJE	QASYVSJ4	Starting or ending a server session
VU	QASYVUJE	QASYVUJ4	Changing a network profile
VV	QASYVVJE	QASYVVJ4	Changing service status
YC	QASYYCJE	QASYYCJ4	Document library was changed
YD	QASYYDJE	QASYYDJ4	DLO object accessed (change)
YR	QASYYRJE	QASYYRJ4	DLO object accessed (read)
ZC	QASYZCJE	QASYZCJ4	Object accessed (change)
ZR	QASYZRJE	QASYZRJ4	Object accessed (read)

> **Technical Note**
>
> As of V4R2, IBM is providing only *TYPE4 formats for new audit entries. In addition, updates to existing audit entries will occur only in the *TYPE4 format.

If you enter the command

```
DSPJRN  JRN(QSYS/QAUDJRN)           +
        FROMTIME(120194 080000)     +
        TOTIME(120494 220000)       +
        ENTTYP(AF)                  +
        OUTPUT(*OUTFILE)            +
        OUTFILFMT(*TYPE4)           +
        OUTFILE(QTEMP/AUDAFFILE)
```

OS/400 places in file AUDAFFILE all the journal entries of type AF that were created for the time period found in the FROMTIME and TOTIME parameters. The ability to generate specific files for specific audit entry types aids the auditing task by letting you focus on particular entry types that are relevant to your situation. For example, if you want to audit the commands a particular user (such as a consultant) enters, you can activate *CMD auditing for that user via the CHGUSRAUD command, then periodically output the entries with type CD to an output file for querying.

Helpful Tools

Auditing security-related events daily is one of the most significant auditing tasks you can perform. Monitoring events as they occur gives you insight into the effectiveness of your security implementation and helps you manage the changes that naturally occur on your system. Listed below are three tools you'll find useful for performing auditing tasks.

Security tool	Description
DSPSECAUD (Display Security Auditing)	Displays or prints a report of the current settings for QAUDCTL and QAUDLVL as well as the journal receiver currently attached to the audit journal
CHGSECAUD (Change Security Auditing)	Lets you set up auditing using one command instead of several
DSPAUDJRNE (Display Audit Journal Entries)	A simplified version of DSPJRN with parameters that pertain only to displaying audit journal entries out of QAUDJRN

Operations Navigator

You can use Operations Navigator (OpsNav) to change the auditing system values. At the OpsNav window, double-click your AS/400, Security, and Policies and then double-click Audit Policy in the right panel. You'll see a screen like the one below, where you can enter auditing system values.

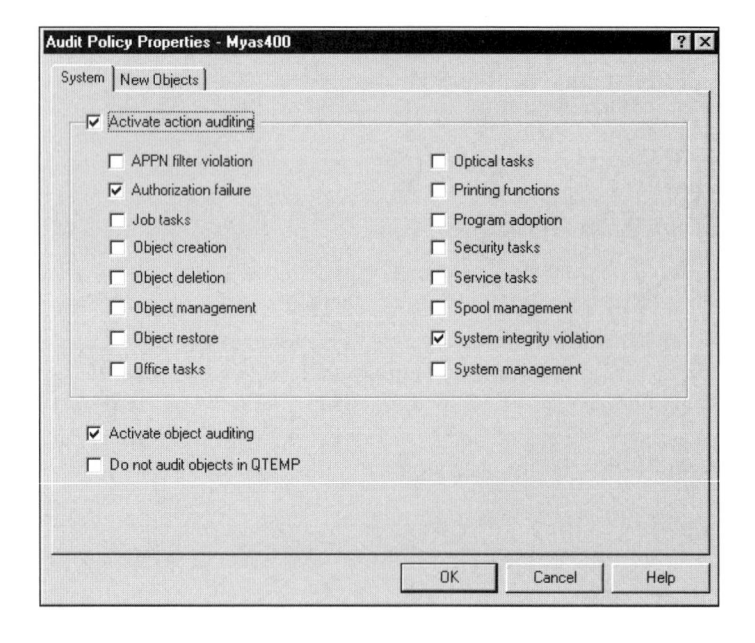

OpsNav also lets you manage the auditing attributes of user profiles. To do this, double-click your AS/400 and then Users and Groups, find the user for which you want to display or change the auditing attributes, and make the appropriate changes.

Technical Note
Although actions taken through Operations Navigator are audited, as are objects accessed through Operations Navigator, Operations Navigator provides no command-string auditing.

Chapter 19

Building a Business Contingency Plan — A Workbook

As we discussed in Chapter 1, contingency planning is the final strategic security issue that you must manage. It involves evaluating your enterprise's business-critical functions and establishing procedures that would minimize the negative effect of a disaster and would ensure that those critical functions can be restored to an acceptable level for the enterprise to survive. This definition contains the building blocks for a good contingency plan: risk analysis, disaster avoidance, emergency procedures, a recovery plan, and testing/auditing the plan. We've organized this chapter and workbook around these building blocks. We say "workbook" because in this chapter, you'll find discussions of concepts, lists of items, worksheets for you to use, and checklists to serve as guidelines. Use them in your organization, and be a part of creating a complete business contingency plan.

Before we discuss the essential building blocks, let's examine a few general thoughts about contingency planning and the leadership required to make it happen.

Have a Purpose

If you already have a contingency plan in your organization, do you know the plan's purpose? Can someone there complete the sentence, "The purpose of our contingency plan is to _____." If no one can complete that sentence, you probably don't have a complete or effective plan. It's essential to produce an accurate statement concerning the exact mission of your contingency plan. Obviously, this mission will vary from organization to organization based on potential risks, available resources, and overall business strategy.

In a one-person consulting business, for instance, your contingency plan might be to have offsite copies of all your records and a tape or CD backup of your PC or AS/400 and then simply to reorder equipment as needed in the event of a disaster. You may need nothing more than that as a plan. However, contingency planning in a larger enterprise has more considerations. When you develop a good statement of purpose for your contingency plan, be sure to

- identify your unique business requirements
- state specific goals
- include statements of responsibility (who will get it done)

Find the Leaders

Unfortunately, many organizations turn to the IT staff for contingency planning. Those organizations are thinking narrowly in terms of IT backup and recovery and are missing the larger effort required. Nevertheless, the assumption that IT handles contingency plans means that you may be the person who must get the ball moving.

First, you must enlist the organization's president or the highest representative at your enterprise location. In other words, you need to involve the person where the "buck stops" — the person who can lose the most financially from some disaster. You should enlist that person in establishing goals, evaluating the risks (potential losses), determining the final scope of the effort (the available money to spend on contingency planning), and approving the plan's implementation. The risk analysis is key to engaging this person. If you can demonstrate that this person will experience significant losses in the event of a disaster without a contingency plan in place (and you'll certainly be able to do this), you'll get his or her attention and support.

Two types of people from the IT area are needed in leadership roles for contingency planning: the company officer responsible for IT operations (the CIO or sometimes the CFO or COO) and the IT manager (this may be one and the same person in some organizations). The former provides the everyday basic leadership for implementing the plan. The latter provides the technical facts required from the IT department and leads in performing the risk analysis for the IT department.

The final group of people you'll need in leadership are the department managers. These individuals are key to providing the necessary information for determining the impact of a potential disaster on your organization's operations and providing leadership for departmental responsibilities in implementing the plan. This may be a hard group to enlist, but you can approach them from two angles. First, if you have the full support of the president (or equal), he or she will give clear signals for managers to give you support. At the same time, you can begin working with those managers with whom you're closest in terms of already having their daily support for IT operations. As they see the necessity for this type of planning, they'll help enlist other managers.

Recognize Reality

As we launch into our discussions of the steps for effective contingency planning, you must grasp several statements of reality. First, a disaster can happen to you! You have to believe this. You may not experience a fire or flood, but you most certainly will experience some type of outage or security breach that constitutes a disaster.

Second, it costs money to be prepared. There is no such thing as a "free" contingency plan. If management thinks the IT department can fully prepare the organization for a disaster cost-free, they're mistaken and you must point that out in some way that gets the message across.

Third, you won't be prepared for absolutely everything. Do a complete analysis, and be prepared for those risks you find.

Finally, you'll probably have to evolve a plan. Rarely can an organization complete a contingency plan all at once. Most plans evolve by engaging one department after another and compiling their ideas into a single, organization-wide plan.

With these thoughts in mind, let's look at the first of the building blocks: risk analysis.

Risk Analysis

"Evaluating your enterprise's business-critical functions" in the definition at the beginning of the chapter describes the process of risk analysis. In performing a risk analysis, you examine which functions are critical or essential to keeping your organization running and the costs of losing those functions. In essence, you examine how much money you'd lose from an outage and whether your organization can survive it.

Identifying Functional Exposures

The first step in performing risk analysis is identifying functional exposures. We classify functional exposures into three categories:

- functions that are absolutely critical to business operations and survival
- functions that are essential to providing management and support for effective operations
- functions that have no immediate impact on the organization but are essential in the long-term picture

Normally, you'll find that the critical functions are functions such as the ability to take orders, the ability to pay employees (they may not be willing to wait for a paycheck, even in a disaster), and customer-service operations. The primary point in common is that each critical function is central to doing daily business; you could absolutely not be without it for even one day.

Before you make the quantum leap into technology here (i.e., what computers and applications your company uses to perform these functions), don't think of these functions in terms of *how* they're done in your organization. Right now, simply identify the most important things.

Next consider the functions that are essential to providing management and support for effective operations. These might include functions such as the ability to pay bills, track inventory, and track daily sales. These functions are by nature not absolutely essential functions but nonetheless are important to the organization and necessary for a smooth-running operation. You can think of these things as secondary in terms of planning and recovery.

The last functions to consider are those that have no immediate impact on the organization but are essential in the long-term picture. These functions include application development and maintenance and general record maintenance (e.g., updating price tables or item descriptions).

Identifying Functional Dependencies

After identifying the functions in your organization and their relative priorities, you should examine the resources these functions depend on — the functional dependencies.

The most obvious types of dependencies for these functions in today's networked and computerized world are IT dependencies. This list includes such items as

- hardware — the actual hardware that works together (servers and clients)
- software applications — applications you've written or bought
- enterprise database — the enterprise data you store and update
- network components — the various technologies and hardware that make up your network (e.g., LANs, WANs, firewall, Internet connections)

After those dependencies, next consider general office dependencies such as

- facilities (the actual office space and fixtures/furniture)
- telephone system (some functions require phone access to and from your customers)
- office equipment (e.g., copiers, fax machines)
- office supplies (e.g., special forms, pencils, paper)

Then consider "hidden" departmental dependencies such as

- location (some departments need access to one another to function)
- flow of information (communication among departments)
- mail
- employees (shared workforce)

Each of these dependencies contributes to the functional exposures you first identified and therefore becomes an essential consideration in your contingency planning.

Identifying Functional Threats

Not all disasters are as catastrophic as a fire or flood. It's important to consider the various forms disasters can take and how each might affect part or all of your organization. You may want to consider the following types of threats:

- General threats
  - catastrophic disaster (loss of entire facility)
  - partial facility loss
  - partial or complete loss of electrical power
  - telephone system loss/line failure
  - loss of employees (e.g., strike or death of a critical person)
- IT threats
  - facility loss
  - hardware failure (CPU or DASD)
  - application failure or corruption
  - data loss or corruption
  - computer virus

- system security breach
- denial-of-service attack
- communications failures

One business Wayne worked for decided to buy a new phone system. The COO didn't involve the IT department in this process and bought and installed a new digital system. After a power loss one day, the operator discovered that the system no longer knew any extensions. The system had been erased, and no one had made a backup copy. You can imagine the havoc this caused while someone rebuilt the system. Something very simple had been overlooked during a change to the business. This is one example of how a small disaster can have a large impact on an organization. Carefully review possible threats as you consider functional exposures and functional dependencies in your organization.

Evaluating Financial Risk — Expenses

Figure 19.1 is fictitious but gives a fairly accurate view, in terms of the general trend, of the dollars you will spend in expenses immediately following some type of disaster. Financial expenses will occur from items such as recovery expenses (e.g., activating the recovery site, travel and meals, consultants), overtime expenses and additional employees, insurance deductibles and noninsured items, and legal fees. This represents real dollars your company will lose beginning on the first hour of the first day of some type of disaster.

FIGURE 19.1
Expenses Immediately Following a Disaster

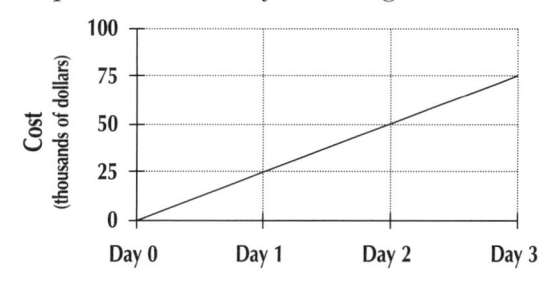

Evaluating Financial Risks — Losses

But wait! There's more bad news. At the same time you're incurring those additional expenses, you're also starting to lose money! Again, Figure 19.2 is fictitious, but the trend is accurate in terms of the dollars you lose following a disaster. Financial losses can occur from productivity losses (i.e., expenses incurred during nonproductive time), production losses (loss of actual value in product and services), loss of sales, and good-faith losses (potential and current customers buying from someone else because they can't reach you or have lost confidence in you during a disaster).

FIGURE 19.2
Evaluating Financial Risks — Losses

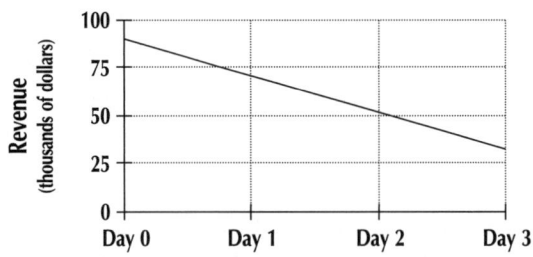

These trends are real and will occur to some degree even with an effective contingency plan in place. However, to ignore them and have no plan is to cede your business to ruin during a disaster. It's important to quantify these financial trends accurately for your organization and then determine — based on them — how much money you'll spend on contingency planning to curb or prevent these losses. The key is to find the right balance between risks and investment in planning.

Identifying Recovery Priorities

Below we examine a practical way to obtain all the risk-analysis information we've been discussing, but first we want to point out that if you do an accurate job with this process, you'll have the benefit of already prioritizing your recovery efforts. Part of a good risk analysis is identifying the key pieces of business to recover first. Many of you may simply believe that you must recover everything before beginning to operate again as a business. This thought process comes primarily from the idea that "everything" is the IT stuff. That isn't true, even in IT. Why recover all data and all programs if the most critical can be done in short order and work can begin while you continue recovery?

If a recovery plan must be implemented because of some disaster, what will be the priorities in the recovery process? Determining priorities is not difficult but is essential in planning recovery. Here are three simple guidelines:

- Priorities must be provided by the management team.
- Priorities should be determined as a result of functional exposures and financial risks.
- Establishing priorities provides the ability to build recovery procedures in order of significance to the overall enterprise.

Getting the Information You Need

Your organization's departmental managers should provide you with the information you need for risk analysis. Using a departmental survey such as the one you find on pages 407–409, interview the managers.

Departmental Survey

Date: _____

Department Name: _____

Contact: _____

What functions must continue in the event of disaster?

_____

_____

_____

_____

What resources would you need to continue those functions?

_____

_____

_____

_____

What would be the impact of losing those functions?

One day: _____

_____

Two days: _____

_____

One week: _____

_____

One month: _____

_____

continued

Departmental Survey...*Continued*

Could your department remain functional in the event of the loss of computer access? Describe the functions that could not be performed or the effect of computer loss on performance over time.

One day: _____

_____

Two days: _____

_____

One week: _____

_____

One month: _____

_____

Do you have any suggested or planned alternative methods for remaining functional in the event of a disaster? If yes, please describe and state how effective you believe these plans are.

_____

_____

Financial Losses

The loss of function in your department would result in what estimated amount of lost sales and revenues (including the ability to collect moneys) over time?

One day: _____

_____ $ _____

Two days: _____

_____ $ _____

One week: _____

_____ $ _____

One month: _____

_____ $ _____

continued

Departmental Survey...*Continued*

The loss of function in your department would result in what estimated amount of lost business due to customer dissatisfaction or loss of service over time?

One day: _____
_____ $ _____

Two days: _____
_____ $ _____

One week: _____
_____ $ _____

One month: _____
_____ $ _____

What are the estimated expenses that would be incurred to remain operational in the event of a disaster (include payroll of personnel who would be employed but might not have a place to work)?

One day: _____
_____ $ _____

Two days: _____
_____ $ _____

One week: _____
_____ $ _____

One month: _____
_____ $ _____

Personnel

What would be the impact if key people were not available after a disaster? Would your department be able to function? Are there others outside of your department who are trained to perform the work of your department?

_____
_____

Sit down with each departmental manager — one on one — and work through this survey. You're looking for functional exposures, functional dependencies, functional threats, and the financial impact a loss of various lengths of time would have on the department. It's important to also understand how this department might function to complete its task during an outage and what the minimum requirements would be to make that happen in both short- and long-term outage scenarios.

When you've completed the surveys, combine the results into a report that serves as your risk analysis. Combine all the financial data in terms of expenses and losses into your own accurate graphs of those numbers. Believe us, you will get someone's attention with those numbers alone. Someone will realize the potential losses of profits and then ask you what your organization can do to minimize these losses. If you don't get buy-in based on your risk analysis, stop — there is no need to continue this process. At this point, you must have the leadership team support or not continue.

Disaster Avoidance

"Establishing procedures that would minimize the negative effect a disaster" in the definition at the beginning of the chapter describes the process of disaster avoidance. There are everyday things you can do to help minimize the effect of a minor or major disaster. These practical steps can save your company money and usually cost very little compared to the potential loss. As you consider the possible threats, you can consider two types of disaster avoidance:

- disaster avoidance through prevention
- disaster avoidance through effects reduction

Avoiding Disaster Through Prevention

There are specific activities you can perform, both IT and non-IT related, that can effectively help avoid certain types of disasters. Below, we look at eight specific areas:

- data center security
- system security
- network security
- fire prevention and natural disaster preparedness
- employee policies
- uninterruptible power supply (UPS)
- records/data-storage options
- preventive maintenance

Data Center Security

As we've stressed throughout this book, you must protect the data center from unauthorized access to prevent vandalism or unintentional harm. You also must protect the data center from dangerous elements such as corrosive chemicals, water, extreme temperatures, flammable substances, and smoke. (Note that the location of the data center in relation to such harmful elements is significant.)

System Security
Similarly, you must protect your system from unauthorized access that might lead to intentional or unintentional damage that causes a loss of productivity.

Network Security
You must protect your communications equipment and your network(s) from access by unauthorized persons.

Fire Prevention and Natural Disaster Preparedness
Fire prevention is both easy to practice and inexpensive. Someone in your organization should ensure that the following tasks are performed:

- Proper heat/smoke detectors and fire sprinkler equipment are installed.
- Regular electrical equipment inspections are conducted.
- Fire-fighting equipment is inspected regularly.
- Paper or other flammable materials are properly stored.
- Proper employee training in fire prevention is conducted regularly.

In addition, your organization should consider having a policy of no smoking except in specified locations to reduce the possibility of fire.

Being prepared for natural disasters requires a little more planning. First, if you don't know already, you should determine which natural disasters are likely to occur in your geographic area. Are tornadoes common? Is there a history of hurricanes? How about earthquakes? Are you located on a flood plain or semi-flood plain?

Once you've analyzed your risk, you can take preventive measures. For instance, in a tornado-prone area, you might put critical operations (e.g., telephone sales) and your IT equipment in the basement of your facility or, at least, in inner office space without any windows. Or, if your facility is on a flood plain, you might put your IT equipment on an upper floor — above the potential water level. Your insurance company can offer other suggestions to minimize the damage from natural disasters — and possibly lower your insurance rates.

Employee Policies
Sudden critical illness or accidental death of an employee is always a tragedy and could be a disaster to the organization if the employee is a critical member of a department or division. With a few additions to your organization's employee policies, you may be able to minimize the effects of such a disaster.

First, you should ensure that the organization has a viable cross-training program for all positions. Such a program provides assurance that a position can be covered in the unhappy event of illness or death. It also provides more flexibility in scheduling vacations.

You might also consider establishing group travel policies. For example, many organizations don't allow members of their senior management team on the same airline flight. Others extend the same policy to include department heads or members of the same department as well as other forms of transportation. For instance, an organization Carol worked for didn't allow critical team members to ride in the same car.

UPS

If a power outage occurs and you don't have a UPS, the time to recover the system (because of rebuilding access paths) could be extensive, causing a significant loss in productivity. Buy a UPS that will guard against lightning, power surges, and unexpected power losses. Program your AS/400 to monitor the UPS to determine whether a system shutdown will be necessary. If it is, automate the shutdown process in case the power outage occurs while the system is unattended.

Records/Data-Storage Options

Here's a question to consider: What records of your business would be left if your entire facility burned down today? The answer you give might have a profound impact on your motivation to perform proper contingency planning. Wayne once consulted for a manufacturing company that relied entirely on existing blueprints (on paper) to begin each process of custom manufacturing. Wayne discovered that these blueprints were all kept in one large room and that there were no copies stored anywhere offsite. Can you imagine the disaster if those blueprints were destroyed?

Items that you should consider for offsite storage include

- drawings and blueprints
- contracts
- production schedules
- payroll schedule/amounts
- financial statements
- tax documents
- office documents
- shipment information
- billing information
- outstanding and completed orders
- IT applications and production data

You have several options for storing documents and records, depending on the item and its current location. One option is simply to store the original item or a duplicate of the original item in a secure offsite location. Another option is to transfer documents to microfiche and store that offsite. You can use optical storage options for storing images or data, then take the disks offsite. You can store tapes, CDs, and actual disks (such as Zip-drive disks) offsite or even copy data to a system at a different location. Whatever you do, don't forget the many items that people have in their individual offices or perhaps on PCs in their offices. There are automatic backup products available for PCs that copy the contents of a PC hard drive to another system, such as your AS/400. The bottom-line question is: What format do you want your documents and records in if that's all you have left?

Here is a sample offsite inventory:

Sample offsite documents

- recent payroll listing for reference if checks must be handwritten
- duplicate copies of tax-related documents and financial statements
- customer listing, inventory listing, and miscellaneous other listings for reference during the interim period when IT resources are unavailable

Sample offsite IT-related materials

- most recent SAVSYS volumes
- most recent IBM distribution tapes/CDs and PTF tapes/CDs
- most recent SAVLIB LIB(*NONSYS) volumes
- recent SAVCHGOBJ volumes
- up-to-date procedures guide (if you use a procedures guide in operations for scheduling specific jobs)
- any special forms required for printing

Preventive Maintenance

Preventive maintenance is still one of the most effective ways to avoid hardware failures. Certain types of equipment (e.g., copiers, printers, disk drives) require some form of preventive maintenance to head off trouble before it arrives and causes unscheduled downtime. This is particularly true of PCs, which take much abuse. Regular preventive maintenance will extend the life of most PCs.

You may take on this responsibility yourself for some types of equipment. For special types of equipment, including most equipment related to IT operations, it's wise to request this service from your maintenance representative.

Avoiding Disaster Through Effects Reduction

Although the discussion above focuses on things to do to prevent disasters, other activities — while they may not prevent a disaster — certainly can help reduce a disaster's effects.

Employee Training

Evacuation-procedures training can save lives. You must do this as an actual physical exercise to ensure that the plan will work and to instill the basic plan in employees' minds.

Basic first-aid and CPR training for some or all employees can prove beneficial and provide a community service to the employees and possibly their families. Specific training about the recovery plan can also help reduce the effects of a disaster.

Alternative Facilities

A disaster might take out your organization's entire facilities. To minimize the effects of this occurrence, you should have alternative operational facilities for IT and other vital business functions. Use the data accumulated in the risk-analysis portion of your planning to determine which business functions are critical and should have alternative facilities. IT is certainly the most obvious but not the only department that could require facilities. You'll probably have to find alternative locations for various departments and ensure that proper furniture and equipment arrive at that location and are installed correctly.

IT Hot Sites

You should plan specifically for securing the use of hot-site facilities so that your IT operations can continue in the event of a disaster. Vendors usually sell these services for a per-month fee. The services may include assistance in your preparation and planning and expert employees who are trained to assist in implementation.

At the hot site, you need a compatible AS/400 model that's at least as large as the system you currently run. You also need

- compatible media-handling hardware
- sufficient workstations and printers to perform necessary operations
- network communications capabilities (rerouting of leased lines or dial-up capabilities) and Internet connections through your Internet Service Provider (ISP)
- PCs that are linked to the system for some vital functions (a growing concern because client/server applications are widely used). Make sure you have access to PCs that are large enough for your existing operations, have the proper networking software and options, and are attached to or have access to any type of printer you currently require for special processing (e.g., laser forms generation).

Emergency Procedures

Emergency procedures include consideration for company material assets, but — more important — these procedures take into account the employee assets in your company and preparation to help employees deal with an emergency and perhaps save lives or avoid injury. Your organization must establish emergency procedures. This includes planning and training for evacuation, proper employee notification, shutdown procedures, and departmental procedures.

Establishing Evacuation Procedures

First, you should produce a master drawing of the building(s) and identify all exits. Then, produce individual area drawings for departments, showing the closest exits and specific routes and including specific instructions about using those exits (e.g., stairways, ladders, which exits are available during which types of disasters). Ensure that each employee can see the area evacuation map in his or her department as a reminder of the planned escape route.

You also must determine how employees will be notified to evacuate (e.g., intercom, supervisor, whistles, horn). In addition, you should designate specific areas outside the facility where each department's employees should meet when the building is evacuated. Then, verify that each existing and new employee has read and understands the evacuation plan. (This could involve some oral or written test performed by the employee's supervisor.)

Establishing Notification Procedures

Make a master list of emergency phone numbers by category and post this list throughout the company so employees can readily call the fire department, poison-control center, utility companies, or medical facilities.

Also make a list of company employees who should be called for various types of emergencies, ranging from power failure, air heating/cooling failure, and system-security breach to general computer failure, flood, fire, or earthquake. The people listed should vary according to the type of emergency, and the list should include primary as well as secondary contacts.

IT should have a special list of emergency numbers: service numbers, offsite storage emergency numbers, and numbers necessary to activate alternative operating procedures should that be necessary.

Establishing Shutdown Procedures

You should also establish which equipment within the company should be shut down if time allows. This typically applies to computer equipment. (Time may be available if you have warning of an impending disaster, such as a flood, a hurricane, or another severe storm that might affect power.)

Establish both the preferred and alternative shutdown methods (such as shutting off the power). Establish how long it takes for each type of equipment to be shut down, and make sure the people responsible know to use their best judgment before executing a shutdown (e.g., leaving time for evacuation). Assign specific people (by position, not name) to be responsible for shutdown under specific circumstances. Obtain the necessary electrical or plumbing diagrams, and make them available to the appropriate people for use during an emergency.

Establishing Departmental Procedures

Because your work environment is typically divided into departments, establishing and publishing emergency procedures for each department is the best way to organize the procedures we've discussed. Such organization will help ensure an orderly process. Emergency-procedures training should be conducted regularly with employees and conducted as part of new employee orientation to the company and department.

A Complete Recovery Program

"Ensure that those business-critical functions can be restored" in the definition at the beginning of the chapter describes the actual recovery planning that many of you are familiar with already. However, one key element to this chapter is that we emphasize that you can't limit your activities to IT recovery — recovery of systems and data. This recovery activity is enterprise-wide (or single-location specific where multiple locations exist).

Building a recovery program includes three essential activities:

- building a recovery-program document
- identifying recovery-program tasks
- assigning recovery-program teams

Building a Recovery-Program Document

Recovery will be performed in stressful times and possibly by people who are not immediately familiar with your particular organization or the task at hand. In a disaster scenario, people who are key to recovery could be injured or unable to perform their jobs. The recovery-program documentation can guide recovery even when a key person is missing.

There should be an overall corporate recovery plan for dealing with disasters. This plan should then be broken down into departments for execution. Each department's plan may also include recovery provisions for emergencies that are not corporate-wide.

The recovery-program document should include items such as contacts and locations for alternative operational facilities for employees and customers, the priorities for recovery, instructions for each team responsible in the recovery operations, and specific instructions for recovery and restoration of vital corporate business records.

Identifying Recovery-Program Tasks

Recovery can be organized by the major tasks that must be accomplished. Table 19.1 lists the general recovery tasks and provides a brief description of each.

TABLE 19.1
Recovery Tasks

Task	General activities
Evaluation	Evaluate the type of emergency to determine whether activation of the recovery program is necessary.
Administration and support	Ensure that all teams are operational and that all tasks are performed and completed.
Operations	Activate and manage the alternative operational facilities for IT and other departments.
IT operations and recovery	Implement backup site operations and restore the system, programs, and data; restore all possible IT operations.
Salvage and facility recovery	Work to salvage equipment and recover any use of the facility possible.
Communications	Establish alternative communications network(s), then work to re-establish the permanent network(s) if possible.

Assigning Recovery-Program Teams

Once the major tasks have been organized, you must assign a team for each task. Team members should be selected from within the company with the possible addition of a few members from the outside who are recovery specialists. Each team should be organized with a team leader and alternates for each position. Each team should meet to determine the list of activities required to perform its task.

One person should be designated as the recovery-program manager. This person is responsible for overseeing the implementation of the entire recovery program. Team leaders are responsible to this person. Good candidates for this job are the COO, CFO, or IT manager.

Here, we've listed each recovery team and its activities. Use the planning form on the next page to help organize your teams.

Evaluation Team Activities

- Evaluate status of the facilities.
- Evaluate status of employees.
- Determine whether the recovery plan should be activated.
- Notify the appropriate team leaders if the recovery plan will be activated.

Administration and Support Team Activities

- Establish a physical control location and establish communications with all the team leaders.
- Coordinate communications, equipment, and supplies for each team.
- Distribute any necessary recovery-program procedure copies.
- Arrange for financial support to teams.
- Arrange for any travel necessary to establish alternative operational facilities.
- Handle other contingencies.

Operations Team Activities

- Activate the appropriate alternative operational facilities.
- Coordinate with the administration and support team to ensure that all the needed supplies, equipment, and people arrive at the alternative facility.

IT Operations/Recovery Team Activities

- Activate the hot-site agreement.
- Travel to the hot site.
- Load the system onto the hot-site machine.
- Restore the applications and data on the hot-site machine.

Recovery Team Planning Form

Team responsibility: _____

Team leader: _____

Alternate team leader: _____

Specific activities in the event of a disaster:

Task	Person responsible	Alternate
_____	_____	_____
_____	_____	_____
_____	_____	_____
_____	_____	_____
_____	_____	_____
_____	_____	_____
_____	_____	_____
_____	_____	_____
_____	_____	_____
_____	_____	_____
_____	_____	_____
_____	_____	_____
_____	_____	_____
_____	_____	_____
_____	_____	_____
_____	_____	_____
_____	_____	_____
_____	_____	_____
_____	_____	_____
_____	_____	_____

- Test the applications and assess program and data loss.
- Re-establish communications where possible.

Salvage/Facilities-Recovery Team Activities
- Evaluate the current condition of the damaged facilities.
- Coordinate with the insurance company for a timely payment.
- Arrange for the removal of damaged equipment.
- Salvage any usable equipment.
- Make decisions concerning the rebuilding or repair of facilities.
- Order any necessary replacement equipment.

Communications Team Activities
- Act as a contact between the organization and the phone company.
- Make sure communications are established at each alternative operational facility.
- Send a previously prepared announcement to customers informing them of the procedures to contact your organization, place orders, and inquire about accounts.
- Assess damage to communications equipment.

Testing and Auditing

"Ensure . . . to an acceptable level for the enterprise to survive" in the definition at the beginning of the chapter describes the testing and auditing phase of contingency planning. The only way you can ensure that your contingency plan will work and work effectively for your organization is to actually test your plan. If your plan isn't tested, it won't work! Believe us on this one. Testing reveals a lot about the effectiveness of the plan, the feasibility of the tasks, the level of training accomplished, and the leadership abilities of those implementing the plan.

Obviously, to test the entire plan all at once would be difficult in the framework of your daily business. Usually, a total-systems test can be performed only once a year, and that leaves too many months for problems to grow. However, it isn't necessary to test the plan altogether, and — in fact — it will probably prove more fruitful to test each component of the plan individually to obtain the maximum benefit of the test and use of time because you can test the pieces of the plan more easily and with less impact upon your daily operations.

The point is that you must develop and implement a formal test plan before you can call the contingency-planning project complete. You can conduct different types of tests. Below, we describe two levels of specific testing you can use for the IT department contingency-plan testing. Use the record form on the next page to record your progress and uncover areas to work on in the future.

Test Observation Record

Test date: _____

Component tested: _____

Goals

What were the goals of the test? _____

_____

_____

Were the goals met? Answer for each goal mentioned above: _____

_____

_____

Observations

What activities were involved with this testing? _____

_____

_____

Specific observations made during the test: _____

_____

_____

Recommendations

Recommendations for corrective or supportive actions: _____

_____

_____

_____

Should the test be repeated? _____

Observer's name: _____

Performing a Level 1 Test

In a level 1 test, walk through a reload of your entire system (with the assumption that you lost your system and had to replace the system with a brand new one). This reload will probably have to be on paper because you won't want to initialize your system and try it for real.

Make notes concerning the current status of the data being reloaded. How current is the data? Did you have all the data? Did everyone involved understand the process? Could you easily find and follow all the instructions?

Performing a Level 2 Test

In a level 2 test, you should travel to the hot site you've secured and actually reload your system and data and establish communications with remote sites (if any). Make notes concerning any difficulties encountered and modify your plans accordingly. Test dial-up capabilities and Internet or other connections.

Auditing Your Contingency Plan

After establishing a working contingency plan, you must maintain this plan so it reflects any changes within the organization over time, especially the changes in employees who are available and trained to execute the plan. Some of the activities necessary to maintain an up-to-date contingency plan are

- ongoing training
- team-employees management
- communication with department supervisors about any changes in recovery issues (e.g., necessary equipment, data, priorities)
- monitoring organization growth to ensure adequate alternative operational facilities are available
- making modifications to the IT hot-site arrangement as IT hardware/software requirements change

Regular testing and auditing will ensure that any changes that directly affect the plan become evident. Then, make sure your organization's top management and IT commits to make the necessary changes to keep the plan current.

Appendix A

Security APIs

To complement the integrated security features and specific security-related commands in OS/400, IBM supplies a set of security-related APIs. These APIs perform functions similar to some of the security-related CL commands, but they perform the functions faster and are friendlier to high-level languages (HLLs) such as C, RPG, and Cobol, which can call an API much more easily than they can execute a CL command. Below is a list of the security-related APIs in OS/400 and a brief description of how you might use each one. For more information about the security-related APIs, see the IBM manual *AS/400e System API Reference*. In V4R5, the security-related APIs are documented in the Info Center online at http://www.as400.ibm.com/infocenter. Go to the Programming topic and then OS/400 APIs. From there, you can search for APIs by topic or name. If you search for the APIs by topic, you'll see a list of topics, and from there you can choose Security.

QGYOLAUS (Open List of Authorized Users)
This API lists information about the authorized users of the system. It provides a subset of the information that the QSYRAUTU API provides. You can obtain the rest of the information through the QGYGTLE (Get List Entries) API.

QGYRATLO (Retrieve Objects Secured by Authorization List)
This API returns a variable that contains a list of objects secured by a specified authorization list. It provides a subset of the information provided by the QSYLATLO API. You can obtain the rest of the information through the QGYGTLE (Get List Entries) API.

QSYCHGDS (Change Dedicated Service Tools Profiles)
This API changes the user IDs or passwords (or both) for the three Dedicated Service Tools (DST) profiles.

QSYCHGID (Change User Profile UID or GID)
You can call this API from an HLL program instead of executing the CHGUSRPRF (Change User Profile) command when you want to change a profile's user ID (UID) or a group profile's group ID (GID). The AS/400 Integrated File System (IFS) uses UIDs and GIDs to identify the process user profile and its groups. You might need to change a UID or GID if you're trying to keep profiles in synch across your network.

QSYCHGPR (Change Previous Sign-On Date)
OS/400 maintains the last successful sign-on date for each user profile on your system. This API lets you permanently modify the last sign-on date and time for the currently running user to the current date and time.

QSYCHGPW (Change User Password)
You can call this API from an HLL program instead of executing the CHGPWD (Change Password) command when you want to change a password. The API's caller supplies the old and new passwords, and OS/400 validates the new password using the password-related system values and a password-validation program if you've implemented one.

QSYCUSRA (Check User Authority to a Specific Object)
This API is similar to the CHKOBJ (Check Object) command in that it checks to see whether the current user has some specific authority to the object named in the API parameter. In other words, you can check to see whether a user has authority to a specific object. QSYCUSRA does not retrieve the authorities but merely returns an error code if the user does *not* have the requested authorities. For an example of how to use this API, see Chapter 5 and sample program CSTMAINT2.

QSYCUSRS (Check User Special Authorities)
This API is similar to the QSYCUSRA API, but it checks only the current user's special authorities. (You name the special authorities to check.) There is no corresponding CL command for this API.

QSYCVTA (Convert Authority Values to MI Value)
Only you "MI-nerds" (you know who you are) need this API. In writing MI programs, you sometimes must obtain a user's authority in MI representation. This API returns those authorizations in the corresponding MI representation. There is no corresponding CL command for this API.

QSYGETPH (Get a User Profile Handle)
This API is normally used with the QWTSETP API to let a user switch user profiles within a job. (Actually, as of V4R4 it switches profiles within a thread.) When using this API, you pass the API a user profile name and password value. If the API verifies that you've given a *valid* user profile and password, the API returns to the caller an encrypted abbreviation called a "profile handle." You can then use this handle to set the current profile of the job (thread). There is no corresponding CL command for this API.

QSYLATLO (List Objects Secured by an Authorization List)
This API creates a list of objects secured by a specific authorization list and places that list in a user space for later retrieval.

QSYLAUTU (List Authorized Users)
This API creates a list of the authorized users on your system and places that list in a user space for later retrieval. The DSPAUTUSR (Display Authorized Users) command is similar except that its output is limited to a workstation or printer. You could use the DSPOBJD

(Display Object Description) command to place a list of *USRPRF-type objects in a file, but the QSYLAUTU API works better if you're writing HLL programs in RPG, Cobol, or C and must access the information quickly.

QSYLOBJA (List Objects User Is Authorized to, Owns, or Is Primary Group of)

If you must know all the objects that a user is privately authorized to, owns, or has primary group authority to, this API is definitely your source. You can use the DSPUSRPRF (Display User Profile) command to retrieve this information, but the command is an awkward multistep process that uses one or more output files. This API creates a list of all objects a user has private authority to, owns, or has primary group authority to and places that list in a user space.

QSYLOBJP (List Objects That Adopt Owner Authority)

The DSPPGMADP (Display Program Adoption) command is similar to this API, but the command is a slow performer compared to the API. This API creates a list of programs, service programs, and SQL packages that adopt an owner's authority and places that list in a user space for later retrieval.

QSYLUSRA (List Users Authorized to an Object)

A companion of the QSYLOBJA API, this API creates a list of all users authorized to a specific object (and those users' authorization values) and places that list in a user space. This API is similar to the DSPOBJAUT (Display Object Authorities) command.

QSYRAUTU (Retrieve Authorized Users)

This API returns a list of the authorized user names on the system and information about those user profiles.

QSYRESPA (Reset Profile Attributes)

Some IBM-supplied profiles can't be changed with the CHGUSRPRF (Change User Profile) command. This API was created to ensure that some important parameters are set the way IBM expects them to be set. When you call this API, the following parameters are set:

Password is set to *NONE

Status is set to *ENABLED

Password expired is set to *NO

Special authorities are set to the appropriate values for each profile being altered.

For the list of profiles being altered, see the online documentation.

QSYRLSPH (Release Profile Handle)
This API releases the encrypted abbreviation (profile handle) that your program previously acquired using the QSYGETPH API. There is no corresponding CL command for this API.

QSYRTVUA (Retrieve Users Authorized to an Object)
This API returns a variable that provides information about the users who are authorized to a specified object.

QSYRUPWD (Retrieve Encrypted User Password)
This API returns a variable that is the encrypted user password for a specified user profile. You can use this API in combination with the QSYSUPWD API to securely synchronize user passwords around a network.

QSYRUSRA (Retrieve a User's Authority to an Object)
This API provides a return variable that lists the authorities a user profile has for a specific object. There is no corresponding CL command for this API. For an example of how to use this API, see Chapter 5 and sample program CSTMAINT2.

QSYRUSRI (Retrieve User Information)
This API is similar to the RTVUSRPRF (Retrieve User Profile) command, except that QSYRUSRI returns the information directly in the parameters to HLL programs such as RPG, Cobol, and C. The RTVUSRPRF command can return variables to a CL program only.

> **Technical Note**
> The QSYRUSRI API is the only means available to retrieve variable-length information (e.g, home directory) stored as part of the user profile.

QSYSUPWD (Set Encrypted User Password)
This API sets the encrypted user password obtained through the QSYRUPWD API for a specified user profile. It also updates the password last-changed date to the current date.

QwtClearJuid( ) (Clear Job User Identity)
If a job is running single threaded, you can call this function to clear the job user identity that was set previously by the QwtSetJuid( ) function or the QWTSJUID (Set Job User Identity) API.

QwtSetJuid() (Set Job User Identity)
This function is used to set the job user identity of the current job to the name of the current user profile of the thread out of which this function was called. The job user identity establishes the user name by which other jobs will identify this job. The intent is to allow a job user identity that remains constant, regardless of whether a profile swap occurs sometime during the job. This API is typically used by OS/400 only for some POSIX-related functions. Note: This API does not change the user in the job name.

QWTSETP (Set Profile)
This API uses a profile handle (which you retrieve using the QSYGETPH API) to switch users during execution of a job. In other words, you can tell the job to run under a different user profile. There is no corresponding CL command for this API.

QWTSJUID (Set Job User Identity)
This API performs the same functions as the QwtSetJuid and QwtClearJuid functions. You can use this API to clear or set the job user identity.

User and Group ID APIs
The UID and GID APIs provide other ways to change the user or group a thread is running under. You'd typically use these APIs for changing the user or first group of the thread when you access objects in the AS/400 IFS. The UID is the numeric representation of a user; the GID is the numeric representation of a group. The UID and GID represent the user and group(s) (rather than the user or group profile names) during authority checking when accessing IFS objects. To fully explain the following APIs, we need to introduce several more concepts from the POSIX standards.

In POSIX, each job has the concept of "real," "effective," and "saved" user and group IDs. The real UID is the user ID of the user under which the job started. The effective user ID is the UID under which the job is currently running (and making access control under). The saved user ID is used by some applications to store a UID when multiple changes are made to the real and effective UIDs. The concepts are the same for the real, effective, and saved GIDs.

These APIs differ from the profile swap (QSYGETPH and QWTSETP) APIs because they change the user and first group independently of each other. For example, when you use the swap APIs to swap to user CAROL, all groups associated with CAROL are also swapped into the thread. As you'll read later, this is not the case with the UID and GID APIs.

qsysetuid() (Set User ID)
This API changes one or more of the UIDs of a thread. If the API is called by a user with *ALLOBJ special authority, the real, effective, and saved user IDs are set to the UID passed to the API. Otherwise, if the UID passed to the API matches the real, effective, or saved user ID, the effective user ID is set to the UID passed to the API. You should note that only the user ID and user attributes such as limited capabilities, group authority, and

group authority types are changed for the thread. The group(s) associated with the thread are not changed. Also note that if the new effective user ID was defined with an attribute of OWNER(*GRPPRF), the set UID won't be allowed if the user's first group profile isn't in the group list for the thread.

qsysetgid( ) (Set Group ID)
The qsysetgid API is similar to qsysetuid, but it changes the GID. When a job starts, a list of GIDs is created from the groups defined in the user's profile. When you run the qsysetgid API, you change the first group in the list of GIDs for the job. All supplementary groups for the thread remain unchanged. This is a way to change the first group the thread is running under independently of how the group was defined in the user's (effective UID's) profile.

qsyseteuid( ) (Set Effective User ID)
This API changes the effective UID of the thread. If the UID passed to the API matches the real, effective, or saved user ID, the effective user ID is set to the UID passed to the API. Otherwise, if the user calling the API has *USE authority to the user profile represented by the UID passed to the API, the effective UID is set to that UID.

qsysetegid( ) (Set Effective Group ID)
This API is similar to qsyseteuid, but it changes the effective GID of the thread. If the GID passed to the API matches the real, effective, or saved group ID or one of the groups in the supplemental group list, the effective group ID is set to the GID passed to the API. Otherwise, if the user calling the API has *USE authority to the group profile represented by the GID passed in to the API, the effective group ID is set to that GID.

qsysetreuid( ) (Set Real and Effective User IDs)
This API changes the real and/or effective UIDs of the thread. If the API's caller has *ALLOBJ special authority, the real and/or effective UID is set to the value(s) passed in. Otherwise, only the effective UID can be changed if it matches the real or saved user ID.

qsysetregid( ) (Set Real and Effective Group IDs)
This API changes the real and/or effective GIDs of the thread. If the API's caller has *ALLOBJ special authority, the real and/or effective GID is set to the value(s) passed in. Otherwise, the effective GID can be changed if it matches the real or saved group ID. The real GID can be changed if it matches the saved group ID.

In addition to these basic security APIs, IBM provides the following security-related APIs.

Digital Certificate APIs

Digital certificates enable several technologies: an alternative user-authentication mechanism (rather than a user ID and password), digital signatures, and encryption. The following APIs let you manipulate digital certificates.

QSYADDUC (Add User Certificate)
This API associates a digital certificate with an AS/400 user profile.

QSYADDVC (Add Validation List Certificate)
This API associates a digital certificate with a validation-list entry.

QSYCHKVC (Check Validation List Entries)
Use this API to determine whether a particular digital certificate is in the specified validation list.

QSYFNDCU (Find Certificate User)
Use this API to find the AS/400 user profile a digital certificate is associated with. (A digital certificate can be associated with only one user profile.)

QSYLSTUC (List User Certificates)
Use this API to obtain a list of digital certificates for a particular user. (A user profile can have more than one digital certificate.)

QSYLSTVC (List Validation List Certificates)
Use this API to retrieve a list of all the digital certificates in a specified validation list.

QSYOLUC (Open List of User Certificates)
This API provides the same basic function as QSYLSTUC and also returns a handle that represents the list of certificates that can be passed to other list-handling APIs.

QSYPARSC (Parse Certificate)
Use this API to parse a digital certificate from Distinguished Encoding Rules (DER) into plain text.

QSYRMVUC (Remove User Certificate)
Use this API to remove a digital certificate from an AS/400 user profile.

QSYRMVVC (Remove Validation List Certificates)
Use this API to remove a digital certificate from a validation list.

Profile Token APIs

The profile token APIs serve the same purpose as profile handles — that is, they change the user the thread is running under. However, profile tokens have a few differences. Profile tokens can be generated in one job, then passed and used in another job. At creation time, you can define them to be multiple use or one-time-only use. They can also expire or time out and can be regenerated when they do.

QSYGENFT and QsyGenPrfTknFromPrfTkn (Generate Profile Token from Profile Token)

This API lets you generate a new profile token from an already-existing one. To regenerate a profile token, the token must have first been created as a multi-use, regenerable token.

QSYGENPT and QsyGenPrfTkn (Generate Profile Token)

You use this API to generate a profile token with the attributes time-out interval and type (single use, multiple use, or multiple use and regenerable). The equivalent profile handle API is QSYGETPH.

QSYGETPT and QsyGetPrfTknTimeOut (Get Profile Token Time Out)

This API returns the time (in seconds) before a particular profile token expires.

QSYINVPT and QsyInvalidatePrfTkn (Invalidate Profile Token)

The API's description says it all: You use this API to make the token unusable. The only action you can perform on a token that has been invalidated is to remove it.

QSYRMVPT (Remove Profile Tokens)

This API lets you perform all the functions found in the next three APIs, which are service programs: Remove all tokens on the system, all tokens for a particular user, or a specific token.

QsyRemoveAllPrfTkns (Remove All Profile Tokens)

Use this API to remove all tokens on the system. You must do this if the maximum number of tokens (approximately 2,000,000) for the system has been generated.

QsyRemoveAllPrfTknsForUser (Remove All Profile Tokens for User)

This API removes all tokens for a specific user. You may want to remove all tokens for a user when the user's password, special authorities, or group profiles have changed.

QsyRemovePrfTkn (Remove Profile Token)

Use this API to remove a specific profile token. QSYRLSPH performs the equivalent function for profile handles.

QSYSETPT and QsySetToPrfTkn (Set to Profile Token)

Use this API to actually change the thread to run under the user (and its associated group profiles) represented by the token. The equivalent profile handle API is QWTSETP.

User Function Registration APIs

Most applications control who can do what by controlling access to a command or program. However, sometimes there is no object to use for access control. In that case, you can define a "function" and then control who can use that function. A function, as defined by the User Function APIs, acts like a pseudo or virtual object to which you can then control access.

QSYCHFUI (Change Function Usage Information)

Once you've defined a function with the QSYRGFN API, you use this API to define which users may perform this function.

QSYCKUFU (Check User Function Usage)

Use this API within your application to determine whether a user may perform a particular function.

QSYDRGFN (Deregister Function)

If you remove an application from your system, you use this API to remove the functions you've defined.

QSYRGFN (Register Function)

Use this API to define a function. All functions are registered and stored in the OS/400 registration facility.

QSYRTFUI (Retrieve Function Usage Information)

Use this API to retrieve information about all registered functions.

QSYRTUFI (Retrieve User Function Information)

Use this API to retrieve a list of registered functions and an indication of whether a particular user may use each function.

QSYRTVFI (Retrieve Function Information)

This API returns a list of users who may use a specific function.

Validation-List APIs

Validation lists are generic objects that any application can use to securely store user IDs and passwords or other user-identifier and authentication information. The authentication information is encrypted in either decryptable or non-decryptable form. Your application, along with the QRETSVRSEC (Retain Server Security) system value, determines whether the authentication information is stored in decryptable form.

In OS/400, validation lists are used to implement the concept of "Internet users" — users known only to Web applications. To create a validation-list object for your application to use, run the CRTVLVL (Create Validation List) command. To delete a validation list, run the DLTVLDL (Delete Validation List) command.

QSYADVLE (Add Validation List Entry)
Use this API to add an entry (user) to a validation list.

QSYCHVLE (Change Validation List Entry)
Once a user is in the validation list, you can use this API to change or update the user's entry.

QSYFDVLE (Find Validation List Entry)
Use this API to find or retrieve the information about a particular user in the validation list.

QSYOLVLE (Open List of Validation List Entries)
This API returns a list of entries (users) in a particular validation list.

QsyAddValidationLstEntry() (Add Validation List Entry)
This function adds an entry to a validation list. It does the same thing as the QSYADVLE API, but is provided as a C function.

QsyChangeValidationLstEntry() (Change Validation List Entry)
This function lets you change or update an entry in a validation list. It does the same thing as the QSYCHVLE API, but is provided as a C function.

QsyFindFirstValidationLstEntry() (Find First Validation List Entry)
This function finds the first entry (user) in the validation list and then returns the information about that entry.

QsyFindNextValidationLstEntry() (Find Next Validation List Entry)
This function lets you pass in an entry identifier and then finds the next entry in the validation list. You can use this function to step through all the entries (users) in the validation list.

QsyFindValidationLstEntry() (Find Validation List Entry)
This function finds a particular validation-list entry (user) and returns the information about that user. The QSYFDVLE API provides the same information.

QsyFindValidationLstEntryAttrs() (Find Validation List Entry Attributes)
This function finds an entry for a particular user and then returns the attribute information about the user. Currently, the only attribute defined for validation-list entries is a digital certificate attribute. This means you can use this function to retrieve a validation-list user's digital certificate.

QsyRemoveValidationLstEntry() (Remove Validation List Entry)
This function removes a particular entry (user) from the validation list. The QSYRMVLE API performs the same action.

QsyVerifyValidationLstEntry() (Verify Validation List Entry)
Use this function to verify that the authentication information is correct for a particular user. For example, you pass in a user ID and password, and this function returns an indication of whether the password is correct for the user.

QSYRMVLE (Remove Validation List Entry)
This API removes an entry (user) from the specified validation list.

Appendix B
Security Journal Entry Types (Detail)

[*Current with OS/400 V4R5*]

Action Auditing

(Actions journaled based on QAUDLVL system value and/or one or more user profile's AUDLVL attribute.)

Auditing value	Journal entry type	Detail entry code	Description of journal entry
*AUTFAIL	AF	A	User attempted to access an object without the proper authority, or a user attempted to perform an operation/function without the proper authority.
		F	authorization error through the ICAPI API
		G	authentication error through the ICAPI API
		J	User attempted to use a job description that named a user profile to which the user did not have authority.
		N	An application tried to regenerate a non-regenerable profile token.
		P	User attempted to use a profile handle that isn't valid on the QWTSETP API.
		S	User attempted to sign on without entering a user ID or a password.
		T	User is not authorized to a TCP/IP port.
		U	invalid user permission request
		V	An application attempted to regenerate a new profile token from a token that isn't valid for generating a new token.
		W	An application attempted to use a profile token that isn't valid for swapping.
		Y	authorization error to the current JUID field while attempting to clear the JUID
		Z	authorization error to the current JUID field while attempting to set the JUID
	CV	E	Connection ended abnormally.
		R	Connection rejected.
	GR	F	Function registration operations occurred.
	KF	P	User entered an incorrect password.
	IP	P	authority failure for an IPC request
	PW	A	An APPC bind failure occurred.
		D	User entered an invalid DST profile name.
		E	User entered an incorrect DST password.

continued

Auditing value	Journal entry type	Detail entry code	Description of journal entry
		P	User didn't enter a valid password for a user profile.
		U	User didn't enter a valid user profile.
	VC	R	Connection rejected because of an incorrect password.
	VN	R	Network log-on rejected because of an expired account, incorrect hours, incorrect user ID, or incorrect password.
	VO	U	A verification failure of a validation-list entry occurred.
	VP	A	APPC bind failed.
		P	User entered an incorrect network password.
		U	User entered an invalid user profile.
*CMD	CD	C	A command was run.
		L	S/36E control language statement was run.
		O	S/36E operator control command was run.
		P	S/36E procedure was run.
		S	A command was run after a command substitution.
		U	S/36E utility control statement was run.
*CREATE	CO	N	A new object was created (excluding creation of objects in QTEMP library).
		R	A new object was created that replaces an existing object.
*DELETE	DO	A	An object was deleted (excluding deleting objects from QTEMP library).
*JOBDTA	JS	A	The ENDJOBABN command was used.
		B	Job submitted.
		C	Job changed.
		E	Job ended.
		H	Job held.
		I	Job disconnected.
		M	Profile or group profile modified.
		N	ENDJOB command was used.
		P	A program start request was attached to a prestart job.
		Q	Query attributes were changed.
		R	A held job was released.
		S	A job was started.
		T	A profile or group profile was modified using a profile token.
		U	The CHGUSRTRC command was run.
	SG	A	Asynchronous AS/400 signal processed.
		P	Asynchronous Private Address Space Environment (PASE) signal processed.

continued

Auditing value	Journal entry type	Detail entry code	Description of journal entry
	VC	E	Connection ended.
		S	Connection started.
	VN	F	Log-off requested.
		O	Log-on requested.
	VS	E	Server session ended.
		S	Server session started.
*NETCMN	CU	M	An object was created by the cluster control operation.
		R	An object was created by the Cluster Resource Group (*GRP) management operation.
	CV	C	Connection established.
		E	Connection ended abnormally.
	IR	L	IP rules were loaded from a file.
		N	IP rules were unloaded for an IP Security connection.
		R	IP rules were read and copied to a file.
		U	IP rules were unloaded (removed).
	IS	A	fail
		C	normal
		U	mobile user
	EV	A	add
		C	change
		D	delete
	GS	G	Socket descriptor given.
		R	Socket descriptor received.
		U	Socket descriptor could not be used.
	IP	A	The ownership or authority of an IPC object was changed.
		C	IPC object created.
		D	IPC object deleted.
		G	IPC object obtained.
	JD	A	USER parameter of a job description was changed.
	KF	C	Certificate operation occurred.
		K	Keyring file operation occurred.
		P	Incorrect password provided.
		T	Trusted root operation occurred.
	NA	A	Network attribute changed.
	OW	A	Object ownership changed.
	PA	A	A program was changed to adopt owner authority.
	PG	A	An object's primary group was changed.

continued

Auditing value	Journal entry type	Detail entry code	Description of journal entry
	PS	A	Target user profile changed during a passthrough session.
		E	Office user ended work on behalf of another user.
		H	Profile handle was generated through the QSYGETPH API.
		I	All profile tokens were invalidated.
		M	The maximum number of profile tokens was generated.
		P	A profile token was generated for a user.
		R	All profile tokens for a user were removed.
		S	Office user started work on behalf of another user.
		V	User profile authenticated.
	SE	A	Subsystem routing entry changed.
	SO	A	Security entry added.
		C	Security entry changed.
		R	Security entry removed.
	SV	A	System value changed.
		B	Service attributes changed.
		C	System clock changed.
	VA	S	Access control list changed successfully.
		F	Access control list change failed.
	VO	A	Validation-list entry added.
		C	Validation-list entry changed.
		F	Validation-list entry found.
		R	Validation-list entry removed.
		U	Verification of validation-list entry failed.
		V	Verification of validation-list entry successful.
	VU	G	Group record changed.
		U	User record changed.
		M	User profile global information changed.
*SERVICE	ST	A	Service tool used.
	VV	C	Service status changed.
		E	Server stopped.
		P	Server paused.
		R	Server restarted.
		S	Server started.
*SPLFDTA	SF	A	Spooled file read by someone other than the owner.
		C	Spooled file created.
		D	Spooled file deleted.
		H	Spooled file held.

continued

Auditing value	Journal entry type	Detail entry code	Description of journal entry
		I	In-line file was created.
		R	Spooled file released.
		U	Spooled file changed.
*SYSMGT	SM	B	Backup options changed using Operational Assistant.
		C	Automatic clean-up options changed using Operational Assistant.
		D	DRDA change was made.
		F	HFS file system changed.
		N	Network file operation performed.
		O	Backup list changed using Operational Assistant.
		P	Power on/off schedule changed using Operational Assistant.
		S	System reply list changed.
		T	Access path recovery times changed.
	VL	A	Account expired.
		D	Account disabled.
		L	Log-on hours exceeded.
		U	unknown or unavailable
		W	Workstation not valid.

Object Auditing

(Actions journaled based on one or more object's OBJAUD attribute value and/or one or more user profile's OBJAUD attribute value.)

Auditing value	Journal entry type	Detail entry code	Description of journal entry
*ALL	YR	R	Document library object read.
	ZR	R	Object read.
*CHANGE	LD	K	Directory searched.
		L	Directory linked.
		U	Directory unlinked.
	VF	A	File closed because of administrative disconnection.
		N	File closed because of normal client disconnection.
		S	File closed because of session disconnection.
	VR	F	Resource access failed.
		S	Resource access successful.
	YC	C	Document library object changed.
	ZC	C	Object changed.

References

IBM Manuals
AS/400 Database Programming Information (SC41-5612)
AS/400 System APIs Information (SC41-5801)
AS/400 Tips and Tools for Securing Your AS/400 V4R5 (SC41-5300)
Client Access Express Host Servers V4R4M0 (SC41-5740)
DB2 for AS/400 SQL Reference (SC41-5612)
DDS Reference (SC41-5712)
Distributed Data Management (SC41-5307)
Integrated File System Introduction (SC41-5711)
OS/400 Security Reference (SC41-5302)
OS/400 SNA Distribution Services V4R4 (SC41-5410)
OS/400 TCP/IP Configuration and Reference V4R4 (SC41-5420)
Remote Work Station Support (SC41-5402)
System API Reference (SC41-5801)

IBM Redbooks
An Approach to Designing e-business Solutions (SG24-5949)
AS/400 e-business Handbook (SG24-5694)
AS/400 e-commerce: net.Commerce (SG24-2129)
AS/400 Internet Security: Developing a Digital Certificate Infrastructure (SG24-5659)
AS/400 Internet Security: Implementing AS/400 Virtual Private Networks (SG24-5404)
AS/400 Internet Security: Protecting Your AS/400 from HARM in the Internet (SG24-4929)
AS/400 TCP/IP Autoconfiguration: DNS and DHCP Support (SG24-5147)
Deploying a Public Key Infrastructure (SG24-5512)
IBM SecureWay Host On-Demand 4.0: Enterprise Communications in the Era of Network Computing (SG24-2149)
Unleashing AS/400 Applications on the Internet (SG24-4935)

IBM Web Sites
http://www.iseries.ibm.com/casestudies/ebiz
http://www.iseries.ibm.com/clientaccess
http://www.iseries.ibm.com/db2
http://www.iseries.ibm.com/ebusiness
http://www.iseries.ibm.com/ebusiness/security
http://www.iseries.ibm.com/firewall
http://www.iseries.ibm.com/http
http://www.iseries.ibm.com/techstudio

Articles from *NEWS/400* Magazine and *AS400 Network*

Beckman, Mel. "Guard Against Internet Invaders with Firewalls," Winter 1996.
Beckman, Mel. "Introduction to Secure Sockets Layer," October 1997.
Beckman, Mel. "Intruders on the Inside," November 1999.
Beckman, Mel. "Your AS/400's Internet Enemies Revealed," Winter 1996.
Botz, Patrick. "Designing Protection Setups for Web Applications," November 1999.
Botz, Patrick. "Making System Value QCRTAUT More Restrictive," December 1998.
Botz, Patrick. "Operations Navigator on a Short Leash," February 2000.
Botz, Patrick. "Security Check for Application Software Vendors," October 2000.
Botz, Patrick. "Wizard Makes Security Configuration a Snap," November 1998.
Heidelberg, Jelan, and Frank V. Paxhia. "V4R1 Security and Your AS/400 Web Server," October 1997.
Madden, Wayne, and Carol Woodbury. "Security at the System Level," June 1998.
Middleton, Dalton C. "Managing AS/400 Network Passwords," September 1996.
Oguine, Azubike. "Using AS/400 Security Auditing," June 2000.
Seiler, Denis. "Keep an Eye on Your AS/400 with Auditing," February 1998.
Singleton, Brian. "Overcoming AS/400 Object Security Exposures," November 1998.
Smith, Barbara. "Using V4R3's Limit Access to Program Function," February 1999.
Steen, Vincent, and Dan Riehl. "AS/400 Passwords: Enforcing New Rules," August 1997.
Woodbury, Carol. "Application Security by Design," November 1999.
Woodbury, Carol. "Don't Let Security Slow Your Apps," March 1997.
Woodbury, Carol. "Master OS/400 Authority Checking," October 1996.
Woodbury, Carol. "OS/400 Security Update — V4R5," October 2000.
Woodbury, Carol. "Policy Is the Best Honesty," October 2000.
Woodbury, Carol. "Taking a Stand with AS/400 Security," *AS400 Network* (http://www.as400network.com), January 1999.

Other Publications

National Computer Security Center. *Trusted Computer Systems Evaluation Criteria*, United States Department of Defense, Standard number 5200.28.

Index

A

Access
  controlling, 6–7
  DDM, 277
  exposures, minimizing, 232–236
  methods, 267
  output queues, 278
  password, hunt for, 236–238
  user profile, hunt for, 236–238
*ADD authority, 65, 108
ADDAUTLE (Add Authorization List Entry) command, 192
ADDCFGLE (Add Configuration List Entries) command, 170
ADDRTGE (Add Routing Entry) command, 278
ADDSVRAUTE (Add Server Authentication Entry) command, 202
Adopted authority, 80–83
  concepts, 81
  hackers and, 238–239
  security measures, 242–243
  security recommendation, 83
  summary, 82
  uses, 80
  See also Authorities
Advanced Peer-to-Peer Networking. *See* APPN/APPC communications configuration security
*ALL authority, 84
*ALLOBJ special authority, 1
  in authorization search progression, 78
  as exception, 7
  non-requirement of, 53
  power, 52
  QSECOFR user profile, 53
  security recommendation, 53
  signing on with, 234
  vendor requirement and, 7
  See also Special authorities
Alternative facilities, 414
ANZDFTPWD (Analyze Default Password) command, 54
  defined, 60
  executing, 222
ANZPRFACT (Analyze Profile Activity) command, 60, 228
Application Administration interface, 181
Application Programming Interfaces (APIs), 16

Application security, 283–286
  APPLICATION category, 284, 286
  categories, 284
  example requirements, 314–315
  PUBLIC category, 284
  recommendation, 284
  requirement list, 285
  requirements, 283–286
  RESTRICTED category, 286
APPN/APPC communications configuration security, 209–213
  controller description, 210–211
  device description, 211–212
  filtering support, 213
  line description, 209–210
AS/400
  as easy prey, 236
  key positions, 269
  key removal, 233
  system unit, 269–270
AS/400 Database Programming Information, 109
AS/400 System APIs Information, 90
AS/400 Tips and Tools for Securing Your AS/400 V4R5, 213, 241
AUDFILE file, 392
*AUDIT special authority, 380
Audit journal, 377–380
  creating, 378–380
  defined, 377
  displaying, 391–392
  entry types, 389–390
  formats, understanding, 387–390
  model files for, 395–397
  monitoring at security level 30, 18
  printing, 392–397
  security recommendation, 279
  standard entry fields, 388
  working with, 387–390
Audit reports, 348
Auditing
  authorization lists, 362
  business contingency plan, 421
  changed objects, 343, 364
  commitment, 9
  communication entries, 363
  consultant/vendor use of AUDLVL(*CMD), 243
  establishing, 7
  event, 375–399
  exit programs, 245, 364
  forms, 345
  group profiles, 348–352
  job and output queues, 363
  job descriptions, 363
  libraries, 244
  lines, controllers, and devices, 363
  object, 353–355, 383–386

object authorities, 359–362
object ownership, 353–355
overview, 344
OVRMSGF use, 244
performing, 7
physical security, 347
resignations, 343
restore operations, 84, 243
special authority users, 243
status, 345–373
system-level security, 347–348
system-wide, 381–382
terminations, 343
trigger programs, 364
user, 382–383
user functions, 362
user profile names and, 48
user profile size, 355
user profiles, 348–359
user profiles with password the same as user profile, 353
users who own programs that adopt authority, 353
Audit-related system values, 38–42
AUT parameter, 71–72
  defined, 71, 131
  modifying, 131
  values, 72
AUTCHK parameter, 131
Authorities
  adopted, 80–83, 238–239
  data, 65
  database file, 89–107
  exposures, closing off, 242–243
  listing example, 337–339
  logical files and, 108, 111
  object, 64–65
  OS/400 checking, 77–80
  ownership, limiting, 245
  physical files and, 108, 111
  printing function, 132
  private, 69
  public, 71–75
  reference, 108, 109
  restoring, 83
  save/restore functions and, 83–84
  search order, 77–78
  specific, 63–66
  temporary, 343
  update, 108–109
  user, 90–92
  viewing, 71
  See also Special authorities
Authority cache, 80
Authority classes, 66–68
  *EXCLUDE, 68
  with generic authority commands, 67
  with QSYS commands, 67

Authorization lists, 75–77
 advantages, 75–76
 assigning user profiles to, 192
 auditing, 362
 authority to, 75
 creating, 75
 defined, 75
 private authorities and, 76
 QPWFSERVER, 178–179
 securing objects with, 76
Authorization models, 249–257
 direct authorization model, 252–253
 group authorization model, 253–255
 library and directory authorization
   model, 251–252
 menu authorization model, 249–251
 profile authorization model, 256–257
 program adoption authorization model,
   255–256
Authorization roles
 communications administrator, 304
 identifying, 291
 network administrator, 308
 operator, 302–304
 programmer/analyst, 304–306
 security administrator, 306–308
 typical, 302
 Webmaster, 309
Authorizations, 292–293
 defined, 292
 defining, 292–293
AUTOANS parameter, 210
AUTOCRTCTL parameter, 210
AUTOCRTDEV parameter, 210
AUTODIAL parameter, 210
AUTOSTART parameter, 189
Auxiliary storage pools (ASPs), 196, 246
Availability, 3–4

B

Backup media, protecting, 279
BLDOWNCL CL program, 354
Bootstrap Protocol (BOOTP), 199
Business contingency plan, 7–8
 building, 401–421
 characteristics, 8
 disaster avoidance, 410–414
 emergency procedures, 414–415
 leaders and, 401–402
 purpose, 401
 reality, 402
 recovery program, 416–419
 risk analysis, 403–410
 testing and auditing, 419–421
 updating, 229
 See also Contingency planning

Business models, 341
Business to business (B2B) models, 215

C

CFGTCP (Configure TCP/IP) command, 190
*CHANGE authority, 286
Changes
 business model, 341
 network attribute, 343
 new product, 342
 object, 343
 operating system, 341–342
 procedural, 342
 role, 342
 system values, 343
 terminations and resignations, 343
 user identification, 343–344
 user profile, 342
CHGACTPRFL (Change Active Profiles List)
   command, 60
CHGACTSCDE (Change Activation
   Schedule Entry) command, 60, 223
CHGAUT (Change Authority) command,
   68, 69
CHGCFGLE (Change Configuration List
   Entries) command, 170
CHGCLS (Change Class) command, 246
CHGCMD (Change Command) command, 56
CHGDEVAPPC (Change Device Description
   (APPC)) command, 170
CHGEXPSCDE (Change Expiration
   Schedule Entry) command, 60
CHGFTPA (Change FTP Attributes)
   command, 222
CHGJOBD (Change Job Description)
   command, 17
CHGLIB (Change Library) command, 25
CHGMODD (Change Mode Description)
   command, 208
CHGNETA (Change Network Attributes)
   command, 166–167, 177
 DDMACC parameter, 168, 182, 183
 JOBACN parameter, 167
 PCSACC parameter, 167–168
 use of, 166–167
CHGOBJAUD (Change Object Auditing)
   command, 384–386
 defined, 384
 prompt screen, 385
 using, 385–386
CHGOBJOWN (Change Object Owner)
   command, 84
CHGOBJPGP (Change Object Primary
   Group) command, 71
CHGOUTQ (Change Output Queue)
   command, 129

CHGOWN (Change Owner) command, 84
CHGOWNER command, 306
 advantages, 306–308
 command definition, 307
 command processing program
   CHGOWNCPP, 307
 creation of, 308
CHGRTGE (Change Routing Entry)
   command, 278
CHGSBSD (Change Subsystem Description)
   command, 246
CHGSECAUD (Change Security Auditing)
   command, 398
CHGSYSVAL (Change System Value)
   command, 12
CHGTELNA (Change Telnet Attributes)
   command, 194
CHGUSRAUD (Change User Auditing)
   command
 AUDLVL attribute, 382–383
 OBJAUD attribute, 283–284, 382
 prompt screen, 384
CHGUSRPRF (Change User Profile)
   command, 13, 45
CL programs
 BLDOWNCL, 354
 CASTOPFT, 333–334
 DSPOQAC1, 162
 PRTOBJAUT, 361
 sample Client Access exit program,
   333–334
 sample DSPT filter exit program, 275–276
 sample password validity-checking
   program, 37–38
 USRFTPLOGC, 184–186
Client Access
 access issues, 178–179
 client, 179
 connection issues, 179–180
 data transfer and remote command
   issues, 180
 disconnection from, 180
 Express, 178
 functions, 180, 241
 limiting function from desktop, 181
 password issues, 179
 PC-based applications, 178
 with resource security, 178
 running over TCP/IP, 180–181
 Web site, 178
 for Windows 95/NT, 178
Client Access Express Host Servers V4R4M0,
   168, 186
CMAST
 defined, 112
 new record format, 113–114
 panel showing all fields, 112
 restricted panel, 113

Index

Command processing programs, 245
   CHGOWNCPP, 307
   DSPOQAC, 137
   PRTCHGOBJ, 366–367
Communications administrator, 304
   authority, 304
   responsibilities, 302
Communications security, 189–213
   APPN/APPC communications configuration, 209–213
   data encryption, 204–209
   evaluating, 261
   Operations Navigator, 213
   TCP/IP, 189–204
   tools, 213
Confidentiality, 2
Consultant security, 309, 311
Contingency planning
   characteristics, 8
   disaster avoidance, 410–414
   emergency procedures, 414–416
   leaders, 401–402
   purpose, 401
   reality, 402
   recovery program, 416–419
   risk analysis, 403–410
   See also Business contingency plan
Control blocks, 20
Controller description, 210–211
CPSSN parameter, 210–211
Crackers. *See* Hackers
CRTAUT parameter, 72–73
   default, 72
   defined, 72
   move, duplicate, restore and, 73
   values, 72
CRTAUTL (Create Authorization List) command, 75
CRTCMD (Create Command) command, 56
CRTDDMF (Create DDM File) command, 173
CRTDEVAPPC (Create Device Description (APPC)) command, 170
CRTJOBD (Create Job Description) command, 17
CRTJRN (Create Journal) command, 379
CRTJRNRCV (Create Journal Receiver) command, 378
CRTLIB (Create Library) command, 25
CRTMODD (Create Mode Description) command, 208
CRTOUTQ (Create Output Queue) command, 129–131
   AUTCHK parameter, 131
   defined, 129
   DSPDTA parameter, 130
   OPRCTL parameter, 130–131
   sample, 133–134

CRTUSRPRF (Create User Profile) command, 13, 45
   AUT parameter, 59, 71–72
   CURLIB parameter, 55
   DSPSNGINF parameter, 57
   GID parameter, 59
   GRPAUT parameter, 58, 71
   GRPAUTTYP parameter, 58–59, 71
   GRPPRF parameter, 57–58, 70
   INLMNU parameter, 55
   INLPGM parameter, 55
   LMTCPB parameter, 55–57
   LMTDEVSSN parameter, 57
   MAXSTG parameter, 246
   OWNER parameter, 58, 71
   parameters, 46–47
   PASSWORD parameter, 49–50
   PWDEXP parameter, 50
   PWDEXPITV parameter, 57
   SPCAUT parameter, 50–54
   STATUS parameter, 50
   SUPGRPPRF parameter, 58, 70
   UID parameter, 59
   USRCLS parameter, 50–51
   USRPRF parameter, 47–49
CSTMAINT2 RPG program
   *IN50, 114
   *IN55, 115
   I-specs, 126
   named constants, 126
   QSYCUSRA call, 127
   source, 115–126
CSTMAINT RPG program, 93–102
   checking for data authorities, 102
   defined, 92
   execution, 102
   indicators, 102
   panel display, 107
   source, 93–102
CUSTDF2 display file, 113–114
CUSTDF display file, 103–106
CUSTLFA logical file, 110
CUSTLFB logical file, 110
CUSTLFNM logical file, 93
CUSTPF physical file, 92
   illustrated, 92
   user authorities to, 106

D

Data authorities, 65
   *ADD, 65
   defined, 63
   *DLT, 65
   *EXECUTE, 65
   *READ, 65
   relationship, 108
   SQL tables and, 128
   *UPD, 65
Data center security, 410–411

Data encryption, 204–209
   AS/400 requirements, 208–209
   Digital Certificate Manager (DCM), 207
   digital certificates, 205
   options, 208
   public key infrastructure (PKI), 204–205
   Secure Sockets Layer (SSL), 206–207
   Virtual Private Networks (VPNs), 207–208
Data file security
   APPLICATION category, 286, 288
   categories, 286
   OPERATIONS category, 286, 288
   requirement list, 287
   requirements, 286–288
   USE category, 286
Database security, 89–128
   data authorities and logical files, 108
   field-level, 108–128
   file authorities, 89–107
   *OBJALTER authority and, 89
   row-level, 128
   SQL tables/views and, 128
   tightening/relaxing, 106
DB2 for AS/400 SQL Reference, 109
DDM
   access, 277
   authorization process, 174–175
   conversation, establishing, 169
   environment, 168
   environment illustration, 169
   files, 169, 173
   requests, 169, 276
   security recommendation, 277
DDM attributes, 170–172
   DDMACC, 170–171
   LOCPWD, 170
   object-authorization-related attributes, 172
   SECURELOC, 171–172
   system-related attributes, 170–171
   user-profile-related attributes, 171–172
DDM security, 168–177
   complexity, 168
   implementation, 170
DDMACC attribute, 168
   modifying, 177
   *OBJECT, 171, 172
   *REJECT, 171
   setting, 173
   target system value, 170
   user-written exit program, 171, 172
DDS Reference, 109
Dedicated Service Tools (DST), 196
   limiting access to, 246
   passwords, changed, 347
Default user profiles, 172, 278
Denial-of-service attack
   defense against, 228
   defined, 3–4
   filling with unwanted files, 196
   mail spamming, 227–228
   safety, 228

Departmental procedures, 415
Departmental survey, 407–410
Device configurations, evaluating, 261
DFTUSER parameter, 277
Dial-back security, 203–204, 235
Dial-up line security, 203–204
   device authorization, 203
   dial-back, 203–204
   line status control, 203
   numbers, 235
   vendors and, 310
Dial-up workstation sessions, 271
Digital Certificate Manager (DCM), 207
Digital certificates, 205
   client-side authentication use of, 225
   defined, 205
Direct authorization model, 252–253
   defined, 252
   illustrated, 253
   management, 254
   problems, 253
   strict implementation of, 253
   See also Authorization models
Disaster avoidance, 410–414
   alternative facilities, 414
   data center security, 410–411
   with effects reduction, 413–414
   employee policies, 411–412
   employee training, 413–414
   fire prevention, 411
   IT hot sites, 414
   natural disaster preparedness, 411
   network security, 411
   preventive maintenance, 413
   with prevention, 410–413
   records/data-storage options, 412–413
   system security, 411
   UPS, 412
   See also Business contingency plan
Display files
   CUSTDF2, 113–114
   CUSTDF, 103–106
   DSPOQAD, 138–139
Display Station Passthrough (DSPT), 271
Distributed Data Management. *See* DDM; DDM security
Distributed Data Management, 117
Distributed Relational Database Architecture (DRDA), 202–203, 241
   conversation-level security and, 202
   defined, 202
   exit-program support, 241
   sending user ID option, 203
*DLT authority, 65
DLTUSRPRF (Delete User Profile) command, 45

Domain Name Server (DNS), 200
DSCTMR parameter, 211
DSPACTPRFL (Display Active Profiles List) command, 60
DSPACTSCD (Display Activation Schedule) command, 60
DSPAUDJRNE (Display Audit Journal Entries) command, 398
DSPAUT (Display Authority) command, 68
DSPAUTJRNE (Display Audit Journal Entries) command, 390
DSPAUTUSR (Display Authorized Users) command, 14, 348–349
DSPDTA parameter, 130
DSPEXPSCDE (Display Expiration Schedule) command, 60
DSPFFD (Display File Field Descriptions) command, 392
DSPGRPLF logical file, 350
DSPJRN (Display Journal) command, 390
   for database file generation, 392
   for displaying entries, 391–392
   FROMTIME parameter, 397
   OUTFILFMT parameter, 392–393
   for printing entries, 392–397
   screen display, 391, 392
   TOTIME parameter, 397
DSPLOG (Display Log) command, 375–377
   defined, 375
   parameters, 376
   See also History log
DSPMBRLF logical file, 373
DSPNETA (Display Network Attributes) command, 166
DSPOBJAUT (Display Object Authority) command, 109, 360
DSPOBJLF logical file, 373
DSPOQAC1 CL program, 162
DSPOQAC command processing program, 137
DSPOQAD display file, 138–139
DSPOQAK Cobol program, 151–162
DSPOQAR RPG program, 140–150
DSPOUTQ (Display Output Queue) command, 129
DSPOUTQAUT utility
   CL program DSPOQAC1, 162
   Cobol program DSPOQAK, 151–162
   command definition, 136
   command processing program, 137
   DDS for display file DSPOQAD, 138–139
   defined, 134
   options, 135–136
   RPG program DSPOQAR, 140–150

sample subfile display, 135
using, 134
DSPPGMREF (Display Program References) command, 288
DSPSECAUD (Display Security Auditing) command, 398
DSPUSRPRF (Display User Profile) command, 350
   OUTFILE parameter, 356
   TYPE(*ALL), 355
   TYPE(*BASIC), 359
   TYPE(*OBJOWN), 354
Dynamic Host Configuration Protocol (DHCP), 199–200
   configuration information, 200
   defined, 199

E

EDTAUTL (Edit Authorization List) command, 75, 109
EDTOBJAUT (Edit Object Authority) command, 68, 131
Emergency procedures, 414–415
   departmental, 415
   evacuation, 414–415
   notification, 415
   overview, 414
   shutdown, 415
   See also Business contingency plan
Employee
   policies, 411–412
   training, 413–414
Encryption. *See* Data encryption
ENDHOSTSVR (End Host Servers) command, 181
Enterprise roles, defining, 291–292
Evacuation procedures, 414–415
Evaluation
   communications and device configurations, 261
   initial programs and menus, 261
   physical security, 258–259
   questionnaire, 258
   resource security, 262
   security level, 259
   system configuration, 259–261
Event auditing, 375–399
   audit journal, 377–380, 387–397
   controls, 380–381
   controls security recommendations, 386
   defined, 375
   general recommendations, 387
   history log, 375–377
   object, 383–386
   Operations Navigator, 398–399
   recommendations, 386–387

Index 447

system and user security recommendations, 387
system-wide, 381–382
tools, 398
user, 382–383
See also Auditing
EXCHID parameter, 210
*EXECUTE authority, 65
Exit points, 182–187
defined, 182–183
documentation, 186
to implement anonymous FTP, 195
Internet security and, 226–227
locations, 182
program code, 184–186
Exit programs
auditing, 245, 364
database file sample, 177
for DSPT, DDM, Client Access function
auditing, 243
implementation example, 333–334
for more authority, 183
passthrough, 275–276
password validity-checking, limiting
authority to, 237
sample, 176
specifying with DDMACC attribute, 171
to stem flood of security exposures, 183
uses, 183
writing, 176–177

F

Field-level security, 108–128
before V4R2, 109–111
program example, 112–128
with projection, 109–111
reference authority, 108
update authority, 108–109
See also Database security
File Transfer Protocol (FTP), 6, 195–196
anonymous, 195
defined, 195
INACTTIMO parameter and, 195
public authority and, 196
QMAXSIGN system value and, 195
remote command submission, 195
session inactive time, 195
Financial risk evaluation, 405–406
expenses, 405
losses, 405–406
Fire prevention, 411
Firewalls, 217–219
breaches, 218
features, 218
illustrated implementation, 218, 219
implementation example, 332
technology implementation, 217
See also Internet security

Functional dependencies, 403–404
Functional exposures, 403
Functional threats, 404–405

G

General system values, 21–32
Group authorization model, 253–255
advantages, 254
defined, 253
drawbacks, 254–255
illustrated, 254
management, 254
See also Authorization models
Group Identification Number (GID), 59
Group profiles, 69–71
audit listing example, 349
auditing, 348–352
authority, 58–59
authority, granting, 71
authority lookup process, 57–58
authorization list comparison, 77
creating with CRTUSRPRF command,
57–59
creating with Operations Navigator, 61–62
GID, 59
multiple, 58, 70–71
parameters, 57–59
passwords and, 57
programmer/analysts, 304–305
sample implementation, 70
security recommendation, 58
using, 70
See also User profiles
GRTOBJAUT (Grant Object Authority)
command, 68, 131

H

Hackers
access, 232–238
adopted authorities and, 238–239
advice on, 247
bypassing/gaining authority, 238–243
Client Access Express functions and, 241
defined, 231
Internet attacks, 247
job descriptions and, 240
ODBC and, 241
profile swapping and, 239
remote command facilities and, 241
resources, 236
*SAVSYS special authority and, 241–242
subsystem descriptions and, 239–240
terminology, 231–232
thwarting, 231–247
Trojan horses, 243–244
viruses, 245–246
worms, 246

History log, 375–377
daily review of, 377
defined, 375
displaying contents of, 375
files, 376
housekeeping, 376–377
illustrated sample, 376
HTTP servers, 224, 225

I

IBM Cryptographic Support for AS/400, 208
IBM HTTP Server for AS/400, 201–202
defined, 201
for secure Web applications, 224
server instance, 202
SSL-enabled, 206
starting, 202
INACTTIMO parameter
FTP and, 195
Internet security and, 221
INETD server, 201
Initial programs, evaluating, 261
Initial-It. *See* Security implementation
example
Integrated File System (IFS), 198
Integrated File System Introduction, 63
Integrity, 2–3
Interactive subsystems, 277–278
Internet Assigned Numbers Authority
(IANA), 190
Internet attacks, 247
Internet Key Exchange (IKE), 207
Internet security, 215–229
business contingency plan and, 229
configuration, 228
control and, 223–224
corporate policy, 216–217
exit points, 226–227
firewalls, 217–219
ISP, 217
monitoring, 227–228
resource security, 223
system values, 219–222
testing, 228–229
user profiles, 222–223
Web applications and, 224–226
Internet Service Providers (ISPs), 217
Intrusion detection, 227
*IOSYSCFG special authority, 53–54
assigning, 54, 189, 235
defined, 53–54
line, controller, device configuration, 166
for TCP/IP configuration/management, 189
IP packet filtering, 191
defined, 191
implementation example, 332

IT hot sites, 414
IT staff security, 301–311
　authorization roles, 301–302
　communications administrator, 304
　difficulty, 301
　network administrator, 308
　operator, 302–304
　programmer/analyst, 304–306
　security administrator, 306–308
　vendors/consultants, 309–311
　Webmaster, 309

J

Job descriptions
　with associated user profile, 240
　auditing, 363
　QDFTJOBD, 240
JOBACN attribute, 167
*JOBCTL special authority, 130–131
JOBD parameter, 277, 278

K

Key
　positions, 269
　removal, 233

L

Library and directory authorization model, 251–252
　defined, 251
　end users/IT personnel and, 251
　illustrated, 252
　public authority and, 252
　See also Authorization models
Line description parameters, 209–210
　AUTOANS, 210
　AUTOCRTCTL, 210
　AUTODIAL, 210
　SECURITY, 209
Line Printer Daemon (LPD), 196
Line Printer Requester (LPR), 196
LMTCPB parameter, 55–57
　functions, 55–56
　security recommendation, 57
　values, 56
LOCPWD parameter, 211
　in APPN environment, 211
　default, 170
　defined, 170, 211
　password, 173
　specifying, 170
　in X.25 networks, 170
Logical files
　authorities and, 108, 111
　CUSTLFA, 110

CUSTLFB, 110
CUSTLFNM, 93
DSPGRPLF, 350
DSPMBRLF, 373
DSPOBJLF, 373

M

Menu authorization model, 249–251
　defined, 249
　failure, 251
　illustrated, 250
　problems, 250–251
　public authority and, 252
　See also Authorization models
MI instructions, restricted use of, 16
Microsoft policies, 181
Monitoring
　critical objects and object authorities, 359–362
　denial-of-service attacks, 227–228
　history log, 375–377
　IBM-supplied user profiles, 353
　intrusion detection, 227
　security configurations, 228
　TCP/IP applications, 363–364
　user list changes, 362–363
　user profiles, 348–359
　See also Auditing

N

Natural disaster preparedness, 411
Network Address Translation (NAT), 191, 217
Network administrator, 308
　responsibilities, 302
　security, 308
Network attributes
　changes to, 343
　changing, 167
　DDMACC attribute, 168
　displaying, 166
　implementation example, 332
　JOBACN attribute, 167
　list of, 166
　PCSACC attribute, 167–168
　recommended settings, 261
Network security, 165–187
　attributes, 166–168
　configuration, 166
　DDM, 168–177
　disaster avoidance, 411
　exit points, 182–187
　implementation example, 332–333
　for PCs, 177–182
　physical, 165
　problems/solutions, 165
　QAUTOCFG and, 166

QAUTOVRT and, 166
　tools, 187
Notification procedures, 415

O

*OBJALTER authority, 64, 65
　in database security, 89
　defined, 64
*OBJEXIST authority, 64
Object authorities
　defined, 63
　*OBJALTER, 64, 65
　*OBJEXIST, 64
　*OBJMGT, 64
　*OBJOPR, 64
　*OBJREF, 64, 65
Object ownership, 84–86
　auditing, 353–355
　IBM-supplied profiles for, 243
　limiting, 243
　report, 355
Object security
　as continuum, 281–282
　flexibility with system organization, 282
　multiple methods use, 282
　purchased software and, 282–283
　requirements evaluation, 283
　tenets, 281
*OBJMGT authority, 64
*OBJOPR authority, 64
*OBJREF authority, 64, 65
　in database security, 89
　defined, 64
Open Database Connectivity (ODBC), 6, 180
　drivers, 241
　security considerations, 182
Operating system updates, 341–342
Operations, 293
Operations Navigator, 42–44
　Application Administration interface, 87, 181
　Audit Policy Properties dialog box, 398–399
　defined, 42
　event auditing, 398–399
　for group profile creation, 61–62
　New Group configuration window, 62
　New User configuration window, 61
　Permissions window, 88
　policies, 44
　policy management window, 44
　privileges, 52
　security wizard, 42–44, 219, 348
　spooled file management, 163
　TCP/IP management with, 213
　user Capabilities window, 87
　for user profile creation, 61–62

Operators, 302–304
　batch job submission, 303
　QSYSOPR user profile and, 302
　responsibilities, 302
　role authorization form example, 330
　*SAVSYS special authority, 84, 303
　*SPLCTL special authority, 303
OPRCTL parameter, 130–131
Organizational chart
　example, 315
　verifying, 362
OS/400 Backup and Recovery, 379
OS/400 objects, direct use of, 239
OS/400 Security–Reference, 131
OS/400 SNA Distribution Services V4R4, 167
OS/400 TCP/IP Configuration and Reference V4R4, 186, 196
Output queues
　access, 278
　auditing, 363
　AUT parameter, 131
　AUTCHK parameter, 131
　changing, 129
　creating, 129
　DSPDTA parameter, 130
　*JOBCTL special authority and, 130–131
　OPRCTL parameter, 130–131
　ownership, 132–133
　sample security implementation, 133–134
　security management utility, 134–162
　security-related attributes, 129–132
　system operator responsibility, 132
Override Display File (OVRDSPF) command, 237
OVRMSGF (Override with Message File) command, 244

P

Passthrough
　exit program, 275–276
　security recommendation, 277
　workstation sessions, 271–276
Password security, 11
　Client Access and, 179
　security level 20 and, 13
　special authorities, 13
Password-related system values, 33–38
Passwords
　change frequency, 236
　changing, 50
　choosing, 14
　different than user profile name, 49
　digits in, 35
　expiration interval, 33–34, 198
　format, 49–50
　group profiles and, 57

hard-to-guess, 236
　maximum number of characters in, 35
　minimum composition system values, 222
　repeating characters, limiting, 36
　rules example, 316–317
　setting to expired state, 50
　validity-checking program, 37–38
PCs
　access issues, 178–179
　connection issues, 179–180
　data transfer issues, 180
　password issues, 179
　remote command issues, 180
　security considerations for, 177–182
　security recommendation, 276
　threat, 276
　viruses and, 182
PCSACC attribute, 167–168
　defined, 167
　and Original Server invocation of exit programs with *REGFAC value, 186
　security recommendation, 168
　See also Network attributes
PGMSTRQS parameter, 212
Physical connections
　AS/400 system unit, 269–270
　backup media, 279
　DDM, 276–277
　dial-up workstation sessions, 271
　direct workstation access, 270–271
　interactive subsystems, 277–278
　passthrough workstation sessions, 271–276
　PCs, 276
　printers and output queues, 278
　TCP/IP applications, 278
Physical files
　authorities and, 108, 111
　CUSTPF, 92
Physical security
　auditing, 347
　computer room, 347
　evaluating, 258–259
　key/console, 347
　need for, 259
　network, 165
　threats, 262
Point-to-Point Protocol (PPP), 191–192
　authentication, 192
　configuring, 192
　defined, 191
　for high-speed connection, 191
　security mechanisms, 192
Post Office Protocol (POP), 198–199
　defined, 198
　IFS storage, 198–199
PREESTSSN parameter, 212
Preventive maintenance, 413

Primary group authorities, 59
Printer access, 278
Printing
　audit journal entries, 392–397
　function authority, 132
Privacy, 4
Private authorities, 59
　authority look-ups and, 253
　authorization lists and, 76
　group profiles comparison, 77
　manipulating, 69
　restoring, 83
　See also Authorities
Procedural changes, 342
Production environment, restricting authorities to, 244
Profile authorization model, 256–257
Program adoption authorization model, 255–256
　defined, 255
　illustrated, 255
　See also Authorization models
Program calls, qualifying, 243
Program security, 288–290
　requirements, 288–290
　swap profiles and, 289
Programmer/analysts, 304–306
　group profile, 304–305
　promotion tool, 305
　responsibilities, 302
　role authorization form example, 329
　security recommendation, 305
Programs
　attaching to database files, 245
　control of, 288
　invoking, 240–241
　modified, restoration of, 17–18
　object authorization requirement list, 290
Projection
　defined, 109
　field-level security implementation with, 109–111
　program example, 112–128
　See also Database security
PRTADPOBJ (Print Adopting Objects) command, 88, 289
PRTAUDJRN RPG program, 393–394
PRTCHGOBJ command
　command definition, 365–366
　CPP for, 366–367
PRTCMNSEC (Print Communications Security) command, 212, 213
PRTCORPG RPG program, 367–372
PRTGRPRPT RPG program, 350–352
PRTOBJAUT CL program, 361
PRTPRFINT (Print Profile Internals) command, 60

PRTPUBAUT (Print Public Authorities)
  command
    defined, 88
    using, 199, 242
PRTPVTAUT (Print Private Authorities)
  command, 360
    defined, 88
    using, 199
PRTQAUT (Print Queue Authority Report)
  tool, 163
PRTSYSSECA (Print System Security
  Attributes) command
    accessing, 42
    using, 348
PRTTRGPGM (Print Trigger Program)
  command, 243
PRTUSRPRF (Print User Profile) command,
  60, 348
*PUBLIC authority, 59
  performance, 286
  for physical devices, 271
Public authority, 71–75
  *CHANGE, 286
  default, changing, 25
  default, using, 73–75
  defined, 71
  determination illustration, 73
  establishing, 71–73
  FTP and, 196
  planning, 242
  too much, 242
  *USE, 286
  use of, 282
Public key infrastructure (PKI), 204–205
  defined, 204
  symmetric/asymmetric keys, 205
  See also Data encryption
Purchased software, object security and,
  282–283

Q

QALWOBJRST system value, 22–23
  *ALWPGMADP value, 22, 23
  *ALWPTF value, 22, 23
  *ALWSETUID and ALWSETGID values, 22
  default, 22
  defined, 22
  Internet security and, 220
  *NONE value, 22, 23
QALWUSRDMN system value, 23–24
  *All value, 23, 24
  defined, 23
  values, 23
QAUDCTL system value, 39
QAUDENDACN system value, 39–40, 380
  defined, 39

*NOTIFY value, 39
*PWRDWNSYS value, 39, 380
security recommendation, 40
QAUDFRCLVL system value, 40, 380
QAUDLVL system value, 40–41, 377
  *AUTFAIL value, 381
  *CREATE value, 381–382
  defined, 40
  *OBJMGT value, 382
  *PGMADP value, 382
  security recommendation, 41
  using, 41
  values, 40–41, 381, 383
QAUTOCFG system value, 24
  Internet security and, 220
  network security and, 166
  turning off, 234–235
QAUTOVRT system value, 24
  Internet security and, 220
  network security and, 166
  turning off, 235
QCRTAUT system value, 25
  *ALL value, 74
  *CHANGE value, 74
  *EXCLUDE value, 74
  objects created in directories and, 72
  *USE value, 74
QCRTOBJAUD system value, 42, 385
QCTL job queue, 246
QDEVRCYACN system value
  *DSCJOB setting, 235
  Internet security and, 220
QDSCJOBITV system value, 26–27
  default, 26
  defined, 26
  setting, 27
QDSPSGNINF system value, 26, 220
QINACTITV system value, 26
  Internet security and, 221
  TCP/IP applications and, 234
  Telnet and, 194
QINACTMSGQ system value, 26, 221
QLMTDEVSSN system value, 28
  Internet security and, 220
  security recommendation, 268
QLMTSECOFR system value, 28–29
  default, 28
  defined, 28, 234
  hacking and, 234
  Internet security and, 220
  for limiting workstation authorization, 270
  for restricting profiles, 237
  security recommendation, 270
  WSG and, 197
QMAXSGNACN system value, 29–30
  defined, 29
  Internet security and, 221

security recommendation, 30
  using, 236
  values, 30
  WSG and, 197
QMAXSIGN system value, 29
  default, 29
  defined, 29
  FTP and, 195
  Internet security and, 221
  *NOMAX value, 30
  Telnet and, 194
  using, 236
QPRCRTPG API, 246
QPWDEXPITV system value, 33–34
  defined, 33
  Internet security and, 222
  security recommendation, 34
QPWDLMTAJC system value, 35–36
  defined, 35
  security recommendation, 36
QPWDLMTCHR system value, 36
QPWDLMTREP system value, 36
QPWDMAXLEN system value, 35
QPWDMINLEN system value
  defined, 35
  Internet security and, 222
  values, 35
QPWDPOSDIF system value, 37
QPWDRQDDGT system value
  defined, 35
  Internet security and, 222
  values, 35
QPWDRQDDIF system value
  defined, 34
  Internet security and, 222
  values, 34
QPWDVLDPGM system value, 37
QRETSVRSEC system value, 30–31
  default, 30
  defined, 30
  Internet security and, 221
  security recommendation, 31
QRMTSIGN system value, 31–32
  defined, 31, 194–195
  *FRCSIGNON value, 31
  Internet security and, 221
  *NAMEPRF value, 31
  *REJECT value, 31, 32
  security recommendation, 273
  with Telnet, 194–195
  *VERIFY value, 31, 32, 274
QSECOFR user profile, 29
  *ALLOBJ special authority, 53
  *DISABLED status, 223
  password, resetting, 233
  production object ownership and, 85
  security administrator and, 306

Index 451

QSECURITY system value, 32, 42, 170, 259
   defined, 11, 32
   Internet security and, 219
   modifying, 12
   setting, 348
   values, 11, 32
QSYCUSRA API, 126–127
   call, 127
   defined, 126
   error code structure, 127
   parameters, 127
QSYGETPH API, 256
QSYRUSRA API
   calls to, 106
   defined, 90
   error code structure, 92
   parameter requirements, 90
   USRA0100 format, 90–91
QSYSETGID API, 256, 257
QSYSETUID API, 256, 257
QSYSLIBL (system library list), 238
QSYSOPR user profile, 302
QTEMP library
   implementation, 20
   level 50 and, 20, 23
   maintenance, 20
QUSEADPAUT system value
   defined, 32
   Internet security and, 221
   values, 32
QWTSETP API, 256

R

*READ authority, 65, 108
Record formats
   file QADSPUPA, 356
   file QADSPUPB, 357–358
   file QADSPUPG, 358–359
   file QADSPUPO, 358
Recovery priorities, identifying, 406
Recovery program, 416–419
   document, 416
   tasks, 416
   teams, 417–419
Recovery team activities, 417–419
   administration and support, 417
   communications, 419
   evaluation, 417
   IT operations/recovery, 417–419
   operations, 417
   salvage/facilities, 419
Reference authority
   defined, 108
   granting, 109
   See also Field-level security

Remote commands, 180
   facilities, 241
   FTP and, 195
   hackers and, 241
Remote Execution (REXEC), 200
Remote Work Station Support, 275
Resource security, 11
   Client Access with, 178
   evaluating, 262
   Internet security with, 223
   support, 14
Risk analysis, 1–4
   financial–expenses, 405
   financial–losses, 405–406
   functional dependencies identification, 403–404
   functional exposures identification, 403
   functional threats identification, 404–405
   information, obtaining, 406–410
   performing, 403
   recovery priorities identification, 406
   See also Business contingency plan
Risk tolerance, 215
RMTCMD (Remote Command) facility, 233
RMTCPNAME parameter, 210
RMTLOCNAME parameter, 211
Role authorizations
   accounting manager form example, 326
   accounts payable form example, 324
   accounts receivable form example, 323
   defined, 291
   documenting, 295
   general ledger form example, 325
   identifying, 291
   inventory control form example, 319
   IT manager form example, 331
   IT operator form example, 330
   order entry clerk form, 296
   order entry clerk user form example, 297
   order entry form example, 318
   order entry/inventory control supervisor form example, 320
   payroll clerk form example, 327
   payroll supervisor form example, 328
   process of, 295
   programmer/analyst form example, 329
   purchasing role form example, 322
   samples, 317–331
   shipping/receiving form example, 321
   time card/order entry clerk form, 298
   user form, 299
Roles, changing, 342
Route Daemon (RouteD), 200–201
Row-level security, 128
RPG programs
   CSTMAINT2, 114–126
   CSTMAINT, 93–102
   DSPOQAR, 140–150

PRTAUDJRN, 393–394
PRTCORPG, 367–372
PRTGRPRPT, 350–352
   sample DDM USER exit program, 176
RRTJOB (Reroute Job) command, 246
RSTAUT (Restore Authorities) command, 83
RSTOBJ (Restore Object) command, 18
RVKOBJAUT (Revoke Object Authority) command, 68, 131

S

*SAVSYS special authority, 53
   hackers and, 241–242
   save/restore functions and, 83
   for system operators, 84, 303
SBMJOB (Submit Job) command, 304
SBMRMTCMD (Submit Remote Command) command, 168
*SECADM special authority
   in security system design, 53
   user profiles and, 45
*SECOFR user class, 189
Secure Hypertext Transfer Protocol (HTTPS), 225
Secure Sockets Layer (SSL), 195, 206–207
   client-side authentication, 207
   defined, 206
   VPN versus, 207–208
   See also Data encryption
SECURELOC parameter, 171–172
   in APPN environment, 212
   defined, 171, 211
   location, 171
   *NO, 172, 274
   value determination, 173
   *VFYENCPWD, 171–172
   *YES, 171
Security
   application, 283–286
   APPN/APPC communications configuration, 209–213
   as business function, 1–9
   communications, 189–213
   corporate policy, 216–217
   data center, 410–411
   data file, 286–288
   database, 89–128
   DDM, 168–177
   dial-back, 203–204
   dial-up line, 203–204
   guidelines, 5
   Internet, 215–229
   for IT professionals, 301–311
   mentality, 5–6
   network, 165–187
   object, 281–283

ODBC and, 182
PCs and, 177–182
physical, 165
planning, starting, 8–9
program, 288–290
purpose, 1
vendor/consultant, 309–311
Security administrator, 306–308
  implementation, 306
  profile, 306
  responsibilities, 302
  security recommendation, 306
Security Advisor, 43, 219
Security implementation
  enforcing, 9
  successful, 6
Security implementation example, 313–339
  accounting manager role authorization form, 326
  accounts payable role authorization form, 324
  accounts receivable role authorization form, 323
  antivirus software, 333
  application administration, 334
  application security requirements, 314–315
  exit programs, 333–334
  firewall, 332
  general ledger role authorization form, 325
  inventory control role authorization form, 319
  IP packet filtering, 332
  IT manager role authorization form, 331
  IT operator role authorization form, 330
  library/object authorities listing, 337–339
  network attributes, 332
  network security considerations, 332–333
  order entry role authorization form, 318
  order entry/inventory control supervisor role authorization form, 320
  organizational chart, 315
  payroll clerk role authorization form, 327, 328
  port restrictions, 332
  programmer/analyst role authorization form, 329
  purchasing role authorization form, 322
  role-authorization samples, 317–331
  shipping/receiving role authorization form, 321
  special authorities listing, 337
  system values, 334–335
  user profile and password rules, 316–317
  user profile listing, 336–337
  VPN connection, 332
Security level 10, 12
Security level 20, 13–14
  defined, 13

special authorities, 13
  See also System security levels
Security level 30, 14–15
  resource security support, 14
  special authorities, 15
  user classes for, 51
  See also System security levels
Security level 40, 15–18
  job initiation validation, 17
  need for, 15
  operating-system integrity, 16
  reasons to use, 18
  restoration of modified programs, 17–18
  running production systems at, 15
  security strengthening, 16
  special authorities, 15
  state and domain restrictions, 16
  Trojan horses and, 18
  use of restricted MI instructions, 16
  user classes for, 51
  See also System security levels
Security level 50, 19–21
  control block modification prevention, 20
  defined, 19
  message restrictions, 19–20
  parameter-passing validation, 19
  pointer removal, 20
  QTEMP library maintenance, 20, 23
  reasons to use, 21
  special authorities, 15
  system integrity, 19
  user classes for, 51
  viruses and, 245
  See also System security levels
Security levels
  changing, 12
  defined, 11
  differences between, 14
  evaluating, 259
  running at, 242
  verifying, 267
  See also specific security levels
SECURITY parameter, 209
Security wizard (Operations Navigator), 42–44, 219, 348
Security-related output queue attributes, 129–132
Serial Line Internet Protocol (SLIP), 192–193
  authentication, 192
  connection authentication user profiles, 193
  defined, 192
  incoming caller validation, 192
*SERVICE special authority, 54, 271
  assigning, 54, 237
  defined, 54
Shutdown procedures, 415

Sign-on
  attempts, invalid, 268
  automatic, 274
  error message text, 236
Simple Mail Transfer Protocol (SMTP), 197–198
  configuring, 197
  defined, 197
  RELAY and CONNECTION functions, 197
  servers, 198
  viruses and, 198
Simple Network Management Protocol (SNMP), 201
SNGSSN parameter, 212
SPCAUT parameter, 50–54
  default, 51
  defined, 50–51
  values, 52
Special authorities
  *ALLOBJ, 1, 7, 52
  assigning, 268
  *AUDIT, 380
  danger, 52
  defined, 348
  granted, 50–54
  *IOSYSCFG, 53–54
  *JOBCTL, 130–131
  listing example, 337
  *SAVSYS, 53, 303
  *SECADM, 45
  security level 20, 13
  security levels 30, 40, 50, 15
  *SERVICE, 54, 237
  *SPLCTL, 303
  use auditing, 243
  See also Authorities
Specific authorities, 63–66
  categories, 63
  changing, 68
  data, 65
  granting/revoking, 68
  object, 64–65
  relationships, 66
  See also Authorities
*SPLCTL special authority, 303
SQL tables, 128
Status auditing, 345–373
  checklist, 346
  defined, 345
  performing, 345
  reports, 345
  use of, 373
  See also Auditing
Strategic issues
  access control, 6–7
  business contingency plan, 7–8
  managing, 4–8
  security auditing, 7
  security mentality, 5–6

Strategy
  changing, 341–344
  current, evaluating, 249–265
  is it working?, 341–344
STRHOSTSVR (Start Host Servers) command, 181
STRPASTHR (Start Passthrough) command, 272
  difficulties, 272
  examples, 272–276
  implementation 1, 273
  implementation 2, 273, 274
  implementation 3, 273, 274–275
  implementation 4, 273, 275–276
  RMTCURLIB parameter, 272
  RMTINLMNU parameter, 272
  RMTINLPGM parameter, 272
  RMTPWD parameters, 272
  RMTUSER parameters, 272
STRTCP (Start TCP/IP) command, 181
  execution of, 189
  SERVER parameter, 190
STRTCPSVR (Start TCP/IP Server) command, 189
Subsystem descriptions, 239–240
  securing, 244
  as Trojan horse opportunity, 239
Subsystems
  change authority, limiting, 246
  interactive, 277–278
Super profiles, 310
Super programs, 309–310
*SYSLIBL, guarding, 242
System API Reference, 186
System configuration, evaluating, 259–261
System security levels, 11–21
  defined, 11
  differences in, 14
  level 10, 12
  level 20, 13–14
  level 30, 14–15
  level 40, 15–18
  level 50, 19–21
System Service Tools (SST), 196, 246
System values, 21–42
  audit-related, 38–42
  changes to, 343
  general, 21–32
  implementation example, 334–335
  Internet security and, 219–222
  overrides, 57
  password-related, 33–38
  QALWOBJRST, 22–23
  QALWUSRDMN, 23–24
  QAUDCTL, 39
  QAUDENDACN, 39–40
  QAUDFRCLVL, 40

QAUDLVL, 40–41
QAUTOCFG, 24
QAUTOVRT, 24
QCRTAUT, 25, 72–75
QCRTOBJAUD, 42
QDSCJOBITV, 26–27
QDSPSGNINF, 26
QINACTITV, 26
QINACTMSGQ, 26
QLMTDEVSSN, 28
QLMTSECOFR, 28–29
QMAXSGNACN, 29–30
QMAXSIGN, 29
QPWDEXPITV, 33–34
QPWDLMTAJC, 35–36
QPWDLMTCHR, 36
QPWDLMTREP, 36
QPWDMAXLEN, 35
QPWDMINLEN, 35
QPWDPOSDIF, 37
QPWDRQDDGT, 35
QPWDRQDDIF, 34
QPWDVLDPGM, 37
QRETSVRSEC, 30–31
QRMTSIGN, 31–32
QSECURITY, 11, 32
QUSEADPAUT, 32
  recommended settings, 260
System-level security auditing, 347–348
System-supplied user profiles, 54
  default passwords, 268
  monitoring, 353
  See also User profiles
System-wide auditing, 381–382

T

TCP/IP
  address configuration, 190
  application servers that autostart by default, 189
  applications, 278
  BOOTP, 199
  Client Access over, 180–181
  DHCP, 199–200
  dial-up security considerations, 203–204
  DNS, 200
  DRDA, 202–203
  FTP, 195–196
  hiding/mapping addresses, 191
  INETD, 201
  IP packet filtering, 191
  LPD, 196
  LPR, 196
  Point-to-Point Protocol (PPP), 191–192
  POP, 198–199
  REXEC, 200
  RouteD, 200–201
  security considerations, 189–204

  Serial Line Internet Protocol (SLIP), 192–193
  SMTP, 197–198
  SNMP, 201
  Telnet, 194–195
  TFTP, 199
  WSG, 196–197
Telnet, 194–195
  defined, 194
  QINACTITV system value and, 194
  QMAXSIGN system value and, 194
  QRMTSIGN system value with, 194–195
  sign-on display bypass, 194
  SSL-enabled, 195
  user access via, 194
Test observation record, 420
Testing
  business contingency plan, 419–421
  Internet security and, 228
TFRJOB (Transfer Job) command, 246
Threats
  competitive information, 264
  data and public access, 263–264
  evaluating, 4
  functional, 404–405
  level, determining, 262–265
  level, questionnaire, 263
  PCs, 276
  physical, 262
  reducing, 4
  source of, 264–265
Transport Layer Security (TLS), 208
Trigger programs, 242
  monitoring, 364
Trivial File Transfer Protocol (TFTP), 199
Trojan horses, 18
  defined, 231
  opportunities for, 244
  planting, 243
  preventing, 243–244
  subsystem descriptions as opportunity, 239

U

*UPD authority, 65, 108
Update authority
  defined, 108
  granting, 108–109
  See also Field-level security
UPS, 412
*USE authority, 286
User authorities
  checking for, 91
  to file CUSTPF, 106
  retrieving, 90–91
User Defined Functions (UDFs), 128
User Identification (UID), 59

User profiles, 45–62
    assigning, to authorization list, 192
    attributes, 46–59
    auditing, 353–355
    for authenticating SLIP connections, 193
    by type, 51
    changing, 342
    classes, 51
    creating, 14
    creating with CRTUSRPRF command, 46–59
    creating with Operations Navigator, 61–62
    default, 172, 278
    defined, 45
    enabled/disabled status, 50
    expanded auditing of, 355–359
    guidelines, 268–269
    implementation example, 336–337
    Internet security and, 222–223
    listing, 14
    management tools, 59–60
    names, 47–49
    naming convention, choosing, 48–49
    planning, 267–269
    purposes, 45
    QSECOFR, 29, 53
    QSYSOPR, 302
    rules example, 316–317
    *SECADM special authority and, 45
    security level 10 and, 12
    sharing and, 268
    special authorities, 50–54
    subset of, 281
    swapping, 239, 256
    system-supplied, 54, 268
    UID number, 59
    See also Group profiles

Users
    auditing, 382–383
    classes, 51
    function, limiting, 86
    sign-on options, 55–57
USRA0100 format, 90–91
USRFTPLOGC, 184–187
    code, 184–186
    installing, 187

V

Validation lists, 225
Validity-checking programs (VCP), 245
Vendor security, 309–310
    dial-in support, 310
    super profile, 310
    super program concept, 309–310
    weaknesses, 309
Virtual Private Networks (VPNs), 207–208
    defined, 207
    implementation example, 332
    integrated support, 208
    as leased line replacement, 208
    SSL versus, 207–208
Viruses, 182
    defined, 231–232
    preventing, 245–246
    SMTP and, 198

W

Web applications
    AS/400 Web server features for, 226
    example, 226
    secure, writing, 224–226

Webmaster, 309
    responsibilities, 302
    security, 309
Workstation Gateway (WSG), 196–197
    defined, 196
    QLMTSECOFR system value and, 197
    QMAXSGNACN system value and, 197
Workstations
    dial-up sessions, 271
    direct access, 270–271
    guarding against hackers finding, 232–233
    locking, 234
    passthrough sessions, 271–276
    signing off idle users from, 233
Worms
    defined, 232
    preventing, 246
WRKAUT (Work with Authority) command, 68
WRKCFGL (Work with Configuration Lists) command, 212
WRKNAMSMTP (Work with Names for SMTP) command, 198
WRKOBJPGP (Work with Objects by Primary Group) command, 71
WRKOUTQD (Work with Output Queue Description) command, 129
WRKREGINF (Work with Registration Information) command, 187
    auditing, 245
    defined, 187

VISIT OUR WEB SITE AT WWW.AS400NETWORKSTORE.COM FOR A MORE DETAILED LISTING OF BOOKS FROM
29TH STREET PRESS® AND NEWS/400 BOOKS ™

New Books in the 29th Street Press® and NEWS/400 Books™ Library

CREATING CL COMMANDS BY EXAMPLE
By Lynn Nelson
Learn from an expert how to create CL commands that have the same functionality and power as the IBM commands you use every day. You'll see how to create commands with all the function found in IBM's commands, including parameter editing, function keys, F4 prompt for values, expanding lists of values, and conditional prompting. Whether you're in operations or programming, *Creating CL Commands by Example* can help you tap the tremendous power and flexibility of CL commands to automate tasks and enhance applications. 134 pages.

DDS KEYWORD REFERENCE
By James Coolbaugh
Reach for the *DDS Keyword Reference* when you need quick, at-your-fingertips information about DDS keywords for physical files, logical files, display files, printer files, and ICF files. In this no-nonsense volume, author Jim Coolbaugh gives you all the keywords you'll need, listed alphabetically in five sections. He explains each keyword, providing syntax rules and examples for coding the keyword. The *DDS Keyword Reference* is a friendly and manageable alternative to IBM's bulky DDS reference manual. 212 pages.

DOMINO R5 AND THE AS/400
By Justine Middleton, Wilfried Blankertz, Rosana Choruzy, Linda Defreyne, Dwight Egerton, Joanne Mindzora, Stephen Ryan, Juan van der Breggen, Felix Zalcmann, and Michelle Zolkos
Domino R5 and the AS/400 provides comprehensive installation and setup instructions for those installing Domino R5 "from scratch," upgrading from a previous version, or migrating from a platform other than the AS/400. In addition, you get detailed explanations of SMTP in Domino for AS/400, dial-up connectivity, directory synchronization, Advanced Services for Domino for AS/400, and Domino administration strategies, including backup strategies. 512 pages.

E-BUSINESS
Thriving in the Electronic Marketplace
By Nahid Jilovec
E-Business: Thriving in the Electronic Marketplace identifies key issues organizations face when they implement e-business projects and answers fundamental questions about entering and navigating the changing world of e-business. A concise guide to moving your business into the exciting world of collaborative e-business, the book introduces the four e-business models that drive today's economy and gives a clear summary of e-business technologies. It focuses on practical business-to-business applications. 172 pages.

ESSENTIALS OF SUBFILE PROGRAMMING
and Advanced Topics in RPG IV
By Phil Levinson
This textbook provides a solid background in AS/400 subfile programming in the newest version of the RPG language: RPG IV. Subfiles are the AS/400 tool that lets you display lists of data on the screen for user interaction. You learn to design and program subfiles, via step-by-step instructions and real-world programming exercises that build from chapter to chapter. A section on the Integrated Language Environment (ILE), introduced

concurrently with RPG IV, presents tools and techniques that support effective modular programming. An instructor's kit is available. 293 pages.

ILE BY EXAMPLE
A Hands-on Guide to the AS/400's Integrated Language Environment
By Mike Cravitz

Learn the fundamentals of the AS/400's Integrated Language Environment (ILE) by following working examples that illustrate the ins and outs of this powerful programming model. Major topics include ILE program structure, bind by copy, ILE RPG subprocedures, service programs, activation groups, ILE condition handling and cancel handling, and more. A CD contains all sample programs discussed in the book, as well as a sample ILE condition handler to address record locks and ILE RPG software to synchronize system clocks using the Internet SNTP protocol. 165 pages.

IMPLEMENTING WINDOWS NT ON THE AS/400
Installing, Configuring, and Troubleshooting
By Nick Harris, Phil Ainsworth, Steve Fullerton, and Antoine Sammut

Implementing Windows NT on the AS/400: Installing, Configuring, and Troubleshooting provides everything you need to know about using NT on your AS/400, including how to install NT Server 4.0 on the Integrated Netfinity Server, synchronize user profiles and passwords between the AS/400 and NT, administer NT disk storage and service packs from the AS/400, back up NT data from the AS/400, manage NT servers on remote AS/400s, and run Windows-based personal productivity applications on the AS/400. 393 pages.

INTRODUCTION TO AS/400 SYSTEM OPERATIONS, SECOND EDITION
By Heidi Rothenbuehler and Patrice Gapen

Here's the second edition of the textbook that covers what you need to know to become a successful AS/400 system operator or administrator. Updated through V4R3 of OS/400, *Introduction to AS/400 System Operations, Second Edition*, teaches you the basics of system operations so that you can manage printed reports, perform regularly scheduled procedures, and resolve end-user problems. New material covers the Integrated File System (IFS), AS/400 InfoSeeker, Operations Navigator, and much more. 182 pages.

MASTERING THE AS/400, THIRD EDITION
A Practical, Hands-On Guide
By Jerry Fottral

This best-selling introduction to AS/400 concepts and facilities — fully updated for V4R3 of OS/400 — takes a utilitarian approach that stresses student participation. The book emphasizes mastery of system/user interface, member-object-library relationship, use of CL commands, basic database concepts, and program development utilities. The text prepares students to move directly into programming languages, database management, and system operations courses. Each lesson includes a lab that focuses on the essential topics presented in the lesson. 553 pages.

OPNQRYF BY EXAMPLE
By Mike Dawson and Mike Manto

The OPNQRYF (Open Query File) command is the single most dynamic and versatile command on the AS/400. Drawing from real-life, real-job experiences, the authors explain the basics and the intricacies of OPNQRYF with lots of examples to make you productive quickly. An appendix provides the UPDQRYF (Update Query File) command — a powerful addition to AS/400 and System/38 file update capabilities. 216 pages.

Programming in RPG IV, Second Edition
By Bryan Meyers and Judy Yaeger, Ph.D.
This textbook provides a strong foundation in the essentials of business programming, featuring the newest version of the RPG language: RPG IV. Focusing on real-world problems and down-to-earth solutions using the latest techniques and features of RPG, this book provides everything you need to know to write a well-designed RPG IV program. The second edition includes new chapters on defining data with D-specs and modular programming concepts, as well as an RPG IV summary appendix and an RPG IV style guide. An instructor's kit is available. 408 pages.

RPG IV Jump Start, Third Edition
By Bryan Meyers
RPG IV Jump Start presents RPG IV from the perspective of a programmer who already knows RPG III, pointing out the differences between the two languages and demonstrating how to take advantage of the new syntax and function. The third edition is fully updated for V4R4 and includes information about the latest H-spec keywords, built-in functions, opcodes, and data types. Also inluced is expanded coverage of RPG's pointer support and new chapters on RPG programming style and what's in store for the future of RPG. 234 pages.

SQL/400 by Example
By James Coolbaugh
Designed to help you make the most of SQL/400, *SQL/400 by Example* includes everything from SQL syntax and rules to the specifics of embedding SQL within an RPG program. For novice SQL users, this book features plenty of introductory-level text and examples, including all the features and terminology of SQL/400. For experienced AS/400 programmers, *SQL/400 by Example* offers a number of specific examples that will help you increase your understanding of SQL concepts and improve your programming skills. 204 pages.

SQL/400 Developer's Guide
By Paul Conte and Mike Cravitz
SQL/400 Developer's Guide provides start-to-finish coverage of SQL/400, IBM's strategic language for the AS/400's integrated database. This textbook covers database and SQL fundamentals, SQL/400 Data Definition Language (DDL) and Data Manipulation Language (DML), and database modeling and design. Throughout the book, coding suggestions reinforce the topics covered and provide practical advice on how to produce robust, well-functioning code. Hands-on exercises reinforce comprehension of the concepts covered. 536 pages.

Also Published by 29th Street Press® and NEWS/400 Books™

The AS/400 Expert: Ready-to-Run RPG/400 Techniques
By Julian Monypenny and Roger Pence
Ready-to-Run RPG/400 Techniques provides a variety of RPG templates, subroutines, and copy modules, sprinkled with evangelical advice, to help you write robust and effective RPG/400 programs. Highlights include string-handling routines, numeric editing routines, date routines, error-handling modules, and tips for using OS/400 APIs with RPG/400. The tested and ready-to-run code building blocks — provided on an accompanying CD — easily snap into existing RPG code and integrate well with new RPG/400 projects. 203 pages.

The A to Z of EDI And Its Role in E-Commerce, Second Edition
By Nahid M. Jilovec
E-commerce expert Nahid Jilovec gives you the practical details of EDI implementation. Not only does this book show you how to cost justify EDI, but it gives you job descriptions for EDI team members, detailed criteria and forms for evaluating EDI vendors, considerations for trading-partner agreements, an EDI glossary, and lists of EDI

organizations and publications. The second edition includes all-new information about EDI and the Internet, system security, and auditing. 221 pages.

BUILDING AS/400 CLIENT/SERVER APPLICATIONS
Put ODBC and Client Access APIs to Work
By Mike Otey

Mike Otey, a leading client/server authority with extensive practical client/server application development experience, gives you the why, what, and how-to of AS/400 client/server computing, which matches the strengths of the AS/400 with the PC GUIs that users want. This book's clear and easy-to-understand style guides you through all the important aspects of AS/400 client/server applications. Mike covers APPC and TCP/IP communications as well as the underlying architectures for each of the major AS/400 client/server APIs. A CD with complete source code for several working applications is included. 505 pages.

C FOR RPG PROGRAMMERS
By Jennifer Hamilton

Written from the perspective of an RPG programmer, this book includes side-by-side coding examples written in both C and RPG, clear identification of unique C constructs, and a comparison of RPG opcodes to equivalent C concepts. Includes many tips and examples covering the use of C/400. 292 pages.

COMMON-SENSE C
Advice and Warnings for C and C++ Programmers
By Paul Conte

The C programming language has its risks; this book shows how C programmers get themselves into trouble, includes tips to help you avoid C's pitfalls, and suggests how to manage C and C++ application development. 100 pages.

CONTROL LANGUAGE PROGRAMMING FOR THE AS/400, SECOND EDITION
By Bryan Meyers and Dan Riehl

This comprehensive CL programming textbook offers students up-to-the-minute knowledge of the skills they will need in today's MIS environment. Chapters progress methodically from CL basics to more complex processes and concepts, guiding students toward a professional grasp of CL programming techniques and style. In the second edition, the authors have updated the text to include discussion of the Integrated Language Environment (ILE) and the fundamental changes ILE introduces to the AS/400's execution model. 522 pages.

DATABASE DESIGN AND PROGRAMMING FOR DB2/400
By Paul Conte

This textbook is the most complete guide to DB2/400 design and programming available anywhere. The author shows you everything you need to know about physical and logical file DDS, SQL/400, and RPG IV and COBOL/400 database programming. Clear explanations illustrated by a wealth of examples demonstrate efficient database programming and error handling with both DDS and SQL/400. 610 pages.

DATA WAREHOUSING AND THE AS/400
By Scott Steinacher

In this book, Scott Steinacher takes an in-depth look at data warehousing components, concepts, and terminology. After laying this foundation, Scott presents a compelling case for implementing a data warehouse on the AS/400. Included on an accompanying CD are demos of AS/400 data warehousing software from several independent software vendors. 342 pages.

DDS Programming for Display & Printer Files, Second Edition
By James Coolbaugh
DDS Programming for Display & Printer Files, Second Edition, helps you master DDS and — as a result — improve the quality of your display presentations and your printed jobs. Updated through OS/400 V4R3, the second edition offers a thorough, straightforward explanation of how to use DDS to program display files and printer files. It includes extensive DDS programming examples for CL and RPG that you can put to use immediately because a companion CD includes all the DDS, RPG, and CL source code presented in the book. 429 pages.

Developing Your AS/400 Internet Strategy
By Alan Arnold
This book addresses the issues unique to deploying your AS/400 on the Internet. It includes procedures for configuring AS/400 TCP/IP and information about which client and server technologies the AS/400 supports natively. This enterprise-class tutorial evaluates the AS/400 as an Internet server and teaches you how to design, program, and manage your Web home page. 248 pages.

Domino and the AS/400
Installation and Configuration
By Wilfried Blankertz, Rosana Choruzy, Joanne Mindzora, and Michelle Zolkos
Domino and the AS/400: Installation and Configuration gives you everything you need to implement Lotus Domino 4.6 on the AS/400, guiding you step by step through installation, configuration, customization, and administration. Here you get an introduction to Domino for AS/400 and full instructions for developing a backup and recovery plan for saving and restoring Domino data on the AS/400. 311 pages.

Essentials of Subfile Programming
and Advanced Topics in RPG/400
By Phil Levinson
Essentials of Subfile Programming teaches you to design and program subfiles, offering step-by-step instructions and real-world programming exercises that build from chapter to chapter. You learn to design and create subfile records; load, clear, and display subfiles; and create pop-up windows. In addition, the advanced topics help you mine the rich store of data in the file-information and program-status data structures, handle errors, improve data integrity, and manage program-to-program communications. An instructor's manual is available. 260 pages.

ILE: A First Look
By George Farr and Shailan Topiwala
This book begins by showing the differences between ILE and its predecessors and then goes on to explain the essentials of an ILE program — using concepts such as modules, binding, service programs, and binding directories. You'll discover how ILE program activation works and how ILE works with its predecessor environments. The book covers the APIs and debugging facilities and explains the benefits of ILE's exception-handling model. You also get answers to the most commonly asked questions about ILE. 183 pages.

Inside the AS/400, Second Edition
Featuring the AS/400e series
By Frank G. Soltis
Learn from the architect of the AS/400 about the new generation of AS/400e systems and servers and about the system features and capabilities introduced in Version 4 of OS/400. Dr. Frank Soltis demystifies the system, shedding light on how it came to be, how it can do the things it does, and what its future may hold. 402 pages.

AN INTRODUCTION TO COMMUNICATIONS FOR THE AS/400, SECOND EDITION
By John Enck and Ruggero Adinolfi

This second edition has been revised to address the sweeping communications changes introduced with V3R1 of OS/400. As a result, this book now covers the broad range of AS/400 communications technology topics, ranging from Ethernet to X.25 and from APPN to AnyNet. The book presents an introduction to data communications and then covers communications fundamentals, types of networks, OSI, SNA, APPN, networking roles, the AS/400 as host and server, TCP/IP, and the AS/400-DEC connection. 194 pages.

JAVA AND THE AS/400
Practical Examples Using VisualAge for Java
By Daniel Darnell

This detailed guide takes you through everything you need to know about the AS/400's implementation of Java, including the QShell Interpreter and the Integrated File System (IFS), and development products such as VisualAge for Java (VAJ) and the AS/400 Toolbox for Java. The author provides several small application examples that demonstrate the advantages of Java programming for the AS/400. The companion CD contains all the sample code presented in the book and full-version copies of VAJ Professional Edition and the AS/400 Toolbox for Java. 300 pages.

JIM SLOAN'S CL TIPS & TECHNIQUES
By Jim Sloan, developer of QUSRTOOL's TAA Tools

Written for those who understand CL, this book draws from Jim Sloan's knowledge and experience as a developer for the System/38 and the AS/400, and his creation of QUSRTOOL's TAA tools, to give you tips that can help you write better CL programs and become more productive. The book includes more than 200 field-tested techniques, plus exercises to help you understand and apply many of the techniques presented. 564 pages.

MASTERING AS/400 PERFORMANCE
By Alan Arnold, Charly Jones, Jim Stewart, and Rick Turner

If you want more from your AS/400 — faster interactive response time, more batch jobs completed on time, and maximum use of your expensive resources — this book is for you. In *Mastering AS/400 Performance*, the experts tell you how to measure, evaluate, and tune your AS/400's performance. From their experience in the field, the authors give you techniques for improving performance beyond simply buying additional hardware. 259 pages.

OBJECT-ORIENTED PROGRAMMING FOR AS/400 PROGRAMMERS
By Jennifer Hamilton

This introduction for AS/400 programmers explains basic OOP concepts such as classes and inheritance in simple, easy-to-understand terminology. The OS/400 object-oriented architecture serves as the basis for the discussion throughout, and concepts presented are reinforced through an introduction to the C++ object-oriented programming language, using examples based on the OS/400 object model. 114 pages.

PROGRAMMING IN RPG/400, SECOND EDITION
By Judy Yaeger, Ph.D.

The second edition of this textbook refines and extends the comprehensive instructional material contained in the original textbook and features a new section that introduces externally described printer files, a new chapter that highlights the fundamentals of RPG IV, and a new appendix that correlates the key concepts from each chapter with their RPG IV counterparts. The book includes everything you need to learn how to write a well-designed RPG program, from the most basic to the more complex. An instructor's kit is available. 481 pages.

Programming Subfiles in COBOL/400
By Jerry Goldson
Learn how to program subfiles in COBOL/400 in a matter of hours! This powerful and flexible programming technique no longer needs to elude you. You can begin programming with subfiles the same day you get the book. You don't have to wade through page after page, chapter after chapter of rules and parameters and keywords. Instead, you get solid, helpful information and working examples that you can apply to your application programs right away. 204 pages.

RPG/400 Interactive Template Technique
By Carson Soule, CDP, CCP, CSP
This book shows you time-saving, program-sharpening concepts behind the template approach and includes all the code you need to build one perfect program after another. These templates include code for cursor-sensitive prompting in DDS, for handling messages in resident RPG programs, for using the CLEAR opcode to eliminate hard-coded field initialization, and much more. There's even a select template with a pop-up window. 234 pages.

RPG IV by Example
By George Farr and Shailan Topiwala
RPG IV by Example addresses the needs and concerns of RPG programmers at any level of experience. The focus is on RPG IV in a practical context that lets AS/400 professionals quickly grasp what's new without dwelling on the old. Beginning with an overview of RPG IV specifications, the authors prepare the way for examining all the features of the new version of the language. The chapters that follow explore RPG IV further with practical, easy-to-use applications. 488 pages.

RPG Error Handling Technique
Bulletproofing Your Applications
By Russell Popeil
RPG Error Handling Technique teaches you the skills you need to use the powerful tools provided by OS/400 and RPG to handle almost any error from within your programs. The book explains the INFSR, INFDS, PSSR, and SDS in programming terms, with examples that show you how all these tools work together and which tools are most appropriate for which kind of error or exception situation. It continues by presenting a robust suite of error/exception-handling techniques within RPG programs. Each technique is explained in an application setting, using both RPG III and RPG IV code. 163 pages.

Subfile Technique for RPG/400 Programmers, Second Edition
By Jonathan Yergin, CDP, and Wayne Madden
Here's the code you need for a complete library of shell subfile programs: RPG/400 code, DDS, CL, and sample data files. There's even an example for programming windows plus some "whiz bang" techniques that can add punch to your applications. The book explains the code in simple, straightforward style and tells you when each technique should be used for best results. 3.5-inch PC diskette included. 326 pages.

TCP/IP and the AS/400
By Michael Ryan
Transmission Control Protocol/Internet Protocol (TCP/IP) is fast becoming a major protocol in the AS/400 world because of TCP/IP's ubiquity and predominance in the networked world, as well as its being the protocol for the Internet, intranets, and extranets. *TCP/IP and the AS/400* provides background for AS/400 professionals to understand the capabilities of TCP/IP, its strengths and weaknesses, and how to configure and administer the TCP/IP protocol stack on the AS/400. It shows TCP/IP gurus on other types of systems how to configure and manage the AS/400 TCP/IP capabilities. 362 pages.

UNDERSTANDING BAR CODES
By James R. Plunkett
One of the most important waves of technology sweeping American industry is the use of bar coding to capture and track data. With so many leading-edge technologies, it can be difficult for IS professionals to keep up with the concepts and applications they need to make solid decisions. This book gives you an overview of bar code technology, including a discussion of the bar codes themselves, the hardware that supports bar coding, how and when to justify and then implement a bar code application, plus examples of many different applications and how bar coding can be used to solve problems. 70 pages.

USING QUERY/400
By Patrice Gapen and Catherine Stoughton
This textbook, designed for any AS/400 user from student to professional with or without prior programming knowledge, presents Query as an easy and fast tool for creating reports and files from AS/400 databases. Topics are ordered from simple to complex and emphasize hands-on AS/400 use; they include defining database files to Query, selecting and sequencing fields, generating new numeric and character fields, sorting within Query, joining database files, defining custom headings, creating new database files, and more. An instructor's kit is available. 92 pages.

VISUALAGE FOR RPG BY EXAMPLE
By Bryan Meyers and Jef Sutherland
VisualAge for RPG (VARPG) is a rich, full-featured development environment that provides all the tools necessary to build Windows applications for the AS/400. *VisualAge for RPG by Example* brings the RPG language to the GUI world and lets you use your existing knowledge to develop Windows applications. Using a tutorial approach, *VisualAge for RPG by Example* lets you learn as you go and create simple yet functional programs from start to finish. The accompanying CD offers a scaled-down version of VARPG and complete source code for the sample project. 236 pages.

FOR A COMPLETE CATALOG OR TO PLACE AN ORDER, CONTACT

29th Street Press®
NEWS/400 Books™
Duke Communications International
221 E. 29th Street
Loveland, CO USA 80538-2727
(800) 650-1804 • (970) 663-4700 • Fax: (970) 663-4007

OR SHOP OUR WEB SITE: **www.as400networkstore.com**

YOU *CAN* HAVE YOUR CAKE & EAT IT TOO!

Join the AS400 Network — the only AS/400 resource you'll ever need!

Your Professional Membership Includes

- ✓ **NEWS/400®:** The #1 AS/400 magazine worldwide, 14 times per year
- ✓ **Tech Resources:** Web-exclusive articles, downloadable code and tutorials and the *NEWS/400* archive
- ✓ **Member Communities:** AS/400 specific forums
- ✓ **Solution Center:** AS/400 vendors, buyers guides, product reviews, and screen tours
- ✓ **IBM Connection:** Find what you need at ibm.com
- ✓ **News & Analysis:** AS/400 news updated daily
- ✓ **Jobs400:** To hire or be hired
- ✓ **Worldwide Events:** AS/400 events searchable by subject or location
- ✓ **Digital Channel:** For AS/400 business partners and resellers
- ✓ **NEWSWire/400:** E-mail newsletters on AS/400 product news, tips, and techniques
- ✓ **Discounts on *NEWS/400* products:**
  - 25% off book purchases of $99 or less
  - 30% off book purchases of $100 or more
  - $25 off any Technical Seminar
  - $25 off any Technical Training Center Workshop

FREE!
ASSOCIATE MEMBERSHIP
Includes e-mail newsletters & access to much more!

Click on www.as400network.com and find out what the buzz is all about. Join today and let us help you work smarter!

☐ **Yes,** sign me up for the AS400 Network as a Professional Member for US$149/year in the United States and Canada. *All other countries US$199/year.*

COPY THIS PAGE AND MAIL TO:

NEWS/400
221 E. 29th St.
Loveland, CO 80538
USA

or fax to
970/663-4007

or subscribe on the Web at
www.as400network.com

Name
Title
Company
Address
City/State/Zip
Phone   Fax
E-mail

BROUGHT TO YOU BY NEWS/400!

AS400 NETWORK ™

NEWS/400

Talk to Us!

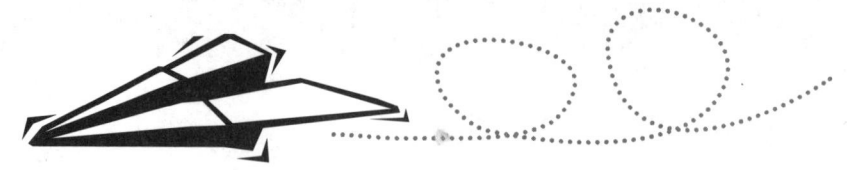

Complete this form to join our network of computer professionals

We'll gladly send you a *free* copy of

- ❏ NEWS/400
- ❏ Selling AS/400 Solutions
- ❏ Business Finance
- ❏ Windows 2000 Magazine
- ❏ SQL Server Magazine

Providing help — not hype.

29th Street PRESS®

Publisher of practical, hands-on technical books for AS/400 computer professionals.

Name _____

Title _____ Phone _____

Company _____

Address _____

City/State/Zip _____

E-mail _____

Where did you purchase this book?
❏ Trade show   ❏ Computer store   ❏ Internet   ❏ Card deck
❏ Bookstore   ❏ Magazine   ❏ Direct mail catalog or brochure

What new applications do you expect to use during the next year?
_____
_____

How many times this month will you visit a Duke Communications Web site (29th Street Press®, AS400 Network, NEWS/400, Selling AS/400 Solutions, Business Finance, Windows 2000 Magazine, or SQL Server Magazine)? _____

Please share your reaction to *Implementing AS/400 Security, Fourth Edition.*
_____
_____

❏ YES! You have my permission to quote my comments in your publications (initials) _____

[00SCXBOOK]

Copy this page and mail to

**29th Street Press
221 East 29th Street
Loveland, CO 80538 USA
OR Fax to (970) 663-4007
OR Visit our Web site at www.as400network.com**